**Dedicated to My Parents**
**and**

**Fran**

# Forward

Now that I have finished my story, perhaps, it would be helpful to a reader if I went back to the beginning to tell him how this autobiography came about. The backdrop to your reading is that I started this project at age 96 and finished with this forward the day after my 99th birthday.

It certainly wasn't on a dare, or a bet, or an assignment in a writing class on composition in a school. If it had been, I would have done some research, gone through the boxes of memorabilia stored in my garage saved when we downsized. I would have taken notes, checked facts, tried to revive long dormant memories.

My approach was far more casual, a belated response to the suggestions of my daughters, and I have relied on my latent memories that were easily accessible, the highlights, as it were. Thus, there has been no searching, no delving, and only minimal checking of facts on Google and Wikipedia: basically to check spelling of place names, I have had my trusty *Webster's New World Dictionary* at my side at all times to use when a word looked "funny" or the meaning didn't feel quite right.

After completing almost 600 pages of easy, and for the most part, happy memories, it is just as well to have used this method. There are many more memories, probably equal in number, buried alive below the surface of my mind that could have been brought back to life, if I had undertaken the project differently.

I am sure this story would have been quite different, both in intent and content. I might have gone into far more detail for the successes in my life, might have found the exact chronology of my medical procedures, might have decided how much of the intimate side of my marriage to reveal, have brought back the few times my teenage terrors reappeared in my adulthood.

The story would have had a different emphasis if it had been written 20 years earlier. Twenty years is s long time to accumulate gratitude. It would have been there, just not as much of it. Most importantly, I think the awareness of the imminence of death that has been growing page by page, would not have been present. I hope its presence now will not detract from a reader's sensing of the author's appreciation of all the goodness in his life and gratitude for having the extra years to recognize his perception of infinity.

I am sure that such awareness was a factor in what kind of memories I chose to recall. Along with a feeling that time was speeding up: 24 hours suddenly felt like 18 hours and there was less and less time to get to the end of the story, the most important part to me, far more than recalling life 100 years ago for grandchildren; would I be allowed to finish the race to the finish line?

After completing the two later chapters, "Credo" and "Music," when I started from page one, I came face to face with the mysteries of the working of memory and before starting with my earliest memory, I set forth some musings on the subject, which I have decided to move from the body of the text to this position that seems more appropriate.

A few musings on the subject of Memory having come face to face immediately with the problems associated with memory, and its importance to autobiography. As I tried to bring back memories and remain truthful, I immediately became aware of the problem of what is true, and can memory be relied on as "truth." Indeed, what is "memory?" Is it really only one or two regions in the brain which light up when called upon, like the storage capacity of a computer? If the storage capacity of the brain is virtually unlimited, why are so many memories so fragmentary? So fragile? And why are memories of significant events remembered by insignificant portions of the event, even trivial or silly fragments?

These fragments can lead to attempts to reconstruct the whole of an event consciously or unconsciously, using logic to reconstruct what must have happened to make the mind recognize it and store it away – so that it will not be forgotten. But, as this process occurs, how "true" is it? Can using logic to reconstruct lead to or equate with embellishment? Or is embellishment a self-aggrandizing attempt to paint a prettier picture? Not even concerned with the truth? Does this mislead the embellisher as well as the reader?

All I can conclude is that memory is wonderful and we could not live without it, but a minefield, and I have already learned after beginning with the two later chapters that I must tiptoe very carefully to come out safely on the other side to arrive at an approximation of the truth (which I will try very hard to do) and will try to point out any attempts at reconstruction with warnings to the reader.

To me, memory is fascinating, awesome, and an enigma.

But all the memories included here should be read as clues as to what I have become, and how, and as signs of my unending search for proof of the existence of Deity, as an acknowledgement of the Presence of God in every stage and aspect of my life, as an expression of profound gratitude for the many examples herein, the culmination of which is to be found in the final pages of the last chapter of my story. Which, you will note does not end with the words "*Finis*" or "The End," but "*Veni Creator Spiritus,*" the endless beginning.

# Table of Contents

# Chapter I

## Early Life to life in the Army

A fine example of this problem is the very first memory of my conscious life. I have always been aware of it and it has been present all my life: this is my memory of seeing what seemed at the time of a large, brown mole on my mother's breast as she breastfed me. How can this memory be true? I do not know how long I was fed that way but, reconstructing, my brother, Russell, was born 19 months after me, so, logically, I should have been 12-14 months old when this memory was generated, and how could a child that young remember something like that? How could I even know what a mole is? Could a visual image have been implanted in my brain only to have been identified years later? But this memory, such as it is, to me is true. It is there in my mind. But I suspect that some of the blanks must have been filled in later. A more sensible memory is that of feeling very warm and comfortable. But this memory is very vague.

I was born at home on W. 34th St. north of Denison Avenue in Cleveland, Ohio, on May 6th, 1921. I was told that my parents, Frank and Lydia (Babe) Schmidt had been married for two years when I arrived; that they had met at a church picnic at Linwood Park in Vermilion, Ohio, a church oriented, gated, summer cottage resort on the shore of Lake Erie, about 30 miles west of Cleveland. How I wish they had recorded the details of their courtship and early life together. How did they arrange to meet: by telephone? Did they even have telephones then? This must have been about 1917-1918. What did they do while getting to know each other? Both had graduated from high school, or were about to, Dad from West Tech and mother from the rival West High in Cleveland. I remember seeing her report cards which recorded the grade numerically, not letters as mine were. They lived two or three miles apart. Dad had a job as a bank messenger and mother worked for an elevator company, the Rossborough Co., as a secretary. What did their parents think of the match? Where was the wedding held? What was it like? It must have been in a church. How did they find their first home? How much was the rent? How I wish I knew. What wonderful lore it would have made!

One very early memory I have is of being pushed in a navy-blue wicker baby carriage and of mother stopping to chat with our neighbor, Mrs. Pollock (sp.), also pushing a baby carriage. I have no memories of the house, interior or exterior, and presume that mother had stopped working sometime before my birth. In later years we paid visits occasionally to the Rossboroughs, her former employers, who lived on Broadview Rd., in Seven Hills, Ohio, and while the elders reminisced, their two older sons introduced us to frozen Milky Way bars. Needless to say, we never objected to these visits.

These memories of carriage rides are very early ones and I wonder why they remain, taking up space, in my memory, and why other more important memories of an awakening awareness have disappeared, or were never considered worth saving in my infant's mind.

The next memory is later: I must have been four or five years old and my parents drove us (when did Dad get his first car and what brand was it?) on a Sunday afternoon - in those early days of the automobile, it was very common to enjoy the adventure, which is what it was, of getting in the car and setting off to pay a visit to relatives or friends, being uninvited was socially acceptable. On this occasion we paid a visit to some distant relatives on the far East Side of Cleveland, the Zierke's (sp.). I remember dreading the visit, expecting to be fondled and kissed, "Ugh!" which is what happened. I was dragged, struggling and screaming up the front walk while being fondled and kissed by the women, and making such a fuss that I was taken back to the car and locked in. I never saw the inside of the house and don't remember how long the visit lasted. And have wondered all my life who those people were. Cousins?

I also am surprised at the total lack of memories of the birth and early days of my younger brother, Russell. His presence in my life is a blank until I was four or five years old. No memories of being encouraged to pat my mother's belly as the delivery day approached. I was only a baby 14 or 15 months old which probably explains this. But, if other early memories survive, why not memories of Russell when he was three and I was four years old? An enigma?

When I was two years old, my parents bought a new house at 1658 Parkwood Road, Lakewood, Ohio. Lakewood is the first westerly suburb of Cleveland, and was classified as a "bedroom" community, 5 miles long and 1 1/2 miles deep. Parkwood Road was only one block long from Madison Avenue which was the southerly east-west thoroughfare to downtown Cleveland to Franklin Boulevard, also an east-west route to downtown Cleveland. Madison Avenue was only paved on the north side of the street as I remember. Lakewood has 5 miles of lakefront perched about 30 feet above lake level and this has always attracted its share of wealthy residents.

The house was a frame Dutch Colonial style, with a tile roof and I suspect was 24' x 24' on the foundation, 2 1/2 stories with full basement. The lot was 40' x 120', a very common dimension at the time. There was a LR, DR, and K with breakfast nook on the first floor as well as a vestibule and a refrigerator room rear door entry at the back of the house. There were 3 BR, and a bath on the 2nd floor with a stairway to an unheated, floored attic which was used for storage. Later a door was cut from the 1st floor landing into the K, and the ceiling of the stairway was modified at the bottom so I would not keep bumping my head on the way downstairs. I was 6' 4 ' tall by the time I was in the 7th grade. The LR had a fireplace with a gas-fired grate where my brother and I played in the cold weather. The LR was large enough, probably about 12' x 22', to have a grand piano in the front corner, next to the entry from the vestibule with its coat closet. The DR was off the LR through an arch and the K was to the rear. The stairway to the 2nd floor started at the K and had a landing halfway to the 2nd floor. It was very handy for sneaking out of our beds to crouch on the landing and eavesdrop on our parents, especially when they had guests. I don't remember ever being caught.

There was a full basement with a coal burning furnace which furnished steam heat to the radiators upstairs (air-conditioning had not been invented yet). There was a coal bin room, and a cold storage room and the rest was open space where my mother did the laundry. Later, Dad had a lavatory installed in the basement, and the furnace was improved with an automatic "Iron Fireman" stoker which drew pea sized coal with a worm into the coal storage room. And after a few years the stoker was discarded and replaced with a natural gas fired burner. This made keeping the house clean easier without the bother of the constant coal dust. And I inherited the coal storage room for my workshop. I had received a wood turning lathe powered with a 1/2 HP electric motor as a Christmas present and had a lot of fun shaping various square pieces of wood into rounded objects.

I remember from this period making round globes from 6" cubes of wood to place on the side yard fence at the home of Dad's boss, Mr. A.D. Fraser, who lived in a very large home on Avalon Drive in Rocky River. He seemed very austere to me at that age but thought enough of Dad to invite the family to come out occasionally on the very hot days for a swim in Lake Erie which was in his back yard. He had a little beach which was accessed by climbing down a narrow ravine on our bare feet. It's undoubtedly why we never saw the inside of the house. I don't remember ever seeing Mrs. Fraser, either. I remember Mr. Fraser complimenting and thanking me, for the fence post globes. I was very proud and felt I had done something to please and help my father.

Another warm memory is my going down to the basement with my father and watching him get the first coal burning furnace ready for the night. He used to shovel enough large lumps of coal into the furnace to last until morning (he hoped) and then made a paste of coal ashes and water and banked this up like a dam just inside the furnace door. This was supposed to keep the coal embers alive until he replenished the coal before leaving for work in the morning. And, if it was successful, this meant he would not have to start a new fire before going off to work. As far as I know, it usually worked. And the whole process fascinated me.

My mother did the family laundry in the basement using a rectangular tub with an electrical motor which moved the tub up and down like a seesaw creating a sloshing effect in the soapy water. There was a hand cranked dryer with two rollers which squeezed the water out of the clothes, which was saved for the next load after the first load had been rinsed. The white things were washed first and then the dark loads were done using the original soapy water. Some of the brands of soap I remember her using were: Lux, Ivory, Oxydol, all in flake form. The damp clothes were hung to dry in the basement in bad weather, or on warm sunny days hung outside on a line stretched from the garage to the rear porch, using wooden clothes pins. There was no such thing as a clothes dryer in those days. There was a laundry chute from the 2nd floor to the basement and I can remember my mother sorting the clothes into piles for washing, from the lighter things to the darker, and presumably, dirtier things. There was a zinc stationary laundry tub against the wall close to the washing machine. The tub had a cover to keep it from splashing and it had other uses, too.

I remember one day when our mother decided we would have a "taffy pull." She made taffy upstairs in the kitchen from a recipe, and then brought the thick, sticky mass downstairs to us, covered the lid of the washer with a cloth and we greased up our hands with butter and pulled the rope of taffy back and forth between us until it was done and then cut it into bite sized pieces. What a neat way for two little boys to learn about candy making, and then to enjoy the fruit of their labors.

I don't remember going down to the basement to play very often; it was unfinished, of course, poorly lit and generally gloomy. Also, knowing what we know today it's probably just as well because the steam pipes to the upper floors were exposed and wrapped in asbestos sleeves. I do remember clearly my first experience meeting and talking to a black person which took place in the basement. I must have been six or seven years old and he was the installer of the coal stoker. I think his name was Jim. He was very kind and patient and explained things to me when I asked the inevitable questions of a curious child. I now realize what a beneficial experience this was in forming my opinions on race, and how limited my opportunities were when growing up since there were no black people and a very limited number of Jewish people living in the entire area west of the Cuyahoga River.

My mother played a tremendous role in our lives and was a living example while instilling the basic principles of integrity and the value of hard work to reach a goal. This was during the period of the Great Depression which started in 1929, when I was eight years old. I remember my father coming home and confessing to Mother that he knew a bank run was coming in advance and had not withdrawn the money they had in the Guardian Bank and it was lost. This meant that we all had to be very frugal and be aware of waste. Nothing frivolous. We had to stretch things and make things do. Dad never lost his job at the A.D. Fraser Mortgage Company, where he became V.P. and Secretary, and he never spoke of it in front of us children, but I am sure there were several pay cuts during the years which did not make my mother's job of managing her household any easier. She was in charge of the finances, never had any household help, other than what she received from training her two small boys, did all the cleaning, cooking, canning, laundry and sewing, and all the other things that go into running a household of husband and four children, because when I was eight years old, my brother, Ken arrived on the scene and two years later, my brother, Wesley. Incidentally, as an indication of how different times were then, neither Russell nor I were even aware that Mother was pregnant. The only thing that might have alerted us was being taken to Grandma Schmidt's house to stay overnight, the only time in our childhood that we did not sleep under the same roof as our parents.

One of the things Dad did to make Mother's life easier was to buy her a mangle about the time I was starting high school, I think. This was used for pressing flat items like sheets, but she could also do shirts, etc. I used to marvel at her skill at handling it. It had a flat surface and a movable upper arm that came down to apply the pressure and steam and was foot operated, like her sewing machine, leaving her hands free to adjust the item she was pressing. I tried to use it only once but couldn't get the knack of coordinating the feet and the hands.

Also, in the basement was the cold storage room under the breakfast nook, which was unheated and where the home canned fruit and vegetables were stored on shelves. Later we kept our homegrown carrots in boxes of sand over the winter, and the huge crock of sauerkraut made by sliding heads of cabbage over a horizontal slicer held over the mouth of the crock with a large plate as a lid to hold the sliced cabbage down in the brine. We grew the vegetables in our large garden at our summer cottage on Tiedeman Road in Brooklyn, Ohio, four miles from the center of downtown Cleveland, and also brought in squash and pumpkins to store in a corner in the basement and hung tomato vines with un-ripened tomatoes on them on the walls for later eating, as late as Thanksgiving. All this in the name of economy with the good, unanticipated side effect of being very healthy for growing boys.

Home canning (water bath, not pressure cooking) was practically a home industry. We had access to black berries and elderberries at our great uncle's farm on Tiedeman Rd., grew our own strawberries and red raspberries, and had a sour Montmorency cherry tree in our back yard on Parkwood Rd. What a messy, dirty job it was picking them. But, oh, the pleasure of the canned juice left after pitting them on the back porch, used in a wonderful fruit punch with an iced tea base made by my mother, and then the canned cherries used in some of the wonderful kuchens my mother made with enriched crust dough from the weekly homemade bread. The elderberries were also used for fillings, but the canned juice was reserved for settling upset stomachs.

Out of the kitchen and basement and back to the bathroom: I remember, while quite young, standing with my chin resting on the edge of the bathroom sink and watching my father prepare his razor for shaving; placing the blade on the base of the silvery, knurled handle; twisting the handle to close the top; and then making a lather with the shaving cream in a mug, and the little shaving brush he used to lather to his cheeks and chin (and upper lip). When I try to remember, I think I can still hear the scraping sounds as he worked away at his whiskers. And then the ritual clean-up.

Another bathroom memory is being taught how to use the toilet when very young, what was then and probably still is called toilet training. I remember being helped up onto the seat but facing toward the tank. I don't know why it was done that way, probably less chance a making a mess, and I wasn't tall enough yet.

While thinking about my growing-up process, I remember the humiliation (and probably the beginning of my father's verbal abuse, due to his frustration at being helpless) of being a bed wetter.

I don't know how long this went on, or the medical reasons for it, but it seemed forever and it was awful: to wake up night after night in the middle of the night and feel once again the cold, wet bedding and to be so helpless. My poor parents were at their wits end. I was their first child, and they didn't know what to do with me, or how to help me stop it. Nothing worked except the passage of time. I do remember no liquids after supper, and, in desperation, handfuls of raisins before going to bed, one of my favorite foods today. But it was no cure then.

Looking back, I am not sure, but I suspect that another unhappy and possibly connected problem began about that time: stuttering. It drove everyone crazy. Especially me. To know the word and the meaning of the word and how to use the word, but to be unable to articulate it coherently, smoothly, was agonizing. My mother kept saying, "Slow down. You're thinking faster than you can make your mouth move." but the more my parents tried to help, the worse it got. I don't know what treatment is used today. Perhaps psychiatry. But there wasn't anything available then. And we couldn't possibly have afforded it then. So, I suffered and retreated into reading and music where it didn't matter. Oddly, I cannot remember it causing me any problems at school and eventually it faded away, probably about junior high school age.

The other childhood ailment which was inconvenient and troublesome was cold sores. I remember when I was in the second grade and developed an especially large and visible blister on my upper lip and being sent to the school nurse who lanced the blister and bandaged it. This caused it to spread and grow even larger and take an extra week to dry up and disappear. My mother was furious that this could be done without her permission as it violated our religious beliefs as Christian Scientists. I believe that she visited the school to register her complaint. I'm sure the school's position was that they were concerned with contagion and the safety of the other students. I don't think they knew much about herpes simplex in those far off days. Recurrent cold sores plagued me all through my school days and interfered with my clarinet playing particularly. They were not painful, but annoying. For a while my, mother thought they were brought on by too much acid in our diet and reduced the amount of canned tomatoes we ate. We learned eventually through experience that the best treatment was simply to ignore the sores and, usually, in a week they dried up and disappeared.

One other incident occurred while I was at Franklin Elementary School which was located on Franklin Boulevard at Lewis Drive, about three blocks from our house. It was probably built about 1900, and is still in use today, with a few improvements I am sure. For one thing our old gravel playground behind the school is now a paved parking lot. Considering the distance of the walk to school, I have a hard time believing that my mother allowed me to walk alone all the way down Parkwood to Franklin and then east past Wyandotte and Elbur to the school at the corner of Lewis Drive. It's all very hazy and hard for me to reconstruct. I was the oldest and tall for my age, yet there were two streets to cross and I was very young. Of course, there wasn't as much automobile traffic then, but still? Maybe my memory is faulty, but I simply do not remember her walking me to school and driving a child to school was unheard of then. After kindergarten, I had to walk home for lunch and back again for the afternoon classes.

I think it was in the 5th grade and there was to be a play, or pageant, of some sort. Being the tallest boy (already) in the school, I was to have the leading role as the Prince, or King. I remember being very excited at this because the Princess (or Queen) was to be a girl named Virginia Hull, who had long brown hair all the way down her back to her waist whom I had a giant crush. As I recall, all went well during the rehearsals, but a few days before the performance I came down with what my mother insisted was swollen glands. But the school nurse said it was chicken pox (another variant of herpes simplex) and highly contagious. I was quarantined. The City nailed a quarantine notice to our front door and I was not allowed to go to school. So, my acting career was ended before it even got started. I remember walking down to the school while the performance was going on and looking at the outside of the building longingly and wistfully. And wondering if it made any difference at all to Virginia Hull.

I remember several of my grade-school teachers very well, more so than my junior high school teachers. Mrs. Rice, 1st grade, seemed very old - probably in her 30s, was very kind and I think she may have detected my color blindness; I skipped the first semester of 2nd grade and have no memory of the teacher. My favorite teacher was Miss McKenna, 3rd grade, whom I loved and would do anything for, especially wiping off the slate blackboard and banging the erasers together outdoors to get rid of the chalk dust. She was so encouraging and kind to me. Miss Montana taught 4th grade, a good teacher; 5th grade was Miss McKewen, also a good teacher, who later married the widower father of two our playmates, the Doty brothers, who lived two doors down the street from us, but I do not remember seeing her while she lived there. Strange!

But my favorite was my 6th grade teacher, Mrs. Henrietta Pagan who was short, overweight and cross-eyed. She was strict but fair and it was disconcerting when one of us was misbehaving to have her scold us while looking in the opposite direction with her crossed eye. By this time, I was twelve years old and almost at my full height, 6' 4", and towered over the other kids. I could run like a deer but had very little upper body strength. In those days, the teachers were all purpose, teaching all the subjects, including phys ed. I remember clearly, Mrs. Pagan coming to my defense when I couldn't get off the floor in gym when trying to climb a thick rope hung from the ceiling. She scolded the others who were teasing me (I may have had tears in my eyes) telling them I was good at other things - like running. I was very grateful and comforted. I think today that maybe her own physical attributes, overweight and eyesight, may have made her especially sympathetic.

One other recollection: my mother had taught me, among many other things, brewing the weak coffee they liked for breakfast in a percolator before they came downstairs; how to darn a hole in a sock; how to sew a square for a quilt; how to cut and peel fruit and vegetables (my Grandma Schmidt taught me how to dismember a chicken when I was eight years old); how to recognize and pull weeds; and how to make baking powder biscuits, pie dough, and bake a cake. Later, if we wanted to have any dessert over the weekend, it fell to me to bake a cake, preferably a recipe calling for less than three eggs for reasons of economy.

For some reason I remember baking a cake and taking it to Mrs. Pagan at school as a gift. I don't think that may have ever happened to her before and she was probably very impressed. If she ate it, it wouldn't have helped her weight problem. I think she liked it, though, and thanked me.

One thing that happened in geography class with Mrs. Pagan was the subject of China. It seemed that she was married to a sergeant in the Army who was stationed in China, and she had many stories to tell us of her adventures while she was there with him. The only one I remember is how to clean a pot that had been used to boil rice and was all sticky afterwards. The secret was to fill the pot with water and let it sit overnight, and then bring it to a boil the next day when it would almost automatically be clean. This was the beginning of my fascination with the Orient, and how odd it is that I ended up studying the Japanese language and the Far East while I was serving in the Army in World War II ten years later.

I think 5th grade coincided with a yearlong celebration of the 150th Anniversary of the signing of the Declaration of Independence. One of my classmates was Jim Fisher who was a very talented artist and Miss McKewen encouraged him to draw a panoramic mural on three or four of the contiguous black boards, which he did. I think he depicted the camp at Valley Forge. At any rate as he drew the outlines of the freezing soldiers huddled around their camp fires in their ragged uniforms with blankets over their shoulders, in front of their lean-to huts, my job was to use colored chalk to fill in the outlines of his drawings. Much later in life I wished the finished work could have been photographed. I think it was of very, high artistic quality for such a young artist. The other teachers brought in their classes to view it. Jim, who later went on to become a commercial artist, was one of the boys' homes I was allowed to stop off at on the way home after school. He lived on Elbur Avenue the street next to the school. The others were: Roger Handwork, Phil Sharp, and Ned Steeb. I suppose we traded stamps for our collections, and marbles, and I can't remember what other activities were of interest to us. Of course, I had to have permission from my mother who kept careful track of my whereabouts, and I had to be home by 5 p.m. It's strange, but I don't remember any of them ever coming to our house, which was much farther from the school.

Grammar school playmates were different from neighborhood ones; stopping on the way home meant playing indoors whereas playing with neighbor kids was usually done outdoors. I do not recall any play sessions indoors ever with the neighborhood playmates. When we couldn't find anyone to play with, or it was raining, we could always practice the piano, or our instruments, indoors. Frequently at the same time. I wonder how the neighbors stood it.

Our next-door neighbors to the south on Parkwood were the Woolseys, with two daughters, Barbara and Polly, whom we played with if none of the boys could come out. I remember playing Jacks on their front porch, and that Polly had some sort of problem which resulted in her crying and screaming in the middle of the night which woke us up and was scary. We had to sleep with the windows open when it was hot because there was no air conditioning. I never heard what the problem was, or whether it faded away with the passage of time. Barbara who was a year behind me in school loved horses and used to go out to Mrs. Parker's Ranch on Mastic Road near the airport to ride and groom the horses. Their father had a nasty habit of surprising Trick or Treaters on Halloween spraying them with a seltzer bottle. He thought it was hilarious and very clever. We didn't.

My mother, on the other hand, made the Trick or Treaters unmask, and had candy for strangers, but slices homemade pumpkin pie for the neighbor kids she recognized. It was a tradition the kids loved.

At the Hannas across the street, you had to go inside down to the basement after unmasking and bob for apples in a big galvanized-washtub full of water which was wet, but fun. Apples can be very elusive!

The house next north of us was the Brown's with one older, very pretty daughter who was a dance instructor. The father, Cliff, had played catcher in semi-pro baseball and sometimes brother Russ and I would pitch to him out on the street after dinner. I remember having sliced the top of my middle finger of my right hand from a glass that shattered while I was drying it. As it was healing, the finger had to be held stiff, pitching to Mr. Brown. The only way I could hold the baseball resulted in my throwing knuckleballs which fluttered and wobbled all the way to the catcher's mitt. He seemed quite impressed. Even after the finger had healed completely, I continued to hold the ball with a stiff middle finger and throw the same slow, fluttery pitches. But I can't ever remember pitching and using it in a game. Mr. Brown got quite a kick out of Russ, who threw left-handed and was fast and quite accurate for his age.

Next to the Browns north of us was the Doty family: father, Orlando, with two sons, Jimmy and Bobby, whom we called "Big Doty" and "Little Doty" just as we were called "Big Schmidt" and "Little Schmidt." These were regular playmates along with two boys across the street: Clarence Hanna, who went to Brown University, and whose father taught English at Lakewood High School and was a Harvard graduate. Their next-door neighbors were the Coopers with a son, David, and a daughter whom we really didn't know at all. Their father was a doctor; and he was reputed to own a sailboat. I was dying to go for a sail and kept waiting for the doctor to take all the playmates out for a sail some Wednesday afternoon, but it never happened. I had to wait for many years after I was married and we went to the University of Michigan Family Camp at Lake Walloon, Michigan, for one week of our vacation where I learned to sail and couldn't be kept off the water.

We used to play Cops & Robbers and Cowboys & Indians using our cap guns loaded with the strip rolls of little percussion caps, choosing up sides, and hiding in the backyards of the houses across the street. For some reason we never used our backyards, probably because we had fences separating them. In the summertime, bedtime was a little later, probably 8:30 p.m. and we would gather to play tag or hide 'n seek under the streetlight in front of the Doty's house. Also, there was a small frame church built at the corner of Parkwood and Madison Avenue adjoining the Walzer's house and it was adventurous for us to go so far away (a half-block) to play around the church which had lots of shrubbery to hide in.

Sometimes kids, non-threatening types, from a little farther away would join us. One was a boy, Bud Chambers, who lived in an apartment, which was unusual for us, at the corner of Parkwood and Madison. He went to a Catholic grammar school nearby, St. Clement's, up through the 8th grade and we all felt very sorry for him because his education was so inferior to ours (none of us was Catholic, of course). He wasn't very smart, but very nice and fun to play with.

On our side of the street south of the Woolsey's were the Duffs who had 2 children, Janet, in my class and a younger brother, Roy, who was too young to play in our gang, whose birthday was two days later than mine on May 8th. My mother always encouraged me to "like" Janet, who was a very nice girl, which meant I automatically resisted even at that young age and never tried to have a date with her. I learned much later that she became an army nurse in World War II in England and stayed there after the War and married an Englishman.

9

One of the causes of feeling so socially inept was that my parents did not teach me - perhaps did not know how (I was their first child, after all) the social graces. I simply did not know what to do in many situations and it contributed to my feelings of inferiority. For instance, I had a terrible time saying a simple "Thank you." I knew I should; I felt the gratitude; but it was never spontaneous and never on time.

However, two girl classmates in high school did teach me two important lessons. At that time, I had the nasty (manly?) habit of expectorating when outdoors especially when chewing licorice, spewing out dark expectorate à la tobacco juice, otherwise plain saliva would do. Janet Duff, who also played the clarinet in the band, at one of our marching band practices on the football field after classes, was standing in formation next to me and I spat and she instantly said, "That's disgusting!" I was shocked to have this called to my attention; realized how true it was and how offensive it was to others and I don't think I ever did it again. Lesson learned.

The other occasion was in my senior year in high school when I took Carol Kuekes, the first girl I was seriously in love with, younger, two classes behind me, very smart, very pretty, extremely quiet voice that drove my parents crazy, on a dinner date at a very fine restaurant, Crosby's, at E. 105th St. at Carnegie Avenue on the east side. I can't recall why we would have gone so far away, or what the special occasion might have been - an anniversary of some sort?

But, while we were eating, at a table with white linen tablecloth and linen napkins and multiple silverware, in public, she pointed out that one was supposed to cut one's meat into small bitesize pieces, one at a time, before putting it into one's mouth. It was a very valuable lesson, never mentioned at home where our mother was trying to feed four voracious young mouths. I was very grateful for this lesson when I got to college and ate with the superbly trained prep-school boys.

Another curious thing involving the Duffs happened when I was much younger. I was outside wandering around one morning and happened to notice Mrs. Duff on her hands and knees planting some flowers in a bed next the foundation of their house and being about six years old and not knowing any better, offered to help her. She knew how little I could help, but wisely said yes. So, I did help, probably handing her the plants and when the job was done and I was back home for lunch, I innocently told my mother all about it. I was promptly scolded with some bitterness for having helped someone else and never thinking to help her at home. This was not true and was not fair and hurt. I loved to help my mother. But even at that early age what she said didn't jibe with what I had been taught at Sunday School. I think now that it may have been the very first tiny seed of doubt planted in my mind.

There were some other boys in the neighborhood I played with or walked to school with a little farther away at the bottom of the hill, a 2-3% grade, on Parkwood: Bob Corbett (a renter) and Clinton Heinbach, called "Heinie" naturally, who later went to the University of Michigan. On my trip freshman year with the Yale marching band to Ann Arbor for the Yale-Michigan football game, I kept my eyes open hoping to see him

On the other side of the street opposite our house were the McCarthy's, the Ross's, and the Walzer's, who lived in the last house next to Madison Avenue. The Walzer's had a son, Billy, who was older and stronger than me and every time our mothers arranged for us to play together, we ended up in a vicious fight, punching, and hair-pulling which I was good at. One time when our mothers had to pull us apart, I ended up with a tuft of his hair in my fist pulled from his scalp. I have no idea what started the fight but suspect it didn't take much to get us started. This ugly trait of losing my temper (I don't know how often it flared up) happened once when I was only five or six years old. We were at Grandma Schmidt's house on a Saturday afternoon. Russ and I were playing on the sidewalk in front of the doorway and I can't remember why, but I think it was the first time it happened and I wanted to hurt my brother so I picked up a toy garden hoe and raised it over my head to hit him with it and was lucky that Mother was there to grab the hoe out of my hand and cool me off. I shudder to think of what might have happened if she had not been there. I could have inflicted some serious damage.

Billy and I came to be friends after I realized that he had not been demoted two grades (whereas I had skipped one) because he was stupid, or inattentive in class. He was actually very smart, but hard of hearing, which the teachers did not pick up, or care about, and since his name started with "W" he was automatically assigned to sit in the last row in the classroom, where it was impossible for him to hear clearly. It must have been discovered about junior high-high school age, where having multiple teachers could overcome the stigma passed on from one teacher to the next of being "slow" in grammar school. It must have been awful for him.

His father owned a sheet metal company and I remember how impressed I was that this "dummy" could draw a pattern on a piece of paper and trace it on a flat piece of galvanized metal and cut it with tin snip scissors, roll it into a pipe shape and repeat the process for a larger pipe, and the two pipes would fit together perfectly, and at an angle other than 90 degrees! I thought it was amazing and never tired of his doing it for me.

Bill had two sisters, Billy and Bobby, and the family had a summer cottage at a place called Cardinal Lake, far east of Cleveland. They took me with them for a day trip once, but the whole trip is very hazy in my memory.

The Ross family across the street had a son older than me, Dick, and two sisters who were college age. He was a "tough" kid and we were glad he was around with us when "our" street was invaded by kids from the south side of Madison Avenue, a classic example of tribal territorialism: lots of bluster and then the withdrawal. The invaders were probably on their way to Detroit Street and had no idea the effect they were having on us.

The one memory of the Ross family implanted forever in my memory is the day I went over to ask Dick to come out and play, and his two sisters were there, much older, and very glamorous in my young eyes. They were grousing because their mother wanted them to bake a cake. Seizing the opportunity to impress not just one, but two, "older women," I volunteered to bake my mother's favorite sponge cake for them. I had done it so many times at home for our weekend desserts that I had the recipe memorized and convinced the girls that I could do it for them; all they had to do was get the ingredients together. All went well and they handed me the final ingredient, one cup of hot water which went into the mix, and then into the oven. I don't recall how we passed the 45 minutes it took to bake, but finally it was time to take the cake out of the oven and it was a disaster. It had not risen. It looked like a 2" thick donut. I had misremembered and used a whole cup of water instead of the proper half cup. I don't know what the sisters did, but I was in a state of total ignominy, and am sure I never set foot in that house again.

Closer to us across the street and with whom we spent much more time were the McCarthy's: Joey and his older brother, John, who was going to Western Reserve University and studying law. John was a big influence on me. He was highly intelligent, only about 5' 6" tall and probably weighed 125 lbs. He claimed that he was the free-throw basketball champ of the whole university. He was the first good golfer, all the more remarkable for his size, that I ever played with. He and his father would go to the "Big Met" course in the Metropolitan Park system in Rocky River after work and if his score was over 65 for the round of 18 holes (unbelievable for me) he would be very unhappy. I only got to play with him once or twice and he taught me a great deal. In those days they always had a bucket of damp sand on the tees, and you could take a pinch of it to make a little pyramid and use it instead of a wooden tee. It was still the Great Depression and you could save some money in that way. I think it was called a "Scotch" tee.

He was the one, possibly because of his stature, who was always seeking a "system" to beat the system, solve any problem, and he was obsessed with efficiency. I observed these traits in him and tried to emulate him. He was a rare, older person who spent any time or took any notice of me. His example has stayed with me to this day. He was the lead navigator in a Flying Fortress or B-17 in one of the mass aerial bombings of Hamburg in World War II and was killed in the raid. I miss him.

Joey, the younger brother, was a fine athlete and larger than John. He really excelled in our touch football games on the street. He had a very easy-going disposition. Strangely, I do not know where he went to high school, one of the Catholic ones, I suppose, and maybe he followed his brother to Western Reserve University. World War II intervened and I lost track of him completely, to my regret.

We (John may have been involved) invented a form of a baseball game which we played in their backyard. There were two-man teams, a catcher and a pitcher, who threw a plastic ping pong ball from about 20 feet to the batter who used a miniature Hillerich & Bradley baseball bat. If he hit the ball as far as the pitcher, it was a single; if he hit it past the pitcher, it was a double; and if he hit it over the backyard fence, it was a homerun. With that skinny 15" bat it was hard to hit even a straight pitch, but it was amazing the spin and curves you could put on the pitch making it almost impossible to hit. So, there were many, many strikeouts. We used to spend hours playing this simple game. I have a theory that I damaged my right arm by throwing such a light object with the same force as a real hardball. I know I could never throw a regular hardball the same ever after that. But it was a challenge and fun, especially if you hit it over the fence.

There were two other boys my age down at the end of Parkwood, close to Franklin Boulevard: Jack Gardiner, who was almost as tall as I was, and who really impressed me by working as an undertaker's assistant after school hours  He never came up the street to play with us. And there was Dick Kelly, a chubby, indifferent student who had moved to Lakewood from Columbus, so he had a bit of an accent. I will never forget the sight of him walking (bouncing?) down Parkwood on his way home singing his signature theme song, "I'm Forever Blowing Bubbles." He never came all the way up to our part of the street to play with us, either. We later became reacquainted when we both ended up living in Parma Height, Ohio, after we were married and belonging to the same bridge club. I learned then that he and Jim Fisher, the grammar school artist, had married sisters. His first job was as a courier for Goodrich Chemical going back and forth between their plants in Brecksville and Avon Lake. His father dropped dead while shaving and, in spite of this and other adversities, including a "C" average in high school he went on to obtain a law degree and ended up with a fine job with Wyandotte Chemical in Michigan.

There was also a group of three or four older boys, probably four-five years older than me, clustered on Parkwood close to Franklin Boulevard. I only remember two names, Don Pagel, a superb clarinetist in the Band who had a badly chipped front tooth which caused him to hold the clarinet mouthpiece at an odd angle when playing, and  Charley Dickinson, and Charley only because I met him doing a menial job handling customer inquiries and complaints for the East Ohio Gas Company which occupied the 1st floor of the building bearing its name where we had our offices on the 14th floor. I learned his name from his nameplate sitting on his desk. What little I knew of him I didn't think he was very smart; he may have been underqualified for the job he held.

Another nameless (could it have been Faud?) boy on the other side of the street close to Franklin Boulevard saw me walking down Parkwood one rainy afternoon and invited me in to watch a chemistry experiment he was working on in his basement. I really didn't know him at all and shouldn't have accepted, but since chemistry was one of my favorite subjects, I agreed. This turned out to be a big mistake because he did something with a test tube and held it up to my nose, told me to take a deep whiff and tell him what I smelled. When I did, I discovered that it was chlorine gas; I got a good lungful and was in big trouble. I don't remember how I got home, but I learned a valuable lesson that day: never go down into a stranger's basement unless you are wearing a gas mask.

Three other Parkwood memories: there was an older boy living in the Duff house after it was sold who had a paper route delivering the *West Side Shopping News* to every house on three or four streets running between Madison Avenue and Detroit Streets. I think his last name was Jones and he asked me to take his route for him while he was away with his parents on vacation. Delivery was only once a week on Thursdays, I believe. I'm sure I got paid but can't remember how much, and it was an easy job in that delivery was to every house, so I didn't have to be careful to find a specific address. I had to start at 6 a.m. and remember how nice it was to be outdoors in the cool, crisp morning air, and it was so quiet and to see the sun rise. It's too bad that later the Army spoiled that euphoria for me.

Directly across the street from us was Mr. Norman, an older gentleman. He hired me to water his lawn while he was away on vacation. I used to go across the street and uncoil the rubber hose and stand there sprinkling away and get paid for it.

The third family, who had no children, were the Frank Selzer's who lived down the "hill" from my playmate, David Cooper. Mr. Selzer was famous to me, although I never met him, because he was the brother of Louis B. Selzer, the Editor of *The Cleveland Press.* At that time there were three daily papers in Cleveland, *The Plain Dealer* in the morning, and *The Cleveland Press* and *The Cleveland News*, with evening editions. My father always brought home the Press which I liked for its comic strips and cross word puzzles. I don't know why my father preferred the Press. Perhaps it was because he grew up in the same neighborhood as Louis Selzer, Bailey Avenue off W. 41st Street, on the near west side of Cleveland. I think they may have said hello in passing in later years.

One highly improbable incident which I remember vividly occurred one morning during summertime when Jimmy (Big) Doty urinated on me from the grass terrace in front of his house at the sidewalk. He was a year younger than me and I had probably done something to provoke him. I flew into an uncontrollable rage at this ultimate insult and chased him into the street, found a heavy paving brick and heaved it at his head. It just missed him and ended up on the front porch of the Durhammer's house across the street. When I realized what I had done, and what could have happened, I was terrified. I think it cured me of my violent streak. I think I began to realize the risk that came with my large size and then and there determined to always be gentle in the days ahead. And, I think I have succeeded. I don't remember ever losing my temper at another person to this day.

After things cooled off and especially after Mrs. Doty died and the sons no longer had a mother, we played a lot with them in our group. I learned later that Jimmy had a "calling" and while very young approached a Methodist Bishop, who was visiting their church, after the service and proudly announced much to his parents' embarrassment that he wanted to be a minister when he grew up. I think he avoided going into the Army because of his calling. I have no idea where he went to school after graduating from Lakewood High School, where he was a very average student. I do know that the younger brother, Bobby, ended up in the Army in charge of a laundry in New Guinea. It didn't seem very fair to me. On the other hand, my brother, Russ, ended up in the Army in the European Theater very much in harm's way while I spent my Army career after Basic Training attending college while learning Japanese in the Military Intelligence Service.

One final Doty memory: Jim did become a Methodist Bishop of Texas, which I find amazing. But then I may be just a wee bit prejudiced. He visited his old church at Summit and Detroit in Lakewood, where I had my first organ lessons, while on a visit to Lakewood in his 70s. It was announced in the papers and Russ and I went to hear him talk about his experiences as a missionary in Africa earlier in his career. We stayed after the service and chatted briefly with him. I'm not sure he even remembered us, or if he wanted to. But he was charming!

Other outdoor sporting activity included kicking the football to each other when there was only one other boy to play with, or playing catch, or going long; when there was a group, touch football with three or four man teams chosen up, where touching the man with the football was the equivalent of a tackle in real football and the end of the play. I don't remember what we used for goals, probably driveways five or six houses apart, but the curbs were the side-line out-of-bounds and beware: Do Not set a foot on Katie Moore's (one of my English teachers) tree lawn. She might call the police.

I remember a newcomer to Parkwood who moved in from Canton, Ohio, down the hill, a short distance which qualified him to become a member on our group, joining us in touch football. I can't remember his name, but he was slender and very fast. He seemed to be able to run through the line without ever getting touched. Very elusive. I learned about the Canton McKinley-Massillon, historic rivalry of these two top high school football teams in the State perennially, from knowing him and this was how I became aware of Coach Paul Brown, the Massillon coach, later of Ohio State and the Cleveland Browns.

We also played hockey on roller skates occasionally. I don't remember much about this, but we did use real hockey sticks and pucks. Roller skates are not hockey ice skates; our game was clumsier; slower and not as much fun so it was harder to get a group organized. We also played marbles when we were younger. We all had bags of varicolored glass marbles and would throw a number of them into a circle drawn on the ground. The goal would be to put in ones we didn't care about or didn't like the size or color, and then take turns shooting, using our thumbs and knuckles, using our favorite shooter to try to knock a marble out of the circle. When that happened, the marble was ours to add to our collection. I don't recall being very skillful but spent a lot of time trying to add to my collection.

When I was younger, still in grammar school, on Saturdays, Russ and I used to put on three or four old sweaters, alternating them frontwards and backwards to simulate real football players' padding. We'd then go over to the football field at the high school on the next street to Parkwood after the Saturday afternoon football game ended, staying close to the street and throw our scruffy football back and forth, hoping someone would notice us. We weren't old enough to go to the game, but liked trying to attract attention.

High school football was played on Saturday afternoons in those days: today's system of reserving Friday nights for high school games under the lights; Saturday afternoons for college games; and Sunday afternoons for the pros came later with the advent of TV which had not yet been invented. The revenues from TV broadcasts have made football a major industry and the networks compete for the right to broadcast a game and have come to dominate the scheduling as the game has become an important source of family entertainment.

From the 8th grade on, I was a part of the "show," marching in the band at half-time at the games. I think we marched at the away games, also, but the school didn't provide transportation, so the parents had to drive us to the games. The Lake Erie League included Cleveland Heights, Shaw and Shaker Heights High Schools on the eastside, and Lorain and Elyria High Schools in Lorain County on the westside. I only remember one trip to a Shaker Heights game when my father drove and Uncle Charlie brought Charles, who was in the class ahead of me, to our house and he had to disassemble his sousaphone to get it into our car and stow it in the corner of the back seat. Then Russ and I and Charles piled in and Dad got behind the wheel and away we went. It was a long trip to the east side, and although I am sure we also went to Shaw and Cleveland Heights, I don't remember any details - where the football fields were located, and certainly not the outcomes of the games. I imagine the marching formations were fairly primitive and have no idea of who devised them. The big climax of the performance was always the drum major throwing his baton over the goal post and what a triumph when he caught it on the way down.

The only drum major I remember was J. Maurice (Maury) Struchen, who played clarinet in the concert band, who strutted well, wearing a tall Shako hat and caught the baton well. He was a quiet individual and having known him later in the business world where he became CEO of one of the major banks in Cleveland, would have seemed to be an unlikely candidate to be a drum major. On the other hand, knowing him as well I did, I can't imagine him taking tap dancing lessons at the insistence of his mother, either. His family was Swiss and like me, but for different reasons I am sure, he neither drank, nor smoked. And he was probably the only CEO of a major corporation in Cleveland who, remaining loyal to his west side origins, lived on the west side of Cleveland all his life, and when we knew him later socially, in a modest home in Rocky River overlooking the Metropolitan Park.

One of the fun things we did once a year was for eight or ten of us to dress up in the original, old-fashioned band uniforms and put on a show between the light weight and varsity team games. We marched out of step and made turns with one of us going off in the wrong direction. Sometimes two of us. While these shenanigans were going on, we were playing an old "oompa" marching tune, "The Jolly Coppersmith." We thought this clowning was hilarious, and I guess some of the football fans who had not gone to the concession stand for coffee, agreed because there was usually loud applause. We did not have a drum major to lead us, either!

Several of us in the clarinet section also brought our ocarinas, called "Sweet Potatoes" because that is what they looked like, to the games. They were very primitive, made of baked clay, and sounded a little like a second-rate flute. I don't know if there is even such a thing today. We fooled around with them during the game and it was all a part of trying to call attention to ourselves in the growing up process.

The concert band and orchestra were more serious and met every day, one after the other, in the auditorium after regular classes were over for practice and preparation for the annual Spring Concerts. Playing in either, or both, earned extra credits which counted on one's scholastic record for as much as an hour of English, or chemistry, so I accumulated far more than the minimum requirements to graduate, or to meet the minimums for college. The conductor was the Music Director for the whole school system, Arthur Jewel, who was not very tall, and not a particularly good musician in our opinions; but he had a remarkably talented group of players in all the first chair positions: clarinet (several), flute, oboe, bassoon, trumpet, French horn, baritone horn. One of the trumpet players, Homer Baumgardner, while visiting Washington D.C. while still in high school, was invited to play with the U.S. Marine Band, considered the finest concert band in the world, at a concert in the White House. We were really impressed. He was really outstanding.

I think my parents came to the concerts which added to my fear of making a squawk or a squeak. But, I do not recall failing to perform well, and it had to be a very beneficial experience and provided me a chance to excel in a group, in public, at a very difficult period of my life while I was struggling to overcome my teenage insecurity and shyness.

We had some very good teachers at Lakewood High School. I remember my college algebra class where Miss Cilda Smith came in early before the school day started to what she called her "Dawn Patrol" to tutor and give special help to those having difficulties understanding the material, voluntary on both parts; Miss Katie Moore in English who taught public speaking and coached the Debate Team. I had her for Short Story writing in my postgraduate semester; both Mr. Waters and Mr. Boruff who aroused my interest in chemistry. I actually read a book on Organic Chemistry outside of class.

And then, there was Miss Bessie Brown, my 11th grade English teacher, who asked me to stay after class one day when we had "book reports. I was always well behaved in class and she was concerned about me because I wasn't paying attention in class and asked if something was wrong or troubling me. I told her there wasn't anything wrong. It was just that I was bored; that I had never heard a book report on a book that I had not already read. She was stunned. The next book report day a month later she appointed me "teacher" to call on the classmate to give his report which I was empowered to grade - which did nothing for my popularity. Of course, I knew whether the book had been read. She then left the room to go to the teachers' lounge where she could relax and probably smoke her cigarette. I recall feeling a sense of power which I had never felt before. It was certainly a neat solution for my boredom and her need to get away from it all.

One nice thing that happened in high school due to my interest in an Ivy League school was that our principal, Mr. Mitchell, arranged for free tickets each year for performances of the Princeton Triangle Club, the Penn Mask and Wig club, and the Yale Glee Club (never any group from Harvard) when they toured the Midwest and came to Cleveland during the Christmas season to put on their annual shows, all written by students. I had never heard of these organizations, except the Yale Glee Club. My impression is that these shows were usually musicals with singing and dancing and since the schools were all male, any female parts were played by men, which was pretty funny.

I wish I had been able to see the Princeton production of *East of the Sun and West of the Moon* which had a wonderful theme song of the same name. The song became a jazz standard and one of my favorites. I was exposed to the fairy tale from which the title came when only five or six years old and read it in one of a set of children's books we had for beginning readers. It made a big impression on me to the extent that I drew the Japanese characters for "East of the Sun" on the account book where I recorded all the expenses which went into building our house in Brecksville, and actually wanted to put a sign down by the road the way the English do with their country homes. I felt it was our theme song since the first words of the song are, "I'll build a dream house of love for you, dear." Fran vetoed the idea. Probably just as well.

I wish I had seen Jimmy Stewart's performance in the Princeton Triangle Club in whatever they did his year, but he was seven or eight years ahead of me. I was privileged to be able to attend these performances, usually held in the small concert hall of the Cleveland Public Auditorium and hosted by the local college club who I am sure provided housing for the visiting performers. The whole scene added to the mystique of the eastern schools in my mind and made the dream of going to Yale, all the more challenging and desirable.

Athletically, my high school experience was a downer and very limited since my mother forbade any of the contact sports, especially football, and since I truly loved the water and Lakewood had a swimming pool and a swim team, logically, that became my choice. Lakewood had a good team and a good coach, Russ Linden (who was reputed to be a good bridge player) and I was accepted on the team. My problem was that I had a severe, chronic case of athlete's foot which never cleared up enough to allow me to use the locker room, let alone enter the water where I could learn how to really swim. So, I ended up becoming the team secretary sitting on the side of the pool, fully clothed, in the spectator's section, keeping records for Coach Linden. I do not even remember attending a swimming meet. All in all, it couldn't have been a poorer preparation for my later career as a swimmer at Yale with its fabulous 1942 swim team.

A final word about the Lakewood school system. I think the school board was exceptional. Two of the members had children in my class: Elaine MacDonald and Brice Bowman, which was interesting. They were treated with a certain amount of deference. But the interesting thing to me was the policies they established: the post-graduate courses I took advantage of, for instance. And allowing non-resident students to pay tuition to attend classes and to receive a graduation diploma, which benefitted my younger brothers after we moved to Brooklyn (I was in college when this occurred) and our parents arranged for them to finish their high school education in the then academically superior Lakewood system. The board also had an arrangement with the City of Lakewood Recreation Department where they allowed school grounds to be used for a summer camp-like program in the afternoons overseen by college student instructors who supervised groups of children, where their mothers could leave them in safety. And then, there were the high standards for hiring teachers which resulted in a very effective faculty, evidenced by the high rate of graduation and the number of scholarships earned at the prestigious eastern schools year after year.

I was always grateful that I was in the smaller January graduating class, as it turned out, because it meant if I enrolled in the post-graduate program, I could round out my education by taking some other earlier electives: Music Theory instead of the 2nd semester of Cicero in Latin, for instance, planning to finish the Cicero in the post-graduate phase. Actually, I had to take the second half year studying Virgil's *Aeneid* instead, which broadened my knowledge. Also, I was able to take a course in short story writing. But the most important, practical courses I took were short hand (to better enable me to take notes in college which turned out not to be useful) and typing which was invaluable and was probably the most useful thing I ever learned in school. I especially liked skipping home room and going directly to class, concentrating on five courses consecutively; no wasted time in study hall and then walking home for lunch and an afternoon free to study or practice the piano. It all felt very adult, mature. I loved school and learning, satisfying my insatiable curiosity. It was one of the happiest periods of my life and I owe a great deal to my parents who encouraged me to follow this path, rather than requiring me to get a short-term job through the summer before going off to college.

From the 8th grade on, there was never any question that I was planning and preparing to go to college, a much rarer event than today. My parents were determined that I should experience what they were denied - and so should my brothers. Thanks to our back-yard neighbor, John Mitchell, the Principal of Lakewood High, I was exposed to the Ivy League, especially Yale, from the 10th grade on, but going there was totally dependent on receiving a scholarship. Realistically, I was prepared to go to Western Reserve University and living at home. I remember being visited in our home one afternoon with my mother present by a representative of Wooster College and being assured, based on my high school record, of financial aid. But I was not interested. We never did investigate Hiram, or Denison, or Ohio Wesleyan, or Kenyon, all very fine private schools in Ohio with excellent reputations, or Ohio University where my Holden cousins attended.

The dream of Yale started with my mother who favored it after hearing a summer replacement radio program on Great American Universities. It became my dream, too, and evolved in an all-my-eggs-in-one basket situation when I failed to remember to go to Western Reserve University to be interviewed and tested one afternoon in February. I felt sick when I realized what I had done. Another example of intelligence doing something stupid for which I was being constantly ridiculed and berated. Of course, it all ended well when Yale did offer the four years full tuition scholarship which I gratefully accepted. I felt I had finally done something to please and impress my parents, to make them proud of me and that it was in some small way a payback for all the sacrifices they had made for me and all they had done for me.

It was always my dream, and would have been the ultimate gift, to have been able to present my mother with a Phi Beta Kappa key or pin to wear as a necklace four years later, but it was not to be. I was at the cut off mark, missing being accepted by one "A."

Another important influence on my life, again thanks to my parents' wisdom, was spending summers at our summer "cottage" on Tiedeman Road in Brooklyn, Ohio, where my Grandma Schmidt grew up and where two of her brothers and a sister still lived.

It was a part of our early childhood with many visits to see the relatives, or for them to care for us while our parents had other places to be. We loved it because there were barns with hay lofts to jump in and play in, and horses and cows and mules to become acquainted with and berries to pick and a creek to wade in and minnows to catch. A different world from Parkwood Road in

Lakewood. Our mother would drop us off at Uncle Louis's or Uncle Irving's to look after us when she had shopping or errands to do.

One exception was her visits to our dentist, Alvarez Nugent, who had his offices in the Central National Bank Building at W. 25th Street and Lorain Road, across the street from the West Side Market. He was very kind and let Russ and me stay with Mother, one on each side of the dentist's chair, holding her hands, while he drilled away at her teeth. It was a great way to teach us not to fear dentistry. Dr. Nugent took care of my teeth until he retired after I was married.

Two things I remember about those days: I was probably five or six years old and was being cared for by Uncle Louis and Aunt Edie, wading in Big Creek over the hill from their house in a one piece white BVD underwear garment, which in that muddy water did not stay white long, and I don't think Mother was ever able to get it really white again. And, on another occasion while being left with Uncle Irving and Aunt Louisa, having a lunch of bean soup with big chunks of pork in it. It was the most delicious soup I have ever tasted. And then to cap it off, being put down for a nap in the 2nd floor bedroom of my three older cousins, Ellsworth, Delbert and Elisha. I can still remember my amazement at the bedsheet which was a Holstein cow hide with the black and white hair still on it. Of course it was a different world for us and very exciting, not only there being big, live animals, but water to drink from a well under the kitchen sink and no toilets in the house, but outdoor privies with Sears catalogs nailed to the wall instead of toilet paper. It was always an adventure and we loved going out to the country.

As I recall, in my 13th summer I went for two weeks to a YMCA camp in Centerville, Ohio, on the far east side on Route 306, and Russ spent two weeks on Uncle Louis' farm where he thought he was having fun doing chores, and learned how to milk a cow. It must have been some sight, him eleven-years-old sitting on a stool, head pressed against the cow's side and pulling away while he squirted the warm milk into a pail. I'm glad I didn't have to drink it.

Sometime during that year my parents must have decided to follow the example of my mother's two older sisters, both of whom had summer places: the Geigers, a cottage at Linwood Park in Vermilion, Ohio, on Lake Erie, with a large beach, and we used to make the long trip from Lakewood two or three times a summer to visit and go swimming and play tennis on the court in their backyard, and softball; and Uncle Herb and Aunt Esther Basil, who lived on W. 134th Street off Lorain Street in Cleveland who had bought a lot on S. Riverside Drive in Berea, Ohio, where Uncle Herb had built an oversized two car garage with a second floor. He used screws instead of nails so he could disassemble it later when he built their brick, permanent home.

My parent's response to these examples, having four boys, was to buy an acre of land from Paul Tiedeman on Tiedeman Road in Brooklyn, Ohio, on the south boundary of his land. It was 50' x 800' and the rear lot line was Big Creek, a tributary of the Cuyahoga River, and was reached by going over the hill via a path. It was probably about 30 feet lower than the street level. A year or two later Dad bought another acre 50' x 800' adjacent. There was no water or gas on Tiedeman Road at that time, so things were very primitive. Uncle Louie Iahn, Grandma Schmidt's older brother, who lived down the road on the family farm homestead, was called on to dig a well for us. It was 12' deep and about 3' in diameter and he lined it with brick. He dug through a strata of blue clay; which he said was very favorable for a well. The dirt he dug up he piled in a crescent shape nearby which my mother turned into a rock garden.

Dad had a business customer named Hymie Epstein build an oversized two car garage, probably 20' x 24' divided into four rooms, with an 8' screened porch opening to the front two rooms with swinging garage doors (it was before the time of the overhead doors of today). Facing the cottage, the front two rooms were the kitchen where we ate, and the living room. Behind these rooms were two bedrooms, one for Mom and Dad, and the other with two bunk beds for the four boys. There was a small closet between the boys' room and the kitchen. You will note that I have not mentioned a bathroom. This function was handled by a two-seat privy located across the cinder driveway in a builder's shed left behind by Mr. Epstein. It was miserable to walk barefoot over the cinder driveway in the middle of the night if the need arose. It was all very simple and primitive, and we learned to live very close to nature. The cottage sat about 150' off the road and was reached over a cinder driveway. There were flower borders along both the lot line and the driveway and a large lawn by city standards which needed cutting and weeding. There were no chemical weed killers then.

I never heard any discussion about doing this, or when the negotiations with Mr. Tiedeman took place, or what my father paid for the land. Today I speculate that he probably bought the land for $100-$200 per acre, and that the cottage may have cost $800 to $1,000 to build. So, for a total less than $1,200, my parents provided (I can't imagine where the money came from - this was 1935, with the Great Depression in full bloom) - for a place to escape the city heat and provide a healthy environment close to nature for their four growing sons out in the country, four miles from downtown Cleveland, the 5th largest city in the U.S.A. at the time, where there were still farms and livestock.

The first two or three years were very primitive. I don't know how my mother coped. She had to use a two-burner coal-oil stove for cooking, had to carry in water pumped from a well for drinking, cooking and laundry. I remember well how lucky I was to be the oldest child when Saturday night came, and two buckets of water heated on the stove were poured into a large galvanized-washtub on the kitchen floor mixed with some cold water. I got to use the fresh water first because I was the oldest.

By the time the "little boys," as I always called them in my mind, had their turn, after a week of outdoor play and working in the garden, if we had been in Lakewood in a real tub, there would have been a real ring left on the porcelain.

A fence separated us from a small farm and orchard owned by Frank Holden, Uncle Irving's younger brother. "Uncle" Frank was very nice, but Mother did not care for his wife, Jesse, whom she felt was nosy, always spying on us from her back door (about 300' away!)

From the rear of our cottage to the top of the hill was all devoted to growing vegetables, and with the addition of the second acre, was probably 3/4 of an acre in size. Here we raised every kind of vegetable imaginable, including eggplant, sweet potatoes, pumpkin, salsify, fennel, watermelon and muskmelon, plus the more usual corn, beans, squash and Irish potatoes. This garden required a lot of attention but supplied us with an amount of produce that lasted until the next planting season and was a big help with the food budget as well as providing freshly picked vegetables for our summer table. We also had red raspberries along the fence, and a large strawberry patch. I wasn't too much help in picking the berries because of my red-green colorblindness and my mother always arranged to pick after me to find the berries I missed.

It was also a source of money for Russ and me. We built a produce stand next to the driveway out by the road and many people would stop on the way home from work. We would run down to the garden and pick Golden Bantam sweet corn, which was the sweetest variety available then, but which lost a large percentage of its sweetness within 30 minutes of picking so our customers appreciated the picking to order, not something that had been out in the sun all afternoon. I think we developed quite a reputation, and Mother always insisted that we give 13 ears for our version of a dozen. One year we sold $300 worth of produce. I can't imagine what the equivalent would be today. We used the money to repay Dad for the Sears garden tractor we had bought to do the plowing and cultivating.

We started going out to "the country," after the school day ended to open the cottage up to air it out the beginning of May, to get the land ready for planting, and to tend to the plantings along the borders. Earlier I had been poring through all the seed catalogs I had sent away for which I loved to do. There were so many possibilities and so many new things to try. Thinking back on it, I have the impression that my mother allowed, maybe even encouraged me, to do this. I know I loved doing it. And it was a big responsibility to pick the right things. A lot depended on it.

So, after making the move to Tiedeman for the summer, the pattern of the days evolved; up at 8 a.m. to see Dad off to work, eat breakfast, do chores, weed the garden or the flower beds, or cut the lawn, usually on Friday or Saturday in preparation for the family or friends who were sure to drop in. It seemed as though we had company every Sunday after church, so the lawn had to be just so. We pushed a reel type lawn mower - all there was in those days - and cut in both directions: up and down and cross ways. It really looked nice when we finished. Then we would rake the cinder driveway. Then lunch. Then maybe a nap.

I wrote a piece for my Daily Theme course in college which was printed in the annual collection of each student's favorite piece he wrote for the whole year. Mine describes one of those afternoon naps. I think it captures a little of the magic (for me) of the whole summer experience. Here it is:

> *It's so easy to lie here on the hammock in the coolness.... Work is done, lunch is done and all there is left to do is sleep. Outside in the sun just a few feet from here on the porch it's hot. If I roll my head over I'll see the heat waves rising off the*

*driveway. And the ground looking so yellow and hard. Everything is brittle in the sunlight today. Out there the breeze is hot and withering. The leaves of the gladioli are drooping and the petals of the petunias in the border are almost closed. But in here it's cool — and the breeze makes music through the screens. When Kenny moves on the glider it makes a music, too, but that music belongs outside because it keeps me awake. The telephone wires out on the road are humming along with the screens, too. It's a trio. Strange how when I was Kenny's age, I hated to take a nap. This afternoon it's very pleasant lying here, waiting to fall asleep. Anyone should want to lie in the coolness and fall asleep. I'm glad King hasn't put his nose in my face yet. He's probably wise and sleeping, too. The kettle of water on the stove throws its queer reflection on the ceiling. It's like a moving mirror. It shimmers and moves palely. The hammock is swaying, too - and the music is ever-changing - but I'm not moving. I'm waiting for my eyes to get heavy and close. The screens don't obstruct the view much - except when I focus my eyes on them and then it only makes the outside darker. I can still see everything—but it's as though a shade were pulled down. Wind on bare legs is pleasant and so is this swaying, tilting hammock moved by the breeze. It's so easy just to lie here....*

I want to pause here for a moment in this plotless narrative to correct a possible misinterpretation of what has gone before. When I started on this section about our summers in the country, I realized that I had mentioned several times earlier how unhappy I felt at home (not at school), how insecure and inadequate, how impossibly shy and how fearful of doing something wrong which would elicit ridicule and/or sarcasm from my father, or incessant, unhampered teasing from my younger brother. Trying to recall all the wonderful things about spending my summers in the country made me realize what a golden period this was - and how basically happy I was.

Suddenly, at this late age, through the cathartic effect of putting my memories on paper, I realized that the above negatives are a common experience for many, if not all, young boys entering their passage to manhood; that the teasing and criticism were not 24/7, and might just possibly have been triggered by some behavior on my part. And in reality, that period of my childhood was on balance a very happy positive one, albeit much of it spent in another world of music and reading, my form of defense mechanism.

To say that I am grateful for this insight would be putting it mildly and is one more reason to thank my daughter, Barbara, for inspiring me to make this effort to tell the long story of all these years.

To resume: other days we used to walk down Tiedeman Road to play baseball with our "country" playmates who were quite different from our "city" friends, a little older, much shorter acquaintance, but good buddies, nevertheless. We played on a large, vacant lot at the corner of Tiedeman and Manoa, the street where Uncle Irving lived and had his small barn where he stabled his mules. I only remember three or four of the boys (no girls): the Clough brothers, Russ and Bob;

"Soupy" Sobczyk; and Rudy Kamm from the other side of Tiedeman, who was Finnish and had an incredibly smooth, unblemished, pink complexion, almost like a piece of wax artificial fruit. There had to be more players in the group, but my memory fails me as to how many, let alone their names.

Thursdays we didn't play. That was the afternoon the Cleveland Public Library Bookmobile, which was a large bus-like vehicle with shelves of books on both sides of the aisle, came and parked on our baseball diamond. We were allowed to take out 3 books per person and I always took out the full allotment - it didn't matter what the subject of the book was. It was something to read. Frequently, brother Russ would only take out one book and he would let me pick out the other two books of his allotment for me to read. I would then have five books due the next Thursday. Usually I had all five books read by the end of the weekend. I was always a voracious reader and read quickly. When that source was exhausted there were magazines to read and crossword puzzles to do. We subscribed to *Better Homes & Garden, Life, Look, Time, Redbook, Country Gentleman, Organic Gardening*, and *National Geographic*. One year someone gave us a large carton of back issues of *Liberty Magazine* which came in a smaller format but was only 5 cents per issue. I went through them all, cover to cover. I suppose I had the time because there were no music lessons; and I didn't have to practice. No homework, either.

However, I was playing the piano for Sunday School and was able to practice on pianos at Uncle Louis's and "Uncle" Frank's. Uncle Louie's son, Harold, had a nice, untrained baritone voice and it was fun to accompany him. Also, "Uncle" Frank and "Aunt" Jesse had an only daughter, Mary Ellen, who was a few years older than me, very pretty and very nice, who was a whistler, which just amazed me. She could have given a concert. Occasionally I would walk across the field to their house, and having asked permission, of course, practice for Sunday School. Sometimes, Mary Ellen would sit on the piano bench to watch me practice. Her ever vigilant, over-protective mother would satisfy herself that I was behaving myself, nothing to worry about as long as she could hear the piano playing. What she didn't know was that I was still working on the left-hand alone piece I later played for the Assembly at Lakewood High School, and, thus, could have had my right arm around Mary Ellen. If I had dared! "Aunt" Jesse could hear the music from the other room and relax. But I can assure you there was never the slightest hanky-panky. Just a wink of satisfaction on both our parts at putting something over on her mother. We knew what was going on

The summer of my senior year at Lakewood High School Uncle Louie's son, Harold, got married and they asked me to play the organ for the ceremony. I had only begun to learn the rudiments of playing the organ, had no repertory of pieces I had learned, and wasn't able to get any special help from my teacher since it was summertime and no lessons. And I can't remember what my mother thought of the idea or if she encouraged me. But I agreed to do it. It was a new experience.

It was not just attending a wedding, but being on the inside of the main event, and I remember the small church on Bosworth Road off of W. 117th Street (our usual route from Lakewood to

Tiedeman Road) and playing *Kamennoi-Ostrow* by Rimsky Korsakov, a wildly inappropriate piece for a wedding. I do not remember playing the "Wedding March" and if I did, if I had as much trouble getting through it as I did many years later when I played for weddings at my wife's church. I do remember the Rehearsal Dinner, not where it was held, or what we had to eat, but sitting next to the Maid of Honor, a much older woman (23-24 years old?) and how exciting it was for me to be a part of a group of adults and accepted as one.

A few of the things I remember about Uncle Louie's house were the gas mantle over the dining room table which burned 24 hours a day (where was the gas well?) provided bright light in the evening and burned natural gas and the pump on the drain board of the kitchen sink, which was made of wood. Aunt Edie seemed very quiet to me. Her son, Harold, had two sisters, Ruth, who was too old for us to play with, and Evie, who was closer to our age and a tomboy. She loved to ride and had her own riding horse. Sometimes we would walk down after dinner and go for a ride with her, she on her horse (I'm sure it had a name but I don't remember it), and Russ and I on Uncle Louie's two plough horses, riding bareback. On one of these expeditions we went riding on a trail on the other side of the creek, and I turned to say something to Russ and the horse walked under a low lying tree limb and left me suspended by my arms on the limb while he continued to amble on. I don't remember but assume when I was clear of the horse's rear end that I dropped to the ground safely. Another time when we returned to the barn after a ride and the horses were tired and hungry, as we entered the barn, the horse was too close to the door and I was brushed off its back. Luckily, again I escaped unhurt. I always thought these experiences explained my distaste for horses and their intelligence and may have accounted for a predisposition to appreciate mules which came to full flower in my Basic Training in the Mule Pack Artillery in the Army in World War II.

It's interesting to me that Uncle Louie's occupation, technically, was "House Mover." He would somehow or other dig under a house, lift it on huge wooden beams with jacks, then dig a basement and reset the house on the new foundation. Sometimes he moved the whole house on the timbers to a different location. This was all done using his team of plough horses. I wonder how much demand there was for his services. Thinking of how it's done today with bull dozers, it's fascinating that he also dug basements for houses to be built. He did this with a team of horses pulling a large scoop with handles which he used to remove thin layers of dirt until he reached the required depth. As a matter of fact, I have a vague memory of watching him dig the basement for the Woolsey house next door on Parkwood Road. I was probably four or five-years-old at the time. He worked from the street towards the rear of the lot, where the dirt he removed was piled. He must have driven the team of horses and wagon with his equipment all the way from Tiedeman Road in Brooklyn to Lakewood, a distance of five or six miles, which would have taken a lot of time. And I now wonder if my father recommended Uncle Louie to the builder, or Mr. Woolsey.

On the other side of the creek at Uncle Louie's, and I am sure our mother never saw it or she would have forbidden it, was a small producing oil well (perhaps one or two barrels per week) which had an open wooden barrel-like vat of cooling water (very stagnant) which was about 8-10' across and 6' deep. On many of the very hot summer days we and the other baseball players from

Manoa would cross the creek and swim in this icky tub of water. Looking back, we were very fortunate that no one drowned because once in the water, there was no ladder with which to climb out. I don't remember how we climbed up to get in the water and am surprised I don't remember how we managed to escape after we had cooled off. I think I realized how dangerous it was and was always relieved while we were drying off on the way home and not telling our mother anything about it.

Over the hill at Uncle Louie's close to the creek there was a field with a long line of blackberry and elderberry bushes and I remember very fondly Mother packing a picnic lunch for Russ and me, sending us off to pick berries (which were free), walking along the top of the hill above the creek, through the back yards of the Tiedemans and the Antles to get to Uncle Louie's farm, stopping to eat our sandwiches in the shade and then going down the hill to the berries and getting down to business. I think we usually came home with a couple of large buckets to eat or to preserve.

One time I accidentally kicked a yellow jacket nest at the head of the berry row (they burrow in the ground to make their nests I learned to my dismay) and they swarmed up and chased me all the way to the creek where I jumped in fully clothed in about 2 feet of water to escape being stung. I think I may have broken the world record for the 100-yard dash.

Paul Tiedeman was about the age of my grandfather and was a very interesting character. He lived with his maiden sister, "Tante" Amelia who kept the house and did the cooking. They had a producing gas well on their property and never turned off their stove oven. She used to dry fruit; and this is where I learned to love dried pears. "Uncle" Paul had many interesting trees planted around the house and barn which he trained from saplings into strange shapes. He also had one variety of pear which was Japanese and was picked after the leaves fell in the fall, hard as a rock, which he stored in their attic until spring when they softened up and ripened and were finally edible.

He owned two 1920 (?) Willy's Overland touring cars, one of which he kept only as a source of spare parts. They were 4-door and had isinglass, the clear plastic of its day, windows which were removable, which made driving in hot weather more comfortable. I remember seeing him and "Tante" Amelia sitting, chin high and proper, chugging down Tiedeman Road on the way to visit friends who lived on Broadview Road far away in Broadview Heights. What a sight!

"Uncle" Paul was interested in our family with the four boys and, particularly, in our gardening efforts which he highly approved of. He loaned us his corn planter at corn planting time, about Memorial Day at the end of May, when the soil had warmed up. This was a device which was about hip high and consisted of two pieces of wood hinged at the bottom with a handle on one of the two upright pieces of wood, and a seed container on the other where the seed dropped down a small tube to the bottom. Every stride down the row the end of the planter was pushed into the soil and three or four kernels of corn were deposited at the right depth and there was no need to go back and cover seeds planted in a furrow. There was a rhythm to it: stride stiff legged, plunge planter into the soil and then on to the next stride. It was fun. This produced a spacing of about 30" to 3' for the seeds to germinate and we used to pull the soil up around the plants when they were about knee high into "hills" which was the style of planting corn in those days. Of course, we only planted sweet corn, but real farmers used the planter when planting their fields of cow corn for feed and silage for their cattle. It was a very efficient tool and made the planting process much easier for us.

He was also very generous in the drought periods when our plants were beginning to wilt. He had a flatbed cart on 6" wheels which we used to transport two 100-gallon (?) barrels of water, pumped from his well, pulling it with our garden tractor across the field. I'm sure it saved our crop several times over the years.

He had a homemade power roller for smoothing the spring frost heaves in his lawn which he made by building 2' wide wooden slats circles which he fitted over the wheels of a Model T Ford. I can't remember if he ever drove it over to do our lawn.

One summer he hired Russ and me to paint his house. I think he paid us $100 which was a lot of money to us. It was a large two-story house with a mansard-type roof; and he suspended a movable scaffolding by ropes from the eaves for us to sit on while we painted the upper sections of the siding. I particularly remember one very hot day when we were painting the front of the second floor of the house above the front door and "Tante" Amelia appeared at an open window and offered us a cool glass of "farmers lemonade," more often used to quench the thirst of the men using their scythes to mow hay. It was made with vinegar instead of lemons, and we thought it was delicious.

"Uncle Paul" Tiedeman used to call brother Ken, eight years my junior, who always had a compact, well developed physique, particularly obvious when he went around wearing only shorts, while operating our garden tractor to cultivate the crops, "Alexander". He never told us why, but it could have been that four names for four boys were too much to remember. Or, I like to think, he was thinking of Alexander the Great from ancient times and Greek statues.

After a few years, Mother, who raised many flowers, always with varieties she could use in her weekly arrangements for the church (two large baskets) became aware of and interested in gladiolus. We went all the way over to the far east side to SOM Center Road in Moreland Hills where H.O. Evans, The Secretary of the Ohio Gladiolus Society, had his fields of the bulbs (technically "corms") for sale. He had a catalog listing the names of the varieties he offered with their descriptions: color, size of blossom, height, blooming season. This was our first experience in named varieties of any flower. Up until then everything we had were the culls from the gardens of friends or relatives. We eventually had about 5,000 corms; ample to supply the church arrangements, and then some. Also, for Dad to drop off bunches of fresh cut blooms at a florist friend, Bill Knoble, on W. 25lh Street near the High Level Bridge on the way into work. "Uncle" Paul's comment, sadly, he couldn't see the beauty, was, "What good are they? You can't eat them."

They were a lot of work: planting by hand individually in the spring every year, keeping weed free all summer, and then digging them up in the fall, cutting off the foliage above the corms, drying and storing the corms over the winter in bags with naphthalene flakes to prevent disease. Then in the spring the cycle would begin again. Only now the corms had to be soaked in a solution of mercuric chloride which was a deadly poison for disease control before planting them back in the ground. After they came up, we prayed we would not have a "thrips" infestation where the insects fed on the edges of the opening buds and ruined the blossoms. So, we sprayed regularly, an all-purpose nicotine sulfate solution, as I recall, from a pump hand sprayer. Pesticides designed for specific insects were just being discovered. When we were successful, we produced some spectacular blooms. However, we never got into exhibiting them in local flower shows or the Gladiolus Society competitions, if they had any.

My only experience with flower exhibitions and competitions came when with my mother's encouragement. I entered some spectacular marigolds in the Cuyahoga County Fair in Berea when I was in high school. I don't remember whether I won a ribbon or not, I did discover a taste for that kind of competition, however, which came into full "bloom" with my peonies much later.

My 18th summer, after finishing my postgraduate high school courses and having been officially notified by Yale of my scholarship, was a little different from my earlier ones on Tiedeman Road. A lot of time had to be spent on getting me ready to go away to school. Basically, it was mostly involved in acquiring a proper wardrobe. I don't remember how we learned what was expected or required. In those days we had to wear a long sleeved shirt, tie, slacks and a sports jacket to every class and that meant more shirts and ties than I had, let alone more slacks and sports jackets, of which I had none  All this had to be done on a tight budget, which became very evident when I arrived and compared what I had with the beautiful things worn by the eastern prep-school boys. It didn't affect me adversely because there were so many other scholarship boys who were in the same economic class as me.

I do remember going to Higbee's Department Store on Public Square in downtown Cleveland and buying a reversible topcoat/raincoat, camel's hair in color, and the rain side was a very silky gabardine. I think we paid $35 for it which was very expensive. But I really loved it and nearly wore it out in the next four years. I recall wearing it reversed, gabardine side out, most of the time.

We also bought a small steamer trunk that would fit on the back seat of the car to transport all the stuff I had to take. There was not only clothing but also bedding, towels, and my clarinet. One important item was the fiberboard Railway Express shipping container (about 18" x 30" x 6"), a distinctive brown color, to ship my dirty laundry home every week or so to save money. I had to carry it down to the New Haven train station to ship it. I think it cost about $1.50, which was a lot less than having the laundry done locally. The system worked well, except for Dad having to stop at the Linndale railroad station, close to Tiedeman Road, to pick it up on the way home from work. The container never got lost or delayed in all the time I was in New Haven.

I think we had to arrive in New Haven three or four days early for orientation and so Dad, Mom and I loaded up the car (steamer trunk behind Dad on the back seat) and the car trunk was full also, including a set of golf clubs. We started off after Dad got home from work. I don't remember, but assume, that Dad stopped off to pick up Grandpa and Grandma Schmidt to stay with and care for the brothers I was leaving behind while they were delivering me to the unknown. There was no Pennsylvania Turnpike then, so we drove all night via Route 20 across Pennsylvania, northern New York State to the Hudson River and through Danbury, Connecticut to get to New Haven, thus avoiding driving through New York City. The one thing I do remember about the trip is that on one of my turns at the wheel in the early morning hours near the Bear Mountain Bridge I dozed off and nearly went off the road into a ditch. Nothing serious happened and Dad took over from there on.

I don't remember what it was like arriving in New Haven for the first time; finding the Old Campus where I was to live my first year in Durfee Hall, fondly referred to as "Dirty Durfee" by my classmates, a dingy old Victorian style 4-story walk-up building. Our room was on the top floor in the entry closest to Battell Chapel which had a loud church bell that rang on the hour and was very hard to get used to at first, but in a short while became unnoticeable. Our room was the width of the building looking down on both the street and the city block size inner courtyard. The Old Campus which covered a city block was used as a shortcut by the townies and had the Yale Post Office in the corner of the quadrangle nearest our entry way which made it easier to pick up my precious mail from home.

That was the first time I met my roommate and his family. We were assigned by the College and had acknowledged each other by letters but didn't know what to expect in person. His name was Gilbert Bronson Hunt; and we were to remain roommates and good friends for our whole four years.

He came from Manchester, Connecticut, a suburb of Hartford, on the east side of the Connecticut River. His father worked at the Cheney Silk Mills and was also the County Delinquent Real Estate Tax Collector. In their system delinquent taxes were collected by individual contractors who were compensated with a percentage of the delinquent taxes they collected, rather than by county employees.

Gil was about 5'8", 165 lbs., olive complexion, narrow face, dark eyes, and had dark hair with a widow's peak. He always wore saddle shoes which I never liked, but never told him so. He had a great sense of humor. We were totally different in our tastes and totally different in the way we treated girls which might have been the result of his growing up with two sisters, Connie and Ruth, and a smaller brother. Their home was in a typical middle-class neighborhood, modest in size and very comfortable. Hartford was only 40-50 miles north of New Haven and I was invited to spend Thanksgiving with them the first year, a blessing for me because they were a very nice family and made me feel very much at home at a time when I was feeling very homesick.

One interesting thing, which didn't mean much to me at the time, was that the senior Student Councilor assigned to me whose role was to be a source of assistance, aid and comfort, to freshmen in the academic and social areas. He was a senior named Hiram Bingham. I only remember meeting him once in those first few days, and never had time to see him later when the time pressures hit me. I learned many years later that he was the son of the famous Yale archaeologist who discovered the ruins of Machu Picchu in Peru.

After getting my room set up and things stowed away, we went to Sears Roebuck and bought me a comfortable, practical easy chair in which I did most of my studying and reading for the next four years. I don't think it was delivered but can't remember how we got it up all those flights of stairs or moved to our residential college rooms where it could be stored during the summer vacation.

My parents had to leave for their long drive home - about 500 miles. I'm sure it was a long trip for them. My memories are vague (once again) but I am sure there were many tears shed by both them and me. They must have been thrilled for me, never having had the college experience themselves; seeing the impressive campus; knowing that this was what my surrounding would be; but at the same time apprehensive to leave their firstborn behind, who had never been away from his family before and whose struggles with feelings of inferiority and shyness they were all too aware of. They did arrive back home safely and our routine of weekly letters, and my new life began.

Freshman year was very difficult for me, not least because of my choices of the courses I took. Based on my performance in high school, I expected to have no trouble with English, French, or Chemistry. But, alas, it was not to be. I found to my horror that I really did not know how to write English and had to rewrite the monthly 3,000 word papers on any subject I chose from what we were studying that month again and again to get my grade up to a "C." This was a terrible blow for me and not just to my pride; I had always thought that I was very good and so did my teachers. The time required to rewrite just added to my overall problem of there not being enough hours in the day. I was fortunate that my instructor was very patient and very kind and I gradually got the hang of it. He was probably the best "pure" teacher I had in all my four years, and I took several other courses from him. His name was Richard Sewall. He was a small man, about 5'8," only an instructor, not yet a professor, receding hair line, distinctive gravelly voice, and reputed to be a terror on the tennis courts. My first exposure to him was in my freshman section of a sophomore level English course, which was a far more interesting and rewarding course than the usual English 101. One blessing in his course was the provision that one could substitute 10 lines of poetry one had memorized, Wordsworth, Shelly or Keats, perhaps, for a question one was unable to answer on the mandatory 10 minute quiz, which counted in one's overall grade. I wish I could remember all the 10 lines I carried around in my head just in case; only a few first lines remain. DO NOT blame him for any grammar lapses, or lacunae in this current project which is being undertaken 77 years after his efforts to train me. Wear and tear do take their toll, as do outside influences.

Chemistry was almost as big a shock. I loved the subject in high school enough to wonder if my future did not lie in becoming a chemical engineer. Unfortunately, or fortunately, I took another advanced course, Qualitative Analysis, (bad choice for a color-blind person). The full professor, Professor Brinkley, in this case was the author of the textbook we used, and although I virtually memorized the chapters assigned for the daily 10 minute quizzes which started each class, I couldn't get a passing grade. There was no way of fooling or bluffing him. It didn't help matters that I liked him and respected his knowledge, and that I could approach him after class with my questions. Although my final grade was a "B," there was never any question of my taking any further courses in chemistry or seeking a career in that field.

I learned quickly that there was no way to ration my time, to neglect one subject for another and then catch up on it later, not with that dreaded 10 minute quiz starting every class and being counted as part of my grade. I had to be prepared in every subject every day (3 classes per week per subject). And the fear of a less than "B" average resulting in the loss of my scholarship and returning home in shame and disgrace loomed over my head constantly. It was a potent motivator. The prep school boys had a big advantage over the public school boys because their senior year in prep school was basically their freshman year in college so they knew the subject matter, what the instructors wanted and had been trained how to study. There was some bitterness on the part of the scholarship boys, including me, because it seemed as if the prep school boys were uniformly handsome, beautifully dressed in expensive clothes, had plenty of money and they were very, very intelligent. It hardly seemed fair.

One of the things I learned early on was the difference in dealing with the teachers, Professor Brinkley, being a good example. In high school often it was enough to be well behaved, cause no trouble in the classroom, and do your homework. That was the formula for getting good grades; to get the teacher to give you the benefit of the doubt; if you didn't do well on a quiz or exam, to make allowances for you: he wasn't feeling well, or perhaps something's troubling him at home, etc., and proceed to give him the grade he should have had. It never happened in college.

In college I learned almost immediately that this system didn't work. Personal relationships, being liked by the teacher, past performance leading to high expectation had nothing to do with the grade received. Everything depended on your performance. It was like a dash of cold water in the face and took some getting used to. But gradually I adjusted to the new system and survived. Actually, I think freshman year at Yale was made especially rigorous in order to weed out any students who were not intelligent enough or dedicated enough to be there in the first place and who had slipped through the admissions process. Gil, who started German, and I both received warning letters from the Dean's office about our low grades just in time for the Thanksgiving break, which we spent with his family in Manchester, and it was a very gloomy occasion. After all, I had never worked harder, never tried harder and had so little to show for it.

After Thanksgiving, things seemed to settle down as I adjusted to the new circumstances, grades on the quizzes and papers improved; and a little relaxation set in. I was able to savor my new surroundings. The time pressures lessened a little; I dropped off the swimming team and marching band ended with the football season. This made a difference and seemed to help, also.

One day in spring when the leaves were beginning to appear, I had, perhaps, my first epiphany. Suddenly I realized that I couldn't be the inept, fearful bumbler that I felt everyone at home thought I was, all in my own mind, of course, but actually that I had to have some good qualities because

Yale was actually paying me to attend. It was a revelation; and that realization grew stronger with each passing year. It seemed to me that the longer and farther away I was from the family I loved so deeply, whom I never doubted loved me, who had to live through my troubled teen years watching my struggles, giving the best help they knew how, the stronger, more self-assured, more self-confident I became. It felt wonderful. Now, looking back, I realize it was my passage to manhood and not all that unusual, endured by every boy, everywhere. I was just very fortunate that mine took place where and when it did.

Part of the new discipline we had to absorb were the new rules of behavior. Only there really weren't any. One did not have to attend class; attendance was not taken; one was free to go to New York, at any time; or to girls' schools for parties on weekends. But, of course, if one did so, one's grades would reflect this behavior immediately and one would surely lose one's scholarship. The one rule indelibly ingrained on us from day one was that any woman, including one's mother, had to register with the porter at his office at the entry gate before going up to a room. And no woman, including one's own mother could be in a room after 6 p.m. Violation of this rule resulted in expulsion and a trip home on the train the next day. I was never aware that this ever actually happened, but the threat was very real in my mind. Less strict rules, more custom, and projecting an image identifying one as a Yale man involved dress. In those days we were expected to wear slacks, shirt & tie, and a sports jacket to classes, and whenever we were out of our rooms. Grey flannel slacks and blue blazer, or tweeds were the mode. Scuffed white buckskin shoes completed the picture. With our limited budget I only approximated this picture, but never felt out of place in the face of the wealthier prep schoolboys, with their expensive wardrobes. After the initial shock, it didn't really seem to matter all that much.

Today, I am disappointed that my memories of those happy, carefree days (except for the ever-present worries about maintaining the necessary grade point average) are such a blur. After freshman year we became wiser in the selection of our courses. The days and hours they were offered entered into our selection process - no Saturday classes. I always tried to pick a few courses which I hoped would be easy for me: no outright "gut" courses in sociology or religion, heaven forbid. I was determined from the beginning to make the most of this opportunity, to explore and receive pure education in the humanities. I was not interested in learning a trade, unless the law could be classified as a trade. I was very idealistic at this point, not seeking the road to riches.

I do remember Classical Civilization in my freshman year which could be substituted for the requirement of taking actual courses in Latin or Greek, which based on my high school experience I knew I did not want to do. I loved the course which aroused a lifelong interest in Greek and Roman history. I even remember the instructor's name: Fink and reading the *Iliad* and the *Odyssey*.

We took five 3-hour courses per year, some only given for one term, so that my total for the four years was probably twenty-four or twenty-five. However, as good as my memory is, I can't begin to remember them all. Some that I do remember, I remember for the subject and its content, others because of the personality of the Professor, or the instructor's teaching skills - some from

Freshman year when I was more impressionable, and some from the later years from some of the famous names which were not available to freshmen.

Freshman year I remember Richard Sewall particularly for both his teaching talent as well as the content. This was a second-year level course given to first year students and consisted of reading one author or source for a month, and then writing a 3,000-word paper on any subject related to the readings. It was far more interesting than the typical English I01. We started with *Beowulf*, followed by the *King James Bible* as literature, Chaucer, et al. I will never forget the day Mr. Sewall read aloud, in his unlovely voice, verses from "Songs of Solomon". He had us all so entranced that the bell ringing signifying the end of class didn't register and he had to dismiss us verbally. He was the teacher who first exposed me to the poetry of T.S. Eliot which made a huge impression on me and is probably the reason for my life-long interest in poetry, both the reading and attempts to write it. If, after I die, I should experience re-incarnation in another form, my first choice would be to reappear as a great poet. Second choice would be as an architect, or cabinet maker. Or peony hybridizer!

I don't remember much about my French class except the surprise and pleasure of reading a contemporary paperback French murder mystery featuring Inspector Maigret, a popular hero of the time: "*La Tête d'Un Homme,*" by George Simenon. It was actually fun to read and to become acquainted with some of the vernacular phrases used in everyday speech - not at all like reading the classic Flaubert or Baudelaire or Montaigne.

One other trivial memory from freshman year was getting used to girls in the classroom. I had already been thoroughly indoctrinated about the female situation, and even though having been exposed in the classroom in high school to girls who were smarter than I was, it was still quite a shock to have girls who were enrolled in the School of Music, not Yale College, in my Music Theory class. I do remember also some of the theory and struggling to compose a one-page composition with the chord structure noted below the staves for my final grade. I still have it, handwritten, somewhere among my collection of piano sheet music. But the most powerful memory is that the class was held at 1:00 p.m., immediately after lunch and the instructor droned and it was almost impossible to keep my eyes open. One of my regrets is that I didn't feel able to continue with Music Theory my second year because that professor was the visiting composer in residence, Paul Hindemith. And I have always regretted that I did not continue with my organ lessons. I felt I was making solid progress under the tutelage of Frank Bozyan and might have become a very good player.

I also felt fortunate to have attended a public high school which was co-educational and thus had the experience of interacting and competing with girls in a classroom setting and seeing firsthand how intelligent some of them were. At the same time I always felt a little sorry for the prep schoolboys who may have had a better secondary education, but because of their economic status not only missed having girls in class, but many spent the school year away from their families at boarding school. All male at that time. It seemed to me to have a sort of artificial, hot house air about their relations and attitudes regarding girls.

I think it was sometime in my freshman year that I decided to major in English Literature. The rationale was that it was a good, basic course exposing me to centuries of writing about the humane in life, as well as a training in how to read closely to determine the meaning of the written word. I thought it was a good fit with my background of voracious reading. There was a vague plan that I might go to Law School, where to be able to determine and interpret language, might be important. It might also be useful in the business world. But the most important reason to me was that the English major did not require a thesis to graduate. Only two days (16 hours) of comprehensive written tests covering the whole of English literature. It didn't seem very daunting three years before the event, but it was an awful ordeal. I got through it but did not distinguish myself.

Later years' courses which stand out in my memory, both for the subject matter and/or the professor would have to include the two popular courses, perhaps "famous" would be a more apt description, given by Chauncey Brewster Tinker: *Boswell's Age of Johnson* and *Romantic Poets of the Nineteenth Century*. I have many memories of Tinker, who was not at all what I expected the first time I saw him. I thought he was the antithesis of my image of a Col. Saunders type of professor: white beard, portly, old, doddering. Tinker was an older man to a twenty-year old student, probably in his late 40s, erect, fairly tall, dressed in dapper tweeds, butch haircut and had only one eye. He did love teaching and his students. He would invite the class to approach around him after his lecture; especially when he would graciously give you your grade after one his famous tests. It was much better than having the whole class milling around the bulletin board in the hall where the grades were posted, according to him.

Seating for his tests was every other seat and every other row in the theater type lecture hall to forestall any attempt at cheating. He always passed out the blue books personally, and the tests had a  different question for the odd and the even numbered seats. The campus mantra was that "Tinker gives a stinker to the odds." Toward the end of the year he had his little joke and got his revenge - he gave his "stinker" to the "evens" and groans went up when it was realized what had happened. The difference in difficulty of the two tests was striking.

I don't think he ever failed to ask me when he was personally passing out the blue books which were used then to write your answers to the quiz or test, bumping knees, whether I had a relative attending Princeton. It was the only notice he ever took of me and I can't imagine how he remembered my name. It was always "Schmidt" not "Mr. Schmidt" as some of the other professors used when addressing me.

In his Age of Johnson class, he would sit and read passages, while lecturing,   from Boswell's *The Life of Samuel Johnson* to illustrate some point or other. I remember the shock and the gasps which were clearly audible one day when two pages stuck together and he couldn't separate them, thus preventing him from turning the page, and in his frustration he opened the book flat on his lap, saying, "God Dammit!" and tore the pages out of the book, separated them, throwing the excess pages on the floor and calmly went on with his reading. I don't remember the passage, but I do remember the event. It was unforgettable, highly dramatic, and attracted a lot of attention to him, not Boswell or Johnson. It also added to his persona on campus and I think I wondered then, and

34

certainly do now, if it wasn't all part of a carefully calculated form of self-advertisement, an act, to try to attract students to take his courses. I know I took the Romantic Poets course immediately following the Boswell, He didn't need the theatrics; I wouldn't have missed his courses for anything.

He was in charge of the Rare Book collection at the Sterling Memorial Library which had 13 million volumes at that time, including a huge collection of priceless books and manuscripts, bequeathed or acquired over the years. Having control over the collection and free access to it, I remember clearly after his first lecture on the Romantic Poets which started with William Wordsworth during which he stroked a small book he happened to have with him. It was a first edition of Wordsworth's *Lyrical Ballads* which had Wordsworth's own changes for later editions marked with pencil in the margins. Tinker caressed this book all during his lecture and then invited those in the class who might be interested to come on the stage to see and handle this remarkable little volume after class. So, of course, I went up and can say that I actually handled a book with Wordsworth's own handwriting on it.

The courses I took were uniformly stimulating and opened up many areas of knowledge which were new to me. There were a few exceptions. I remember a one term course in Roman Government because it was so utterly boring, not a very good reason for remembering something and I think the way things are done today, I might have quit the course after a week or two and switched to something more interesting.

One reason for remembering the course is that it was given by the son of Eugene O'Neill, the famous playwright. He invited me to his home for dinner one  night with my organ teacher, Frank Bozyan who was his close friend.  I remember nothing of the evening, but do remember the final exam which had 4 questions, essay type. which I knew practically nothing about.  I think I wrote one or two sentences for each in the blue book, turned it in, and O'Neill gave me an A.

On the other hand, I remember taking a course in English history which I did not enjoy but could not have quit and switch because it was required for the English major. I am ashamed to confess that the names and dates came so fast that it was impossible to take good  notes and that  I found Dryden and Milton, very great poets, boring. An English major should love all poetry, and I don't.

I took a one term course on Chaucer, an even earlier poet, whom I do love. It was given by one of the stars in the English department, alongside Chauncey Brewster Tinker, Robert Dudley French, who was the Master of Jonathan Edwards residential college. His endearing idiosyncrasy, of which I am sure he was completely unaware, was to end every sentence with a loud, very satisfied smack of his lips. We used to keep track of the number of "smacks" with tick marks on the edge of the notes we took. This took nothing away from his scholarship or from the beauty of his reading of Chaucer's *Troilus and Cressida*, the first psychological novel in verse form, from which our modern term "to pander" comes. In this course we had more time to explore the glories of *The Canterbury Tales* to which I had been exposed in freshman year in Mr. Sewall's class.

Professor French was particularly effective in his reading of "The Miller's Tale." Lots of real juicy smacks!

In my junior year, I took a beginning course in psychology. My roommate and a mutual good friend had both taken the course the year before and it enabled them to predict and explain my behavior and reactions with uncanny accuracy; I had to take the course in self-defense. It may have been the most practical course I took, just as typing, was the most useful course I took in high school. Psych 101 introduced me to the principles of "Goal Responses" (commonly known as satisfaction) and the "Frustration Aggression Sequence" which proved to be very helpful tools in dealing with my roommate and friend, and are useful to this day in understanding the behavior of others. This was the only class I ever sat in with my brother, Russ. I do not ever remember discussing it with him, or what effect it may have had on him, or what his final grade was. An "A" or "B," I am sure.

At one point our instructor, Professor Sears, came into class very excited and proceeded to tell us of experiments he and his wife, who was also a professional psychologist, were performing on their newborn child. The experiments involved pricking the infant's extremities with a needle and recording reaction times to determine the rate of development of its nervous system. We were all horrified and he made no friends in class that day. But it was unforgettable.

In my senior year in the summer term caused by our entry into World War II, I took two "practical" courses in preparation for my entry into the military. I had enlisted in the ERC, the Enlisted Reserve Corp, where my colorblindness made no difference, and other requirements were very minimal, but which delayed induction until after graduation. The courses were in map reading and drawing, and a freshman course in mathematics. The map reading course involved learning to draw a map of terrain showing elevation contour lines and was not too difficult. We used land over by the Grove Street Cemetery on Science Hill. It was interesting but proved to be of no use in the Army. The math course made me wish I had just a little more talent for a subject I have always had a great interest in, but do not have the basic intelligence to understand, only up to a certain point. Bad combination: fascination but not enough intelligence. Actually, I was never able to find out how much talent for the subject I really had because of the shortened term which came to an end just as we were taking up the subject of Calculus. This course proved to be of no value in my military career. However, I was tantalized by what I learned from reading, much later, Korzybski's *Science and Sanity*, a great text on Semantics, which has a chapter on calculus late in the book which expanded my understanding somewhat.

I also took a one term class in Shakespeare's Tragedies given by Samuel Hemingway, another renowned name in the English department. This class was different. Because of the small number of students, it allowed Professor Hemingway to teach it in his rooms at Berkeley College seminar style, the only class that I had not in a classroom. Again, I am ashamed to say that I have never been a Shakespeare fan. I do appreciate the greatness, but I do not go back to the plays again and again, as some do. My favorite is *King Lear*. I regret never having studied his "Sonnets." I think now that I should have taken a course concentrating only on them.

One of my fond memories from my English major courses was a one term class on the English novel given by Professor J.B. Adams. I derived great pleasure from the early novelists, Fielding, Richardson and Defoe, but really loved reading Laurence Sterne, the Bronte's, Anthony Trollope, and Jane Austen. Professor Adams was retiring, and this was to be the last class he taught. I was thrilled to receive an invitation via a postcard addressed to R. F. Schmidt, Esquire, the first time I had ever been addressed in that fashion. It made a huge impression on me. If possible, I was to join him for lunch at the Elizabethan Club, an eating club located on the main campus in an elegant old early American style house, with the same sanction from the University as the Secret Societies. I don't remember any of the specifics of the lunch, or the conversation - only the feeling that perhaps I had learned how to be a gentleman, at last. It was a very warm feeling, and I thank Professor Adams for it to this day. I much prefer to use Professor Adam's salutation today when addressing a letter to a male friend, rather than the pedestrian "Mr." I took it as a mark of honor then and it is what I intend when I use it today.

I also had a one term course in American poetry given by Mr. Sewall. I am ashamed that I don't remember it more specifically. I didn't care as much about American poets when comparing them to Wordsworth, Shelley, Byron or Robert Browning, or the lesser poets of the nineteenth century. We did read Vachel Lyndsay, and Poe, and Walt Whitman, whom I actively disliked. I was also surprised to learn that Ralph Waldo Emerson wrote poetry. I discovered Emily Dickinson who took my breath away. We never read anything by Ezra Pound so I have no opinion of his work, but we did spend a good deal of time reading T. S. Eliot, whose poetry made a profound impression on me, and who is the one poet I would emulate, if I could.

Another one term course I enjoyed which later played an important role in establishing my credentials as a "linguist" after my basic training in the Army was the course I took in French: Romantic Poets of the Nineteenth Century. I was exposed to poets I had never heard of before. I still have many of their cheap, soft cover books in my library. Two or three names that stick in my memory are Paul Verlaine, Arthur Rimbaud, and Stéphane Mallarmé, whose poems are so far out that I could never decipher them. I struggled with them and they remained unintelligible. It was a very small class, only six or seven students, and our professor was Professor Seronde, a very important name to remember as it turned out.

Although I always felt I could spend the rest of my life limited to going back and forth between the Sterling Memorial Library and the 9-story Payne Whitney Gym, there were, of course, many other activities other than going to class and studying. There was a social side which included going to movies and plays, bowling, and playing bridge, which I did as frequently as possible. I will never forget what it meant to be invited to a party weekend at a girl's school in the springtime. And there were the sporting events: football and basketball which I preferred to tennis, or crew, or soccer. My main interest was swimming (brother Russ spent his time at the gym with the boxing team!) and the swimming team had a much better win-loss record than the football team and was a source of great pride among the students. After learning how to really swim freestyle in freshman year, I "went out" for and was accepted on the varsity swimming team under its famous coach, Robert J. Kiphuth. He was a brilliant coach, ahead of his time in his training methods, a strict disciplinarian, who benefitted from having a group of superbly talented swimmers while I was there. I had no business being among them. They set many school records and many world records, and ran up a record of 1,500 consecutive wins in dual swim meets

The facilities at the gym were outstanding. A separate exhibition 25 yard pool with special gutters which made it very "fast," steep spectator seating, and a separate locker room was available for the visiting team. Our team practiced in this pool. There was also a 50 meter practice pool with a movable bulkhead on the 3rd floor, reputed to be the largest suspended pool in the world where I would go between classes in the morning to swim laps alone. Sad to say, because of my late start (today's competitive swimmers start instruction and training at eight or nine years of age) I was ten years too late and never able to catch up with the more experienced members of the team. My stroke compared very favorably with the other teammates, but I just couldn't go fast enough, no matter how hard I worked. I always felt that Coach Kiphuth was very benevolent and very patient with me to allow me to remain on the team, and enjoyed being able to eat my meals at the training table in the Ray Tomkins House near the gym during swimming season. I was very pleased when Fran and I visited New Haven the year after my 65th Reunion to find a photo of the 1942 Swimming Team with me in it on the wall just outside the entrance to the Exhibition Pool.

I did get to swim the 100 yard freestyle event in two or three meets over a period of three seasons where the opposing team was weaker and whose best 100 yard freestyle times were slow enough that my best times (about 53-54 seconds) gave me some chance to win the event. I have no recollection of how I finished or even who the opposition was.

One memorable thing that Coach Kiphuth did was to include me with a small group of teammates to visit Vassar College, all women at that time, of course (my only trip there) in Poughkeepsie, New York, about 50 miles west of New Haven. I don't remember the transportation method. We were to put on a swimming exhibition. I was never told why I was included, certainly not because of my limited ability. Perhaps a reward for all the hours of hard work in the 3rd floor pool where Coach had his office? I don't remember any of the details. We were not there long, arriving about dinner time and back home the same night. I think each of us was assigned a coed as "hostess" to have dinner with and mine was very nice, but I never saw her again.

One of the recurring memories in my dreams for years was my first day in the 3rd floor pool trying out for the freshman swimming team and meeting Coach Irving Newton, the freshman swimming coach, for the first time. He was a very fine coach and teacher and was a good friend of mine all my time in New Haven. He was used to dealing with the already well-trained prep schoolboys and must have known right away that I posed a challenge. He put me with the slowest members of the team, fortunately in the lane closest to the edge of the pool, and then gave his unforgettable command, "Swim 10." I looked up at him and said, "You mean you expect me to swim back and forth 10 times?" He looked at me sternly and repeated, "Swim 10." And this was expected from someone who had never swum more than one 25-yard length in his life. Somehow or other I managed to do it, struggling with every stroke to pull myself through the water and barely managed to finish. I think they had to help me out of the water; I may have vomited. But this was the beginning of many miles of swimming with arms only and kicking with legs only; I learned a new skill whose benefits I think I am still enjoying, and, for the first time I was a member of a team, although swimming is a very solitary sport.

At one of the regular Sunday afternoon teas at the Master's House, I learned that the Master's wife, much loved by all the members of the college, attended all the intramural sporting events, but had never seen a swimming meet. I brashly, I thought, offered to take her to one. She accepted gladly, which was a great honor for me. I think it was very seldom that a student was able to spend a whole afternoon, one on one, with the Master's wife. She was very popular with the students because of her interest in the boys, most of whom she knew by their first names, and their families, and their status with their girls. The students loved her for her interest in them, and for her wonderful, plenteous sandwiches always on hand at her Sunday teas.

As it happened, there was a meet a week or so later with Army where I was not required to dress or sit on the deck with the team. So, I escorted Mrs. Wolfers, walking from Pierson to the Gym, a fair distance, where she saw the interior of the Exhibition Pool for the first time. She was very impressed but expressed alarm when the Army team removed their sweats, revealing some very brawny, heavily muscled men. The Yale swimmers with their long, smooth swimming muscles looked hopelessly outclassed, a classic example of David vs. Goliath. I reassured her that she need not worry and tried to explain the difference in training philosophy; that Yale's method was to build long, lean muscle as opposed to weight-lifting type bulk muscles which hinder rather than help swimmers. Yale went on to win the meet, taking 1st and 2nd place in every event.

This was the occasion, while describing my family and answering her questions as to did I have a girlfriend, when I said yes I had a girl back home who was a Senior at my high school and I had, in fact, invited her to my Junior Prom, (a major social event in eastern college circles, like Dartmouth's Winter Carnival) and her mother had granted her permission to come. The plan was that I was to go to Grand Central to meet her train, we would go to the Metropolitan Museum of Art, and after dinner, would go to hear Gershwin's *Porgy & Bess*. Then back to New Haven where I had a room for her at the York Hotel on York Street. Mrs. Wolfers instantly said: "No. She must stay with me. Why didn't you ask me? Of course you wouldn't, but plenty of others would." I said, "I wouldn't dare to presume such a thing." She said I was too nice and insisted that my date, Carol Kuekes, with whom I was very much in love, should stay with them. I don't know how many other girls were also invited. But a nice middle class high school girl from a middle class family in Ohio spent the weekend as a houseguest at the beautiful Master's House of Professor Arnold Wolfers, Sterling Professor of International Relations, with a delightful, youngish Swiss wife, being pampered and looked after by the Wolfers' "Swedish couple", the butler and his wife. What an experience that must have been. I would have loved hearing Carol tell her mother and her friends at school all about it. I still feel grateful for the indirect compliment paid me that such kindness would be extended to a friend of mine.

One of the disastrous experiences I do remember vividly is my first and only, as an undergrad, encounter with the Yale Golf Course which is located in the hills of West Haven, a fair distance from the main campus in downtown New Haven. It is a beautiful, challenging course and at that time was ranked among the top 10 courses in the U.S.A. We brought a set of golf clubs to New Haven freshman year and in Spring just before the end of the term, on a beautiful sunny Saturday afternoon, I played 18 holes with a fellow scholarship student, John Schulman, from White Plains, N.Y. I usually scored between 80 and 90 at home, but I had never seen a course like this before and ended up with a score of 139 strokes; John who was more experienced did equally poorly. I took the clubs back home and never played the course again until I started attending my Class Reunions. I was a better golfer by then, better prepared, had a better set of clubs, and thoroughly enjoyed it. Never got a decent score until the round played after my 65th Reunion when I shot in the 80s. I was probably lucky my first experience was so discouraging because golf is very time consuming and if I had fallen in love with the course, I couldn't possibly have been able to find the time for it - in any of the four years.

One other memory connected to the Exhibition Pool concerns a Life Saving Course I signed up for my junior year. If I was successful, it might help in getting a job as a lifeguard. The course was given by my old freshman swimming coach, Irv Newton, and the certificate awarded upon successful completion was Instructor, not just Lifesaver. It was fun to work under the watchful eye of Coach Newton again after two years had lapsed. Now the "Swim 10" held no more terror for me. We learned the various approaches, surface and underwater, the various holds, and how to protect ourselves from a panicky victim. There were about ten men in the class and we worked in the water crosswise in the pool. The biggest men in the class were a senior named Trudeau and me. Naturally, we were paired off in the training sessions. He must have been about 6' 2" and weighed about two hundred twenty-five pounds; very solid, heavy bones, little buoyancy. He was not on the swimming team and had no swimming muscles. Unfortunately for me he was physically unable to float, and I had to haul him back and forth across the pool. It was exhausting. Coach Newton bet Trudeau a steak dinner that he could make him float and spent at least a half hour in the water with him and failed. Trudeau would slowly sink to the bottom. I imagine he really enjoyed his steak dinner. It didn't take any effort to earn it after all. Since he came from Lake Saranac, N. Y., where the famous T.B. Sanatorium was located and operated by the Trudeau family, I now think he must have been related to the famous Doonesbury cartoonist who used the great quarterback from St. Ignatius High School in Cleveland, Brian Dowling, as a model for his character in the comic strip, "B.D."

One little addendum: I passed the class and got my Instructor's License with Newton's signature on it, still have it somewhere. This led me to my answering an ad posted on a bulletin board at Yale Station and applying for job as a guard at a swim club in Old Greenwich, Connecticut, on the rail line from New Haven to N.Y.C. I made an appointment to be interviewed on a Sunday afternoon and duly boarded the proper train, hit the books on the way, got absorbed in my reading and missed getting off the train in Old Greenwich. It wasn't like riding on a city bus where you could get off a few blocks ahead and turn around and go back; more like missing an exit on a turnpike and being trapped until the next exit. I stayed on the train all the way to Grand Central and waited for the first train I could take back to New Haven. I never even saw Old Greenwich, let alone the swim club and pool. I often wondered what changes there might have been in my future if I had gotten the job and met an heiress. Greenwich was a very wealthy community, along with Stamford and Darien. Who knows?

I did get a job back at home as one of two lifeguards in the Metropolitan Park System pool (West Branch of a polluted, Rocky River) in Strongsville, Ohio, at the foot of the hill on Pearl Road. The pay was $139 per month, which with my $400 per year Bursary job at Yale, reduced the amount of the contribution my parents had to make and left that much more for my younger brothers' education, something that was always on my mind. This was a very satisfying experience; I got along well with the other guard, Leo Abood, an Ohio State student who lived in the Birds Nest neighborhood in eastern Lakewood off Madison Avenue where his parents operated a small grocery store. We had only two "pullouts" (rescues) the whole season, whereas the previous year when there were three guards they had thirty-one. I think we were more alert and more disciplined. The only pullout I had just happened to be performed before the eyes of my boss, Chief Hoy, chief of the Park Police who had dropped in one evening on a surprise inspection. It was simpler than anything I ever did in class with Coach Newton. I think Chief Hoy was impressed. He couldn't have appreciated how easy it was. The young lady I "saved," who was a nurse, certainly appreciated it as did her date and her brother whose horsing around, tossing the date off the diving board into the deep water to the brother waiting below, caused the problem in the first place.

I started the season about two weeks late, just in time for the July 4th holiday and hadn't been on the job two hours when a young couple came up to the guard stand carrying a small child about three-years-old who had been wading in the wading pool and cut her big toe on a piece of glass. It was bleeding profusely. I didn't think I was equipped to deal with the situation and recommended that they take the child, who was crying as well as bleeding, to a hospital. After they left, we closed the wading pool and the main swimming area, and Leo and I got on our hands and knees and tried to find all the pieces of glass from the Pepsi bottle someone had deliberately thrown into the pool. I was appalled that someone would do something like that. Eventually we reopened the big swimming area; and the day came to an end. It was a great way to start a new job. I never heard if the little girl was OK, but I am sure she needed many stitches.

This section of the park was patrolled by a mounted park policeman named Don who used to stop and chat and became a friend. At the end of the season when our job was over, Leo's mother invited us to their home for a Mediterranean meal and included Don and my brother, Russ, as well. It was my first experience with hummus and stuffed grape leaves and lamb kebob, which I thought were different and delicious. I think that was the last time I saw Leo and am sorry that our friendship had to end.

The lifeguarding part of the job was made easier because the month of August was very rainy and very cold. We spent most of our time trying to stay warm, wrapped in towels, and shivering. After I had been on the job a week or so, Leo had spilled the beans about my going to Yale and the swimming team and some of the local kids overcame their shyness and started hanging around the Guard Stand, which was on an old unused bridge over the dam. They had seen me kicking laps on a board when we weren't busy and wondered why I was doing it and after I explained and offered to instruct them, wanted to come mornings and take swimming lessons. The boys quickly dropped out and most of the girls, but there were three or four who stuck to it. One was Vivian Orchard, who spent so much time in the water that she developed a serious ear infection and another was Arlene, who was smaller and had had ballet lessons. She had a wonderful freestyle kick. I ran into her on the bus to downtown Cleveland after the War was over, and she still recognized me, but was still small but older and I would not have recognized her if she had not had the courage to ask if I was that Lifeguard. Sunday afternoons they would swim up and down the length of the "poo;" and the other swimmers would get out of the water and gather on the edge of the pool to watch them. I was always sorry that I didn't know about the Greater Cleveland Swim Meet held in the Cumberland Pool in Cleveland Heights earlier because I could have tried to enter "my" three speedsters in the shorter freestyle events. Without ever having taken their times, I knew they were fast, and I think they would have had a chance to win. Wouldn't that have been fun to tell Kiphuth!

Of course, there was a social side to life at Yale. There was a bonding between the scholarship boys, who faced many of the same problems: mainly fear of losing their scholarships and a lack of money. This was especially evident freshman year where my recollections are of endless bull sessions and going to the movies Saturday night rather than saving money by staying home and studying. There was always something that needed to be studied. The makeup of the moviegoers varied with different boys searching for a regular group to coalesce. I don't remember specifically, but I suspect my roommate was part of most of the shifting combinations who came mainly from fellow workers at Freshman Commons.

This changed in sophomore year when we moved into our permanent rooms for the next three years in our residential college. I think we were allowed to choose which of the ten colleges we preferred, but, if this is true, I don't remember how or why we chose Pierson College, which with its neighboring Davenport College was not built in the Gothic architectural style, but done in red brick white trim Williamsburg style. I didn't realize it at the time - a part of my general unawareness of many things at that age, but the residential colleges were only five to ten years old and in practically new condition. They seemed very luxurious and were.

They were in the form of large quadrangles which provided privacy from the street, but large grassy courtyards to look out at and play on. Each college had its own Coat of Arms, repeated on its silverware and china and available as a patch on the ubiquitous blue blazer, the preferred "dress up" jacket. Each college had its own Dining Room, Common Room and small Library and a home in one corner of the quadrangle where the Master and his family lived. Masters were usually full Professors and were appointed for a term of five years. Students' rooms and suites were accessed from separate entries; there were no long halls such as are found in hotels. And each room had a real fireplace. The showers were in a large room on the entry landings; the basement level had storage and activity rooms; and in our entryway, two squash courts.

No formal classes were taught in the colleges, but other instructors were appointed as Fellows and did not sleep there but had offices for their own work or for counseling students. They ate many of their meals in the Dining Room, and we could ask to join them. It was all part of turning us into gentlemen. Their influence was never overt, but very subtle, and, I think, very effective.

The Common Room in Pierson had a grand piano which could be used for practice (I never did) and was used for programs of various kinds. I remember particularly a lecture given by the great poet, Robert Frost, one evening after dinner, with the room filled to capacity, probably 100-125 people. I was one of that audience, and remember his bushy eyebrows, but not what he read or recited, but did shake his hand at the reception afterwards.

Another, lighter event, was a marvelous performance of Gilbert & Sullivan's *Iolanthe*. It was done by our Pierson classmates (brother Russ, who also chose Pierson, was one of the chorus). Of course, all the female roles were played by male students which made it all the funnier. One of the Fellows, James Leybum, provided the musical background on the grand piano. One of my brother's classmates was very ingenious and fashioned the female wigs, all very blond and shiny, out of short lengths of one-inch hemp rope. He also was noted for putting fizz into wine with compressed carbon dioxide turning plonk into a form of cheap champagne.

Each college's common room and dining room were distinctive, and I always admired the Early American style of Pierson: simple, plain but elegant. We had an hour window to appear for each meal of the day and when we appeared were greeted by our hostess, Molly, who then seated us, perhaps with a new classmate she felt we should meet, if we were alone, and handed out the day's menu. My recollection of the food is that it was varied and quite good, except for Saturday lunch, and Sunday dinner. We were served by waitresses in black dresses and white aprons. It was school policy that after freshman year classmates should not act as servants by waiting table for their fellow classmates and assumed that table manners would be elevated through observation to an acceptable level.

One thing that was not under control: one sunny Saturday during football season while I was in my band uniform eating lunch before the game, one of the upper classmen brought a date into the dining room. She was absolutely gorgeous, wearing a mink coat, high heels, and if she wasn't a model she should have been. The thing that really caught my eye was the ring on her finger, square cut, that I think may have been a real topaz, and it was about an inch square. They may have taught us how to use a knife and fork, but they didn't teach me how not to stare.

There were things on the menus that I was not familiar with, such as swordfish, which I had never tasted before and instantly became my favorite fish and have loved ever since. I continued my habitual breakfast at home and had Grapenuts every day for four years, and sometimes for lunch when I didn't see anything I liked on the menu for the main course. Another discovery was canned Queen Ann cherries, and canned figs, which are hard to find today. I think it's interesting that although my parents drank coffee at home, it was not permitted for us as growing boys (might stunt our growth?) but when I was "grown up" and away from home, I drank hot tea with every meal.

Since there were three classes dispersed in each college with a one-third turnover as the seniors departed and a new crop of sophomores appeared to take their places, there were many chances to meet new people since we all lived and ate together. I never thought about it at the time but since a whole class usually numbered between 1,100 and 1,200 men and there were ten colleges waiting to receive them, one tenth of the class would amount to 110 to 120 men and there would be a total of 330 to 360 men per college. I thought it was a wonderful system and made college life much more enjoyable.

We occupied two single rooms separately even though we were classified as roommates, Nos. 1480 and 1481.They were entered from a tiny lobby off the entry stair landing. Across the landing, opposite our rooms, was a luxurious suite with a living room, two bedrooms and two large closets. At the head of the landing was the shower room which was spacious. It had huge shower heads which delivered a deluge of water. There were no tubs. During swimming season I remember starting and ending the day with a long, relaxing shower, as well as taking before and after showers after two practice sessions at the gym which added up to a total of six showers per day plus being in the water in the pools for almost two hours. It's no wonder I developed dry skin. But I was clean. The swim team supplied olive oil by the gallon to combat the chlorine in the water and the perchlorate used to sanitize the towels. I rubbed it on my dry arms and legs but was never sure if it did any good.

Our rooms were probably 12" x 15": we arranged them with one room for the beds and study desks, and the other, the one facing the courtyard, as a living room with a couple of overstuffed chairs and a shabby, used sofa bed in case an unexpected guest dropped in. Which happened to me. This was where we played bridge and did what passed for entertaining. Our circle of friends, (Hunt, Rosenberg, Hilbert, Cardon, McKinney, Kehoe), are a few of the names I remember, did not do much drinking, although there was a lot of it in our entry. But the scholarship boys simply did not have the money to pay for the booze. I was amazed that the two men across the landing, one of whom owned an airplane, a Lincoln Zephyr, and oil wells in Butler, Pennsylvania, consumed $300 worth of liquor by Thanksgiving. It was an early contrast in styles of living. Since I could never see how the drinking I observed increased happiness or conferred any other benefits, and with my religious convictions at the time, our non-alcoholic style of entertaining suited me just fine and I did not feel out of place at all.

On the other hand, senior year when I was no longer playing in the band, I went to the football games with my roommate as an ordinary spectator for the first time. Alcohol was forbidden at the Bowl and I was always amused to see Gil prepare for the game by making a "Zombie" which consisted of vodka, lemon juice and powdered sugar, put it in a hip flask, conceal the flask in a breast pocket, and sip it through a straw during the game.

Also, after the Harvard game senior year some of our friends organized a Brandy-Milk Punch party, the recipe supplied by our N.Y. social arbiter, Dick Kehoe, in one of their rooms across the quad from us. I bought a gallon of sweet cider on the way home from the game and took it to the party. While the others were downing their punch and cheering Yale's victory, I downed the whole gallon of cider (with no ill effects whatsoever), and we all went off to dinner in the Dining Room at 7 p.m., where we all ate a very dignified dinner and played bridge afterwards. The end of a perfect day. Especially with World War II staring us in the face. This was November 1942.

My brother Russ, who I always thought was brighter than me, was the winner of a Yale scholarship the year after me, upholding what had become a Lakewood High School tradition. Looking back, I find it curious that we saw so little of each other. In spite of his teasing, there was a very real bond between us. I still had the feelings in me instilled by our parents of being his, as well as the two younger brothers, protector and champion and mentor. Perhaps this feeling is common among all oldest siblings. I know our parents inculcated it and stressed it, directly and indirectly. I do remember feeling it was important that I should respect his privacy and independence, and encourage him to make his own choices, make his own friends, and follow his own interests as they developed. I think I succeeded in doing this. But looking back I wonder if I didn't overdo it. To not know where he lived freshman year, did he also work in Freshman Commons, what courses did he take, was it as hard for him to adjust to the new ways of studying as it was for me? Was his choice of Pierson a cry for more interest on my part which I misread? He never came to me for help of any kind. I can't remember him ever playing bridge with us, but one of his classmates, Bill Hilbert, did. He lived in the second entry next to ours, but I don't remember ever seeing the inside of his room, or who his roommate was. This is deeply troubling to me today. I don't know where the balance lay. I can't even remember how our parents got the two of us to school his first year in New Haven. I now wonder if both of our college experiences might not have been richer if we had done more together.

In my junior year our parents loaned us their second car, a six-cylinder Chrysler Royal, and we found three other classmates as passengers who paid us enough to cover expenses. The Pennsylvania Turnpike was completed from Pittsburgh to Harrisburg, which made the trip a little easier. I don't remember who our three backseat passengers were, or where we stopped along the way. I'm sure we switched drivers every hour or so and drove straight through. After our safe arrival we had to find a garage to store the car and found one near the gym within close walking distance. We never used the car for local trips but I did use it once or twice for trips to girls' schools for weekend parties, Smith College in Northampton, Massachusetts, or Connecticut School for Girls in New London, Connecticut. Gil went to Tufts College in Boston alone for a party, but I don't know how he got there, by train, no doubt. We did not loan him our car. At the end of the year we made the reverse trip home to Cleveland with three backseat passengers, one of whom was the diver on the swimming team who lived in Hammond, Indiana, and had to hitch hike the rest of the way after we dropped him off in Cleveland. On one of my trips to Smith College I had a passenger who responded to my bulletin board ad seeking someone looking for a ride to Smith who was part of the Wiss cutlery (scissors and toenail clippers) family. I had never met him before, but we got on well together.

One amusing visit to Smith which turned into quite an adventure involved the only time my roommate Gil, and I ever went to one of these parties together. I don't remember who his date was, or how it was arranged, but we had the usual good time and after lunch on Sunday in the Park

House (my date Liz Dawson's dormitory where the dance had been held the night before) we bid the girls a fond adieu and took off for New Haven. It was a bright, sunny afternoon and we drove on and on, chatting and reminiscing, and suddenly saw a road sign which read "Vermont border, 2 miles ahead." So, two college seniors with Yale scholarships had been driving with the sun, which was still shining brightly, on their backs instead of through the windshield. We had been driving north instead of south. It was embarrassing! We had to turn around and the only route we could take back was the same one which meant we were going to pass through Northampton again, and just about dinnertime. So, we decided to stop at Park House to see if we could eat with the girls again, which is what happened. We were the only two men in a large roomful of girls who were very gracious but must have also wondered about our sanity. We were very brave and said our second farewells and got back to New Haven well after dark with a fun story to tell.

The more organized activities available to undergraduates included fraternities and the mysterious secret societies. There were only six fraternities, perhaps the best-known being Delta Kappa Epsilon (Deke), who always snagged the football captain (and I think both Presidents Bush) Sigma Chi and Chi Psi. Freshmen were forbidden to rush or join fraternities until sophomore year which I think was a wise policy. As I remember, rush took place early in the fall and we visited all the houses which were located on Fraternity Row, a short "L" shaped lane off York Street, only a short distance from the entrance to Pierson. I think the houses were all built about the same time to fit in with the colleges' architecture and had no sleeping rooms. A member could eat meals there, but, if he did so, had to pay for his uneaten meal at his college. Of course, there was a bar and plenty of room for lounging and dancing. I remember one wild night when I opened the window in my bedroom and went to sleep listening to the Count Basie band which had been hired for a party at one of the houses. The Band was top ranked and one of my favorites. I thought they sounded much better live than on a shellac record and I didn't call to complain about the sound volume. What a way to drift off to sleep.

Gil and I decided to participate in the rush just to see what it was like and one evening toured the houses to be chatted up by the upper classmen who tried to sell us on all the advantages of fraternity life; the connections we could make that would be important in later life; how they could improve our social graces, how to impress a girl (very important,) how to handle drinking, and even tutor and mentor. After our exposure, we both were dubious, but maybe tempted just a little. End result: Gil was not invited for a second visit by any of the fraternities and I received one from the fraternity ranked sixth in the list of six in campus scuttlebutt, Alpha Phi Sigma. I actually was flattered at first, enough to go back and hear the final sales pitch. But, after hearing the same benefits again and all they promised to do for me, on the way back to Pierson I realized there was nothing they claimed they could do for my personality, or social graces that I couldn't do for myself, and, most importantly, I could not justify asking my parents for the additional $300 per year in fees which might have jeopardized the chances for my two youngest brothers being able to go to college. So, I turned the offer down, politely, I hope.

Secret Societies were a different matter. There were also six of them, the most famous and the most mysterious was "Skull & Bones." There were all kinds of rumors about what they were and what went on behind their closed doors. The selection day was known as "Tap Day" and was early in May. Each Society selected fifteen members of the junior class, 90 men from a total of 1,143 in our class so it was quite exclusive. No one knew what the criteria were for being picked, only that they did the picking, unlike fraternities where everyone offered himself to be chosen. There was enough chatter and curiosity that I estimate 90% of the class were curious enough to subject themselves to the process and assembled at the appointed hour at the Woolsey Hall plaza outside the doors to Freshman Commons. Gil and I both went, milling around, looking up at the clouds drifting by, not expecting the "Tap" on the shoulder by an unseen senior, approaching from the rear which signified you had been chosen and were to go directly to your room, followed closely by your "tapper." Upon arrival you had to signify whether or not you accepted the invitation to join. Each Society had prepared a list of selections and competed for the same man in some cases: the football captain, or Editor of the Yale Daily news. They did not want to lose their first choice to a competitor. Needless to say, neither of us was "tapped" and the mystery continues to this day.

The University approved of this system and allowed the construction of the Societies' meeting places which are known as "Tombs," having no windows, to be built on land owned by the University. The Societies are reputed to have large endowments which ensures their independence, and this could be expected, I suppose, given a system where wealthy members pick their successors.

Of course, I was a member of the marching band, but I was never interested or had the time to investigate the Glee Club, directed by Marshall Bartholomew, a famous conductor. This was, and is, an outstanding college a cappella chorus, all men in my day. The talented "Whiffenpoofs" famous for their signature song were also a rich part of the musical scene on campus and were very popular. I mention later the impression they made on me when hearing them return from their evening rehearsals. I always thought the Whiffs' method of selecting members was interesting. The departing seniors chose their successors. Apparently, the pool of singers is large and fairly constant in quality. I do not know whether my brother Russ, who had a year of vocal training in high school and a deep interest in music, ever tried out for the Glee Club. I hope he did.

Even though life grew easier as we grew older and learned how to play the game in our sophomore and junior years, there wasn't much in the way of local dating. Some of the men dated the girls at Albertus Magnus, a Catholic girls' school in New Haven (I have no idea where it was located.) The thing that one looked forward to, the highlight of a whole year, was, if you were lucky enough to know someone, to be invited to one of the eastern girls' schools for a weekend party and dance. I was one of the lucky ones and was invited to Smith College, an all-girls school, in Northampton, Massachusetts, three or four times. My date/hostess was Liz Dawson, who also had a scholarship, and was one of the nicest, smartest girls in our high school class. The parties were held in her dormitory, Park House, and were wonderful. The girls all seemed to have the knack of instantly making their guests feel relaxed and at home, everyone was so glad you could be there. Liz had a roommate from Hartford, Lee Deming, whose date was a fellow waiter from Freshman Commons, James Foster Collins, also from Hartford. We were invited to parties together several times, stopping at his parent's home to borrow a car from his father to drive the rest of the way to Northampton. The dances were "formal" which meant I had to acquire a set of tails, white shirt with studs, white bow tie, and cummerbund and patent leather dancing shoes. At least the costume was the same for every party, not like the girls who had to have multiple long evening dresses. I was not a good dancer, as I explain in my later chapter on Music, but the girls were so gracious I never felt awkward or embarrassed, and thus could enjoy myself.

On one of those weekends, Jim and Lee left early Sunday morning to go skiing in Vermont but returned early in the afternoon. Lee had fallen on the slopes and injured one of her knees. Jim and I applied some sort of liniment to the injured knee, taking turns rubbing it in - under the very close supervision of the House Mother who hovered over us every second. All turned out well because they later married. He later became the U.S. Ambassador to Panama and retired to teach at the University of Miami. It is true that many fairy tales have happy endings.

I think I was invited to the Connecticut School for Girls twice, which was different from Smith but the same in all the important aspects. My date was a girl from Patterson, New Jersey, whose name was Jane Storms, better known to her friends as "Stormy" which was hardly appropriate, but understandable. She was very nice, and I'm sure we exchanged letters, but nothing ever came of it. The format for the entertainment the girls arranged was very similar to that at Smith. One thing the Connecticut girls did differently that I really liked was their custom of electing twelve senior girls, who dressed in long white evening gowns with red sashes draped over their shoulders down to their waists. They roved around the dancing couples, cutting in, the initiative being with the girl and not a possibly shy boy, thus ensuring a thorough mixing of partners. No one was to dance the whole evening exclusively with his date and no girl would have a dance card with blank spaces on it. Thus, it was that I was cut in on, and danced with one of the roving seniors who happened to be the daughter of Henry Wallace, Vice President of the U.S. My recollection of her is very vague: tall, dark hair, pretty, and that she was very gracious and very charming.

I think I was somewhat remiss in the reciprocation department. I can only recall inviting my Smith College friend, Liz Dawson, to come to New Haven once. I don't think it was a special occasion and am certain it was not for a dance, but probably for a football game. I can't remember where she stayed or what we did. It didn't help that no matter how nice she was, or how smart, there simply was no romantic spark. And I don't think I ever invited "Stormy" to come down from New London.

I should get fairly high marks for hospitality, however, for my suave aplomb, my imperturbability, when one Friday night after dinner there was a knock on our door and it was Dave Bortz, one of my least favorite Sunday Schoolmates from Lakewood, now attending Dartmouth College in New Hampshire, just dropping in, hoping to find a place to sleep. I couldn't believe he would travel that distance without making some prior arrangements for a place to lay his head before the game. What if I was the only person he knew at Yale, and I already had a friend staying the night, or was out of town? I don't know how he ever found my address. We were not close at home, nor were our families. With that kind of nonchalance, he probably had a fine night's sleep on our sofa bed, but I don't remember taking him to breakfast the next morning. I was involved with the marching band and never saw him again. Nor did I receive a thank you note. Dartmouth always was considered to be way up North in the wilderness.

We had to go to school during the summer of senior year in order to delay induction in the Army and with World War II in full swing, the whole country was fully mobilized. Even my father at age 45 or so had to register for the draft and I remember going with him to the Parma, Ohio Town Hall to register. It was very different from the usual summer at home where I'm sure I could have gotten a job as a lifeguard again, maybe even gotten paid more than $139 a month. And I would have spent every minute I could with my sweetheart, Carol, who was more precious every day. When I think of the movies we could have seen, the drives we could have taken without destination, her sitting close and handling the shifting of the gears, timing her shifts perfectly with my using the clutch. How perfect it could have been!

In New Haven, we were still an all-male society and the girls' schools did not have summer sessions, not that I would have been able to date and remain faithful to Carol. However, we did manage to amuse ourselves after classes. After all we were seniors! For instance, we built a horseshoe court in an area between two of the Fellows Offices and Fraternity Row and had fun that way. One of my best friends, George McGoldrick, from Meriden, Connecticut, was uncannily accurate with his pitching technique and unbeatable. The horseshoe didn't rotate but went to the pin head over tail which increased the probability of it flipping on to the pin for a ringer. I tried to copy his style, but couldn't, but I kept trying.

One of our other scholarship classmates, Ralph Ottomar Fuerbringer, bought an old beat-up Model A Ford which was equipped with a valve which allowed the driver to switch fuels from gasoline to kerosene. I think he may have paid $25 for it. I think gasoline was already rationed, and kerosene was not, so this extended the range he could travel, and on weekends he used to take a group of us for trips up and down the coast. It was always an adventure. We never knew where we would be going, or if we would be able to get back home. We visited many scenic spots on the coast, but today I can't tell you where we went. In many ways it was an idyllic time, the last semblance of a normal life for us as we embarked on a more than usual unknown future.

In later years I became aware of occasional ads in the New Yorker by a Manhattan photographer styling himself as "Ottomar", who specialized in portraiture, and I am sure he was our "Furby" since while in school his passion was photography. He always had his camera, an expensive Speed Graphic, with him, even bringing it with him to meals in the Pierson dining hall. He surprised me after breakfast on the way to class one morning and captured me, unshaven, in one of my all-time favorite photos. I have never taken a good picture - never have known how to put on a happy smile. But he caught me.

Another thing which made our separation from our families (and girlfriend) more tolerable was that on two or three occasions, one of my English professors, Ben Nangle, who was also one of the Fellows of Pierson College, invited a group of us to spend the weekend with his family at their summer place on Branford Sound. Sleeping on an open sleeping porch was very nice and being on the water was a nice change from the urban setting of our College. His wife was a Radcliff graduate and they had two sons and a very smart Cocker Spaniel named "Albert." Mr. Nangle would gather us up after lunch on Saturday, and the three or four of us would ride with him in his Lincoln Zephyr out to the cottage. It seems strange to me that I can't remember who the others were because we had such a good time.

One of the things we did was to go clamming in the Sound close to the shore. The technique was to go out to a depth of about 6' and then bob up and down with the waves, maintaining a vertical position so we could feel the sandy bottom with our feet for the clams which were just lying on the sandy floor of the Sound. The variety of clam found was fairly large, 5"-6" in diameter, and just lying on the bottom, waiting to be picked up. When we felt one, we surface dived down to pick it up and deposit it in a mesh bag. Given their size it didn't take too many clams to fill the bag which we took back to prepare for dinner. The more buoyant salt water made it easier than it would have been in Lake Erie. When we got back, we would pry open the shells, extract the clams, and Mrs. Nangle used them to make the best clam chowder I have ever tasted. Mr. Nangle confided that it was the only thing she knew how to cook, and being a Radcliffe girl, it was probably true. After dinner there would be lots of conversation, followed by bridge, then to bed. On Monday morning Mr. Nangle would gather us up and we went back to the grind and he went off to his teaching duties. The memories of those weekends are warm and memorable. It was all so adult and glamorous for a middle-western schoolboy,  a different culture, a different world.

One humorous thing occurred on a Saturday morning in the Pierson courtyard. It was after breakfast and Professor Nangle and Albert were talking to a group of students, one of whom was a genuine German prince, Eugene (I can't remember his last name). I had never seen him before at Pierson; he was probably a grad student. He was moaning that his family couldn't get their money out of Germany because of the Nazis; that they had to return to Germany and spend it there; and they assuredly did not want to do that. I may be wrong, but I faintly recall that he was related to Senator Hamilton Fish of New York, who was the only senator to vote against the U.S. declaring war on Germany.

Eugene was about to leave to drive up to a boy's prep school in Massachusetts to be interviewed for a job teaching English. He was looking for someone to go with him and it ended up being me. He had just bought two German Shepherd (naturally) puppies who were frolicking around our feet. They momentarily quieted down; and wise old Albert calmly walked over to them, lifted his leg and peed on them. Eugene was furious and embarrassed. It was really funny. I hoped it was an omen.

It was a warm spring day and we drove up to Massachusetts with the top down on his convertible and while he was off for his interview, I was minding the puppies for him. It was at the edge of a large pond and he had closed the dam so that it could fill enough so I could swim if I cared to. I had brought homework for my Philosophy class with me and remember the assigned reading was Henri Bergson, a well-known French philosopher. Eventually it was time for a break, the pond had filled from the cold, running stream water to be deep enough for me to dive in which

I did. It was the shock of my life: I had never been so cold so fast before. I was numb. I couldn't breathe and in one body's length, I had turned and jumped back on to the rocks. I couldn't stop shivering and did all the way back to New Haven. I never heard if Eugene got the job. He was the only royalty I ever met. I never saw him again. It was a very strange day but an interesting one in many respects.

I probably should report on one important part of my college experience: the requirement that all scholarship students be assigned a "Bursary" job provided by the school which paid for the food portion of the annual fees, which were $267 per year for three meals per day. I just figured out that this amounted to about 30 cents per hour, not much by today's standards, but very significant for scholarship boys' families in those days. Needing a minimum of $1,000 a year to get by, $267 plus the $450 Scholarship, a total of $717, was a significant portion of the total bill, and another $200 to have a semi-luxurious experience would only have required a contribution from parents of about $500, surely a manageable amount, one would think. A different world from today. Although Yale boasts today that no student accepted in their admissions process would be unable to attend for financial reasons; the school would provide any amount needed above the parents ability to pay, enabling the student to graduate without student loan debt. Yale's financial aid to students in 2016 totaled $163 million dollars, an amount I find astounding.

As I have already written, I worked as a waiter in Freshman Commons my freshman year. Sophomore and junior years, I was assigned to work as an assistant to a professor, doing a completely different, much more genteel type of work, also, a little more interesting. I do not remember how this was accomplished, what the criteria for the appointments were, probably in response to requests of the various professors, or how I was notified.

Sophomore year I worked for Henry Hutchins, an English Professor from the University of Michigan who tried to teach English to engineering students in Sheffield School of Science, the equivalent of but separate from Yale College, which concentrated on the classics and humanities. Students were free to select courses in either undergraduate school, and I always felt sorry for the Sheff men because their studies were dominated by required courses and they had very few electives. On our side of the fence, I felt our courses were far more varied and interesting. We in Yale College were only required to take one or two courses in the sciences, and these could be in easy, survey, "gentlemen's" courses where you couldn't get less than a "C" if you showed up for class and kept your eyes open. To satisfy my science requirement, I took Qualitative Analysis Chemistry which was a different story altogether.

Professor Hutchins's job for me was to complete typing a handwritten manuscript left to him by a Professor Trent of the University of Indiana. The previous bursary student had probably finished about 60% of the transcription of the manuscript. The title of the book was *A Definitive Bibliography of the Works of Daniel Defoe*. The "manuscript" was in the form of individual sentences cut out of his hand-written subject matter and then rearranged and pasted on pages of a lined letter sized pad in their final form. These edited pages were stored in Manhattan Shirt boxes which were stacked along one whole wall of Professor Hutchins's office where I did my work.

Typing three hours a day, I actually finished that job, and thank goodness, Prof. Trent's handwriting was easy to read. Then the job became more interesting. Professor Hutchins had me go to the Rare Book Room in the basement of the Sterling Memorial Library and drag out dusty bundles of old, old original publications of DeFoe's writings. I had to locate those mentioned in Professor Trent's manuscript and compare the title page of the original with what Prof. Trent had written. This was tedious, exacting work, but it was fascinating and certainly fit in with my love of reading and literature. And my English Major.

Professor Hutchins was a very nice employer who explained what he wanted and then left it up to me to perform in my own way. He sometimes talked to me about his private life. He was probably about 40 years of age and married. He told me they desperately wanted to have a child. He told me, of all people, about having seen a fertility specialist who put him on a special diet which featured lots of oysters, and long walks for exercise. I recall his coming into his office one day, jubilant: they were expecting. I was very glad for him because they were so desperate, and he really was a nice person.

Junior year I worked for George Heard Hamilton, a Professor in the School of Art. He was also very nice to work for. He was one of the Fellows at Pierson, fairly small stature, wore glasses and had a sort of bulb on the end of this nose and pink cheeks. I think he was quite an authority in his field: The Impressionists. He later became the Director of the Williams College Art Museum, in Williamstown, Massachusetts, which we visited on one of our trips East and were quite impressed at its collection, anchored by the gifts of one Alumnus.

My job was to catalog his personal collection of books on art in his office, and after telling me what he wanted and showing me how to do it, he left me on my own. I remember nothing about the job itself, or even where his office was located. It should have been in the Art School on Chapel Street, but I don't recall ever setting foot in that unusual building. What little I knew about art I had gained from reading, not trained viewing of paintings and sculpture; works on appreciation by Berenson and the poetry of Robert Browning, for example; all I knew was a few of the great painters' names. So, it was a revelation for me to be exposed to a library of books on art and painters. I probably spent at least 50% of my (his?) time reading and studying the texts of the books I was supposed to be cataloging in his office, and not getting very much cataloging done. I don't think I finished the job. He had too many books, and I was too curious. I also suspect he may have known, and since it wasn't his money, didn't care.

Many years later he came to Cleveland to give a lecture at the Cleveland Museum of Art and we went to hear it. It was on one of the early French Impressionists I had never heard of before but was important for his early contributions to that school of painting. Prof. Hamilton had aged somewhat, naturally, but I recognized him immediately: the distinctive nose and pink cheeks. After his lecture there was tea and cookies in the lobby and it was possible to speak to him, which I did. I think he may have faintly recognized me (after about 30 years and 3-4,000 students) and I told him about my very real feelings of guilt through all the years for having really cheated him in my labors, but how much I had gained in knowledge and appreciation of the world he so obviously loved. He chuckled a bit and said to forget it, saying, "Go and Sin no more!"

He is another person I wish I had had in class and wish I had known better. I don't remember ever seeing him in Pierson or his office when I was there "working," and I never had time to take a class in Art Appreciation in spite of the interest aroused in that office. There simply was not enough time. I really needed about ten years to satisfy the curiosities aroused by those academic surroundings.

Senior year differed in one more way, not just going to class in the summertime. I was offered the job of Athletic Secretary, in charge of the Pierson intramural sports program, as part of the scholarship student administrative team involved with overseeing student affairs on behalf of the Master, Professor Wolfers. Looking back on it now, I wonder if Mrs. Wolfers after attending the swimming meet with me in the Spring of Junior year and having hosted my date for the Junior Prom, might not have had something to do with my appointment.

My responsibilities were to recruit from among the Pierson talented residents', teams to compete against the other nine colleges in the various sports: football, baseball, touch football, basketball, tennis, swimming, soccer, etc. I also served as a referee for touch football and soccer, about which I knew nothing. The college teams could be fleshed out with willing varsity team members in their own sport, or another, if needed. I cannot remember how I found the players, or how, in the case of football, they were coached, or secured their uniforms. I, as Secretary, was allowed to participate and did in swimming and touch football. The best part about the job was the pay: $400 which reduced the amount needed from my parents even further, which made me very proud.

Things I particularly remember were playing on the Pierson touch football team, swimming backstroke in the swim meets, and refereeing soccer matches. The touch football was eastern style, not what we used to play at home and took a little getting used to. For one thing the playing area was not confined to the width of a city street. It was played on full sized fields out near the Bowl. I always thought eastern style was basically basketball without hoops, only outdoors. Teams had to score a touchdown within five downs or the ball turned over to the other team; forward and lateral passes could be thrown from any place on the field without reference to the line of scrimmage; no blocking and a simple tag anywhere on the body ended the play.

Pierson's touch football team had two outstanding members: the former captain of the freshman basketball team and the star quarter-miler on the track team. They were a devastating combination. The center would pass the ball to the quarter-miler playing quarterback standing farther than usual from the line of scrimmage so that if he were blitzed by the opposing rushers, he was fast enough that he could elude them and then throw a pass to the former basketball star who, I swear could catch anything within 10-15 feet of him, high or low.

The talk of the other colleges by the end of the season was the game we played against Berkeley College. I hope that was one game that Mrs. Wolfers, who came to most events to cheer us on, did not miss. Pierson scored a touchdown every time it had a possession or intercepted a pass and ended with a score of 132 to 12 (22 touchdowns). It had to be some sort of record, and when I was refereeing other games, I could overhear the other players pep talking: "Remember what happened to Berkeley!"

There were two members of the Ford family, twins, on the Pierson team, one married to a cousin, Josephine Ford, who I think was a daughter of Edsel Ford. The twins were cousins and not involved with the manufacturing side of the family. I remember being supplanted in the championship game by one of the twins and being bitter because I thought I was the better player; and I was much taller than he was. I did get to play in the last quarter and did catch one pass for a touchdown. I can't remember which of the colleges won the championship, which qualified them to play against the champion Harvard "House" (they had Houses, not Colleges) team, which was a part of the Harvard-Yale weekend festivities. And, today, I can't imagine not knowing more about such celebrities. As members of the Ford family, I knew absolutely nothing about what they studied, or where they lived, one in Pierson certainly. The married couple must have had an apartment somewhere nearby. I suspect the other twin may have lived in Pierson's "Slave Quarters," the most exclusive living quarters in all ten of the colleges. Still I should remember how I recruited them for the team or seeing them even once in the dining hall. But I don't. At that age other things were more important. I don't remember a lot of them, either.

However, I do remember freshman year when we were young and impressionable, looking down from our room in Durfee Hall, to see young Henry Ford's red convertible Lincoln (we never saw him) parked across the street at the entrance to Berkeley College at lunch time. He would have been a junior, in his last year at Yale - he never graduated - and we only knew of his presence on campus by his signature automobile.

My memories of my senior year are diffuse today, but that it was a relaxed, mellow time, except for the cloud of World War II. I had enlisted in the Enlisted Reserve Corps (ERC) and knew I would be going into the army which was a fear inducing unknown, but I had survived college and learned the system and found a group of good friends who accepted me for who I was, warts and all. And as with every senior in college hated to see it all come to an end.

These feelings were intensified when on December 7th, 1942, a Sunday, just nine days before our accelerated graduation, I was in my room studying at the end of a sunny afternoon, getting ready to go to dinner, with the radio playing, when I heard an announcer alerting listeners to a message from the President. Then the somber voice of Franklin D. Roosevelt telling us of the surprise attack on Pearl Harbor, and that we were at war with Japan, that this was "a day of infamy," etc. When I entered the dining room later, I remember how quiet the room was, how hushed. Everyone knew that we were facing an unknown future where many of our lives would be lost - far different from that of one facing a graduate in peacetime.

I remember my parents coming to my abbreviated graduation ceremonies and their pride and joy at their realization of their dream for their first son, for whom so many sacrifices had been made. Sadly, graduation lost its full impact on me. I remember practically nothing of the actual ceremony because I had witnessed too many graduation ceremonies of other classes starting in high school while playing in the orchestra and having heard the same old platitudes and exhortations

I do remember forcefully hustling my parents off to bed wherever they were staying so I could get back to those last few precious moments with the friends I might never see again. It was hard being tom between the two loyalties: the underlying love of family and the group of friends who were my support in my maturation process and leaving the warmth of the nest of my childhood.

After graduation, I don't remember, but we must have packed the car with my accumulated belongings (how did we dispose of the stuffed chair and sofa bed?) and reversed the process of the trip four years earlier, driving back home to Tiedeman Road, to a different house. At some point in those college years, while my father was establishing his own new mortgage loan business, my parents had sold the house in Lakewood (to my former homeroom teacher in Emerson Junior High, George Webb) and converted the cottage on Tiedeman Road into a permanent, year round residence. A basement was dug and the cottage structure was moved on to it (by Uncle Louie? and if so, I missed watching him do it), plus new construction in the form of an addition plus a second floor single dormer style bedroom for the four boys. Most gratefully, the first floor opposite the new master bedroom had an INDOOR bathroom! The cottage was transformed into a modest, very functional home. Also, they built a two-car garage across the driveway and the original builder's sheds remained for tool storage and chicken coop.

My induction notice arrived, I was to proceed to Fort Hayes, Columbus, Ohio, on February 15, 1943, to begin my army career. So, I only lived in the new house on Tiedeman Road for 57 days, and, as it turned out that was a lifetime total. It also meant the end of any influence I might have had in normal times on my younger brothers who were only twelve and fourteen years of age when I left. They lost any benefit they might have gained from observing an older brother's character and problem-solving ability. I also feel I missed out on not observing the way they developed and being more a part of their lives.

To toughen me up a bit after a largely sedentary life at college after the swimming season ended, my father found a job for me with Tom Kirk, a member of Fifth Church, and good friend. Tom owned a coal company with a coal yard on Berea Road on Cleveland's west side, next to the railroad tracks. I had to secure a chauffeur's license in order to operate a truck, and proceeded to drive a 5 ton dump truck, loaded with lump soft coal by hand (shovel) from piles in the yard which was next to a railroad siding. Deliveries were made to customers who lived mainly on the west side and the coal was shoveled from the truck into basement coal bins. We also delivered loads of pea sized stoker coal to the Federal Reserve Bank in downtown Cleveland on Rockwell Avenue at E. 6th Street. This was a much more desirable job because the truck was backed into a large open room at the rear of the building under the watchful eye of a guard with a machine gun (!) in his guard booth next to the door. Once in position the truck bed was elevated, and the coal was dumped onto a steel grid in the floor which opened onto a bin in the basement. This was the best part of the job because it was so easy, and relatively labor free, at least on the delivery end.

It was terribly dirty work. Coal dust is grimy and greasy, and it permeated my skin, my hands, my nostrils and ears and I felt as if I would never be clean again. It didn't seem to matter how long I spent soaking in the tub or under the shower. My poor mother must have gone crazy trying to get whatever clothes I wore clean. I only worked there for about six weeks, but it certainly left a lasting memory with me.

I remember three specific things about this short-lived career: 1) the immense pride I felt when I presented my mother with a $25 War Bond purchased with my first paycheck. (I don't remember how much my pay was - it may have been $25 or $35 per week); 2) having a delivery in my Grandma Schmidt's neighborhood and calling her to see if I could pay her a visit. I parked the truck at the curb in front of the house I had loved in my early childhood and we visited and then she gave me a lunch of homemade chicken soup with her homemade noodles. It was the last meal I ever ate at her house, although there were other later visits, I know she saw me in my army uniform when she came to Detroit with my family for my wedding; 3) and the really dramatic memory of a delivery to the Federal Reserve Bank when going down the hill on Berea Road approaching Detroit Street, I felt something wrong with the steering and brakes. I looked out the window to the rear and was horrified to see the wheel had spun out from the truck about three feet and was bending, making the truck body loaded with pea coal start to tilt. The load might spill, and I had no brakes and Detroit Street, which had a streetcar line and bore heavy traffic, was very near. I was pretty panic-stricken and didn't know what to do. Luckily, I came to a stop before reaching Detroit Street. I must have dismounted from the truck and found a phone at a nearby business and called Mr. Kirk, who sent another driver with an empty truck so we could shovel the coal from one truck to the other. The new driver then completed the delivery. I'm sure Mr. Kirk arrived to survey the damage and it was probably he who got me back to the coal yard. It was such a shock for me that perhaps it's not surprising that I don't remember all the details surrounding the incident: how many other trucks and drivers did Mr. Kirk have; did the police come to the scene; did I have to fill out an accident report; did I ride with the new driver to the delivery and then back to the yard, rather than Mr. Kirk getting me back there after surveying the damage; how did he get the truck repaired; did I ever drive that truck again? I just know that I was very lucky.

During the period when this "dirty" work was going on, the induction date arrived in the mail, but I don't remember what it felt like to have a date certain at last. That surprises me today. I am sure I spent as many evenings as possible and weekend time on dates with my high school sweetheart, Carol Kuekes, a relationship classified as "going steady", now three years old, which had developed into talk of marriage and our being privately engaged. I actually picked apples for 50 cents an hour in the New Haven area in the fall of 1942, to save money for an engagement ring. Neither set of parents would acknowledge nor accept this situation and thus nothing formal ever happened.

Parting from her and my family made induction into the army doubly difficult. I remember what must have been our last date: don't remember what we did, but saying goodnight, goodbye on the gravel driveway of her home at Laurel Lake in Solon, Ohio; driving away only to turn back when half way home; returning to her home and somehow getting her attention without arousing her parents; her coming back out to the car and my open driver's window so we could have one more farewell kiss; and then the long drive home, 10-12 miles, and being greeted at the front door by my Dad who was worried because it was now about 3 a.m. and he was concerned something might have happened to me; my reassuring him there had been no car trouble or accident. Just that I had never felt such a physical ache in my chest in the heart area before.

One other very poignant memory of this time was Dad waiting in the car impatiently for me to say goodbye to Mom who was standing on the porch in the front doorway. Ours was not a demonstrative family. I think my parents in their unspoken philosophy of child rearing, especially in light of their children being all boys, felt that outward displays of affection, or emotion, might be construed as, or lead to, signs of weakness. Such displays could not be allowed if their boys were to grow up to be stalwart and manly. Therefore, there was never any hugging or kissing or patting on the cheek or shoulder in general day-to-day life, or on special occasions. Of course, I never passed brother Russ and he never passed me nearby without slugging each other on the upper arm, but that was not the same thing. So, it was a monumental experience for me when my mother with tears in her eyes kissed me on the lips as we said goodbye. I can still feel it. A chapter of our lives had just ended, and I was now on my way, even more so than entering college, to a new, far more unknown and hazardous future. This was repeated a short time later at the railroad station in Linndale, Ohio, when my father who always seemed so remote, so critical, shook my hand and hugged me, saying goodbye, tears in his eyes, and saying he would give anything if he could only go in my place. It was February 15, 1943.

I remember few details of my swearing in at Fort Hayes, Columbus, Ohio, which was near the downtown and if still there, I would not know how to find it today. I do remember a huge, gymnasium-like room where 300 inductees slept on cots and where those nearest the windows insisted on keeping them closed. I estimate that within 30 minutes after lights out the atmosphere turned into a classic definition of a "miasma". You could feel the humidity in the air and within a day or two everyone developed raging head colds. I remember blowing my nose constantly into the one handkerchief I had brought with me and having to wash it in the latrine with hand soap. After it dried it was stiff as a board and hurt to blow my nose again. (If only they had had Kleenex then.) It was all so new and bewildering and scary. College did not prepare me for this.

Memories are blurred but I know we had physical exams after sitting around naked on a cold stone or marble bench, freezing, for what seemed like hours; finally being issued GI uniforms and underwear and socks and army boots; and a barracks bag to stow it all in. Then we had to take the Army General Comprehension Test (AGCT), after which we were eventually interviewed by a Corporal, who had the test results in front of him, and this I do remember clearly. He asked in a very kindly, solicitous way if I knew where I would like to serve in "this man's Army". The scuttlebutt was that the best deal in the whole army was the Air Corps Ground Crew. You were far behind the front lines and best of all, the Basic Training was in Miami Beach, which sounded very good to me. So I told the friendly Corporal my choice and he replied that this sounded like a wise choice to him, that with my test scores and the fact that the Army needed men in that branch of the service that that was undoubtedly where I would end up. It was the first time since I left home that I felt relaxed.

I think the processing took four or five days and finally a group of twelve or fourteen of us, utterly ignorant of the military, not even knowing how or when to salute, under the command of another inductee, equally ignorant, appointed as an "acting" corporal with a large brown envelope under his arm which contained our orders, train tickets, food vouchers, etc., boarded a train. It didn't take long, probably as far as Springfield, to realize we were not heading for Cincinnati, but going westward, the long way to Miami Beach. Everyone in the group (we could hardly be called a squad yet) had been assured by our friendly Corporal at the Induction Center that we would soon be doing close order drill on the warm sands of Miami Beach, so we were a little confused. Our hopes were somewhat raised when we disembarked about dinnertime in St. Louis. We straggled (no marching yet!) past a train waiting next to the boarding platform which had "Flamingo Express," St. Petersburg, Florida, printed under the windows on the side of the car. The thought flashed through my mind, "Aha - secret troop movement." Why not? There were signs everywhere warning "Loose Lips Sink Ships."

We had to eat before the next leg of our journey - to the Promised Land - and had supper at the Harvey's Restaurant in the station. These memories are very sharp and quite detailed. Everyone had the same meal: a large slice of ham with a cherry sauce, one of my favorites, and all paid for by vouchers from our acting corporal. We all felt pretty good with a full stomach after the long day on the train.

We then boarded another train with Pullman Sleeper Cars, not the Flamingo Express, but my first experience sleeping in a berth and not sitting up in the coach section was not all it could have been. There were not enough berths so each of us could have a single, so I ended up in a lower berth with a bunkmate, sleeping head to toe. His is one of the few names I can remember of all those I met and lived with in Basic Training: Petersen. He was a "good guy," an eastside Clevelander, whose family owned a dry-cleaning business on Scranton Road, down in the "Flats" by the Cuyahoga River. They specialized in dry-cleaning lady's fancy kid gloves.

This was my first experience traveling on a train with sleeping facilities and after an endless night of blowing noses and hacking coughs, hearing the clacking of the train wheels, we all woke up the next morning with a serious case of the "GIs," army parlance for diarrhea. We were heading south close to the west bank of the Mississippi River, not eastwards to St. Petersburg, and looking at a map we had found, the only posts we could find were Fort Smith, Arkansas, and Fort Sill, Oklahoma. We clustered in a group as close as possible to the rest room at the end of the car, and occupied it, rotating, all day long. It was a miserable day. I don't remember ever having ever had anything like it before. As the day wore on we became aware of two officers (I later realized that they had to be in the Field Artillery and returning to Fort Sill) who snickered at us every time they looked at us or passed by muttering "Mule Pack," which sounded a little ominous but didn't mean anything to us at the time. A couple of us were tall and I'm sure this is what drew their comments, that and our obvious rawness.

Eventually the train arrived at Oklahoma City, where we transferred to a school bus for the 100+ mile trip to Fort Sill, Lawton, Oklahoma, our only possible destination. We all realized immediately that there was no toilet on that little bus. It was a desperate bus trip with only one stop about half-way at Chickasha, Oklahoma, the hometown of the famous New York Yankee pitcher, Allie Reynolds. It was easy to see why he would want to escape to the big time. Chickasha was just a crossroads town with a gas station, and a little general store, but did have a one story adobe hotel (at least that's what the sign called it) where we scrambled in desperation for the restroom just off the lobby. We were all in the same straits and were dismayed to find that every stall was Pay Only Enter, requiring a dime in a slot to open the door, and there were three or four doors. None of us had a dime. Our solution was to hoist a smaller man over the top of the door which he then opened from the inside and all turned out well. After a very long day, we eventually arrived at Fort Sill after dark, were fed, and led to bed in a temporary barracks where we stayed until we received our final assignments. We started our new lives the next day.

We learned early on that this was a serious business. One of our group was really sick, far more than a head cold, and was taken to the base hospital where he died a few days later. We speculated that it was probably pneumonia. We realized for the first time that in the army death didn't only come from an enemy bullet or artillery shell.

I don't remember all the steps of our processing but do remember that on the second or third day the taller men were marched to a room where we were examined by an army doctor, a Major; we had to stand on a hospital type scale with its height measuring arm fixed at six feet, and if you had to duck under it in order to be weighed and if the weight exceeded 165 lbs., you went on to the next step. This consisted of removing your shoes and socks and holding your feet up off the floor so the Major could look at them. He looked and then asked each of us in a kindly manner if we had ever had any trouble with our feet. Not being flat footed, and my athlete's foot having cleared up years earlier, I innocently answered that my feet were fine. That is how I ended up in the mule pack artillery training program. It was the easiest test I ever took, and I had a perfect score.

Basic training lasted 13 weeks and our barracks were close to the stables and stable yards close to the perimeter of the camp. It was all so new and confusing I don't remember many of the details of our exact location in relation to the rest of the post, nor do I remember the order in which we learned the basic military skills, which, for the most part, was done by our cadre: army courtesy - how and when to salute; how to address an officer; how to march in close order drill; how to clean and reassemble our weapons - our weapon was the carbine, much lighter in weight and shorter in range; how to fire the various other weapons, the Garand rifle, the Lee-Enfield rifle, the Browning Automatic Rifle, and the 45 caliber Browning automatic pistol. We went to various ranges to fire the weapons and after practice, were graded. I was always impressed with the safety measures and the care with which the cadre kept track of the ammunition. There was no chance of stealing even one round, if you had any inclination to do so. I think my army records put me in the "Marksman" class. I was more accurate with the carbine and BAR than the machine gun or pistol,

In addition to all the ordinary duties: such as KP, working in the mess hall in preparation of the food; cleaning up after meals; cleaning a shower room (latrine) and scrubbing the floors to pass inspection; keeping our footlockers tidy and beds made properly was not all that different from what I had learned how to do at home from my mother (who did not wear a uniform with stripes on its arms). We had to learn to work with the mules: groom them, feed them, lead them (never get behind a mule), clean up after them in the stable yard. This was different. Although my great Uncles Louie and Irving had farm animals, I had never had anything to do with them directly.

Along with all the other college boys, I learned and used a new vocabulary which was a far cry from that used in French Poetry of the 19th Century. I think it was the only language the mules understood. It was very common at all levels in the army. Considering the levels of frustration at the army way of doing things and the hazards we were exposed to, it being an all-male environment, it's not surprising. However, I was happy that when I left the army the foul language disappeared over night. If it had become a habit, I worried what I would do in civilian life. I wince these days when I hear young women using the same words and expressions which is very common. That kind of language is really only appropriate in an army barracks.

There were 4 squads of 12 men each which formed 1 platoon, and 4 platoons in our Company under the command of a Captain whom I do not remember ever seeing. Our training was done under the direction of a Sergeant Comstock, from Detroit, whom I ran into in front of the May Company store on Euclid Avenue in downtown Cleveland, with his new bride long after the war was over, and Corporal Knoke. They were under the command of a Master Sergeant whose name I do not remember. He was an enlisted man in the pre-war army when the total number of men in the entire armed forces was 40-50,000 and when the size of the army expanded, so did his rank which was the highest rank an enlisted man could rise to. With his background he had very little use for college men, and we knew it. We set out to prove that college boys could perform whatever jobs they were given faster and better than ordinary draftees. Sergeant Comstock was strict but had a sense of humor. Corporal Knoke was serious at all times and definitely did not have a sense of humor. I remember appreciating the professional way they did their job of preparing us for the field. They really knew what they were doing, but I'm not sure they had ever seen a real battlefield.

Our Company was a little unusual because it had the first influx of college men who had been allowed to graduate, mixed with the regular draftees, resulting in a mixture of men with two different levels of education and economic background. We had a lot of redneck hillbillies and farmers. They made excellent soldiers. I also remember after the early morning reveille at 6 a.m. waking up to loud, twangy, country western singing. It wasn't my favorite way to start the day.

Our barracks were typical army post two story frame, long buildings with a door at each end. The Sergeant's office and sleeping quarters were located at one end on the building on the 1st floor. The floors were wood and were scrubbed on hands and knees with brushes every week, and the walls were not insulated. Oklahoma gets very cold in the winter and equally as hot in the summer. We had cots, not bunks, and a footlocker at the foot of each bed, which was inspected frequently for tidiness. The latrine and the mess hall were in separate buildings. All these areas had white glove inspections every Saturday morning, and if anything was deficient it had to be corrected, or the punishment would be confinement to barracks, and no movies, or ice cream at the PX. It took a little getting used to.

KP duty was assigned by rotation and listed on a bulletin board which it was wise to keep track of. There is a picture of me dressed in my GIs (work clothes,) wearing a helmet liner wool cap, sitting at the back door of the mess hall peeling potatoes with another draftee, a classic army picture. My memories of the food are good. But the different tastes of the college boys versus that of the farm boys was obvious. Boiled navy beans were served with most meals and never touched by the college boys. There was wonderful grapefruit from Texas and Jell-O with fruit cocktail which were never touched by the other half. Uneaten food was disposed of in large metal containers by the exit door. Rather than letting good food go to waste, I saved the grapefruit by squeezing each half into a cup and devouring the Jell-O combination by eating as much as I could right from the big serving dish, until I couldn't spend another minute, before having to fall out for formation for whatever the activities of the day had in store for us.

One thing that was inedible was the pancakes for breakfast. I remember being on KP, getting up at 5 a.m., staggering over to the Mess Hall still half asleep, and putting the pancake batter mixed by the "chef" on the grill, and when they were done depositing those beautiful, tender, fluffy pancakes, one by one, in layers in a tall metal, 50 gal. container where they sat until 7 a.m. when breakfast was "served." By then they resembled pieces of a cold, soggy desk blotter. It was a major crime, but the way the Army did it!

Because of the number of men in the Company, I think I only had KP duty three or four times for the duration of our training. One thing I hated was having to wash dishes with the army's version of soap which looked like large lumps of yellow cheddar cheese. I was convinced it had an extra heavy portion of lye in it for hygienic reasons. We had to cut it into slivers, put it into the very hot water, in the large sinks and after stirring to get suds, begin the scrubbing, up to the elbows in the scalding water. There were no rubber gloves in those days, of course, and it did wonders for my skin. Also, since extra KP was one of the forms of punishment the cadre could inflict, after one tour of regular KP and learning what that entailed, it was a great incentive to follow orders, no matter how unpleasant.

Considering the impact of the training, and the pride of being in a mule pack outfit which developed very quickly and has lasted to this day, it's surprising to me that I don't remember more of the details of our daily routines and our surroundings. We were told what to wear every day; which pair of boots to wear (we had two pair and they were the most comfortable shoes I ever had, and interestingly, size 11 1/2D, not my usual 12B); listened to lectures on military law and how to salute, and when - only when approaching an officer, never an enlisted man; calisthenics and close order drill; how to march in step; all this to establish conformity and discipline on a group of young men who were carefree civilians. They had to be made into obedient soldiers quickly for their own survival, and that of the country. Looking back on that period I have to say that the Army knew how to do it. It certainly worked on me. I think I turned into a pretty good soldier. I know I was proud of my uniform.

Training for the mule pack was different in some respects from that of the other artillery men, and different from the infantry, or tank corps, or the air force. We had to learn how to care for our real, live mules; how to groom them and how to feed them. Our sentry duty was different. We did not walk a sentry post guarding our camp at night, but had stable guard duty, taking care of the mules' needs. It paid to be very careful if you had to enter a stall. One poor GI, probably half asleep, walked into a stall directly behind an irritable mule which kicked straight back with both hooves and crushed his chest and killed him. One of our other duties was the housekeeping chore of using large 6" bristle paving brooms to sweep the stable yard daily, push the debris into piles which were deposited in large bags and carted away. We had a "battery" of twelve white (actually gray) mules, which made us a little different from the other squads.. These were the only mules we worked with, so we became familiar with a lot of their quirks. One thing I learned was that mules loved to have their necks scratched, and behind their ears even more so. And the way to control them if they became frisky was to grab an ear and twist it. It was the only way I ever saw to control them. I always liked to work with one particular female (Jenny) mule whose identifying brand on her left haunch was 7K47. She was gentle and even tempered and never tried to bite me or kick me as some of the others did. I always tried to have a handful of linseed meal in my pocket to give her as a treat and when I approached the stable yard before a training session, would whistle and she would trot over to the fence to get her goody. That made it easy for me to claim her to use in our training. I never forgot her number and my wife would later claim that she was a rival, teasing, of course. 7K47 became a by-word in our house.

We had to learn how to load a mule using a pack saddle made of wood similar to the support of a very small picnic table without the tabletop fitted to the mule's back, 2 "x 4s," with a bar between them, to which the loads were fastened with rope. We learned the "Double Diamond Hitch" which was more secure and used for longer hikes than the "Squaw Hitch" which was simpler and faster. Both hitches involved two men, one on each side of the mule who hoisted the load, 60 pound bags of grain in our case, up to the saddle and then tossed ropes over the object being loaded securing the load to the saddle and then tied the knots which gave the hitches their names. I wish I could say that I remembered how to tie the knots, but it was a long time ago. We usually had twelve mules per squad, tended by two men each, four squads per platoon and four platoons per Company. Stretched out in single file it was quite a sight. Six of the squad mules carried the 75 mm howitzer, "our gun", broken down into six loads: breach block, tube (barrel) wheels, axle, frame, and tail piece. The other six mules carried the artillery rounds. There was also a herd of about 20 pack mules following, carrying the bulk supplies, and herded by a mounted cadre soldier. His job was made easier because he led a female mule, or horse, which was in heat and all the male mules kept trying to make her acquaintance.

At the end of our training we had a competition to see which squad could load a mule the fastest. We started with the disassembled gun parts on the ground and had to saddle the mules, load the parts, and dash 100 yards to the finish line. The college boys did it in less than 2 minutes, which amazed me, and which frustrated the cadre, especially our Master Sergeant, who, not surprisingly, was rooting for the farm boys.

Compared to the 105 mm or 150 mm howitzer batteries, whose trainees rode trucks to their firing ranges, (we walked) and which I never saw fired, our 75 mm gun looked very puny. However, our squad was chosen to demonstrate the new "High Burst" shells before an audience of observers: visiting field artillery officers from our allies, as well as U.S. officers and trainees, all seated in a small grandstand behind our guns.

The range was a large, open field about 500 yards distant with carcasses of ruined tanks and trucks scattered about, used as targets. We set up our four guns very precisely about 30 feet apart, and when our sergeant was satisfied, an officer dialed in the proper timer setting on the nose of the shells for the distance to the range where the targets were located. The shells were then inserted into the tube, the breech block closed, and upon a signal of the officer, all four of the lanyards were pulled simultaneously. I was sitting directly behind one of the guns and was amazed that I could actually see the shell all the way to its zenith, probably because of its high trajectory and relatively low velocity. This feeling turned to horror when I saw the shells burst, simultaneously, all at about the height of a telephone pole over an area comparable to a football field, where the shrapnel created a cloud of dust, shredding everything in its path. Suddenly I realized that no ordinary fox hole would provide any protection whatsoever. It was a very sobering morning.

We spent the first five weeks of training on the basics of being a soldier with minimal contact with the mules, and then got into the real training for our specialty: climbing mountains while tending our mules. Sgt. Comstock advised us one day at the end of week five that we would take our first "walk" the next day; we would be walking out to Rabbit Hill, a distance of 18 miles. I was incredulous. No one could walk 18 miles in one day - especially a sedentary college student, but we did it. We did not march in formation, as in close order drill, or moving as a squad somewhere on the base. Once we had loaded the mules, we walked in what was called "route step" which was at your own pace, which in this case was dominated by the mule you were walking beside. A word about the speed: *The Army Manual* states that a mule walks at 3 miles per hour. This is not true. Our mules walked at 4-4 1/2 miles per hour, and if they did, so did we. Also, it was a steady pace, up-hill and down-hill, and I learned it was easier going up than coming down. By the end of the 13th week, I couldn't walk any slower than 4 mph and keep my balance.

After the adventure of the walk to Rabbit Hill, our real walks, or hikes began. Fort Sill is located at the base of the Wichita Wildlife Game Preserve, a small mountain range with mountains as high as 3,500 feet and naturally rugged but hardly the Rockies. The WPA built several lakes in the range during the Great Depression, and it was used for recreation. This range was clearly visible from our stable yards and was very beautiful to me. I thought of the Old Testament Psalm, "I will look unto the hills, whence cometh my help" often, and it provided an odd comfort for me. Having grown up in the part of Ohio, which was very flat, looking at hills was something new for me. Later when we built our house in Brecksville, a very hilly area south of Cleveland, my army experience played a part in our selection of the building site.

For the next 7 weeks, typically starting out at 7 a.m., mules loaded, we left barracks and stables behind and walked and climbed with full 30 lb. backpack and carbine. It was early spring with a few days in the 80s and I do not recall any rainy days, which would have complicated things considerably. We went up and down the mountains, tending our mules, never allowed to sit and rest, a distance of 30-35 miles (!) usually arriving at our campsite about mid-afternoon. There we pitched camp, dug slit trench latrines, dug sump holes for the camp debris, and picked a spot to sleep and pitched our pup tents, although we usually didn't bother, simply spreading the tent on the ground to provide a barrier to moisture rising during the night while we slept under the stars. After the struggle with the rough terrain, there was always a truck waiting for us with our food on it which I thought was ironic. We covered this distance in 8 hours or less. We had a 10-minute break every hour which was used to check the loads on the mules and their cinch straps. I don't recall anyone checking us, other than to be sure none of us was sitting down. The second day we broke camp and hiked a short distance, probably about 10 miles, and set up camp all over again. That was the day we actually set up our guns and learned the use of "firing poles" which were used to orient the gun position to a compass. Then on the third day we packed up and hiked home, another 30-35 miles. Recalling all this I can't believe we did it.

It was beautiful country with things turning green in the spring and the weather gradually warming which brought snakes out of hibernation. I do remember on one of the hikes hearing gun shots and learned that Sgt. Comstock, who was riding a mule (something I never did,) shot a 6' rattlesnake, which must have been fun for him. I also remember stepping on a low-lying cactus and one of the needles penetrated the instep of my boot. The pain was so intense that I couldn't walk so I sat down (the only time I ever did that on a hike,) unlaced my canvas legging and took off my boot. By this time Sgt. Comstock was looking down on me very sternly, not a good omen, He saw me pull out the needle so there was no punishment, and the pain stopped immediately. I got put back together and had to run to catch up with the column.

I learned the importance of keeping my feet dry after our first hike when Sgt. Comstock, riding on his mule high and dry, led us through a shallow stream and I had the only trouble with my feet in all our hikes. The Kiwi polish I used for waterproofing my boots did not keep all the water out, and my feet became very tender. We learned to find stones to cross the stream; or a narrow stretch we could jump over going a 100 yards out of our way if necessary. Anything to keep our feet dry. The terrain was so rough and rocky that I wore out the heels of one pair of my boots on one hike and had to get a new pair from the Quartermaster.

One of our later hikes, probably May 1st, 1943, occurred on payday (we were paid $50 per month less a deduction for part of a War Bond and laundry) and that was always done right after breakfast, and usually took a couple of hours. After passing the "short-arm" inspection, we had to stand in line, present ourselves in turn, and receive the balance of our $50 in cash. Thus, we did not start out our hike until after lunch when the temperature had risen to about 80 degrees.

I remember starting down a narrow defile and hearing the distinctive snap of a recoilless 75 mm rifle which had a very flat trajectory and was used as an anti-tank weapon. It was mounted on the rear of a Jeep, making it very mobile. It was being fired at a target on a hill the other side of the defile, right over our heads, several yards above our heads, to be sure, but scary all the same. Then, a little farther on, we were walking close to a road when an officer with a beautiful girl drove by in a convertible with the top down and you would have been impressed by how the whole column smartened up.

Another memorable walk was the one, when because of the heat, all the men had emptied their canteens which held probably a quart of water and had consumed all their candy bars and their mouths had turned to cotton. We had more than half-way to go, "Over Hill, over Dale," until our 8 hours came to an end at our campsite where the truck was waiting for us with our food. I don't remember how we made it, but several of the men had severe cramps, and others were throwing up. But not me. After setting up the camp, digging latrine, sump hole, and cleaning up after eating, we discovered that some of the mules had developed "bunches." These were large blisters caused by chafing of the girths holding the saddles and aggravated by the heat. They were raised and about 5-6" in diameter. The bunches had to be rubbed out by hand, and I remember standing next to my mule with my head against its side rubbing by hand his hairy coat in a circular motion until the swelling subsided and the mule could carry his load the next day. It usually took about an hour to clear up and the mule would get restless and irritable. Time to be on the lookout for a forward kick.

On one of the hikes when it was very hot, and after we had discovered that instead of candy bars, the smart thirst quencher was to slip into the mess hall storeroom and "borrow" 6 or 7 lemons to store in our back pack, in the area where our mess kits usually were kept (our packs were never inspected when we were out in the field, luckily). We had found, I don't know how, that biting into a lemon and sucking out the juice, cleared all the cotton out of the mouth and made the walking much easier. They actually tasted sweet!

At twilight we discovered one the lakes created by the WPA, who had made many improvements, roads etc. It was a park for the public, and many of us went swimming which was incredibly refreshing. The water was very clear and just the right temperature after enduring the heat of the day. Also, there was a large well with a pump and I will never forget how sweet and delicious that water was. It all lingers in my memory to this day.

The weekly hikes were all the same format - endurance tests producing well-conditioned soldiers. Until the final test which was a short two day walk to where we did an RSOP, Reconnaissance, Selection of Position. It was only a distance of 12 miles. We set up the guns ready to fire with specific imaginary targets, using aiming posts, then disassembling everything and moving the next day to a nearby location and setting up all over again. In a way this was our final exam. This was also the hike after we had run out of meat the previous hike. So, the army made up for it by serving wonderful, thick pork chops for every meal, five meals in a row, including breakfast on our final outing. After lunch we broke camp and started back to our stable yard twelve miles away about 4 p.m. I was very lucky and was assigned to the lead communication mule, the first mule in the column, whose load was two large spools of wire. The mules had not been fed and the cadre had dates since it was Friday night, so there was no restraint in the pace. We were back in the stable yard at 6 p.m., having covered 12 miles in 2 hours, and the column was stretched out behind me for what seemed like a mile. The men behind me dog-trotted the whole way. I am still amazed at the whole thing.

After our marathon march, I don't recall how our basic training ended. There may have been some sort of formal parade and passing in review of the commanding officers which I know we did once, but it may have been earlier. I think we were all promoted from Private ($50/month) to Private First Class ($54/month), still a private, and given a three-day pass prior to our next posting. At this point in time, the influx of college graduates was so large that the OCS (Officer Candidate School) for every branch of the service was closed; it was recommended that we try to qualify for a new program, the ASTP (Army Specialized Training Program) which might lead to becoming an officer without ever having to attend an OCS. It seemed like the best deal by far for me. Certainly, better than signing up for Saddle Maker's School at Camp Carson, Colorado.

The ASTP offered courses at various colleges in either science/engineering or languages. Since I had had French since the 8th grade all through college, up to reading the *French Romantic Poets of the 19th century*, I went for an interview to try to qualify for French. The interview took place on the base in another building with an inner and outer office, where the applications were filled out, handed in to a Corporal who checked to see if they were filled in properly and then sent us in to be interviewed by an officer.

The form I filled out asked three questions: was I fluent in reading, writing, and speaking? I felt confident that I was quite fluent in both the reading and writing areas. But questioned whether I was in the speaking department. I had never spoken French outside the classroom, never even having visited Quebec on vacation where, I might have heard real day-to-day French spoken. I went up to the Corporal and asked him how "fluent in speaking" was defined. He looked over my application forms and asked me who my last professor was, and I told him: Professor Seronde. He promptly said, "You're fluent."

He was a fellow Yale graduate and recognized the professor's name and the level of the courses he taught. So I checked "fluent" in the speaking box, and went in to be interviewed (this part of the episode I don't remember at all - not even the interviewing offer's rank), I walked out with orders to report to a STAR (Separation, Training & Replacement) unit in Stillwater, Oklahoma, home of Oklahoma A &M University.

Before reporting for this next stage in my Army career, the whole company was granted a three-day pass, our first in the army. This pass was good for 72 hours and limited to a radius of 100 miles. No chance to go home. This meant that the only large city that was legal was Oklahoma City. I applied for and was granted my pass by an officer whose name I do not remember. In the meantime, I had received an invitation arranged by the Christian Science Chaplain to spend my three-day pass weekend with a Christian Science family in Tulsa, Oklahoma, which was well beyond the 100-mile radius. This would be the next best thing to being with my family whom I really missed in Cleveland. I wanted very badly to go to Tulsa but feared being caught by the MPs.

I was in a quandary. Another Christian Science officer in the Christian Science organization on the Post offered to forge a pass for me and urged me to accept the invitation, pointing out that I would only be exposed to the MPs on the way to Tulsa; there would be a ride for me in a private car to return to Fort Sill.

After a lot of soul searching, I decided to take the risk and go. But I was afraid to go by train for fear of being found out by an MP patrolling the aisles of the cars and asking to see my pass, which could result in my being sentenced to a stockade after a court martial. And I thought I was a sophisticated army man! So, I decided to take a bus. No patrolling MPs on buses. I carefully placed my legitimate pass in my left breast pocket, and the fake in my right pocket and rode in the front seat of the bus all the way to Tulsa, where, upon arrival, when I got off the bus I walked right into the arms of an MP. Before he could challenge me, with my fake pass in my hand, I babbled that I was late, in a terrible hurry, had to call someone, and where was the nearest pay phone. He pointed it out and I dashed to it and never had to show the fake pass to the MP. It was quite a relief.

I called my hosts. They came to pick me up. Their name was Levorsen and they were very nice and lived in a lovely home. Their daughter was away at college, so I stayed in her room. After getting settled, I went downstairs and sat down at the piano in the living room and found something to play, the first time I had touched a keyboard in what seemed a very long time. There were two other army guests expected, both officers, and while I was playing, they arrived. To my utter dismay one of them was the officer who had signed my valid pass. I think I was thoroughly terrified! After introductions and getting acquainted, I confessed and the officer whose name I cannot remember got a good chuckle out of it, and said not to worry, he wouldn't tell our Captain about it until I was off the post.

Saturday night we went out to a restaurant for dinner, and while there were relatively few servicemen in Tulsa, I remember walking down the street afterwards and being embarrassed when I automatically returned the salutes given to the officers I was with. Enlisted men do not salute each other. My officer friends found it very amusing.

Sunday we all went to church and then came home to a fabulous chicken Maryland-style dinner, creamed, with mashed potatoes and gravy, followed by delicious, homemade pecan pie, which I had never had before. After three months of army chow, it had to be one of the most wonderful meals I ever had.

All turned out well. I think it was the officer who had signed my fake pass who drove us back to Fort Sill where we arrived on time. And, I had spent time in a normal family setting and done normal things. It was a welcome decompression before going on to my next posting.

I do not remember how I got to Stillwater, but there was probably another secret troop movement of twelve or fourteen enlisted men under the command of another acting Corporal, and I do not know where it is in relation to Fort Sill, geographically. One of the things I regret is my lack of interest in the places I was stationed. I now wish I had had a map to keep track. It would have helped to be able to retrace steps. Stillwater was a small town but the home of a state university and, apparently, had virtually no Army presence on campus. The STAR center did not seem overly large and, therefore, the citizens had very little experience in dealing with large numbers of enlisted men. We saw some men in naval uniforms so there may have been some naval program at the University.

The contrast with Lawton, Oklahoma, the old, small town near Fort Sill which swarmed with uniformed men, which the residents had to put up with for years, was startling. I only went into Lawton once on a Sunday to go to church, I think, and the people outside of those in church, mostly tradespeople, treated the servicemen like dirt. They had had years of dealing with the riff raff element among the servicemen; so perhaps their attitude was understandable. It didn't make it any more palatable for me. I couldn't get back to Fort Sill quickly enough and I never went back until the day we left.

The people in Stillwater on the other hand couldn't have been nicer to us; were appreciative of our service; greeted us from their front porches after dinner; and generally tried to make us feel at home. It was a welcome change.

We were in Stillwater for about two weeks and after the rigors of basic training at Fort Sill, it was a dream. Our only duty was to make our beds and go for a 45-minute walk every day. No inspections. No KP. After our mule pack walks our new 45-minute walks were a joke. Our group from Fort Sill quickly learned to gather at the head of the column and would simply take off, leaving the rest of the men far behind because of our 4 1/2 mph pace. We would reach our destination, the University pig farm, and wait for the rest of the men to arrive. Then, we repeated the process on the way back to our quarters.

Stillwater had a large municipal swimming pool; and I don't remember how, but I met a very cute coed who belonged to a sorority, and I spent as much time as I could with her. Her name was Carmelita Smith, from Texas, studying I don't know what. Everyone called her "Carmel". She was very petite, probably 5' or 5'1" tall. We used to go swimming in the evening and walk from her sorority house to the pool, several blocks distant. It must have been quite a sight to see her trotting behind me, trying to keep up with my long legs doing 4 1/2 mph. I couldn't keep my balance if I went any slower.

She was the first girl for whom I was moved to write a poem. It was hard to say goodbye, knowing I would never see her again. I was beginning to sense a drawing apart from Carol at Rensselaer, from her infrequent letters which kept mentioning someone named Jim, and I was becoming receptive to other possible futures. I really liked Carmel. The result was a farewell poem I called "Green Grapes", which I still like. But I don't remember if I ever sent it to her, or if I did, if she liked it. Chronologically, it is at the front of the poems in the collection of poems I have written over the years, most of which were inspired by my need to express something important to me, better said in writing than fumbling around verbally.

Eventually we received our orders and once again a group of twelve or fourteen PFCs under the command of an Acting Corporal, boarded a train for the long trip to Minneapolis and the

University of Minnesota. We traveled northward near the west bank of the Mississippi River and the contrast of the red soil and burnt out landscape of Oklahoma as we traveled northward through the lush greener and greener landscape of Missouri and Iowa was a revelation. It was almost as though we were going home.

We arrived in Minneapolis about 5 p.m. and our Acting Corporal used the tokens from his packet of papers to pay for our trolley ride out to the campus of the University of Minnesota. I am a little surprised that I do not remember the names of the men, selected from all the units at Fort Sill, and sent to study French. I also do not remember much of the train trip which must have been at least 1,200 miles. Were we on a sleeper? How were we fed? How did we pass the time? Which cities did we pass through?

What I do remember vividly is the shock that awaited us upon arrival. We sat on the terrace in front of a two-story brick building with a sign designating it as the "Continuation Center," across the street from the Armory, where our Corporal went to report our arrival. After a short while, he returned with a Lieutenant who had been drinking and who looked to be about 40 years old (and still a Second Lieutenant?) and whose name is the only one I remember: Lt. Barlow. I don't think we ever saw him again. In a slightly slurred voice, he proceeded to welcome us to Minneapolis and the University. He then delivered his bombshell: The ASTP program at the University did not offer French! We would be given two choices to elect our preference for a different language, from German, the Scandinavian Languages and Japanese. I think I felt a little chill when I heard Japanese. My first and second choices were German because my brother Russ was already fluent in German and until now we had no common second language; my second choice was Swedish because it was purported to be the easiest of the Scandinavian languages.

With the exception of the five or six west coast Nisei in the group, no one elected Japanese. The Army's solution was to take the highest 120 AGCT test scores and assign them to the Japanese program. I was in that group along with several other Ivy Leaguers, who gravitated into a very close inner circle and became lifelong friends. In my case, they supplanted all but one or two of my college friendships. At that time there were only a handful of people in the entire U.S. who had any knowledge of the Japanese language and after just a few weeks our group became very important to the war effort. I have always thought how fortunate I was that an apparent disaster turned out to be a specialty that may have saved my life.

In peacetime the Continuation Center, which we now occupied exclusively, was used for special groups seeking advanced knowledge in specialized areas, perhaps PhD candidates or senior scholars attending a colloquium, seeking the latest developments in their field. It was a self-contained unit which had classrooms, sleeping rooms, lounging areas and a dining room which suited the Army very well. It was certainly very convenient for us and a total contrast to the typical army installation we had known before. It was great having all our activities under one roof. It was actually close to being luxurious, even if we had been civilians. It was a total contrast to the typical army installation we had known before. It was great having all our activities under one roof.

The educational program was in the charge of a civilian named the Reverend Hepner, an older man who had lived in Japan for many years as a Lutheran missionary and was fluent in the language. He devised what is known as the "Romaji" system for Anglicizing the Japanese alphabet and words. He was not a large man, wore glasses, and was missing the end joint of his right forefinger. When he wished to make a point while lecturing, he would remove his glasses, with the stub of the finger pointing the glasses and the finger at us. This gesture was caught perfectly in a cartoon drawn by one of our classmates, "Obie" Oberholzer, a commercial artist in civilian life. "Obie" also did a remarkable job capturing the transformation of our female sensei (teachers) when their drab, native hair styles were replaced with modern western styles performed by another of our classmates, "Jacques," who had a salon on Michigan Avenue in Chicago. I always felt that the Reverend Hepner, having lived with people of uniformly smaller stature for so many years was just a little intimidated being surrounded by our much larger servicemen in uniform.

The language classes were strictly conversational Japanese, which has no tricky, foreign to us, verbal pronunciations to learn, such as the French "u", or the Italian trilled "r". Other than learning a totally new vocabulary with no clues derived from other Western languages, it wasn't too difficult… Luckily, we were all blessed with exceptional memories, and many of us were musical with trained ears. Our sensei (teachers) were all Nisei, second generation Japanese, born in the U.S. and therefore, U.S. Citizens, unlike their parents, Issei, first generation, who had immigrated to the U.S. in the 1920s. As we got to know them, we heard the stories of their forcible relocation from the West coast, with one or two-days-notice in many cases, at tremendous financial loss, and terrible family disruption. Working with these people every day our hearts went out to them. It seems ironic today that people, who were suspected of disloyalty and treachery resulting in something as drastic as relocation to concentration camps, would be the source of the recruits to teach their language to the "enemy" Army Intelligence Service. Of course, the Nisei proved their loyalty over and over, whenever and wherever they had the opportunity.

In addition to the language studies we also studied in English, of course, the culture of the Far East, stressing Japan: their history, their religion, geography, political structure, economy. These classes were taught by regular University faculty. One outstanding class was Economics taught by Professor Harold Quigley. My other memory of the Caucasian teachers was our geography instructor. He seemed timid and unsure of himself, totally uncomfortable with a roomful of giants in uniform, but in spite of this, did a very good job. When we finished his class, I knew more about the geography of Japan than I did of the U.S. Sadly, I have forgotten most of it, as well as his name.

We were divided into 12 classes (sections) of ten men each and ranked academically by test scores from the weekly Saturday morning exams. We moved from classroom to classroom and thus had a variety of different teachers and accents to cope with every day. The University gave credit for the work done in the English language classes. My recollection is that our Nisei teachers were uniformly excellent, perhaps surprising since none of them had graduated from a teachers' college. As we got to know them, we quickly came to sympathize with their treatment by the U.S. We heard some very troubling stories: Endo-san, about 50 years old, was separated from his family and had to sell his small drugstore chain in Los Angeles on two days' notice, realizing about 10 cents on the dollar. I could detect no signs of bitterness on his part, but perhaps understood a little when we learned the meaning of a colloquial Japanese phrase he used: '*Shikata ga nai*" that we found very useful, which means "It can't be helped."

Another unforgettable teacher was Ruby Sakota, very petite, Mongolian features with perpetual pink spots on her cheeks and a wonderful twinkle in her eyes. She taught me how to use chopsticks the first night. I was invited to join a group with some of our instructors at John's Place, one of the best Chinese restaurants I have ever eaten at. She later married one of our other instructors, Inamoto-san and died in childbirth before we left Minnesota, which devastated the entire Company, which went into mourning.

One of the popular sensei was Yoshiko Arimatsu, young, pretty (especially with her new hairdo) voice student at U.S.C., who settled in Chicago after the war and with whom I corresponded for years. We visited her in Des Plaines after one of the APS Peony Exhibitions we entered. When we took her to lunch, her mother, who lived with Yoshiko, came down the stairs to check out the "*gaijin*" (foreigners) who were stealing her daughter away from her. She was very diminutive and after the introductions relaxed a little. Yoshiko married an outdoorsman, Tommy Uragami, who went out fishing off the coast of Costa Rica in a violent storm and was presumed drowned. All Yoshiko's efforts to find out what happened were unrewarded and it caused her years of anguish.

One unusual event, which interrupted our regular classes, was a talk by a Captain, recovering from wounds received in battle, on a speaking tour sponsored by the Army. His talk was on the battle to take Guadalcanal from the Japanese, and the importance of accurate intelligence, accurate information of the strength and location of the enemy. Apparently, Guadalcanal was a horrible place; a large island covered with jungle and bougainvillea which is a large bush covered with vicious thorns. The particular action he told us about involved a Japanese army division with a strength of about 5-6,000 men who planned a surprise dawn attack on the U.S. position. Our Nisei scouts overheard the plans and reported back to our headquarters. The Japanese were very confident and thought they were attacking a U.S. regiment strength force (faulty intelligence) while in fact the U.S. had a whole division, about 10,000 men, including division strength heavy artillery. Fifteen minutes before the Japanese attack was scheduled to begin, the U.S. artillery opened fire with high burst shells, and when the barrage ended, the U.S. troops entered the jungle where even the trees were stripped of their leaves. They never found a whole body of a Japanese infantryman. It was a very sobering talk and made us feel that our studies were important.

We settled into a regular routine: fall out in the early morning to the street in front of our building (Ridiculous! Who would run away from such an army life in wartime?) then breakfast, followed by classes where we quickly learned what we were up against in the language (many flash cards in chow line.) The other classes presented no problems.

During our free time we played a lot of contract bridge in the Lounge, and we discovered a famous ice cream parlor just off campus. After our tests every Saturday morning and the lax inspections of our rooms and latrines (they were clay tiled bathrooms,) we were free and could go to downtown Minneapolis which was a lively place with several movie theaters and many fine restaurants. Among these was "John's Place" on the 2nd floor of a building between Hennepin and Nicollet, the two main streets. Here, Ruby Sakota, one of our sensei, taught me how to use chop sticks, and which Chinese dishes to order. Frequently, two or three of the sensei (teachers) would invite several of us to go with them to John's Place which we were flattered to do. We would order one dish per person and then share, family style - the more people the more variety. After eating, we would usually go to a movie and then visit the USO to check out the hostesses and maybe dance, and at the very least sample the free donuts and coffee. Then the trolley ride home to the Continuation Center. I remember we had a classmate, a sergeant, named Jim Burke who had contracted malaria at Camp Shelby, Mississippi. I thought it could only be caught in the tropics, or Africa. He would fall asleep while standing, holding on to the hand straps or support poles on the trolley on the ride home. It was unnerving, and we tried to stay close so we could catch him if he fell. He also could not control falling asleep in class. Another of the classmates I remember was "Swede" Lundberg, who was married and was a Sergeant.

Distinction in rank meant nothing if you were a student. The higher ranks had no authority to give orders. They were only a reminder of the Army policy of a student being frozen in rank as far as his monthly pay was concerned. Thus, sergeants, and we even had one Master Sergeant among us, received much higher pay than we lowly PFCs. whose weekly test scores were invariably higher than theirs. All of us were doing the same work, with no incentive whatsoever for us to study even harder. There was no way to get a raise in pay. From the Army's point of view, it made sense. But it was counterproductive if the aim was to produce language specialists as quickly as possible.

The circle of Ivy Leaguers who gradually gathered together consisted of: Alex Norton, Yale '44, Junior Phi Beta Kappa, perfect score on the AGCT test, the most brilliant mind I have ever encountered and one of the most unpretentious; Hermon Wells, Yale Law School, Quaker, affectionately called "Orson", another brilliant mind. After the war he went to Geneva, Switzerland, and earned an advanced degree in International Relations, taking his classes in French!, which really impressed me; Sidney Mishcon, University of Pennsylvania, Jewish (it took us a while to be sure because of his fair complexion, reddish hair and blue eyes), one of the nicest, finest men I have ever known. He called his mother every weekend no matter where he was stationed; Phil Kazon, Harvard, Leonard Bernstein's roommate one year; Del Zucker, Columbia, Manhattan attorney in the real world; and also included in the "circle", Lou Gelfand, University of Oklahoma, Journalism major and our Mr. Malaprop; Chuck Steiner, University of Detroit; and Hugh Nash, Reed College, Oregon, brilliant mind, who grew up in China and whose father was the leader of the World Federalist movement.

Various combinations of us would find things to do together. There was always someone to play bridge with or go for a soda or downtown to a movie. I think the bond between this group of men was something out of the ordinary, especially in an army where transiency was the norm.

One of Alex Norton's roommates comes to mind: he was a Nisei, a Corporal, named Trueman Kennichi Oshima and was on the fringe of our group, played a lot of bridge with us. I remember the unusual number of slams he bid and how unlikely it was that he made so many of them. We could hear him across the hall starting every day with three tremendous sneezes.

I found a Christian Science church within walking distance (after the mule pack, what wasn't within walking distance?) and met a lovely, older lady, Mathilda K. Schmid, who befriended me and used to invite me for Sunday dinner at her apartment after church services. Her family had brought her to this country as a child and she had only an 8th grade education, but her study of the *King James Bible* had made her truly literate. She was socially active and was a fantastic cook. I don't know how she did it with the food stamp rationing that was in effect during the war. She couldn't have been kinder to me.

She was happy when I met a beautiful coed at church (a twin of the movie star, Maureen O'Hara, in appearance) after church services one Sunday and started to date her. I have always been amazed that I cannot remember the name of such a beautiful girl, or what we did on dates, or even how many dates we had. All I remember is that she came from Montana and was an English/Drama major. I helped her with one of her papers and it did nothing for my respect for the quality of instruction at the University, not very high to begin with after the men we had in the classroom, except for Professor Quigley. As far as I knew she was a pretty good student, but I felt her work would not have been acceptable at Lakewood High School. And she was a junior! It all ended badly. I have been ashamed of myself ever since because at this very time I discovered the novels of Thomas Wolfe and their effect was so profound that I simply lost interest in her. She had done absolutely nothing to provoke this. I tried to explain but, she could not understand. In effect I "dumped" her, something I had never done before. I still look back on the episode with great regret.

One of our instructors in Japanese was a white Russian, Mme. Surabyovski (sp), whom we always addressed as Mme. Suro, probably in her 40's, who had a son about 9 years old, Sasha. She had been a tobacco trader in Mongolia during the Japanese occupation. We all took advantage of her predilection for Ivy Leaguers, having learned almost immediately that she always gave us the benefit of any doubt as to our work. I could never understand, with her background, where such a prejudice could have come from. She was our only non-Nisei instructor. She did many nice things for us outside the classroom socially.

One time she invited four or five of our inner group to her home for dinner. I don't remember the food, but have never forgotten the two Oriental (not Persian) rugs on her floors: both plain colors, one royal blue, the other blood red, one 10' x 12', the other 6' x 9', both with a "V" border, carved into the surface about a foot from the edge, and both had a huge rose blossom in one corner woven into the rug. I had never seen anything like them before, nor ever have since. They were her prized possessions and she had managed with great difficulty to keep them with her in all her travels.

The other memorable event of the evening occurred before the meal when her son, Sasha, with no provocation, attempted to stab mild-mannered, inoffensive, affable Del Zucker with a pair of scissors. He failed and I think Mme. Suro sent him to his room. We ate her meal without him. Mme. Suro also arranged for our group to spend a Sunday afternoon as guests of Laurence and Alexandra Schmeckebier in their home near the campus. He later became Director of the Cleveland Museum of Art. Mrs. Schmeckebier was also a white Russian, very cultured and attractive. They had a grand piano in their living room and there were some Scriabin Preludes on the rack which I proceeded to play; she was probably surprised that a man in uniform could play the piano, let alone Scriabin whose preludes really appealed to me. I obviously enjoyed playing, which I missed. When they came to Cleveland after the war for him to take up his appointment, I contacted them and since I was in the mortgage business, offered to help them in their search for their new home. They thanked me; seemed to remember a serviceman and Scriabin, but nothing came of my offer. They had plenty of advice from members of Cleveland's 400. We used to visit the Museum of Art infrequently and never ran into the new Director.

Come to think of it, we really were an unusual group. I wonder if there was any other unit in the entire armed forces which had such a concentration of Ivy Leaguers with such diverse talents who stayed together as a group for three years. I was very fortunate to be included.

On another occasion Mme. Suro arranged for us to attend an open house at the Frank Lloyd Wright designed home of Malcom Wiley, V.P., of the University. The house was perched on a bluff overlooking the headwaters of the Mississippi River. It was my first exposure to Wright's architectural thought and made a lasting impression on me. After the war I sought out examples of his work during my lunch hour in the reading room at the main branch of the Cleveland Public Library which was located across the street from our offices. Traces of his influence show up in the house we built in Brecksville.

I don't remember too much about the Wiley house, done in Wright's Prairie Style, one floor, no basement and nestled into the landscape. It had an unusual, high window which took its shape from the end of the gable roof and light from it filtered into the living room. There was a long row of built-in cabinets, hip high, lining the corridor to the sleeping area, a typical Wright feature. I didn't realize what I was looking at, having no interest in house plans at the time. That came later. The Wiley house was included in the issue of Architectural Forum devoted exclusively to Wright's work which I read at the Cleveland Public Library, and, I recall recognizing it and having spent a Sunday afternoon there.

The occasion was an open house hosted by several University coeds to whom we were introduced, and being told of my mule pack background, one of them, obviously not a farm girl, innocently inquired if I were involved in the breeding of mules. This was the highlight of the afternoon and caused some mild hilarity among my comrades who were always on the lookout for a good laugh.

The one other social Sunday afternoon that I remember took place when a group of us was invited to the home of one of the members of a Jewish sorority (I think it may have been a girl Del Zucker met at the U.S.O.) whose parents owned a home on Lake Minnetonka. I can only remember that the hostess' nickname was B.J. Most of the entertaining took place in a long narrow glassed-in porch overlooking the lake and I remember hearing a Benny Goodman Trio recording of "Soft Winds" which was new to me and immediately became one of my favorites. We learned that we were the subjects-objects needed for the girls to earn "Brownie Points" for a sorority project to "Entertain Our Servicemen." Since there was no personal interest in us as such, it spoiled the afternoon somewhat. They asked us if we appreciated what they were doing for us! Not that the girls were unattractive, nor the food inedible, and I did love the music. It wasn't a total waste of time by any means.

On our Saturday night expeditions to downtown Minneapolis, we invariably stopped by the U.S.O. before or after dinner or a movie. Sometimes the donuts and milk took the place of dinner depending on how close to payday it was. And there were always young girl hostesses, about our age, there to talk with or dance with, which was an additional reason to check out the scene. It might even lead to a date!

On one of these occasions, when I was feeling blue and neglected, possibly from not having a letter from my hometown sweetheart, Carol, or maybe from having one mentioning "Jim" again, and not being able to do anything about it since I was in Minnesota and she was in New York, I was sitting against a wall and must have been projecting a feeling of profound sadness, because a very pretty, very young lady came over and sat next to me. She wanted to cheer me up and we talked and ended up dancing and sharing a donut. I asked her out several times after that. I cared for her up to a point. She lived with her family whom I never met, fairly far from the center of town but easily accessible by trolley. On one of the dates I missed the last trolley home, and it was a very long walk back to the Continuation Center.

This is another example of my spotty memory. As much as I liked her, I cannot remember even her first name. However, I was interested and became concerned for her when Dennis Morgan, the Hollywood singing movie star, made an appearance in Minneapolis and visited the U.S.O. where he spotted my friend. He singled her out for his personal attention and tried to get her to join his traveling troop on the road. She told me this and I cautioned her against the idea vigorously. As I recall, I wasn't too happy about such stiff competition. Luckily, nothing ever came of it.

One of the advantages for us in our surroundings was the number of small lakes in Minneapolis, some easily accessible by trolley. Minneapolis was a city of extremes: bitterly cold in the winter and equally as hot in the summer. Frequently, some of us would take the trolley to Lake Calhoun, the nearest to us, to swim on the weekends during our free time. The lake was fairly large, had a public, sandy beach and changing facilities. Alex Norton and I went once on a sunny

Sunday afternoon, changed into our swim trunks, stretched out on a blanket, swam when we got too hot, read, and dozed. Eventually we dressed and trolleyed back to the Continuation Center. We were both severely sunburned and about ten days later I happened to look into Alex's room on the way to Roll Call to see him with one leg propped up on his window sill peeling off the dead skin from the back of his right thigh. It was probably 6" x 10" in one piece and was shocking. It could have been used for a lampshade.

One of the unusual things that happened to me that eventful year was receiving an award that was a reward for good grades. We had tests in all subjects every Saturday morning and if one's grades were at the top of the class, one was awarded a "Blue Star" patch (not a gold star on a blackboard) which was to be sewn onto the cuff of the left sleeve of the dress uniform jacket. What really made it important was that it meant one could take Wednesday night off from study hall, and go downtown for dinner in a restaurant, or go to a movie at a time when there were virtually no servicemen there. One had the whole downtown all to one's self. One of the weeks I was awarded the Blue Star and remember going downtown and how strange it felt - so different from Saturday night - where did all the soldiers go? I only remember going downtown in the middle of the week once, don't remember what I did, and suspect the privilege was only granted for one week, unless the following Saturday's test scores were again high enough to qualify.

We found various ways to amuse ourselves above and beyond the flash cards with the new vocabulary words, constantly displayed in the chow line at the mess hall while waiting in line for our food. Some of the pranks were pretty juvenile. For instance, one evening when there wasn't anything to do and not very many people around, one of the men, having been urged, but not resisting very strongly, was persuaded to call Northwest Airlines, headquartered in Minneapolis, on the pretext of conducting a survey, to ask the question as to how the airline disposed of solid waste while in flight; surely they didn't dump it over the countryside. The "joke" fizzled. It wasn't very funny in the first place.

Then there was the time when Alex Norton and I stole into the room where one of Professor Quigley's tests was to be given after lunch. We erased Quigley's questions which were printed on a blackboard and replaced his questions with some of our own. They were essay type and asked for impossible answers. Many of the men when they arrived early saw what was on the blackboard and rushed back to their rooms to look for answers. I can't remember exactly, but one of the questions we devised asked something like: Compare the roles played by the Samurai and the Pope's Swiss Guard and how they might achieve their mission. Unfortunately, Professor Quigley was out of town that day and the test was administered by a Proctor who merely glanced at our questions, never even reading them, promptly erased them and we took the dull, regular test. But Alex and I always suspected that Quigley, being the man that he was, might have let our questions stand, and we could all take the fake test - and suffer the consequences. He might never have had so much fun reading answers to a test. The rest of the Company was not amused and spent a lot of time trying to find out who the jokesters were. They never found out. And now it's too late.

An aside: Professor Quigley was the only teacher we encountered at the University of Minnesota who approached the quality of the men we routinely studied under at Yale. He was able to recognize true intelligence and, to this end, he read Alex Norton's Blue Book Test answers aloud to the rest of the class. I have never heard of such a thing, before or after.

One of the things we found amusing, and looked forward to, was the Sunday night "settling up", the reckoning. This took place after dinner. The Jewish men in the Company gathered in the lounge area and reconstructed their weekend in town. They decided who had paid for what, and who owed whom how much to balance the books. Their usual pattern was to go downtown and rent a suite in one of the big hotels and relax. Lots of food, lots of drinking, lots of soaking in the tub, but no girls. This went on for two days and it was pay as you go. No one ever wrote anything down; it was all done in their heads. I never heard a challenge, or a disagreement. Just plans for the next weekend: a different hotel, perhaps? This is where we learned for sure that Mishcon had to be Jewish, in spite of his appearance. He was the paymaster, having advanced most of the money, and the others were Zucker, Kazon, Teitlebaum, Nussbaum and Neidelmeier. The last three never became part of our group. We were always amazed at the performance; who needed live theater? And we felt fortunate to live with them and to learn from them.

I think the Army's lease of the Continuation Center ended the first of the year because we moved down the street to Shevlin Hall, another university building, where the quarters were a little more Spartan and in keeping with being in the Army - we had not become completely spoiled as yet. It did take a little getting used to: for one thing everything was painted pink - walls, furniture, closets, everything, maybe even the doorknobs. Apparently, our space had been occupied by girls enrolled in some program similar to the Curtis Wright Air Cadettes. Now we even had to sleep in bunks. I don't remember much else about it; where we ate, and if we had our classes in the same building. I'm pretty sure we did. I do remember that Sidney Mishcon's bunkmate was an otherwise nice Princeton man, John Miner, who was not interested in our group, an excellent classical pianist. He was surly when getting out of his bunk in the morning and refused to speak until he had his first cup of coffee. So, I, a bunk away, observed Mishcon plodding away daily to find a cup of coffee, I know not where, but after the coffee, Army life could begin for the day.

We had one non-ASTP class taught by Army officers at the Armory: Military Science, which we all thought was an oxymoron having observed the workings of the Army after 3 or 4 months of service. We had been studying Japanese for approximately 6 months and most of us ordinary students were beginning to realize how hopeless it was to think we could ever become fluent in the language and we had not yet even been exposed to the written language. The Military Science lectures we had to endure were ludicrous and had to be attended by all the language students on campus. The European language students were not as disillusioned as we were and still highly motivated. We quickly created a system, to the disgust of the non-Japanese students, of appointing a "note taker" who would take notes on the lectures so the rest of us could go back to doing our cross word puzzles, or reading our detective stories. After the first month's test, we learned that the Army instructors would read the questions and give us the correct answers for the next day's test - this to a group of men with phenomenal memories. Our German and Scandinavian fellow students were scandalized by our attitudes and took it all very seriously. On test day we would gather around our "note taker" and shamelessly copy any answers we couldn't remember from the previous day. It seemed the Army wanted successful, high performance and at least the Japanese students didn't let them down.

At the end of the year, all of us having come to love all that Minneapolis had to offer, the people, the amenities, if not the climate, we received our final grades and received official credit for our non-language courses from the University of Minnesota (the transcript is somewhere in my papers.) In the final two weeks of our stay, the men in the top two sections were interviewed by an Army officer, and we learned that twelve of us had been selected for further study at the University of Michigan in Ann Arbor in the pre-OCS MISLS (Military Intelligence Service Language School) and were to report there after a week's leave. This sounded like good news to me since Ann Arbor was much closer to Cleveland than Minneapolis, and I would have a better chance to see my family.

I do not know what happened to those we left behind. They never arrived in Ann Arbor while we were there, and the entire ASTP program was canceled in April of 1945, with the exception of the Japanese language studies. All the European language students (my brother Russ, fluent in German and with three years of Russian at Yale, thanks to the ASTP studied Turkish at Indiana University) ended up at an Infantry Replacement Training Center, and were then thrown, inadequately trained or equipped, into the Battle of the Bulge where the U.S. Army suffered some of its worst casualties. I learned later that there were 150,000 men in the ASTP program when it was cancelled, the equivalent of 10 divisions.

In the fall of 1944, my romance with Carol Kuekes was on the rocks. She was studying engineering in a government program at Rensselaer Polytech in Troy, New York. She had met "Jim" who was a fountain of information about the symphony and our letters were becoming more and more strained. On one of our quarterly 7-day leaves, against my parents' wishes, I spent two of those days going to Troy, New York. My parents were terrified I would marry Carol. The trip was a last attempt to arrive at a final understanding to see if our relationship had a future. I promised my parents I wouldn't do something stupid. The meeting took place; my memories of it are almost non-existent for something so seemingly important, and I could tell it was all over, that this was not where my future lay. I do remember walking up a hill to a park and lying on a bluff overlooking the Hudson River and just talking, very quietly, very sadly. The result was a poem I wrote, sitting on the lawn, back against a tree on the campus of the University of Minnesota after my return from my leave. In it I tried to convey my regrets at having to say goodbye, as gently as I could. I called it "Troy" and used the modern city's motto, *"Troia est, Ilium Fugit"* as a subtitle. I think it may be the best thing I have ever written.

Our new class was recruited from other ASTP Japanese language units from other colleges, University of Minnesota, Yale, University of Chicago and I do not recall the other schools. Other than the University of Michigan, whose men had the advantage of being in Ann Arbor for a year already. The members of our Minnesota contingent that I remember were Alex Norton, "Orson"

Wells, Sidney Mishcon, Hugh Nash, Chuck Steiner, Oberholzer, and me. It seems strange today that I don't remember the others. As it was, it was a blessing that so many of our Minnesota group were able to stay together. We remained tightly knit but also got to know many other bright men from the other schools, particularly the Univesity of Michigan. It was an outstanding collection of exceptional talent and was largely ignored by the University of Michigan. I don't think the University had any idea of what they had in their midst or cared. They had other problems trying to run a major institution in wartime.

The academic program was now to be all language, not just conversational Japanese, but also the written language. The program was under the command of Col. Kai Rasmussen for the military side, and Prof. Joseph Yamagiwa, a noted Japanese scholar, for the language side. The teachers (sensei) were all Nisei, once again recruited from the far West concentration camps. Oddly, I do not recall their names as well as I do those in Minnesota. We had seven hours of classroom instruction and two hours of compulsory study after dinner in our rooms or the Law Library, 5 days a week; tests were given every Saturday morning as well as the usual inspections of our living quarters. We were free from 9 p.m. to 11 p.m., which was lights off time and one of our classmate Sergeants was required to do a bed check. We also had free time Saturday afternoons and Sundays; and could leave Tyler House in East Quad to savor the delights of campus town.

I think that I was promoted from my rank of PFC to Corporal T5, probably upon arrival in Ann Arbor, along with all the other PFCs, and received a pay raise to $65/month. This would be my rank and pay as long as I remained in school, no matter how hard I worked, or how much of my free time I spent trying to improve my Japanese. It was galling to realize that the lowest two sections (classes), the poorest students, contained all of the students who were already officers (there were about ten of them) who had no military duties and lived off post, but received their, to us, princely pay. We never got to know any of them because we were never in class with them. I suspect they were misfits in their regular outfits, and their commanders found the school program a convenient place to dump them, Col. Rasmussen was helpless in the matter.

The spoken language classes took up where we left off in Minnesota, but the writing was all new. It was horrendous. Every *kanji* (character, or pictograph) was different, unrelated to anything in our experience, and required sheer, brute memory to learn. With a few exceptions, they bore no resemblance to anything we were familiar with. It is commonly accepted that a basic vocabulary of 2,500 characters is needed to be able to read a Japanese newspaper, but at the end of the year in Ann Arbor, when I supposedly had learned 2,300 kanji, plus additional combinations of 2 or 3 characters to express a more complex, recent word, there was no way I could read a newspaper, let alone a novel or a captured document from a battlefield. Even the newspapers in Japan printed meanings next to unusual characters using their formal alphabet *katakana* to indicate the sound and help the readers' understanding. It was utterly discouraging to go home on a 7-day leave and return to Ann Arbor to find that I had forgotten 30% of all that I had just learned; and to have to go back and review and relearn.

In Japanese and Chinese, writing is not from left to right as in the European languages we are familiar with. The columns of kanji (I will use this term rather than "character" or "pictograph" in this discussion of the language) are read from top to bottom starting from the top right side of the page. In addition to the kanji, there are two written alphabets, the *katakana* and the *hiragana*, which correspond to our large cap printing and cursive style of writing. The Japanese alphabet has 52 characters. The 5 vowels, in Japanese order: a, i, u, e, o; but they do not have single letters for the consonants as we do. Each character combines a consonant sound with one of the vowels. Thus, there is: ka, ki, ku, ke, ko., pronounced as in English. There is no sound for "1". And the list of sounds in the regular vocabulary can be expanded by placing a small circle, or other diacritical mark to the top right of the character. It would probably be more correct to think of drawing kanji since originally the writing was done with brush and ink. Of course, we used pencils or pens and lost most of the beauty and symmetry of the kanji by doing so, which could be expected, since our efforts were about the level or a five or six-year-old child without much muscular control.

The katakana and hiragana are used with the kanji, following them in the column, to denote subject, object, prepositions and verb tenses. The common sentence structure is: subject, object, verb. To further complicate matters for us, the kanji were originally imported from China with the arrival of Buddhist monks and retained their Chinese sound and meaning, which was further complicated by retention of one of the three or more sounds for the same kanji, depending on which province of China the dialect came from. In addition, anything but the simplest words or concepts required two or more kanji and the correct pronunciation could be a combination of sounds of two different provinces. So, the Japanese learned the meaning of a Chinese character and attached their native word for it. They adopted and adapted a foreign language to express themselves in writing.

There was no uniform system to help us; everything was a special situation, and we had to rely on our memories to keep it all straight. There are actually two or three different vocabularies which are used in situations where there is a difference in rank between the speakers. The vocabulary at home between family members was totally different from that used between a civilian and a government employee, or between a boss and his employee. We had to learn all these distinctions in order to function properly.

Above and beyond all this complexity, the Japanese used an informal style of writing between family members, or sweethearts, or just friends. It was rather similar to the shorthand used by the stenographers in the Western business world at the time. It was called *sosho* or "grass writing", and that would have been impossible for us to learn. It reduced complicated kanji to what looked like vertical scribbles.

I quickly developed a taste for the abstract beauty of the kanji. The sensei would draw their top to bottom columns of writing on the blackboard, each in his own style, just as no two of our handwriting was the same, and I thought it was beautiful. I spent a lot of time with a pencil and pad of paper trying to emulate them, trying to make my characters as elegant as theirs, but never succeeded. I always wished they had tried to teach us how to use the brush and ink the way the

Japanese and Chinese do, if they had the skill, but there simply was not enough time. If our childish efforts with pen or pencil could be deciphered by our sensei, that was sufficient.

We were issued a Japanese to English dictionary: *A Beginners Dictionary of Chinese-Japanese Characters and Compounds*, by Arthur Rose-Innes. I have a copy still and it contains about 8,500 characters. Luckily, the sensei supplied us with daily mimeograph printouts with the new words and we did not have to use the dictionary. It is not organized alphabetically as our English dictionaries are, but by the number of brushstrokes contained in each kanji. All but the simplest kanji are made up of two or more "radicals" which are words in and of themselves with their own sound, which when combined with the other radical, produces a new sound and meaning. When two or three kanji are combined to make a word, they are referred to as a "compound."

To find a word it is necessary to pick the radical which may be the right, left, top or bottom part of the kanji, with the smallest number of brushstrokes and proceed to that section. At least the Rose-Innes is organized numerically by brushstrokes. It was important to know not only the number of brushstrokes, but the order in which they were drawn because every kanji had to be drawn in that order every time it was used. The order was usually top left to right, then right and down, bottom last, followed by tear drop little strokes to finish off the kanji, if called for. Rose-Innes lists the most used common kanji in larger print, followed by varying numbers of other kanji used in combination with it, each of which is a word itself, below the main kanji without repeating it. It is hard to imagine a more cumbersome, time consuming process than this.

When I started to describe these intricacies, I wondered if I remembered how to use the Rose-Innes. I found the book and tried to look up the verb, *hiku,* which is a two radical kanji meaning "to pull." The left half of that kanji is the character for cart, or *sha,* and the right radical is *ban* which means "evening." This kanji takes its sound from the right radical, pronounced "bam" which is the first kanji in the compound in combination with the character for *umu,* horse, a single kanji. This was the nickname *Bamba,* which means "plow horse," which stuck to me for the rest of my army career, and later in life, after I first used it in retelling an old folk tale in class one day. I spent more than an hour searching for *hiku* in my Rose-Innes and never found it.

Before I leave the subject of the language and its complexity, two examples remain in my memory in addition to remembering how to say "Hello" and "How are you" (to which the reply was in those days: *Genki desu,* translated as "My spirit is strong!") and how to count from 1 to 10 and draw those characters. One example is my favorite piece of calligraphy, 5 characters "painted" with powerful brush strokes by an Imperial Court calligrapher, in the 1850s, black ink on brown paper, which hangs in my hallway and gives me goose bumps every time I study it: *Matsu nashi ko kon iro,* the meaning of the characters in order is: Pine tree - is not – past - future- color. The meaning is poetic "It is evergreen." It's almost a Zen kōan.

The other is a famous saying which is complicated enough to make me wonder why it would stick in my memory when so many other simpler things have fled. There is a famous shrine or temple in the city of Nikko, a Buddhist religious center, and the saying is: *Nikko made miru wo kekko to iu na.* The literal translation of these words in order is: Nikko - until - {*wo*= object preposition} - you see - splendid - to say - do not! We would probably translate as: "Don't use the word splendid until you have seen Nikko." Having never been to Japan, nor seen Nikko, I don't know why I remember this. It must be the catchy sentence structure.

All of this was very strange to us, totally unrelated to anything we had ever known before. I felt then and still do that the younger one is, the easier it is to grasp a new language; we had several men who were in their 30s, some with wives and children with them living in private housing off campus and some even older (very old to us recent graduates) and they struggled. The strain to perform must have been very severe. I have only included these memories of the language to give a feel for what we faced for 2 1/2 years and can only hope that my descriptions have not been too confusing - or too boring.

It was not all work, of course. I remember one Sunday shortly after our arrival in Ann Arbor. We skipped lunch at Tyler House, and our group from Minnesota stopped at a Deli for picnic supplies on the way to Barton Pond, formed by a dam on the Huron River, a short distance down State Street near the campus. We planned to celebrate our arrival and have our own little picnic (*pikiniku* in Japanese). We found a boat livery where we rented two canoes, loaded up our supplies and books and cards and set off to find a suitable spot to place our blanket and settle in. We found a little bulge in the shoreline perfect for beaching and launching our canoes. We must have picked a desirable spot because while we were eating an obnoxious group of noisy students, who were following a path along the shoreline, decided that they wanted the spot and demanded that we leave, as though they owned the place. Needless to say, it was a skirmish we won. We had a great time, but I don't remember ever doing it again.

We soon discovered that there were many shops, not really a surprise, that catered to students within easy walking distance from Tyler House. Campus town was somewhat removed from the downtown Ann Arbor business district and I was never aware of any town-gown friction. Borders Books main store was located on the edge of the campus along with other shops specializing in cameras, music stores, expensive men's and women's clothing stores, restaurants, places for students to hang out, a large movie theater; just what one would expect for a major university with probably more than 30,000 students. I loved Minneapolis's large downtown, but much preferred the small-town atmosphere of Ann Arbor near the campus.

One of the large university buildings, Angell Hall, was located on State Street across from the Men's Union, which had the quaint rule by today's standards of not permitting women to enter by the front door. It was a large building, had a cafeteria on the lower level, lounging areas, a ballroom where students had their dances, always with a live band, and sleeping rooms on the upper floors. There was a 25 yard swimming pool in the basement; where I used to go after my last class at Angel Hall for a swim workout. I even went to a lumberyard and bought a piece of 12" x 18" board to use as a kickboard. I could swim a mile, dress and get back to Tyler House for lunch before the lunch line closed. This was very beneficial because I regained much of the physical condition I had lost while at the University of Minnesota.

The retail area was west of Tyler House; one of our frequent destinations was to the north, Lydia Mendelsohn, the Women's Union, where we spent far more of our free time. It was smaller than the Men's Union and seemed more welcoming. It had a smaller restaurant, conference rooms, lounge areas, and sleeping rooms. It was the sort of place a single woman scholar attending a meeting, or a mother visiting a child would feel very much at home.

It also had a movie theater; this is where we were marched every Friday afternoon to view an authentic Japanese movie, filmed in Japan, made for viewing by a Japanese audience as a boost to morale and to encourage the war effort. Our sensei would preview the movie and then would extract vocabulary which we would not be familiar with in our regular classes; would teach us the new words and we would enact the key scenes in our classroom. These movies did nothing for our morale, however, unless you place some value on a three-hour nap in an uncomfortable seat, but cozy darkness.

It was utterly humiliating, in spite of the extra preparation effort and supposedly on the threshold of fluency in the ordinary day to day speech, to sit there in that darkened theater and to listen to professionally trained actors with superior diction and not understand one word. If we were lucky one of the characters might say: *O-hayo de gozaimasu!* (Good morning!). That we could grasp. But only that. And in the early days, really trying, straining to pick out the words we had just struggled to learn, I didn't think it was a very good idea to pursue a policy which led to such frustration on our part.

Many of the movies were historical with exaggerated gestures and loud declamations, seeming rather silly, similar to seeing one of our early silent movies made in Hollywood. The language used was archaic. It would be like to going to a Hollywood movie which used Chaucerian Old English. Trying to learn this old Imperial Court language was a complete waste of our time

The one exception in the whole year was a Western style melodrama which took place in Shanghai. The dashing young hero (in modern dress) waded into a river to save the life of the beautiful heroine, carrying her out of the water in his arms, and KISSING her. We couldn't believe it. Public displays of affection were forbidden by the culture. And kissing! Unthinkable. The theme song was playing in the background and it was very Western. It could have been playing in the U.S. I think its title was the same as the movie's: *"Shina no Yoru",* which means "China Nights." This was popular with the men and quickly became the Company's signature song. We learned the words and frequently would burst out in full voice while marching to class, adding to our reputation of being a very strange group. I wish I could remember more than the first words and melody which I can still sing.

After our evening compulsory study hours, during which we were not allowed out of our quarters, our group used to go to Lydia Mendelsohn for snacks and soft drinks. I remember vividly one night when on the way, Mishcon, in his hoarse, crackly voice was singing his favorite tune "I Can't Get Started with You," which was very popular, but would never have reached its success if it had to depend on his voice. Our form of protest in self-defense and only "horsing" around, was to run him and push him into some bushes at the edge of the sidewalk. No harm done, but there was no more singing in the future?

While enjoying our snacks, we used to play a word game probably invented by Norton or Wells. Each of us had to find an esoteric word, and taking turns, had to present it to the group, spell it, pronounce it and then demand the meaning which the others in the group had to determine from the clues within the word, in many cases a Greek root. We found some amazing words, using *Webster's Dictionary*, and I was always surprised how the combined efforts of the rest of the group could derive the meaning of the word. Now I don't remember any of the words and thus can't provide an example of this exercise.

One of the waitresses was named Claire: young and pretty, probably not long out of high school, definitely not a coed. She rapidly became our favorite waitress and we always sought out her table. She took an interest in us and developed the habit of "forgetting" to include any additional charges for things we ordered the second time around - the way to a man's heart!

We learned that she was having trouble with her landlord and felt very uneasy when he insisted on collecting her rent in person every Sunday morning; she felt as if he were coming on to her and she didn't know how to defend herself.

We were incensed and concocted a scheme wherein one of us would be present on the next Sunday when he arrived, jacket off, unshaven, in a T-shirt and stocking feet, reading the paper, perhaps a cup of coffee in hand, right at home. She would answer the door, invite him in, and then introduce him to the landlord as her boyfriend from her hometown, home on leave from the army. Naturally, the landlord would be intimidated and leave Claire alone in the future.

We tried this idea out on Claire; and she was thrilled and relieved. The next question was who would be the one picked to play the role of the boyfriend? After considerable discussion, the others decided the only one she would be safe with was me and I was elected. I'm not sure it was a great honor, but secretly was pleased that the others in our group perceived me as honorable and that she would have nothing to fear from me taking advantage of the situation.

I showed up on time at her one room apartment in time to prepare for my role; even had time to get the cup of coffee in my hand as I relaxed waiting for the knock on the door. When the knock came, Claire answered the door, introduced me (at my full height) to her landlord, and he learned to his disappointment that she was off limits. Up to this point my memory is clear. But I cannot recall the aftermath. I think our little plot was successful and that sometime later Claire must have moved away because she no longer worked at Lydia Mendelsohn and we missed our "freebies."

There was a U.S.O. not far off campus in an old house and occasionally, when the others were busy studying or out on a date, or washing their socks, I would drop in. I remember one time playing bridge with a JAG officer for my partner who had never played before which, made for a very strange and exciting game. It was like playing "Pin the Tail on the Donkey" at a children's birthday party. I also met a nice young lady there whom I dated a few times, taking long walks and going to the movies. I think her name may have been Helen Mruk, which I only remember because the last name was so similar to the last name of a family on the other side of Tiedeman Road, where we spent our summers before the war. One year we watched their barn burn down on the 4th of July in daytime, but it was still a spectacular display with the flames from the burning hay shooting high into the sky.

There were a substantial number of other servicemen at the U. of Michigan in various programs. One night after returning from Lydia Mendelsohn in time to beat the 11:00 p.m. curfew, there was an officer waiting for us at the entrance to Tyler House taking down the name of every returning man. Later, at midnight, we were awakened from a sound sleep, ordered to dress in the same uniform we had been wearing earlier, and to report to the basement. A coed returning to her dorm had been terrified by a man in uniform who jumped out from behind some bushes and exposed himself. She reported the incident to her housemother who in turn promptly informed the military authorities, who also reacted promptly. Every serviceman whose name had been noted upon his return to quarters had to appear in a line-up and parade before the girl, who was in a dark alcove and invisible, to see if she could identify the offender.

It was very frightening. One of our men was an older man, a prominent attorney from Pittsburgh, Solus Horowitz. While we were waiting our turn, he told us of the dangers of a false identification; that in rape cases the girl's word was almost always taken as true, even if, as in this case, she was a nearly hysterical young woman who only had a very brief glimpse of the man on a dark street. Sol impressed on us the seriousness of the consequences if she had picked out one of us, even if we were able to prove we were all together the whole evening. We went back to bed, shaken, after it was all over, to an uneasy sleep. We never did learn the outcome, or if the offender was discovered.

One of the advantages of being stationed in Ann Arbor was its proximity to Cleveland, much more favorable than Minneapolis. It rarely took more than 4-5 hours to hitch-hike, and if lucky, possibly only three or four different rides. Of course, there were fewer cars on the road because of the gas rationing in effect. But civilians seemed very willing to stop to pick up a man in uniform and help him along on his way. There was also excellent train service between Cleveland and Detroit. I remember "hitching" down to Milan, Michigan, then east to Dundee, then south to Toledo. From Toledo many times even without the Ohio Turnpike which had not been built yet, it was only one ride all the way to the outskirts of Cleveland where my parents could pick me up. Going home my arrival time wasn't critical; but returning had a time deadline with consequences, and that was when I used to take the train to Detroit, where I had the choice of taking a bus, or hitching the rest of the way out to Ann Arbor.

We continued to have one week leaves every three months; but could apply for a 3-day weekend pass if there was something special we wanted to do. Special permission had to be requested, and if the pass was granted, it was issued by the sergeant in charge of the Company office, Sgt. Brubaker, an older man.

After my break-up with Carol (from which I recovered nicely,) I dated a girl from Rocky River, Nancy Graham. Our parents knew each other, both sets of parents attending Fifth Church. Nancy was blond, very attractive, and had a great sense of humor. She was a commercial artist, and when I was home on a pass or leave, we started going out to dinner, or to see a movie, or listen to my jazz collection. Jazz was something new to her and she grew to love it. She was delightful to be with and it was sad that no romantic feelings ever developed on my part. We did correspond regularly and, since she had an assignment to provide a series of paintings of tropical fish for a calendar, it was simple for her to practice her fish paintings on every page of her letters, as well as on the envelopes. The envelopes caught the eye of Sgt. Brubaker who passed out mail at mail call and asked if I would save the envelopes for him. He was a tropical fish enthusiast. I did save many of the envelopes for him and it may or may not have had something to do with the frequency with which my requests for passes were granted. I think the Captain asked for his Sgt.'s recommendations. It couldn't have hurt.

I remember on one of those passes going with Nancy and my parents (very unusual) to see Walt Disney's *Fantasia* at the Granada Theater at Detroit Avenue and W. 117th Street. It was probably the largest and most ornate movie theater on the West Side, built in the style of the movie palaces in downtown Cleveland. It was a great movie, and afterwards we all went to Kaases, a very popular, nearby ice cream parlor featuring homemade ice cream. The others ordered typical sundaes or sodas, but, I, having become habituated to ice cream by the pint at the Fort Sill PX, asked the waitress to simply bring me a pint box of ice cream and a spoon (I don't remember the flavor.) This caused a mild furor.

I think we dropped my parents at home, and then continued on our date, doing what I do not recall. Our relationship, one sided as it was, came to an end later that spring, and she returned the box of records I had loaned her. And, alas, there were no more beautifully decorated letters.

There was great excitement in our group when Chuck Steiner married the girl he spent all his weekends with in Detroit, his hometown, so nearby, so convenient. He invited the group to the wedding, and we all attended. I remember nothing of the service, which was Roman Catholic, a first for me, with strange rituals and Latin language. Nor the reception following. But I do remember our using masking tape to spell the Japanese words for wedding "*Kekkon shimasu*" on the side of his get-away car. Being in school we didn't have access to the traditional tin cans to attach to the rear bumper.

Eventually, about the first of June 1945, after fulfilling our duty with a lot of hard work; still worrying about the progress of the war; suffering the disappointment of the University of Michigan's refusal to grant an advanced degree to those of us who sincerely believed they deserved it, we were gathered on a bright Saturday morning at the Rackham Auditorium and sat through a graduation ceremony. John Miner, Mishcon's old bunkmate at Shevlin Hall, played a spirited version of Ravel's *Bolero* for us, which did nothing to overcome my distaste for the piece. I remember nothing of the rest of the ceremony. I had met Fran five days prior and my mind was in a sweet turmoil.

We had received our orders to report to the IRTC (Infantry Replacement Training Center) at Fort McClellan, Alabama, for a nine-week refresher Basic Training course. The idea was to prepare us for the physical demands of the expected occupation of Japan, and to restore some of the physical conditioning lost in two years of sitting in a classroom. Being in Alabama for the months of July and August without air conditioning would be a big step in that direction.

We had two weeks' leave before we had to report, but our parting and separation was going to be hard to endure. I go into more detail of our meeting in my later Chapter XIV "Credo." Also, more detail of the formation of the Company's Jazz Quartet, The Sunnysiders, that started in Ann Arbor can be found in my later Chapter V "My Musical Life."

I visited Sidney Mishcon in New York the first week where we toured the 52nd Street jazz scene until the wee small hours, returned to Ann Arbor for Fran's Senior Prom, went in to Detroit to meet her mother, and Fran took the train down to Cleveland to meet my parents and brothers. It was a very sad parting when she left to return to Ann Arbor to take her finals. However, this was the beginning of our regime of writing a daily letter which we had agreed to do and was the only way we could "court" and get to know each other. The men in the Company couldn't understand my daily letter writing, but after only 21 "dates," they must have contributed something to a marriage that lasted 69 years.

We wrote almost every day - long letters which were journals of our daily activities. Fran numbered all our letters next to the postmark and the final number was 263, including those letters written after we married and were parted by her visits with the children to her mother in Detroit, or my rare out-of-town business trips. We trusted each other completely and felt free to express our deepest feelings which was very revealing. I bless Fran for saving all those letters which contain so much of our history, and which are stored in an airtight plastic container in the garage.

The letters I wrote provide a vivid record of the rigors of the training we received at Fort McClellan; in some respects, a repeat of the endurance test I underwent at Fort Sill. Without my letters to refresh my memory, McClellan would have just been a blur: awfully hot and humid and very demanding physically. But when I read these letters now, the reality of the experience is there, face to face and hard to believe. However, it was nothing compared to what the men had to undergo who were actually in the field overseas. And we knew it.

I do not remember how I got to Ft. McClellan after leaving the Birmingham, Alabama, RR station, or the distance from Birmingham to Anniston, the closest town to McClellan, which I think is to the east. I was travelling alone this time, not as part of a group, and that was different. I think I was reimbursed for my travel expense on the next payday. I do remember the shock of seeing drinking fountains and restrooms designated "For Blacks Only" in the RR station, something I had never encountered before. I thought it was wrong and it bothered me, especially after my childhood experience of Jim, who was black and so nice to me when installing the new stoker for our furnace, and having lived with another minority group, the Nisei, in the Army, and having minority Japanese Nisei teachers. These were real people, not stereotypes, and very likeable.

The only blacks I had seen in uniform were a black company of Engineers (they may not have been issued rifles) who had barracks across the street from us at Fort Sill. We used to see them take off marching to their training sessions and marveled at the way they marched. They had a swagger and a strut- they were "swingers" and it was inspiring to watch them. But we never had any contact with them or spoke to them.

After arriving at Ft. McClellan and getting settled, I found that all the others in my "group" were in another barracks; I was among a totally different group of the arrivals from Ann Arbor. This took a little getting used to. In what little free time we had, I just didn't see as much of Norton, Wells, Mishcon or Nash as before except for the occasional trips to a movie, or the PX for ice cream, or the swimming pool. From Fran's point of view this may have been a blessing. It meant far less distraction during my free time which could be better used writing to her. The other men couldn't get over how much time I spent writing, often in the latrine after lights out where there was some peace and quiet. I remember once when Dick Thomas stopped to chat while I was in the midst of writing and had one of Fran's letters open for reference in answering her questions, and he exclaimed, "My God! Even your handwriting is the same - such tiny letters!" Our handwriting was similar. Both of us wrote in tiny script and crammed a lot of words on every page. It was very beneficial for me because it was almost the same as being in the same room with her and talking to her. It helped reduce the stress of the day.

You ask, "Why didn't you just telephone her?" Because there were very few phones available for servicemen, and long-distance calls were expensive. Even $1.50 to $2 for a 3-minute call was an item on our limited income. We did manage two or three calls. I had to wait my turn for an hour or more in a line of other soldiers waiting to place calls on the single pay phone nearby and to have made arrangements by letter to be sure when Fran would be there to answer the phone. It was very cumbersome, but it was wonderful to hear her voice. It was all so new and so impossible. Pure bliss.

The training was tough and thorough. The cadre did their best to prepare us for the worst. We had weapons training, breaking down the guns, how to clean them, reassemble them, proper technique for firing them and finally actually firing them on the range; physical training, close order drill, distance marches with full field pack; and two or three night exercises in black face (which turned out to be fiascos.) We never reached our objectives in the wooded hilly country, and our non-com cadre were disgusted with us. We stumbled around in the dark looking for a machine gun nest in the woods and none of the squads found it. The exercise ended at midnight, back where we started, and we rode back to the mess hall where they gave us dessert. It couldn't have been a reward for a job well done.

I remember after one particularly hot and dusty afternoon's exercises, perhaps crawling on our bellies up a hill through a hay field, our attitudes were less than enthusiastic. When we returned to our barracks for our evening meal, after being dismissed by our non-coms, we were called back into formation by one of our fellow students, one of the officers, Captain Maxwell Flapin from Camp Maxey, Texas, who proceeded to give us a tongue lashing for being such poor soldiers, whiners and complainers, when someone in the rear ranks heckled him. He flew into a rage, demanding to know who had spoken, but before the incident went any further, the commandant of the company, another Captain, arrived who had been in battle in North Africa while Flapin was in a classroom, and who had the real authority over us, ordered everyone to calm down and, in a very quiet voice, said that when he was dissatisfied with our performance, he would let us know. The wind went out of Flapin's sails, and on our part his behavior was never forgotten.

After one of these exercises in the field, I acquired several chigger bites. Chiggers are small, almost invisible insects and the female bites through one's skin and lays her eggs to hatch later and feast on a built-in, near-by blood supply. The bites produce an intolerable itch. Some of the men would light a cigarette and hold it just over the bite to draw the chigger out of hiding where it could be disposed of. Another method was to cover the bite with nail polish, which would seal the bite, the chigger would die; and the itching would stop. One of my letters to Fran begged her to send me some of her nail polish, clear or colored, which she did. I survived.

I remember we had several marches with full packs, but I don't remember what the destinations were. Fort McClellan covered a very large area, probably several thousand acres, much of it hilly and heavily wooded, so we may have never left the base. I don't remember how far we went or how long we marched but it was nothing comparable to our mule pack walks. I do remember how hot it was and having our cadre pass out salt pills while we were in formation and ready to leave. This was a first for me and I had a difficult time swallowing the pill without water. The first time I accidentally crunched down on the pill with my rear molars which flooded my mouth with an instant highly saline solution and I almost vomited.

Several of our men had trouble with the heat, especially the older married ones. We actually had an army ambulance following the column to care for the men who couldn't make it and had to fall out of the formation. One of those was named Jolly, from S. Carolina, I think, who had a more serious problem. The marches in high temperature and with full backpack caused him to have blood, and a lot of it, in his urine and he was actually put in the ambulance and got a ride back to the base hospital. When it happened again on the next march, he was excused from any future hikes. I don't remember the outcome of this - whether his condition was ever diagnosed or what happened to him.

I didn't like the heat and the sweating, but after the mule pack hikes at Fort Sill, didn't think the infantry marches were very difficult even though the full packs we carried on our backs were heavier.

The weeks passed slowly and Fran's letters told of her worries about her final exams; then the exams and their outcomes, which were very favorable and proved her worries to be needless; then the packing up of her belongings and getting them home to Detroit, thanks to a friend of her mother's giving them a ride in their car; getting used to the struggles with rationing firsthand; her determination to learn how to be a homemaker; fun with three of her close childhood friends, giving each other dinner parties, playing bridge afterwards; visits back to Ann Arbor and her understandable instant nostalgia for her four years of freedom; her befriending a sorority sister's husband, who was trying to come to grips with having his marriage annulled after three days which was very mysterious; and caused a great deal of discussion about our own marriage plans - where, when (how soon), children, a house - but what kind?, religious accommodations, drinking. All topics which I am sure were common to most couples at that time when the war with Japan was coming to an end.

The other thing I remember is the "combat village," a form of final examination which lasted a week, living under field conditions: an exercise where we charged up a hill in the dark firing our rifles which were loaded with blank ammunition in order to simulate the sensation of firing and the noise, everything but being fired at. This was done earlier when we crawled on our bellies under chicken wire while machine guns were firing live rounds over our heads. We were aware that even though we were not firing real bullets, the mere discharge would foul up the rifle barrel with the carbon residue and would require cleaning (a very difficult job) to pass inspection. Many of us did not fire at all and did not have to clean our weapon. Very unsoldierly. But a lesson learned in the Army.

While we were in the combat village (this was the first week of August 1945) we heard rumors that a new kind of bomb had been dropped over Hiroshima and that this would bring the war to an end very quickly. Our officers ordered us not to listen to the radio, or read newspapers, and above all not to believe or spread these rumors. They emphasized that we could still look forward to wading ashore in Japan up to our knees in blood. I remember being confused, not knowing what to believe. But at the same time being thankful that maybe I would be spared having to witness the worst horrors of war. However, based on what we knew of the fanatical defense of Saipan and Okinawa, we all breathed a sigh of relief.

When the rumors proved to be true, we blessed President Truman for having the courage to give the order, I still bless him to this day for undoubtedly saving thousands of American soldiers' lives. I felt then and do now that it made no difference to the Japanese dead, whether death came as a result of an atom bomb, or death from a fire storm after the firebombing of Tokyo.

We all believed the occupation of Japan after the end of hostilities, which I expected to be a part of, would still be miserable and dangerous, with guerilla type attacks by hold-out Japanese army soldiers, and could go on for years. But still preferable to a mass slaughter similar to the D-day landings in France.

After the week of exercises ended, we returned to barracks to prepare for our next move to Fort Snelling, St. Paul, Minnesota (almost like returning home for me after my year at the University of Minnesota.) Fort Snelling was the location of the Japanese Military Intelligence Language School OCS, and we could finally look forward to becoming officers, with all their privileges and higher pay. I was happy that I would be somewhat closer to Detroit and Fran, and to Cleveland and my family, and planning for our wedding could proceed. We still had no idea whether I would have to go to Japan, or if so, for how long, but felt it would be better to go as a married man (officer) because if it was a long occupation, at some point, when peace and order was thoroughly established, wives might be allowed to come over to join their husbands; but the Army would never sanction girlfriends going to join their boyfriends.

Our letters of this period reflect a lot of confusion and uncertainty, but also a sense of determination. We were told we would have a week off duty after cleaning classrooms and before classes resumed. Fran made plans, changed many times in the making, to come to Minneapolis to spend the week with me, staying in a very respectable hotel, and we would spend every minute of my free time together. This became part of our mythical 21 dates prior to our marriage, some of them longer in duration than others. After this week, our determination to marry was stronger than ever; the confidence in each other strengthened by our faithful correspondence, and in fact our marriage did take place in Detroit, about 60 days later after many "Alarums & Excursions." It was 158 days after our first meeting. I had finally reached adulthood.

# Chapter II

## Family, Relations, Friends, et al.

An important part of my growing up process was my exposure to the large number of relatives who lived on the west side of Cleveland. It seems now that we were always getting in the car to go visit, more often than not, relatives of my father's family, perhaps because there were more of them than on my mother's side. We went regularly on Saturdays to my Grandma Schmidt's house on Woodbridge Avenue between W. 25th Street and Fulton Road while my father took the streetcar downtown to work until noon. I always loved that neighborhood and remember some of the names of the nearby streets: Trowbridge, Sackett, and Marvin, which had big houses and many trees. It was very quiet and one time I remember seeing an older lady riding by in a Baker Electric motorcar and steering it with a horizontal tiller, rather than a steering wheel. She was wearing a hat in the fashion of the time and in my naiveté, I remember wondering if it could be Mary Baker Eddy, Founder of Christian Science. I remember how silently it moved.

Another time, I was allowed out alone on one of the neighboring streets and a small truck, ringing a bell, with open sides was selling fresh waffles dusted with powdered sugar. I think they cost 5 cents each and I bought one. It was delicious. Especially the powdered sugar.

There was another occasion, which I now believe was more serious and wonder what the problem was, when my mother visited a Christian Science Practitioner, Mrs. Weidenthal, in her home on Trowbridge Avenue (I believe) and took me with her. I was probably five or six-years-old. While the consultation was going on, I stayed out in the parlor which had tall, narrow windows down to the floor with drapes which went from the ceiling to the floor which I had never seen before. This produced a very cool, quiet, peaceful feeling. I never learned why my mother went, but there must have been some physical problem she needed to overcome.

Woodbridge was within walking distance , a long distance, of the West Side Market at W. 25th Street and Lorain, and there was an icehouse nearby. I can remember walking there with Grandpa Schmidt holding my hand while I pulled a small wagon on which to load the 25 lb. block of ice for their icebox. I wonder now how much of the ice melted on the way home. I think it was quite a fair distance and I don't know whether I did it more than once. I think he had to resupply the box once a week. It was a rare enough event that I have remembered it. I do not remember Grandpa paying very much attention to me. I think he was uncomfortable around small children. I was probably about six-years-old at the time.

I was always fascinated by Grandma and Grandpa's house. I don't think it had a basement but was a two-story frame, long, narrow rectangle with a round porch on one corner where the front door was. I remember how impressed I was that Grandpa had made trellises of ½" round lead pipe to support vines and mounted them on both sides of the porch. We never used the front door, which opened into the front parlor, but walked down a sidewalk along the side of the house about halfway to a door that opened onto their dining room. Next to that door was a door and separate stairway to the second floor where Grandma rented out sleeping rooms. I never saw them and was always curious about the floorplan. I wondered if they had a share bath and whether Grandma rented two or three rooms. I know my grandparents needed the income. I think Grandpa, who had been a foundry worker but was retired when I first knew him, may not have had much of a pension, if any, and there was no Social Security at that time.

When we climbed the steps to enter from this side door, we were in the dining room, which had a round table and a chest of drawers against the far wall with a three panel still life colored print of fruit hanging over it which I remember always liking. Grandpa's rocker was in the corner of the room next to the door with his spittoon (I hated the smell) on the floor next to him, and there was a built-in cupboard above his head with a glass door where the baked goods from the Fulton Bakery were kept. I always checked out the contents greedily. They were "store bought" and tasted so good. The kitchen, which was about 6' x 9', adjoined the dining room and had a sink, stove (fuel?), ice-box, and a counter where I watched Grandma Schmidt make her bread and home-made noodles, rolling out the dry dough and cutting it into strips. This is the counter where she taught me, at the age of eight, how to dismember a chicken.

Chickens were brought home from the market, freshly killed and wrapped in newspaper, and then dipped in boiling water before plucking off their feathers, trying not to leave any "pin feathers." I used to be fascinated by the skin on their feet which was peeled off including the claws and after the boiling water dipping process, saving the remaining bones, which had practically no meat on them, for making soup. I was also fascinated by the chicken's gullet, which was a pouch at the base of its neck through which its food passed before entering the stomach. It was filled with fine gravel for grinding up the food. All my life, I have never liked chicken liver, perhaps I associated it with the gullet. On the other hand, I remember peeling off the lining of the chicken's stomach and really liking the taste of the meat, either served alone, or in chicken soup.

Going from the dining room to the front of the house, there was what I would call a living room where most of the family activity took place and at the far end of that room, the front door and another living room, or formal parlor, which I think was used only rarely. The house was divided in half, roughly, from front to rear. Grandma and Grandpa's bedroom, with its own bath, opened off the dining room. Aunt Clara's bedroom, which I do not remember ever entering, opened off the living room. I think it, too, had its own bath, (we always used the one in Grandma's bedroom) and, if the plumbing was stacked with similar rooms above, there may have been two "rental suites" on the second floor, each with its own bathroom, rather than three or four rental rooms with only one bathroom to be shared by the roomers. There was no central hallway; rooms simply opened into other rooms. (The FHA would never have approved.)

Our activities usually took place around the dining room table after supper, when Grandma played games or taught us drawing and coloring while Grandpa, Aunt Clara (Dad's older sister), and Mom and Dad retired to the front room to play pinochle. I used to love to go to that room after we arrived and made a "bee-line" to the window seat under the windows where the books were kept. I remember one book of Teddy Roosevelt's African safari with a picture of him standing next to a rhinoceros he had shot, holding his rifle upright with his left hand and his right leg resting on top of the Rhino's head; and the other book I always looked at was probably called something like "Wonders of the World" and the one picture that made the biggest impression on me at that age was of a giant squid rearing out of the sea with its tentacles gripping the prow of a big steamship. These books were both well-worn. There was also a stereo opticon which really fascinated me: I used to hold it up to my eyes after loading it with two stiff photographs on a tray-like holder, look through the eyepieces, and marvel at the 3-D effect. I have never gone to a 3-D movie today and wonder if I would be as impressed with the magic of the 3-D effect now as I was then. I think there was also a kaleidoscope which I loved to look through marveling at all the patterns which resulted from every turn of the tube.

I remember one time when my mother went on a weekday morning to be part of a group of ladies doing some sort of craft in that living room. They sat around a card table in a corner of the room and I have a recollection that they were decorating satin squares of cloth on which they stitched outlines of something and then painted the stitches with white paint. I remember crawling on the floor and ending up under the table and getting all tangled up with all the legs there and Grandma's high laced black boots.

Grandma and Grandpa's house was so different from our house on Parkwood Road. For one thing, there was an alley about 10' wide, paved with brick and sloped to a gutter down the middle, behind their house running parallel to Woodbridge. There was also a second house at the rear of the lot next to the alley about 30 or 40 feet from the main house. I speculate that it was built for Aunt Clara and her husband, Will Smith (whom I barely remember) who had mental problems. He had been in the Army in World War I, had never left the country, but was always described as "shell shocked". Their daughter, Marian, who was a couple of years younger than we were, with whom we played when we were at grandma's, lived there too.

The house was at the rear corner of the lot and was a small bungalow with two small bedrooms on the second floor. It was quite small, probably about a total of 700 or 800 square feet for both floors. There was a walkway between the house and a small garage that I remember as having some kind of metal siding, which was entered from the alley and was where Aunt Clara kept her car. I remember that she had an Auburn, one of the more expensive brands. Aunt Clara was probably teaching school at this period, I think second or third grade, there having been enough money to send her to Kent State Normal School (now Kent State University) for her teaching certificate. There was not enough money to allow my father to go to college, which based on my experience of the benefits of college life, both socially and academically, would have made his life easier. I always felt this was very unfortunate.

There were two other things I remember about Grandma's house. Once we stopped off on the way home to Lakewood one afternoon after a heavy rainstorm. The house had just been painted and I am sure it was done with a lead-based paint, perhaps Dutch Boy, and the raindrops had gathered together into large droplets which were clearly visible on the siding. My most powerful memory is of the freshness of the air that day and the smell of the paint. I don't think I have ever encountered a combination of odors anything like it ever since. It was so refreshing and distinctive.

The other memory is of a quite elaborate "glider" which suddenly appeared on one of our other visits, either on my birthday, May 6, or very close to the day. It had two wide seats facing each other to seat six, a roof like the surrey with fringe on top to provide shade and had to be stepped up onto a floor about six inches above ground. It was suspended on half circle wheels, which made it possible to rock back and forth when seated, which I thought was neat, especially when I was alone. It was placed on a new six-foot square slab of cement right next to the sidewalk and opposite the side door to the house. Without air-conditioning it was a great place to escape from the summer heat. I always considered this glider to be mine since it appeared on my birthday and was undoubtedly meant for me. Again, I speculate that it may have been a gift for my Dad's parents, bought and paid for by him. I think I was 6 years old at the time.

In those days, the 1920s, one of the favorite family pastimes was going for a ride. Automobiles were becoming popular since Henry Ford had made them affordable, and more roads were being paved; but it was all very primitive and going for a drive could be quite an adventure. Especially when we heard the "pop" of a flat tire, which had to be changed and was a major undertaking. Tires had rubber inner-tubes which developed leaks or running over a nail could result in a puncture, which could be patched while on the road. We always had a kit which had patches, rubber cement, and a device which was used to rough up the surface of the tube where the leak was, to improve the adhesion of the patch. Of course, no automobile went anywhere without a jack to raise one side of the body of the automobile off the roadway to be able to remove the tire from its axle, and a hand operated tire pump to re-inflate the tire, which I learned how to use at an early age.

It was no surprise, then, to hear the familiar words, "Get ready. We're going for a ride." Or "We're going to see Aunt Lizzie." Sometimes, on hot summer nights, after supper, Dad would pile us into the car and off we would go for a ride down in the valley of the Metropolitan Park System next to the Rocky River where the difference in elevation, being a deep, broad valley, and the sun going down, caused the air to be cooler with all the windows rolled down, speeding along at a steady 25 miles per hour. If we had been good, and begged hard enough, we might stop for an ice cream cone treat, which cost a nickel.

It seems to me, now, recalling those rides with relatives as a destination, that by far the most numerous were those to relatives on my father's side of the family. I can remember some of the names but probably never knew the connection to my immediate and most familiar relatives. More than once we dropped in to see Uncle Will and Aunt Lizzie who lived on W. 94th Street north of Denison Avenue in a small frame house. I do not know if they were cousins of my father's parents, or brothers or sisters. When I was 5 or 6 years old, we called everyone my parent's age and older either "Uncle" or "Aunt." I think Uncle Will was an Erhardt. But I'm not sure. "Uncle" Will and

"Aunt" Lizzie had a daughter, Maud, who married Fred Blank, whom we saw quite often. Fred had a slight stature and poor eyes, wearing glasses with lenses like the bottom of Coke bottles. I think he was a bookkeeper. He liked to play pinochle with Dad as his partner opposite Russ and me. They couldn't get over it when Russ and I beat them. They had two children, Don, who was sardonic and critical of his father, and a younger sister whose name I do not recall. She was young enough that we never played with her. They lived off West Boulevard south of Madison Avenue, near the Industrial Rayon factory, which emitted a very distinctive odor that permeated the neighborhood. We were usually invited to the Blanks for a meal and did not just drop in on them, the way we did with the Haemerles, another distant relative.

The only Haemerle I can remember is Eila, a very nice lady who always seemed glad to see me. I think she may have been a nurse and may have been living with her mother. They lived in the Clark Avenue neighborhood off W. 65th Street, sort of on the way home. I don't know if she had a husband. There was also a Norman Haemerle, probably a brother, who had a son, but my memory of them is very faint.

The one relative I do remember and can still picture his face is Bill Erhardt. He never married but had the same girlfriend for years who was very nice. I could never understand why they never married. I remember that the girlfriend tatted beautiful lady's lace handkerchiefs and gave them as presents. Mom and Dad used to invite them over to our house to play bridge, which is why I remember them.

I don't think any of the others, except the Blanks, ever came to our house. I remember not understanding why Don had so little respect for his father. I remember my mother standing at the dining room window waiting for our Dad to come walking down the street after his street car ride home after work, and being taught to welcome him and to be thankful for his providing our home and the money that bought our food and clothes. We were indoctrinated at a very early age to feel gratitude, and I wondered if this was something missing in Donald Blank's early childhood as an explanation of his attitudes. He seemed very negative and sour to me. He wasn't fun to play with and left me feeling uneasy. How could one not love and look up to one's father?

We paid far more visits to my father's relatives who were clustered on Tiedeman Road in Brooklyn, Ohio: Uncle Louie and Aunt Edith, Uncle Adolph and Aunt Nell, and Uncle Irving and Aunt Louisa. These were actually great-uncles and great-aunts but at age five or six it made no difference. Most of our visits were utilitarian. When we were left in one or another relative's care, it was free baby-sitting and allowed my mother to go shopping or do other errands, while the children were free to play in hay lofts, or pet large animals, or use a privy, always under the watchful eye of an adult relative. I don't remember playing with any other children in the early years. On other occasions we would just stop to visit and didn't get to play. Only Uncle Louie and Uncle Irving had children, and only one of them was our age: Cousin Evie. She was a real farm girl and rode her own horse and we had good times with her.

Uncle Irving's youngest son, Elisha, was a year or two older than me. I remember his taking Russ and me with him one day when he practiced his marksmanship with a .22 rifle down in the Big Creek valley behind their house. I can't quite remember but think he might have let me try to pull the trigger and hit something, just one time. It was pretty exciting. Uncle Irving came from Virginia and didn't farm any land near his home, which was actually on a city street, Manoa Avenue. It did have a small barn where he kept his mules. He preferred mules to horses, and after my army experience, I admire him for that. He was tall and gaunt and I can see him with the leather lines from the mule's mouth wrapped around his shoulders while he controlled a cultivating tool, trudging down the rows of his crops, hollering "Gee" or "Haw". He was a hard worker.

I have strong memories of the time Mother had left us with Aunt Louisa, who served bean soup with chunks of pork for lunch which may have been the finest tasting soup I have ever had. She then put Russ and me down for a nap in the cousins' bed on the second floor. The sheets were real cow hide, Holstein, I think, because they still had the black and white hair on them. It was quite a contrast to our house in Lakewood.

We visited Uncle Adolph and Aunt Nell only infrequently. Uncle Adolph was taciturn, unsmiling; Aunt Nell was small, plump, and from the "James" family, which was an important name in Brooklyn, Ohio history. They lived across Tiedeman Road from Uncle Louie's farm in a small bungalow-type house and, as far as I know, Uncle Adolph made his living by running what would now be known as a "convenience store" by selling sundries from the front room of his home. I remember a glass showcase in their living room. I can't imagine how he made enough to live on. They had no children, so we really had little interest in them. I think all three siblings, Louie, Adolph, and Louisa, were older than Grandma Schmidt.

We spent far more time at Uncle Louie's house on Tiedeman Road, situated about 200 feet from the road at the base of a long "U" shaped driveway, both before and after we had our own place down the road because it was a larger piece of land, a real farm to us, and there was so much more for growing boys to do. We could play in the hayloft, all dusty and soft; help harness the work horses; help Cousin Evie muck out the cow stall; Russ learned how to milk a cow (I didn't); learn what to feed the horses and the cow; follow after Uncle Louie as he rode the horse-drawn mower cutting hay; raking the fresh-cut hay into windrows; how to make corn shocks. We learned so much and had such fun. We went for rides on the draft horses after dinner with Cousin Evie, in the lead, on her riding horse.

Uncle Louie allowed Russ at age ten or eleven to drive his Ford Model T truck down his long driveway once. He forgot to tell Russ that to come to a stop, the clutch had to be depressed to act like a brake, which resulted in a minor crash when the truck came to a halt by poking the handle of the hand crank through the garage door at the end of the driveway. It was very exciting to be riding in the open body of the truck with Uncle Louie yelling excited instructions and Russ frantically trying to comply. All ended well. I don't think anyone ever told our mother.

Another memory of Uncle Louie, which impressed me, was the time I was following him while he was mowing hay, and the cutter blade, which slid along close to the ground, caught a rabbit and cut off its hind legs. Uncle Louie stopped his horse, got down on his knees and hit the rabbit on the head with a wrench, putting an end to its suffering. He felt sorry for what had happened. I liked his philosophy of planting an extra row of corn so there would be enough for the wild animals. He was a wonderful example of what a man should be for a young boy to emulate.

I remember one hot summer Sunday, after church, driving west on Memphis Road with Mom and Dad, stopping to pick up Uncle Louie walking home from his church, Epworth Evangelical Methodist, which was located at W. 25th Street and Memphis Avenue, about five miles from his home on Tiedeman Road. He had his sleeves rolled back, his suspenders holding up his pants, and his coat jacket neatly folded over one arm. His cheeks were pinker than usual, but in spite of his age, heat, and fatigue he still had a twinkle in his eye. He was always jolly and was glad for the lift home. It may have been an answer to his prayers.

I remember how my brother and I looked forward to an event that occurred in Uncle Louie's front yard, which was very large: the annual July 4th Picnic of Uncle Charley Geiger's Ebenezer Evangelical Church, which was located a few miles away on W. 65th Street. I never heard how the church found out about the Iahn farm, or how suitable it would be, but the picnic was held there every year. Somehow or other my brother and I were invited, or allowed, to attend. It was a very nice group of people, probably 75 or 80. I remember the cold pop, especially the grape Nehi, in washtubs filled with ice and we could drink all we wanted. I don't remember joining in playing softball or the other typical games played at church picnics. I do remember Russ and me depleting our joint savings from our odd jobs and weekly allowances of 25 cents each to buy fireworks. We joined the Geiger cousins later in the afternoon and used to put cherry bombs in tin cans. It was a highlight in the summer and was nice because it was so close to our summer cottage and we boys could easily walk to the picnic.

One name that I remember, which has always puzzled me because it is associated with Grandma Schmidt, is George Meyers. He used to bring Grandma in his car to visit her brothers and sister, the Iahns and Holdens, on Tiedman Road, always on a weekday, two or three times every summer and they would also stop to visit us. He was about my father's age and I thought it was very kind of him to see that Grandma Schmidt got out of her house to visit relatives and get some fresh air. He may have been a member of her church, or a distant relative.

I remember that Uncle Louie's house had a melodeon, a keyboard instrument, similar to a piano in the living room that sounded more like an organ. It had two pedals that had to be pumped to produce the sound, rather than strings. When I was playing the piano for Sunday School, I would take my music and practice on the melodion which was convenient for me. I also accompanied my cousin, Harold, Uncle Louis's son, six or seven years older than I was, when he sang. He had a good, untrained baritone voice, loved to sing, and sang loudly. After I had one year of organ lessons my senior year in high school, Harold asked me to play the organ for his wedding which was an interesting and exciting event in my young life.

The visits to my mother's relatives were to her parents, John and Sophie Gaede, who had five children: Esther (Herb) Basel; Ottilia "Tiel" (Charley) Geiger; my mother, Lydia "Babe" (Frank) Schmidt; David (Elsie) Gaede; and the youngest, Elmer Gaede. We visited the sisters, who lived nearby, the most frequently and Uncle David, who also had five children, four daughters and a son, very rarely because they lived in North Ridgeville, next to Elyria, Ohio, which was a very long drive in those days.

We stopped to see "Cousin" A1 Thran, occasionally,  he was the son of Grandma Gaede's sister, Katy Thran. They lived in Lakewood, north of Edgewater Drive on Rosalie, a short street ending at the cliff overlooking Lake Erie. The house was on the east side of the street about half-way to the cliff overlooking Lake Erie. I don't remember ever seeing the inside of the house, which looked just like the other houses on the street. I think it was dark brick and there were shade trees which made it seem gloomy to me. I remember Aunt Katy as being very diminutive and always dressed in black. I think I only saw her once or twice.

Cousin A1 was also small, with a receding hairline and small, beady eyes like his mother. He was always very nice and the thing I remember most about him is the huge bunch of keys he always had attached to his belt. He owned a small four suite apartment house nearby off Clifton Boulevard and hired Russ and me to spread gravel on its driveway one spring when we were in high school. He lived with his mother and took care of his younger brother, Ed, who had a mysterious mental problem and could not be left unattended. Ed was docile but scary to us when we were young because we didn't know how to behave when he was there. I remember that he liked to draw pictures.

Cousin A1 was the only relative other than Uncle Herb Basil and Aunt Esther who ever came all the way out to Brecksville to inspect our house when it was under construction. Cousin Al's visit was on a Sunday afternoon when the house was in its early stages but closed in, and the approach was over a very rough slag driveway an eighth of a mile long. He did a thorough inspection and then asked me why we had chosen to build so far from the road and why on the edge of a ditch, this after having looked out at the far away hills from the big window in the den and looking down into the valley from the living room windows. I think I replied politely that if I had to explain, he wouldn't be able to understand. I suspect he thought we were out of our minds. It did not affect his regard for us, because many years later, when he died, he left us a small legacy that was very much appreciated coming at a time when it was badly needed.

My impression of visits to relatives includes holiday family get-togethers, and it seems to me that we saw the Gaede sisters more often than father's side of the family. I remember Uncle Herb's roast goose which he carved with a razor-sharp big knife into slices as thin as a piece of paper. He had a coffee grinder mounted on the wall of their kitchen and ground coffee beans to make his coffee. My parents were satisfied with the Eight O'Clock brand from our A&P grocery store.

My aunts established a rotation for the holidays with one hosting the occasion with one of the other sister's families and including Grandpa Gaede and Uncle Elmer so there would be ten or twelve people at the table. I think the occasions were very similar and remember eating so much turkey that I had to lie down on the sofa with my hands on my stomach after dessert. At that age it was a challenge to over-eat, which Russ and I never failed to meet. It formed, or was the result of, some very bad eating habits which lasted for years.

I remember one Thanksgiving or Christmas when it was our turn to have the family. This year it was the Geigers, plus Grandpa Gaede (Grandma Gaede had died and he had not yet remarried) and Uncle Elmer. Uncle Elmer was the youngest Gaede and we all felt he was indulged by Grandma Gaede. He was very bright but vulnerable and my father and Uncle Charley (Geiger) did not have a very high opinion of him. During the meal they began to razz him unmercifully, pointing out how pathetic he was. He was unable to defend himself and his older sisters did not try to protect him, nor his father who sat there and watched the verbal destruction of his son. I was so ashamed of the behavior of the adults and having endured similar abuse on occasion from my own father, that I almost got up and left the table. I think even my seven or eight-year-old youngest brother, Wes, felt the same. I felt so sorry for Uncle Elmer, and I have never forgotten.

One other holiday meal I remember, somewhat more amusing, was the Easter when it was Aunt Esther's turn to have the family. Once again, Grandpa Gaede and Elmer were included. This may have been the first time I was introduced to the thin sliced goose, and once again Uncle Elmer was teased unmercifully. After the meal, in order to escape the ordeal, Uncle Elmer asked my mother if he could take me to a movie. At this point, I was probably thirteen or fourteen years old, and my parents had not allowed us to see very many movies - they did not want us to be over-stimulated or cause nightmares. I only remember one or two of the movies we did get to see: *The Barefoot Postman*, the story of the postman who walked the length of Florida along the east coast barefoot in the surf most of the way, and the *Cuban Love Song* with Lawrence Tibbets, who was a classical singer and sang a song that I can still hum, the theme-song tune: "Peanuts". It took place in Havana and I have no idea what the plot was, but I remember the song.

My mother gave her permission (younger brother Russ was not invited) and we went to a movie theater on Lorain Street and W. 117th Street, the "Variety." The movie was a Boris Karloff horror movie, was in black and white, and very graphic and very dramatic. I think I may actually have had some nightmares after seeing it. When my mother learned what Uncle Elmer had done, she was furious and gave him a severe tongue lashing. I wonder now what his motivation was to select such a picture for such a young, impressionable boy - on Easter Sunday, of all days; revenge for some of the humiliations he had experienced at family gatherings? I like to think that it was just a movie he wanted to see and since I was taller than he was, he thought I was old enough, and wanted someone to go with him to the movies. I think he was a very lonely man all his life, always seeking acceptance and approval from his peers, and never quite succeeding.

My memories of Uncle Elmer, many as they are, are inevitably incomplete, but I have often thought his life would make a good case study in a psychology textbook. He was the youngest of five siblings, arrived late in his mother's life, and was fussed over and doted on by her. He could wheedle anything he wanted from her. His older sisters may have thought this behavior cute at the time, but as they grew older and had children of their own, disapproved loudly. The effect of his mother's indulgence, her favoritism must have had an effect on the others in the family, especially on the hardworking, serious older brother, David.

The end result of this indulgence was Elmer's persuading his parents (Grandpa Gaede was always subservient to Grandma Gaede) to buy him a motorcycle when he was a junior in high school. He liked athletics, but was no athlete, and was reduced to reporting games for the high school newspaper. Perhaps he felt a motorcycle was a form of compensation for slights he had to endure and would raise his esteem among the members of the football, baseball and basketball teams that were denied him because of his lack of athleticism, reducing him to writing about the exploits of the other boys.

I don't remember hearing how long he had the motorcycle, but he was out riding it one evening and was caught in the blind spot of a double-decker bus in use at that time on Clifton Boulevard, not far from his home, and was sideswiped and severely injured: concussion, compound fracture of one leg, left arm rendered useless for the rest of his life, broken jaw and one ear almost torn off his head. It was a week before the doctors could operate on his leg. He was taken to the nearby St. Johns Hospital and we were not allowed to visit him for two weeks. It was my first visit to a hospital and to see Uncle Elmer, almost unrecognizable with a black and blue face, heavy bandaging of his head, his leg in a cast and suspended on a pulley at the foot of his bed made a huge impression on a ten-year-old and mother used Elmer as a bad example for years. Elmer was seven or eight years older than me and had always been kind to me. It hurt to see him in this condition. I think we only visited him that one time.

There was no money for college in the family and when he was recovered, his interest in sports became his life and he became a sportswriter for *The Cleveland News*, one of the two evening newspapers. This turned out to be to my advantage, as he took me to many sporting events, free and very preferred seats. Thus, he went on to make a career in the newspaper business for the rest of his life, never married, and a large portfolio of news clippings he had with him at all times became the wife and children he never had.

I remember Uncle Elmer very fondly, with all his faults, and always felt a little sorry for him. He was very bright and had talent, but never seemed able to reach his potential. He never had the benefit of a college education, going into the newspaper business after high school. I remember my mother dropping in with me at what was probably his first apartment after leaving home. It was a small building at the southeast corner of Franklin Boulevard and W. 117th Street and is still there. My only recollection of his apartment is of its small size and his pride in it. I suspect my mother was on a scouting expedition for herself and her two older sisters who wanted to be sure that baby brother, Elmer, was safe.

Having become a sportswriter for *The Cleveland News* meant that Uncle Elmer was able to meet many famous athletes and have favored seats at many sporting events. I remember that he took me to a Cleveland Indians game and after the game was over, we went into the locker room and I was introduced to Lou Boudreau and Ray Mack, the best shortstop-second base combination in baseball at the time and I got to shake their hands. Elmer knew this would get back to my parents, and then the sisters and their husbands and then to Grandpa and Grandma Gaede, and maybe impress them just a little.

Uncle Elmer was also a steady source of broken baseball bats from the Cleveland Indians, which we taped back together, and used in our own baseball games. The bats were always manufactured by Hillerich-Bradley and had the signature of one of the players burned into the barrel part of the bat. I remember one we taped up with the name Joe Vosmik, one of the Indian's outfielders, etched onto it.

One of the other sports thrills for which Uncle Elmer was responsible was his taking me to the basketball game between UCLA and Marquette at the Cleveland Public Auditorium. In spite of my height, I was never recruited for basketball in high school at a time when a height of 6' 4" was an asset and never played it at school or our back yard very much. I was a very poor shot. Today, I can't imagine how a game between a west coast college and a midwestern school was ever scheduled. This was long before travel by airplane and the game must have been part of a tour during the holiday season. It was heavily promoted because of the UCLA star player, Hank Luisetti. Our seats were directly behind the basket backboard on the ground floor, so we very close to the action. This was the game that Luisetti scored a record breaking 50 points personally, in spite of being double teamed and repeatedly fouled, and before the advent of the 3-point basket. I remember one shot right in front of us when Luisetti was double-teamed and fouled, and while horizontal on his way to the floor somehow was able to get his shot away and it went in. It was very exciting to be so close to the action and seeing history being made.

I have a few other memories of Uncle Elmer. While Russ and I were living in Pierson College at Yale, he visited us. We took him to lunch in the elegant Pierson dining room with its distinctive china and waitresses. He did something which I cannot remember, but which Russ felt worthy of reporting to our mother who then berated him for embarrassing her boys. He knew who had tattled and never spoke to Russ again.

He also invited me to join him in Detroit, where he was working the police beat for *The Detroit Free Press* to see a Detroit Tigers baseball game in Briggs Stadium. I was stationed in Ann Arbor at the time, so it was easy to get to Detroit. I remember seeing the hotel room Elmer was living in, which was tiny; stopping in at the police station on the way to the ballgame, and meeting one of his sources, a Major, in the central police station; and going through the tunnel under the Detroit River for the first time to Windsor, Canada, (I assume a passport was not necessary if one was in Army uniform) to have dinner with an old newspaper colleague from Cleveland, Isi Newborn, who reported on the bowling scene in Cleveland when Elmer worked there.

After the war I had little contact with him. He was never in one city for very long due to his constant job changes. He had graduated from reporting to assistant editorship posts by this time. I have a vague memory of a visit he made to Cleveland, he may have visited our home on Oakes

Road and we were privileged to see his portfolio of clippings, which he obviously regarded as his most precious possession, clutching them to his chest, his useless left arm hanging at his side. He had no wife, no children, only his clippings. Sad.

My memories of my mother's mother, Grandma Gaede are very faint. I do not remember a happy expression on her face, but a severe hairstyle, and dark clothing. My mother was dutiful and did pay visits, but nowhere as frequently as to Grandma Schmidt. I always felt that Grandma Gaede was very intelligent and was the one who managed the family finances and as long as she was alive, the family was moderately successful. Grandpa Gaede, on the other hand, was very outgoing and gregarious, but not very practical. He had a mechanical talent and was granted several patents. He invented a saw tooth setting device for handsaws (no power saws or tools then) and had a small manufacturing shop on the West side of Cleveland in the Franklin Boulevard W. 65th Street area where he produced the tool. I remember the only time I saw the shop was the time my mother stopped to see him and have him sharpen her ice skates. He later had a larger shop on W. 130th Street south of Brookpark Road. Both of these businesses failed, perhaps due to poor marketing, or cost controls.

Grandpa and Grandma Gaede owned two two-family houses, back to back, on Clifton Boulevard and Lake Avenue where they crossed each other. I remember how impressed I was that both houses had underground garages, which I had never seen before. They also owned the triangular piece of vacant land between the houses and the intersection. This was a valuable piece of commercial property. There was heavy traffic on both streets, which had bus lines and heavy automobile traffic, especially at rush hour, when downtown workers returned to their homes on the West side. These were two of the most important routes to the West side from downtown Cleveland. The first Gaede real estate venture, after owning the two two-family houses where they lived in one of the ground floor suites and we visited them, involved the vacant triangular lot. I remember being in the kitchen; mother and grandma talking about something and getting my chin pinched by the dropleaf in the kitchen table by Russ, who didn't realize what he was doing, which left a scar; I do not remember any of the other rooms, or ever eating a holiday meal at their house; the other three suites must have produced rental income, which would have been important to them. They built a restaurant on the adjoining triangle of land. I cannot remember its name (it may have had "Rooster" in it) but the competition from the larger Poschke restaurant across the street, who sponsored a Class "D" baseball team in the Cleveland Recreation Program, was too much and it failed after a few years. I still remember Mother stopping in when the equipment was being disposed of and bringing home a box of tall, amber colored soda glasses. We used them for years.

The restaurant venture was followed by building a Sinclair gas station. I scarcely remember it at all, but faintly remember mother stopping once on the way home for gas and that Uncle David, her younger brother, wiped the wind shield, and checked the oil after filling the tank. I don't know how long the gas station was open or what happened to it. I think that within a short time after Grandma Gaede died, Grandpa Gaede floundered and in a short while lost everything, the houses and the gas station and his manufacturing business.

I remember with some bitterness that he came to my mother to borrow money to help pay for Grandma Gaede's funeral. Mother took the $300 my brother and I had saved through a program promoted by the Society for Savings Bank on Public Square in downtown Cleveland, where students were encouraged to make weekly deposits into their own savings account books in their homerooms, which made it easy, not having to go to the bank downtown. The program was promoted by the Society for Savings to instill in young people the habit of saving. She loaned all of our savings to him. Not surprisingly, knowing Grandpa Gaede, he never repaid the loan, money borrowed from ten and twelve-year old grandchildren. He was still able to visit us occasionally with a jolly smile on his face and marvel and how big we had grown. He also married a very nice widow named Chilcote. I have no memories of how that worked out.

Many years later, after we were married, Fran and I visited him in a nursing home in North Royalton at the top of the S.R. 82 hill. I think it was called Royal Crest. I wonder how he managed to pay for his care. I'm sure his children did not get together to make regular contributions. He eventually died of cancer, probably at a time when we were in Florida because I know we did not attend his funeral service.

Uncle David, the fourth Gaede child, and probably five or six years younger than my mother, was always a mystery to me. I do not remember much about him - an impression of a serious, intelligent, ambitious person, determined to be more successful than his father. I do not remember his being included in the family gatherings at either our house or that of the other aunts. He may have been old enough to tend the gas station while the others, including the favored Uncle Elmer, were invited. I really did not get to know him at all.

I do remember being taken to his wedding to Elsie, a pretty, vivacious girl with a complexion flawed by what I now suspect may have been eczema. I do not recall anything about the wedding other than the white dress the bride wore, and that the church was on the far East side, in the E. 185th St. area on St. Clair Avenue.

I have no idea where they lived in their early married life, but they had five children, four daughters and one son. I was always bothered by the way my mother and my aunts treated Uncle David's family. I felt they were treated like second class citizens and could never understand why: was it because Uncle David was too independent and insisted on going his own way, or was always under scrutiny for signs of his father's failings, or that they moved so far away to North Ridgeville, Ohio, almost as far as Elyria, Ohio, which was like a foreign country? While we visited the Geigers frequently at their summer place in Linwood Park, in Vermilion, Ohio, which was about the same distance from Lakewood, we stopped to visit Uncle David very rarely. I may have been oversensitive and the reason for not stopping may have simply been that North Ridgeville was located on Center Ridge Road about 12 miles south of Lake Road and it was too far out of the way at the end of a long day at the beach.

He had bought a fair-sized piece of land at the southwest corner of S.R. 83 and Sugar Ridge Road, built a house there by himself, and an ice cream stand at the corner, later followed by a gas station. It seems to me that the only time we ever stopped to see them was when my father had bought a new car and he ostentatiously showed it off to Uncle David while having him fill it with gas. I was sure this was intended to point out my father's superiority. I know I cringed. On one of these infrequent stops, Russ and I helped Uncle David harvest the corn he had grown on the back, westerly part of his land. One other memory of Uncle David is that he was the Executor for Cousin Al's estate, and it was he who sent us the check for the legacy left us by Cousin Al.

Much of what I know of David's family I learned many years later when young David, the youngest of the five children, who should have been spoiled by having four older sisters who adored him, and wasn't, visited us at our condo in Florida in Bradenton with his wife, Terry, and we had lunch and visited. I remember one year when young David's visit coincided with our cousin Jean Basil (and Bob) Ridenour and her sister Virginia and her husband, Jack Fischrupp's annual vacation on Siesta Key. We all went to a large pizza parlor for lunch in Ellenton, Florida, nearby, where the big attraction was a mighty theatrical model Wurlitzer organ, one of two remaining in the U.S.A. So, in addition to a large selection of pizzas and other foods available, picked up at the rear of the room and brought to picnic style tables to be eaten, at the appointed hour, the organ rose to stage level and one of the two staff organists played a concert.

I learned more of my David Gaede cousins after making contact with the oldest sister, Marilyn and Don Bayer, who sent us Christmas cards from their home in Seminole. Florida. I used to go to the Bay View V.A. Hospital in St. Petersburg to get my prescriptions filled to save money, and it involved having to have a physical examination in the morning by a V.A. doctor assigned to me, then waiting until after lunch to pick up my prescriptions. When I discovered that Seminole was only about a mile away from the hospital, I called Cousin Marilyn and suggested meeting them for lunch. It was very pleasant to be with them, and once, at Christmas time, they invited me to their home for lunch with other members of their singing group. They were very active in their church choir and gave many concerts during the year. I remember how amused I was the first time I saw Marilyn's husband, Don, in his Elvis Presley costume. It made me wish I could have attended one of their performances.

The first home of Aunt Esther, who was my mother's oldest sister and her husband, Uncle Herb, which I can remember was on W. 134th Street north of Lorain Avenue, in Cleveland. It was a bungalow and all I can remember is the kitchen where Uncle Herb had his coffee bean grinder mounted on a wall, which fascinated me, and the living room. I remember Aunt Esther, a former schoolteacher, as stern and demanding; she was a gardener and horticulturist: I thought she knew the Latin name for every flower in her borders - which Uncle Herb planted and maintained. I think Aunt Esther was the only Gaede to go to college, and, as in the case of my father's sister, Clara, she obtained a teacher's certificate.

Uncle Herb worked for Detroit Diesel on Clinton Road off West Boulevard in Cleveland. I never learned what he did there, but he was very meticulous in everything he did. They bought a large lot in Berea, Ohio, on Riverside Drive where he built an oversized two story, two car garage which they lived in until he replaced it with a conventional single-family house. I remember the garage but not the house. I remember that on one of our infrequent Sunday afternoon visits, my brother Ken who was about six years old, fell down the stairs from the second floor and cut his knee severely on the rim of a 5 gallon kerosene container. After getting him bandaged up it was felt serious enough for us to take him to see Dad's cousin, Eila Haemerle, who was a nurse, (not a doctor, of course) to be sure the wound had been treated properly.

On another visit after their house was completed, I remember watching Uncle Herb, who was the most meticulous man I ever knew, sifting soil through a large screen and then wheeling it into place on the front lawn he was preparing. It wasn't the sifting process that fascinated me, but that he was using a surveyor's transit to get the level and slope of the land the way he wanted it, wheelbarrow by wheelbarrow load. He was a very patient man. He amazed me because he was surrounded by women, a wife and two daughters, but every other word he uttered was a swear word. I never understood this, but it was good preparation for me when I was in the Mule Pack in Basic Training in the Army where the words didn't sound so out of place.

Uncle Herb was the only relative who came out to Brecksville to help me while we were building our house and frantically trying to get it livable in time for the beginning of the school year. When he saw that I might not make my deadline, he came on a Saturday morning and made sure that our daughters had shelves in their closets, if not doors to their bedrooms. Before that, in the early stages, he had come with Aunt Esther, to inspect my progress. When they were leaving, Aunt Esther had to pull hard on the front door, which was three feet wide, solid wood and very heavy, and had the knob installed in the middle of the door. The door didn't open immediately so she gave it a jerk and it opened suddenly and slammed into her head, almost knocking her down. I do not remember her reaction, a little scream, perhaps, but I still wonder what she thought of the whole house. This was after my mother's death so she could not report to my mother.

We did go to the Basils for holiday meals and they came to our house on Parkwood Road in Lakewood. It was all done on a rotation devised by the three sisters. We also visited them in the summertime and I remember once going over the hill at the rear of their property to a small branch of the Rocky River to swim and splash around - it was far too small an area to swim in and not much fun because the water was so muddy.

We spent by far the most time visiting the Geiger family; I remember the many, many visits to their house on Hilliard Boulevard at the corner of Niagara Avenue. Aunt "Tiel" (Ottilia) was my mother's older sister, the middle of the three Gaede girls. She was always smiling, jovial and outgoing, traits which stood her well when she helped Uncle Charlie in his haberdashery business in Lakewood. I think she worked full time in the store, which suited her well because I remember my mother being critical of her housekeeping. I think Aunt Tiel wanted to be out meeting people, not doing household chores. She was particularly critical of Aunt Tiel's laundry schedule. Aunt Tiel allowed laundry to pile up and did it once a month. Shocking. This was possible because Uncle Charley, who was very dapper and a sharp dresser had to display all the latest men's fashions, and the boys always had something new to wear. They were walking billboards at Lakewood High School, publicizing the family business. Aunt Tiel was always there at the cash register to greet customers and help solve problems. It was a family business and has remained so to this day.

There was an underlying tension between our two families that I was aware of when I was growing up. There were three boys in the Geiger family and four boys in the Schmidt family. I do not remember specific instances of comparison, but I think the older Schmidt boys got better grades in school than the oldest Geiger son, Charles, who was about a year and a half older than I was. He went to a church affiliated small college in Naperville, Illinois. Both older Schmidt brothers won scholarships to Yale. I remember my mother always making a point that material things (like fancy clothes) were not as important as intellectual things. The Geigers bought clothes and the Schmidts bought music. On the surface, things were always peaceful and friendly, but under the surface I always was aware a slight tension.

There were other similarities: Uncle Charley and his brother, Howard, had had a haberdashery business in the Hotel Cleveland on Public Square in downtown Cleveland and it went bankrupt in the Great Depression. He and his brother started new separate haberdashery businesses, Howard at Kamm's Corner, Lorain Avenue at Riverside Drive on the west side of Cleveland, and Charley at Detroit Avenue at Warren Road in Lakewood. Shortly after this, my father started his own mortgage loan business in a small two room office in the Leader Building at Superior Avenue and E. Sixth Street. In both cases they were starting business from nothing, and in both cases, the wives helped the fledgling businesses with Aunt Tiel acting as a salesperson, and my mother as a secretary. I am sure that both men hoped that their business would grow to a point that they could provide jobs for their sons. And I am equally certain that there was intense curiosity as to how successful the other's business was financially. I know that my father was dying to know how Uncle Charley was doing, and could never understand why Uncle Charley would not give his mortgage business to us; of course, Uncle Charley would have had to provide his financial statements to us, and that he could not do.

I remember the store very well. It was located on the north side of Detroit Avenue between Warren Road and St. Charles Avenue, which was the heart of the Lakewood business district. It was a double store front in a two-story brick building and had a basement. This was where I had my first paying job and received my Social Security number. I remember I was sixteen and worked during the Christmas sales season on weekends and during the week while we were on vacation from school. My duties were menial: sweeping the floor, going to the basement to bring up fresh stock, washing the front door windows, and replacing stock left on the counter after a sale to a customer. I remember vividly, once, having replaced several shirts on the shelves, standing between the counter and the shelves on the wall, when a lady customer asked me to show her (I was not allowed to deal with selling) that *green* shirt. Being red-green color blind, I couldn't tell which shirt she wanted to see, and in a panic, I pulled down the whole stack of shirts, six or seven, and spread them on the counter for her to choose, at which point Uncle Charley came to my rescue and all ended well.

I don't remember how much the pay was, not much, but it was welcome. The only non-family member who worked at the store full time was a very fine salesman, named Bill Fritz. I remember how nice he was to me (nepotism awareness?) and that he had a moustache. On the other hand, the time I spent doing housekeeping chores was time gained for the salespeople to spend more profitably, selling.

The thing I remember most fondly was the Chinese restaurant, The Bamboo Gardens, across the street where I discovered egg foo yung. In those days of the waning Great Depression, it was exciting to eat a meal in a restaurant. Chinese cooking later became one of my favorite cuisines, especially after being trained on what to order by our Japanese *sensei* (teachers) in Minneapolis in the Army. I also remember a Dairymen's ice cream parlor two doors away from Uncle Charley's store where I discovered milk shakes. I remember going with Cousin Charles on our breaks and having my very first chocolate malt shake. Then two or three shakes a day for two or three days in a row, getting to a point where I could not look at a milk shake. It was years until I had another one. Working for Uncle Charley was a far cry from an internship at a law firm, but I loved the experience, and after two or three years of helping out part-time at the store was actually allowed to sell to a customer, which was quite an achievement for what was still a very shy individual.

I remember many, many visits to the Geiger family home. This was only a short distance from our house on Parkwood Road in Lakewood, which made it easy for family get-togethers. When the two families did get together whether for a meal, or a drop-in visit, the two outnumbered women would retreat to the kitchen, leaving the rest of the house and yard to the seven boys. The two dads who were usually sitting in the front room discussing business, with my dad trying hard to sniff out how well Uncle Charley was doing. I remember we were always welcomed warmly, and it was a good feeling to be part of a larger family.

I remember the house quite well. It was a 2-story frame Dutch colonial on a corner lot and had a nice front porch (later enclosed). Uncle Charley raised tea roses on both sides of the walk from the kitchen door to the garage, which was entered from the side street, Niagara, and I now wonder if his roses could have planted the early seed for my later obsession with peonies.

The house had a full basement, which seemed to me to very cramped. It had a big, fat, hot air furnace and there were 12" circular galvanized metal pipes hanging from the ceiling, which had to be that large to supply the necessary volume of hot air needed to rise to the upper floors. There was no electric motor blower fan. The heating system was known as a "hot air gravity" system, and I think it used natural gas for fuel.

They had a ping-pong table under those pipes, and ping-pong was an acceptable activity in their church. I remember having to duck under the pipes to hit the ping-pong ball, which didn't help my game. The only time we ever played ping-pong was at the Geigers, and I always lost. I wasn't very skillful, but the pipes were a handicap.

I used to feel sorry for the Geiger cousins; their religious beliefs (Evangelical) forbade not only drinking and smoking, but also playing cards, gambling, dancing and even movies. Our Christian

Science teaching forbade only drinking alcohol and smoking, and any other substance that would affect the functioning of one's mind. I always thought we were the lucky ones. We could play cards and call a card table a card table; our cousins had to call a folding card table a "picnic" table, and as far as I know, never saw a movie, or attended a school dance, or played a game of hearts or rummy. And, I do not know, but suspect, that this rigid discipline held up through their college years and adulthood.

The only unpleasant memory I have of growing up with the Geiger cousins was the time we were playing out in the back yard on Niagara, tossing a football, and playing some form of tag. Charles, who was a year and a half older than I was and stronger, tripped me and I fell to the ground with my back on the grass and he held me down by kneeling on my biceps and grinding them back and forth. It was very painful, and I have never forgotten the experience, nor understood the underlying cause.

We also spent many happy hours at the Geiger's summer cottage at Linwood Park in Vermilion, Ohio, about 30 miles west of Lakewood. Linwood Park was founded in the late 1880s by an Evangelical Church group, modeled somewhat on Chautauqua in New York. It had an entry fee to keep out sightseers, a small hotel, a tabernacle used for church services and other intellectual events, about 150 summer cottages, and was situated on a bluff overlooking Lake Erie. It had a wonderful, extensive sandy beach, which made it popular with vacationers from Cleveland, Columbus, and Pittsburg. There were many mature trees providing shade for the cottages on both sides of the narrow streets, which bore only local traffic so small children could safely roam. I used to love to go to Linwood. There was a small children's play area in front of the hotel, which was demolished in the '30s and I only remember faintly, and I can remember the teeter-totter, and the whirligig, and the slide. I used to spend a lot of time as a six year old polishing the slide with the wax paper wrappers of candy bars to make the surface slipperier and the ride down the slide, all six feet of it, faster and more exciting. And then there was the water. Digging holes in the sand and building sand castles near the water's edge; we could go into the water and splash each other and paddle around pretending we were swimming. My parents had a hard time getting me to come out of the water, which I loved so, to go to supper.

I remember on one of our Sunday visits, when we were down on the beach with the whole family, and I walked along the edge of the water all the way West to the Vermilion River without telling anyone where I was going. The banks of the river where it entered Lake Erie were lined with huge sandstone blocks and I was contemplating swimming from one side to the other, a distance of probably 30-40 feet. I knew I hardly knew how to swim, and the river looked dark and very deep and awfully wide, which frightened me. Luckily, I turned and walked back to the family.

I had caused a furor; everyone, including strangers, was all lined up, holding hands in a line, chest deep in the water working their way to shore, feeling for my body with their feet, when I suddenly, nonchalantly, appeared strolling down the beach. There was great relief, some tears, a hug; and then a severe scolding and, although I do not remember it, one of the few spankings I ever received. I do remember promising never to do such a thing again.

Other memories of the beach: the time we were all together with Aunt Tiel and the boys, and out of the water resting between swims, and Aunt Tiel fell asleep, gently snoring with her month open. I saw a large housefly fly into her mouth and out again, several times, which I thought was hilarious. I remember teasing her about it, and her indignant denials.

On another occasion, after we were married, we were invited to Linwood for a Labor Day family picnic. The annual Labor Day Air Show, which was held at the Hopkins Airport then. It was coming to a close and was to feature an over-flight of a squadron of the Strategic Air Command huge B-36 bombers. We were all down on the beach standing at the water's edge in anticipation. I remember, and can still feel, the rumble of the engines as the huge planes approached from the West. The flight of three planes flew by at an altitude of about 300 feet a quarter mile from the shore. This was during the Cold War and it was very impressive. When they had passed, I stepped back to sit on the low bank of sand and misjudged the distance to the ground and sat with a thump. I thought nothing of it at the time, but, in fact, had fractured my coccyx. This turned out to be a very painful experience. It was impossible to sit on a chair comfortably and even hurt when lying in bed. We had made a mortgage loan to an orthopedic surgeon, Myron Pardee, who lived in Parma, but had offices in Lakewood and practiced at Lakewood Hospital. I went to see him to find out what was wrong and why it was still so painful after two weeks. I remember his asking me to stretch out on a table and his pushing his thumb against the base of my spine and my nearly shooting off the end of the table from the excruciating pain. He then diagnosed the fractured coccyx and recommended a donut cushion and warm soaks in the bathtub. There was nothing else he could do. It took a month or so before the pain subsided, and the fracture eventually healed. That was probably sixty years ago, and I am still cautious when taking a seat.

I have other memories of Linwood. I remember Dad's exasperation at having to stop at the gatehouse and identify us as guests of the Geiger's, thus avoiding the entry fee, which, if he had had to pay, would have annoyed him even more. I remember the cottage which had bedrooms on the second floor and a comfortable porch across its entire front. The park's tennis courts were behind the cottage and the hole in the fence between Linwood and the small amusement park, Crystal Beach, which we sneaked through to get into the park was on the other side of the courts. I always enjoyed Aunt Tiel's cooking which was slightly different from my mother's, and admired how she (she was unflappable) could put together a meal with very short notice, sometimes driving to downtown Vermilion to get something she needed after the guests had arrived, and sometimes bringing back bakery sweet rolls, or donuts, which were treats we never had at home.

On one Sunday when we were there, we attended a vesper service at the Tabernacle because the twins, Donald and Douglas, were going to give a concert, playing their trumpets. The only thing I remember is their playing a duet of the famous show piece, "Carnival of Venice," which has a lot of intricate triple tonguing, something which cannot be done on a clarinet. I think they played well, but the thing I remember the most is the turmoil of deciding what they were to wear. We were in the cottage when it came time to get ready for their performance, and their bickering was comical. They always dressed identically to emphasize their twinness and argued constantly over which outfit to wear until they finally arrived at a consensus.

I have other memories of the City of Vermilion: there was a small hotel on the west bank of the Vermilion River close to the Lake. I remember going there for lunch when I was about six after church one Sunday, climbing the steps up to the dining room, and eating chicken and mashed potatoes with a wonderful gravy. It was so unusual, quite a treat for one so young and that accounts for the retention of that memory.

This rare visit to a restaurant may have preceded a visit to a friend of Grandpa Schmidt, whose name was Kobbs. They lived in Vermilion in a house on a street south of the railroad tracks. Walter Kobbs, his son, was a friend of my father's and for several years we took Grandpa and Grandma Schmidt on a Sunday afternoon to Vermilion for a visit with his old friend. I remember a small garden at the side of the house, and a Victorian style house with curtains drawn making it dim inside, and the smell of lavender, which pervaded the whole house. The smell of the lavender remains with me. I think it is my favorite scent.

I remember that my mother and Aunt Clara had a nice relationship in my early childhood. They were interested in Christian Science which was very new and a serious interest in common for them. They did craft things together and ice skated at Brookside Park where the Cleveland Zoo was located at Fulton and Denison Roads. I sat in the natural amphitheater seats while they glided over the ice; Grandma Schmidt was entrusted with my baby brother Russ while we were gone. I remember one trip home late in the afternoon when Mother had to drive in a blizzard, following the street car on its tracks to see where she was going, having to stop every time the street car did, which made it a much longer trip.

I remember in the days before the annual Home and Flower show in the spring, Aunt Clara and Mother took me with them to its predecessor, the Cleveland Food Show, at the big Cleveland Public Auditorium where there were booths and booths displaying the latest kitchen gadgets and the newest recipes. I remember how tiring it was to trudge from stall to stall. Free samples were offered and carefully stowed in shopping bags to carry home. I remember Aunt Clara as being innovative and eager to try new things. Unfortunately, one Thanksgiving she did the turkey with a pineapple glaze and stuffing and it was terrible, but we had to eat it.

I do not remember Grandpa Schmidt having anything to do with religion. But, both Aunt Clara, who had become a Christian Scientist tried to interest Grandma Schmidt in going to her church, Third Church, located on W. 25th Street, a long white frame church with Grecian columns on the front. She was unable to lure Grandma away from her Pilgrim Evangelical church, nearby in the Tremont district. Grandma went to two services every Sunday: the first sermon preached in German (I question how much she understood); the second sermon, in English. She tithed faithfully as I learned later when, after we were married, I helped her do her income taxes.

A large majority of my memories are happy ones, ones I get pleasure from revisiting. Not all of them, however. One concerns Aunt Clara. My early memories are of an older relative who cared for my mother and for me. This changed when my parents announced the impending birth of their fourth child. Aunt Clara, who must have been an early feminist, and further, had issues caused by being limited to one child because of her husband's mental illness, burst out with some remark comparing Mother to wild animals who had no control over their reproduction. I did not actually hear this. But I saw the effect it had on my mother and it hurt her. She was very sensitive in any case and it affected her deeply. I don't think she ever spoke to Aunt Clara again. Our Saturdays spent at Grandma Schmidt's house ended.

For many years, we children were cautioned by my parents, of Uncle Will's illness, which might be inheritable, never to use the word ''crazy' or "idiot" or "moron" in the presence of either Aunt Clara or her only child, Marion, whom we played with, joined by Grandma Schmidt at the dining room table after the dishes were done after Saturday night supper.

Cousin Marion was highly intelligent and did well in the advanced classes she took in the Cleveland Public School system, which was highly regarded at that time. She, too, was denied college for financial reasons, married, had two children. She was divorced by her husband, remarried a high school sweetheart and moved to the West Coast. She played tournament duplicate bridge, something I never accomplished, in spite of my love of the game. I remember her stopping to see us at our condo in Florida at Vizcaya when she was on a visit. I remember her blonde hair pulled into a tight bun, still wearing glasses, dressed very primly. I had not seen her since her mother's funeral visitation when I brought her a beautiful tree peony blossom. We never exchanged Christmas cards, but I always seemed to be aware of where she was. She lived in Palo Alto, California. On our one trip to California, our time was so limited we did not have time to look her up and see where she was living.

When I was old enough to drive, brother Russ and I were allowed to drive by ourselves to visit Grandma Schmidt, which we did, loving to be with her. Aunt Clara, who lived with Grandma and Grandpa at different times was often present and was pleasant with us. I think that depending on the state of her finances, she alternated living alone with Cousin Marion in her little bungalow or moving back into her room, which was always waiting for her in Grandma's house. Russ and I were always tense and very cautious if Aunt Clara was present when we visited, and carefully omitted mentioning seeing her to Mother when we returned home. It was a very touchy subject and I always felt the situation was very sad.

Another unhappy memory involves Fran. We had been living in Brecksville for some time, the house furnished, the pond built, the children thriving, two cars, a circle of friends, finances secure. And I was very content. One morning I went into our bedroom before leaving for work to kiss her goodbye. I remember it was a sunny summer morning, and I found her lying in bed in tears. When I asked what was wrong, had I done something to bother her, she insisted everything was alright. I knew this was not the Fran I was accustomed to and I persisted in questioning her. She was obviously very disturbed. I pointed out all the good things in her life, things that other women would love to have, which should be providing a solid foundation for her happiness, how much we had to be grateful for and how fortunate we were. She tearfully admitted all this.

Gradually she revealed that she felt inadequate; that I was constantly correcting her, many times before strangers; that I interrupted her constantly, finishing her thoughts and sentences with what I thought they should be. This may have seemed charming at the beginning of our marriage as proof of how we were meant for each other, that we were able to complete the other's thoughts, but had long since lost that charm. This was happening not just in private, but in front of our friends; that she had no independent life; that she always had to ask me for money, and on and on.

To me, with my Christian Science background, where I was taught that my mind was in control of my thoughts and that Mind was a synonym for God, it was hard to understand why Fran's mind did not control her thoughts and emotions. She freely recognized all the positive things with which I was trying to reassure her and comfort her. She seemed to be helpless and telling herself how much she had to be grateful for did not seem to help; her mind could not control her emotions. Help had to come from elsewhere.

I remember feeling alarm when I remembered the situation in the first serious romance of my life, Carol Kuekes, two years my junior. Her mother had married an older man and after ten or twelve years of marriage, she felt she had married too young, before she had had any experience of life and what it could hold for her; that she was stifled; that her older husband was dominating her very thoughts. Her solution was to divorce him, to gain her freedom to be herself. I only remember meeting her once or twice, and that as Carol and I left for our date, after my first meeting with her mother, she said *à bientôt*, which made a big impression on me. I did not want to be the cause of something similar to her marriage in my own marriage.

As I tried to reassure Fran and comfort her, that bit of history flashed through my mind: had my behavior in those first few days after our meeting in Ann Arbor been so filled with the fear of losing her by doing or saying the wrong thing, that I dominated her and she was swept along by sheer romance and the improbability of it all? I didn't really think so. We were both older, more experienced and seeking a lifelong companion. She had been looking for someone for four years on campus. She was not a sixteen-year-old high school girl. The feelings we discovered were real and we had the evidence to prove it.

The first thing I told her was that there were going to be some changes made in my behavior, now that I was aware of how my unthinking, insensitive actions affected her. I would try hard to stop doing these things, which would probably not be easy, but I would work at correcting these unlovely habits; that I knew I could change; it was too important; that I had always dedicated my life to making her happy. The first thing I was going to do that very day was the easy thing, which should have been done years before, was to go to The Cleveland Trust Company, a different bank from the one we used, and open a checking account in her name alone and fund it, even with only a few hundred dollars, and this was to be hers alone to do with as she wished, replenished when necessary; no need to justify how she was spending her money. I remember the checkbook in its light blue pseudo Morocco leather holder which she carried in her purse for years.

The sequel to this scenario was that things did improve although I never did completely overcome my tendency to correct her statements or break in to finish her sentences. As the years passed my lapses were implemented by my boring her more and more by having to listen to my stories when out in company, ones that she had heard over and over, which you are seeing here for the first time.

At some point in our oldest daughter Nancy's first marriage, when she was trying to cope with the verbal abuse she was enduring from her husband, she went to see a psychologist, which she found helpful. The details are very hazy, but Fran ended up seeing the same man. I don't know if she felt he helped her cope with what I now feel was the early stages of depression which persisted even after I had had some success in curbing my share of the cause for her feelings.

Still desperately seeking help to regain her old self, this chapter in our lives ended with her seeing a psychiatrist at the Cleveland Clinic after we had moved back to Lakewood. He prescribed anti-depressant medication, which did little to help her, and he never tried to explore her conflicted feelings about her father whom she adored and who, effectively, abandoned her at the age of eight.

The depression she suffered, which was manageable at first, deepened upon the death of Nancy, our daughter, in 2003, at which we were both physically present, a first for both of us, and I began to notice a loss of interest in many activities which she formerly enjoyed, and her spending alarming amounts of time in her bed to a point which began to affect her muscle tone. I talk about this time more in Chapter XII.

In 2010 after our return to Ohio, she had to be hospitalized because of extreme weakness and while she was in rehab for six weeks, I spent every afternoon and evening with her, a lot of the time reading when she was napping.

Barb and Pete bought me a small portable refrigerator which we placed on a table in Fran's room and stocked, so I had my evening meals with Fran in her room. She never ate in the dining room with the other residents until she was at Kemper House, and then only for a short time.

This was when we discovered that she enjoyed having me read aloud to her. I was reading the Lawrence Sanders "Archie McNally" series and she particularly liked "Archie" and his adventures and was able to remember the characters and where the story left off, which I found encouraging. This was before we learned of her dementia. I am so thankful to Genworth Life, who provided the insurance which covered most of the daily room charges. I certainly did not regret having paid long term care premiums since 1988, at this time.

When she was released from rehab, we returned to our new home in the Del Webb community, Prairie Ridge, to a house which was cluttered with unopened boxes in Fran's bedroom which had been there for six months and a dining room table covered with small items waiting to be placed on tabletops, and no pictures hung. Fran, who was a meticulous housekeeper, was able to walk by this unsettled mess, on a daily basis without concern. It did not matter that things, which would normally have required her approval as to placement, were not being done. It was a further sign of the coming diagnosis of dementia. In the end, I had to make all those decisions and it was particularly disturbing for me to have to decide which pictures to hang and where they should go. She had no interest in my problem. I could only hope that when family or visitors came, they would think that I had made decisions that would have been the same as if Fran had had been involved. I have made no changes in the seven years I have been here and have a comforting feeling that she did have a hidden hand in my decisions. After 68 years of marriage it could hardly be otherwise.

More detail of Fran's final months are to be found in Chapter XII, which covers our final return to Ohio from Florida, memories which I relive almost daily when drifting off into sleep. This is one of the three pre-sleep scenarios I run through my mind when I am trying to fall asleep.

Briefly, we received a our first diagnosis of dementia, which caused a change in my care since I now knew that her behavior was not under her control and had not been for some time; two serious falls with trips to the ER; an early morning "stroll", followed by a short period of lucidity when Fran suggested that perhaps it was time to think of an assisted living facility since I was no longer physically strong enough to care for her; the move to Kemper House in Olmsted Falls, and six months later her unexpected death.

This is another time when I am not pleased with my memory. It seems that I can remember the unimportant details, but, as we sat in the conference room together in our shock at the unexpectedness, the thunderclap, the finality of this sudden death, the emotions I felt, and the immediate thoughts I had are blurry. I remember feeling a sudden great gap in my life, a sense of physical loss, but no great sadness. Rather, I was overcome with a great sense of relief that my partner in life, my great love, had been released from her suffering at last. I had recently seen a picture of a large bird that had been brought back to health after having suffered a broken wing, being tossed into the air by a Forest Ranger to regain its lost freedom. This image that occurred to me was a source of great comfort, feeling as I did that Fran had now been released from her prison.

After a while the staff asked whether I would like to go to our room to view the remains, and, at first I did not think that I wanted to, or could; but Barb did, and I decided to go with her. When we entered the room, I noticed immediately that the bed had been moved from its position next to the wall so that it was at right angles to the wall. It was hard not to believe that Fran was not sleeping. Her hair had been brushed and her mouth was slightly open, just as when I arrived for my daily visit. I sat in a chair on the right side of the bed, and Barb sat at the foot of the bed. After a half hour or so of contemplation and reliving memories, it was time to leave. I got up and leaned over to kiss Fran's forehead for the last time, and, remember the shock of feeling the coldness of her skin, and the film of moisture I felt: such a contrast to the night before.

After that I remember none of the technical details of funeral arrangements, or of the legal requirements. The children would not let me drive home and insisted that I stay with them for a few days. I think one of Pete's brothers helped him move my car to their driveway. I stayed in what I came to think of as "my room" and had my meals with them sitting around the island in their kitchen. I don't remember how long it was before the children felt it was safe for me to drive home but the day came and my life resumed in much the same pattern that it had had before Fran had to go to Kemper House. I was alone in our house on Prairie Moon, but in a sense, I had been alone when Fran was still with me there. She spent all her time in bed in the master bedroom with the blinds drawn, and other that giving her pills and feeding her meals, and checking in on her to see if there was anything she needed, I spent my time in my office on the computer, or in evenings in the living room watching TV. I had been in preparation for living alone for several years before Fran's death. If her disease had not been dementia, one could almost believe that she had been preparing me for a life without her. I do not remember how long it took me to recover from the initial shock and to come to terms with a life that had to go on. About six weeks later, I went back to play bridge with my new friends at Pioneer Ridge and got through the evening in control of my emotions and no outward signs of grief. It was a beginning.

One new thought that occurred to me at this time was my recollection of our wedding vows, the part where we promised to care for each other "'til death do us part". Suddenly I realized that although death is a physical parting, like one partner leaving for a long trip with an uncertain time of return, death is not a true parting. It is not an ending. I believe the bond of love reinforced by a life lived together with all its memories remains unchanged and continues on.

My memories of a funeral and later memorial service are spotty. I remember Barb, who was such a rock throughout this whole experience, contacting St. Matthews Episcopal Church in Brecksville about arrangements and our going to St. Matthews, where Fran had invested so much of her love and service, for the Palm Sunday Service, four days after her death. Many of the older members offered their condolences, among them, Harry Bartels, "Skip" Smith, and Ceil Clarenbach. The minister was now a lady priest whose name I do not recall, only her warmth and compassion and her willingness to travel all the way from Brecksville, a distance of about 25 miles, to Lakewood Park Cemetery in Rocky River to accommodate the family and perform graveside rites.

I think there were two visits to the cemetery, one a memorial when the weather was bad. A canvas shelter was erected to shield us from any rain. I remember walking very gingerly down the slippery slope to the grave. A weekend was picked when all the family could gather, including the grandchildren from out of town. The other was the interment of the ashes, some of which I scattered around to feed the Japanese tree peony, "Hana Kisoi," which I had received permission to plant about 15 feet away from our daughter, Nancy's grave. This was when I realized that our gravesite was head to head with Nancy's, and was glad the tree peony, which will live and bloom for 100 years was so nearby, standing vigil over our graves.

Whenever I am in the area, I visit my two graves and recall what the presence of two such exceptional women in my life has meant to me. This is the spot where my vision of Nancy occurred, described in the later chapter "Credo". Many years later when the plant had matured, I picked a blossom of "Hana Kisoi." It was surely the most beautiful flower in color and shape I have ever seen in all my years of raising peonies and seeing the thousands of blossoms at the peony exhibitions we attended. The symbolism is very potent for me: a sign and a reminder that beauty and life are eternal.

I have to concentrate deliberately when I watch my TV screen in the living room, not to look at the blank wall between the screen and the ceiling, because I see Fran lying in her bed, the bed at right angles to the wall in the room, as I first saw her upon entering the room after receiving the terrible news. It has now been almost five years, and I wonder how long my memory will keep that image alive. Part of me wishes it would disappear and part of me is glad it is still with me and I can count on its reappearing.

The passing of Nancy eleven years earlier was no preparation for Fran's passing. The process was far shorter and far more brutal, involving cancer, as it did. It was in the time period when we were spending our winters in Florida, and when we were living in the third condo we had bought in Bradenton, named Vizcaya. One of our bridge playing friends put their condo on the market and we told Nancy about it. She and her husband, John, had both retired from their teaching jobs in Rocky River and Lakewood, and had visited Florida often enough to know that this was where they would like to settle. Nancy flew down to Bradenton the next day and bought the condo on the spot and arranged for its financing before her return home three or four days later. It was located about 80 yards from our front door in a building on the circular drive through the development, which provided the necessary privacy between our two units.

In short order they sold their house in Rocky River and moved into their new home, Unit F in Building 26. John played more golf, which was his passion than he ever had before and Nancy joined him often and did her best to arouse his interest in tennis, which was her passion. Once their condo was furnished, and she had done all she could with their small patio garden, in order to avert boredom, she found a job where she learned to be a picture framer and became very proficient. She also became involved in committee work for the condo association. She chaired the committee for revising the condo By-laws and Rules and Regulations. One of the members of the committee told me that he had never seen a committee run so efficiently. I remember how good it felt to have her drop in to visit us on her way home after committee meetings. Life was good.

I remember one afternoon when John was playing golf and she stopped in and complained that she was having trouble breathing. This was very unusual. It was obvious to me that she was in some distress. I insisted on driving her to the Blake Memorial Hospital emergency room. I left her there after John arrived, and when Fran and I returned for visiting hours, we found that they drained a liter of fluid from the lining of her lungs, and she had to stay in the hospital with a tube inserted which drained fluid constantly. Once again, I go in greater detail in Chapter XII.

I remember that the reports of her progress were very hopeful, and that she felt strong enough while undergoing her chemo therapy treatments to take a paraglide ride over the Gulf of Mexico with one the neighbors in our building. I would have liked to have seen that. There is a photo somewhere of the two of them, sitting side by side on the bench under the parachute, waving, far above the waters of the Gulf, taken from the speedboat towing them.

We had a Christmas tree in the living room, all decorated with pink bows, which Fran had painstakingly tied, and the floor was covered with presents which were to be distributed after dinner. Our traditional Christmas dinner happened to coincide with the day of the appearance on national television of a high school basketball star, LeBron James from Akron, Ohio. John, Nancy's husband, was an ardent basketball fan, and I remember, with some bitterness, that he insisted the TV be on so he could watch the game which totally disrupted the opening of the Christmas presents, and both Fran and I had unspoken fears that this might be Nancy's last Christmas, in spite of her prognosis. I couldn't understand Nancy's husband's insensitivity, since there was another large screen TV in the master bedroom on the other side of the living room wall, where he could have watched the game without disturbing the rest of the family. At one point, John walked through the group to go out on the patio to complete a phone conversation on his cell phone, complaining loudly that he wasn't being allowed to watch the game. The evening finally came to an end, and Fran went directly to bed, weeping with tears that would not cease.

I remember calling Nancy to tell her the effect of her husband's performance and detected the first signs of her acceptance of her fate when she said, "Don't talk to me, talk to John. I'm just so tired." I could hear the deep fatigue in her voice, and I had a sinking feeling that this was the beginning of the end game. I felt it was a rebuke to me, and a plea for understanding. Now, I believe John's behavior was the first sign I detected of his efforts to come to terms with the enormity of his inevitable loss of the most important person in his life and his fear that he would not be able to cope with it.

Nancy's birthday was May 19th, and in spite of her being bedridden and semi-comatose, we planned a mini-celebration and went to their condo after dinner with a small, 6" birthday cake, hoping that she might be able to get one biteful down her throat.

Gamely, she tried, but it was impossible. Fran had written a long letter to Nancy and I had finished a poem started years earlier, which we hoped to read to her, but we felt it was better for us to return home.

A huge regret on both Fran and my parts is that we never knew if Nancy was able to read these final communications from her parents, or to understand them if she did, or if John had been able to read them to her, or if he even attempted to do so, given Nancy's condition and his state of mind. My poem was found, after her death, at the bottom of a pile of magazines on her bedside table. Fran's letter was never found. I think Fran's fear that she had not had this final communication with her daughter understood by her, haunted her and was the beginning of her own deep depression with its own awful aftermath.

On June 6th, eighteen days after Nancy's 56th birthday, about one o'clock after lunch, I remember John callings us, saying that he felt the end was near, and we should hurry over. We dropped everything and rushed to be there and stood around her bed. Fran held her right hand, John her left, and I was at the foot of the bed, touching her foot. At 2:15 p.m., John announced very quietly that her suffering had ended.

We joined the support group who had been waiting in the living room, said a few words and returned quietly to our condo to begin living with our great sense of loss. Later that afternoon John called and asked if we wanted to return for one last time before the body was removed for the mortuary. Neither of us felt we could do this.

The following days are a blur. We packed and returned to Ohio and were shocked to learn that John was not planning a memorial service. He was coming to grips with his loss, and I am sure, with emotions he had never known were possible. Fran and I told him that a simple funeral service was not sufficient, and that if he felt that he could not arrange for a memorial service, we would and he could attend, if he felt able.

John established an endowment in Nancy's name with the Rocky River Education Association to provide an annual college scholarship to a worthy Rocky River High School student. I believe the initial amount subscribed totaled about $20,000, and scholarships have been granted every year since, many to the University of Michigan, Nancy's alma mater, in amounts ranging from $1,500 to $2,000. I receive a report published by the RREA every year.

Nancy was an exceptional teacher, a legendary one. I know many of her students look back on her classes as places with a fresh approach to learning, more than just facts and figures from a textbook, but how to live a life. Many benefited from being in the groups of students she led on trips to Europe during summer break, part of a program which established student exchanges with high school students, first in England, and later, in France. I wish there had been such an opportunity when I was in high school.

The deaths of my wife and my oldest daughter left large holes in my life, which can be realized when reading the foregoing accounts of the events and the amount of space needed to recount the many memories. In such a long life, there are many recollections of death and funerals; all being important; some more personal and moving than others. Some might say that I was fortunate because of the 30 years of winters spent living in Florida. We did not subscribe to *The Cleveland Plain Dealer*, and if not on a list of those to be informed, were not aware of many funerals I would have otherwise attended, a cause of minor embarrassment on some occasions when a name came up in conversation, only to learn that the individual had died a year before.

In the case of my mother, my memories of her death are scanty, it seems to me, but understandable. While we lived in the same city, my parents had a full church and social life of their own. We were raising a family in a suburb 20 miles distant. My first inkling that something was wrong with my mother's health came while we were attending my brother Wes's graduation from Yale in June of 1953. As we were ascending the broad, shallow-stepped staircase to the second-floor balcony of Woolsey Hall for the Baccalaureate service, Mother had to pause every five or six steps to rest and catch her breath. She barely made it to the top. I had never seen such a thing before; it was so unusual for such an active person. She never stopped working; she was always busy; the tasks she set herself were, literally, never done.

I didn't say anything to anyone about what I had observed. I don't remember where Dad was during the climbing episode, certainly not at Mother's elbow helping her. There had been no signs of weakness on the car ride from Cleveland to New Haven.

After we were home and back at the office working, we got reports every morning from Dad: Mother was seeing a Christian Science Practitioner. She had also seen a doctor (!) and she had to go to Lakewood Hospital and stay there. She was a terrible patient, proudly resisting the treatment they were trying to administer, being uncooperative with the nurses. The Practitioner was calling on her in the hospital (!) and advising her to ignore the doctors' instructions. This was not unexpected in view of her ardent belief in the teachings of Mary Baker Eddy.

I believe she refused further treatments at the hospital and insisted on going home. We brothers continued to receive daily reports from Dad as to her progress. I don't recall even knowing what the problem was. He used to leave early in the afternoon every day to visit with Mother. I remember it was early summer and we were planning a week's vacation with Paul and Marge Hacker, members of our Parma bridge club, and their children, at a cottage of a friend of theirs on Pigeon Lake, about 60 miles north of Toronto. I was concerned about being gone that long and so far from civilization with a wife 6 months pregnant. I called the doctor, a heart specialist, who had been treating mother and was bitter about the interference from the C. S. Practitioner.

When he heard of our plans, he advised us to go, by all means; he felt that Mother would be fine while we were gone; it was safe for us to go. Our vacation plans also included a second week in the Adirondacks with another couple, Bob and Dorothy Demuth from the same bridge club and their two daughters. They were neighbors on our street in Parma Heights, and our children were playmates. I found a resort in the Fulton Chain of Lakes, advertised in the Christian Science Monitor. It was to be two weeks of relief from a very stressful summer.

On Thursday or Friday of our first week, the mailman told us that there was a phone call for us and to call home from the General Store about a mile away, which had the only telephone in the area. I hastened to the little General Store to call and was told that Mother had been rushed back to the hospital, but not to worry and not to even think about shortening our vacation and coming home. At this point there was nothing we could do. Reluctantly I agreed and we finished our week, then went on to the Adirondacks, entering the U.S. at Canandaigua, New York.

One of my memories of this hectic summer is of our experience at the resort on Seventh Lake (?). It was a very nice facility, the food was good, rooms comfortable and our two daughters and the two Demuth daughters, ages 6 to 8, were well behaved and having a wonderful time swimming and playing on the grounds. After the second or third day, Bob Demuth, who was an easy-going gentleman, and I were called into the Owner/Manager's office and asked to leave. He was concerned that his repeat customers were unhappy with the presence of young children and might not return the next summer. Bob and I were speechless - and furious. The owner told us he had arranged for us to stay at a hotel farther down the lake, and that they would pack up all our belongings and transport us to the new location. We did not make a fuss and agreed to leave. It wasn't easy to explain what happened to either of our spouses or our children.

When we left, the dock was full of the other guests, many of the women in tears, hating to see us go. But it all worked out well. The hotel (I don't recall its name) had a two-story frame annex with twelve or fourteen rooms, and a living room/lounge area with a wood-burning fireplace on the ground floor. It was empty so we had it all to ourselves. We tossed coins and won the first floor. The food was good; the girls could play in the water; and the adults played bridge every night we were there. We kept cumulative score and got so far ahead that it created a little tension. We escaped by driving alone, exploring, and drove all the way up the chain of lakes to the first of them at the highest elevation. It was a beautiful drive and I marveled at the clear water.

On our drive back home on Sunday afternoon, as we approached a long, straight incline into Warren, Pennsylvania, the brakes on our Studebaker Landcruiser froze, and it was a hair-raising descent into the town, complicated by the fact that it was a small town and a Sunday afternoon. How were we to get repairs done? We were hurrying home to an ailing mother. I do not remember how, but we found someone to fix the brakes and arrived safely back in Cleveland after dark, too late for visiting hours. I never saw my mother in the hospital.

During her second stay at Lakewood Hospital, I was told that she was a changed person; that she was very cooperative and open to any new procedures proposed; that she hoped that what they found out might help others. They were draining fluid from her lungs daily which was not a pleasant experience. I do not remember how many days this stay lasted, but not too many, before she was allowed to return home. She had had what was probably a little stroke and could no longer swallow. She could still talk clearly but had lost the ability to swallow food or liquids My father had to feed her liquids through a tube inserted through her throat with a funnel at the top. I feel fortunate that I never had to witness this. Mother spent her days lying in the living room on the chaise longue brought in from the patio, from where she could watch the lake through the picture window. This is where I would find her when I visited her after dinner. The other three sons were out of town: Wes, on duty on his naval mine sweeper in the Mediterranean; Ken, on duty in his Army enlistment center in Richmond; and Russ out of town on vacation.

I only remember one of my visits, I think the last, when I played her favorite hymns on the piano in the sunroom, and then knelt on the floor next to her chaise. We talked, and I told her how proud she should be, having four sons so loyal to her training, and so loving. She confided that she always thought that I had been the son expressing the most gratitude. I was deeply moved by this revelation. I never saw her again after that lonely visit.

Shortly thereafter, she had to return to the hospital for more liquid drainage procedures, and one afternoon about 3:30, there was a call from Dad at the hospital telling me that we had lost our mother that afternoon. Apparently, the strain from the drainage procedure was too much for her heart which simply stopped beating. I do remember calling Jonathan Alder, a high school friend who lived nearby on Ridgewood Drive and asking for ride home, since I had taken the bus to work that day. I remember virtually nothing of the following days: how the funeral arrangements were made (since there are no funeral services prescribed in Christian Science), I assume, readings from scripture and the C.S. textbook were done by one of the Readers from Fifth Church), and sometime later actual burial took place at the mausoleum at Sunset Memorial Park.

I remember asking the undertaker if he could put a small brooch I had given Mother for her birthday and which she wore frequently and said she liked in her coffin with her, and he said he would, which was a real comfort for me.

Later I started writing an account of these days for the benefit of my brothers, none of whom had any part in her final days. I have always felt guilty that I was never able to finish it. Perhaps it was all too fresh in my memory, or too painful. I felt a different sense of loss from anything I had ever experienced before. It was as though I felt the umbilical cord being cut, separating me from my ancestors who had gone on before, and I felt a strange sense of loneliness. I had lost my direct connection to my past. In the midst of my family, friends, and my active life, I was now alone.

Mother loved flowers and was in her glory when she did the flower arrangements for church during the summer months, using flower from her own garden. I did not have my Brecksville peony collection yet but try to take tree peony blossoms from those I now have when in season to Sunset Memorial every year, in her memory. I know that she would have loved their beauty and being faithfully remembered in that way.

Memories of my father's death are far fewer. We were spending the winter in Florida in a rental condo in Holmes Beach when we received a phone call from Nancy that Dad had fallen in the kitchen while shining his shoes before going out to dinner. He had lost his balance or fainted and fallen, hitting his head on the floor. He did go out to the restaurant for dinner with Mary, his second wife of many years, and while at the table experienced symptoms which suggested concussion from the fall. They returned home and Mary called Nancy, asking what she should do. Nancy immediately took over, called Dr. Malm, the family internist who rushed him to the Lakewood Hospital emergency room.

A brain specialist was called in who confirmed a massive hematoma. By this time, he was in a coma and died two days later. There was nothing that could be done for him, at his age 88, and Dr. Malm, himself, called me and urged me not to come back to Ohio to be with him. We did fly back for the funeral services, renting a car and staying in Brecksville until our return to Florida after the funeral services. Again, I am shocked to realize how few memories I have of the details. He lies next to Mother in the mausoleum at Sunset Memorial. I always take a tree peony for him as well when I visit Memorial Day week. Until his fall, he was in good health, but had low blood pressure, and still played a good hand of bridge. Physically, he appeared to be 20 years younger than his actual age. His fall has instilled in me a fear of falling, and I do all I can to avoid any risk of falling. Today, the fear of falling almost dominates my daily activities.

One other memory involving my father happened a week or so after my mother's death. We were walking down E. 9th Street on our way to the parking lot after work. He was going home for dinner with his sister, Aunt Clara, who had come to stay with him the first few weeks after Mother's death. He was lost without Mother and in the deepest period of his grief he complained of chest pains and said he felt he would be joining Mother very soon. He didn't know how he could survive without her. I remember my response to this, which came from the depths of my 32-year old wisdom: I told him that I didn't think it would be as easy as that.

I urged him to see a cardiologist, which he did, who told him he was in good health and suffering from stress which explained his symptoms. A year later he became reacquainted with the daughter of the couple who had introduced him to my mother at Linwood Park. Mary Louise Gehlke, who had never married, and was about 20 years younger than he was. This was a happy marriage for both parties. She had been raised by her grandmother and led a very sheltered life; now was able to enter a world she had never known before and had the advantage of the financial security and experience offered by an older man. He had the pleasure of the companionship of a very attractive, younger woman (she would have been about 35 years old then) and the opportunity to be the leader in a marriage, which had not been the case until then. We brothers were delighted at the match, and Mary was very good to our families and was good for him.

I knew all four of my grandparents and always felt surprised when someone mentioned: "Oh, I never knew my grandmother, or my grandfather." I just took it for granted. However, I remember little of their deaths. I think Grandpa Schmidt was the first to go. He had cancer of the throat and I remember a whole summer of watching him starve to death. My father would take delicacies from the West Side Market to entice him to try to eat: kosher dill pickle spears and slices of watermelon, two of his favorites. But it was useless; his throat was so restricted by the ever-growing cancer that he could not swallow. I remember how gaunt he became; it was scary for a teenager to see.

I had overheard quiet conversations between my parents about Grandpa Schmidt's verbal abuse of Grandma and his mistreatment of her. She was my favorite, and being young and idealistic, I boycotted Grandpa's visitation at the funeral parlor, and his funeral service, sitting in the car outside the church. I felt it would have been hypocritical of me to honor someone who had mistreated my beloved Grandma. I do not know how my behavior was viewed by my parents, but it couldn't have made things easier for them. I think he is buried in Riverside Cemetery off W. 25th Street in Cleveland.

Grandma Schmidt died at age 83, about 20 years after the death of Grandpa Frank. I remember picking her up on a Saturday after we were married and living in Parma Heights and taking her downtown for an appointment with her podiatrist who was located in the Colonial Arcade. Fran helped her into her appointment while I circled the block until they were finished; and I picked them up to return home. On another occasion we visited Grandma at home to find her suffering from a heavy head cold, and Aunt Clara, who was living with Grandma at the time and who was a practicing Christian Scientist, disparaging an over-the-counter cold medication as "dope," knowing that Grandma would refuse to take anything that was a narcotic.

Fran and I were appalled at Aunt Clara's cruelty. We went to a drugstore and bought a bottle of Privine nose drops, which we both used regularly and found to be the most effective product to clear our nasal passages. We brought the drops to Grandma and I remember Fran administering them to her and what a relief it was to her, within minutes, to be able to breath easily again.

I do not remember what the cause of her death was but heard the word gangrene used and assumed it was a circularity problem. It did not prevent her from hanging wallpaper in one of her upstairs rental apartments a month before her death. I am surprised that I do not remember more of the details surrounding her death. I remember how frustrated my parents were to find all of the nice underthings they had given as presents over the years, little luxuries, in a drawer, the packages unopened. Grandma felt they were too nice to wear and should be saved for her to be buried in.

One thing I remember about that time is that Grandma left me a small, inexpensive gold pocket watch with an engraved lid that popped open. It was broken and could not be wound up and was useless, but it was something of hers and she gave it to me so I would remember her. I kept it for years. This was the only personal remembrance I ever received from any of my forebears and it made me wish that my mother or father had selected something personal to leave me that would have been a symbol of their love to help me keep their memories alive.

I remember nothing of the deaths of Grandpa and Grandpa Gaede, my mother's parents. They had fourteen grandchildren, whereas the Schmidt grandparents had only three; hence the Gaede's affections were more widely distributed. I didn't feel as close to them, saw them far more infrequently, and consequently did not feel the same sense of loss that I did when Grandma Schmidt died. The only thing, other than Grandpa Gaede's borrowing my brother's and my savings to pay for Grandma Gaede's burial, that I remember is Mother taking me with her to tend to her mother's grave in the Spring. I would watch while she got on her hands and knees and dug out weeds and then planted small flowering plants in front of the grave marker. I do not recall the name of the cemetery, which was located on the west side of W. 73rd Street south of Denison Avenue. I think I could still find it and wonder how well kept it is today.

Of the many other funerals, I attended, very few affected me enough to retain specifics in my memory. Attending memorial services for two disturbed young men who committed suicide remains with me. I remember how bitterly I lamented such a waste, and how helpless I felt, realizing that if I could have spent time with the boys prior to their deaths, hoping to find the magic words that would change their outlook, knowing that it would have made no difference in the outcome. And the enormity of the loss for the rest of their loving families.

The first, Sandy Patterson, oldest son of one of the architects for our Brecksville house, was very idealistic and had a vision of a perfect world so powerful that it drove him to do missionary work on the streets of Chicago, trying to convince strangers on the street to help him change the imperfect daily world we are all trapped in by following the teachings of Christ. He was very gentle and very sincere. I think he knew the impracticality of his mission which only reinforced the pressure he lived under to deliver it. His parents were all too aware of his troubled mind and did everything in their power to get him the professional help he needed; several earlier suicide attempts were averted. They stood by helplessly when Sandy successfully ended life in far-away Chicago where he was staying with a loving family.

We went to the memorial service which was held in their church on Chagrin Boulevard in Orange Village, and since it was June, I was able to take a peony for the altar (Clyde, his father, painted a water color of the peony which we hung on the wall in our entry hall next to the front door) and I also wrote a short poem, more a prayer, which is included in the collection of my poetry. It was a truly sad occasion for me. Words spoken about "a better place" and "not in vain" were a mockery to me that day.

The other suicide was the death of the oldest son, Charlie, of our next-door neighbors, the Hills, who were originally from Nova Scotia. Charlie was very polite and always addressed me as "Mr. Schmidt," which was hard for me to get used to; did yardwork for me. With his two younger brothers, Brian and Eric, he created a banner about twenty feet long proclaiming in large letters "Good Luck, Nancy!" which was stretched under our kitchen windows. It was the first thing our out-of-town guests saw as they drove up the driveway for Nancy's after-wedding celebration.

I was told there was some sort of friction between Charlie and his father and after his graduation from high school he returned to Canada and, I believe, lived alone. He found work in Toronto as a postman, and then as a bus driver. On one of his visits to Brecksville, he spent some time with me, and he talked of his search for the true meaning of life. I was surprised and a little uneasy that he could talk to me, a virtual stranger, about such intimate thoughts, which were obviously very important to him. He gave me his book of the writings of Meister Eckhardt, a 14th century German priest and mystic, to read. Perhaps he felt with my higher education I could help him understand, or even convert me to his own beliefs. The writings were very mystical. Charlie tried very earnestly to explain Eckhardt's thinking to me, and what it meant to him. I thought it was delusional nonsense, but did not say so, of course. I thought he needed professional help but did not feel I knew either him or his family well enough to suggest it. Therefore, it was a shock, but not a great surprise, when his mother, Shirley, obviously devastated, told us Charlie had taken his life. I never heard what funeral arrangements were made or where he is buried.

There are some funeral services I cannot forget. Among them was that of Charlie's father, George Hill, a wonderful neighbor, fellow gardener and good friend. He died of cancer and his funeral was the first in the modern trend that I attended where members of the congregation were invited to stand and share memories of the deceased with those present. I assume the theory is that this practice will be an additional comfort to the immediate family. I shuddered and thought it was barbaric.

I had a similar reaction to an earlier funeral, that of a cousin of my fathers, Ed Erhardt, who was another virtual stranger. I cannot remember the reason why, but I was elected to represent the family at the funeral, which was held at a church in the West Park neighborhood of Cleveland. My memories of the funeral are of an open casket at the altar and of the pastor, after completing the service, adding a personal tribute to the deceased, who was his brother-in-law. He related how years of active membership in all the lay roles of the church in the service of his God had transformed a shy, insecure individual into a mature, confident servant of God. He had become an example of what it meant to be a Christian to his fellow church members. It was a very moving story and I am sure meant a great deal to the family. But, with my mixed religious background, all I could think of was of Ed's reward for his years of service, his God allowed him to die of stomach cancer, one of the most painful ways to die. It was hard for me to understand the connection of this ending with an all-powerful God of Love. Bad things happening to good people is still a problem for me.

Another memory, which is hard to forget, is the death of the secretary who did my work at Schmidt Mortgage Company. Her name was Marilyn (can't remember her last name) and she had a twin brother. She was young, petite and pretty and was willing to stay late to finish the typing of a loan submission for me, whenever it was necessary to meet a deadline. After several years with us, she left to take a job with one of our developer customers, Julius Paris, and I never saw her again. I heard that she had moved on from her job with Julius Paris and moved to Tennessee where she died very mysteriously. She was very young, still in her 20s, I believe.

I was elected to attend the funeral as a representative for Schmidt Mortgage Company, one of my more unpleasant duties, and remember joining the congregation in passing the open casket at the end of the service. I remember how life-like she looked: no signs of a debilitating disease. It was hard to believe she was simply not alive and sleeping. We never learned the cause of her death.

There are a few other memories associated with the subject of death, a subject which does not dominate my memories in spite of the amount of time and space I have devoted to it. I remember our taking dinner to Bob and Helen Hendrickson in Rocky River shortly before Helen's death from breast cancer. They were members of the Gamma Phi Beta dinner/bridge club and Helen was one of our favorite people. I remember the three of us eating while Helen lay on her side in her hospital bed in an alcove watching us: not a pleasant memory. And no memories of the funeral.

Another unusual occurrence was when Aunt "Tiel" Geiger was in the hospital recovering from a hysterectomy and Uncle Charlie died of a heart attack. For fear that the news of his death might have had an impact on her recovery, she was not told of his death until after she returned home, and he had already been buried. I never understood how she would not have missed his daily visits to the hospital. I do not remember Uncle Charley's funeral, which I attended. I assume that it was held at Ebenezer Evangelical Church on W. 65th Street, but do remember that at the end of the service, the family was invited to view the body in the open casket and that the twin sons, sobbing aloud, kissed their father farewell in front of rest of the congregation who were waiting to pass by and pay their final respects. I felt embarrassment to witness such a final farewell, which might well have been more private.

Part of my duties playing the organ at St. Matthews was to play for funerals, the most notable funeral being that of William Stinchcomb, father of the Cleveland Metropolitan Park System, whom I had never met. This made it much easier for me than when I played for friends, with whom I had had a personal relationship.

I remember the first of these "difficult" occasions at St. Matthews being the service for the wife of my insurance agent, bridge playing friend, Bob Busha. He was a young man at the time of his first wife's death from Hodgkinson's Disease and was left with a young eight or nine-year old daughter. Bob gave a very moving eulogy at the service which I could never have done, and wanted me to play their favorite song, "The Impossible Dream" from *The Man from La Mancha*. I refused to play it on the grounds that there was no arrangement of the piece for the organ; that I did not possess the skills to improvise from piano sheet music; and that I felt strongly that it would be very inappropriate to play a Broadway show tune at an Episcopalian funeral service.

Later, I found it very difficult to play the organ for Dave Terry, another member of St. Matthews, the husband of one of Fran's good friends, and sometimes bridge partner, Diane. He drowned in the first sailboat race of the season, out of Port Clinton, when the lake water was still very cold. He was in his old, wood-hulled, small sailboat which disintegrated when it hit rock bottom between crests of waves in Lake Erie near Sandusky. It was very stormy with waves six to eight feet, in very shallow water; no-one was wearing a life jacket, the hatches were open, and the boat was so slow they were dead last in the race so there was no one nearby to be aware of the accident, or able to go to their assistance. Not only did he put his own life at risk, but he had two of his sons and one of their college classmates for his crew. The younger men were able to find life preservers, and the college friend was found washed up on the shore of Cedar Point Bay beach the nest morning, almost dead from hypothermia and exposure. The two sons were picked up and saved. It was foolhardy, foolish, unnecessary and a terrible tragedy for Diane. Not a fun funeral.

Another unforgettable funeral for me was that of Rudy Kutler, former Director of Athletics at Kenyon College in Gambier, Ohio. His wife, Dorothy, was a close friend of Fran's and a music lover. They attended the Cleveland Symphony's Thursday morning dress rehearsals as part of the Brecksville Music Appreciation Group. Rudy was a very reticent man, very proper mannered, very courtly, and always addressed both Fran and me as Mrs. or Mr. Schmidt. He knew us fairly well and knew how close Fran and Dorothy were, but he could not overcome his shyness and call us by our first names. Having been involved in college administration and dealing with so many people, I always found this interesting and endearing in an age of over-familiarity.

Rudy was diagnosed with cancer and struggled with the disease for a year or more. During that time, knowing that I would be called on to play for his funeral at St. Matthews, I wanted to play the J.S. Bach "Passacaglia and Fugue in C minor" which has a repeating bass figure for the entire 20 minute length of the piece. It builds to a shattering climax as it comes to the end. I thought it would be a perfect tribute to his final days and would like to have it played on a grand organ at my own funeral. I was able to master most of the upper staff passages which are based on the bass line, and was gaining confidence that I could do an adequate job at the funeral, when, unfortunately Rudy died, and I was not yet quite prepared. This meant I had to find something else suitable for a funeral service, something special for Rudy for many reasons. I don't remember how I discovered it, but I had stumbled on Widor's "Suite Latine," which is actually a 5-movement symphony, similar to the other organ symphonies he wrote. He is most well-known for the final movement of his Fifth Symphony, the Toccata and Fugue.

I felt the second movement of the "Suite Latine" was within my capabilities and was able to master it in time for the funeral. There is a passage about midway through the piece where there is a descending melodic line with a brief, just a few notes, abrupt change to a minor key, which is very moving. It reminds me of a similar passage in Bach's "St. Matthews Passion." I hoped that any feelings of grief it engendered would be washed away with the hopeful/ peaceful ending. I do not remember any specifics of the funeral except that I vaguely recall Dorothy telling me afterwards that she loved the music, which was a relief.

The point of telling this story is that I had to play for another funeral, which Dorothy attended, two or three years later and played the Widor again. I will never forget Dorothy rushing up to me after the service with tears in her eyes, exclaiming, "That was the same piece you played for Rudy's funeral, wasn't it?" I knew then I had made a good choice in what to play, if she had been able to remember it after such a long passage of time. This was the first and only time that something like this happened to me: a genuine compliment on my playing. The piece had to have been very effective. I still love it and listen to it on YouTube when in the mood.

I do not want to neglect my memories of the events surrounding the death of Fran's mother, Fanny Bell Thompson, who was an ideal mother-in-law, unobtrusive, patient, always showering us with love. She suffered from asthma and had heart problems. She moved to Brecksville after a disastrous medical event while on a trip to Scandinavia with two friends. She had to be rushed to a hospital in Oslo and after being stabilized was able to fly home to Detroit, where we went to meet her at the airport. I will never forget the look of relief in her eyes that she was back home safely, and we were there for her. It soon became apparent that she should not be living alone in a second-floor walk-up apartment in Grosse Pointe, Michigan. Fran begged her mother to buy the small house next door to the east of us on Oakes Road, which had come on the market, so she could take care of her.

She agreed to buy the house next door and I arranged the mortgage financing with the Cleveland Trust Company, Ohio's largest bank, and was very proud that the signing of the mortgage papers, which took place in his private office, was presided over by the head of the mortgage loan department, Tom Clutterbuck, who normally handled million dollar deals. He was one of my bridge-playing friends and had taken a personal interest in the case. When he met Mrs. Thompson, he immediately recognized that she had an air of old-world gentility about her, not seen very often in his world at that time. I think Grandma Thompson knew the special attention she was receiving and the honor it was. I think it was only a $28,000 mortgage, hardly worth his attention.

It was a great relief for us: she would be able to continue to live alone, maintaining her independence, and would only be minutes away; the grandchildren could stop in on the way home from school; Fran could take her shopping and get her out daily; and take her to her doctors' appointments. Although the house was "next" door, it was 300-400 feet distant and hidden from our house by the dam of our lake, only the tip of the gable from the addition we put on the house visible from our bedroom, so we could rest easy when the light from her bedroom went out every night, knowing that she was safe. The house was basementless with a radiant heated floor ideal for an older person, and had a wood burning fireplace, two bedrooms and one bath, and a one car attached garage. It was only eight years old, architect designed and custom built, and the interior was in terrible condition. She allowed us to take charge and we had a small addition added on the back of the house, doubling the size of her bedroom and adding a family room, and then completely rehabbed the rest of the interior for her with us doing all the finish work.

She insisted that she pay me; and we argued (our only disagreement in all the years I knew her), finally settling on allowing her to pay me for the hours I worked. I fudged the hours so that they happened to be just enough to pay for a professional paint job on the exterior of our house next door, which was badly needed;

We spent many additional hours working on her house that she, still living in faraway Grosse Pointe, did not know about or pay for. I was trading hours of distasteful labor on the exterior of our house and exposing myself to the risks in painting the high places for the much more enjoyable, risk free interior finish work which I found so satisfying. I was very pleased with this arrangement.

The job turned out beautifully and Grandma Thompson was thrilled with her new "little house." After years of renting, she was so proud of the only house she had owned since 1931, that after she moved in, she invited the postman and other strangers who came to her door to come in to see her new home.

I found working on a smaller project with a short time span for completion and no financial pressure such as we had at 5320 Oakes very pleasant. It was a small way to repay Fran's mother who had accepted me sight unseen and allowed me to marry her daughter, without ever voicing an objection, or concern over possible religious issues, her only family, and take her far away to a strange city. She had been unfailingly kind and generous to me. Every hour spent working on her house brought me quiet satisfaction. Seeing the improvements take shape was an added bonus and was visible proof of my appreciation to her. I think she knew that.

After the move to Brecksville, Grandma Thompson continued to have breathing problems and saw a specialist at the Cleveland Clinic regularly. She used an inhalator and I associated the very unpleasant odor of the propellant, with her suffering. She was now eighty years old.

One Sunday in February, I went over to her house after church (she attended St. Matthews regularly, but not this Sunday), to shovel the snow from her front walk. When she did not come to the door, as she usually did, I went around the back of the house where I could look in on her bedroom, and saw her lying in her night clothes in an awkward position on her bed.

Alarmed, I hurried home to get Fran, who had a key to the house; and we went in to find her struggling to breath and groggy. We packed her up and brought over to our house where Fran could care for her and installed her in the guest bedroom, which had been planned for just such a situation. She stayed with us during the week and her condition was not improving. I remember seeing her sitting on the edge of the bed, hunched over, chest heaving with exertion, gasping for breath and using the inhalator far more often than allowed, which filled the room with that awful odor I hated.

One of the things I loved about Grandma Thompson was her love of owls. I knew I could always make her happy on any gift giving occasion by finding a figurine of an owl, or, perhaps a painting, and presenting it to her. It simplified my hunt for something to please her. I came to believe that the owl was her totem, or talisman. I have one of the pictures of an owl I gave her hanging on the wall of my office (which I just looked up at as I write this).

One evening while Grandma Thompson was staying with us I decided to light a fire in the fireplace, and went out to the woodpile, which was located at that time just beneath the window of the breakfast nook at the rear of the house. As I was gathering the logs, I happened to look over my shoulder and saw a large owl perched on the lowest thick limb on the white oak extending toward the house. He was motionless, staring at me with his huge eyes. I stared back at him, and after what seemed like an eternity, but was only a few seconds, he spread his wings and glided majestically into the ravine, and I never saw him again. He was the only owl I ever saw in the 44 years we lived there. It was eerie and made a big impression on me. After Fran's mother's death, I was moved to write three haiku in her memory, which are included in the collection of my poetry. The first of these is as follows:

> *The Owl*
>
> *Owl, why art thou come?*
>
> *Without "who o o o " or blink or stir.*
>
> *"Go: Naught here for thee! "*

Fran's mother's condition worsened, and we took her to the Cleveland Clinic the Thursday of that week, visited with her, were sent home and almost immediately called by the Clinic and urged to return, only to arrive too late. Grandma Thomson had died. And we were left with our grief. It was especially hard for Fran, who consoled herself with the knowledge that her mother had spent three of the happiest years of her life living next to us in a house we had prepared for her.

I remember taking Kathy and Barbara (Nancy was away at school in Ann Arbor) to the Dillow and Wood Funeral home in Brecksville, who handled the arrangements, for a final viewing of their grandmother. Reverend Wrenn of St. Matthews accompanied the coffin in its hearse on its trip to Lexington, Michigan, about two hours north of Detroit on the shores of Lake Huron where he conducted the services which were held in the Episcopal Church. Actual interment could not be done at the time because the ground was still frozen. Later, we visited the grave, which is in the Lexington Cemetery in the family plot, next to the other Niggemans, her maiden name. I think we were able to visit the grave every time after that when we visited friends in Detroit. I also remember how alarmed I was on our trip home after the funeral when we had a tire blowout about midnight on the Ohio Turnpike as we neared Brecksville. We had dropped Nancy off in Ann Arbor, but both Kathy and Barbara were with us. A State Trooper pulled up behind us on the side of the road within minutes and he changed our tire. I was never so glad to see a State Trooper

Another sign of the passage of time was the death of my close friend and golfing companion, Ted Billings, longtime member of the Brecksville Duplicate Bridge group, sailor, and one of our inspirations to buy a condo in Florida. A memorial service was planned to be held in June in Ohio, where most of his closest friends and family lived. His daughter, Cricket and son, Johnny, approached me and asked, *pleaded* with me to deliver a eulogy. I had never done anything like that before; I felt I could probably write an acceptable eulogy, but it was the delivery that was my concern. I had been a terrible speaker in Miss Moore's Public Speaking class in high school and did not feel that speaking during my stints as an officer of several business organizations over the years had improved my performance. Eventually I agreed to take on the responsibility and set about writing the remarks that I would deliver at the ceremony.

This was not a simple task. I faced a dilemma. Ted was a more complex person than most, and I wanted to stress all his positive aspects, although I disapproved, silently, of many of his beliefs and the way he did things. Furthermore, he was not a churchgoer, and this was a quasi-religious service.

How to present a positive, comforting picture of a man who was a good friend; an honorable, ambitious, successful businessman with an engineer's approach to solving problems; who adored his wife and never remarried after her death nine years earlier; generous to his family; who had all the outward trappings of success. But who tried to force his brilliant son, Johnny, to follow his footsteps as a builder and give up his true love, music, by never giving him music lessons; or ever hearing him play as an adult member of a professional Bluegrass band; who preferred a Sunday afternoon of golf with our wives at Pine Hills golf course, followed by a cookout at our house, to being with his teenage daughter on her birthday; who would kick a cat if it got in his way; who loved the killing part of hunting; who overcompensated for his feelings of inferiority due to his ethnic background in relation to his socialite Akron wife, whose father was the Chairman of an Akron bank; his ever-present struggle for acceptance into their world; who made no provisions in his will for his unmarried sister who had given up her own home to make a home for him; and . . . . who never approached me for mortgage financing for any of his projects (!).

It was not an easy task, but I finally finished the composition. I do not remember where the event took place, only that there were a large number of people there: among them friends from the Brecksville duplicate bridge group, his extended family, business friends. To my dismay, seated in the rear row, but the first face I saw before I began my remarks was that of Dr. Richard Hilfer, Ted's oldest friend and personal physician, who had grown up with Ted; a John Adams High School classmate and fellow member of their Reunion planning committees; and who I thought should be standing where I was, delivering remarks based on an even longer friendship. When it mercifully came to an end it was apparently successful and the children had heard what they needed and expressed their gratitude. In later years Cricket and her husband approached me for financial advice: seemingly, they now perceived me as an alter paterfamilias.

I am sure I saved a written copy of this speech, which I would like to read again today, but I have no idea where it might be. Since I never throw anything away, it is undoubtedly buried away in one of the many boxes of cards and mementos stored in my garage.

One other funeral with bittersweet memories is that of Elden Papke of Wichita, Kansas, a businessman I met in connection with the financing of the purchase of two oil wells in Oklahoma. He was one of two civilian men I met after World War II who compared to the men of my "group" in the Army language program. He died very unexpectedly of an aneurysm in the groin. I flew to Wichita on the Saturday morning of the funeral and remember very little of the actual ceremony. I do remember the embarrassment of having the seam along the seat of the pants in my brand new navy-blue blazer suit rip out as I lifted my leg to get into the car of the person who picked me up at the airport and the frantic search for a men's store where I could buy a pair of slacks that fit, and get me to the church on time. I also remember meeting Elden's parents and a brother, from Wisconsin, and being given a homemade venison sausage to take home with me. I stopped off at the St. Louis airport on the way home to visit our newly married daughter, Kathy, in nearby Alton, Illinois, where her husband, Stephen, the Assistant Director of the Alton library, had recently been attacked by a deranged customer wielding a butcher knife, which caused serious damage to my newlywed son-in-law's left arm.

The final comment on my memories of death and funerals is to mention the death of a soldier in Basic Training at Fort Sill who, while on stable guard (the mule pack artillery equivalent of walking guard at a regular army post) in the middle of the night made the mistake of entering the stall of one of the mules from the rear to calm him. The mule, startled, instinctively kicked straight back and crushed the soldier's chest, killing him. He was in a different training company, so it did not affect us directly, but our sergeant told us of it as a warning, and it did seem to make what we were doing a little more serious. It did not take a bullet or piece of shrapnel to get oneself killed in the army.

There were also the suicides of two classmates in our Company in our first year of studying Japanese at the University of Minnesota: one by gunshot and one by hanging. One man was Master Sergeant Reinhardt, who was one of the older men and married; the other was Furman Keyes of South Carolina, one the brightest men in the company. There were many rumors that both had been involved with the same "black widow," a young woman who watched the grisly deaths, but was not charged with complicity. She was advised to leave the Twin Cities area, or face charges. We were all very disturbed because these were fellow soldiers and none of us could understand how a young woman could affect two such intelligent men that they would take their own lives. I recall how subdued the Company was for several weeks afterwards.

I am not unhappy to leave these memories and am sorry to have devoted so much time to them, but the memories are there, mingled among other sunnier ones, and this account would not be complete without them.

My memories of the early days of our marriage are an interesting mix of great happiness, a sense of tremendous gratitude for having found and secured the love of my life; the adventure of starting a new life with another person; of something as simple as furnishing an apartment; of beginning to learn a new business for which I had no training. This feeling was only marred by watching, helplessly, the suffering of my new bride. Fran was in constant, debilitating pain in her lower back and her left leg. I think I was still administering shots of B-12 with a hypodermic needle as recommended by Dr. Parsons, the allergist recommended by Fran's mother in Detroit and flinching every time 1 had to push the needle into her hip.

She was so uncomfortable sitting that I remember spending hours lying on our living room floor on our stomachs doing jigsaw puzzles. I don't remember how the shopping, or laundry got done. I think it must have fallen to me to do these chores. I remember Fran doing the cooking, and the small stove with a warped oven door, which made it difficult to control the heat when using the oven. There must have been days when there was some relief in the pain. I don't remember how, or exactly when, we found a doctor, a neurologist, or who recommended him, or his name, but his office was located near Lakewood Hospital, and we finally learned what the problem was: Fran had what was then called a "slipped disc", and there was nothing that could be done about it. We stopped the B-12 shots, mercifully. and Fran struggled on.

We took our first vacation the second year of our marriage spending a week at the Geiger cottage at Linwood Park, renting a room on the second floor. I don't remember how we got there since we had no car until the third year of our marriage. We spent a lot of time on the beach and swimming. One of the other activities that was very nearby was tennis. The Linwood courts were in the Geiger cottage backyard, and there were racquets stacked in a corner of the kitchen. On one of the days after swimming, I suggested that we go out and hit a few balls back and forth. Fran said, "Are you crazy?" I said I would be careful to hit the balls directly to her so she wouldn't have to move around on the court. She probably couldn't hurt any more than she was hurting at the time. So, she reluctantly agreed, and we went out to play some tennis, something neither of us had ever done before. All went well until I hit a ball well to her right and low. Instinctively, she moved to her right, bent over and stretched to reach the ball, and something "popped". Apparently, her vertebrae moved in such a way that the disc cushion readjusted, took the pressure off the nerve, and most of her pain disappeared. Our life was much more pleasant after that. She still was very careful in doing any activity where her back muscles were involved for the rest of her life.

One delightful thing for me in all our married years was Fran's urging me to have male friends, and join in male activities, such as golf, and sailing, and bridge. My mother had always kept very careful track on my father's whereabouts; he did join the Masons and a bowling league, but otherwise, when he wasn't working at the office, he was with her. It took a little getting used to for me to learn that my wife actively encouraged me to have activities of my own which did not involve her. I was always aware of the time spent away from the family and the number of hours involved. Golf and sailing were half day minimums away from them. When I began to explore this freedom on Ridgewood Drive in our first home, I tried to arrange for my golf on Saturdays so that I would be home in time for lunch. I could tend to the garden, cut the grass, etc. and the children would know that Daddy was at home with them. Fortunately for our children and Fran, my work did not require travel, so I was not a weekend husband.

I remember how unusual I thought it was that on our "stretch" of Ridgewood Drive that we had all German names: Demuth, Stancel, Schneider, Schmidt, Werner, Schlientz and Schultz. I thought the house was a bargain at $13,950, and so must our second-generation German neighbors. Germans probably outdo the proverbial Scotch in their frugality.

We had a regular foursome who left for Seneca Golf Course in Broadview Heights every Saturday morning at 6 a.m., weather permitting, so we were able to get home by noon. I do not remember who all the others were, except Schultz. I remember him only, because he walked ahead of the tee box, as one of the others, not me, hit his drive. It was a low ball to the left and grazed Schultz's head on the right side which knocked his glasses off and broke them. He never forgave the one who hit the ball because he refused to buy him a new pair of glasses. I thought Schultz was the guilty one who could have been killed by his foolish breaking of one of the cardinal rules of playing golf: do not get ahead of anyone hitting the ball. I must say that I do not remember much about the many rounds we played at Seneca but do remember the sense of relief in not having to get up at 5-6 a.m. every Saturday when October finally arrived.

I do not remember how we moved from Lakewood to Parma Heights, but we must have hired movers. I do remember Nancy, our oldest daughter, who was about four at the time, walking around the empty house and patting and kissing each wall. I have memories of Kathy, our second daughter, three years younger than Nancy, struggling on her hands and knees on the living room floor, rocking back and forth, trying to crawl and how frustrated she was when she made no forward progress. I also remember one sunny afternoon taking a picture of Kathy in her stroller on the front sidewalk with her wonderful, infectious grin that lit up her whole face (and which still does) with her fine hair rippling in a light breeze in its early growth, still in a butch cut style, holding a giant marigold blossom out to the photographer (me). It is a wonderful slide which I still have somewhere probably in a somewhat faded condition. She must have been about six months old and was wearing a pair of light blue corduroy overalls.

I remember the day I came home from work and walked in through the garage, as I usually did. We had purchased a 13 cubic foot top opening Harder freeze chest and placed in the corner of the garage next to the overhead door. I was shocked to see two pig tails of hair, still braided and with the ribbons still attached lying on top of the freezer. Without warning me, Fran had cut Kathy's hair, of which she had enough by this age, into a Dutch bob. Fran had a little trouble cutting the bob in a straight horizontal line, and it had a slight slant when she gave up. She cut off the entire pigtails at the top, still braided, which, thankfully, she saved. It was still a shock and one of many memorable events I did not get to witness as the children grew up.

Fran's mother visited us frequently, always a welcome addition to the family. Fran would take the children up to Detroit for visits frequently, to be with her mother, which allowed the children to play with the children of her closest friend, Evelyn Montgomery, whose children were about the same age. The Montgomery's lived in Grosse Pointe Park which had its own pool restricted to residents and guests and a swimming area on Lake St. Clair and playground, which the children loved. They also took the children to the Children's Zoo on Belle Isle, a huge island park in the Detroit River opposite downtown Detroit. The children got to pet baby animals, and watch shows by Charley Menzies, a trained chimpanzee, which were famous. I would drive them up, stay the weekend, and then drive back to Lakewood Sunday night. By this time we had a real car, a 1951 Studebaker Landcruiser which was a very fine automobile; a far cry from the old Pontiac which we loved so well because it was our first personal transportation and our ticket to freedom.

Our first house on Ridgewood Drive, Parma Heights had three bedrooms, the smallest of which was 9'6" x 14', which is very small. Nancy and Kathy slept on twin beds in the second bedroom, and Grandma Thompson slept in the small bedroom when she came to visit, usually for a week or so. This arrangement was fine as long as there were only two children. But when Barbara arrived and had to be put into the small bedroom it became too cramped for space when Grandma visited.

Our housing agenda had been to stay in the apartment a maximum of three years, then buy a house and live in it for another three to five years, saving money to accumulate enough to make our dream of having a larger house on a bigger piece of land come true. This is basically what happened. However, each period of time lasted longer than we had planned on and after Barbara's arrival we really started our serious search for our final destination. For many reasons, the house on Ridgewood Drive was no longer large enough.

We had done everything we could to the landscaping and the garden, had screened in the rear patio and I think the final thing we did was to widen the driveway with two 15" strips of concrete on each side. I remember doing the prep work and then having a concrete mix truck deliver a yard of concrete on a Saturday morning. That was when I learned how heavy concrete is and how much effort it takes to move it around.

I remember another picture I took at this time which ranks right up there with the one I took of Kathy. This is one of Fran holding Barbara in her arms the first day she came home from the hospital - in those days a new mother was allowed to stay in the hospital for a week before returning home to face a new reality. Her mother had come from Detroit to take care of the older girls while she was in the hospital and would stay for a few weeks after to help with the new baby. Fran was displaying the new baby to all the small neighborhood playmates who were lined up peering in the living room windows to marvel at the new baby. Barbara tells me she still has this photo, which is very touching.

We started to accumulate furniture when we lived on Ridgewood Drive. All we had to start with in the Lakewood apartment was a cranberry colored love seat and an old dining room set we brought down from Detroit, plus two unfinished kitchen chairs we bought at Sears & Roebuck, and Fran's maple three-quarter sized bed.

I remember going to one of our customers who had a small factory on Superior Avenue around E. 23rd Street, where he manufactured sofas and easy chairs. We bought our first large piece of furniture from him: an easy chair covered in a gray and yellow striped fabric. 1 remember how shocked my mother was when she saw we had painted the walls in our house in a warm gray color, had a plain gray uncut pile carpet on the living room floor, the large yellow and gray armchair, *and* yellow shantung ceiling to floor drapes! This was not her idea of decorating.

Shortly after we moved in, we bought a Magnavox console combination radio and record player. It was blond oak and very handsome, I thought. I was finally able to hear the records in my growing collection with some clarity and fidelity. This was where we placed the first TV we ever had, an Admiral 14" black and white. It sat atop the Magnavox cabinet. I remember how amazed I was at the magic of seeing free entertainment in one's own living room. We did not have to go out on Saturday nights anymore to find entertainment. We had Sid Caesar and Milton Berle and Ed Wynn at our fingertips and later Jackie Gleason and Jack Benny.

A few other memories of our time on Ridgewood Drive: I faintly remember a visit from my dear friend from my days in Minneapolis, in the Army, Mathilda K. Schmid. It is a vague recollection. I struggle to remember the details. I remember her having to walk around the shallow, portable wading pool we had set up in front of the garage, and the two older girls playing in it. Was she on her way home from a wedding in the East and took the opportunity to stop off in Cleveland to see where we lived? Did she stay for a meal? Did I pick her up and take her back to the airport? I know she did not stay overnight. I visualize her in her dark blue suit, fur stole, and hat, limping on her deformed leg, injured when she disembarked from the ship on which she emigrated to the U.S. when she was a child. She was so kind to Fran when we arrived in Minneapolis after our marriage, inviting her to stay in her apartment the three days I had to be in classes at Ft. Snelling, until we could move into our rented room on November 1st. For many years she sent us one of her wonderful plum puddings at Christmas time.

I remember the shock I received when I returned from one of the regular golf games on a Saturday and was met at the front door by Nancy, seven or eight years old at the time, who excitedly told me that Mommy had cut her finger off. I rushed in to find Fran holding her left hand, heavily bandaged, elevated, and learned that a heavy glass vase she was carrying to the kitchen to wash had shattered in her hands and had sliced the tendons of her ring finger. When it happened, she went next door to our neighbors, the Schneiders, for help. Luckily, George was home and rushed her to the emergency room at Parma Hospital. After the wound healed, she had to have an operation performed reattaching the two ligaments which control the movement of the finger. The finger was usable but never the same. It was truly a freak accident.

I also remember the evening on one of Grandma Thompson's visits when she invited us to go out for dinner at the "Surf and Turf," a favorite nearby restaurant, which was something she often did. After loading Grandma and the two girls in the back seat, we set off driving west on Ridgewood Drive, turning north on York Road to Pearl Road, where it ended, and then going west again on Pearl Road past Stumpf Road, where we ran out of gas! It had to be one of my most embarrassing moments. Fortunately for me, if I had to pick a spot to run out of gas, I picked the perfect one because there was a gas station directly across the street. So, it wasn't too inconvenient. However, it did do some damage to my "amour-propre."

The route we took on that occasion took us past the parent's home on York Road of one of Fran's sorority sisters, B.J. (Miller) Trebbe, with whom she had reconnected. B.J. was a graduate of Ohio Wesleyan College, where she met her husband, Bob. They became good friends and we played bridge with them frequently in their one-story redwood modern home, which her father, who was involved in real estate had built for them. It was located on Pleasant Valley Road just east of West 130th Street not far from where we lived. I remember every time I drove by the parent's home on York Road, I thought how strange it was that I was driving by the place where B.J. grew up. Eventually, when we were ready to build in Brecksville, we used the same architect.

Although they are earlier, I have many memories of our early days, freshly married, at our apartment at 17540 Madison Avenue in Lakewood, Ohio. This was a very convenient location at the end of the streetcar line, so I was always assured of a choice of seats when I took the streetcar to work in downtown Cleveland. I don't remember how much the fare was. The timing was a little tricky on the days when my father arranged to pick me up in front of the Superior Avenue entrance to the Leader Building where our offices were located, to go with him on a trip to appraise a house or an apartment building. My brother Russ had worked at the office during summer vacations and was already expert at the servicing part of the business. Logically, I was to be trained to inspect and appraise mortgage loan inquiries. Fortunately, I enjoyed that part of the business.

I remember the custodian (janitor) couple who lived at the rear of the building in an English basement suite overlooking the parking lot and rear entrance to the building. Their name was Fanslau and they were very nice to us. Of course, they knew we were the owner's children, but they were very competent and helpful. Mrs. Fanslau gave Fran a recipe for pumpkin pie which we used for years.

Among the tenants, I recall are the Parks, who were our next-door neighbors on the southeast corner of the building, overlooking Madison Avenue. I remember that Tom, the husband, who was a journeyman bricklayer, insisted on red meat, preferably steak, for his evening meals. I assumed this was a symbol to him of his success in life. They had a baby daughter who suffered from hydrocephalus, whom I only saw once lying in her crib and cannot forget the sight of her grotesquely swollen head. I think they were only there our first year and I do not know what became of the child, or of them.

I have a vague recollection of my cousin, Charles Geiger, newly married to Virginia, living on the third floor on the opposite side of the building, but I cannot remember how long they were there, or why we never did anything with them. They did not play cards and we may have been in their apartment only once.

We did form a friendship with another young couple, Hubert and Virginia Schmidt (not a relative) who were a little older than we were, and who also lived on the third floor, possibly in the suite the Geigers vacated. Hubert was a very interesting person and a landscape architect with the Cleveland Metropolitan Park System, Virginia was a secretary. I can still remember their faces: he with a butch haircut and she, square-jawed, with a lop-sided grin. They were fun to do things with and we were both in the same financial boat. They had an old car and one Saturday afternoon we went for ride west along the lake and saw a tree in an open field quite close to the road loaded with small yellow apples with greasy skins. I think we all looked at each other, jumped out of the car, and picked all the apples we could, improvising some sort of container to get them home. After we got home, we made applesauce, in an effort to stretch our budgets. Unfortunately, the applesauce was not very good. In fact, it was inedible, and we wasted a lot of time peeling and a lot of sugar. After a year or so, Hubert was offered a job in San Francisco and we lost touch with them

I remember that in our first two years at 17540 Madison we had out-of-town visitors twice, which was very exciting for me who grew up in Cleveland surrounded by relatives and friends. To see someone from out of town, or to visit someone in another city was unheard of when I was growing up; my parents never could understand why neither Russ nor I could find a local girl good enough to marry. To this day there is something special for me to have a visitor from another city in my home, or to visit and stay in someone's home in another city, and it adds an element of a special kind of excitement to my life.

Our first overnight visitors were Annabel Danhof and Sam Hess, who were engaged, and came from Detroit for a weekend. Annabel, who graduated from Wellesley College, was one of the four girls with whom Fran grew up, who were in the same class at Highland Park High School. Sam was an Amherst College graduate and went to the University of Michigan Law School.

Those were the days of propriety and the sleeping arrangements were for the girls to share our bedroom, and Sam and I slept on the Murphy pull down bed in the living room. Timing the use of the single bathroom with the four of us must have been tricky, but it all worked out. After all, it was only one night. We splurged and I remember Fran cooking a delicious standing rib roast of beef with all the trimmings and ice cream for dessert. For a newlywet it was a remarkable feat and a meal I have never forgotten. Afterwards we went to the Homestead movie theatre on Detroit Street near W. 117th Street to see one of today's classic movies, but I can't remember its name. It was a very successful visit, the first of many; we felt a sense of accomplishment and contentment.

Sometime later, as I recall, I had a phone call one Saturday morning and the voice asked for *Bamba* which could only have been one of my Army friends as no one in Cleveland knew my Army nickname. I was very excited because I recognized the voice immediately. It was Del Zucker, an attorney in Manhattan, who had been a good friend in our first years in the ASTP at the University of Minnesota. Del, who was still unmarried, was at the Cleveland airport on his way to

St. Louis to attend a wedding and was wondering if he could pay us a visit on his way home after the wedding. This would be the first time I saw anyone from "the good old days" and I was overjoyed to say yes.

He did stop and came to our apartment and brought a very attractive young lady with him named "Babe." They brought a gift for Nancy, a little yellow summer jumper suit, which I am sure "Babe" picked out for her bachelor friend. She was so nice that I hoped Del might settle for her and that might create the possibility for more visits in the future. This did not happen. Many years later Del married a widow, a fellow Manhattanite, named Frieda. She was very special. I was happy for Del.

One memorable event during our days in our apartment was the evening we invited my old high school friend, Bruce Hardy and his wife, for an evening of bridge. I had run into Bruce by chance at the corner of E. 6th Street and Euclid Avenue on my way back to our office after lunch. After reliving memories of our high school days; of playing clarinet in the marching band; when he was the Captain and I was his Quartermaster; we discovered that both couples enjoyed playing bridge. A date and time were agreed upon, and Bruce and Doris, arrived promptly. Bruce was two years older than I was, and I later learned that he was very precise, almost prim, in everything he did. He was a true Renaissance man:  he golfed, he sailed, he sang in a chorus, acted with a local playhouse group,  played a wonderful clarinet with a group of doctors in a Dixieland band, wrote poetry, and was just all around modest about his accomplishments.

After our wives got acquainted, we settled down for what turned out to be one of the longest evenings in our lives. Bruce was so talented in so many things: golf, sailing, writing poetry, painting, play acting, had a wry sense of humor, that it was a shock to see how inept he was at the bridge table. He agonized over every bid, and the play of every card. He obviously had no "card sense". It seemed to take a half hour to play each hand. And they did not know when to go home. As I recall, it was 4 a.m., when they finally said goodnight, and even then, lingered at the door. It was the longest night of bridge we ever endured.

The Hardy's lived on Bunts Road, south of Lakewood Heights Boulevard, over the line in Cleveland, in a small post-war bungalow, not far from us, and we went back and forth many times playing what passed for bridge. It was never an evening we looked forward to, and when we were their guests, we made it a point to go home before midnight.

Considering how important it was to us, I am surprised I don't remember more details of the purchase of our first car. We were anxious for our independence, and were chafing not to have to ask to borrow one of Dad's cars, to say where we were going and what time we expected to return, to continue to feel like a teenager with a curfew. I know now these were feelings on our part and not justified. My parents, who were living at 16414 Madison Avenue down the street from us a short distance in an apartment managed by my father and owned by his friend, Bill Steudel, owner of a Dodge agency, were always gracious and uncritical. Reconstructing, I know we did not buy our first car from a dealer. I think I must have answered an ad in the newspaper and remember meeting the seller at the Sohio gas station at the corner of W. Clifton Boulevard and Detroit Avenue after work. ( the gas station is still there). I probably took the Detroit streetcar rather than the usual Madison one. I remember doing the transaction alone without any help or advice from my father, which I am sure was a disappointment to him. I know he was appalled at the outcome. It was hard for him to swallow that one of his sons, one of his employees, could be seen in such a car.

The "car" was a 1938, 4-door straight, 8 Pontiac sedan, stick shift with a tricky clutch, red, faded to a splotchy pink, with many miles on it. It proved to be a useful form of transportation for three or four years. It was used for all the usual trips locally. I'm sure I continued to use the streetcar to go back and forth to work much of the time, and do not remember using it for any appraisal trips for the office. But having the car gave us a fine feeling of freedom. I remember driving to Detroit to visit Fran's mother more than once. On one of the early trips to Detroit, which took almost 5 hours pre-Ohio Turnpike, we despaired at baby Nancy on the back seat in her crib, on her stomach, who would not go to sleep. She kept raising her head to watch the oncoming headlights the whole trip with her large eyes, wide open and glistening.

The two most vivid memories of our first car was our trip to Detroit to attend the wedding of Annabel Danhof and Sam Hess. They had visited us at our apartment in Lakewood while engaged, and now their big day had arrived. Annabelle's father was General Counsel for the Michigan Central Railroad and President of the Detroit Country Club, a very conservative Hollander from Grand Haven, Michigan. He drove a mid-size Ford. The large wedding, with over 200 guests invited, was to take place at 7:30 p.m. at their Presbyterian church, followed by a reception and dinner at the country club. It turned out to be the most-posh wedding we ever attended.

We pulled up at the front entrance to the country club in our faded red, old Pontiac, in a light drizzle, where I dropped off Fran and her mother. The attendant who opened the doors to help the ladies promptly came to my window and offered to park the car for me. I insisted on parking it myself, explaining to him that the car had a balky clutch which took some getting used to - which was true - but the real reason was that I had seen the other cars in the parking lot, nothing but Cadillacs and Lincolns, it seemed, and was ashamed at what we were driving. I found a parking place some distance from the entrance and retrieved the car myself at the end of the evening.

I will never forget the end of the wedding ceremony. Sam had a booming voice and, as large as the church was, and without a modern amplifying system, when he said, "I do," it resounded all the way to the back row where we were seated. Then when he was advised that he could kiss the bride, he did so, and the loud smack of his kiss could also be heard in the last row.

It wasn't only the car that was an embarrassment. This was a 7:30 evening wedding, and we were the only people in attendance who were not in formal attire. It had simply not occurred to Fran, her mother, or me that formal dress was required. I still had my "tails" from college hanging in the closet and Fran still had several long formal dresses, any one of which would have let us blend in with the other guests. No one made any comment; no one seemed to be staring at us; and I thought we carried off our gaffe with aplomb. Very few people saw the car we were driving. The sit-down dinner with white tablecloths and served by waiters, was delicious.

After having driven the Pontiac several thousand miles, on the way home from one of our trips to Detroit, the car broke down on Lake Road in Bay Village. I had to call my father to come to our rescue, to bring us and the baby back home. Although no sarcastic comment was made and he was glad to help us, I am sure he felt vindicated and assumed I had learned my lesson. I do not recall what the problem was but think it may have been overheating of the engine caused by a broken fan belt. I have no recollection of the logistics of getting the car repaired. We drove it for a while longer, but I knew we had to upgrade. We ended up buying a Studebaker Landcruiser, which was their top model and very luxurious. I remember it had a "hill holder", which automatically applied the brakes when coming to a stop on a hill so the car did not start to roll back downhill before applying the gas pedal to go forward.

I have many memories of the period of Fran's first pregnancy. Her slipped disc problem seemed to abate. She was able to cook and climb the stairs to do the laundry. I think we saw more movies during that period. The Hilliard Square movie theatre was within easy walking distance, and I think we did fewer jigsaw puzzles. I tried to be of help in my clumsy way. I remember carrying a load of clothes to be washed down to the laundry in a large wash basket, and missing the last step, spraining my ankle badly. But we were searching for a car then, and I took the streetcar to the westerly end of Lorain Street, which was automobile row at that time, and walking (limping on the bad ankle) about two miles to West Boulevard, stopping at every car dealer and used car lot along the way without success.

Fran was under the care of Burdette Wylie, M.D. for all three of her pregnancies and we used Paul Crohn, M.D. as our pediatrician for all three children. I can remember Dr. Wylie's appearance: he was portly and had a moustache. I remember Dr. Crohn, who lived on Story Road in Fairview Park, more because of his hobby: he raised tuberous begonias and had a spectacular display of them in his front yard. I thought both men were outstanding physicians. I had only met Dr. Wylie once when he held up the newborn child for my inspection, assured me that she was perfect, and had to tell me it was a girl. I had never seen a naked baby before!

As her due date neared, we were invited with my parents, for a Sunday supper at the Geigers, on a Sunday afternoon. I do not remember what we had to eat, but Fran ate a very hearty meal, with seconds. She had a black maternity dress given to her by one of her sorority sisters, which was very stylish, and disguised the pregnancy. People could not believe that Fran, who weighed 118 lbs. (people accused me of starving my new bride) at the start of her term was pregnant a week before the birth.

We arrived home after dinner at the Geigers about 9 p.m. and Fran laboriously climbed the three and a half story flight of stairs. About midnight she told me she was having labor pains and maybe we should think of going to the hospital, which we did. Three or four hours later I was told to go home and get some sleep; they would call me if I was needed. No call ever came; and I slept well. I went back to the hospital the next day and waited and waited. Finally, in the late afternoon I was called and learned that we had a new little girl, whom we named Nancy Elisabeth. She was beautiful, but had virtually no hair, which caused many people to exclaim, "Oh, what a cute little boy!"

When it came time for Fran to come home, I was instructed to bring a dress, among other things. I picked out one of my favorites: a light blue cotton print with pale yellow daisies sprinkled all over with a script below each flower which said, "He loves me; He loves me not." Fran wore it home, but never again, and never forgave me for picking out something with that sentiment for that occasion. Of course, I didn't know what I had done.

Just as I wish we had had a better camera I wish I retained more memories of that wonderful first child. She had such large eyes, and was such a bright, happy child. I remember Fran reveling in her role as a new mother. I remember devising a method of burping the baby after feeding her: rather than spreading a towel over my shoulder and holding her up over my shoulder and patting her back, I would hold her in the crook of my lap, and after she had finished her bottle, put my right hand on her tummy, left hand on her back, and bend her forward, and she would burp copiously. There is a great picture of this process with me sitting in our chair in the corner of the living room, the baby looking very happy and Daddy looking very proud, but with a large hole in the heel of his sock.

At first she seemed to fuss more than she should have, and finally, Fran called Dr. Crohn who told her he suspected that Fran, who wanting to experience all the aspects of motherhood and was breast feeding, was not producing sufficient mother's milk. We should supplement with Similac in a bottle. Nancy was simply hungry and letting us know the only way she could, by crying. This solved the problem.

Nancy started to walk at a very early age. She never crawled or toddled. She just started walking. She even climbed the stairs to the apartment without help. She also did not like to be held and cuddled. Her independent nature asserted itself very early.

She was very inquisitive and when she was about six-months-old and already walking around the apartment exploring, she touched the radiator in the living room and burned her hand so severely that we took her to Lakewood Hospital to have it treated. I remember that we brought her home with a heavily bandaged hand, put her to bed in her crib, and woke the next morning to find that she had unwrapped all the bandage which was about six feet long and was playing with it in her crib.

I remember how Grandma Thompson doted on Nancy. She bought her one outstanding piece of clothing or another constantly, things we could never afford on my salary at the time, and she derived such pleasure from the giving. One outfit I remember especially: it was a pink woolen winter coat with matching leggings, and I took little Nancy, reaching up to hold my hand for a walk to a nearby store on a very cold Sunday afternoon. When we got back Fran was waiting for us in the parking lot. At that point my parents pulled into the lot in a brand-new light green Dodge sedan which my father had to show off, making a silent, pointed comparison to our faded pink Pontiac. This was in the winter of 1947-48, and I had only been working in the family business less than three years, which was still a sole proprietorship, still earning only $50-60 per week, and very aware that every increase in my salary came directly out of my father's pocket.

Being the firstborn, I'm sure Nancy received more attention form both of us than her sisters did. When the later children arrived, there wasn't as much time available for their play and learning. Not that they were neglected. They received added attention from their older siblings, as well as more efficient attention from the parents who had learned a thing or two from their experience with the first child.

I do not remember Fran and me ever sitting down and discussing a philosophy of child rearing. We were true amateurs. We only knew we felt a love we had never known before. I think we agreed that we would try to recognize the needs caused by the difference in personality of each child - we could see differences almost immediately - and would respect each little person as an individual. We never talked baby talk to them. The only rule on which I was adamant, based on my own childhood, was there would be no teasing. I am sure Fran thought I was uncharacteristically ferocious about this. But then she did not live through what I did at home. I always felt from the beginning that the children were not "mine" but that they belonged to Deity, and that I had a caretaker's responsibility to tend to their needs and to encourage their talents.

Nancy grew into a very tall girl, almost 6'. Her obvious intelligence caused great expectations from us and from her teachers, perhaps more than her actual age would warrant. I remember when she was seven or eight-years-old, while still living in Parma Heights, driving her over to Berea after work to take ballet lessons at the hall of the Episcopal church on Bagley Road. She was too tall for a career in ballet to be possible, but gained skill in control of her body, and a certain gracefulness. Mrs. Vera Yanko came to the house to give all the daughters piano lessons, and there was summer day camp at the Greenfields in Brecksville, on Stadium Drive, and the Girl Scouts. Because our house was so isolated, not part of a dense suburban development, after- school play had to be arranged by the Moms who had to drive the children back and forth. Nancy's particular friend was Danette Gentile, a high school classmate, who lived on Oakes Road close to Brecksville Road. This became a lifelong friendship.

I remember one of the annual Memorial Day parades, which started at the center of Brecksville and proceeded west on Rte. 82, passing a reviewing stand and a crowd of proud parents and friends, led by the high school band, and followed by the Boy Scout troops and the Girl Scouts, who would lay flowers on the graves of the many Revolutionary War graves at the two city cemeteries. As the band neared the crowd of onlookers, I came to attention with my hand over my heart when the Colors passed. Standing next to me was "Charlie" (I can't remember his last name), who had substituted at bridge one or two times, and who had terrible posture, featuring a potbelly tummy. I said to him out of the corner of my mouth: "For God's sake, Charlie, come to attention when the Colors pass." His reply was to hiss: "I am at attention!" I can still see him standing there.

We were fortunate that we had two older ladies, grandmothers, living across Oakes Road who were available for babysitting. The one I remember most is Grandma Bahr. I think the fee then was 50 cents per hour. For longer stays when the sitter lived in the house while we were on a trip to Europe, or visiting on a weekend out of town, we could rely on Grandma Butts, who was born on the Isle of Mann, and was excellent and very reliable. We could feel that the children were in good hands and safe while we were gone. There was also a local Brecksville woman named Carolyn, who was very reliable, except that she had an older Polish boyfriend, who kissed Fran's hand every time he met her, and taught the children how to play poker.

One of the most important criteria for us in selecting the suburb in which we would like to raise our children was the quality of the school system. Fran checked with some of her sorority sisters who were teachers in the area and Brecksville was at the top of the list. Once the children were enrolled in the system, Fran followed up by visiting every class for each of the children's courses, involving driving many times to the various schools during Teacher's Appreciation Week sponsored by the P.T.A. There was only one other mother who showed such interest and concern for the quality of the teaching.

There were other interactions with the school hierarchy. We insisted that since Latin was in the curriculum, that our daughters be allowed to enroll, even if it was not offered at their school. Since the classes were only given at one location, this meant that Nancy and Kathy had to be bussed to a different school building for that one class in the middle of the school day. I do not remember if we subjected Barbara to this special attention. I'm sure that this did not endear the Schmidt family to Mr. Wiesnieski, the Principal of the high school, but the Schmidt family felt that the study of Latin was an important part of their daughters' education, even though it was considered a "dead" language but we persisted.

Another example of the friction we caused, occurred when Nancy was a junior in high school, and we learned that there was to be an eastern private girls' schools fair held in downtown Cleveland at 3 p.m. on a regular school day. Each college would have a booth manned by a graduate and a school representative who could explain the benefits of attending their school, narrowing our search, possibly saving miles of travel.

I had been alerted to this event by one of the young men, E. W. Bush, in the Aetna Life Insurance Company Mortgage Loan Department to whom I enjoyed sending my loan submissions. He was easy to work with. He was a Dartmouth graduate, single, lived with his mother in an old farmhouse built in the 1700s outside of Hartford. His roommate at Dartmouth had married, gotten a job in Cleveland and lived in Shaker Heights.

On one of our regular inspection trips by the Aetna to view recent loan approvals, I arranged for us to stop at his roommate's home and "Ted" ran in to say hello to the wife, who had gone to Smith College. Obviously, he had mentioned to the wife that we were in the college selection process, which was very kind. He came back to tell me of the upcoming College Fair to be held in the Higbee Department Store auditorium in downtown Cleveland and that Smith College would have a booth and urged me to have Nancy attend and to mention the wife's name. They would be on the lookout for Nancy.

A week before the Fair, Nancy came home to tell her mother that she could not go to the Fair. She would have to miss her final class of the day, French, and if a test were given, she could not make it up because her failure to take it would be treated as an "Unauthorized Absence." When Fran called to protest, Mr. Wiesnieski, the Principal, suggested there might not even be such an such an event, although it had been announced in the local newspapers.

I had never seen Fran so furious and upset. She insisted that I call on Mr. Wiesnieski and persuade him to rescind his decision. The next morning, I called on him in his office. He deprecated the entire matter; dismissed our concerns for securing the best education possible at any cost for our daughter; pointed out that there were many fine colleges in Ohio, which would cut down on travel time to visit their campuses. I could not believe what I was hearing, and from an educator! His decision was final: if Nancy attended the Fair (he grudgingly admitted there might be such a thing) and skipped her last class of the day, it would be counted as an unauthorized absence, with a possible consequence of a lower final grade. This was such a contrast to my experience with my high school principal who was so encouraging, and in my mind, more than a little responsible for my receiving my scholarship to Yale.

Nancy did attend the Fair and I recall that she was very impressed with the people she met and the interest they took in her. The class she skipped was her best subject and there were no lower grade consequences. In contrast to her principal, her teacher was directly involved in Nancy's education and development as a person, and had encouraged Nancy to attend.

In June of that year we took one of our best family vacations ever: we went college hunting. We toured the East and visited the campuses of Cornell, Wells College, Smith College, Radcliff College, Wellesley College, and Connecticut School for Girls. We also stopped in New Haven and Fran and the girls were able to see where I had spent four of the most important years of my life, visiting the residential Pierson College where I lived in room No. 1480. The colleges were closed following graduation and reunion weekend, but we were allowed to wander over the quadrangle courtyard and get a glimpse of the Common and Dining Rooms. It was all nostalgia for me, and of no importance to Nancy in her search because Yale was still all male at that time.

Later that fall we took Nancy with us for a weekend in Ann Arbor for the Home Coming football game at the University of Michigan. I don't remember where we stayed, but she got a taste of the Big Ten atmosphere. We visited friends we had met at Camp Michigania, who lived in Ann Arbor, who were close friends of the Culligans. Bill Culligan who held the school record for the longest run from the scrimmage line at that time, introduced us, (we were in the kitchen), to an All American tackle teammate, a very large, impressive man whose name I do not remember, who was also visiting and reliving old times.

Nancy was part of the crowd of 100,000+ people at the game, saw a big-time football team for the first time, and the large, impressive marching band in the huge stadium. We walked back to the campus after the game with the crowds of people and went to the Women's Union, Lydia Mendelsohn, where I had spent a lot of time while studying Japanese in the Army. We unexpectedly watched from the lounge, a race between teams of fraternity boys pushing bed frames down the street bearing a sorority girl, emitting sparks from the wheels all the way to the finish line. It was exciting and fun and part of the campus atmosphere. Before the game we had already seen East Quad where I lived while in the Army and visited the Gamma Phi Beta sorority house where Fran had spent three happy years, and where we met for the first time. I remember meeting the Culligans for dinner at Webbers after the game, a well known restaurant off campus famous for its food and its dimly lit, warm ambience. It was quite a weekend.

A week or so after our return, I remember I was standing at the kitchen sink, when Nancy approached me and announced that she had decided that she wanted to attend the University of Michigan. She knew this would be a big disappointment to me since she knew I hoped she would like Smith College, but Michigan had a fine teacher's training program which was her lifelong ambition; to become a schoolteacher; she really wanted a bigger school and, besides, it would be a lot less expensive. I remember being proud of myself for not showing any disappointment over her decision and remember telling her that I was pleased with her decision and that the monetary aspect should not play any role in her choice. That was my problem, which I would solve, and that I only wanted her to get the best education possible, and to do her best at all times.

When Nancy's graduation from Brecksville High School drew near, Mr. Wiesnieski had to watch at Honors Night (which Nancy had not told us anything about and we learned of at the last minute) the girl he had refused permission to miss one class, be named the Outstanding Senior in all categories, except French in which she truly excelled, but that honor had to be given to another girl because it did not seem right that one student should receive all the top honors. We were stunned and I think Nancy was also. I vaguely remember that Nancy was awarded a small scholarship from the Brecksville Women's Club, perhaps two or three hundred dollars. And to think that we might have missed her triumph had we depended on her to call the event to our attention.

So many other memories, so little space. I remember how caring she was, especially for her sisters. When they were young, she used to "mother" them, and they seemed to accept her attentions. I remember very clearly when Grandma Thompson would take us out to dinner at a restaurant, how Nancy, age nine or ten and Kathy, six or seven would make her selection from the menu, and could hardly get it out of her mouth before Kathy would chirp up, "Me, too!" Nancy grew impatient with this and tried her best to give her order last, but never quite succeeded.

We had so many out of town friends and relatives on our mailing list that we took photographs of the growing family which we printed ourselves at home as an economy measure and enclosed with our Christmas cards. Those far away could keep up with the children's development. Taking the pictures was quite a production. The photo flood lamps had to be set up and the girls dressed nicely, or in costumes, on occasion. Then came the ordeal of getting two or three little ones to sit still, and to smile, in unison. Sometimes harsh words had to be spoken. I recall my frustrations and feeling lucky if one or two of the exposures out of a roll of 36 were usable. But many of the distant recipients appreciated being kept somewhat up to date with the children's progress, and told us that they saved every year's photo, and looked forward to them and complained when we no longer performed the annual ritual.

We also, as an economy measure, in the early days of our marriage, baked Christmas cookies to send as Christmas presents, using my mother's German recipes - we used lots of butter and sugar and as little flour as possible: *pfeffernüsse* "pepper nuts", which had to be "aged" on the stairs to the attic when I was a boy, *springerle*, anise drops, butter cookies cut into shapes with cookie cutters and frosted, and also a recipe Fran found that was Swedish and used only confectioner's sugar, whipped egg whites, almond flavoring, no flour at all, and melted in the mouth.

We used to package these and send them to the out-of-town relatives, hoping they were not all crumbs upon arrival. There was bitter disappointment on their part when we discontinued doing this. They were the best Christmas cookies I ever ate in my humble opinion, much superior to the authentic cookies given to us by our German, native-born, cleaning lady, Martha. The daughters were allowed to frost the butter cookies with colored icing of their choosing which they mixed themselves without any supervision. The results were spectacular, but still edible and it established a tradition.

My recollection is that Nancy's college years were happy ones, without the stress of having to maintain grade levels to keep a scholarship. She did not come home to "Momma" on weekends, but we made the easy trip to Ann Arbor when there was an occasion to do so. I am ashamed to say that I do not remember what her major was; nor do I remember the majors of the other daughters. I think Nancy's must have been French literature.

I remember the empty bedroom on the lower level, packing the car, getting the sitter and the long drive to Ann Arbor to install Nancy in her first dorm room. We stopped for lunch at a restaurant at Rte. 23 and Washtenaw Avenue, Bill Knapps, which became a tradition on our many trips to Ann Arbor. She lived in one of the large dormitories her freshman year and I do not remember getting her things up to her room, or what the room was like. I do remember a lump in the throat when we waved good-bye and left her on her own. I'm sure it was nothing like the emotions my parents felt when they left me in New Haven the first time.

Fran was disappointed that Nancy, in spite of being a legacy and other strong recommendations from alumnae friends, was not pledged by her own sorority, Gamma Phi Beta, but she was pleased when she pledged the Pi Beta Phi sorority, which was highly regarded on campus. The Pi Phi's always had a Father's Day on one of the football weekends and, of course, I was invited. It was a great weekend with all the daughters lavishing attention on their dad's. I recall that the fathers got together for a private meeting and voted to contribute to a fund to buy a new and larger TV for the house. I remember having our meals in their dining room, but do not remember where I stayed. Do not remember the football game other than the festivities and huge crowds. The most vivid memory I have of that weekend was that before I left on Saturday morning.

I had to get up early to get to Ann Arbor in time for the game. The night before, I had set a muskrat trap on the far side of the dam for our pond, and when I looked out the bedroom window to see what the weather was like - it was clear and beautiful - I saw something thrashing in the water where I had set the trap. It had to be my first muskrat. I had not considered what I would do if I actually caught something. I hustled out and found that it was a good-sized muskrat, which had almost chewed off the leg caught in the trap. I could see bone. It was obviously in a lot of pain, and the only solution I could think of was to go up to the garage where I had an old rusted chipping iron golf club (I did not own a gun, or bow and arrow) and return to try to hit the animal's head - not easy. It took several blows - to put an end to its suffering. This is how I learned that trapping is an ugly way to kill anything. And, what a way to start a happy weekend!

One touching memory I have of Nancy is going downstairs to kiss her goodnight one night and finding her in tears, probably sometime in her junior year in high school. I got on my knees next to her bed and tried to get out of her what was troubling her. I was glad it was not something we had done, or she had been teased. She was disturbed that she had refused an invitation to a party that she knew we would not have approved of and had refused without even asking our permission. I remember trying to console her and apologizing for the training in idealism we had instilled in her. I feared that there would be many similar situations in the future where she would find herself saying no while a part of her wanted to say yes, because she had learned the difference between right and wrong at her father's knee, and observing her parent's daily lives.

The sequel to this memory is the morning during summer vacation during her sophomore year in college when Nancy knocked on our bedroom door before we were up and asked to come in. This was a first and very unusual. Although we had trained the children to knock before entering if a door was closed, it had never happened before. This must something of great importance.

She stood at the foot of our bed and declared that now that she was an adult, she wanted more freedom to come and go as she pleased. She spent some time describing what freedom meant to her. When she finished, I exploded with the only barrack's room expletive I think any of the children ever heard from their father: "B..1 S..t!! I pointed out that all of us, including her, might think we were "free," but we were not. We were trapped by the ideals and morals we had learned as children, and there was no way to escape. These lessons learned in childhood lasted a lifetime. I think she was shocked at my vehemence and left the room quietly. I do not remember Fran's reaction to my automatic response, but it was not a crisis and life went on much as it had before. And, in fact, she was free.

There were few opportunities in my recollections of the period when the children were growing up when I had the opportunity to make a specific teaching point. For one thing, I never considered myself an authority figure, a fount of wisdom, in either my family or business life. But I know that I had a chance to respond to a specific occasion to write a personal, "Papa" letter to each of the girls. I must have copies somewhere, and I hope they were well enough written and said the right things that the girls would have wanted to keep them in their own archives. It was not ever anything we spoke about, and I don't know if any of them told their mother about the letters.

One opportunity arose at the time of the J.F. Kennedy funeral ceremonies. I had taken the day off and been glued to the TV set all day; watched the procession with the rider-less horse and the two children holding their mother's hands as they walked behind in the procession; the grace and dignity exhibited by Jackie. It was all very serious and somber, and about 4 p.m. I had had enough. I had to get out.

Our youngest, Barbara, was due for a haircut and Fran called the hairdresser to see if she was open for business. She was and I gathered Barb up and we took off. It was a beautiful, clear day with no traffic on the roads. The hairdresser's shop was at Broadview and Wallings Road. There is a steep hill, down and up, as the shop is approached. My mind was elsewhere, reliving all that I had seen that day, and when I got to the top of the hill, I noticed a flashing red light in my rear-view mirror. I pulled into the parking lot of the Faulhaber Funeral Parlor and the Chief of Police of Broadview Heights wrote out a ticket for speeding. Having an 8-year-old, wide eyed passenger sitting beside me, I was very polite, but pointed out the visibility, road conditions, lack of traffic, and my preoccupation with the events of the day.

When he handed me my ticket, he asked if I knew the Mayor of Brecksville. I replied that I did and served on the Planning Commission in Brecksville and the Mayor attended all our meetings. The Chief of Police, not a patrolman, suggested out loud in front of a child that I should tell our Mayor about the incident, and the ticket would probably be "fixed." I thanked him and said that I would be sending in my check for the fine.

That evening at the dinner table I used the incident as a rare opportunity to explain to the family that what had happened to me that afternoon, the lack of respect for the law, the assumption that I would use a relationship to evade my responsibility for a few dollars, taken to the extreme, could lead to what we had witnessed that day, the funeral of an assassinated President. Perhaps not a very good analogy, but I hoped the children would see the point and remember.

I remember it must have been Nancy's junior year at Michigan when she met Paul Burstadt, an aeronautical engineering student, from Beverly Hills, Michigan, a suburb of Detroit. We met him for the first time on one of our visits to Ann Arbor. He was good looking, very clean-cut and very polite. I think Nancy had her heart set on him as soon as she met him, although Fran had some misgivings about the pace of the romance. I remember both of us being happy when Nancy had an opportunity to spend the summer in Rouen, France, living in a boarding house and studying the language in the classroom and using it in her daily living in the real world. It was the beginning of her lifelong love affair with things French, and a huge boost to her fluency and mastery of the language in her career as a French teacher at the high school level. It's strange that I do not remember how the trip was arranged. Both Fran and I felt the separation, a whole summer, from Paul for such a length of time would be beneficial. She loved the experience and thrived on it.

One amusing thing that happened when she came home for Christmas break that year was my meeting her at Cleveland Hopkins Airport after work. She flew the Gray Goose Airline, which flew small 6-8 passenger planes and only commuted between Cleveland and Detroit, about a 45-minute flight. It was very cold. The airport terminal was undergoing improvements. We had to stand in a temporary baggage pick-up area outside the main building which had overhead infra-red heater lights and shelter from the wind by a temporary wall of vinyl fastened to 2 x 4s. The lights were about 7' above the ground, and I was wearing a hound's-tooth cloth fedora style hat. We had probably been standing there, shivering, for about twenty minutes, when one of the bystanders pointed out that my hat was smoldering, about to burst into flames. I was so glad to see Nancy that I was oblivious to everything else. I liked the hat, wore it all the time, but it had to be discarded after that little adventure.

Most of the memories of the excitement surrounding the engagement and marriage of our first child are a large blur, and once again, the memories that are clear are trivial. I remember the weekend when Paul hitch-hiked from Ann Arbor to Brecksville, arriving Saturday afternoon. It was the start of the pro football season; the Cleveland Browns were scheduled to play the New Orleans Saints Sunday afternoon. I think this may have been their first meeting after the long separation caused by Nancy's summer in France. It may have been the weekend they announced their engagement. I'm sure it was the first time he saw our house on Oakes Road.

I remember it was a very hot, sunny Sunday afternoon and I had spent three hours mowing the lawn; I was sweating profusely and over-heated. Within 10 minutes of finishing the job, I felt as though I had been jabbed with a red-hot poker on my right ankle. I was wearing navy blue ankle sox and never saw what had stung me. I was brave and shook the sting off and finished the mowing. As I was putting the tractor away, scraping the clippings off the underside of the mower deck, suddenly everything became blurry and I felt dizzy. When I looked up toward the top of the oak tree, the branches were swirling in a big circle, I felt euphoric, and I wondered if this was what a heart attack felt like. I tottered over to our nearby woodpile, and stretched out for a few minutes, and then became aware I had to get to the bathroom as fast as possible to avoid a serious accident.

It was a fair distance from the back yard through the kitchen, entry hall and hall to the bathroom. As I passed through the entry hall, I was able to call up to the family, who were watching the football game, that something was wrong and then reached my destination in time. The next thing I knew, Paul was rubbing the back of my neck and I was looking down at the loafer shoes he was wearing. I had passed out. They helped me into bed. Fran went to call Dr. Vigor our local family doctor, who happened to be home. He said it sounded like heat stroke, and that Fran should get some large bath towels, soaked in cold water, and use them to lower my temperature.

About this time, I became aware of severe pain in the area of the sting which I had failed to mention previously. My sock was removed and there was a red circle the size of a half-dollar with a puncture mark in the center. Fran hurried to call Dr. Vigor again. He said that it was not heat stroke, but anaphylactic shock. If I was still conscious, I would survive. Fran was to be sure to remove the barb of the stinger, but there was no stinger in the wound, so we assumed it was a hornet sting. The previous Fall, I had received multiple yellow jacket stings, which probably used up all my immunity. This first new sting triggered the shock response.

It was pretty scary. Dr. Vigor told us that he had lost one of his patients when the husband had been stung by a bumblebee in his backyard while viewing his garden after dinner. By the time his wife went back to the house to get baking soda and returned, she found him dead. Before the next spring, I visited Dr.Vigor twice a week to receive injections to restore my immunity to bee sting venom, and carried an anti-bee-sting kit with me at all times when I worked outdoors, or played golf. I was very, very wary.

I remember how much we liked Paul's parents, Irving and Phyllis. "Irv" was a graduate of the University of Illinois, receding hairline and wore glasses. He was rather serious and was very gracious. Phyllis had a tart sense of humor, came from Lennox, Massachusetts in the Berkshires and had French ancestry. There were a younger sister, Claire, and brother, Billy. Irv worked as a salesman for Westinghouse in the atomic power plant division. They were about our age and we got along well together.

Since this was our first wedding, everything had to be done by the book. The wedding service was performed by the Rev. William Wrenn of St. Matthews Episcopal Church in Brecksville for whom I was playing the organ for the regular Sunday services. (I retired the Sunday before the wedding). For this special occasion we were able to secure the services of Warren Berryman, my organ instructor from Baldwin Wallace College, and he played the Trumpet Voluntary and Purcell for the march down the aisle and the recessional. The organ never sounded better. I must have walked the bride, who was never more beautiful, down the aisle, but truly, I do not remember the emotions I felt on that long walk, or when I gave away the bride.

Prior to the wedding, there was a bridal shower given by Nancy's best friend, Dannette Gentile, at which her father took many photos which he continued to do after the wedding at the reception and gave the photos and negatives to the newly-weds, a wonderful gift and informal record for them to have. I had never heard of doing this before and thought it was a great idea and did the same for several of the future weddings we attended as guests.

The wedding was followed by a reception at the University Club in downtown Cleveland and included a sit-down luncheon. I do not remember the menu - or the centerpieces. After the reception, the out-of-town guests who did not leave for home immediately after the ceremony, and who would have had a long, empty evening in a strange city, were invited back to our house in Brecksville to spend the evening with the families and the newlyweds. There were Fran's childhood friends from St. Louis, Chicago and Detroit, two generations of sorority sisters, Fran's and Nancy's, the grandparents, my parents and brothers, members of our Brecksville Duplicate Bridge group, and so many others I cannot recall. I think the number of guests totaled about 60; it was the largest party thus far and the house accommodated everyone very comfortably. I remember lamenting that it was over all too soon. There were many guests I hardly had time to speak to, and I wished there had been some way to make it a three-day celebration. Perhaps chartering the "Goodtime" sight-seeing cruise ship on a three-day cruise on Lake Erie. Nancy had parked her Volkswagen (named Wilhemina), given to her for her practice teaching, at the head of the driveway; and everyone gathered to throw rice as they departed. Only, we couldn't find the rice.

When they were ready to leave for their honeymoon, about 10 p.m. Nancy and Paul were showered with dry lentil beans. Probably a first, which later sprouted in the cracks between to stone flagging. They had to be harvested later, but I don't remember getting any beans for soup.

I remember how wistful I felt as I waved goodbye and they set off down the driveway for their honeymoon.

I remember, after their marriage, that Nan (as I always called her) and Paul found jobs in Cleveland: he at NASA where he spent his entire career, and she as a French teacher in the Rocky River School system. Their first apartment was on Webster Road near the airport, and that was where we were invited to have our first meal cooked by Nan as a married woman. I don't remember anything about the meal, or the apartment, except that it was a typical one with a balcony, and it was on the second or third floor.

In the second or third year of their marriage, Nan moved up to the Rocky River High School teaching French to older students. She remained there until her retirement. She loved her students and loved teaching. I have the journal she started the year she decided it was time to retire. It was very difficult for her to give up something she so loved, which fulfilled her childhood dream.

After a year living in an apartment, they moved into the first floor flat of a two-family house, which was very common in that neighborhood, on Bunts Road south of Madison Avenue in Lakewood. I remember being invited to dinner in the summertime when Fran was in Detroit visiting her mother with the children. I do not recall what Nan served, but I do remember the discussion that took place after dinner. It was the first and only time any of the children ever availed themselves of the knowledge I had acquired in the mortgage business. I was still spending most of my time financing residences, appraising seven or eight houses of all types every week and Nan and Paul wanted to know what they should look out for, and what the criteria were for the financial side of the equation. With their incomes, how much house could they afford?

At that time, the maximum residential loan we could obtain from the Aetna Life Insurance Company was $20,000 and the interest rates had risen to four and one-half percent. The cash down payment had declined from one-third of the purchase price to twenty percent. Monthly mortgage payments should not exceed one-third of their joint incomes. We talked about other aspects of owning a home, and they thanked me profusely for sharing so much information with them; said that it was the first time I had ever talked to them about something so serious, or shown any interest in their affairs. My feelings, always, were that the children's financial lives were private, and we would intrude only if asked. We never inquired as to any of their incomes, and never would think of equating financial success with the other intangible elements of their lives and marriages. I thought they were happy, which was all that mattered

I must confess that I always felt a little hurt when one of the children bought a house and did not take advantage of my knowledge or seek my advice. And I think both Fran and I were always curious as to exactly how much money the children were making.

I remember the first house that Nan and Paul bought some time after my educational seminar on Bunts Road. It was in the Beach Cliff neighborhood in Rocky River, developed in the 1920s; was a well maintained, mature, desirable section of Rocky River and within walking distance of Lake Erie. It was bungalow style and had a detached garage. Paul used the driveway to work on an old sports car he had bought. The yard was not large enough to provide much space to satisfy Nan's gardening desires, but I recall feeling good that they had found such a nice, reasonably priced home. Of course, following our family tradition, they never told me the price, and I never asked, or tried to find out.

I remember seeing Nan in her classroom, which was on the second floor of the high school facing Detroit Road, only once when I had to deliver something to her, and very jauntily addressing the class with a hearty *bon jour,* the limit of my ability to speak French at that time. I'm sure they admired my pronunciation.

One of my regrets is that I could observe first-hand so little of her accomplishments. She was a truly dedicated, old-fashioned teacher, and played a huge role in the school's extra-curricular activities. I was only able to see Nan in her role as basketball coach once. In my defense, the distance from Brecksville to Rocky River was sufficient to make the trip impractical to see her games regularly. Nan had initiated the girls' basketball program in Rocky River and learned to be a fine coach. It was interesting to watch her in action, employing strategy from the sidelines, encouraging her players, making substitutions, challenging referee's calls.. I think she was before her time and may have been the only lady coach in the league; I know that she was liked and respected and helped by some of her male rivals in her learning process. The game we saw was refereed by John Mihocik, an English teacher at my old high school, who became Nan's second husband after her divorce from Paul. One form of encouragement Nan employed was to treat her players to a home cooked spaghetti dinner at their home after they won a game. I wonder if this would not be illegal today?

I remember many occasions when Nan and Paul came to Brecksville for dinner and an evening. When they arrived, we would notice that Nan's eyes were red, as though she had been crying. We never mentioned this at the time. After they had been married thirteen years, Nan called and asked if she could take us to dinner at a restaurant by herself. I don't remember which restaurant.. After eating, she told us that she had decided to divorce Paul. After thirteen years of increasing verbal abuse in her own marriage, and observing the toxic deterioration of Paul's parents' relationship, she had no desire to end up in a barren, bitter relationship in her retirement years. Her decision was a shock, but not really a surprise. Paul wanted to try to "save" the marriage and agreed to go to counseling in hopes of getting Nan to reconsider. She encouraged the counseling knowing that her decision would not change, but it might help Paul have a better chance of a successful relationship with Nan's successor, whoever she might be.

We accepted Nan's decision with some sorrow. We finally understood her red eyes. And, I had played golf with Paul and witnessed samples of his temper. However, it was the first divorce in my side of the family, and it took a little getting used to. My father was outspokenly opposed to the idea of divorce and risked his relationship with Nan with his own version of verbal abuse. To him it was simple: just learn to put up with whatever it was, try to change, and let time do its work. In his mind the responsibility for this failure was Nan's, it was up to her to make whatever changes were necessary to save the marriage. I remember Nan telling us of her encounters with my father during this period. He couldn't see what Nan lived with privately, and, based on what she observed with Paul's parents, had every reason to foresee for herself: a lonely future with an increasingly hostile, bitter partner. She felt she had a right to a happy retirement, and we agreed.

I do not remember when Nan's troubles began. The purchase of their house was a happy event. They walked down to my father's house after dinner, or Dad and his wife, Mary, walked up to their house. They took vacations in France, bicycling all over the country and had many adventures and obstacles to overcome. I remember being worried about their personal safety in the nightly campgrounds. I remember that on one of their trips, while they were in London, Paul passed out at one of the monuments and it was determined that it was a case of low blood sugar. Paul did some of the work on the space shuttles, and they went to Cape Canaveral to watch one of the lift-offs, which was exciting. On the surface they appeared to be happily married.

As I recall the divorce was reasonably amicable, but Paul ended up with the house, which seemed a high price to me, but was worth it to her if it meant her freedom. She moved into a basement apartment in Rocky River, and again, I worried about her safety, but she seemed unconcerned. She lived in the apartment long enough to learn that she could handle her affairs and be happy alone.

Then, through her coaching the high school girls' basketball team, she met John Mihocik, of Slovak-Finnish extraction, divorced with one son of high school age, good looking, fellow teacher (English and golf coach at Lakewood High School), graduate of Wittenberg College and Ohio State, sports fanatic, and a 6-7 handicap golfer. We played a lot of golf over the years, and it quickly became my ambition to play one round where I bested him. It never happened and the older I became, with our twenty-five-year age gap, the more impossible it became physically.

We played as couples at many of the public courses on the southwest side of Cuyahoga County. Working on her second marriage, Nan really started to learn golf to be able to spend time with John and made quick progress. Fran had been playing for a long time, although both she and Nan preferred tennis, and John was impressed with Fran's distance off the tee and her putting skill.

I remember one of these occasions when we were playing at Pine Hills Golf Course in North Royalton, on a short par three hole, Fran hit the green from the tee, her ball landing about 6 feet from the hole. John and I both missed the green, he to the left and me to the right. My approach chip shot hit Fran's ball and knocked it three or four feet closer to the hole, and John then proceeded to chip and also hit her ball knocking into the hole. In all our years of playing neither John nor I had ever seen such a thing before. The big question: Did Fran score a hole in one? I don't think we ever found the answer.

One of the things I remember about Nan was her birthday cards for me. They were always witty and clever, usually involving a pun. I don't know where she found them. But the most touching card she ever sent me was dated November 18, 1986, which was the first anniversary of my quadruple by-pass surgery. She added to the card her short message: "So glad you are still with us!" Something I shall never forget.

One memory involved with Nan's marriage to John was the reception held at The Clifton Club after the ceremony, which took place on a Friday night at the nearby Methodist Church on Detroit Road in Rocky River. The Clifton Club was an exclusive, private eating and meeting club at the westerly end of Lake Avenue at the mouth of the Rocky River and Lake Erie. I had never been there before. I think the date was June 23rd, well after the peak peony bloom season. At that time, I think I only had about 100 plants. As an experiment I had cut about two dozen stems with tight buds showing a little color and wrapped each stem individually in newspaper, never putting the stems in water, and dry stored them in our refrigerator. The night before the reception, I took the blossoms out of the refrigerator and they looked terrible: limp and dead. Following the instructions, I had read in the peony literature, I recut the bottom of each stem and plunged them into a vase of tepid water up to the unopened bud. I went to bed praying a lot that night. The next morning it was obvious the experiment had been a success. Peonies could be cut dry before the blossoms had opened and kept refrigerated for several weeks and then revived using this method.

I took the flowers in to our local florist to whom I had sold peonies previously and paid her to make a centerpiece arrangement for the dining table, which turned out beautifully. The blossoms not used in the centerpiece were displayed, unarranged, in one of our own vases in a corner of the room. For me, at any rate, the flowers added something special to the wedding, as did the presence of two young, vivacious granddaughters. And Nan, following in her father's footsteps, developed a love for the flower and planted many peonies in the yard of the home she and John bought on Erie Road in Rocky River.

We took the flowers home with us. We had been invited to a dinner party the next night, Saturday, at Brecksville friends, the Hoffmans. Mary Hoffman was one of Fran's bridge playing friends. The center piece from the night before was still beautiful and Fran asked Mary if she would like to have us bring it along for a dining table decoration. Mary said yes, so we took all the flowers with us and, Mary, who was quite a gardener, was very grateful. She later told Fran that they were still beautiful and usable a week later. Considering their treatment, I thought it was amazing.

I have fewer memories of our younger daughters, Kathy, born in 1950, and Barbara, born in 1953, but it was obvious from the start that the daughters had different personalities, and although children of the same parents and sharing the same upbringing, were individuals requiring different responses to their differing needs. Nancy was a tall girl and a leader, very intelligent, and did not want to be restrained; Kathy, was more outwardly affectionate and loved to be cuddled. I remember vividly the time she toddled over to her mother in the kitchen, and spontaneously, threw her arms around Fran's knees and exclaimed: "I wuv me mommy." Barbara was quieter and more introspective. It troubles me that I do not recall more incidents of the younger girls' childhood, or their college years and life as adults. One explanation that occurs to me is proximity: after college and marriage both Kathy and Barbara started their marriages far away in St. Louis and Columbus. Nan, on the other hand, spent her adult life in Cleveland, much closer to us, except for a post-graduate year in Ann Arbor with Paul.

I remember how hair-raising Kathy's birth was. After Fran's long labor with Nancy, I thought there would be ample time for the trip to the hospital. This was not the case. Fran's mother had come to Cleveland before the due date to help before and after the hospital stay. I took the bus to work as usual on what turned out to be "B" day. I had no sooner arrived at the office than Fran's mother called and said that I had better hurry home as Fran's contractions had started. Now I wished I had driven to work. I did not even take my coat off, rushed through the Taylor Bros. Department Store arcade, and was lucky to catch the No. 98 route bus to Parma and Ridgewood Drive, as it was pulling away from the bus-stop on Huron Road.

Even at that time of the day the trip took 45 minutes, which seemed interminable. I arrived to find Fran with her coat on and eager to leave. I helped her onto the back seat; and we started off for Lakewood Hospital another 45 minutes away. Every corner turned, every bump felt, brought forth groans and yelps of pain. At one point as we were nearing Lakewood, I noticed a fire engine and asked Fran if she wanted me to stop for help. She said, "For God's sake, NO. Just get me to the hospital!" A few minutes later we arrived at the Emergency entrance to the hospital and I rushed in to get help. Nurses brought out a gurney. When we got to the car, Fran announced that her "water" had just broken, which flooded the back seat and ruined her favorite winter coat. I went to park the car as she was being wheeled into the hospital. When I returned to the hospital less than ten minutes later, I was taken up to the maternity ward where Dr. Wylie, Fran's obstetrician, awaited to present our newborn second child to me, who had been delivered while I was parking the car. As all babies are, she was adorable, and unlike Nancy, had a full head of hair. From the very beginning she was a happy child, plump, cuddly, loved to be held and had an infectious smile. She was easygoing and very photogenic; it is a shame that better cameras were not available yet in 1950, because many, many photo opportunities were missed. We named her Kathy Ann; and I loved her happy approach to life.

My memories of Barbara's arrival are much more sketchy; same doctor and same hospital, and lots of beautiful red hair when she was born, which I reported to her mother as being "orange" before the nurses brought the child for her to hold for the first time .The moment she first saw her, Fran loved the color of her hair. Of course, my perception of anything in the red spectrum would be flawed due to my colorblindness. My mother had always wanted to have a red-haired grandchild and missed her opportunity by only a few weeks, having died in August before Barbara's arrival the first week in October of 1953.

My memories of Barbara's first few months are not happy ones because she cried incessantly and was obviously in great discomfort and we did not know how to help her. She had difficulty in digesting milk and suffered from severe gas bloating. Her little tummy was as hard as a basketball constantly and must have been extremely painful. We experimented with all the different varieties of milk that we could think of. Nothing helped. At one point I drove to Berea to a goat farm on Bagley Road to buy unpasteurized fresh goat milk. This only eased her discomfort for a few days but provided a clue. We still took turns jiggling her bassinette every night in a half-awake state until she could finally fall asleep.

I don't remember how I learned of it, but I discovered powdered goat's milk, which was very expensive, and came in cans in a health food store in the Old Arcade, which was only a short distance from our office. This had to be reconstituted with distilled water, fed by bottle, and seemed to give Barbara some relief. As I recall, when she was about six-months-old, her stomach apparently started producing sufficient digestive juices that she could finally digest milk and the swelling in her tummy subsided and she started to sleep the night through. It was a great relief for her, and for us, too, seeing her happy and comfortable at last and we were able to get a good night's sleep again.

Barbara was different from her older sisters, growing up in their shadows, quieter, and winsome. Her red hair was beautiful and drew comments from strangers constantly. She was obviously very intelligent, well behaved and a quick learner, but had trouble with her schoolwork. Fran drove her to a tutoring company on Brecksville Road for help in reading and math after school two or three times a week. It wasn't until her high school years when her academic advisor, the football coach Mr. Vadini, a very fine coach, very male oriented more attuned to boy's problems, questioned Barbara's even attending college. He questioned her chances of success, if she did. This was when we discovered that she suffered from dyslexia, which explained the cause of many of her problems, and her lack of interest in reading which was difficult for her.

There was never any question of her going away to college. She elected to attend Indiana University, an indication of her spirit of independence. She chose to break a family tradition and not follow in the footsteps of her sisters, who both followed their mother to the University of Michigan and where her grandparents had received degrees.

I remember how pleased I was at her selection. Indiana University had a reputation as a conservative institution in a conservative state at that time. I would have been worried had she chosen the University of Wisconsin or even the University of Michigan. This was the era of student activism, of the SDS (Students for a Democratic Society.) Furthermore, the President of the University was one of my Japanese language Army friends, Joe Sutton. The only drawback was the distance: Ann Arbor was a three-hour drive; Bloomington, Indiana, was eight to ten hours.

I still remember the shiver I felt when Kathy called us one night during her sophomore year to ask for our permission to accept an invitation from a classmate on her floor at the dorm to spend a week in Montreal where the girl's brother lived. The girl was very active in the SDS and was black. Kathy faced the problem every morning of whom she could speak to the rest of the day. Her roommate, Sandy Smith, from Kalamazoo, who was the younger sister of Nancy's sorority sister, was very conservative. If Kathy said hello to the black girl, Sandy would not speak to her the rest of the day. And vice versa. Kathy had told us about this situation earlier, and it was hard for her to tiptoe such a fine line every day at a time when she was adjusting to the demands of college level studies.

As I recall, we equivocated: we would get back to her; there were a lot of considerations; was her passport still valid; where was it, etc. We didn't know what to do. I only knew I did not want to have my daughter spend a week in a foreign country with a radical black family. We quickly contacted Tides Inn, a very fine resort hotel at the mouth of the Rappahannock River in Virginia where we had stayed once or twice and found that we could get a reservation for three people the same weekend as the proposed Montreal trip. We concocted a story that we had been talking about a trip with Kathy all to ourselves for a week, to this elegant hotel where they had a sunset cruise on a converted Canadian naval ship, and cookies and milk on the way to bed every night, and then a side trip to Williamsburg, and she could decide which trip she would prefer..

Fran called Kathy to tell her of this plan, and Kathy was thrilled to go with us, and it was a wonderful experience. One that I will never forget. And a great relief. I do not remember the resolution of Kathy's problem of choosing up sides every morning, but it resolved itself when she pledged the Pi Phi sorority her sophomore year, following her sister's lead. Her relationship with her roommate, Sandy, remained strong and we visited her and her family at their summer cottage on Gull Lake, Michigan, for a week's vacation, twice.

Kathy's experience with radical activists who were tolerated by the school authorities helps explain why I was so comfortable with Barbara's choice.

I remember Barbara's otherwise happy time at Indiana University, being marred by the presence of her cousin, Debby, my brother Russ's daughter on the same campus. They had been good buddies through their high school years and gone back and forth to play although it was not easy because of the distance between Lakewood and Brecksville. I don't remember Debby ever sleeping over at our house, although Barbara assures me that the two girls spent most weekends sleeping over at one or the other's house. My memory is blank about this and I wonder how the transportation problem was solved. In her senior year of high school, Barbara was invited to accompany Debby and her family on a driving trip through Europe celebrating Russ and Dot's 25th Wedding Anniversary, where they planned to visit places where Russ had served in World War II.

The cousins lived on different floors in the same dormitory freshman year, but with her Christian Science background, Debby, or her parents, realized after the first year that the big college atmosphere was not right for Debby and she did not return.

One of my most powerful memories of Barbara as a college student is of her return home for the Christmas break after having been away, on her own, for what seemed like forever. She had elected to major in Journalism, which seemed a little strange then but now, knowing of her dyslexia, makes perfect sense. An English major, which gave me such pleasure in my days at Yale, would have required far too much reading for her to struggle through. She brought home with her several journalism article assignments she had written, and I was absolutely astounded at the quality of her writing, this from a child who had done as little reading as possible all through her school years. Where did she learn the style, the use of an extended vocabulary, the felicity of her phrasing? I could not get over it. I only hope those papers have been saved. They were amazing. I wish Coach Vadini could have read them.

We did not make the long trip to Bloomington very often. The first time was for orientation and to get her installed in her dormitory room. I recall stopping in Centerville, Ohio, overnight to stay with friends from Camp Michigania, Jim and Doris Abby, whose daughter, Lynn, was also starting her freshman year at I.U. Jim was an insurance agent and took us to see a client's orchid greenhouse that he had insured. It was a case of a hobby that had grown into a business. The greenhouse was built specifically for orchid growing and had programmed heat and humidity controls and was very impressive. It was obviously successful because the orchids were in full bloom and very beautiful.

My memories of other visits to Bloomington are hazy. I think we went to visit Barbara her sophomore year for Parent's Day, leaving about 4:30 on a Friday afternoon after work. The route was easy driving, interstate highways almost all the way: 1-71 to Columbus; 1-70 though Springfield and Dayton to Indianapolis, then leaving the Interstates on the more dangerous two-lane road, Route 64 through Martinsville, Indiana, to Bloomington. It was an eight-hour drive, which meant sleeping in a motel overnight and the natural stopping point, about half-way, was Richmond, Indiana, which is just west of the Ohio border. I remember a large manufacturer of school busses on the south side of the road with a parking lot full of yellow school busses waiting to be delivered and finding a tearoom type restaurant for dinner.

I remember how impressed I was with the campus, one of the most beautiful I have ever seen. The contrast with the Yale campus, crowded and essentially built around the Public Square of a downtown business district is striking. Indiana University was situated in a natural setting; spacious, with many beautiful buildings, mostly built with Indiana sandstone, which has a distinctive shade of beige, seen everywhere in the state.

I do not remember very much about Barbara's sorority house, Alpha Gamma Delta, except that it looked impressive and yet welcoming at the same time. It was located on fraternity row on the edge of campus. It surprises me that I do not have more specific memories of Bloomington compared to my memories of Ann Arbor, which we visited far more often. I do not remember how Barbara entertained us, where we had dinner, or what planned entertainment there was for celebrating Parent's Day. I think we spent the Saturday afternoon, a warm sunny day, at a small town nearby in Brown County, which was filled with antique and souvenir shops and crowds of people. I do remember that we left Sunday for Brecksville after lunch with Barbara and drove all the way home without stopping so I could report in to work on time Monday morning.

Kathy joined Barbara at IU for her graduate work in Library Science after her graduation from the University of Michigan and this is where she met her future husband, Stephen Kershner, who was also seeking his graduate degree in Library Science. So, we had reasons to make more than one trip to Bloomington. On two occasion as I recall, we stopped over with Irv and Phyllis Burstadt, the parents of Nancy's husband, who had been moved to Indianapolis by Westinghouse. Their basementless ranch type house was different from the house they had in Beverly Hills, Michigan, where we first met them. It was in a good neighborhood and I remember taking a walk before dinner with Irv, who had had by-pass heart surgery a few weeks before we arrived. Irv was one of the first children in the U.S. to be diagnosed with diabetes, which I believe made his surgery more than just routine. This was my first experience with a survivor of a heart attack and it was alarming to see him sitting in an easy chair, pressing a pillow firmly to his chest in case he sneezed or coughed, which might have broken stitches (not true I learned later from personal experience.) As we went for a walk in the neighborhood, he walked very slowly and gingerly. On our stroll Irv pointed out the home of a famous NBA basketball star who had a home a few streets away. One other memory is that every time we drove through Martinsville, I thought of one of our early bridge club couple friends, Paul and Marge Hacker. Marge came from Martinsville. I recall feeling that being able to break up our long trip to Bloomington by staying with friends/relatives made the long trip much more palatable.

Barbara's graduation and her relationship with Kathy who was on the same campus at the time are a blur to me. The one memory that persists is packing the car with all her belongings and the long trip to Brecksville, with no stop overnight, driving our car with Barbara and Kathy following in Kathy's Opel; finally reaching the 1-271 shortcut in Ohio, and stopping at a state rest area. I think we got home well after mid-night after a grueling trip.

My recollection is that, after her graduation, Barbara lived with us for a time while searching for a job. She was discouraged with her search as the days dragged by. I do not recall if she looked into job opportunities at our local newspapers, or Penton Publishing, but at some point she looked into banking which was not surprising considering her father's occupation, and that was where she found her first job. I remember lying in bed, unable to go to sleep, until I heard the front door open and knew that she was safely home from a date. I don't think she ever brought a young man in. I thought it strange that I never worried about her in that way while she was far away at college, but now that she was an adult, a college graduate, I worried as though she were a teenager.

I think her first job was with Central National Bank in the main office in downtown Cleveland. One of her duties was to prepare the corporate loge for entertaining favored customers at the Cleveland Cavalier's professional basketball team headquarters, located in Richfield, Ohio, in a large, freestanding building half-way between Cleveland and Akron. It had little to do with actual banking and I do not think she was ever allowed to see a game. But I suspect she felt it was a great way to get out of the office, just as I felt about my appraisal trips, which usually consumed half of a business day.

After she found a job, she found a place to live in Lakewood. As I recall, the first place was the downstairs flat of a two-family house on Harlan Avenue, west of Nicholson Avenue and just south of my junior high school, Emerson. All I remember is the location, north side of the street, middle of the block. While she was there, she invited us in for dinner. It may have been the first time she entertained as an adult.

Sometime after that she found an apartment on Clifton Boulevard in a "U" shaped building, on the second floor, and I remember going in one evening to do some repair work in the bathroom. This was a very convenient location for her getting to work. I think the bus line was No.51, reputed to be the fastest bus to get to downtown Cleveland on the west side. I think by this time she had changed jobs and gone to work for Society National Bank in the mortgage loan department (surprise, surprise) where the chairman of the board was my old high school friend, Maury Struchen, and Schmidt Mortgage Company had a working relationship, servicing the mortgage loans we originated for the bank.

The next step was Barbara meeting a young man named Peter Pappadakes at a party, their falling in love, and deciding to marry. I can't remember our first meeting him, whether Barbara brought him out to Brecksville, or invited us to a dinner she prepared at her apartment on Harlan Avenue in Lakewood.

I liked Pete immediately, detecting in him traits I associated with our only Greek customer, Jimmy Watson, who owned a small apartment building in Lakewood, which we financed. I always looked forward to his coming in to make his payments because of his sunny personality and his warmth.

Pete's parents insisted on a Greek Orthodox ceremony. I think they felt the children would not be truly married if the wedding was not performed in a Greek Orthodox Church, so, as parents of the bride, we deferred, feeling it would help Barbara be accepted in a foreign culture. But we did insist that the reception would not be held at the Pappadakes's church, St. Demetrius, in Rocky River. We would control the time of the wedding, the reception and luncheon afterward, which was held at the Cleveland Athletic Club in downtown Cleveland. A Saturday morning wedding was unheard of in Greek circles, but we persisted, probably establishing a precedent.

Originally the children had hoped for a Decoration Day date for the wedding, but had to settle for the week following, Saturday, June 7th. When this came about, I realized that peonies would be blooming, of which I had about 100 plants at the time. We prevailed on the florist, Michael's of Lakewood, whom we chose because of his work at the Struchen wedding we had attended earlier, to use our peonies exclusively for the flowers at both the wedding and the reception following. He had no experience with peonies and had never used them before and was highly dubious. But his arrangements for both the church and the reception were a huge success, and the Greek guests never forgot the flowers, and associated me with peonies thirty years later. I always wondered if Michael incorporated peonies in his repertoire for later arrangements; and was glad we had been so persistent.

After our two earlier weddings with the old, comfortable Episcopal service, the Greek ceremony was a mystery. The language was literally Greek, and the ritual totally different. We had not been given a program by the ushers so we could not tell at what precise moment in the ritual

Barbara and Pete officially became man and wife - was it while they processed around the altar? Nevertheless, it was ancient and beautiful.

The one thing I do remember is that James, Pete's father, who was sitting on the aisle across from us, was sobbing and snuffling throughout the entire ceremony. I actually leaned across to him and whispered, "For Heaven's sake, James, get control of yourself." He was a deeply emotional person, and I'm sure was worried about the future of the first of his sons to be married - and not to a Greek girl and not of the Greek faith.

After the ceremony I remember standing in the courtyard outside the entrance to the church in a reception line and then all departing for the luncheon reception party at the Cleveland Athletic Club in downtown Cleveland. Here the flowers were truly spectacular, and the whole party was enlivened by our two little granddaughters, Kathy's five and two-year-old daughters, Elizabeth and Katy, who were dancing with each other in all their excitement, stealing the show.

Michael, the florist, had erected an arched arbor opposite the entry to the lounge area outside the dining room and we have a photo of the smiling newlyweds looking at the guests as they arrived, beaming over two beautiful large baskets of peonies. It was a very happy occasion for me. I don't remember the menu. I think Fran had decided on a small basket containing a live African violet plant for the center pieces. The Club was closed weekends the month of June, and I felt the flowers would be wasted if left there, so I asked the Manager if we could invite the guests to take a blossom home with them. He agreed and all the arrangements quickly disappeared. One of our friends from the East side, Bill Kraus, got lost between the church in Rocky River and the CAC, a wrong turn, and my bridge playing friend, Bill Braman, was simply late, arriving just in time to sit down; he warned us that he dodged some rain drops on the way in, and that a storm was approaching.

There was a violent storm, but it dissipated before we had to leave to return to Brecksville where we had invited the family and all of the out-of-town guests to join us for the evening. We did not want them to be stranded in a strange city before leaving for home the next morning. Many unexpected local Greek guests arrived, very welcome, of course, and they all came bearing gifts - we were not wary at all - and I never saw so many silver trays of *baklava* in my life. I didn't count but think the total number of people who attended was about 70, and I remember a feeling of pride that the house we had planned and built functioned so well.

I remember seeing and listening to Barb and several of her sorority sisters standing close together, arms around each other, quietly singing sorority songs in front of the tokonoma in the dining room, which was emotional for me. Also, watching Pete's grandmother, Yaya, who had emigrated to America 50 years earlier  sitting in the middle of the sofa in the living room like a queen, observing all the comings and goings. It was a wonderful party, as were all of the post wedding parties, and I felt sad and frustrated to see it come to an end. There had simply not been enough time to spend with our friends individually.

Both Fran and I had been concerned from the beginning about the danger to the marriage that could come from Pete's mother's attempts to control their lives. She was very forceful and a real estate agent. My attorney who had dealt with her said she was the most intelligent businesswoman he had ever met. But above all she was a mother. Before the wedding she had already picked out a house for the children to buy, located on W. 104th Street, between Clifton Boulevard and Baltic Road, in an older section of Cleveland's West side, which had been developed in the 1890's. The houses were still well kept-up but were a generation older than what I grew up in Lakewood, and while close to downtown and public transportation, would require increasing maintenance. I thought the idea was totally inappropriate and unacceptable. So did Barbara.

At that time, I owned two large apartment properties with 304 units in Columbus, Ohio, and there were always a fair number of vacancies. I took it upon myself to investigate and found that Pete could transfer the credits he had earned from courses he had taken at Cleveland College to Ohio State University without the loss of any credits. Society National, where Barbara was working had a branch in Columbus, and theoretically, she could transfer her job. So, our proposal/suggestion to the newly married couple was that they start their marriage in Columbus, 120 miles away from either set of parents: Barbara was to find a job in Columbus and Pete was to enroll at Ohio State, and as long as he attended classes and until he graduated, they could live rent free in one of my vacant apartments.

This worked out well although there was no job available at Society National. After a misfire at Buckeye Federal, whose Chairman I had known when he was with Union Bank of Commerce in Cleveland, and whose S&L had arranged the FHA financing for my Columbus apartment projects, she eventually found a job at Huntington Bank, which supported them while Pete finished his education. I remember reading a paper he wrote about insurance finance, and how impressed I was with it, how well-written it was, and after getting his degree, he did indeed, go into the insurance business.

At some point after his early learning experiences in the insurance business, he found a job with State Farm and was moved to Cincinnati to head their Claims office. Barb's boss, whose name was Starbucks, was able to arrange for Barb to do her job at home in Cincinnati with a weekly trip back to Columbus. I think by this time several challenges had been successfully met and the marriage was well under way.

I remember vaguely that their first apartment was on the west side of Tamarack Road where 80 of the 240 units were located, and where we had a suite, also, for the business trips I had to take every month to inspect the properties. I remember that at least once, Fran accompanied me, and we saw the children, but I do not remember anything about the suite they lived in. After Pete's graduation they moved to another apartment project, and I remember visiting them there, but not any details. I think it was an English basement type suite, and they may have had the first of their many cats.

I do remember stopping to visit them in Cincinnati on our trip home from Florida for the summer. We stayed at a motel in Lexington, Kentucky, and the next morning drove about 50 miles southwest to Pleasant Hill, a Shaker community, had lunch, toured the grounds and buildings and heard a hymn singing performance which was most interesting. It was a side trip well worth taking.

We timed our leaving Pleasant Hill, using the Interstate round-about Cincinnati to arrive at Barb and Pete's house (no more apartment living) after their workday. I do not remember the house very well except that it was in a newer subdivision and there were no trees, and I do not recall where we ate.

The next day, Saturday, we drove down the hill on I-71 to downtown Cincinnati, which we had driven through many times before on our way to Florida, but never stopped to visit. I remember passing a large General Electric manufacturing plant, where one of our Brecksville bridge club member's son, Bill Cullers, worked in management. This was our first tour of the city. All I remember is Fountain Square and an interesting department store, The Parisian. It seemed to me then that Cincinnati had much more "character" than Columbus, and still does.

I remember Barb and Pete taking us to a famous restaurant located in the oldest hotel in the State of Ohio, The Golden Lamb in Lebanon, about 25 miles northeast of Cincinnati for dinner. After an excellent meal, we were shown the private dining rooms and the bedrooms on the upper floors, where several presidents and many other famous people ate and slept. It was a memorable evening.

I have many memories of Kathy's wedding, also. Her marriage took place in August, so there were no peonies involved. There were a few other mundane details that needed to be attended to: St. Matthews had finally been able to replace the folding chairs used for services in the early years with real, wooden pews. They arrived the Wednesday before Kathy's wedding and our whole family went to the church after dinner and helped unload the pews, which were a huge improvement, from the truck and arrange them in the sanctuary. At last it looked like a real church, and just in time.

I was also very aware that all the upper glass above the entrance was grimy and needed to be washed. I elected to take my equipment for washing the windows at home down to the church and do the job myself. Washing the glass above the entrance to the church, which was essentially a large "A" frame structure, involved climbing a ladder to reach the roof of the portico over the doors, and then use my improvised aluminum extension tubing on which the brush and squeegee were attached and which extended my reach about 12' to do the washing. This was easy to do when standing on level ground at home, but not so easy at the church in such a restricted area, standing on a level (thankfully) 4' x 6" portico, 10' above the ground. Today, looking back, I must have been crazy to take such a risk. The job did get done, and I was grateful when it was finished and that I had suffered no mishaps. It may not have been as well done as by a professional, but I thought it was a big improvement. And Kathy would not have to be ashamed of her church.

On the day of the wedding, which was scheduled for mid-afternoon, with a reception to follow in downtown Cleveland at the University Club, the women went off to the hairdressers to get their hair done and while they were gone I decided to clean up the floating algae which had accumulated on the surface of the pond at the shallow south end. Where the pond was less than four feet deep and the sunlight could penetrate to the muddy bottom, a form of algae grew and formed a crust. Gasses would develop, trapped under the crust of algae, eventually the gas would expand, and patches of the algae would pop up onto the surface and accumulate at the edge of the pond. At first, I thought this would make a good form of mulch, but when applied around plants it dried into a hard crust, which repelled rainwater rather than conserving it and it was unsightly.

To get at the algae I had to squat on the downside of the dam close to the surface of the water, bracing myself with my toes, and use my pond skimmer to scoop the algae off the surface and spill it into my wheelbarrow and then, when it was full, spill it over the hill. It was hard work and after an hour of this activity, I could feel my thigh muscles tightening up and it was hard to regain my feet. In addition, it was a hot, sunny day. I was in my work clothes, hot and sweaty.

It was at this point, unexpectedly, that a large mobile home came up the driveway, which was filled with the groom's family, the Kershners, who wanted to be sure how to find the house in the dark after the reception, and to inspect the house, which I am sure Stephen had described to them. They came over to see what I was doing, and then we went up to the house. My appearance was a far cry from that of the dignified, well-dressed host at the Rehearsal Dinner the night before which was held at Broglio's, one of our favorite eating places near the cloverleaf interchange on Brecksville Road in Independence. The only thing I remember about the dinner was Stephen's father, Bob, remarking that the roast beef was the best he had ever had.

I remember having some difficulty getting dressed in my rented morning coat, some problem getting tangled up in the suspenders, running out of time, and Fran being annoyed at having to help me. By now my right leg was stiffening seriously and I had some difficulty walking. The stiffness seemed to be increasing every minute.

I remember the contrast for Kathy, who, at Nancy's wedding had been the Maid of Honor and had to walk down the aisle on the white runner, having had an operation on her left knee six weeks prior and was fearful that she might fall, and, today having to worry about her father: would he make it to the altar to give her away? I walked by swinging my rigid right leg forward from the hip with each step, and was thinking of the painting of the drummer, the piccolo player and the flag-bearer at the head of one of George Washington's armies. It must have been quite a sight.

The ceremony was performed by William Wrenn, who came from Boston to officiate. The organist was Warren Berryman, my old instructor, who had played for our oldest daughter, Nancy's wedding. After we had christened the new pews, used for the first time, and mingled in front of the clean windows in front of the church, everyone drove to the University Club for the Reception dinner.

The University Club was housed in one of the dignified, old mansions on Euclid Avenue, east of E. 30th Street. It was a fine place to have a wedding reception and Kathy and Stephen's was a joyous affair. All went well until the main course was served at the sit-down dinner, which turned out to be beef stroganoff instead of the sirloin beef tips, which Fran had ordered when making the arrangements. No explanation was given for the switch. Fran was very upset because the stroganoff was not very good, and when it came time to settle the bill before we left for the post-reception party back in Brecksville, Fran voiced her complaints to the Manager. I don't remember whether any adjustment was made.

On the other hand, the post-reception party back in Brecksville was very successful. I think the groom's grandmother sat in the middle of the sofa in the living room in the same spot where Peter's grandmother, "Yaya," sat several years later, as the eldest member of the party, presiding over the festivities. I remember the warm feeling I had after the newlyweds left for their honeymoon and the other guests had departed. It was the kind of party that I wanted to never end. And, again, the few words spoken, the handshakes in the reception line, standing next to the bride after the ceremony was over could not take the place of real conversations with distant friends and relatives not seen for years. It was all over too soon; there was not enough time to spend with individuals. I remember having these same strong feelings of regret after each of our three weddings.

Stephen's first job as an Assistant Library Director was in Alton, Illinois, an old grain terminal town on the Mississippi River, about 20 miles north of St. Louis. I remember the shock we felt when Kathy called, only married four months, to tell us that Stephen had been attacked in his library by a deranged man wielding a butcher's knife, and while Stephen was trying to protect the other customers, he suffered a long slash on his left arm, which caused severe nerve damage. After recovery, he only regained partial use of the arm. Unfortunately, he is left-handed and this meant learning to write right handed for the rest of his life; fortunately, he had worked as a sheriff's deputy summers while in college, and this training may have saved his life. It was a terrible shock for Kathy, and a poor way to start married life.

I remember stopping off in Alton to visit the "children" on the way back to Ohio after calling on one of our insurance company lenders in Galveston, Texas. They were living in an old-fashioned house, converted to apartments, in a ground floor suite, which I thought was cramped and not in very good condition. I remember that Stephen had saved his old beat-up, overstuffed easy chair from his college days, and it was one of the few pieces of furniture they had. I can't remember if I stayed overnight and flew back to Cleveland the next day. It was long ago, and details are very hazy.

I don't remember the timing, but Kathy found a job as a Children's Librarian in St. Louis and sometime in their second year we visited them and got to see all the sights in Alton: the barges lined up to pass through the locks on the Mississippi, the campus of Principia, the Christian Science college nearby, and the Illinois River which enters the Mississippi just north of Alton. Kathy's job was at one of the smaller branch libraries on the north side of the city and she had to drive a long distance back and forth to work, crossing the Mississippi River. After all I had heard about the mighty Mississippi and having seen it while in Minneapolis in the Army at its headwaters, I was not that impressed. It was muddy and just didn't seem very mighty

I remember being concerned not only by Kathy's long drive to work over a very high, long, bridge but also because her library was in a predominately black neighborhood, and she was the only white employee at that branch. We visited her at work and met her manager who was very personable, and I felt somewhat reassured. We had lunch at an old and famous Italian restaurant. While we were there, we must have visited Fran's childhood friend, Julie (Slocum) Matthey who lived in Town & Country, a westerly suburb of St. Louis. The Mattheys came to Kathy's wedding, but I can't recall our visiting them while we were in the St. Louis, area. I can't imagine not seeing them.

I remember how excited we were when Kathy called after Stephen's recovery from his injury to say that he had taken a job with the Cuyahoga County Library System and his new job would be in charge of the library in Warrensville Heights, Ohio. Earlier, on a Saturday morning, Kathy had called and got us both on the line; I remember I was sitting on the side of our bed and she told us she was pregnant and the baby was due in July. We were both very excited, but Fran was the one who burst into tears. They were anxious to leave Alton with its ugly memories and were fortunate to find a position so much closer to family in Ohio. Fran set about trying to find an apartment for them and located a very modern one in the old section of Brecksville, where two members of St. Matthews, Lowell and Margot Kiester, and Noel Wynn, lived. When the time came to move, I flew to St. Louis on a Friday where Stephen picked me up, and we loaded a trailer hitched to his car and drove to Cleveland. It was a nice trip with two drivers spelling off each other. I remember stopping for dinner at a well-known restaurant in Effingham, Illinois, and then resuming the trip straight through to Brecksville, where two of Dianne Terry's five sons (she was a friend of Fran's from St. Matthews) were waiting to help us unload. I remember how excited Kathy and Stephen were with the newness and floor plan of their new home.

After a stint as the Branch Librarian at the Chagrin Falls Library, Stephen found a new job as Director of the Geauga County Library System, east of Cleveland. They bought a small Cape Cod house with detached garage in Chagrin Falls on the border of Geauga County. I remember going over on Saturday mornings to scrape the old peeling paint off so Stephen could paint it, yellow, as I recall. We did it by hand using scrapers. It was impossible to avoid patches of the original paint which adhered to the wood, so that when Stephen painted our finished prep-job he could not leave a smooth surface. It would have been much easier if we had been able to use a power sander.

It was a quiet neighborhood and our granddaughters, Elizabeth and Katy, had playmates nearby. There was a boy their age who lived on a side street whose backyard adjoined theirs. His father was an artist, and we had one of his paintings of the entrance to the cathedral in Rouen, France, which we had seen and I had taken many photo slides of on one of our vacations in France. We hung it in our house in the entry hall.

I do not remember ever appraising any homes in the city of Chagrin Falls, which was a very old early American community with a triangular town square, and many century homes. The Chagrin River, which flowed on its way to Lake Erie through the edge of the business district and was dammed to create the "falls" (about 8-10 feet high) was crossed on a bridge. I remember there was a famous ice cream shop on the west side of the street right next to the bridge. It was a favorite destination for weekend visitors. The city also had a high-end furniture store, Brewster & Stroud, on the square, and a psychiatric nursing home up the hill from the business district. This was an area that I felt I should take more interest in for business reasons, and I was glad that Kathy and Stephen had increased my exposure to it. Although I did not know it at the time, Chagrin Falls was the home of Tim Conway, the famous comedian on "The Carol Burnett Show" and of Bill Watterson, creator of the comic strip "Calvin and Hobbs."

One of my memories of this period was the Saturday we all visited the Geauga County Fair. I don't remember any rides, or entertainment, but it had a Midway which was lively and fun, and I do remember it was the first and only time I ever had "funnel" cake, which was delicious, but not very healthy.

After several years Stephen moved up the ladder and secured a position as Director of the Baldwin Memorial Library in Birmingham, Michigan. I remember how we wondered how we could cope with having the grandchildren so far away. We were very spoiled. The move was a big step forward in Stephen's career. The Baldwin Library was a large one, in a very high-end economic and social area. Birmingham was Detroit's suburban equivalent of Shaker Heights in Cleveland. They bought a sprawling, basementless house in Bloomfield Township on a large lot not far from Telegraph Road and the famous Oakland Hills Country Club. I remember continuing my tradition of buying a tree peony for the front yard of their new home. I think the blossom was purple and may have been named *Iphigenia*. We had already done this for Nancy when she bought her house in Rocky River with her second husband, John. There was a large backyard where I remember the family and friends gathered for a cookout after Elizabeth's graduation from high school. It was large enough that I could practice my golf chip shots. Again, Kathy was able to get a job in her specialty, Children's Librarian, nearby in the West Bloomfield system.

These were golden years as far as proximity was concerned. It was a short drive from Cleveland via the Ohio Turnpike to Detroit to visit Fran's childhood school friends, and Kathy, who had given us two granddaughters. We took advantage of this and visited as often as we could. I remember the "kick" I got out of traveling to a different city and, for a short time, sampling a different culture where the flavor was different from Cleveland. After a stifling childhood limited to Cleveland where all the relatives lived, and no one ever came from out-of-town to visit or stayed overnight in our house; it was always refreshing for me to experience some new place. It was a feeling that I never outgrew, an added dimension underlying the more obvious pleasure I felt from being in a different place. I always loved being a guest, or a host.

Both of our granddaughters, Elizabeth and Katy, were a joy and it was great privilege to be able to observe, and photograph their early years, while they lived in Chagrin Falls. I remember the perfect example of the kind of children they were, their character. Although I am somewhat shaky on the details, Elizabeth, then in high school in Birmingham, called us to enlist our help in a plot the two daughters had concocted to surprise their parents on their 20th wedding anniversary. Elizabeth was a senior, and Katy three years behind her, and their plan was to surprise their parents with a night in a downtown hotel, luxury room, lavish meal and bed clothes spread out on the bed, and a bottle of champagne to round off the occasion. The hotel reservation and dinner menu were not difficult to arrange, but they were not old enough to enter a liquor store to buy the champagne. Could we help? We did, glad to be a small part of their surprise. Kathy and Stephen were overwhelmed, and I have always thought the whole concept of such a celebration was remarkable for two teenagers. It made me very proud to be their grandfather and is one of my happiest memories.

Stephen ended his Michigan library career and moved on to be director of a smaller system north of Chicago until he became worried about the politics of funding public libraries in Illinois, and found a job as Director of the Pasco County system in Florida. Kathy found a position with the adjoining Hernando County library; for the first time in her library career she was not a children's librarian responsible for decorating the children's section, reading during story hour to three and four-year-old children, dealing with mommies looking for a free babysitter while they did their shopping. She now selected and purchased materials for the whole system, adults as well as children, and her hours were 9 to 5, no more evening hours or weekends.

They bought a house with a pool in a modest priced subdivision about midway between their two jobs on the Gulf coast in Weeki Wachee, about 50 miles north of Tampa. This was an easy two-hour drive from our condo in Bradenton, which made visiting easy.

I think their love of Florida started with their yearly visits to our first condo in Cortez (Bradenton) during the children's spring break. I remember visits to the beach where Stephen, who had a very fair complexion, deliberately acquired a horrendous sunburn every year (I thought it was very foolish) to display to the plebs back home in the dreary North.

Stephen loves horses so we spent an afternoon watching the white Lipizzaner horses practice their dressage formations and jumping in their winter quarters south of Sarasota. We had seen them perform in their royal quarters on our first trip to Vienna so we knew what to expect, but it was a first for Stephen who had a passion for horses dating from his early boyhood; there was the obligatory three day expedition to Disney World for the benefit of the grandchildren and all I remember is Katy's piteous complaints after the first day that her legs were too short, she was tired, and couldn't we go home to our swimming pool; and I remember, vividly, at the end of one visit while we were waiting for the departure of the flight back to Detroit, Stephen's back "went out" and he was in terrible pain and had to be helped into a wheel chair to get on the plane. I do not remember the outcome but imagine many trips to a chiropractor before his return to normal.

Memories of our three daughters coalesce into a picture of three wonderful, unique persons, each different in her own special way: Nancy, born teacher, linguist, and more athletic than her sisters, a leader; Kathy, loving, caring, talented seamstress and needle worker; and Barbara, analytical mind with a way with words put to good use in her business career. They came of age in troubling times of great social change without ever giving either parent a moment of worry. I give credit to Fran, who bore most of the daily responsibility for the children's care and training. And, I have told many people in my business world that they could learn more that was critical about me from spending an afternoon with my daughters than reading my credit report.

There will be many memories of Fran sprinkled elsewhere in other chapters, but there are one or two that give me pleasure very time I think of them. I remember what a thrill it was to live with a woman! After twenty five years of an all-male existence, to buy gifts for a girl, to observe the grooming rituals of a female, to observe the grace and charm when entertaining, to help her get dressed to go out, straightening the seams of her nylons, all these little things were new to me and the source of daily, little pleasures. I loved her sense of humor, perhaps intensified by living with my own quirky ways. I learned early on that Fran took me seriously, and when the right opportunity arose, I would tell her something in a grave manner, something that everyone knew was "true", and when she innocently accepted my outrageous statement, would give her the knowing wink, and she would say, "Oh, you," initially upset, than burst out laughing. She learned well from me.

A fine example: I remember coming home from work one evening when we were living on Ridgewood Drive, and Fran telling me that a man had come to the door selling cemetery lots. He had a lengthy spiel, which she listened to patiently, and when he was finished with his presentation, she told him in all seriousness, with a straight face, that we would not be interested. We were building a home on 12 acres of land in Brecksville and had already picked out the spot where we wanted to be buried, side by side, on our own land. The salesman sputtered and replied, "You can't do that. It's illegal in Ohio." Fran couldn't tell if he knew she was putting him on. I congratulated her and told her she had been living with me too long, already.

I remember her skill at planning and perpetrating surprise parties. The first time it happened to me was while we were living on Ridgewood Drive and I came home after work as usual. It was May 6th, my birthday. Fran met me at the door, handed me the newspaper and said dinner would be late. I assumed she had made some special, complicated recipe as a treat. It seemed to take a long time and when she finally called me to come to the table, I found it was set for four people. I happened to look out the small window on the front door and saw Bill Braman and Bill Carter waiting to come in, followed by Doyle Robbins, regular bridge playing friends. In a flash I realized that this was a surprise birthday party, something that had never happened to me before.

As I recall, the meal was spectacular, but I don't remember the outcome of the bridge game that followed. I don't think Fran was able to arrange for me to win. The children had been fed and stayed in their room, and Fran spent the evening in our bedroom reading. When the "boys" left, I thanked her for the most memorable birthday in my life, which was slightly bittersweet because her role in it has been almost like that of a servant. It was hardly the more typical couple getting all dressed up and going out to an expensive restaurant for dinner, which I think we did a day or so later, just the two of us. I never forgot it and can still see the faces of the two tall Bills through the window in the front door, waiting to come in.

Fran arranged an even more elaborate surprise for my 50th birthday. May 6, fell on a Saturday in 1971, which also happened to be our regular Brecksville Duplicate Bridge night and there was a problem because one of the couples was out of town. Therefore, I was surprised when our doorbell rang on Friday night about 9 p.m. - no one ever came to our door at that time of night - and looked out to see Bill and Ev Montgomery peering in. I assumed that Fran had called them in Grosse Pointe to come down to help me celebrate one of the big birthdays, my 50th, and, as a bonus, fill in for our missing couple at bridge. They played bridge but we never played with them when visiting in Michigan. I didn't think they enjoyed the game or were very experienced with Duplicate. So, after getting over the shock of seeing them, I babbled on about how good of them it was to come all this way to help me celebrate my birthday and how fortuitous it was since they could help us out as substitutes in our bridge game, and assured them they would like the other people. It was a very friendly game with no criticism of partners, or opponents. And off to bed they went in the guestroom downstairs.

Bridge on Saturday night was to be at the Adair's house on Oakwood Circle off Fitzwater Road in Brecksville. I paid no attention to the unusual number of cars parked in the driveway and street, had no idea of what was going on until we went in the front door and I saw Bill Braman standing in the living room. He was one of my bridge partners, but had no business being here, unless… suddenly I knew I was the guest of honor at another surprise party.

We actually didn't play any bridge that night, so the Montgomery's were not put to the test. But it was the start of a wonderful party with many friends, with lots of joking and good-natured teasing. It ended up in the basement recreation room where everyone sat around a couple of ping-pong tables with paper tablecloths. After eating, going around the circle and ending with Fran, presenting me with a card or small gift, all with small jokes or good-natured teasing. When it was Fran's turn, finally, she presented me with an album she had constructed over a period of months, working quietly in her bedroom while I was sleeping innocently next door. She couldn't believe that I had not heard her working, snipping away. She got her idea for the album from a regular meeting of a monthly book discussion group of seven or eight couples we were a part of in Lakewood. Books to be read the next month were proposed by individuals, while simple refreshments were being served after the discussion, and the criteria were the number of pages to be read, and the price of the proposed book, which was then voted on. It was a very intellectual group; it was far more fun choosing the book than reading it.

On this occasion the format was a little different. The meeting was on a Friday night at the home of Bob and Betty Carr on Webb Road in Lakewood north of Lake Avenue. When we entered the living room we were confronted with a pile of old magazines, blank albums, scissors and scotch tape. One of the couples was moving back to Pittsburgh and to keep alive the memories of the group, each couple was to use the magazines from the pile to cut out ads and cartoons, and paste them, into an album with their name on it. The album was to tell the story of their life using the cut-outs from the magazines. At the end of evening, Charlie and his wife would gather up the albums and take them with them to their new home in Pittsburgh and never forget us. I thought it was a very clever idea. All the other couples took their assignment very seriously and produced sober stories. Fran and I decided to have some fun and found ads and cartoons which told our story in a humorous way. Everyone thought we did a great job with our album. Years later I like to think it may have been the only album that recalled a true picture of the most interesting couple in the group.

With this background, Fran constructed a wonderful album, telling the story of the first 50 years of my life. It has baby photos, favorite photos of me on Tiedeman Road, in my college room, posing in my lifeguard bathing suit, in uniform in Fran's backyard in Detroit, at her Senior Prom, and many, many magazine ads and cartoons. Under each item, she pasted a typed caption, which gave a humorous explanation of the item above. It was a remarkable effort, and revealed her wonderful sense of humor in the telling of my story and at the same time a great deal of the reason for my great love of her: the time and effort spent, her love of me, her gentleness and her wit.

I think this album is my most prized possession. I check it out frequently, and every time marvel at it (some of the captions are coming loose). I was glad to have it displayed at my 90th and 95th birthday parties here at Pioneer Ridge. I wanted the children in the family to see a side of their mother and grandmother they might not have suspected, and for the new friends here at Pioneer Ridge, who never had a chance to know her, to see how blessed I was and what they missed.

Over the span of sixty-nine years of marriage a tremendous number of memories accumulated; the ones associated with our daily routines are blurred and the highlight memories are quirky. In our early days, I remember when visiting Fran's mother, the many times she treated us to dinner at the Women's City Club in the downtown business district of Detroit, not far from the great department store, Hudsons. The food at the club was outstanding, and the club published a cookbook with many of their landmark recipes. Fran bought one and used it; or, perhaps, Fran's mother gave her a copy. It is still in Fran's cookbook library. My recollections of the Club are of wonderful meals and bringing home their famous cinnamon rolls. After all, I had been living on Army chow for a long time. One nice feature of the Club was a 20 yard swimming pool, but I never saw it or swam in it. I combine memories of the City Club with the nearby Sanders shop and bringing home their wonderful coffee cake and famous fudge sauce.

At that time Fran's mother lived at 2254 Calvert Avenue in a two bedroom flat on the second floor and shared expenses with an old college friend, Aunt Kate, who was a prickly roommate in some respects, austere and overbearing. But the sharing of housing expense was the only way Fran's mother could provide a decent home for Fran, since her income was so limited. Aunt Kate seemed to like me and I remember one Saturday morning she invited me to go on a ride with her and we drove some distance to a large cemetery, White Haven, where she showed me her gravesite. I remember thinking this was little unusual. She was a grammar schoolteacher in one of the poor neighborhoods in Detroit, and nearing retirement.

I recall how hard it was for me to get used to Fran's mother's and Fran's shopping habits which were so different from my mother's. In my family when clothing or a gift was bought and brought home, it was expected that it was final; we were expected to like it and wear it! We never took anything back, even if we didn't like the item. In Detroit however, clothing, especially, was paid for, brought home, tried on in the home setting, and as likely as not, nine times out of ten, would be returned to the store for credit. And the search would go on for something more suitable, or reasonable. It took a little getting used to and I remember accompanying Fran many times to return something to Hudsons, or Himmelhoch's, or Siegals, or Russeks, all high-class merchants.

One of Fran's mother's favorite shops was Kay Cooley's. I remember being with Fran when she picked out one of her favorite dresses, designed by Claire McCardle. It had a light background and dark brown lines which formed a geometric six-inch cross-hatching. It was very smart and led to finding a new pair of shoes. I remember the amount of time we spent looking for a pair of real alligator high heel pumps; every girl had to possess a pair of alligator pumps in those days to be *au courant*. Fran was hard to fit, had a very high arch, and her left foot was a half-size larger than her right foot. She allowed me to help selecting her shoes, which I enjoyed very much. I think she agreed that this was one department where my taste was better than hers.

Often, Fran's mother, as a gift, would send Fran downtown to find something Fran needed with a limit on how much she could spend. Fran would find something, bring it home, and she and her mother would decide if it was "right." If not, back to the store it went. It was fortunate that the house on Calvert was only a block from the streetcar line on Second Avenue, and such a short distance to downtown because there were many such trips.

I remember one of Fran's mother's little tricks: she would go shopping and find something plausible for herself, I recall one very expensive brown wool suit from Himmelhoch's which was very stylish which she bought and brought home. When she tried it on for Fran's approval, it was obvious it was a style for a much younger woman (she was in her 70s at the time) and did not look good on her at all, and she was well aware of it. So, not for the first time, she had Fran try it on and it was perfect fit and very becoming. Thereupon, she would say we'll keep it and it'll be yours. She used this little ploy many times. It was fortunate for Fran they were both the same size.

I remember Fran telling me that Kay Cooley, the owner of their favorite dress shop, once suggested that Fran's mother come and work for her as a salesperson. It would have been a good occupation for Fran's mother, who had impeccable taste. Being of her generation and upper class, she was totally unprepared to support herself. She was easy to talk to and was trained to love entertaining, music, sewing and art. She decided against it and nothing ever came of it. I thought it was a sign of the kind of relationship they had with Kay Cooley: they were more than just good customers. Grandma Thompson's generosity was also evident in her deep love for her only daughter and her grandchildren. The closeness, which I observed was wonderful. And beautiful.

I remember how generous Grandma Thompson was with me, especially at Christmas time. She gave me gifts of the quality I had always yearned for and would never dream of buying for myself.

One Christmas she gave me a dress shirt from Saks Fifth Avenue which was a light blue with French cuffs, monogrammed, and felt like silk. It was so nice I didn't dare wear it. She also had wonderful taste in cuff links, and I acquired quite a collection over the years. I also remember the first custom-made suit I ever owned. I think the occasion was one of my birthdays. I went to Slavin Tailors at Euclid Avenue at E. 6th Street to be measured and fitted and select the fabric. As I recall, it was a brown wool tweed, three-piece. And it was so well made that I got tired of it because I wore it so much and it never wore out.

This led to our first business dealings with the Slavin brothers; there were three of them, Louis, Max and Ben, all in business together. In addition to their original military officers' uniform business, and, after the war years, men's custom tailoring, they also invested in real estate. They may have liked doing business with us because we were a family business - father and four sons - and our offices were only a short distance away on E. 6th Street. The oldest brother, Louis, asked me at one of my fittings if we made commercial mortgages and I said, "Yes." He said they might be looking for a piece of real estate to buy. When I got back to our office, I told my father of this conversation, and he couldn't believe I hadn't asked how much money they had to invest. He was very upset with me. In my defense, where I came from (Yale), one did not ask intrusive personal questions like how much do you earn a year, or how much money is in your bank account of virtual strangers, or especially, family. Louis came to our office and sat down with Dad and we learned they had $500,000 to invest, a large amount at that time. They found a shopping center for sale located on Euclid Avenue in East Cleveland east of Monticello Boulevard, and we financed the purchase. It's hard to foresee what a gift may do for you.

I remember how grateful and pleased I was with the way our social life developed. When we started our marriage in the apartment in Lakewood after the war, Fran was coming to a new city and knew no one. I had been away from Lakewood, effectively, for seven years, at school and in the Army. I had never had many friends while in high school and by the time I returned to Lakewood, the few I had known had scattered. We did meet a couple, the Hubert Schmidts, in our apartment building and I did run into an old member of the high school marching band, Bruce Hardy, who was two or three years older than me. This could hardly be called a circle of friends.

I now began to appreciate the value of membership in a fraternity, which had been touted when I considered joining one of the fraternities at Yale: the instant network of friends, no matter where one was located. Fran was a member of the Gamma Phi Beta sorority at the University of Michigan, where I met her. There was a Gamma Phi alumnae group in greater Cleveland, and through her attendance at their meetings, we found a true circle of friends; young couples, about our age, just starting out after the war, starting their families, buying homes, starting their first jobs, and, in those days all the wives were at home being homemakers. The wives arranged the dinner parties, and the entertainment, bridge games or movies, all with the same limited budget.

This was the source of what became a circle of friends. The women organized a monthly "potluck" dinner bridge group, which met on a Friday after work at one of the homes. The host was responsible for the meat course and the beverages, and after eating the bridge game began. There were the Trebbes, BJ & Bob; the Cuntrymans, Ralph & Jean; the Hurdlebrinks, Mike & Peg; the Hendricksons, Bob & Helen; the Wadleighs; Lee & Hope; the Moores, Barb & Tom; and my brother Ken and his wife, Pat. I remember looking forward to our meetings; they were the highlight of the month.

I remember in the early days of our social life Fran pleading with me to be able to serve alcohol. At first, I refused because of the rigid teachings of Christian Science. I could not drink alcohol in any form and even having it in the house would be abhorrent. This was ingrained in my thinking from my early childhood onwards where there had never been even a bottle of beer in our house. At Yale it was a different story. There the drinking was very heavy and nothing I observed made it attractive. Freshman year one of the members of the swimming team who lived in our entry came home, after an end-of-the season victory celebration, drunk, unable to climb the stairs to the 3rd floor unassisted, covering the floor of the shower room with vomit, the odor, ugh! It was quite a spectacle for a young teetotaler from Lakewood, Ohio. I also remember vividly, one of the upper classmen from St. Louis living in our entry at Pierson College, always impeccably dressed in a three piece pin striped, expensive, suit going to dinner just before the doors closed at 7 p.m. with two of his friends who lived on the ground floor of our entry. They were Junior Phi Beta Kappa's: one the son of the Episcopal Bishop of Washington, D.C., the other, later in charge of the China Desk in the State Department; all heavy drinkers, but brilliant. Half way to the dining hall, in the twilight, our friend from St. Louis, tripped on the flagstone paving pieces of the walkway, bruising himself and ripping a large hole in one of his trouser legs at the knee, ruining his suit. These were examples that reinforced my feelings that drinking was not for me. I could not square what I observed, with an increase of happiness, or giving up control of one's behavior.

This was the easiest of all the Christian Science disciplines for me to follow; observing it did not make me feel virtuous; it was something accepted by society that was forbidden to me. Besides, I was aware that my great-uncle Bob was an abusive drunk and I had heard whispers that he beat his wife, Aunt Dorothy. I knew just enough of Mendel's genetics to be aware of genes skipping generations, and I did not dare take a chance on a behavior which could be addictive and affect the workings of my mind.

I remember Fran, whose family background was so different from mine and her experience at the University of Michigan preparing her for acceptance of drinking at social occasions, bringing up the subject and voicing her concern that if I could not learn to accept having liquor in our home and serving it to our guests, we would isolate ourselves and be excluded socially. Any friends we might make would not feel welcome or accept our invitations. It was a very hard decision for me to make, compromising and betraying a lifetime of training, but finally, realizing that I was not responsible for other's behavior. I agreed so long as I was not required to participate, and if she felt that we had something to serve, and one of us was participating, that would suffice.

I still remember the strange sensation I felt when I bought my first six pack of beer and brought it home. Later, wines and whiskeys were added to the array. I then determined that although I could not be part of the crowd, guests in my home would be treated to the finest brands on the market -

one extreme to the other. Names that come to mind are Tuborg Beer from Denmark, J&B and Cutty Sark Scotch, Canadian Club, Old Grand Dad Bourbon, Jack Daniels, Noilly Prat Vermouth, Harvey's Bristol Cream Sherry, and B&B and other Liqueurs for after dinner drinks. I also remember having to buy a copy of Stouffers Recipe Book for Mixing Drinks. I always felt slightly ridiculous when filling an order to have to refer to a recipe so as not to disappoint a guest or offer him something undrinkable.

One of the duties of the host at the monthly Gamma Phi potluck dinner/bridge meetings was to serve a mystery cocktail and have the guests try to guess the ingredients in the concoction. On one of these regular meetings at our house, I was pretty sure I could stump Mike Hurdlebrink and Bob Hendrickson, both experienced drinkers, if not connoisseurs. I had found a recipe in my trusty Stouffers recipe book for a "Jack Frost" cocktail, which had as its main ingredients Calvados, a French apple brandy, and maple syrup, with lemon juice and crushed ice, "shaken, not stirred". I measured out each ingredient very carefully and remember vividly standing in our living room and passing around the drinks and waiting for the guessing to begin. No one could guess the magic ingredient, which was the maple syrup, but all agreed it was very tasty and I could serve it again at the next gathering. It was a triumph, and, I thought, very ironic.

A few more comments on the subject of drinking, and I promise not to mention it again. I always found it very objectionable for us to be greeted at the door by the host with a drink in hand for the wife, always the wife, urging it on her, before she even had her coat off. It seemed to me to be carrying hospitality a bit far and many wives were intimidated and accepted. I also always had a slight feeling of resentment at the thought that my presence was not sufficient in itself, but that I had to be "loosened up" a little before my company was tolerable. I'm sure my being the only non-drinker made it awkward for the host, who did want me to have an enjoyable time while under his roof.

I remember one of the meetings of the Brecksville Duplicate Bridge group at the Sutherland's home. Probably a little more alcohol had been consumed than usual during the meal, and there was more than the usual silliness and disputation after the meal, so I left the table and went up to the living room to shuffle the cards and set up the boards for the game. One of the wives, Win Culler, who was a lovely, gentle person came up to join me as I was finishing my chores, and asked me how I could put up with such a group. As I recall I replied that they were all that I had. I really had very little choice in the matter. It seemed that all the people I could call "friend" were at that table, and that I was lonely.

Other than my parents, my brother Russell and his family, my Grandma Schmidt and Aunt Clara, the Geigers, my old friend Maury Struchen, Chairman of the Society National Bank, were the only other people in my lifetime that I knew who did not drink. My father was very awkward in social gatherings such as Mortgage Bankers' banquets or conventions, where he would announce in a loud, clear voice that the did not "use" alcohol, when offered a drink. It took some persuasion on my part to point out to him he should simply get a tall glass of ginger ale and no one could tell what he was drinking and if he already had a glass in his hand, no one would offer him a drink. I always knew that an Ivy League education would pay off.

The two occasions when I tasted alcohol (not the same as drinking it) happened in Wichita, Kansas, at the Petroleum Club when, before going in to dinner, a group of eight or ten of the principals in the purchase of two oil wells for which I had secured the financing were celebrating the closing which was to take place the next day. Elden Papke, who became one of my closest post-war friends, ordered drinks all around and ordered a "Horses Neck" for me, which can be made with or without bourbon whiskey. Unfortunately, since all the other drinks contained alcohol, so did mine, which I did not discover until I tasted it. Elden was aware of the strange look on my face and knew immediately what had happened; called the waiter over, apologized to me, reordered and no harm was done. Religious indoctrination, or not, I really disliked the taste.

Another time I recall unexpectedly tasting alcohol was after our daughter Nancy's wedding. The bridge group friends were given a key to the house and preceded us after the reception at the University Club while the wedding party photos were being taken. They couldn't find the champagne flutes (which were sitting on the back seat of Nancy's V.W. at the head of the driveway in preparation for their honey-moon getaway) and ransacked our cupboards to find every juice glass in the house. I was standing in the kitchen before joining the others and picked up one of the glasses, thinking it was gingerale, and knew instantly from the taste I had made a mistake. I knew about the cult of champagne, the great names and the great vintages, but thought the actual taste was terrible and, luckily, was in the kitchen so I could spit it out

The last recollection is gathering together at the Sutherlands for dinner and bridge to celebrate New Year's Eve which fell on a Saturday night one year. We had grown old enough that going out to a restaurant to eat didn't seem as important to any of us as when we were younger, and then returning to one of our houses to play bridge until midnight, when the couples would arise to greet the new year, leaning across the bridge table to smooch his spouse, then sit down to finish playing the hand.

Marge Sutherland was not only a fine bridge player, but a wonderful cook. I, therefore, deliberately skipped lunch in preparation for a gourmet meal. The group gathered in the family room before dinner and it seemed to me the cocktail hour went on and on, and I was getting hungrier and hungrier, until, finally, it was 8:30 and Marge announced dinner was ready. My stomach was growling, it needed food. I was not very polite and ignoring the ladies first rule, made a beeline for the dining room where dinner was laid out buffet style. I was dismayed to see the main course was what turned out to be Shrimp Creole in a pastry shell. I cannot stand the taste of shrimp, so I only took one and later took it out to the kitchen and surreptitiously put in the disposal unit. I was somewhat heartened to see the next course, which was a huge salad bowl. I love salads, but this one had suspicious white chunks all through it, and when I asked, had my suspicious confirmed: the little white chunks were Roquefort cheese. I dislike intensely, all the varieties of "blue" cheese, so I was not going to be able to fill up on salad. Things were looking really grim and my stomach was beginning to growl loudly. Luckily, the next course was chutney, which I really like, so I filled my plate with that. And, all was not lost, because dessert was a beautiful, large angel food cake loaded with icing. I felt I was entitled and proceeded to cut myself a very large slice. To my utter dismay, it turned our Marge had used sherry wine for the liquid in the cake and also in the icing. Sherry is high on my list of disliked flavors. I had learned by this time to appreciate the use of wine in cooking, which was permissible in my belief system because all the alcohol was burned off in the cooking process, and in my later years I learned to enjoy the subtle added flavor wine imparts to French and Italian cooking.

All the others thoroughly enjoyed Marge's New Year's meal and her offering to be the host couple out of turn and were very complimentary. When we got home, I remember Fran's comment to me, "Poor baby."

I remember how fortunate I felt I was at one of Fran's characteristics, which was utterly different from what I had observed in my parent's marriage. When I was growing up, my mother seemed to be working every waking hour. She refused to have another woman in the house to help with the housecleaning and laundry, etc. An unfortunate consequence was that we all had to be busy at all times. The rule was that only when Mother was not working, could we relax and have fun. However, this rule did not apply to our father. He was working very hard out of our sight and was the source of our home and our food, and we were taught to be grateful to him for all his hard work. But Mother did not encourage his having any real outside relationships with men. He did join a bowling league a few times and did become a Mason which meant one evening a month away from the family, and possibly an occasional meeting of some committee at church in the evening. But, today, I feel that my mother had deep-seated feelings of insecurity, especially competition for Dad's affections from other women. She wanted him near at all times and luckily for her mental health, Dad's business life did not require that he be on the road. He was home for dinner with his family every night. She wanted his family to be his whole life.

Fran, on the other hand, urged me to have interests beyond the family. She encouraged my relationships with golfing and sailing friends and bridge, activities which consumed large blocks of time away from the family. I think she felt confident enough in our marriage that outside interests for each of us only strengthened our relationship and posed no threat. I reveled in my freedom to be away from the family on a short business trip, or a service club convention or to be able to accept an invitation to go on an overnight golf outing. It was so different for me, such a different atmosphere. I think it would have been hard for my mother to understand how I could be away from my wife and daughters physically and never feel closer to them, wishing they could be with me to experience the new sights and places and interesting people. It was the antithesis of the old saying: out of sight, out of mind, and I had years of such freedom, and the subsequent joys of coming home to a loving wife and children.

I do remember one thing that caused a problem: Fran could never understand why, if I was in a business meeting, or some other group of men, and I was going to be later getting home than I had promised, I could not break away from the group to call her to warn her. I fear that I caused her unnecessary worry on many occasions and, she was understandably upset with me. The fault was mine; I did not want to be perceived as a "mama's" boy having to report to the authorities at home and I suffered a certain degree of coolness when I did get home eventually. There were no cell phones then, and it would have required excusing myself to leave the room, announcing that I had to call home to say I would be late, the only one of my peers who felt the necessity, thus diminishing myself in their eyes. So, there was an element of pride involved on my part, and not a very attractive one.

This type of situation happened often enough - I did not seem to be able to learn my lesson- that Fran finally said, "Don't tell me when you'll be home. Just get here as soon as you can." and this solved the problem.

I remember one of the many things I loved about Fran was her loyalty to her relatives in Midland in spite of the way they treated her mother when her father divorced her in 1931, and the role that the difference between Roman Catholicism and Episcopalianism played in it. In spite of this, there was love and loyalty, which I observed all the years of our marriage. We stopped in Midland on the way to the Michigan Alumni Camp at Lake Walloon in northern Michigan every summer for 25 years to visit the Thompsons: Aunt Maud and Aunt Myra, spinsters who made a home and cared for Fran's older brother, Mark, Uncle Frank and Aunt Lizzie, who lived next door, and Uncle Bill and Aunt Rose. This was always a chore for me, but a chance for Fran to relive happy memories of her early childhood, when she was the apple of their eye, and to let her relatives meet and know our children. It was more than just duty for Fran, and I admired her for it.

I remember how fortunate I thought Fran was to have her group of four lifelong friends, the equivalent of the powerful bond I felt for the group of friends I found in the Army. These were girls whom Fran joined in the third grade who all graduated together from Highland Park High School, Michigan.

Evelyn Lough, who lived across the street on Farand Park Avenue; Julia Slocum, possibly her best friend, during their school years, whose father was a dentist with offices in downtown Detroit; Annabel Danhof, whose father was General Counsel for the Michigan Central Railroad, and who was the only one of the five girls who went out of state to go to college at Wellesley College in Massachusetts; and Nancy Northrup, whose father was a physician.

After marriage they scattered to Detroit, St. Louis, Chicago, and Boston. Naturally we visited the Montgomery's (Evelyn Lough) in Grosse Pointe more frequently because they were the closest to us. I remember the whole group gathering for the wives' 25th High School Reunion, which was held at Cobo Hall in downtown Detroit. Fran was a little upset when she picked up her I.D. tag and the girl behind the desk who had been a good friend in high school exclaimed, "Franny Thompson, you haven't changed a bit. I would have known you anywhere!" Fran was sure her appearance had improved with her weight gain and hair style change in the intervening years.

I remember that two of the husbands, Bill Montgomery and Sam Hess, were also graduates of Highland Park high school in the class a year before the girls, and all five of the couples attended the husbands' 50th High School Reunion which was held at a tennis resort on Ford Road near the

Ford Motor Company, Willow Run airport. I thought it a little strange that non-members of the class would be welcomed at such an event, but we were. The five old childhood friends had a wonderful time catching up on their latest doings and the status of their families and started anticipating their own reunion the next year.

The next spring, we waited for an invitation to Fran's 50th Reunion which never came. She decided to call Ev Montgomery in Grosse Pointe to see if they had received their invitation and the date. I remember being present when Fran made the call and her surprise that the Montgomery's also had not received an invitation, but had learned that the President of the Class, who was the son of an Armenian immigrant who had come to the U.S. to work in the Ford Motor Company Rouge River steel plant, had cancer and did not have the strength to organize a reunion and there was not going to be one.

At this point in the conversation I intervened (Fran's version is slightly different, taking credit for the idea.) I remember clearly that I suggested that the five girls hold their own private reunion at one of their homes. After all, at the regular reunion the five would spend 90% of their time together; this way, all five could be together exclusively. I proposed that the first "Polar Bear" reunion (the Highland Park High School mascot) be held at our house. And that is how it all started, all ten years of private reunions.

This was agreeable to all and thus began an annual event, one of the highlights of the year for us. The format decided upon was that the meeting would take place in the host couple's home town: Boston, Detroit, Cleveland, Chicago or St. Louis; would last three or four days; the visiting couples would all stay in a nearby motel; the first evening meal would be at the host's home; subsequent dinner meals would be at a restaurant chosen by the host; all would gather at the motel for breakfast; and then the whole group would explore the host's city with the host as guide. A final farewell breakfast would take place at the motel the day the group dispersed.

I remember how interesting it was to visit the various cities and to visit places we would not have normally seen if visiting on our own. I remember ascending the Saarinen Arch in St. Louis and visiting the St. Louis Arboretum where I was thrilled to see two of Sir Peter Smither's enlarged photographs (4' x 5') of tree peonies displayed in the entrance lobby. We had met Sir Peter who was an associate of Ian Fleming in World War II at one of our peony conventions. I can't remember all of the interesting places we visited or sights we saw in the various cities. One of the years we met in Grand Haven, Michigan, where the Hess's, who lived in Mt. Prospect, a Chicago suburb, had a summer cottage on Lake Michigan (almost too cold to swim in) and we visited the famous Baker Furniture Company museum in Holland, Michigan. This was interesting to me because Grandma Thompson had a classic Baker 7' sofa with a one-piece goose down cushion that I slept on once or twice - utter comfort. We visited the Meijer (grocery chain) Gardens in Grand Rapids with its huge bronze copy of the statue of the Michelangelo prancing horse, about 16'-18' feet tall. In Boston I remember walking the historic trail; lunch at the famous Durgin Park restaurant, across the way from Faneuil Hall; stopping in an old manufacturing town, Lowell, Massachusetts, to tour an old water powered weaving mill museum next to a mill pond, where the power was transferred by 6" inch wide leather belts stretched twenty feet apart between rollers, from one floor to another, a fascinating way to transfer the weight of falling water to individual looms. Of course, there was no electricity when the mill was built, and it was interesting to see how Yankee ingenuity solved the problem. Then we were on our way to the Jarnis's summer place in Eastman, New Hampshire, near Dartmouth, where we had lunch, the only time I ever saw the Dartmouth campus, where my Sunday school friend, Dave Bortz, attended and our good friend, Phil Sutherland, member of our Brecksville bridge group graduated. In Detroit I remember exploring the Ford Dearborn Museum and lunch at an Arab restaurant in Dearborn, being fascinated to watch unleavened bread baked on a globe while we watched - it was delicious; also delicious was our evening meal at the famous Dearborn Inn.

The first meeting of the Polar Bears, our name for our group, which took place in Cleveland, was the year of the Supreme Court Justice Clarence Thomas's Senate hearings. I remember that Sam Hess and Lee Matthey, both very politically minded, elected to stay glued to the motel TV set while Jack Jarnis and Bill Montgomery and I went off to Canton, Ohio, about 50 miles south, to tour the National Football Hall of Fame Museum, which I had passed many times, noticing its unusual shape - of a vertical football - and was never interested enough to explore. However, I was surprised at how interesting the displays were. We met the Director, Ray Elliot, brother of Bump Elliot, head coach of the U. of Michigan football team with whom I had the pleasure of playing golf at Camp Michigania. Ray Elliot, who was very gracious, was a member of the Canton Brookside Country Club where Phil Sutherland, our bridge-playing friend was also a member. On the way home, we had lunch in Akron at the Diamond Grill, famous for its steaks: the finest I have ever had anywhere in all our travels.

Other memories of the Cleveland Reunions are of playing golf at Sleepy Hollow Golf Club near our home on Oakes Road, visiting the Cleveland Zoo, University Circle with all its cultural institutions, a boat trip up the Cuyahoga River to see all its bridges from water level, and a trip on "Lolly the Trolley," a fun way to do a sightseeing tour without walking. I was surprised at what I learned about my own hometown.

Alas, the reunions started to fall apart as we grew older and experienced health problems; the real jolt came with the death of Lee Matthey, the oldest of our group, followed by our most intelligent member, Annabel Hess, suffering from dementia and Bill Montgomery, a stroke. It was no longer feasible to drive between the widespread cities which we had always done; although Ev Montgomery and Julie Matthey did fly to the last meeting we had in Cleveland. As I write this, only three of us are still living of the original ten. I remember feeling as the years passed how fortunate we were to have had such an interesting, compatible group in our lives, and I missed the witty poems Nancy Jarnis composed for each occasion.

I remember admiring and envying Fran's ability to relate to and become friends with, establish a relationship with people in all walks of life. I recall her fondness for Bessy, the colored woman, who did the housecleaning for Fran's mother, and followed her from the Calvert Avenue location in near downtown Detroit all the way out to Grosse Pointe where Fran's mother moved after her financial situation improved. I heard mention of Bessy often in conversation but think I may have met her only once in all the years we visited Detroit. Eventually I heard that she retired because of her age and this caused distress for both Fran and her mother.

Fran was very fond of her mother's landlady on Calvert Avenue, Miss Buhrer, who was a Christian Scientist, and constantly brought home-baked goodies up to their front door. She also met and liked Mrs. Randolph, her mother's landlady in Grosse Pointe on Harcourt Road off Jefferson Avenue. They had an unspoken agreement that she would keep an eye on Fran's mother who was approaching her 80th year and would notify Fran if she noticed any health problems in Fran's mother. I thought the rental situation was a little unusual. Mrs. Randolph's husband was in the dental equipment manufacturing business, but Mrs. Randolph seemed to be in charge of the rental and maintenance of the apartment. She was the one who called Fran to alert her when Grandma Thompson fell, breaking he arm, which led to her move to Brecksville, where she bought the house next door to our house on Oakes Road.

I remember admiring how Fran's relationship with Corunna Feuerhahn, her Hudson, Ohio, seamstress became more than a business one; we had dinner and played bridge afterwards with them for many years. And, similarly, we visited our Brecksville cleaning lady, Martha LeJeune, a German immigrant (who claimed to know nothing of the Nazi atrocities), who married a Belgian cabinetmaker, Fred LeJeune, after her first husband died, both at their home in Middleburg Heights, on the Metropolitan Parkway, and, after their retirement, the long drive to Carrolton, Ohio, close to the Pennsylvania border to see the house they bought there. Fred's cabinet making skills were very evident in the improvements he made to that house. Martha always brought us authentic German Christmas cookies, and came to Fran's funeral, and still sends me Christmas cards.

I remember how pleased and proud I was at Fran's skills in making friends which I envied, that began after we bought our first house in Parma Heights. There were the neighbors which led to the formation of a regular group we met to play bridge with: the Demuths, the Hackers, the Leyavas, and the Kellys, all close to us in Parma Heights. There was a more geographically diffuse circle of sorority sisters, which became a second bridge group, which gradually supplanted the earlier Parma Heights friends. If this social activity had been left to me, it never would have happened. As much as I would have liked to have the ease and openness that was second nature for Fran, something in my background prevented it. The process of becoming close to another took me much longer. Except for Fran, herself.

After moving into our new home on Oakes Road in Brecksville, the circle of friends widened again, like the ripples in a pond, to include members of the newly founded St. Matthews Episcopal Church, which started as a mission church with only nine members, of whom Fran was one. She became close friends of Aurel Ostendorf, (who lived on Whiskey Lane!) Noel Wynn, Janet Ellenberger, Margot Kiester, Ceil Clarenback, and, especially, Dorothy Kuttler. Fran was very active and was the first lady member of the Vestry. We both felt very close to Bill and Nancy Wrenn, the first minister at St. Matthews, where Fran worked in the office mimeographing the weekly notices and programs, and I became the organist. We also helped lay the asphalt tile flooring in the new church, and painted walls. Although I never felt I could become a member, or take Communion because of my religious upbringing, I had more time invested physically in the church than many actual members, and perhaps I was a member - ex officio. It was always a silent comfort to me; made me feel good.

I remember how pleased I felt with the social relationships which developed as we became old-time residents of Brecksville. The most important and constant were the duplicate bridge group. In addition to our monthly Friday night meetings, the men played golf together frequently. Three of them, Ted Billings, Phil Sutherland and Mike Hayes were members of private country clubs and invited the others to play as their guests. I think I was always included.

One of the things that bothered me was to observe the hurt Fran felt when she told me of a phone call, typically from Micky Billings, an excellent golfer with whom we were good enough friends to go on a golfing weekend in Cambridge Springs, Pennsylvania, and share a sailing weekend at Sandusky, Ohio, where they docked their sailboat, Cygane, at the Sandusky Sailing Club. Micky would tell Fran that she and Marge Sutherland and Neola Hayes had been at lunch after a shopping trip and had mentioned as they were finishing lunch that they should have included Fran. She just wanted to let Fran know that they had not forgotten her! This happened more than once and Fran could never understand why she had been excluded?, overlooked?, forgotten?, slighted?. And neither could I. After all, they were close friends and always glad to see each other.

There are many more memories of Fran in the chapters on "Golf," "Bridge," "Music," "Gardening" and "Vacation/Travel" that follow.

I think of some of the memories in connection with my parents, which surprise me but shouldn't, because they were simply highlights of an unwavering background of love and pride; they create a picture of them that I cherish. I remember my father's calm acceptance of my failure to pass my Driver's Test (straight A's in high school!) when I reached the age of 16: no sarcasm, no ridicule on this occasion. The test was given at a License Bureau in a very old building on the west side Warren Road between Detroit Street and Franklin Boulevard in Lakewood. It surprises me that I remember so little about such an important event in my life. For instance, there was no Driver's Ed course at the high school in those days: did my father teach me how to drive, and if so, where and when? My mind is blank. I do not remember any road test after the written test, either. I think the license, which was granted to, a sixteen-year-old, restricted driving to daylight hours. After failing the drivers' test, we returned home and I spent a half hour studying the material issued by the License Bureau and we went back to the Bureau and I passed the test easily. The license issued required that there be an adult in the passenger's front seat whenever I was behind the wheel, but I do not remember what I had to do or how old I had to be before I could drive alone.

During this probationary period, I remember one afternoon when I was behind the wheel and my mother was in the passenger seat. I had only picked up my license a week or two earlier. We were driving east on Memphis Road in Brooklyn in a section where there were residences with garages and driveways on the south side of the road, which was six or eight feet higher than the surface of Memphis. Suddenly, I became aware that there was a car, which had no driver, parked at the top of one of the driveways and was rolling down the slope to Memphis, and if I didn't do something, I was going to run into it. I remember freezing for a moment and then tramping on the accelerator. I think that our car was a 1936 Plymouth, not known for its acceleration, but it responded and the driverless car rolled across the street, barely missing the rear of our car, and came to a halt against the curb on the far side of the street.

When we told Dad about the narrow escape, he surprised me again by complimenting me for my quick thinking. I could not get over how calmly he accepted our news, and that he praised me instead of criticizing me. It felt wonderful.

I remember the burden of being the oldest child, tall for his age, and precocious. From an early age I was indoctrinated with the responsibility of caring for my younger brothers, protecting them from harm, that this was what "family" meant and was, therefore, good.

I remember one Saturday afternoon when I was probably twelve years old and my parents entrusted me with looking out for my brothers. I think it was the first time they had ever done this. They were going somewhere, probably shopping, and would be gone an hour or so. They put all four of us down for naps in our bedrooms, and I was to be in charge if we woke up before they returned. I sneaked out of bed before they left and remember looking out the bathroom window as Dad backed the car out the driveway and a terrible fear swept over me that our parents no longer loved us and they were leaving us to start another life somewhere else. How was I going to take care of my brothers and earn enough money to make the mortgage payments and buy the food? I was only twelve years old. It was overwhelming; an exaggerated, morbid fear in an overactive imagination. But I still remember that first feeling of real fear in my life as I went back to my bed, obediently, and covered my head with my blanket.

This feeling of responsibility for the well-being of my siblings started that day and was still present years later when I was an adult and we four brothers were working together in the mortgage banking business started by our father when I was a sophomore and Russ was a freshman at Yale. I eventually became the commercial loan man in the company where the loan amounts were larger and the commissions earned were larger and it was always my dream to make the one deal so big that my brothers, who were working very hard at the more mundane residential part of the business, could relax and know their future and that of their families was secure. The failure to close the exotic oil well deal in Kansas which would have earned our company, and for which I was solely responsible, $60,000 per year for 19 years, 23% tax free, was all the more bitter for having these feelings, childish as they may have been. I was so close to being their hero.

Not all my memories are happy ones; the most devastating one was of the morning after breakfast as I was preparing to leave for my morning classes in my postgraduate year of high school. We were alone in the kitchen, and my mother suddenly burst into tears as I was going out of the door, and with no warning or explanation cried out, "I'm sorry I ever had you." I was stunned and flared back, "Well, I didn't ask to be born." I had done nothing to provoke this outburst, no misbehavior, no backtalk, nothing. I could see she was very disturbed but could not understand why. This was something worse than withholding love, or approval, or disappointment in me, as a means of motivating me. As I recall, I rushed out of the house and walked slowly down Parkwood to Franklin Boulevard, with tears in my eyes, muttering to myself, over and over again, "I didn't ask to be born into this world, I didn't ask to be born into this world."

I remember nothing else about this incident. I don't remember how I got through the morning classes, or what happened when I got home for lunch. I wonder now if the only thing serious enough to have precipitated such an outburst might have been some imaginary threat to her marriage; that she suspected my father of some infidelity, the very idea of which was ridiculous; his every minute of the day was accounted for. We all knew she was the most important thing in his life. One of her problems that I was aware of was her feelings of inferiority and her suspicions of other people's motivation, which I used to marvel at because she never had time to read novels where she might have discovered the world of farfetched plots. I do not remember ever seeing her even read a newspaper! But temptation lurked in the form of beauteous secretaries in the exciting world of business. The whole flare-up incident was a puzzle I was never able to solve.

My memories of my last time alone with my mother, when I visited her after dinner on a weeknight before her final trip to the hospital, dispelled any doubts I might have had that she had a deep love for me and was proud of me, her efforts to raise me a success. I still remember, achingly, holding her hand while kneeling at her side as she lay on the chaise longue in their living room, telling me that she had always felt that of the four of her sons, I had shown the most gratitude and appreciation for all they had done. Long after her death, loyalty to her principles and attempting to live up to her ideals are powerful motivators for me. Much of what one sees in me is her.

# Chapter III

## The House of Dreams

I am not sure that the subject of this chapter of my life, the planning and completion of the construction of the house we built at 5320 Oakes Road, Brecksville, Ohio, is not the most significant thing that I ever did, other than my marriage and the birth of our three daughters. I don't think anything else I ever attempted was comparable to that achievement, or better evidence of the maturity I had attained, or meant as much to my personality in terms of confidence or self-worth.

Searching through old memories of either Fran or my early homes provides no explanation of how we arrived at the concept of 5320, as I think of the house whenever it comes to my mind, so modern, so ahead of its time. which it often still does in my early morning waking dreams. I can find no predisposition. We never lived on either coast where modern architecture could be found. I did note articles from time to time, after I was married, about the Bauhaus school, about Marcel Breuer, about Philip Johnson and his glass house in Darien, Connecticut; Fran lived in Midland, Michigan until her 8th year, which was where Alden Dow, a student of Frank Lloyd Wright and a member of the founding Dow Chemical family, practiced architecture and was noted for his many "modern" structures. Neither of our childhoods reveals a source of strong memories of the homes we were brought up in that would carry over to adulthood, and I cannot find any adult likings lingering from childhood such as a love of sweet corn, or playing cards. No, I think our love of modern architecture was not a result of childhood influences but was learned much later by study and then observation, and an occupation that forced me to see all types of housing. Our minds were open to the new ideas arising in a booming housing market trying to satisfy the pent-up demand created by World War II and the millions of men leaving the army to enter a normal civilian life.

It was surprising to me when I found and re-read the letters that Fran saved that from our very earliest daily letters to each other that she was already thinking of what kind of house we would build after we were married. Perhaps on the shore of a lake? I don't remember either of us having any particular style in mind; but very early in our relationship there was a craving on both our parts to create our own home, before we even knew where or when we could be married. I do think that traces of what provided a sense of security and comfort in our childhood homes found their ways into the home we eventually built in Brecksville.

It was fortunate that my father had bought a 24-suite, 4-story walk-up apartment building in Lakewood, Ohio, as an investment just before World War II, and an apartment was available for us when we returned to Cleveland after my discharge from the army in the Spring of 1946. Our apartment was on the top floor, and was a little unusual because it had a living room with gas grate fireplace, a self-storing "Murphy" bed in a closet, and a separate large dining room; being a corner apartment on the top floor had many advantages, better ventilation and no noisy neighbors overhead, but it was a long way down the back stairs to the laundry room. We were grateful being spared living in a rooming house. It was where we started the 69-year adventure of our life together.

We had our first daughter, Nancy, in 1947, while living in the apartment, and a year later when Fran started having trouble climbing the stairs to do the laundry or go shopping (she was suffering from the pain of a slipped disc) we started looking for a house to buy. Building our own home was completely impossible financially. Luckily, by this time, I was appraising 7-10 homes a week, mainly on the East side of Cleveland, exposed to many different types, decorated from modest to lavish. One of the new styles, which were becoming popular, was the "Ranch"; usually 1,000-1,500 square feet, all the rooms on one floor, with or without a basement, frequently, with an attached garage. This type of house required a larger lot, and the standard became a minimum 50' to 60' frontage. The style was probably a commercial builder's adaptation of Frank Lloyd Wright's "Prairie" or "Usonian" innovations, but without the individuality of his designs that were tailored to the needs of his clients. It was my first exposure to Wright's thinking

After some searching in the westerly suburbs of Cleveland, I became aware of a development getting under way in Parma Heights, Ohio, on Ridgewood Drive which was part of a promotion of the Revere Copper and Brass Company The builder was Precision Housing, owned by Harry Fishman, who had an excellent reputation. We looked at the model house and were impressed with it and bought our first house for $13,950, financed with a $12,000 low rate/long term first mortgage, using my VA loan guarantee. The 25-year term, 10% down payment, and 4% interest rate were far more favorable terms than the 33% down, 4 1/2%, 15-year term conventional mortgages prevalent in the market at the time. I remember that our monthly payment was $83 per month including real estate taxes. Such a low monthly payment was necessary because of my low monthly pay at that stage of my business career. It was the only way we could afford our own home.

The house was interesting. It was basementless and had copper piping buried in the concrete floor which made the entire floor surface a radiator in the wintertime. The hot water was pumped from a small furnace located in the attached garage which was heated the same way. It was an ideal heating system for a family with small, crawling children, which we were. The house was 25'x 36', 900 sq. ft., and had a remarkable floor plan which provided a 16' x 16' living room, Pullman kitchen - dining area 8'x 16', and three bedrooms and a bath. The living room faced the rear of the lot and had four large Thermopane windows over awning type windows at floor level for ventilation and a rear door to a patio behind the garage, which was offset 6 feet toward the street. It was an extremely efficient, livable plan. The other copper feature was copper downspouts, no surprise in a house sponsored by Revere Copper. It was well-built and held its value well. We sold it five years later when we moved into 5320 for $18,000, and the daughter of one my good friends (golfer and bridge partner) bought one of the same models 30 years later for more than $80,000.

Our plan was to stay in this house for three years while trying to amass enough money by doing things ourselves and bonuses from the family business to buy a piece of land and build our own home, designed by an architect to meet our family's needs. This was the dream. It did not work out quite that way; we lived in Parma Heights for five years and when our third daughter, Barbara, arrived, 900 square feet was no longer enough for us. This was especially true when Grandmother Thompson came to visit from Detroit, which happened several times a year, and was always a happy occasion: good for Fran, who was very close to her mother; good for the girls who adored their grandmother; good for me, she was very good to me and I couldn't do enough for her.

Also, I had improved the garage by building in storage cabinets (very primitive carpentry at that stage), screened in the patio and built in an upholstered bench behind the garage (also primitive); widened the driveway, and couldn't find room in the yard for any more plants. I was bored already, and ready to move on to bigger and better things.

For a long time, we had admired Bay Village, the third westerly suburb of Cleveland on Lake Erie's shoreline, after visiting some of Fran's Gamma Phi Beta sorority sisters who had located there after the war. We had saved enough money at this point to buy a 40' lot on Huntmere Road, south of Wolf Road, an important east-west thoroughfare in Bay Village. When we bought it the entire west side of the street was wooded and undeveloped. Within a year a developer acquired the lots and proceeded to erect very cheap, all alike, poorly built post war Cape Cod bungalows with unfinished second floors; I remember looking at the house across the street from our lot and was shocked to see bark on some of the rafters, the only time I ever saw such a thing, and no garage. It was a very common practice then, a time when the only way many young couples with very limited means could find a place to live was to buy a house and finish the second floor after they had lived there a year or two. The street was spoiled for me and I no longer wanted us to live there. We were fortunate in our timing that our building plans were still dreams and had not proceeded to the building stage.

However, we did own the lot long enough for me to start spending lunch hours at the Cleveland Public Library, which was across the street from our office, and begin my study of the latest architectural thinking in the many magazines in the Reading Room: the most important being *Architectural Forum, Architectural Digest, Architecture* and *Interiors*. I remember how excited I was when I realized that there were far more interesting styles of housing being built in other parts of the country than what I was encountering in my appraisal trips for our office. Before assigning a value per square foot, or per cubic foot, I was required to measure the exterior dimensions of the house, put them on a graph on the appraisal card supplied by the Aetna Life and then enter the house and draw in the floor plan, inspecting the amenities, mechanical equipment, and condition as I went along, from the basement to the third floor. Not many young prospective home buyers had that kind of training in their search for their first home.

One of the *Architectural Forum* issues I found at the Library was devoted entirely to the work of Frank Lloyd Wright, the most famous architect in the U.S. It included his major works, including the Imperial Hotel in Tokyo and the drawings for the Guggenheim Museum in

Manhattan and I remember the impression these buildings made on me. I wondered if Wright was a visitor from Mars - his ideas were so far out. But the impact on me in the world I was living in came from the many examples of the residences he designed for individual clients to fit their needs, and his philosophy of the influence a residence could have on its occupants' lives; that the land dictated the shape of the structure erected on it. I felt this was true and had no trouble digesting it. It would govern my search for our dream house.

I now wished I had been more aware of what I was seeing, like nothing in my past or what I was seeing in my appraisal work, when I actually spent an afternoon in one of the famous Lloyd Wright houses, the Wiley home in Minneapolis, where I was stationed in the Army for a year and a half, and, regrettably, much too young to appreciate what I saw.

At the library I found a Prairie style basementless house in one of the architectural magazines that I thought might fit on our 40' lot in Bay Village. I remember being quite excited about it and rushing home to show it to Fran. The house had been built in California and was long and narrow and would sit at right angles to the street. It had three bedrooms in the front, followed by the LR, DR & K with the entrance between the sleeping and living areas, and before the attached garage. I think I could draw the plan from memory today. It was just a dream, however, which we never pursued. Instead, we found a buyer and sold the lot for which we had paid $1,000 for $1,500 and were happy to escape from the Huntmere scene.

I remember the thrill of stopping on the way home from work at the office on Madison Avenue of the buyer (I do not remember his name), and watching him draw the check for payment of the lot and the way he wrote the dollar amount. He did not use a horizontal line under the cents and over the 100, but a bold diagonal downward slash at a 45-degree angle, left to right. It must have made a big impression on me because I do my "cents" on my checks the same way today, 70 years later.

Now, with our profit in hand, we searched for another building lot in Bay Village. The new lot had to be larger; having found that 40' was too small and confining and bored with living on a 50' lot for five years, we hoped to find something with a 75' frontage, or larger. We finally located a vacant lot on W. Oviatt, farther west in Bay Village, south of and parallel to Wolf Road, and a short distance south of Huntington Beach Park with its beach for swimming which was an added attraction.

Indeed, the lot had 75' frontage, and 160' depth and had a large tree in a very interesting location about the middle of the lot. The street was well developed with attractive ranch type, postwar construction houses. The other side of the street was largely developed so we knew what we were getting into this time. One of the houses directly across the street was very distinctive, painted a soft yellow, and was built by Krumwiede Builders, noted for the quality of their houses. We bought "our" lot for $2,500, but once again I do not remember any of the details of how we found it, whether a broker was involved, or how the closing was done.

We were excited and hired a young architect, George Calvin Means, a member of my church. We impressed on him the restrictions imposed on his design efforts by the limitations of our budget: we could not afford to invest more than $18,000. We simply did not have enough equity. Being in the mortgage business I knew we could not qualify for a mortgage larger than $16,000. Working with these restrictions in mind, George designed a remarkable house. Again, I think I could draw the floor plan from memory today. It was as unconventional as the plan I had found for the Huntmere lot.

It was "H" shaped, basementless, shed-type roof with the two long legs of the "H" parallel to the street and the crossbar providing the entrance and hallway from the living areas in the rear wing and the three bedrooms on the front wing facing the street. This created a fairly large courtyard between the two wings and happily saved the large tree which became a focal point. It was a very livable, charming solution to our problem. The garage was located next to the kitchen; the north walls of the living and dining rooms were largely glass and looked out on the courtyard and, perhaps, the most intriguing feature was the proposed heating fuel: anthracite coal! This would have been pea sized, stoker fed to a hot water furnace which would pump the hot water into a baseboard radiant heating system. Anthracite was much preferable to bituminous coal from a cleanliness standpoint.

Then it was our turn: we submitted the working drawings to several reputable west side builders and could not get an offer to build for less than $20,000. I remember our feverish attempts to find a way to reduce construction costs: reducing overall size; conventional hot air heating system; scrapping the wood burning fireplace; having a carport rather than an enclosed garage. All to no avail. We had to give up the dream, and I remember how sad it was to notify George that we had failed. We had to face the fact that we could not afford his wonderful house. (Which I would have loved to have seen built). We made an appointment to drive to North Ridgeville after church and pay him for his services, $300, as I recall. He lived on Center Ridge Road in a really tiny house, which I am still trying to identify on my way to the grocery store, if it is still there.

I have spent this much time going through old memories of our housing experience, trying to understand where the passion that led to 5320 came from, and hoping the picture here contains clues for the reader. It is surely very complex, a combination of my occupation which was a great preparation for the subject of housing, and then the two searches for land as our tastes were maturing, and the hours of study at the library of the architectural magazines; just the general getting older and the kind of family we were - three daughters and no sons which had a bearing on what kind of environment we wanted for them to grow up in. All these factors contributed to the final product, 5320 Oakes Road, East of the Sun in my mind, the house of dreams.

Now that we had the profits from our earlier lot purchases in our pockets, we started our search for an even larger piece of land. Fran had always wanted a house overlooking a lake, a vestige from her early years with vacations in a cottage on Lake Huron. I knew that we could not afford a lot overlooking Lake Erie where the minimum lot size was 100' frontage, and the going price was $100 per front foot. We didn't have that much money. Nevertheless, I remember driving up and down Lake Road from Rocky River to Sheffield Lake looking, and having Fran write down phone numbers from For Sale signs, which finally convinced her, after calling several, that her dream of living on Lake Erie was impossible.

I then suggested that we look into hilly land which is found south of Cleveland. I had loved looking at the low mountains at Fort Sill where I had my Basic Training. She agreed and we began spending evenings after dinner driving through the hilly areas in North Royalton, Broadview Heights, Brecksville, Richfield, and Hinckley. We never were able to find just what we were looking for, and eventually ended up in the hands of a real estate agent who specialized in land sales, Inez Hoffman, of Independence, Ohio, a former schoolteacher. I do not remember who recommended her. She was very petite, probably about 5' tall, and mannish. We told her we were looking for a larger piece of land, possibly as large as an acre, but it had to have some sort of view, and it had to be in a good school system. Fran had learned from some of her sorority sisters who were teachers that the Brecksville system was the best. This narrowed down Inez's search somewhat.

One night at dinnertime, Inez called and said she had two properties for us to look at, both on the same street, Oakes Road, across from each other; one was overpriced and the other a great bargain. She urged us to look at them soon.

We called our friends, Bob and Dorothy Demuth, neighbors and members of our bridge club, and invited them to go for a ride while we looked at these two properties. It was a Friday night, because I remember I had an early morning golfing date with 3 of the neighbors early Saturday AM. We picked up the Demuths and it was twilight by the time we identified the lots. The first was on the north side of Oakes Road, 160' frontage and uphill from the street. It was later bought by Carrie Cerino, owner of the Brecksville bakery and a well known restaurant. The other lot was on the south side of Oakes Road, 289' of frontage and very deep. It was owned by an architect who had split it down the middle so that friends of his wife's could build on their half of the land. When one of the friends died, the whole parcel came on the market.

Bob and I got out of our car and in the middle of the frontage trudged down a slope where we crossed a small stream about 150' from the road, which I learned later carried raw sewage, and then climbed through an old apple orchard through an open area until we came to a fallen down line of grapes and found ourselves on the edge of a ravine. By now, it was almost dark. We could hear a stream gurgling but could not see it. We turned and went down the west side of the lot, our feet kept dry by a primitive bridge over the little stream made of railroad crossing ties, and back to the car. He looked at me. I looked at him. And we shrugged shoulders and raised eyebrows. I think I remember returning to their house and playing bridge for the rest of the evening.

The next morning I woke up an hour before the alarm was set, wide awake and think I may have had my first epiphany: I knew we had to buy the land we had seen the night before, where the house should sit, "T" shaped, and even a ham-shaped pond in front of it. I got out of bed very quietly and found a pad of accounting paper, very large, no longer used by the Aetna, which I had brought home for the children to draw on. I sat down at the dining room table and drew two long parallel lines which represented the lot lines and sketched the house at the edge of the ravine, reached by a driveway along the west side of the lot with a circle in front of the house, and the "lake" in front of it. I still have the drawing somewhere in my papers. I scribbled a note to Fran telling her that we had to go back to see the land immediately before someone else beat us to it, and quietly placed it on her dressing table next to the bed. The page of paper was so large it covered the surface of her table. Then I tiptoed out to the garage, gathered my golf clubs and went off to play in our regular foursome.. I was so excited by my vision that I don't think I played very well; I couldn't wait to get back home to see Fran's reaction to my vision.

When I arrived home sometime after lunch, I rushed in and grabbed Fran by her shoulders and asked what she thought of my idea. She replied, "What idea?" In her haste to get the children up and fed, she had not even seen the top of her dressing table. We did go back to look at the land that afternoon, made an offer, and we did buy it. It turned out not to be 1 acre but 11 acres, a little more than we had asked Inez to find for us. But we bought it for $5,500.

My memories of the next step are not clear. I don't remember how long it took us to locate an architect, but think he was recommended by Bob and B.J. Trebbe, another of Fran's sorority sisters. His name was Clyde Patterson, about my age, who taught architecture at Kent State University, as well as having a private practice. He had designed the Trebbe's one story basementless house in a contemporary style with redwood siding. We had played bridge in their home and gone to parties there many times and liked the house. It was located near Pleasant Valley Road and W. 130th Street, not too far from our home on Ridgewood Drive.

After showing us some of his drawing for other houses he had planned which were impressive, we gave him the commission to design a house for us. He brought in a partner named Robert Gaede, whose name by coincidence was the same as my mother's maiden name but was not a relative.

I proceeded to write a letter outlining what our needs were, what our style of living was and the fact that it would be three young daughters who would be living there. Also, I pointed out my Army study of Japanese and requested that they incorporate as many Japanese housing ideas as possible, while still staying within the realm of practicality. I hoped these ideas would be subtle and unobtrusive, and, along with the other goals I had laid out in the commission letter would result in a simple, elegant, low-key home which would leave a visitor asking himself what was so different from the more typical houses of the day and why did a lover of Early American style, or of French Provincial, find it so comfortable and memorable.

I did not want a home designed as a show place for others, but a source of beauty and comfort for our family. By the time we found our architects, I had already drawn two or three layouts, based on my experience in my appraisal work, trying to utilize the special features of the lot; its high vantage point, a quarter mile from the highest elevation in Cuyahoga County; overlooking the Cuyahoga River valley to the northeast; and its proximity to the ravine, an eighth of a mile from the road. I don't know if any of my feeble attempts, which had possibilities and were not all bad, have survived in my archives, but when we saw the concepts of the architects, they were so far beyond my amateurish attempts that it took my breath away.

I don't think we were typical clients, however. I think Patterson and Gaede were a little shocked that we did not jump at the first drawing they brought for our inspection. I think they had unexpected input which spurred them on. It was the third set of drawings they presented, which took my breath away: "T" shaped as in my epiphany, with 4 levels nestling into the land. We accepted the plan immediately as the answer to our search. Even then we suggested changes; the original drawing for the final plan had the living room to the front and the master bedroom suite located above the children's bedrooms, which was very practical with the plumbing stacked. However, I wanted the living room and den located on the highest level in the house to take advantage of the view of the distant hills of the Cuyahoga River valley, and it was not too difficult for the architects to make the switch. They had our budget in mind when sizing the rooms, and the only change I could have wanted would have been to make the overall house six feet longer and four feet wider. But that would have been too costly; we were already reaching the limits of our budget. I wish I could remember what the dollar part of the equation was. My memory seems to retain the physical aspect, which was the vital part, much more readily than the down-to-earth question of how much the cost would be and how could we solve that problem, without going to my father for help.

When the final drawings were completed, the architects included a "Van Dyke" print of the first floor. I had never seen a "Van Dyke" print before, which is a form of blueprint where the background is black instead of blue. It is far more interesting, and our copy was mounted on hard board. I remember waking up morning after morning staring at the print of "our" house displayed on a chest of drawers at the foot of the bed, and the excitement I felt. I do not know how to convey to others the power of the feelings aroused by this print. It consumed my thoughts and became a near obsession. The plan was begging to be built and I was the one chosen to do it. Everything in our past had conspired to bring us to this point. I simply had to make it happen.

The next step was to find a building contractor. Once again, I am frustrated by the holes in my memory of the details of such an important part of my life. I think that perhaps the man, William J. Rehker, a 65-year-old retired carpenter from Berea, Ohio, may have built our friends, the Trebbe's house and they recommended him, or possibly there was a Christian Science connection since I believe Rehker's daughter went to that church. He had a partner, another 65-year-old carpenter, Lou Fuller, and they had built a log cabin style house out of old telephone poles in the Cuyahoga River Valley in Brecksville, and another large house on Brecksville Road in Independence. I do not think I even went to look at these two references before deciding that Bill Rehker would be our contractor. I was so impressed by his obvious integrity, and by his manner.

On his side, I think when we met at the site and Rehker saw the working drawings and the site itself, he wanted the job. I do not think we put our agreement in writing, and he agreed to work on an hourly basis, paid every Friday afternoon based on hours worked. His work ethic was simple:

start at 8 a.m. on the dot (he had an old fashioned railroad watch); stop all work at noon when the town whistle blew, and sit under the big oak tree behind the house to eat lunch and study the plans for the next step; resume work at 1 p.m. exactly and work until 5p.m. Close up the job for the night and study the plans for work to be done the next day.

He admired the plans and the architects, and the architects admired his work and told me it was a shame their rough carpentry work had to be covered up. I wish it had turned out that I could have seen what their interior finish carpentry work would have looked like. The architects visited the site regularly to inspect the progress of the work and approve work done and offer help with any questions. I, of course, stopped by every opportunity I could find. This arrangement meant that no General Contractor's fee was added to the cost and worked very much to our advantage, because Rehker actually performed many of the duties of a General Contractor, and always had my best interests in mind. I still find it amazing that a pair of 65-year-old men could erect a 3400 square foot, complicated plan to architects' specifications, subject to the architect's inspections, ready for interior finish in three months. I don't know how they did it.

The financing had to be arranged before the work could begin, I had to arrange a "takeout" loan commitment with our lender, Aetna Life Insurance Company, on whose good offices the livelihood of four families depended, and I remember nothing of how this was done; whether my father wrote the submission letter, or I did; what the loan amount was, $20,000 or $24,000; what the interest rate was or if it was more than a 20 year term. I don't even remember what the estimated cost of the construction was. We would have had to use our company bank line of credit to make the advances, against Aetna's takeout upon completion. For all I know my father may have guaranteed the loan personally without my knowledge. I often wondered what our "boss" in Hartford, Doug Swinehart, V.P. of the mortgage loan department and extremely conservative, thought of the plans and what he may have said to my father privately. I think the length of the commitment was one year, a hopeless deadline as it turned out. I do not recall any difficulty or resistance on the part of my father or any comments or reservations he may have had about the style of the house, or the scope of the project for which I will always be grateful. While there was no physical help on the project from my father or my brothers, there was no resistance on the financial aspect, which was a blessing.

I do not remember, and a great regret associated with the whole Brecksville house is whether my mother ever saw the plans for the house. It was the last summer of her life and the month construction began, July 1953, she spent much of the time in Lakewood Hospital. I am sure she would have admired the plans; she had drawn the plan for their home overlooking Lake Erie in Rocky River, and had them done formally by an architect friend of my father's, Bill West, so she would have appreciated the whole process. I think she would have admired our building site. I think if she had lived to see the finished product and been aware of my efforts to complete the project, she would have been proud.

I don't remember at what point, but it wasn't very long after the beginning of construction, that I realized with a sickening feeling that we did not have enough money to hire Rehker and his partner to finish the interior of the house so that all we would have to do was move in our meager amount of furniture and start living in a completed house. We were still living in Parma Heights and making mortgage payments there, as well as paying interest on the advances on the construction loan in Brecksville. The only solution was for me to step in and do the completion work personally, just as our customer, George Weisz, had done on York Road near us in Parma Heights. The big difference was that in his case, his builder had absconded and abandoned the job; in our case it was a simple insufficiency of funds. However, the solution was the same: finish the job yourself, praying that your own labor will equal the cash insufficiency.

I remember having seen a house on my appraisal travels to the far east side of Cleveland which I admired and taking Fran for an evening drive to look at it again. It had vertical siding and a color I liked. We stopped and talked to the owner and learned that the wood was vertical tongue and groove cypress, very unusual in the Cleveland area. It was stained with Cabot's Medium Gray, No. 43, creosote shingle stain, with white painted wood trim. We decided this was what we wanted. If we could find the cypress.

I discovered that there was a lumber company in the Flats along the Cuyahoga River in Cleveland named Rock-Daoust that carried cypress, which solved that problem. I think our order was for 3,800 square feet, tongue and groove, random width, and random length. As an additional point of interest, I learned that Mr. Rock was the son of the lady who cared for my mother and me when I was born. She performed the same practical nurse functions for all four of my mother's sons, who were born at home, not in a hospital. For many years we made an annual trek out to Butternut Ridge Rd. in North Olmsted to call on Grandma Rock so she could check on the progress of "her" four boys.

Construction finally began in July 1953, a hectic summer for us. Fran was pregnant with our third child, who was due in October; I went with my parents to see my youngest brother, Wes, graduate from Yale, and learned when climbing the stairs at Woolsey Hall for the Baccalaureate service, that there was something seriously wrong with my mother who had to stop to catch her breath; and almost couldn't make it to the top; our Canadian vacation with our friends, the Hackers when we learned of my mother's hospitalization; and, all the preparatory work for the start of construction at 5320 Oakes Road.

The excavation work was done by the Henry Mieze Company, of Peninsula, Ohio. I remember looking at the enormous hole and wondering what they did with all the dirt they removed. It must have been hauled away and used for fill dirt elsewhere. It was not a simple large rectangular hole because of the multiple levels of the house. I wish I had been there to see how they determined the location and determined the various levels. It was very impressive. I also remember being impressed that the architects did not automatically site the house on the land parallel to the road, but pointed it slightly to the northeast so that the amount of roof overhang would permit the winter sun to enter the house and help with fuel bill; at the same time it would prevent direct sunlight from entering in the summer. There were 46 pieces of glass (which took three hours to wash on the exterior) that were designed to bring the outdoors into the house which they did very successfully.

Every window, even the bathrooms, looked out on something natural. The view from the large window in the dining room looked down into the ravine, which after a heavy snowstorm was particularly pleasing.

After they were finished, the masonry contractor, Norman Dieckman, came with his crew and put in the footers and did the cement block foundation work. We did not face the cement block above ground with brick in order to save money. His contract included constructing the double fireplace in the living room and den called for in the drawings. This was the first time Bill Rehker stepped in. He detected a flaw and insisted the flue on the fireplace facing the living room be redone because the flue box had not been properly constructed, something I would never have realized until it was too late. I also was pleased with our selection of Baby Roman shaped brick, thinner and shorter than standard Roman, for the four foot exterior wall leading to the front entry, extended into the entry hall, and used to face the fireplace and exterior portion of the chimney. The architects had specified Crabapple Orchard stone from Tennessee, and had shown what it would look like on the exterior elevation drawings, but for some reason, although it was very popular at the time and I had seen it many times in my appraisals, I didn't like it for our house.

I remember being excited to see these first stages of the realization of my dream and glad when Dieckman's work was done. I was not impressed with the quality of the man he used to mix the mortar, which they did by hand in a large mortar boat, I suspected he was a drunkard and showed up for work on one of the days when he should have been home sleeping off a hangover because several years later I noticed serious deterioration of the mortar joints in the wall area between Nancy and Kathy's bedrooms. Fortunately, the erosion of the mortar joints was shallow, and I was able to scrape it clean and replace with fresh mortar then covered with Thoroseal to match the rest of the foundation wall.

After Dieckman's work was finished I started installing the drain tiles around the foundation, which I had planned on doing since it was unskilled labor which would be unseen after it was finished. The 3" diameter unglazed tile were laid on gravel next to the footers with the joints left open, with a "fall" of 1/8th inch per foot. This was to intercept any water that approached the footers and might threaten the integrity of the foundation of the house. After laying the tiles they were covered with gravel I hauled in my wheelbarrow and a second tile system, 4" glazed, slip seal pipe connected to the downspouts was installed. Both systems had to be laid with care, maintaining "fall" from the high point, the garage, to the southeast corner of the house, where the two lines met in a drainage vault I had to build to receive the water and direct it via 6" slip seal pipe over the hill to the stream below.

I had dug a trench about 8' long and 3' deep from the corner of the house to the top of the hill, and as I was standing at the edge of my trench, contemplating my next move, the edge of the trench gave way and in an instant I was lying on my back on the bottom of the trench looking up at the tree leaves overhead and the sky. It happened so quickly that I had no time to feel any vertigo or tottering to regain my balance. I think I let out a loud woof, then checked myself over and found no damage and continued with my work. It was a Saturday and I cherished the 10 hour stretch of time to finish whatever job I was engaged in, rather than the later, shorter 3-4 hour stints on week nights after work when I was busy doing the finish work, working in the dark all alone. My only damage from the fall was a large bruise on my inner right thigh. I was lucky. My little vault didn't look very professional but held up and did its job. Of course, it was fully covered up so no one could see it, and it didn't have to pass any inspection.

I also had to consider what kind of septic tank system we would use since there was no sewer on Oakes Road at that time. I had been thoroughly indoctrinated by my Uncle Louie in "green" practices long before Rachel Carson. I decided to use a double tank system which called for a 1,000 gallon-tank, plus a second 500-gallon tank, discharging into a filter bed, 50' x 60', with a 60 tons of gravel. The second tank would have a submersible sump pump which would be manually switched on for 60 seconds each week to flush out the joints of the tiles laid in the filter bed. It was common knowledge that after a few months service, the first 4 or 5' of the joints of the tile clogged up thus rendering 80% of the filter bed useless.

We went to considerable extra expense to install this elaborate system, far beyond what was required by regulations, but I was always proud of the crystal clear, odorless effluent which discharged over the hill into the stream below.

Later in the building process, as Bill Ranker and his partner were finishing applying the cypress siding and laying the roof shingles, (we didn't use a roofing contractor in order to save money,) when they were within 5 or 10 square feet of finishing the siding, and the last 50 square feet of roof shingles, they taught me how to do those two jobs. I was interested that they used aluminum nails to nail in the cypress, explaining that there would be no chance of rusting steel nail heads disfiguring the appearance of the siding. They didn't like the aluminum nails which were softer and didn't have the holding power of the regular steel ones.

It was also interesting that the shingles we selected were especially made for low-pitched roofs. Our slope was 1' for every 3' of rise, which was flat enough that a strong wind driven rain could lift the edge of an ordinary shingle and allow water to invade the interior of the house. The shingles we chose were tapered and the exposed bottom edge appeared to be almost twice as thick as the top edge of the shingle; heavy enough to withstand the power of the wind. Furthermore, they were supposed to be self-sealing. The heat of the sunlight was supposed to meld the edge of the exposed shingle to the one below. I don't know if this happened in our case. We chose a light gray color. However, the theory may have been good, but in the real world, the shingles failed, and we had to cover them with a tar and gravel surface. The original plans had called for white marble chips over felt and tar, to help reflect sunlight and keep the house cooler in the summer. The shingle solution was an economy measure.

Eventually, we replaced the tar and gravel with a rubber product that came in rolls like carpeting, was light weight and could be patched if necessary, like an old inner tube in the early automobile tires. It was a new product, widely used in commercial installations and was available in white, which was our choice, returning to the architects' original concept. Its drawback was that the rain leached the coloring from the surface of the rubber and it washed down and collected in the gutters; I had to go up on the roof once or twice a year to scrape the goo out of the gutters. I do think it was very practical and wish that we could have started out with it. It would have saved a lot of work and money.

One of the Japanese "influences" the architects specified was to have the roof overhangs be tongue and groove cedar over exposed outriggers whose exposed ends were cut at a 30 degree-angle, all to be painted white. The painting required a lot of extra effort and was miserable to do; we had to suspend scaffolding between ladders and it's hard to work with a brush over one's head. Fran, bless her, took part in all of this difficult labor. Eventually we replaced the open oriental effect by installing a simple soffit with the flat plywood connecting the edge of the roof and the building walls at right angles, which could be painted with a roller.

Very early I began to realize how long it took to do even the simplest jobs when doing them alone. I think I began to realize that I had grossly underestimated the cost of the project, and that I would be faced with completing the house basically by myself. The time/money equation was inexorable. With the Aetna commitment expiring in another eight or nine months, I decided we had no choice but to hire the work done that, originally I felt I could do, but I would run out of time. So, I gave up the idea of drywalling the house by myself, probably physically impossible without a helper, especially considering the high ceilings; and doing the insulation work by myself, which I knew I was capable of, but would also be too time consuming.

I remembered that we had a customer who was a journeyman plasterer, Eddie Piunno, and he agreed to do the job at cost. This was a wise solution because real plaster is far superior to drywall. After the United Insulation people finished installing the 4" flameproof cotton (not fiberglass) on the upper floors, finished installing ceiling and exterior walls, and I finished the lower level with 3 ply aluminum insulation where the exterior was cement block, we called in the lathers in preparation for the plaster. We nailed the ¾"x ¾' plaster grounds at the floor level. Fran on her hands and knees with me, and then learned that Piunno and his men were going to Canada on a 10-day fishing trip. It was very frustrating. But they did return, and they did a superior job; and we had a better house for it.

Prior to their work, we had to have the electrical work done, and once again, I turned to one of our residential customers, Bill Eyerdam. He had come to our office desperate to find financing for a home. He was widowed with five children and had married a widow with five children. They were all living in his mother-in-law's basement in Parma Heights. The living conditions were impossible; and he was slowly going crazy. I was able to get a VA guaranteed loan for him: 10% cash down payment, 4% interest rate and 25-year term. He said I might have saved his life, and if he could ever do anything for me, to call him. Which I did. He came to our house on Ridgewood Drive one evening after dinner and we sat cross-legged on the living room floor while he studied the plans. He was a master electrician and was one of men who had worked on the Ford Motor Company automated production line in the engine plant in Brookpark, Ohio. He was also a jazz harmonica musician, and a very good one. We sat on our living room floor, cross legged, listening and swaying to a jazz record I had just bought, Vic Dickensen's "I Cover the Waterfront" while he studied the working drawings. Fran did not find this spectacle very reassuring. Bill was thrilled with the plans and the chance to do something for me in appreciation for what I did for him (which I would have done for any customer). He said that he would really love to do the job but wouldn't unless he could get permission from his union and be allowed to place a union stamp on the finished job. When the union heard his story, they granted their permission.

Eyerdam assembled a crew of his brother, Roy, his father, Tom Rohrbach, who later became one of my favorite bridge partners, John Bitto, whose wife was a teller at my bank, and Frank, the pipe bender.

They were amazing. They improved on the architects' specifications, increasing the electric service to 200 amps, unheard of in a residence at that time; insisted on a phone outlet in every room, and wired one in, including the bathrooms; installed hi-hat light fixtures in ceilings; put two lamp receptacles in the living room floor in the middle of the room to accommodate possible furniture arrangements in front of the fireplace; used Sierra silent mercury switches; and installed a master switch in the master bedroom which turned on all the exterior lights under the roof eaves at once which improved our security. They kept running out of wire and I had to stop on the way home from work and bring more to them. They used a mile and a half of black and white wire. They also installed three branch panels in addition to the main panel in the garage, also unheard of in an ordinary residence. We became very good friends and saw each other in later years. I got Tommy Rohrbach interested in bridge again, and because of the bridge, his wife believed, he stopped his drinking which was becoming a problem. His wife, Dorothy, was very grateful.

After the plastering and wiring were done, it was time to tackle the rough plumbing work. All the interior waste and drainage piping had to be cast iron in those days which meant cutting the 4" heavy cast iron pipe to length with a hack saw, fitting the ends into the bell of the prior piece, tamping the joint with Oakum, and sealing it with molten lead heated in a pot with propane gas. It was complicated and tedious. I was always grateful that I never burned myself with the hot lead during the process. There were the kitchen and utility sink drains, and the four bathrooms. I was very happy when that part of the job was done, and once the cast iron left the house under the guest bedroom wall, could be hooked up to the slip-seal clay tile to the first septic tank, which was much easier to use.

I remember one Saturday afternoon when Bill Rehker visited to see what progress I was making. He taught me how to "sweat" a joint on copper tubing which we used for the water supply to the sinks and showers and tubs. After World War II copper began to replace galvanized steel and lead piping, so it was relatively new when I began my learning process. I had never done this before; and I liked it much better than the cast iron work. I had to learn to scrub the two ends of the copper pipe that were to be joined with steel wool until they were shiny, put them together, heat them with a propane torch (my neighbor, Ed Paulsen, across the street from us loaned me a large cylinder tank of propane which saved a lot of time and money), and when the joint was hot enough, to melt the solder wire into the joint by touching the wire to the hot metal void between the two pieces of pipe. I could see and hear the joint sucking up the solder, and then wiping the excess off. Needless to say, I was thrilled the first time we tested the piping with water pressure, after installing the water softener, that there was only two flaws: one was a poor solder joint of mine that had to be replaced. It was in the kitchen in an accessible spot, a 45 degree-bend  the other was a flaw in a ¾" elbow at the top of the water softener, a pin prick hole in the fitting, not the soldering. (I used a lot more solder than a real plumber would have, just to be on the safe side).

I think, as an amateur, I did many things to excess because so much of the work would be covered and inaccessible, and the house might have to last 100 years. My thinking was that if I spent a little more on materials, the additional cost was covered by the free labor I was providing.

I really did not like plumbing work; there was too much pressure from the uncertainty of not being able to test until everything was hooked up - what if the hot and cold lines were mixed up? Or a leak developed behind the walls?

Once the rough work was done, the finish job began. I set up shop on the highest level in the living room; built a crude stand for a DeWalt Power Saw which I bought and was invaluable. The finish lumber was stored in piles in the den. We used the finest lumber, poplar for the baseboard and window trim, walnut for the dining room cabinet, and solid cherry from near-by Peninsula, Ohio, for the wall in the living room-den. The kitchen cabinets had cherry plywood doors, and the cabinet in the dining room, walnut plywood with walnut trim. The stair treads to the living room were 1" oak, with the leading edge tapered 30 degrees, another probably un-noticed Japanese influence, and the bottom step extended along the planter in the entry hall to the bedroom wall. The entry hall walls were paneled in the same cypress as the exterior but left natural with a clear oil sealer stain. We used a different cypress, pecky and tongue and groove in the rec room in the lowest level. The bookshelves in the den were cherry planking. All the doors except the front and rear door were Gold Coast Cherry. The baseboard and window trim were painted, but all the other wood was left natural and, after power sanding with #0000 emery paper, coated with "Deft", a synthetic varnish which was a combination primer, sealer and finish. It had a peculiar odor which I can still smell today if I close my eyes and sniff. We spent a lot of time picking out the hardware for the drawer pulls in the kitchen, bathrooms, and dining room and used Schlage tulip-shaped handles for the doors, rather than the typical round knobs.

There were soffits along the exterior wall in the girl's bedroom level which covered the hot air ductwork to the living room/den area above the bedrooms. The heating for the lower levels was supplied by 8" galvanized duct pipes buried in the concrete floor. I was there when the floor was poured and watched the ready-mix truck back down the slope to the girls' level and tear off a major lower limb on the big white oak tree at the rear of the house. I remember the shock of hearing the ripping sound and seeing the limb fall to the ground. Luckily, it did not do any permanent damage to the tree which was a very important backdrop to the house.

I think I decided the next step before starting the carpentry work was to do the clay tile work in the bathrooms. In the 1950s, Cleveland was a very strong union labor town. The unions had almost monopoly power and could demand that union labor be used, at union rates, and if a contractor tried to use non-union labor, could shut down the job, and even resort to violence. It made building significantly more expensive and I always thought resulted in very unattractive, barracks-like apartment buildings, and manufacturing plants. I felt it helped explain the type of sterile architecture seen in the new subdivisions springing up on both sides of town. One outstanding builder, a Purdue graduate, was Bob Schmitt of Berea, Ohio. He produced more housing per square foot per dollar than any other builder in Greater Cleveland. His houses sold for less than the FHA appraisal value and were custom designed to order by his brother, Ed, an architect. A prospective buyer could walk into Ed's office, outline his needs, and move into the completed house in six weeks. All his houses were basementless and provided ample storage which he said he could produce above ground for less than digging a basement. My brother, Russ, who lived in Berea at that time knew Bob Schmitt, serving on the School Board with him, and our office did a fair amount of business with Schmitt, even financing the undergrounds on two of his subdivisions in Strongsville and North Ridgeville.

I mention this because Schmitt used non-union labor, prefabbing cabinetry in his own shops, and using three or four-man teams of inter-disciplinary workmen. I was aware of his success, which depended partially on his access to building materials, such as clay tile for bathrooms. In spite of my concerns about offending the unions to a point where they might pay a visit to our house to make their displeasure known upon finding that I had purchased materials for a "non-union" house, I had no choice but to proceed, and finally found a tile supplier on Fulton Road, on the west side of Cleveland, where I could order the tile I wanted: 6" square, rather than the usual 4", oatmeal color for the upper bathrooms, and pink for the lower level, buy the adhesive and grout, and the necessary tools. So, I had solved that problem, and in my mind, I budgeted four weeks to complete the job, working weekends and four weeknights, until midnight after finishing supper at home. I would use the DeWalt with an 8" carborundum cutting wheel which produced clouds of ceramic dust coating everything for the fine fitting work. Another optimistic estimate: the job took eight weeks but turned out well and held up well. I even tiled the ceilings of the stall shower and tub enclosures while I was at it. I was very pleased with the outcome and there was no union trouble.

I remember that early in the building process, the driveway was three to four-inch slag and, I thought, very hard on tires. My solution was to find a used car that we could use for going to and from and for hauling necessary supplies. I cannot remember where we found it, but we bought a used Kaiser for $150, a post war off-brand, produced briefly by a new automobile manufacturer, the Tucker Company. Mr. Tucker also named a higher class, more expensive model the "Tucker". Our Kaiser was in poor condition. It was a 4-door sedan, but instead of a trunk, had a 5th door which made the whole interior accessible for hauling supplies, much like a station wagon. Two things I remember about it were the driver's door had to be propped up with the left hand while closing it, otherwise the door would not latch; and the tires were snow tires which did not have deep treads, but raised rubber circles about 1 inch in diameter. It served us well during the construction period, and when the job was finally completed I took it to a junk yard at Brookpark and Pearl Roads, on the west side in Cleveland where they paid me $35 for it because it could be driven in, not towed.

I think I should spend some time describing the floor plan of our house of dreams and the thinking behind it before getting into the actual building of the cabinets, etc. In our letter to the architects commissioning the job, I tried to lay out my philosophy of what a house should do for a family. It should be more than simply shelter; it should be a place providing serenity, but excitement; it should be simple, but elegant; it should be subtle in achieving it effects, not extreme or blatant; it should accommodate our style of living. It should be a positive influence on our lives together.

I advised them that we required a separate bedroom for each of our three daughters, with their own bath; that we wanted a master bedroom suite with its own bath and separate stall shower; that we wanted a guest room for Fran's mother for her visits, and in case of illness; that we wanted a large separate dining room because much of our entertaining involved dinner parties; we needed a living room and den with wood burning fireplace, large enough to accommodate three or four card tables for our bridge clubs; a separate recreation area for our piano and where the children and their friends could play without having adults passing through their space, where practicing their piano lessons could be done in private; space for a future dark room, and a cold storage area. We hoped they could come up with a plan where in our later years we could live on the ground floor level, when climbing stairs might become a problem; and a three-car garage, the extra stall for all the grounds keeping equipment I anticipated needing. Above all, they were to provide for as many large plate glass windows as possible to bring the outdoors into the house, and they were to be aware of opportunities to include Japanese features. I hoped there would be a simple, overpowering logic to their design.

The final plan they devised, with which I fell in love instantly, managed to provide a very tidy solution to the problems I had posed to them. Its exterior was a "soft" modern style with a pitched roof, not the, to me, ugly cubic, boxy, flat roof ultra-modern style. It was sited at the highest point on the property at its southwest corner close to the edge of the ravine, surrounded by trees on the south and west elevations with an unobstructed view to the northeast of the Cuyahoga Valley. Except during the winter snowstorms coming directly from the north, the trees provided a windbreak, which was very welcome, and added to our sense of being sheltered from the storm.

To describe the floor plan: the 3' front door, surrounded by plate glass from floor to ceiling, with a centered door-knob, opened on to an entry hall about 14' x 18' with a slate floor and sloped ceiling following the roof line and 14' above floor level at its high point. It was the central distribution point for all the rooms in the house. There was a copper lined planter (3' x 12') along the east wall, which was six panels of plate glass,(unfortunately our budget did not permit Thermopane in the Entry Hall), next to the stairs on the right up to the living room and down to the girls' bedrooms and recreation, furnace and storage rooms. There was unfinished storage area above the stairwell. To the left, a short hall led to the guest room (12' x 14'), and master bedroom (12' x 20'). All upper level flooring was unfinished plywood to be carpeted; all bathroom floors were 3" hexagons in the same color as the walls; the kitchen was floored with expensive Robbins rubber tile, and the concrete basement level floors were covered with asphalt tile, later carpeted. To the right was the coat closet and entrance to the dining room (12' x 20', which was open to the living room, about 4' above the entry hall level, which could be closed off with Japanese sliding *shoji* panels; it also had a pseudo *tokonoma* alcove on the wall between the kitchen and the dining room. The kitchen-breakfast nook-utility area (16' x 24') was reached from the corner of the dining room and had the rear door and a door to the garage. The garage and kitchen areas had a flat "pond" tar and gravel roof which theoretically kept the rooms below cooler in hot weather, but it failed and leaked and had to be replaced with a slightly pitched surface to allow water runoff.

From the entry hall one climbed four steps to the living room (20'x 20') level which was divided from the den by a double fireplace. The wall facing the ravine had two large fixed-glass panels looking down into the ravine, flanked by two operating Pella windows. The north wall was solid cherry in the living room with a slit window at the top of the stairs, and in the den a 6' x 10' Thermopane glass window with Pella awning type windows below for ventilation, looking out on the Cuyahoga valley with its light display on the distant hills after dark. The fireplace on the den side had a raised hearth, cherry paneling above the mantle and a cabinet for the TV, opening to both the living room and the den, and bookshelves between the fireplace and the wall,

Going down the stairs from the entry hall led to a hall with three 10' x 12' bedrooms for our daughters, in two of which the position of the closets allowed me to build built-in desks next to their closets, and the bath and lavatory were located along the north side of the hallway. The girls appreciated it when we were able to carpet the asphalt tile floor. Up near the ceiling was a remote listening device which was connected to the master bedroom, so we were able to hear if the daughters needed help or were delaying closing their eyes. There was a grade door at the lower level landing on the way down to the lowest level, where the recreation room was located and the furnace room, storage room, and dark room/storage room. Only the rec room was finished with pecky cypress paneling. I built a bench below bookshelves on one wall, and there were three Pella awning type windows which opened onto the Japanese stone garden between the house and the ravine, to provide light and ventilation. The furnace room was under the entry hall and unfinished. It was interesting to me to see the exposed joists which were 2"x 6" but on a 12" rather than the usual 16" spacing used with 2'x 8's. The 2-inch difference provided the depth needed above for the mortar bed for the slate entry floor and the closer spacing allowed for the heavier than usual weight caused by the slate. It was a very crowded room with two Perfection hot air furnace, (the best money could buy) the hot water tank, and the water softener with its brine tank. There was also access to the concrete paved crawl space under the master bedroom wing.

So, there were four levels: the daughters' bedrooms were on the level under the living room/den; the rec room/furnace rooms were under the entry hall, dining room and kitchen. It was a very practical utilization of space, very compact and very efficient, providing enough square feet for us live in on one floor in our old age. It would have been nice if we could have afforded a full basement under the master bedroom, but the budget would not permit it.

Now is the time to recall as much of the detail of the various finishing tasks I had to perform as I can remember. There were so many and spread over such a long time that I am sure many will be neglected, and probably be of no interest to the reader. Bill Rehker was certainly qualified to teach me how to "sweat" a joint, but really excelled in his specialty, carpentry. He taught me how to use a level; how to stretch a line when building a soffit; how to use a plumb line; how to build a cabinet base; how to install a doorframe; how to hang a door; how to build kitchen and bath cabinets and drawers; how to select a piece of wood to find its natural bow and then how to use a wedge to force it into place, straightening it to fit over its neighbor's groove; how to use a coping saw to cut a profile on a piece of trim obviating the need for a perfect meeting of two 45 degree angles; how to stay on the right side of the measuring line when using the DeWalt. And much more which I cannot dredge up from my memory. Between him and my neighbor from across Oakes Road, Ed Paulsen, who loaned tools to me and offered solid advice, by the time the job was completed I was on the way to becoming a fairly competent carpenter. I had learned that nothing is naturally straight or level and how to compensate for nature's shortcomings.

I built the cabinets in the bathrooms first, I believe, and covered the surface around the sinks with the same tile used on the floors, 3" hexes. This process then moved to the kitchen where the base cabinets were anchored to the wall with nails, the kitchen and utility room counter tops and sinks were stainless steel which came from Chicago, and we had to wait for their arrival, and used oil cloth over 1" x 10" planking and a temporary sink loaned to us while waiting for the stainless steel. I think it was more than a month before the stainless steel arrived. It wasn't easy for Fran to function. In the corner opposite the doorway from the dining room, we had side by side stainless steel Thermidor ovens. The kitchen counter had a row of windows its entire length which gave a commanding view of the front door, and of the pond which we built later. There were hanging cabinets suspended from the ceiling over the base cabinets separating the working and eating areas. We used cherry plywood for these cabinet. The doors were cut from the sheets of 3/4 inch cherry plywood which were in serial order, which, when hung with concealed hinges, maintained the natural order of the wood grain. We used Deft to finish the doors which were smooth and unornamented. There was also a large window looking out at the beech and oak trees, a shallow pantry cupboard, and a slit window next to the rear door. The utility room had the same finish and had the laundry equipment backed up to the kitchen plumbing. The utility sink was 12" deep which proved to be useful. The utility area was on the same slab as the garage and had no basement under it.

I took a little time off after the interior of the house proper was finished and we were living there before finishing the garage. I think it was about a year and a half later when I drywalled it, a miserable job to do alone, and put up two storage shelves which ran the length of the garage. I also thought it was ironic that when I no longer needed it, I built a nice home for my DeWalt saw on my workbench in the garage.

All this learning process preparation culminated in the walnut dining room cabinet which was built-in and covered the width of the dining room. I was fortunate that even although the width of the room was 12' 2" or so, with the picture framing trim around the top and sides of the cabinet, a sheet of 12' x 3' walnut plywood would cover the area, allowing for the seven saw blade width cuts that had to be made to make the cabinet doors, this after cutting the 12' sheet of plywood into three widths length-wise for the top of the cabinet, the showcase above the cabinet, and the doors. This was a very delicate operation trying to keep a uniform width over that length, without a really proper work bench providing stable support in the living room shop. I remember Bill Montgomery, who was on one of his infrequent visits, standing down in the dining room, receiving and supporting the cuts of the plywood as I made them. It was tricky, but we managed to get it done and with the correct dimensions. I think the cabinet was 42" high and had a 12" display cabinet on top next to the wall which was at floor level with the living room and provided the base for the *shoji* panels. This was divided into four sections and was enclosed with sliding glass panels; the interior was painted Chinese red. We bought four simple authentic *shoji* panels made of walnut and rice paper from a company in San Francisco that I found in the magazine *Interiors*; they were hung on tracks fastened to the opening from the living room looking down into the dining room, and all four panels could be stacked in a pocket at the head of the stairway to the girls' rooms on the lower level. When the four panels were pulled closed, they made the living room and dining room into two separate spaces, but we found we preferred having one panel stationary at each end of the opening, preferring the open feeling. I do not remember how the panels were packed for shipping (they were fairly fragile) such a great distance, nor how much we paid for them. The sensation of sitting at the dining room table, looking out toward the little pond and ravine, under a sloped ceiling 12' high, and looking up into the living room with its cathedral ceiling gave me great pleasure.

I remember the amount of time it took me to learn how to install a door frame and hang the doors. Doors and frame were not prefabbed when we built the Oakes Road house, but came in three pieces separately which had to be cut to fit, plumbed vertically and shimmed to fit the doors, which were hung after the frame was in place. Rehker advised allowing a "nickel" of additional width in the frame so the door could close easily. Both the door and the frame had to be notched for the hinges, and the door had to be drilled from the edge to receive the latch, and the face had to be cut with a circular keyhole saw using a 1/4 hp electric drill. For my first attempt I chose the small coat closet near the door to the garage. It took me a whole Sunday afternoon to put together the frame, drill the holes in the door and install the hinges. It seemed very complicated.

The large openings for the closet doors in the bedrooms were no easier to do. If I count in my memory correctly, I believe there were fourteen doors to be hung, plus one sliding-pocket door in the lower level bathroom, which was very complicated, plus fourteen closet openings with sliding slatted closet doors. However, at the end, I did the final nine doors in one day. I was pleased. And it is true: practice makes faster, if not perfect.

We could not afford readymade cabinetry, and I wanted to have as much storage space built in as possible, so it fell to me to build the cabinets, and the drawers in them. These were located in all the baths, the kitchen and utility room, and between the fireplace and the outer wall in the living room. In that cabinet I built a sliding shelf for the TV, which could be pulled out, so the TV could be viewed from either the den or the living room, I also built an upholstered bench in the den, and a plain one in the rec room, both with book shelves above them. The provision for every day storage was ample, but the accessibility of the dead storage above the stairwell and the master baths required a ladder which was not very convenient but worth it. One innovation of mine was to build three sliding shelves in the middle section of the dining room buffet for storing table linens, which pleased Fran. All in all, the storage aspect of the planning was excellent; the one oversight was not providing an easy way to get at our folding card tables. We had to dig behind the coats on the coat closet in the entry hall to find them which was a nuisance.

The finish work was very satisfying; every time an element of the work was completed there was a sense of satisfaction; every time a whole room was completed and the concepts shown on the working drawings became three dimensional and tangible, it created a state of almost euphoria. So many of the jobs in themselves were unexciting and time consuming; fitting the trim around the windows; putting down the baseboards, for instance; the final painting or the "Defting" of the wood paneling; the completion of the cherry wall in the living room and over the fireplaces; constructing the two cherry mantles; the surfaces sanded smooth before applying the three coats of Deft, rubbed with fine steel wool between coats of the satiny Deft, which produced a surface comparable to that of furniture bought in a store; of making the drawings come to life and be true to them, were triumphs which no one but myself could really appreciate.

The cherry wall in the living room posed a problem, initially. Bob Gaede, the architect, prepared drawings of several different ways it could be finished to provide interest, and we finally decided the simplest way: random length, random width, and simple tongue and groove would be the best. We would rely on the natural beauty of the wood grain and its rich color to keep the expanse of wall from being boring. The actual job was exacting; five horizontal l" x 2" stringers had to be nailed horizontally at floor and ceiling level and three evenly spaced between them to which the pieces of cherry would be nailed; then the cherry had to be selected, and, when the length was less than 8', had to be cut to measure, using the fine tooth saw blade on the Dewalt for smooth end cuts, leaving carefully saved scrap pieces; bevel the ends with a plane to match the grooving where the two ends met; and, then, the tricky part, the nailing.

I was taught to use 4 penny finish nails, and every nail hole had to be drilled because cherry is a very, very hard wood and will bend the nail and split the wood if not drilled, even when the nail is greased with plumber's wax, as I was also taught. I drilled a hole in the handle of my hammer and melted the wax into it and inserted the nail in the wax before nailing a piece of cherry into place. Even then some of the nails bent. And I don't how many drill bits I dulled and burned out. The cherry was nailed from the tongue side at a 45 degree-angle after sliding it onto the tongue of the previous piece; if the piece was bowed, it was necessary to nail a piece of wood temporarily onto the stringer and drive a wedge between it and the piece being nailed to straighten it in order to make a tight fit for the next piece to be put in place. But all the effort was worth it, it was so beautiful when it was finished.

Another vivid memory was the laying of the slate in the entry hall. I had helped my good friend, Roy Hausheer, V.P., Land Title and Guarantee Company, and a regular luncheon companion, with some work on his house in Olmsted Falls, Ohio, and when he heard I was about to lay the slate, he offered to help. He had no idea what he was getting into. Neither did I. The load of slate was delivered a couple of days before the weekend which I had allocated for the job; I do not remember where we purchased it, but it was Vermont slate, fairly light gray and in irregular shapes and thicknesses, not cut into the regular 4" x 6", or 8" x 8" squares used in Ashlar patterns, which would have made it a much easier job. On Friday, before Roy came on Saturday morning, I laid out the slate outside the front door in a pattern, carefully marking three sides of the adjoining pieces of slate with chalk so we would not lose the pattern, (somewhat similar to doing a jigsaw puzzle,) when we carried each piece in to be set in the cement mortar which we mixed by hand in batches and transported into the house with a wheelbarrow.

Roy arrived about 8:30 a.m. and we got started. We began by laying the slate in the corner of the entry hall between the bedroom hallway and the planter, an area about 4' x 5' which consumed the first load of mortar, spread about 1-2" thick, varied for the thickness of the slate, which we leveled as we progressed. But when we got to the second load of mortar, we lost the pattern, and my chalk marks did not help us. We would have been much better off had we started with a narrow strip of slate the length of the planter to the stairway and worked toward the front door. From that time on it was a nightmare, making up the pattern as we went along, trying to find pieces of slate which would fit together without leaving too large an area between pieces to fill with cement grout after the slate had set. I think it took us until 6 or 7:00 pm to finish. I felt as though I had fishhooks implanted in my temples and someone was pulling on the lines. Roy stuck with me to the end and I could never repay him for his help. A day or so later I mixed up grout using Pozzalano cement from Pittsburgh, which was a light gray and made a pleasing contrast to the slate. The floor held up; did not develop cracks, and was very practical, removing dirt, etc. from shoes before entering the carpeted areas of the house. The only maintenance was to put a coat of wax on it every spring.

That was the day when Fran came out to work on painting the fascia of the kitchen and garage. She was working on the fascia above the garage door, on a ladder that was, unknown to her, sinking into the unpaved, mud apron of the garage. She was wearing an old brown sweater and a worn-out pair of pink corduroy slacks, when suddenly, the ladder slipped below the fascia board which had been supporting it, and the bucket of cold, wet white paint spilled towards her and covered her in paint. She came into the Entry where Roy and I were struggling with our job, adopted a Charlie Chaplin pose, holding the pants out to the side, pants cuffs filled with paint, seeking some sympathy. I guessed what had happened and she had obviously not fallen from the ladder and was unhurt, so I uttered the immortal words, "How much paint did you waste?" These kind words were not well received. But the opportunity for a "straight line" couldn't be passed up. We found an old pair of pants of mine, which we had to use a length of rope to hold up on her, and bless her, she went back and completed her job.

Putting up the cypress in the entry hall was simple compared to the cherry wall in the living room. Cypress is a much softer wood and could be nailed straight without drilling or wedging and when finished with a natural oil stain gave a very warm appearance. I was pleased to add another Japanese touch by finding a piece of cypress that was darker than the others and using it for the lintel over the hallway to the master bedroom. I was able to slant both ends at 30 degree-angles, which was an echo of Japanese *torii* entry archways, which are found at Japanese temples.

The ceiling of the Entry also proved to be troublesome. It sloped to match the roof line and started at about 10' at the low point and ascended to 14' at the ridge beam. It was to be finished with ordinary 1' x 6' tongue and groove yellow pine, which is another very hard wood, and exceptionally warped and curvy. I had to work on scaffolding, all the work overhead, getting up and down from the scaffolding, and working upside down, and found it to be very tiring. It was to be painted white when finished and at least I did not have to sand it when the job was finally completed. It was one of least pleasant jobs in all the finish work.

I do not remember how soon after finishing the entry hall floor, I started working outside on the stone pavers in front of the garage and the kitchen, which were the approach to the front door. We had another Japanese touch at the front door; in a typical Japanese home, the stoop at the front door is usually a large round flat river stone. In our case we used a piece of sandstone about 3' x 5' and 4" thick. The hidden base for this entry stone made it seem to float, and the 4" step up from the grade level of the house was an easy transition.

The stone we chose for the entry approach was called "yellow stone", a form of sandstone found at a quarry in Amherst, Ohio. It was delivered in pieces about 2' wide and 6-7' long, rough at both ends. I had to learn to use a large square and score the surface with a steel stylus, being sure to break the surface with my line. When that was done, the stone would snap and separate. I would cut one of the rough ends first, making sure that the cut was a right angle, snap it and then measure to 3' and score another cut, snap and repeat at the other rough end. I would end up with two pieces of stone 2' x 3', very glad it could be done so simply without any sawing. I remember how hot it was and using two or three of Barbara's old diapers, which were very absorbent, to wipe off my sweat. Each piece weighed about fifty pounds and had to be picked up and laid on a bed of sand with one inch spacing all around to maintain the geometry of the pattern. These voids were later filled with sand. I remember how pleased I was when the job was done; I loved the simple geometric pattern of the stone; I had realized another part of my dream.

One other memory associated with the entry to the house remains. I was painting the final coat of white paint (we used the Cabot brand, the same manufacturer as the stain, for the first finish work) on the overhang at the front door. I had to use a ladder on both sides and an expandable walk board stretched between them to paint the outer edge of the overhang which meant I could not brace myself on the wall for balance. The board was somewhat springy, and I had to maintain my balance while painting overhead. It was then that I realized that I was no longer comfortable with heights. I thought what a disaster it would be to fall from such a height - the rear side of the entry hall was even worse - and end up crippled, or dead, after having worked three years without a serious accident. In the future, we would pay a contractor to have the painting done.

To make matters worse, Fran had driven to Detroit with the children to visit her mother over the 4th of July weekend, and I was alone, expecting to get a great deal accomplished because we had not told anyone that I would not be with the family in Detroit. While I was on "the high wire,' bouncing around, the phone rang. I would have to move from the middle of the walk board to get to one of the ladders, lower myself to get on to the ladder to climb down, and hurrying, get to the phone inside the house in the kitchen before it stopped ringing. I debated whether I should take the risk. And finally decided to do it. It could be Fran calling, needing help, or one of the children might be sick. Or car trouble.

The phone kept ringing and I made it down safely and when I answered it I learned that it was Bruce Hardy, the only high school friend I still knew, former Captain of the Lakewood High School marching band. We played bridge with him and his wife, Doris. He was calling to tell me that Doris, who was only 38 years old, mother of three, had died suddenly from an aneurysm in the brain. He was obviously very emotional, knew I would want to know, and that I would be a great support for him. I tried to be of help to him, of course; went to the visitation at the Baker Funeral home in Berea, and to the funeral at one of the churches in Berea a day later. This was my first experience of a death of a peer my age, and I was very upset; until I was driving home when I suddenly realized what a hypocrite I was; that I was not really grieving for my friend's wife, but for myself because I had suddenly realized that if it had been me, life would have gone on and in a few weeks the world would not know I had ever existed. It was a thought I had never had before. And it had nothing to do with a newfound fear of heights.

We moved into our new home in time for the beginning of the fall term of school at Highland Elementary three years after starting the job, Nancy was 8, Kathy was 5 and Barbara 2. Unfortunately, this was the only time in the whole building process that I didn't feel well. I came down with what seemed like the 48-hour flu the day before the move. I was desperately trying to finish laying the rubber tile on the kitchen floor so the refrigerator could be put in place and so we wouldn't have to be walking on the underlayment felt. I took Friday off from work to try to get the job done and worked until midnight and still did not have it finished when I just had to go home to bed. The next day the movers came and I simply sat and watched them load the van and then go out to 5320, sitting on the top step to the living room, holding my head in my hands, watched them unload our meager pieces of furniture. I never felt so useless. Luckily, Fran's mother had come down from Detroit to help and she looked after the children.

The living room was still my workshop, and we used the dining room for our living room temporarily. The kitchen counter was wood covered with oilcloth; the girls' bedrooms did not have doors yet; Uncle Herb came over two or three times the week before the move and put in shelves in their closets, which was very kind. He was very competent and meticulous, and I wanted his approval of my work very much. Fortunately, we did not have adventurous sons; and I did not have to put my tools away every night, because the girls were girls and not interested in the carpentry-work I was doing. I think we lived this way for another year or year and a half before the job could be called done, and we could finalize the much-extended loan commitment from the Aetna.

We had had trouble finding a buyer for the house in Parma Heights, and finally, after 18 months of making two mortgage payments, by a complete fluke, I was overheard by an older lady sitting at the same large round table in the Blue Boar Cafeteria, talking about our house on Ridgewood Drive with our credit report supplier, Harold Trattner. I had run into him unexpectedly and we had lunch together. Being in the soliciting side of his business, he had to listen to me lamenting and not understanding why no broker could find a buyer for such a nice house and we hadn't had any success, ourselves, and the price was right, at which point a little old lady sitting opposite us at the round table for eight, spoke up and said she might be interested and gave me her pack of cigarettes and asked me to write down my telephone number - she might call me.

When I got home that evening, I told Fran about this strange encounter and we thought no more of it. The next morning, Saturday, at 8 a.m. the phone rang. It was the little old lady. She wanted to know if she could bring her daughter and see the house that afternoon. We said, of course, and the deal closed at our full asking price of $18,000 at her bank at Warrensville Center and Cedar Roads the next Thursday. She was really very nice and asked me if I would paint the living room walls, which I was glad to do. There were one or two other small things I helped her with. She had a German name, I think Schwachter and her husband had been a jeweler on Pearl Road at Lorain Street. When he died, she took over the business, so she had the experience that allowed her to make a quick decision. One never knows where lightning will strike.

At this point, now might be a good time to clarify my role in this building process. In all the years since building the house at 5320 Oakes Road, when the subject came up I would say that after the plasterers and electricians finished their jobs, that there was not another paid worker involved; it was implied always that it was "I" who did all the work and you may have noticed how often that pronoun has been used in these recollections, but that was not strictly true. We hired a man to install the glass door in the stall shower in the master bedroom, and we hired another man, a paperhanger from Berea, to hang the Japanese grass cloth wall covering in the dining room. There was other help, also, provided by friends. The neighbor across the street, Ed Paulson, who walked over to check progress almost every time I came out to work, was a great source of good advice on how to do the new things I was learning and had many tools in his little barn workshop which were always at my disposal.

Also, my brother, Ken, spent an afternoon shoveling fill sand into the foundation under the utility room; Roy Hausheer was a tremendous help in laying the entry hall slate floor; and Wilson (Bill) Townsend contributed more hours of free labor than anyone else. He was a friend of one of Fran's sorority sisters, Ginny Heun, who lived in Chicago. Bill had been moved by his employer, Home Lines, a Greek shipping company, to open a one-man office in Cleveland. Ginny called Fran and asked her if we could invite him for dinner since he knew no one in Cleveland, was single, and very lonely. He accepted the invitation instantly and showed up on a Saturday night with his box of carpenters' tools in the trunk of his car, as I recall.

Bill was about 5'8" tall, fair complexion with a tuft of curly hair in a widow's peak, and very agreeable. He was a graduate of Rutgers University and fit right in with our family. When he saw the house, he loved it, and when he learned that I was doing all the finish work, offered to help, and claimed to have the necessary skills. His claims proved to be true, and thus began a relationship which lasted until well after the house was completed. Almost every weekend he would come to Brecksville after work, change into the work clothes he had left there, and undertake whatever task I was involved with at the time. He would sleep over in the guest room and became a part of the family. I think he liked our daughters and they liked him, and he got along well with Fran who made regular reports to Ginny back in Chicago.

I remember Bill out cutting the "lawn" (still the original vegetation) with the Gravely mower which was powerful and hard to handle, being thrown around off his feet while desperately holding onto the handles of the tractor when he had to turn around at the end of a swath. It was like watching a bucking bronco.

My most vivid memory is when we were doing the finish cypress work in the entry on the stairs to the living room, and Bill was shaping a small 6"piece of cypress on a planer at the head of the stairs; I was working nearby, when I heard an ominous "thunk". He had been careless and pushed a very short piece of wood through the planer, not with a "push- stick", but with his hands. The piece of wood bucked and drew his right forefinger into the blade and sliced the end of his finger off to the first joint. I remember the awful sound and looking up and seeing blood splatter sprayed on the ceiling above. It was late on a Sunday afternoon (when the few mishaps we experienced always seemed to occur), and we bandaged the stump of his finger as best we could and went to Marymount Hospital emergency room to have it taken care of. I think he stayed with us a few days before going back to work, and for a few weeks I used to go to his office, nearby on Euclid Avenue, after work and type his correspondence. There was no infection and after a short time, he resumed his regular routine and continued his invaluable assistance. I always felt a little responsibility for the accident; after all the premises were mine, although it was his carelessness with its little touch of characteristic bravado which caused it.

The fact is he became like a fourth brother to me and I was sorry when he was moved again to the Home Lines home office in New York. We lost touch after his move except for Christmas cards and I do not know if he met a girl, or married, and built his own home. He never came out to Cleveland to visit the finished product to which he had contributed so much. My final contact was not with him, but with his parents who were living in a small town in New York state where I dropped off a few of Bill's things he had left behind when I was on my way to New Haven for one of my class reunions.

Once we moved in, it was a time for relaxation, for getting used to our additional space, and to begin to observe the subtle influence the house exerted on us, which was what I had so hoped for. It wasn't hard to do. I did odds and ends, created a vegetable garden in front of the house where the pond would later be constructed, finished the garage interior, finally was able to get the driveway paved with asphalt by a contractor who quoted a price much too low based on my experience as an appraiser, and who begged me to agree to pay more when they were on the last truck load of asphalt, which I refused to do. The fact that the asphalt was much thinner down near the road turned out not to matter. I think it was about this time that we had an overhead door opener installed on the heavy plywood garage door. I used to jokingly say that the two best parts of the whole house were the paved driveway and the garage door opener. I was constantly pinching myself in disbelief that everything worked; that nothing fell apart, or leaked, or fell down. I couldn't accept that a person, me, who never completed even a model airplane as a teenager, could have had the patience and tenacity to spend three years of his free time completing as large and complex a job as our House of Dreams.

The house functioned so well; it was great for entertaining, both friends and large family gatherings, our largest being Barbara's wedding after-reception party. I remember looking for Barb and finding her in the lowest level in the rec room, (her version is that they were gathered at the *tokonoma* in the dining room) teary eyed, singing with her sorority sisters songs from their songbook. The daughters loved having their own rooms and their own bath. For the first few years the entire family, including Fran's mother, always, gathered in Brecksville for Thanksgiving or Christmas, twelve around the table in the dining room, and the rest at the table in the kitchen. It helped having two ovens with such large numbers to feed.

I loved having people in for bridge when I would play my favorite jazz things softly in the background and didn't care too much how good the cards were. I felt that people enjoyed being in such a home, so different from the conventional homes they were used to; if they were accustomed to Early-American, not quite understanding why they felt so comfortable. Ownership of this house was immaterial; it was a validation of my theories, and a tribute to our architects.

Moving into the new house, and living in it, brought a new set of problems. We had very little furniture, just enough to furnish a 900 square home: easy chair, love seat, black lacquered maple cocktail table I had built myself, a blond oak TV cabinet for our first 14" black and white Admiral TV, slippery elm drop-leaf dining room table, and beds, of course. We were expanding into 3400 square feet, and in spite of building in as many things as possible, we needed new living room and dining room furniture, a dinette set for our daily meals, among other things.

I had spent many hours at the library studying the magazine *Interiors* which featured contemporary designs, now known as "Mid-Century Modern." The work of the designer, Paul McCobb: appealed to me the most for its timeless simplicity and elegance. I remember how pleased I was when I learned that there was a furniture showroom at E. 40th Street and Prospect Avenue, The Tom Sinks Company, who carried his work. Fortunately, Fran and her mother had been exposed to this type of furniture, the antithesis of the bloated, overstuffed things common at the time, while living in Midland, Michigan, where modern furniture was preferred in the homes they visited. There was no resistance to my evolved tastes, utterly different from that of my parents, and, Mrs. Thompson, Fran's mother, paid for our selections. I cannot believe that I can't remember the details of an expenditure of that size, for something so important, and which meant so much to me.

For the living room, we bought a Paul McCobb 7' sofa covered with a yellow fabric, a couple of easy chairs, two small square leather top coffee tables used in front of the sofa, a large 4' McCobb circular white vitreous coffee table flanked by a McCobb easy chair and two T.J.

Robbisjohn-Gibbings slipper chairs, gifts of Fran's mother, and another leather covered end table. We already had two square JBL walnut speaker cabinets which sat on the floor at both ends of the sofa and acted as end tables for lamps. All these pieces were arranged around the perimeter of the room which was 20' x 20', leaving the central portion open, and we never used the two electric outlets seated in the floor in the middle of the room which had been provided by our electricians for a possible seating arrangement in front of the fireplace. However, I used them for practicing my putting in the dreary winter season, the green carpeting an adequate substitute for bent grass, so their over-planning did not go entirely to waste.

After thirty or so years later, we had thought of ways we could make a perfect house even more livable than it had been for a growing family of five, and make it more suitable for us to be able to live entirely on the ground level as we grew older. We employed Clyde Patterson, solo this time, to prepare drawings for additions to the house, which totaled about 600 square feet. We ended up having a contractor, recommended by Clyde who was a wannabee architect himself, whom I got to know well. But I only remember his first name: Claudio. He prepared working drawings for the tiniest details for his crew every day.

We added a family room 12' x 26' on the kitchen wall as wide as the space between the dining room and the garage, entered from the original rear door in the dining room, and with a new rear door onto the concrete apron behind the garage. The ceiling was sloped and had exposed beams, all stained natural, and all three walls were Anderson glass. The room was like living in a tree house. The original breakfast area wall between the kitchen and the new room was removed, opening up the kitchen area that was completely remodeled with new natural beechwood cabinetry imported from West Germany. I remember how impressed I was that the order was received at the Port of Baltimore 6 weeks after it was placed and how precisely everything fit together. My old cherry cabinets and the old island were removed, and a new island cabinet placed where the new stove top was installed. It was interesting that the new room was built over a crawl space, and that the stove vented downward under the floor to the rear of the new room. We found two circular ceramic sinks which were placed at a 45 degree-angle at the corner of the new Formica counter tops. Before, the kitchen was open to the utility room; now, a wall was built creating two separate rooms. We also discovered multicolored Mexican terra cotta 12" square pavers for the kitchen floor. The new family room had its own furnace located in a corner of the garage and was also used to heat the kitchen which had always been a cold room because of the amount of glass on the north wall. Now we had three separate heating and cooling zones. It was all very efficient and a big improvement. And I thought most attractive.

The other improvements were in the master bedroom/guest room wing. We replaced the windows in the master bedroom overlooking the pond with Anderson sash to within 12' of the floor so that the pond could be seen while lying in bed; and another addition, 8' x 30' was added to the east wall. This enlarged the guest room to 12' x 18' and created space for a new bath at the corner of the house which was entered from the master bedroom by removing the center section of the closets where the chest of drawers had been located, and from the enlarged guest room from a new doorway in the addition. The big attraction for us was a 6' fiberglass sunken whirlpool bathtub which we discovered at the Home & Garden Show at the Cleveland Public Auditorium. It was manufactured by Pearl and could be ordered in a custom color, in our case a light green to match the green tile walls. We purchased it from the Wolf Plumbing Supply Company in Medina, Ohio; with glass windows on two sides to tub level it afforded a wonderful view of the pond and a great place to soak away the cares of the world in complete privacy. We used a one-piece white sink top in a non-marbleized pseudo Corian material. Also, the new toilet fixtures, which included a Kohler bidet were in the same color of green as the tub. I always thought it was one of the nicest rooms in the house

Before we solved the furniture problem, we had to solve the carpeting problem. I remember an evening meeting at the house while the living room was still being used as a workshop. Two carpeting salesmen who owned their own company, Morrie Herskowitz and Ted Wahl, spent a whole evening educating us (and entertaining us) as to the merits of various types of carpeting (it was almost like a Kirby Vacuum Cleaner salesman pitch) and we ended up looking no further and ordering a one piece, seamless, 20' x 30' beige cotton carpet woven in India. The cutouts for the fireplace and the den bench were used to carpet the stairs leading down to the girls' bedroom level. I remember coming home from work the day the carpet was laid and rushing in to see it and kneeling on the top step of the stairs to the living room and remember the feeling of brushing the surface with my hand, caressing it. It was our first wall-to-wall carpeting and another milestone.

Several years later the original carpeting was replaced with one of the standard brands manufactured in the U.S, with seams, and in a soft, light green color; I don't remember if we went back to Herskowitz. It was the start of our "green" period for flooring which lasted as long as we owned our own home. Fran loved pastels: the light greens, the pinks, the corals and used them extensively, feeling that they formed the background for a bright, cheerful but restful living space. This was particularly true in Brecksville where we had so many windows bringing the outside in and allowing us to be outside while inside.

As I recall, it was at this time that we were finally able to carpet the girls' level and I think, although they never complained, that they were glad not to have to pad to the bathroom in their bare feet over cold asphalt tile any longer. I always felt that their rooms in a so-called English basement with windows at grade level looking out at nature (they saw a fox once, and a mother quail leading her hatchlings along the foundation, another time) with their built-in desks and now carpeted were very cozy retreats for them from the world, from school and from their parents

I remember the many, not all by any means, parties we had at 5320; the three after-wedding reception parties when we invited the out-of-town guests who otherwise would have been alone in a strange city to the house for the evening and how disappointed I was when they left all too soon; my not having been able to spend more time with each of them.

1 also remember the bridge group taking time from the bridge table to gather in the den and watch Neil Armstrong take his first step on the moon; the somber, silent daylong vigil watching the pageantry of the J.F.K. funeral; the all too few visits of out of town friends; three of my Army

friends did see the house, Norton, Wells, and Ray Kiser and his wife (Norton referred to the pond as "Lake Eerie"); the year the Camp Michigania group chose to drive all the way to Cleveland at our urging, for our annual mini-reunion after a football game in Ann Arbor - all the others lived in Michigan nearby, or Toledo, so it was a special effort to come all the extra distance.

I reserved a tee time at Sleepy Hollow Golf Club, which had become a public Metropolitan Park golf course thanks to the efforts of Senator Metzenbaum, for Sunday morning and do not remember who was in my foursome, but I do remember "Skip" Gross, Dick's wife, who were members of a private country club in Toledo, imperiously ordering the starter to put her bag on the cart and his look of amazement. I was embarrassed, but the starter had a look of satisfaction on his face while he watched her load her own bag on her cart.

Our house was headquarters for the first meeting of the Polar Bears, (the Highland Park High School mascot) a group of five girls who met in the 3rd grade and grew up together in Highland Park, Michigan, went to high school there, and then to the University of Michigan, after, with the exception of one who went to Wellesley, and who remained close friends the rest of their lives.

When their 50th high school reunion could not be held, I suggested that the "Fab Five" (Fran Thompson, Evelyn Lough, Julia Slocum, Annabel Danhof, and Nancy Jarnis) hold their own private reunion with their husbands at our house. This became a tradition with each couple hosting a three day get together in their home city: St. Louis, Chicago, Detroit, Boston, and, of course, Brecksville. Not much was needed in the way of entertainment - it was enough for the girls to be together and relive their early days. This pattern went on for ten years until the first death occurred, Lee Matthey, Julie's husband, from St. Louis. After that, the meetings changed a little, and the activities slowed down. Time was taking its toll. There was a little less emphasis on the sight-seeing, if it required walking.

I think the first meeting at our house took place during the Clarence Thomas Supreme Court hearings, and I remember watching the proceedings on the TV with the men while the women were away shopping. I also remember taking the men down to Canton, Ohio, to the N.F.L. Hall of Fame and how impressed I was with something I had dismissed before; meeting Ray Elliot, the Director of the museum, brother of Bump Elliot, and former head coach of the University of Illinois football team; and then taking our group to the Diamond Grill in Akron on W. Market Street for lunch afterwards and being disappointed in my steak.

I had never forgotten our first visit to the Diamond Grill, many years earlier when I had a 32-ounce Porterhouse steak, which was the finest I had ever tasted, before or since. It was hard to believe a restaurant with such a shabby exterior could serve such high-quality food. But then, Akron was a city of 125,000 people and the headquarters city for four billion-dollar corporations, plus other Fortune 500 companies in nearby Canton and Barberton. There was plenty of financial support for fine eating establishments.

We had very few unexpected guests. One Sunday afternoon when the Montgomery's and Bakers from Grosse Pointe were visiting in connection with one of the big sailboat races, Bill and

Julie Culligan, our friends from Camp Michigania, who lived in Hillsdale, Michigan, and who were on their way home from a wedding in Pennsylvania, left the Ohio Turnpike at Exit 11 and dropped in on us. It was great to see them although they only stayed a short time. It was also a little embarrassing because there was a power outage and without electricity the pump in our well could not function, which put a crimp on using the bathroom. Fortunately, we had a large fresh water supply in our front yard and had gotten a big white plastic 5-gallon bucket filled with water; and had it in the house so the situation was under control.

On another occasion Marilyn Brooks, another Camp Michigania regular and who was a docent at Meadowbrook Hall, the old Dodge Estate on a satellite campus of the Michigan State University, dropped in without any warning. She knew we had plenty of room. She had a very generous nature and would have expected us to do the same. She had come to Cleveland to attend a conference for docents and needed a place to stay. Fran took it all in stride and I think Marilyn only stayed two nights and was busy the rest of the time attending lectures, so we didn't have to entertain her. Just a bed somewhere to lay her head at the end of a long day. I recall that she had met Mrs. Seiberling, of the Seiberling Tire Company of Akron, widow of the founder and brought her to the house to meet us. I think Marilyn was proud of our house.

One night I received a phone call which started by the caller asking for *Bamba*, which meant it had to be one of the "boys" from the army Japanese Language Program since that was the nickname by which I was known in the company. It was Ray Kaiser, calling from Chicago, his hometown before retiring to Palm Springs, California. One of the things they did to escape the summer heat in Palm Springs was to return to Chicago for a month or two. They were on their way to Pinehurst, North Carolina, to meet some golfing friends. It wouldn't be too much out of their way, and he was wondering if they might stop and pay us a visit. I immediately said yes and they had to stay overnight. He said they couldn't, it would be an imposition with such short notice, and on and on. My reply was to say they should stop, that we had plenty of room, and if, after they saw the house they thought they would be imposing on us, I would take him to our local motel for a room for the night. They did stop and we had a fine visit. He had been in the ASTP program at the U. of Michigan; was selected to stay for the pre-OCS program where I met him. He was the guitar player in the jazz quartet, the "Sunnysiders", which formed there. I think he knew what to expect when he called because before his phone call, Marilyn had bought a beautiful oriental vase as a thank-you gift, which I still have.

There does not seem to be much left to say about 5320; I hope I didn't forget to mention the story of the digging of our well with its 49 grain hard water and submersible pump – I wanted to be as independent of public services as possible - and Rehker's having fun with me by delaying until the last minute the news that the well was a success, 60 gpm at 52'. It was a wonderful, beautiful home and a source of immense pride for me. We raised our daughters in it; it was their background; they married and hated to leave on their honeymoons after the after-reception parties; Fran's mother got to experience the house while living next door in her own home for three or four years and spent her final days in the guest room we called for in the original plans. In those days, a home was also used for entertaining, far more so than nowadays, and we used it for family, and friends, and on several occasions for business entertaining. It was a superbly logical realization of the dreams we shared when Fran and I first met in Ann Arbor.

However, as we grew older and after my heart attack in 1984, we were living in Florida six months of the year in a condo with 2,300 square feet with the expense associated with that, and maintaining another residence in Ohio with 4,000 square feet with the expense associated with that, I came to realize that we were spending too much of our limited income on housing.

This was brought to a head in 1998, when my investment in Columbus real estate, which had started out so well and provided so much tax shelter, due to a change in the apartment market, resulted in a foreclosure in which I lost $1,100,000 of equity and could have faced bankruptcy depending on the IRS treatment of my depreciation account. To protect the family interests, we placed the house on Oakes Road in a Trust, and all my other assets in Fran's name. It turned out that it was not necessary, and our fears of the IRS were groundless. But upon the advice of our attorneys and C.P.A.s, we were committed to selling the Oakes Road house.

In addition to being a wonderful home, the house proved to be a good investment due to the increasing prices in real estate in general. We were able to sell the rear six landlocked acres of the land south of the ravine to a developer who needed the land to complete a small subdivision of very expensive homes for $135,000. We had paid $5,500 originally for the entire plot, plus another $1,500 later to give us 300' feet of frontage so we could sell off two building sites on land hidden by the dam for the pond (which was never attempted, just planned for.) The land sale obviously produced a large profit. It took place three or four years before we had to sell the house sitting on the remaining 6 acres of land. We had trouble getting a reasonable appraisal made to act as a guide for our asking price, and my memory of this period is surprisingly hazy. One would think the details would be crystal clear in my memory, but they are not. The house was now in the Trust, and I remember my bitter disappointment when the builder Bob Schmitt's daughter, who was a real estate agent, came to see the house and seemed very unimpressed. And in spite of a very favorable review of the house in the real estate section of the Cleveland Plain Dealer, we had great difficulty finding anyone interested in buying. It may be hard to believe but I do not remember how long it took, or who the buyers were, or what they paid. I think the sales price may have been $345,000, but I am not sure. The answer is in my attorney, Bernie Mandel, who was co-trustee's, files. The whole episode is still too painful for me to ask him to go back in his files and find the answers.

I do remember that during this period, I went back into my records of all the costs associated in building the house and the large maintenance (new roofs) items, and the addition, and was surprised that, in spite of the three years' labor I had performed at no cost, the total came to over $200,000. I don't know where the money came from, but refinancing the mortgage, details of which I also do not remember, was probably part of the source, that plus regular bonuses from our mortgage business. I have often wondered what part psychological repression may have played in suppressing such painful memories of this period of my life. So many memories are clear of the good things: the achievements during construction and the many happy social gatherings over the

40 plus years we were able to live in the same house, which I remember clearly, that I feel repression is probably the most logical reason.

We faced old age; we were now in our 70s; there was the inability to find or afford the help needed to maintain the property to my standards, our hopes to live out our lives in the house thwarted by the financial realities; the growing realization that the house could never have the same meaning for another person, not having created it or watched it reach its current state; all this made it possible for us to part with a physical place where we had been able to make a dream come true.

I do not remember the name of the first buyer except that he was single, came from the West coast, and had a large dog. I remember preparing a list of the people who had provided services over the years since he was new to the area and passing along a set of the working drawings for the house for reference, if needed. I do not recall any response to this gesture.

I was happier with the second buyers when I learned of a subsequent sale - again I have no recollection of the sales' prices. But I do remember the name: Radigan. He was related to the Radigan McGilly Moving and Storage family who operated their business on Brecksville Road near Snowville Road. "Our" Radigan had his own sporting goods business in Ohio and Michigan, was married and had two teen-age daughters. And another large dog. I was glad that he had daughters who might experience the same pleasure from having their own bedroom suite that our daughters had enjoyed.

The first purchaser apparently did not pass along my tip sheet and I contacted and met Mr. Radigan only twice when I arranged to go out and remove two of the tree peonies in the flower bed outside the guest room addition so I could plant, them around the patio of the Bob Schmitt condo we had bought in North Ridgeville, Ohio, in our down-sizing move. I remember that I had to go out to Brecksville on the morning after having just been informed of the death of my brother, Russell. I think the year was 1998. That Fall I went back to Brecksville to meet with Mr. Radigan to show him how to care for the remaining peonies. I had the impression that he was not much interested in yardwork.

I was not invited in to see the interior of the house, and that was the last time I set foot on the property. We visited our old neighbor, Shirley Hill, several times in later years and I always walked up to the top of the driveway and looked at the house from the Hill property, something Fran could not bring herself to do. I was not happy with the way the yard was being maintained. Twice I drove up our old driveway, hoping to see Mrs. Radigan, hoping she might invite me in to see our old house, but it never happened. I was always greeted by the large, seemingly, ferocious dog when I tried to open the door of my car and I drove away. Shirley Hill seemed to know very little about her new neighbors, so we just had no further connection with our house, which is typical in residential real estate transactions.

The only remainder of this era is the recurring dream I have of the house in early morning dreams. It is always the same dream. We are having a family picnic on a Sunday afternoon; the whole family is there and it is before the addition was built which covered the area behind the breakfast area; the left-over slate from the entry hall covers the ground and we are seated at the picnic table I built; we suddenly realize that it is late and we have to leave before the new owners catch us trespassing; we rush to straighten up the inside of the house (how could we have a key?) so they will not know we have been there; clean up the back yard; and in our several cars rush down the driveway and disperse in both directions just as the new owners are approaching to turn up the driveway. Very strange. But always the same dream. It has been recurring for more than 20 years.

*Sic Transit Gloria!*

# Chapter IV

## Reading & Writing (no 'rithmatik)

My love of reading started very early in my childhood. I don't remember, but assume instruction began as early as the 1st grade, when I believe we learned that letters of the alphabet had sounds associated with them which helped with saying words on the page. The first books my mother bought was a set of six books, good sized volumes with colored illustrations on the outside cover. It is tantalizing that I cannot remember the name of the set. The books were numbered from 1 to 6, ascending in difficulty. I don't remember much of the content, other than Mother Goose, Grimm and Aesop Fairy Tales in the earlier volumes. But I remember the pleasure associated with reading, sitting on the floor on cold wintry days reading those books in front of the gas grate in the living room; being transported to faraway places where it was warm and the people were different. The books were practically worn out by the time I reached Junior High School. At some point, I learned what a library was and now a much larger world was available to me. The Lakewood Public Library was a very good one and within walking distance of our home. I spent many hours there. It seems strange to me now, but I do not remember my mother ever reading to me. With my growing skill in reading, I was chosen by my Sunday school teacher, whose name I do not remember, but that she was pretty and wore lipstick, to read stories from the *King James Bible* to the class; I think this was because I seemed to be able to recognize the words, pronounce them correctly, and comprehended what I was reading. I was probably ten or eleven years old.

I vaguely remember a small library at my Junior High School where I could borrow books. I was exposed to many authors new to me, writers other than those we were assigned to read for classwork. I do not remember how old I was, perhaps the 5th or 6th grade, when I discovered the series of historical novels written by Joseph Altsheller; which featured the adventures of Henry Ware, the protagonist, who was a young frontiersman of high school age with very high principles and was with the first group of settlers to arrive in Kentucky. He became my hero. I tried to emulate him and attribute much of my sense of honor and faithfulness to the depiction of his character. I also found that I loved reading about the Revolutionary War, much preferring this period of our history to that of the Civil War.

My reading helped me through a very troubling period in my teens. It was a means of escaping from the torments of dealing with my feelings of inferiority and insecurity, and above all, the fear of failure. As I got into my high school years, I read much more widely. I discovered Raphael Sabatini, Dumas, the French Revolution, dueling and swordplay, honor and intrigue. I also discovered H.G. Wells and the world of science fiction; also *Lawrence of Arabia*, *War and Peace*, and *The Last of the Mohicans*. I remember my extracurricular reading far more than what we were assigned to read in English class. All this reading expanded my vocabulary and I even loved to read the dictionary. One word whose pronunciation I remember as my nemesis was "society" which left my mouth as "soshity". It took years to overcome this foible.

As time went by, I began to be fascinated by words themselves; to associate both color and sound with them; to be aware of the rhythm combinations of words could produce. When they were skillfully used; they added another dimension to the author's work. I remember consciously trying to use this quality when choosing one word of several, with the same meaning, to express my meaning for some of the writing assignments in college. For instance, I read somewhere that "velvet" was the softest word in the English language, but I don't remember ever finding a way to use it in a composition. If it's true.

I read the few magazines we subscribed to from cover to cover except for the Saturday Evening Post, which I never liked. Dad brought home *The Cleveland Press*, Cleveland's evening newspaper every night and I read the comic strips avidly, following the story lines of "Little Orphan Annie," "Captain Wash & Easy," the "Katzenjammer Kids," "Major Hoople," "Terry and the Pirates," and "Buck Rogers," among others. I remember single, large soft cover books of some of these characters, which recounted a single adventure, which I received as a gift, particularly Buck Rogers and his comrades, Wilma Dearing and Dr. Hugo; also Little Orphan Annie and her cast of characters, Daddy Warbucks, Punjab and the Asp, and of course, her faithful dog, Sandy. I read them over and over when I had run out of anything else to read.

When I arrived at college, the reading skills I had developed became very useful because of the sheer volume of reading required in our various assignments (really three hours preparation per classroom session.) I think I used to be able to read about a page a minute with comprehension and retention of meaning. Now, I read more slowly, understanding what I am reading, appreciating the plot and the skill of the author. But because of the sheer volume of the reading with the immediate distraction it provides, can't recall what I have read, one book to the next, unless it is something truly exceptional, which doesn't happen very often. It is just as important that I have a constant supply of reading material. I have my *New Yorkers* in the bathroom, numerous different things to read stacked next to my recliner in the living room, and a stack of magazines on the kitchen table where I eat my meals. It rather reminds me of going from one classroom to the next in junior high school. I always have a book to read if I am alone at a restaurant, which is most of the time. I have also discovered that I usually can't sustain my interest in most non-fiction books beyond one or two consecutively. After plodding through one, I turn to a mystery or spy thriller for relief and excitement. I think I am grateful that my mind won't, or can't store 90% of what I read today. Nowadays, even when I am reading something I know is not well written, or poorly plotted, I am still grateful that I am able to satisfy my craving for distraction and my innate curiosity; and can continue to occupy my mind with an activity I love, which has extended over many thousands of books.

At Yale I majored in English Literature and was required to read all the classics. I was also exposed for the first time to the world of Poetry which was a revelation, a real exposure to the power of words and their ability to reveal new meanings. At that period of time, the faculty in the

English department was exceptional and it was unfortunate that I was unable to sample each of their teaching. I was grateful for the insights and stimulation I received from the men I did have. I will never forget Chauncey Brewster Tinker, Richard Sewall, or Robert Dudley French.

I feel like a traitor when I confess that so little of the content of what these remarkable teachers taught me remains accessible in my memory. Perhaps, if I had the energy, to locate the box of notes saved from the courses I took, which I have saved but never looked at, some cherished memories might return. In general, I just remember how much pleasure I derived at the time from the many authors, new to me, that we studied. I do recognize their names, fiction writers, essayists, poets; the important thing for me is knowing that I could read them all again, and still derive great pleasure from the experience. I think the pleasure would be even greater now, and different, because of the perspective afforded by my age. I would like to have the leisure time to explore that possibility.

A few of the authors and books which have influenced me in my post college "adult" reading, which stand out in my memory are: *Psychotherapy East & West* by Alan Watts, *Science & Sanity* by Alfred Korzybski, *The Uses of the Past* by Herbert J. Mueller, *History of the Jews, History of Christianity, History of the World to 1970*, all by Paul Johnson, *In the Wet* by Nevil Shute, *Economics in One Easy Lesson* by Henry Hazlitt, *Europe and the Jews* by Malcom Hay, *The Terrible Secret* by Walter Laqueur, and especially, *How to Think About God* by Mortimer J. Adler, and many others. Bits and pieces of the ideas propounded in these readings came to rest in the persona with which I viewed the world in which I had to navigate.

However, fiction is easier and more fun; and since my curiosity is, and always has been, insatiable I read many, many contemporary writers, among whom I recall offhand: Graham Green, Raymond Chandler, Dashiel Hammet, A.E.Clark, John O'Hara, James Lee Burke, Alan Furst, John D. MacDonald, Dick Francis, Alexander McCall Smith, Ian Fleming, interspersed with Jane Austen, the Bronte sisters, Thackery, and Tolstoy. Light, distracting reading prevails; the ratio of light to serious may be as high as 100:1. This may not be admirable, given the education I was privileged to receive, but it is the fact. Another confession: I could not get past the first fifteen or twenty pages of *Moby Dick* and felt the same way about *Alice in Wonderland*.

All this reading may provide an explanation for the writing I have done, which started with the course in "Short Story Writing" given by our neighbor on Parkwood, Katy Moore. This was one of the courses I took in my postgraduate spring at Lakewood High School. The last story I wrote was called "The Brothers Scaporelli" and contained a lot of Italian/English dialogue as in Brooklynese. I can't imagine where it came from. I revised the story and used it as the last paper due in Mr. Sewall's freshman English course. This was the only time we could choose to be creative and not be tied to a subject chosen from the prior month's reading. I remember Mr. Sewall gave me a B+ with the comment that it was a "Good effort." Many years later I came across the story and was surprised that I could produce something that interesting at such an early age

The next step in my learning the writing process was taking the "Daily Theme" course in my junior year at Yale. The discipline of having to produce three original pieces of writing every week and having them read critically with suggestions for improvement could not have been anything but helpful. An example of one of these daily themes (I thought it my best) appears in an earlier chapter.

My exposure to poetry in my college years led me to attempt to write my own poetry. I feel not having had any formal training comparable to the Daily Theme course was a handicap; it would have been easier to have been trained in the fundamentals and not having to deduce them from my reading assignments of the great Romantic Poets of the Nineteenth Century, Emily Dickinson, and T.S. Elliot

The stimulus for my first attempts was the anguish caused by the breakup of my first serious romance, and in the years following, a response to the urge to express the feelings aroused by special events in my life continued. But the inspiration was sporadic and I cannot explain why many of the most important events in my life did not inspire me to undergo the discipline to force myself to sit down and not get up until I had produced a poem. One would think that the unexpected death of my mother, which was a tremendous shock and a terrible loss; or the births of our three wonderful daughters; or a response to some of the wonders we saw on our travels; or the awe produced by the mysterious beauty of one of my peony blossoms might have caused an irresistible urge to create a poetic response. It happened very rarely. I was never able to generate a steady stream of poems as part of my daily life, or extract poetic truths from everyday events or surroundings, and as much as I would have liked, to have been a true poet. I do not think I have the talent to qualify as such. This is not to say that I am not pleased with some of the poems I have written over the last 75 years. Some of them amaze me. Especially the age at which they were written.

At the urging of my cousin, Caroline (Sue) Gaede Bauer, I gathered all the poems I had ever written over the years. She edited them and had them professionally bound and printed. The unexpected consequence for me was the pleasure of seeing 75 years of experience all in one place and to be able to read this record as a whole. It was a mixture of wonder and pride. There are only 29 poems, not much to show for a lifetime, and the last two were written at the age of 90 and 92, which was a big surprise to me, that any spark of creativity remained at that age.

The next body of writing was the series of letters written to Fran before our marriage, and after, which thankfully, have been carefully preserved. These have brought back many happy memories when I have gotten out the plastic box they are stored in and reread them after I have finished my income tax prep work. I have done this every year since her death in 2014.

Writing was also important in my business life. In addition to the Application Forms, the Appraisal Forms and the photographs of the subject property, every loan submission, whether residential or commercial, required a submittal letter. It presented a description of the property and its surroundings, for a life insurance company 600 miles distant, who were relying on the eyes and experience of their local loan correspondent to give them the facts they needed to make their decision whether to approve or decline the loan.

I am sure the training in how to write I had received was helpful when I was experienced enough to be allowed to compose these letters, the commercial loan cases being far lengthier and more critical. Writing these "submission" letters and the "explanatory notes" which accompanied them became a very important part of my duties, both to our insurance company investors and to our own business which supported four families. I have sometimes wondered, vain as I am, whether the quality of the prose in those loan submissions made the difference between a yes or no answer. I hope it did.

The culmination of all this lifelong writing is what you are reading here. Once again, an unexpected result is the amount of pleasure I am deriving from recalling all these memories and committing them to writing, and to be physically able to do so at the age of 97. I have never written anything of this length before and had no idea when I started that it would be so extensive; or that I would end up writing for myself, for my own pleasure, in a way validating my own ego. Any other reader's interest or pleasure in this story would be a huge bonus - and one I would love to be here to witness.

# Chapter V

# My Musical Life

My earliest musical memories are of a mahogany cabinet Victrola spring driven record player with a crank handle with music and record storage space in the lower portion of the cabinet. It stood in a corner of the dining room. I vaguely remember playing big heavy records of *Il Trovatore*, Caruso singing and some Wagner. I remember my mother singing to herself while she worked in the kitchen or cleaning in a lovely clear voice: "I Love You Truly" and her favorite hymns.

She was the one, middle class family, very talented, the third of five children, insecure, longing for a better life, without a college education as was common at the time who was determined that her children would have a musical education which would open the door to popularity for them and be a sign of a higher class background. However, in that pre-electronic, age when families provided their own entertainment or listened to the radio, usually all together; spontaneously being asked to play for a group never happened. Rather, music was for family entertainment. Music as a source of popularity for her children never occurred.

As is often the case, good intentions lead to unexpected results. In my case, music served, along with reading, as a place of escape from the verbal abuse, the ridicule and sarcasm used as teaching tools or punishment by my father, who loved me dearly, I know, but suffered from his own unwarranted feelings of inferiority. An added burden for me at such a young age was the incessant, cruel teasing by my younger brother which further intensified my insecurities and shyness. (I was the oldest child and the first to attempt anything new. Woe, if there should ever be any failure.) And my mother was unable to intervene. Music was my salvation. And later, reading.

Mother started us on piano lessons when I was 6 years old. We had a baby grand player piano which played music from perforated paper rolls. It was a very poor instrument. But Dad could load a roll into it and the keys would go up and down and produce music and that fascinated me.

Our first teacher was Miss Naomi Gratz. I have no idea where or how Mother found her. Possibly through a church connection. But she was satisfactory for beginners and she drove to our home on Parkwood Road in Lakewood. She only charged $1 total for 30-minute lessons for both me and my brother. I can still remember the first instruction book. Just big whole notes on the staff. No black notes. Miss Gratz had scheduled a recital for her students which I feared and which I avoided by breaking my left wrist on the first day of our family vacation at Devil's Lake, Michigan.

Dad was furious because it happened while I was being disobedient, trying to mount a pony too soon after lunch prior to a family horseback ride. I never got to see my mother and father try to ride a horse! A sight I always regretted because I am sure neither had ever been on a horse before. I learned to dislike milk that afternoon after being given some fresh from the cow's udder with the foam still on it - to settle my stomach, after what I have always thought must have been a local veterinarian mis-set my wrist. To compound my Dad's rage at losing his whole week's deposit of $50, he had to witness me having my wrist re-broken in a doctor's office and reset later that summer. Ether was used as an anesthetic in those days (1927) and I had a dream I have never forgotten of digging gold coins from the sand at Edgewater Beach in Cleveland near Grandma Gaede's house, or the scent of ether, either. At any rate I avoided the recital and never had to prepare for another. Possibly as a result, I have never learned how to memorize a piece of music. I am unable to sit down and play without a sheet of music before me.

At a certain point, probably when I was in the 7th or 8th grade, Miss Gratz retired (she got married?) and my mother located another teacher, Jay Bevington, older, very fine player in spite of his stubby fingers. He was very gentle and lived in the Hilliard/Madison area with his two daughters, and so was able to take the streetcar down Madison Avenue. to our home. So, we continued to receive our lessons at home. By this time the player piano was long gone, replaced with a Chickering baby grand, a fine piano, still located at the front window of the living room where, with great longing, we could watch our playmates having fun playing all sorts of games in the street and their front yards. We hated to practice, and Mother had to threaten punishment to force us to practice. I will always bless her for having the tenacity to not allow us to quit and for her faith in the power of music for good that kept her from letting us quit. It would have been so much easier for her and made us so much happier - at the time; also have cost so much less money at a time when it was scarce. (I don't know how much Mr. Bevington charged). But her persistence resulted in a positive force in my life for the rest of my life and I bless her for it

Mr. Bevington had us do the standard exercises (Hanon, Clementi, etc., and he brought old (very old) issues of a monthly musical magazine, *The Etude*, for which he charged 25 cents, which had instructional articles by prominent teachers on technique, which I don't remember ever reading and by well-known artists with their personal instructions on how they played one of the pieces featured that ,month. Each month the pieces were by various composers and usually included one or more of the great composers. The pieces were graded 1-6 in difficulty. I remember one I particularly liked (it fit my big hands) "Melodie" by Rachmaninoff. I played it to audition for my organ lessons at Yale.

*The Etude* usually included a duet, and soon my brother and I were playing duets: Russ always played the flashier Primo and I the lower, more inconspicuous Secondo, in keeping with my inferiority complex. I did control the pedals, however. I think our favorite was an arrangement of the *Fifth Symphony* by Beethoven! We also liked *Invitation to the Dance* and *Scheherazade*. One interesting insight our mother had was that she insisted that other than the duets, we would never learn or play the same piece, thus avoiding any friction or sibling competition. This might never have resulted in any case since Russ loved loud, showy things and I loved the slow, sad, lugubrious pieces. I often wonder what our mother thought as she listened to me practicing the slow, sad things; if she had any idea of how unhappy I was. It was so hard for me to have a family I loved -

there now were two more younger brothers- but feel freakish because of my height and my religion. And the feeling that I could never do anything right, or be told that I had done something right and pleased my parents.

I clearly remember Mother showing off her "prodigy" sons' skills by the nod towards the piano when guests arrived, invited or drop-ins, which was common in those days. Before they could be seated at the other end of the living room, we would be hammering away at Beethoven's Fifth, and after about 2 minutes of music, their conversation would start and we might as well have been playing in an empty room. We never had a request for an encore, either! It could be that we weren't quite as good as Mother thought we were!

My brother and I used all sorts of strategies to avoid the hated daily practice and it was a small triumph when we succeeded, but this ended for me, when in the 11th grade, Mr. Bevington gave me the Mozart *Fantasia* to learn and suddenly by reading the notes I knew absolutely what was in Mozart's mind, what he wanted to say and how to say it. I spent hours on the first two pages trying to achieve his intent and fell in love with the piece. I couldn't stay away from the piano. It wasn't "practice" anymore but being able to produce real music. Now my mother had another reason for scolding: neglect of my chores! I consider this my awakening to the world of music and I note that as with learning a foreign language, it took five years to get to the starting line where true appreciation and comfort begin.

While my mother's dream of the piano as a pathway to popularity never occurred, I did end up playing as a public service where piano music was needed on a public occasion. This started with my playing the hymns and the before, and after music for Sunday School. I have always suspected that, at that age, the necessity of learning three or four new short pieces every week suitable for playing in a church contributed to my skill in sight reading and explained my inability to memorize. There was never enough time to spend on any one piece of music to memorize it.

I find it interesting that I do not recall any undue nervousness or fear when I sat down at the piano to play before an audience at this age, when I was almost paralyzed with doubt and fear in so many other areas of my life. Music was my key to overcoming fear: not pep talks or religious belief.

Later, after my army service, I played for church services at Sixth Church, Christian Science, in their temporary location in the auditorium of a junior high school on Lorain Street at Kamm's Corners for which I was paid $30 per month. This was a significant amount for newlyweds living on $50 per week. It was difficult to get there having no car and required three transfers on the streetcar. Unfortunately, after two years, I was fired by a classic letter "knowing that I would find greater opportunities elsewhere." I have saved the letter somewhere in my archives. The problem was with the First Reader who was obsessed with being on time, and two weeks in a row my prelude music did not end precisely at 11:00 a.m.

I also recall playing for a Christian Science lecture during this period in a school auditorium filled to capacity, this by someone who could not face playing with other students in a piano recital. I think I played the Mozart mentioned above, and shudder today at my chutzpah to play Mozart in public. The end result of my mother's dream was not popularity, but service.

Another fond memory of my high school days was playing duets after school at his house with a classmate, John Wyman, who played oboe in the high school band and orchestra. He studied at the Cleveland Institute of Music and was a better player than I was. But we had fun and played duets. I have a vivid memory of working on Rimsky-Korsakov's *Scheherazade*.

Another high school memory, even more vivid, is of being asked to play a solo on the stage in front of 1,200 students at the induction into the Honor Society ceremony in my senior year. I was terrified. But at least I did not have to memorize and could use the sheet music. I have large hands and could easily stretch my fingers to play 10ths, two keys more than the usual octave (8 keys.) I had always been fascinated by music written for the left hand alone and I had learned an arrangement by Ralph Kirkpatrick, the harpsichordist, of "Song to the Evening Star" from the opera *Tannhauser* by Wagner. I found it in one of the old *Etude* magazines.) It was not a show-type of piece: no flashy runs or arpeggios, no bombast, but rather quiet and relying on the lovely melody. I felt playing with the left hand alone would provide just enough interest and showmanship, or so I suppose my thinking went. It was only one page long and lasted probably 3-5 minutes, or so, and so I didn't have to worry about turning pages, even though I would have had my right hand available.

It all went well until, for some reason my mind wandered, and I lost my place on the page. I froze, broke into a cold sweat, and just sat there, frantically trying to find my lost place. When I did, after a long, pause, I finally finished and tottered off stage.

Later that day I ran into one of my old English teachers at my junior high, now teaching at the high school, Miss Edna Kleinmeyer, tall, erect, stately, very prim, eye glasses and hair done in a bun, who rushed up to me and said, "Oh, Robert, I loved your playing and especially that pregnant pause in the middle of the piece. It was so dramatic, so effective." Just goes to show: " you can fool some of the people some of the time."

Also, during this time frame, bearing in mind the paucity of entertainment available compared to our electronic age today, we had to provide our own entertainment, and music was one form. We used to see our cousins, the Geigers, who also lived in Lakewood nearby, frequently and many times the occasions would be Sunday suppers. Often, after finishing supper, Uncle Charley would get out his fiddle and scrape away, leading the family "orchestra": me on clarinet; brother Russ on saxophone; and our cousins, the twins, Don and Doug, on trumpet with older brother, Charles, on Sousaphone. I can't imagine where the sheet music for such a disparate group of instruments came from and shudder to think what it must have sounded like to our poor captive audience, the two mothers.

Grandpa Gaede was a Mason and on one or two occasions arranged for Russ and me to be the program after their meetings at their Lodge on Franklin Boulevard in what, is now known as Ohio City. I don't remember too much about this, but think Russ and I played the piano, both solo and duets. I can't remember whether the Geigers were included in the programs. I have to assume we performed acceptably but doubt if the other Masons were as pleased as Grandpa Gaede presumably was.

To conclude the keyboard section of my musical life, in my senior year of high school, my mother arranged for me to take organ lessons, no doubt hoping that someday I would be the organist at Fifth Church, Christian Science, where we attended and I had played piano for the Sunday School.

I remember taking the lessons on the organ at the Methodist Church at Summit & Detroit Streets in Lakewood, within walking distance of our home on Parkwood. But I do not remember either the organ or the name of my lady teacher. I do remember wearing heavy crew socks instead of shoes, which is not a very good way to play the pedal keyboard. I was able to practice on the Wurlitzer theatrical organ, which had many unusual stops, at the Hilliard Square Movie Theater at Hilliard and Madison Avenues, also within walking distance of our home on Parkwood Road. I was able to do this through the good graces of the manager of the theater, a business friend of my father.

 The culmination of my musical training and, indeed, of my understanding of pure music, such as it is, came the following year as a freshman at Yale, where I auditioned and was accepted to take organ lessons. I had followed a Lakewood High School tradition of winning one of the many Ivy League scholarships each year. In keeping with my determination to gain an "education in the humanities," as the oldest of four brothers and the first in the family to be able to attend college, I took a heavy five course load of subjects, none of which turned out to be easy for me based on my performance in high school, even English, French and Chemistry, to an extent that I was in danger of losing my scholarship by Thanksgiving because of my poor grades. High school was no prep school for me.

In addition to the heavy course load I had to work three hours per day, required for scholarship students and chose to work as a waiter in Freshman Commons, where the Freshman class ate all their meals,. I worked as a waiter seven days a week, 3 hours (2 meals) a day, went out for the freshman swimming team and joined the marching band, which meant riding in an Army truck to the Bowl every Friday night to practice the formations for the game the next day. And I took an organ lesson every week which meant practicing an hour a day and there were not that many hours in a day. Those were interesting times.

My organ teacher was Frank Bozyan, one of the top two or three organists in the U.S. in his day. I took my lessons on the big organ in Battell Chapel which was a thrill. Practicing was done a hour a day on a small reed organ in the basement of Sprague Hall where the School of Music was located; and where I also went for my Music Composition class, which was deadly because it was at 1 p.m. right after lunch. The instructor droned and it was very hard to stay awake.

I don't remember much detail of my lessons but do know I learned more real music from Professor Bozyan than from any other music teacher I ever had. He spent a lot of time working with me on Bach's *St. Anne's Prelude & Fugue* which I finally mastered to some extent. At least I was able to play the Prelude at St. Matthews Episcopal Church, where both Fran and her mother worshipped, for the Sunday service the week after my dear mother-in-law's burial 25 years later.

As an aside, I have always remembered fondly being invited to dinner with Professor Bozyan at the home of Eugene O'Neill, son of the great playwright and a Classics professor at Yale. I had him for a one semester class in Roman government, which was extremely boring. He did have an amazing bass speaking voice and sang in the Battell Chapel choir on Sundays. (I never attended or heard him sing). This must have been in my sophomore year after I was no longer taking lessons from Professor Bozyan and spoke to him after one of his free afternoon concert series in Dwight Chapel, where he performed the entire organ works of J.S. Bach every year. I believe their friendship must have developed because of Professor Bozyan's playing for the Sunday services at Battell Chapel.

Along with all of this keyboard training and my growing love of classical piano music, my mother thought it might be a good idea if my brother and I learned to play an instrument. It's interesting that our three male cousins who also lived in Lakewood never had any keyboard lessons but did learn to play brass: tuba for the oldest and trumpet for the younger twins.

We went the other direction: reeds. Our mother's younger brother, Uncle Elmer, had an old metal clarinet which Mother "persuaded" him to give to me in about the 6th grade. I started taking group lessons from Harry Parks, a retired symphony clarinetist, in the Chamber of Commerce Building at the south-east corner of St Charles and Detroit Avenues, where we learned how to fasten the reed to the mouthpiece and proceed to make terrible noises, all six or eight of us together, and how to cover the keyholes with our fingertips to be able to play scales.

After a year of this, I started taking private lessons from Mr. Parks in his living room on Lakeland Avenue between Clifton and Detroit once a week on my way home from school. At Mr. Parka's suggestion, we threw away Uncle Elmer's terrible instrument and replaced it with a new, metal Silver King clarinet manufactured here in Cleveland - a huge improvement.

By the 8th grade, I was 6' 4" tall and playing in the Lakewood High School marching band for the football games, which was under the direction of Arthur Jewel. He was about 5' 4" tall,. He directed both band and orchestra for the entire Lakewood School System. I was issued a uniform and the trousers which had a stripe down the out seam had to be special ordered because of my height, which was the reason for Mr. Jewel's recruiting me at that age. I remember my measurements: 34" inseam, 45" out seam. The trousers were new, had never been worn by anyone else, and were very nice, I thought.

I remember our first band uniforms at Emerson Junior High School which consisted of our own white "duck" pants and white shirts plus a school cape we wore at concerts. The only concert I remember is when we walked (marched?) the three or four blocks west on Clifton Boulevard to Taft Elementary school and played a "concert" for the younger students. I have no idea of how long we played, or what the songs were - or how they sounded but my imagination makes me wince.

However, I do remember that at this time I was introduced to popular dance music by playing in Mr. Herman Gannet's (he was the Metal Shop teacher!) Dance Band at Emerson Junior High, which played once a month for the Friday afternoon teacher chaperoned dances for the older students. I recall that we practiced regularly, all 8 or 10 of us, in the metal shop, and it was fun, a bit of an ego trip, but only realized much later that while my peers were learning valuable social skills and how to dance, I wasn't, which certainly was no help for my inferiority complex and shyness, and was a handicap the rest of my life.

I seemed unable to make my body move to the "beat" I felt, which was frequently missing in the ordinary dance bands we heard locally, and this became a *bête noire* for me all my life. Later, after marriage, swallowing my pride and taking dancing lessons more than once, once as late as our living in Florida when I signed us up to take "cha-cha" lessons for a new dance craze) I never overcame my lack of confidence or added to my skill. I loved it but couldn't perform. (Fred Astaire was my hero.) It was humiliating and a source of embarrassment.

I remember one occasion when we were part of a group of people we didn't know well and went to a dance held at the American Legion hall on Brookpark Road in Brookpark, Ohio. The women were terribly excited because there was a live band, the big attraction. I think there were 6 or 8 couples. The band was terrible, and I was not a good sport. I remember actually developing a headache, rare for me, and never set foot on the dance floor. It must have been very rude because I never asked any of the other wives to dance and didn't even dance with Fran. It was a long evening, and a long ride home. I don't recall facing that extreme a situation ever again.

Fran loved to dance and was very good. I always felt it would have added to her pleasure if I could only let my body relax and go with the beat, if there was one. It was especially hard for me, who considered himself to be a musician.

After my discharge from the army and return to Cleveland we started our real-life marriage, after our two month "honeymoon" in the frozen North. We were fortunate to have a father who owned a 24-suite apartment building at the end of the Madison Avenue streetcar line in Lakewood, Ohio, at a time of extreme housing shortage. We were able to rent an apartment in his building on the 4th floor. The rent was $50 per month. And we were very grateful to have a place of our own to live.

When the opportunity came to play the piano for the Sixth Church, Christian Science, services after the birth of our first child, Nancy, I needed a piano on which to practice and found a big, old, ugly upright piano which was in good tune and had a good sound. I don't remember how I found it, but vaguely remember paying $50 for it. I don't think I was there when it was delivered but would not have liked to have been one of the men who had to struggle with that monster, lifting it all the way to the fourth floor. It sat against the outside wall in the dining room.

A very fond memory is of Nancy who was just old enough to stand, standing in her crib/bed next to the piano, holding on to the edge of the crib and swaying to my playing with her eyes wide. It provided a very warm feeling to have such an appreciative audience.

It had to be at this time that I discovered that the Cleveland Public Library, where I spent many a lunch hour researching the architectural magazines in the reading room, that I discovered that the Library had an extensive collection of all kinds of music, including classical piano sheet music which could be taken out for a 30 day period. This solved my problem of finding a source of material for playing for the church services and at no cost. I also became aware of many composers I had never heard of before and started my explorations with Albéniz, working my way through the alphabet. Two of my favorite discoveries were Gabriel Fauré and the Russian composer, Scriabin. Fauré's barcarolles and nocturnes and Scriabin's preludes seemed particularly suitable to me and were very musical. My theory in selecting what to play was always that I would rather play something of high quality and interest poorly than something easy and meaningless perfectly, like Ethelbert Nevin pieces.

After I retired from playing the organ for St. Matthews, I called the Library to see if they would be interested in the collection of organ music I had accumulated. Amongst this miscellany were things I had found in music shops in Paris and Venice on two of our European vacation trips. The music was from unfamiliar publishers and composers, inexpensive and both suitable and within my skill level.

In due course I delivered the music to the library and received a nice letter of thanks which pointed out that 85% of the items donated were new to their collection. Sadly, in 1996 when I wished to donate most of my piano music, some of it from the 1890s from Grandmother Thompson, they no longer accepted donations. I do not know if one can borrow music from the library any longer.

I think we moved the old upright piano when we left the apartment in the fifth year of our marriage to our first home on Ridgewood Drive in Parma Heights, Ohio. It had a radiant heating system created by hot water being pumped through copper piping embedded in the concrete floors, including some in the attached garage floor so it was possible to put the piano in the garage and it would not lose its tune. I could practice in reasonable comfort in cold weather. I don't remember its ultimate disposal.

Three years after moving to Brecksville, when we were settled in, I was anxious to have another piano, not only for myself, but also for our three daughters so they could also have piano lessons, as I did. I started my search and ended up at the Mattlin-Hyde Piano Studio at Lee & Mayfield Roads in Cleveland Heights; I probably noticed the store on one of my appraisal trips to the Eastside where I appraised many homes.

I remember vacillating between two spinet style models of Steinway and Baldwin, the two most highly regarded brands at the time. Then the salesman took me to the other side of the room and had me play a few chords on a piano I had never heard of before, a Haddorf, a very handsome spinet. I liked the sound much better than either the Steinway or the Baldwin. The salesman said the secret was the Haddorf was built with a bridge similar to the bridge connecting the back and front panels of a violin, between the main sounding board at the rear of the instrument to the "skirt" on the front below the keyboard. This increased the total square feet of resonating surface to that of a baby grand piano. It was remarkable. Later they were forced to discontinue selling Haddorf or lose all the Steinway and Baldwin products. So, I bought the Haddorf, but don't remember the price, probably $1,200-$1,500. When I got home and told Fran, she was dubious. Her comment, "I hope you know what you're doing!"

Later that summer we were invited to our next-door neighbors, Sid and Vera Stadig, for a cookout. We were good friends, but on this occasion may have been invited to gain access to my jazz collection. I remember taking a big box of records suitable for dancing over to their house and helping Sid move their TV/record player downstairs to their rec room where there would be dancing later. He was an engineer at one of the TV stations, and the guests were mainly studio people.

Among them was a wife who was one of the most highly esteemed piano instructors in Shaker Heights. During the course of conversation, the subject of our new piano came up and she remarked, "Oh! That's a wonderful instrument; it's the one preferred by piano teachers who live in small apartments and have space limitations." Fran overheard this comment and was reassured. She looked at me and said, "You lucked out this time!" And I did luck out. That piano was a constant source of pleasure for many years.

We also had very nice time dancing to my music. One of the women asked me where this kind of music came from and I told her it was easily available, but she would never hear it played on her husband's station.

While living in Brecksville and after playing the organ for Fran's church for 3-4 years, I got tired of having to go out after dinner to practice at the church three or four nights a week: to open up the church, turn on the power and lights, climb up to the choir loft where the organ was situated, practice for two or three hours and then reverse the process, turn off the lights, lock up and drive home, even although it was only a short distance. We decided we had room in the lowest level recreation room where the Haddorf sat and we ended up buying a basic, full pedal keyboard Allen Organ. Now I didn't have to leave the comfort of my home to do my practicing. The Allen wasn't very exciting after playing the larger organ at church; just as practicing on the simple reed organ in college was after taking my lessons on the huge organ in Battell Chapel. Fortunately, my dissatisfaction did not last too long because about a year later, I resigned my position at St. Matthews - actually the week before Nancy's wedding in that church, when the organist was my Baldwin Wallace College instructor, Warren Berryman. The organ never sounded that way when I played it. I still don't know how he did it.

The Allen sat, basically unused, for several years until we downsized and sold the house, a very hard thing for us to do. We had a lot of trouble trying to dispose of the organ. There was no market, either institutional, or private, for selling it and we couldn't even find anyone to take it as a gift. Finally, a small storefront Black church on the near east side of Cleveland accepted it. I don't remember how we were led to them.

They came on a Saturday morning, a small crew and somehow or another, moved it out of the basement, around the bends in the stairs and out the front door onto a trailer. I found an old piece of carpet for them to use to protect the finish. The Pastor said his wife who had been playing the piano for their services would now become their organist (at which my eyebrows raised slightly). They were all extremely nice and the Pastor remarked what a wonderful spot this would be for church retreats, (at which my eyebrows twitched again, slightly). They were extremely grateful. A few weeks later the Pastor stopped on the way to drop off his daughter at Kent State U. to return the rug and was again effusive in his thanks.

Our Allen Organ story ended in 1996, and the reason for including this story is the great contrast to a recent funeral I attended at a (white) community church in a shopping center where there was no organ at all, just an electronic keyboard on a stand and a drum set on the stage. Of course a church organ is far more expensive today than it was 30-40 years ago, but I find it difficult to compare the quality of service music for worship in my day to what is current in the more popular community churches today. At my age today, I could never attend a church service where the music was not provided by an organ with all its grandeur and inspiration.

In 1996, at age 75, the Haddorf ended up in the laundry (music!) room at the Bob Schmitt condo we bought on Cedarbranch in North Ridgeville. I still admired the sound it produced and enjoyed playing it occasionally. One of the few sad memories I have is playing for my brother Russ after a strenuous Sunday afternoon while he was resting across the hall. He had not heard me play as an adult and had never heard me play the organ at St. Matthews, being occupied Sunday mornings playing the organ for his own church. We had had a good visit and conversation, warm and conciliatory, while waiting for our wives who were inspecting a model home in the Bob Schmitt subdivision where our daughter, Barb, now lived. It was a great shock the next morning to learn he had been rushed to Lakewood Hospital and died there that same day. There was great sadness but also some good memories for me.

One other piano oriented memory took place at our Florida condo in Vizcaya of Bradenton. There was an active Social Committee, headed at the time, by Joan Schneurke, a very persuasive German immigrant. The committee arranged to buy a Technics digital piano which was placed in the great room in the clubhouse where it could be played by any of the residents, including me. This was my first experience with this type of piano. It was spinet style and thus did not take up much space and only needed an electric outlet for its power. I was pleasantly surprised by the quality of the sound and believe it was achieved by blending digitally the sound of a Steinway and Baldwin concert grand piano. There were many other sounds available, also, including organ. But the only one I ever used was the concert grand piano. I used to take my music with me and go early to the afternoon bridge game and practice.

After the 1st year the Social Committee decided to have an evening musicale piano concert where any resident who wished could perform. I was asked to play but refused, pleading that I had not played in such a long time and needed much more practice to regain even some of my skill. But I promised that I would be a part of the program the next year if they had a second concert. This promise was an incentive and I practiced much more regularly and was well prepared when they did stage a second concert, well attended by probably 75-100 people, including Fran and our daughter, Nancy and her husband, who had their own condo nearby in Vizcaya. I ended up being the last performer. The others on the program usually played a single piece, and for the most part it was just short of embarrassing. I played three or four short pieces by Fauré, Scriabin and Rachmaninoff and got through them in pretty good shape; received many compliments afterwards with the coffee and cookies. But I do not recall any special comments from the family and have no idea what the other listeners really thought of the kind of music I chose to play which was so different from the previous players' choices. It was the last time I ever performed in front of an audience and I think of it as my Swan Song.

While in high school, I acquired a used E flat alto saxophone which was somewhat similar in technique to the clarinet, and although I never had any lessons, could play it well enough to become a double threat in the two or three extracurricular dance bands I was invited to join. This was not a money-making proposition, because other than the school sponsored after school "tea" dances, I don't ever recall playing for hire (or free) at a local dance. I did meet some very nice boys who became friends, Bob Radefeld and Herb Seitman, and it was fun to get together to "rehearse" after school at the leader's home and make music. I remember one of the better groups being organized by "Skeets" Whittaker who lived on St. Charles Ave. between Franklin Blvd. and Madison Avenue, who played the drums, and in later life became a professional music educator.

During this period, having progressed in my ability on the clarinet, my parents somehow or another found the money to buy me a wooden Selmer clarinet, I remember it cost $150, manufactured in France, which was supposed to be the instrument of choice among symphony clarinetists. It had a superior tone and I loved to practice in our tiled bathroom which was a great enhancer of the sound. I wished I could produce that tone out in the real world.

In high school, I played the clarinet in the marching band for the football games from the 8th grade on, basically because of my height, of which Mr. Jewel was well aware. I also played in the concert band and orchestra. Both groups had outstanding players in all the first chairs.

The band, both concert and marching, competed in mid-western competitions, once in Cleveland, where the marching competition was held in the Cleveland Stadium and the concert competition at Severance Hall, home of the Cleveland Symphony Orchestra. I don't remember what composition we played but do have a vivid memory of sitting in the left balcony while the Joliet, Illinois, band (competition we feared) played. They were unusual in that the band was all male except for one girl, elected from the student body who simply sat on the stage on the right in front of the band, not in a uniform, but a pretty dress, acting as sort of a mascot, I suppose. She was striking and beautiful and we spent all our time ogling and never heard what was being played.

Another small band came from Mason City, Iowa, the home of Meredith Wilson, the composer of *The Music Man*. Their marching style was very high stepping with very sharp breaks just popping into their formations. These two bands are the only thing I remember of the entire competition.

We also competed in 1939, I think, at Elkhart, Indiana, where we stayed overnight in the homes of private residents which was very hospitable. With the number of bands competing, it must have enlisted most of the households in the small city and required a tremendous amount of organization. We marched well and played well. We felt should have come in first place which would have meant another medal to wear on our uniforms. We waited and waited for our name to be called, and when it was, the final name called, we were disqualified because a couple of our wilder male members of the band were caught drinking hard liquor, transported in their suitcases, in their host family's home. Unbelievable. After the close of the judging, I remember walking the city streets for what seemed like hours with Barbara Peebles, our second chair oboist, a very pretty girl with a great figure, who cried and cried in her disappointment, using my handkerchief to dry her tears. She lived on Clifton Boulevard and I remember clearly walking her home one afternoon after our return in shame and her returning my laundered and pressed hanky, which she must have kept in one of her dresser drawers where it picked up a delicious feminine scent. I kept that hanky under my pillow the whole summer!

I never entered any of the contests for individuals, but my brother Russ, who also had a Selmer saxophone, did, and made amazing progress while I was away at college my Freshman year.

The closest I came was to compete in a clarinet trio, where all three of us had Selmers, which we felt produced a superior sound mix which we hoped would give us an edge in the competition. I remember painstakingly transcribing the three parts of the piece we played onto lined musical paper so we each had our own separate part for practicing at home. Of course, I cannot remember either the name of the composer of the piece or its name - or whether we won.

The other members of the trio were Fred Bowditch and Ken Kettering, both members of the Band and in the class behind me. Fred went on to become an executive in GM's engineering department, and Ken, who was the nephew of the famous Kettering of GM, committed suicide while a freshman at Baldwin Wallace College in Berea, a terrible shock and very sad. This was my first experience of a suicide and very hard to accept.

Playing an instrument probably was one of the plus factors in my receiving the Yale scholarship. I played in the marching band for three years. The band was small, about sixty men, and I didn't think compared with my high school band. I became first chair clarinetist within weeks, which should give you some idea. Freshman year I went with the Band by train from New Haven to Ann Arbor where we played on a very uncomfortable, cold day for the last football game ever played between Michigan and Yale. We played Cole Porter arrangements of the Michigan songs and were a big hit. Of course, I don't know what kind of an impression sixty men without even helmets for their uniforms could have made as opposed to a 180-man organization the University of Michigan put on the field. The whole experience was a big thrill for me, of course.

The band also traveled to Cambridge, Massachusetts that year for the final game of the season against traditional rival, Harvard. I arranged to meet Doug Fentom, son of my favorite Sunday school teacher and winner of the M.I.T. scholarship that year, for dinner and an evening at his fraternity house afterwards. After only two months at Yale, I will never forget how shocked I was that there were girls allowed on the upper floors of Doug's fraternity. I don't remember who won the game but remember going out on the field after the game and playing "Bright College Years," Yale's college anthem, on the field after the game for all the loyal Yalies who waved their hankies back and forth in unison in time with the music. It was a pretty emotional event for a lowly, mid-western freshman. I don't remember who won! I do remember the score of the Michigan-Yale game: 39-6.

Both my high school and college football teams were consistently second rate and there was little to cheer about, especially when getting soaked in the perennial rainstorm at the Brown University game. Finally, in my senior year I retired from the marching band and watched my first games with my roommate as an ordinary civilian, sitting in end zone seats in the Yale Bowl.

While at Yale, I also played in a small pep band at basketball games. (Never an away trip). I was invited to play in a small, three or four player, peasant, costumed group in a play staged by the Yale Drama School. I have no recollection of what the name of the play was, but it was an interesting experience. I do not remember the rehearsals, or how many performances there were.

I think it was in my senior year when I became aware of a U.S. Government program, the C.Y.S., College Youth Symphony (?). One could audition and if accepted become a full-fledged member of a professional symphony orchestra, under the baton of an European conductor, who was the best conductor I ever worked under and whose name I have been trying to remember for years.

I know of no connection of the government program with Yale. I must have seen a notice on a billboard which aroused my interest and caused me to apply. At the concert we prepared for, I do remember that the major piece was the *Second Symphony* by Cesar Franck. This I remember well because in the slow movement there is an exposed clarinet solo, not difficult to play, but in 3/2 time and I have always had problems with 3/2 or 5/4 time and I was terrified I would fluff it. I don't remember where the concert took place - off campus I am sure - or what the other pieces we played were. But I do remember how relieved I was when it was all over, and I had successfully gotten through that brief passage satisfactorily. An added benefit was that the U.S. Government paid us $30 per month, a significant amount for a scholarship boy on a very limited budget. It meant that much less I had to ask my parents for, and indirectly that much more available to my brothers in the future.

Reading this thus far, you may be aware that all the emphasis up to this point has been devoted to classical music. However, in my junior year in college I was exposed to what became a near obsession for me: Jazz. Obviously, I had some exposure to non-classical music since I had played in some dance bands. Also while buying sheet music, I bought some books of piano jazz arrangements by some of the great players of the 30s & 40s: Art Tatum, Teddy Wilson, Mary Lou

Williams, Billy Kyle, Count Basie and Duke Ellington; none of whom I had ever heard on the radio, let alone live in a theater or at a dance. There were only a few of the songs in their piano albums which were easy enough for me to play but I kept trying. I didn't realize at the time how lucky I was to be alive during the Golden Age of the American Song Book and the birth of Jazz, to awaken at the peak of the age. However, because of my family's religious background where drinking was forbidden and night clubs were where this music was performed; plus my ignorant prejudice that "black" players were undisciplined and immoral, I would surely have been classified as very "square." As an example of my ignorance and flawed judgment, I looked down on Benny Goodman, who happened to be white, because his "tone" wasn't what a clarinet should sound like. In my youthful wisdom I knew what that should be. What opportunities I missed before my awakening.

In my junior year (1941), the Yale band accompanied the football team on its biennial visit to Princeton. We went by train a day early to give a concert at the Yale Club in Manhattan and stayed overnight at the Commodore Hotel, where I was one of the lucky ones who was assigned a single room. After the concert, a small group of band members talked me into going with them to the Savoy Ballroom in Harlem to hear the Erskine Hawkins Band play. It took quite a bit of persuasion to get me to go: What would I tell my mother? Go to a black dance hall in Harlem? Where a white college boy had been stabbed a week earlier; and to listen to "uncivilized", "black" music? But I did go. It was a revelation: all well-dressed young black couples; no liquor sold, only set-ups - you had to BYOB; some mixed couples; all very respectable. And the music. I had never heard anything like it before. I stood up near the bandstand, transfixed, and just absorbed it. This was not frenetic, undisciplined noise but highly organized arrangements of popular songs for dancing, beautifully performed by The Hawkins Band and the house band, The Savoy Sultans. There were no breaks, one band sliding into the other's seats at break time so the music was continuous. They finally closed up shop at 3:30 a.m. and we got back to the Commodore about 4:00 AM, There was no way I could fall asleep; I simply lay on the bed with the music still going on in my head, never closing my eyes, reliving the experience until it was time to report to the lobby for the rest of the trip to Princeton. I have always regretted that there was not enough time to explore the campus, and, also note that we played Cole Porter arrangements of the Princeton fight songs. Wish I had been smart enough to keep those arrangements. They would be interesting to see today. The Savoy Ballroom experience changed my life. It opened up a whole new realm of music for me: Swing, Big Bands, and Small Combos. Even an occasional Country Western. My musical world had suddenly widened enormously.

After marrying Fran and settling in Cleveland after World War II, which did not do much for my newfound desire to hear live jazz in addition to attending the Thursday night performances of the Cleveland Symphony Orchestra, which we eventually shared with my brother, Wes, each choosing the programs he preferred and then tossing a coin to decide the remainder, we also attended concerts featuring choruses (I have always been partial to vocal music), glee clubs, opera and light operas.

I never was very enthusiastic about grand opera, probably because of my first exposure. This took place when a very nice high school friend, Emma Able, who lived only one street away from us, invited me to go with her and her parents to hear a matinee performance by the Metropolitan Opera Company, on one of their annual "opera weeks" at the Public Auditorium. They performed in the large end of the auditorium which (I believe) seated approximately 8,000 people; and with their six or seven evening and one or two matinee performances, appeared before more people in Cleveland than in their entire season at Carnegie Hall in New York. The "Met's" appearance was a big event in Cleveland's cultural life, and also a highlight annually in the higher social circles.

Unfortunately, the opera I heard was *"Louise"* by a second-tier French composer, Charpentier, and it was long and boring and had not even one memorable aria. The afternoon was a blur and I hope my boredom was not too obvious to my hosts. I now wonder if my interest in opera would have been greater if that first exposure had been to have heard *Aida*, or *Porgy and Bess*, or *La Bohème*.

There were two or three later experiences when I was older and more appreciative. One was hearing Beverly Sills sing *"Thaï"s* by Massenet the year before her retirement. She no longer had the figure to play a slender young girl, but listening to her beautiful, soprano voice made it easy to overlook.

I did get to see *Porgy and Bess* with the original cast while a junior in college and went into detail about that occasion in my chapter on my college years. That was the time when Tinker had announced a test on the day I was to meet my senior high school date at Grand Centra, and Tinker had a hard and fast rule that he would not permit make up tests for those who missed the regular exam. I had an idea and went to see him in the Rare Book Room and asked if I couldn't take a make-up test, would he consider letting me take the test in advance. I think this was something new for him, and he looked at me and said: "Schmidt, you are the crafty one!' and allowed me to do just that. However, I will say that was a memorable experience in and of itself, and many of the scenes are still sharp and etched in my memory. So many singable, beautiful songs.

I also have a vivid memory of a Met performance of Alban Berg's *Lulu*. It was done live on TV and I really didn't want to waste my time on 12-tone music, which I thought, with my traditional background, was very "far out" (too hard to understand). I knew I wouldn't like it but thought I should give it a chance. If it was as bad as I thought it would be, I could always change stations and switch to one of the sitcoms. I was amazed at what I heard and after five minutes was totally engaged; I listened to the very end and couldn't get over the power of the work and how the music captured and expressed the deepest emotions. This is one opera I would like to hear in live performance.

Another opera I found I really enjoyed was Puccini's *"Madame Butterfly"*, which had additional poignancy for me because of my study of the Japanese language in the Army.

The final operatic experience which comes to mind started out with a French "noir" movie I happened to see, *"Diva"*. This concerned a very reclusive opera singer in Paris, a beautiful black girl, played by Herminia Fernandez, who refused to be recorded, but sings one aria to herself repeatedly and in recitals. It says something to me that after seeing the movie 35 years ago, I remembered the name of the movie and was able to find it on Google and Wikipedia. I know at the time that I thought the melody of the aria was haunting.

Many years later while wintering in Florida, the Sarasota Opera Company, on a sunny Saturday afternoon, gave a performance of *"Le Wally"* by Catalanti, a very obscure composer, which contained the aria from the movie, *Diva*: "Ebben? Ne andro lontana," and it can be heard on YouTube. Naturally, I couldn't miss the opportunity to hear it in a live performance. This turned out to be as big a disappointment as my first opera, *Louise*. It was long, dull and very boring; well performed and done very professionally, but overall a second-rate piece of music, and easy to see why not performed regularly. The only worthwhile thing in the whole long afternoon was the aria!

To complete my operatic history, on our first trip to Vienna with the University of Michigan travel group, we took a side trip to Salzburg through the beautiful lake country. There, one evening, we heard Mozart's *Magic Flute*. I know I was supposed to like anything by Mozart but am somewhat ashamed to confess I did not like it. And on one of our last trips to Europe, on a University of Michigan tour, we visited Vienna again and went one evening to the famous Opera House and heard an opera by Richard Strauss, probably *Electra*, and once again, in spite of the beautiful surroundings and the very polished performance, my only recollection is that I didn't like it, and would certainly never try to see it again.

One other comment I would like to make before concluding this chapter is how grateful I am to my wife, as a youngster a would-be ballerina, for introducing me to the Ballet. When I was twelve or fourteen, I went with my brother and the gang of guys to the Hilliard Square Theater for the Saturday afternoon double feature. Once or twice between the movies, the management allowed a local dance studio to stage a recital. The sight of those young girls in their tutus trying to be graceful was too much for us. We made such a disturbance that I think we were ejected at least once, and missed the second feature, undoubtedly a cowboy movie. Maybe, Hopalong Cassidy.

Contrast this with a young married man 30 years later being "persuaded" by his wife to take her to see Moira Shearer dance in Tchaikovsky's *"Swan Lake"* at the Public Auditorium. Even though I was familiar with his music and loved it, nothing prepared me for the experience of seeing and hearing a third dimension added to the language that is music; to see a series of stylized, disciplined body movements used to convey and add to the message contained in the music was a revelation to me. The performance was by the Sadler Wells Company with their own orchestra. From our seats in the front row of the balcony at the end of the horseshoe we were as far as possible from the stage but with an undisturbed sightline to the stage. I think the distance added to the magic. I later saw Margot Fonteyn do *Swan Lake,* which was her most famous role, but I preferred Moira Shearer's interpretation.

This was my first exposure as an adult to a wonderful art form and we saw as many more ballets as we could over the years. Nothing ever surpassed that first experience

This led to a great love of the Tango. We saw several of the professional Argentinian groups perform, and also bought movie DVDs centered on the tango. If there is such a thing as reincarnation, I would like to reappear as a professional Tango Grand Master!

Once again, and finally, one of the things we found to do in our summers in Ohio, in addition to visits to Blossom Music Center for special events that interested us, was to travel down to Wooster, Ohio, about 30 miles south to listen to performances of the Ohio Light Opera Company.

This started out as a 10-week season of all Gilbert and Sullivan, produced by James Stuart of Kent State University. Originally, they put on their productions at the Porthouse Theatre on Steele Corners Road off S.R. 8 on the way to the main entrance to Blossom Music Center, summer home of the Cleveland Symphony. As their popularity grew, they moved their productions to the Freedlander Theater on the campus of The College of Wooster. This was a much more desirable location: seating for 300 people, larger stage, better acoustics, movable pit (the orchestra - no longer simply a piano - rose from patron seating level to stage level to lead the singing of "God Save the Queen" when the play was to be Gilbert and Sullivan; always a big hit with the audience, putting them in the mood for what was about to come, and a good sized lobby where the cast could mingle with the audience after the final curtain came down. The performers were all professionals. James Stuart was not just the producer and manager of the operation, but loved to perform in the comic, pompous roles which he did very well, especially the brilliant patter songs.

As time passed the range of operettas expanded into more than just Gilbert and Sullivan. The Company branched out into other classic operettas by the likes of Strauss, Lehar, Kalman, Romberg, Victor Herbert, et al. In the 2017 season they even did *"The Music Man" by Meredith Wilson and "Anything Goes"* by Cole Porter. These were all done up to Broadway standards in every respect in a little college town between Cleveland and Columbus, a real opportunity for mid-westerners.

We used to try to sample things we thought we would like, pick the dates out of the Repertory calendar and make the long trek to Wooster in time for lunch at the Wooster Inn nearby, where the food and service were very good, and then go over to the Freedlander for the performance. We spent many a happy summer afternoon that way. I note that after James Stuart's death, the summer program has expanded into the Broadway productions of the 30s, including musicals by George Gershwin, Cole Porter and Irving Berlin, which are hard to find done professionally elsewhere. How I wish I had been able to attend in recent years.

The next step in my development after the Savoy Ballroom experience occurred at a very fine record shop on campus, David Dean Smith, where I went to buy a popular new record by Skinnay Ennis and his Band, with him singing in his unique, breathy voice "I Don't Want to Set the World on Fire." As I was paying for it ($0.35?) I noticed on the counter a small display of very expensive 12" Bluenote label records ($1.50) and took two of them into the demo booth, which all record stores had in those days, and was stunned by what I heard. This was the first small jazz combo I had ever heard. The artists were people I had never heard of before: The Edmond Hall Jazz Quartet consisting of Edmond Hall, a New Orleans clarinet player; Meade Lux Lewis, a widely known boogie-woogie pianist, playing the celeste on these records; Charley Christian, the 23-year-old guitarist, who played with Benny Goodman and originated playing melody on the guitar rather than simply strumming rhythm chords; and Israel Crosby, the bass player from the Cab Calloway Band. I believe the two records were produced in 1937, which makes them 80+ years old today and I believe they are as fresh and interesting as they were when they first appeared on the market. I wore out two or three sets until they were finally released on vinyl and believe they can now be found on YouTube. They were the first true jazz records I ever bought and led to a collection of about 1,300 records collected over a period of 50 years. Along with these, another collection of classical records accumulated totaling about 800. These were acquired one by one and were far from comprehensive regarding any one category. I only bought according to my own taste and preferences and frequently learned of new things from reading the reviews of Whitney Balliot of the *New Yorker*, a fine critic, and from reading *Stereo Review*, and other catalogs from record companies. For instance, many would think my "neglect" of the brass players shameful, but I preferred reeds and piano - Frank Sinatra was in a category all his own - but with a background of playing reeds which helped me appreciate those skills, it's not hard to see why.

My main interests from the beginning were the small groups rather than the big bands, some of which created small groups from their own personnel, i.e., Benny Goodman, Tommy Dorsey and Duke Ellington, for example. I felt then (and still do, to some extent) that there was more clarity and creativity and precision in the small groups, to say nothing of originality and improvisation. No chance of "faking" it in a small group. Exceptions were found in the big bands who could afford superior arrangers, who provided original ideas to popular songs which appeared almost weekly, some not very good, and leaders who did not tolerate sloppy playing: Goodman, Shaw, the Dorsey brothers, Basie and, of course, Ellington come to mind. There were many other big bands who crisscrossed the country playing in theaters, amusement parks with dance floors, night clubs, anywhere a dollar could be made. Alas, after the war and a disastrous strike of the musicians' union which stopped the recording industry cold, the changing times after World War II virtually destroyed the big band business. This, plus the power of the promotion, prepared the way for the rock-n-roll era, and the following generations were basically deprived of the experience I had with jazz, a genuine form of art originated in the U.S.

Thus, my horizons widened, both classical and jazz during the years of our marriage. Fran was already well-steeped in her appreciation of classical music - and Tommy Dorsey - but widened her taste to include my kind of jazz after our first date, which was a first time experience for her when we danced in her sorority parlor to my small group jazz. However I would love to know her true, initial reaction to the first present I ever gave her upon my return to Ann Arbor for her Senior Prom, after my visit with Sidney Mishcon in New York, when I proudly presented her with a 12" Signature label record of the Coleman Hawkins Quartet, playing "The Man I Love." She really wanted and was expecting perfume! But that record ended up being worthy of inclusion in the Smithsonian Jazz collection, and her tastes developed and improved over the years. I always wondered what the Brecksville duplicate bridge group thought when they played at our house because I seized the opportunity and had my jazz records playing in the background. They couldn't hear that kind of music anywhere else.

In addition to small combo jazz, I became enthralled with the wonderful piano players of that time beginning with Art Tatum, the blind pianist from Toledo, Ohio. I knew the name because I had bought a book of his arrangements while still in high school. They were far beyond my ability except for one song: "Don't Blame Me." When I got into record buying, I soon discovered him and bought as many of his things as I could afford. Constant source of amazement. Dazzling technique with a fabulous left hand, and the ability to make anything he played his own. If I had to pick only one of his records as my favorite, I would probably choose his Art Tatum-Ben Webster Quartet on the Verve label. Pure pleasure, and such easy listening. Two older gentlemen ruminating on life.

The other pianists I admire and never tire of listening to would include, in no particular order: Dick Hyman, Teddy Wilson, Count Basie, Dick Wellstood, Ralph Sutton, Oscar Peterson, Johnny Guarnieri, Paul Smith, Marian McPartland, Sir Charles Thompson, Eddie Higgins, Mary Lou Williams, Fats Waller, Dave McKenna, John Bunch, Mark Shane, and my most recent obsession, Stephanie Trick, a 28 year old stride pianist from St. Louis whose pure joy shows on her face while playing and the way she keeps time with her feet. She recently married a fine Italian pianist, Paolo Alderighi and they have a remarkable 2 piano version of "The World is Waiting for the Sunrise," accessible on YouTube. Anyone who has ever taken a piano lesson has to be impressed with the technique displayed by these people and impressed with their improvisational skills. And be a just a little bit envious.

Since that was my case and having played piano (No solos!) in a Nisei dance band in Minneapolis in the army at USO dances - my pay was $3 per gig which was a significant amount when we were first married and I was earning $65 per month before deductions. I was frustrated and felt there had to be some system that I could learn which would free me from the notes on a sheet of music and enable me to improvise. It was much too late to develop the skills of the above list, and I was hampered by a very limited amount of talent, but to be able to play even one piece in an original interpretation, all my own, was a deeply held dream. Therefore, somehow or another I found a teacher in the E. 105th St. and Euclid Avenue area, who had a studio on the second floor. Every Tuesday night I would stay late after work and drive out there, parking somewhere a block to the south near Carnegie Avenue and, I shudder to think of it today, walk to my lesson. I am ashamed that I can't remember the teacher's name but I think he was fairly competent and I was beginning to get the hang of it when it all came to a halt when St. Matthews, Fran's, church needed a substitute organist. She asked me if I could try to step in. I pointed out that it had been 20 years since I had touched an organ; and I didn't know the order of service. And I didn't want to embarrass her.

I agreed to try and sometime later became the permanent organist. I ended up taking my final music lesson, an organ lesson, as a tired businessman from Warren Berryman, member of the faculty at Baldwin Wallace College. He was a fine player and instructor, and very patient with me. Thinking of the comparative satisfaction derived from becoming a church organist as opposed to a competent jazz pianist playing in some smoky bar, I believe I made, I know I made the right choice. Serving a congregation for five years as I did was probably the most satisfying thing I ever did in my whole life, far more satisfying than the selfish thrill of being able to sit down without music and improvise on a standard ballad or swing tune would have been. I think of it occasionally but without any regrets whatsoever.

I also felt and hoped my playing for her church was a form of redemption in Fran's eyes for my earlier shameful outburst when the church was being formed. And I can still listen and marvel at the wonderful jazz geniuses of my day whose work is readily available on YouTube on my computer; I feel truly sorry for others, young and old, who are unable to experience for whatever reason what I do while listening to my Golden Age music.

I think I was very fortunate to grow up in a period of time when technology was making the Golden Age from the 1920s to the 1950s more accessible and affordable. The music could be heard live on the radio, then TV, and on the constantly improving sound systems following the transition from shellac to vinyl, long playing records which allowed the performer to escape from the 3 minute 78 RPM limitations, and to have more time to explore their musical ideas. The final improvement was the advent of the compact disc, CD, where the time limit expanded far beyond that of the LPs.

One of the ways musicians put food on their tables was to be hired to play at private parties. Probably the precursor of the jazz party/festivals we enjoyed so much later on. My room while in college was located right off fraternity row and I remember well a party one of the fraternities gave where the band they hired was the Count Basie Orchestra. I didn't get much studying done that night! Many years later, while living in Brecksville, we hired Chuck Braman, the son of my best friend, a genius percussionist and his small combo to play for us and a small group of friends on a Sunday afternoon. He set up in the dining room and we all sat up in the living room looking down on the performers. I wonder what our guests thought of the music they heard.

Early in the era Tin Pan Alley flourished and many young aspiring musicians made a living playing the latest songs in music stores to promote the sale of sheet music: George Gershwin, Irving Berlin, and Fats Waller among them. They went on to write some of the great, timeless songs and to create musicals for Broadway. Movie theatres hired dance bands to play for a week as an added attraction to entice more people to see the movies they were showing; recording studios were busy churning out various versions of the new songs by the big bands; Hollywood jumped on the "bandwagon" and produced both original and their own version of Broadway hits. I remember going down to the Palace Theater on Euclid Avenue which had a live performance of some sort every week, which competed in a way with the movie being shown, to see Ted Lewis and his band do his famous "Me and My Shadow" routine.

Also, I remember going out to the Euclid Beach Park, which was purported to have the best dance floor in the State of Ohio as well as the fastest roller coaster, to hear big bands several times. I remember going way down to Chippewa Lake, about 30-40 miles southwest of Cleveland, a vacation cottage community with an amusement park and a dance floor to hear the Will Bradley Band who were famous for their drummer, Ray McKinley's version of "Down the Road Apiece," a piece I loved to listen to while studying in my room in college.

I should point out that classical music flourished on records with their longer playing time and the scope of the music available increased many fold; many lesser known composers and artists became known to the record buying public. I took advantage of all this to the extent I could, both jazz and classical. Others were far more deeply involved. While my collection of records and CDs grew to total 2,300 over a period of 50 years, this was modest compared to many who had collections of 8-10,000, or more.

Those living in the New York area, or the west coast, had far more access to live performance, especially New York. There were limits imposed on me by money and family responsibilities. But I feel fortunate to have enjoyed the opportunities that presented themselves and that I was able to take advantage of.

After all this background, now is the time to recall some of the experiences that made a lasting impression on me beginning with my high school and college days. I recall two shattering musical experiences in high school. The first occurred when we were allowed to leave school early one day to go to Severance Hall to hear an afternoon rehearsal of the Cleveland Symphony conducted by Artur Rodzinski. They played *L'Après-midi d'un Faune* by Stravinsky. I now realize that although I had played in my high school orchestra, this was the first time I had ever experienced the power of the sound produced by a professional symphony orchestra. I had never heard anything like it before, the gorgeous sound. I remember standing up on the streetcar all the way home at rush hour and feeling sicker and sicker and when I got home, going to bed for a couple of days. I don't think I even came downstairs for meals. Maybe it was the effect of the music. But it could have been the intestinal flu.

The other high school experience, probably my senior year, was when my parents allowed me to go alone to downtown Cleveland at night to the small concert hall at the Cleveland Public Auditorium to hear a piano recital given by Sergei Rachmaninoff, one of my favorite composers. I was overwhelmed by his technique and his austere presence seated at the piano. One of the pieces he played was an impromptu by Schubert which I had been working on and his playing was magical. The result of this experience was that I didn't touch our piano for about two weeks. What was the point? There was no way I could ever approach such perfection.

Also, thanks to my high school principal, Mr. Mitchell, I was able to hear the Yale Glee Club, and the Whiffenpoofs live. I had never heard anything like that before, either. Later, in my Freshman year at Yale, we would open our windows on the fourth floor in Durfee Hall and listen to the Whiffenpoofs singing on their way home after practicing (at Mory's?) in the soft, spring air and it is simply unforgettable. How fortunate!

While at Yale, I went to an organ concert given by Marcel Dupré, one of the great living French organists. He improvised a symphony based on five original themes provided by School of

Music students, which was impressive. But the most memorable thing was shaking hands with him at the reception afterwards and being amazed at how cold and flabby his hand was.

I also went to a recital by Artur Rubenstein at Woolsey Hall and didn't like his playing, or the liberties he took with the music he played, copies of which I had brought with me. I thought he was demeaning the largely student audience. It bothered me that he didn't play the notes the way the composer wrote them. He was physically flamboyant, emphasizing himself and not the music. Absolutely no comparison to the Rachmaninoff performance I had heard earlier.

I played hooky one afternoon and went to hear the Jimmy Lunceford Dance Band, very popular at that time, playing a weeklong engagement at one of the two movie theaters in downtown New Haven, the Roger Sherman. I think I sat in the last row of the balcony and my ears still hurt from the volume of sound they produced. Strange memory.

During the war years while at the University of Michigan, four of my friends formed a jazz quartet, the Sunnysiders, and became very popular. There was no specific leader, but they were all from the U. of Michigan ASTP program. They were Dick Thomas, piano; Ray Kiser, guitar; Bud Klauser, drums; and Ken Pierson, trumpet. It was Pierson who set up my blind date with Fran. Occasionally another U. of M. ASTP-er, Bill Corkery, a fine Irish tenor, would sing vocals with them. When we finally got to Fort Snelling, Minnesota, they played for USO dances. They were quite a contrast to the high school or retiree-old men bands, uniformly weak playing, and not very good. It was war time and all the regular young men players were in uniform. When the Sunnysiders were on the bandstand, everyone in the room was on his feet dancing.

The outstanding member was Dick Thomas, who played the piano and became a very good friend. He was a Princeton graduate who majored in Arabic and was one of the outstanding Japanese language scholars in our group. While at Princeton, he used to go up to Manhattan on weekends and play as an amateur intermission pianist at one of the 52nd Street night clubs.

He had an amazing experience one night when he was playing. Maxine Sullivan, a famous girl singer, known for her recordings of "Loch Lomond " and "Comin' Through the Rye", came up to him and asked if he would like to accompany her in some Gershwin. He said he almost fainted, but did play and was complimented, and loved it.

Many years later Maxine Sullivan, who was one of my favorite singers, and the reason we went to our first jazz party at Conneaut Lake, said, when I spoke to her, that she remembered him. Could that be true? After 15 or 20 years?

The men in the company used to ask Dick to play for us after dinner at Tyler House, East Quad where we lived. He usually agreed to play and then would play his own improvised versions of the popular songs of the day for 30-40 minutes, holding us all spellbound. What a wonderful experience and memory. He was very modest, and gentle. He was also very popular at least one of the sorority houses. I went with him once, not Fran's house unfortunately, or I might not be telling this story, and he played for the girls who were enthralled. I think it may have been the Chi

Omegas and have often wondered if any of those who heard him realized how rare it was to hear such talent and did those evenings become part of their treasured memories.

Many years later while he was living in Washington, D.C., and working at the VA, he played regularly for a wonderful, relatively unknown girl singer, Joyce Carr, who lad a lovely, clear soprano voice and superb diction. He gave me a record she had produced privately where she was backed by the Bob Vigoda Trio (Bob was the nephew of Abe Vigoda of the famed *Barney Miller* TV series). Dick sat in and played for two of the songs. The one I like best is "You Don't Know What Love Is," a haunting ballad. I was instrumental in interesting the Heritage Jazz Society to publish the album and put it in their catalog and distribute it (a small claim to fame!) It was quite successful for an unknown singer, I was told. Dick was very grateful to have Joyce's name more widely known. I would have loved to hear her sing live.

At the end of our stay at Fort Snelling, before scattering after our discharge from the Army, the Sunnysiders had two 12" LPs recorded by the Rudolph Schmitt Company of Minneapolis, a recording studio. I paid $5 each (a fortune in those days), for both and eventually had them reproduced as CDs, and gave copies to each of the members of the group. I was told that after hearing the recordings, a nightclub in Chicago offered the group $300 per week to play there. If true, this was a huge amount for men who were paid $65 per month by the Army at that time. But they all had other plans - two of them were already married, the others had careers to begin. It never happened.

Two other musical memories of the time spent in Minneapolis/St. Paul were the occasion, I have no recollection of the details, how or why it happened, but I was one of a committee to meet and deliver Vaughn Monroe, a very well-known singer/band leader and escort him by cab to a concert he was giving. Tantalizing not to remember more details, since he was very well known for his nasal baritone voice.

Fran and I went to a concert given by Art Tatum, the incredible pianist, the only time I ever heard him live. I don't remember a thing of what I am sure at the time I thought was unforgettable; he played or how. But I do remember (I always remember the important stuff) him arriving at the concert hall the same time we did, and it was cold and rainy, and I held the door open for him to enter. Ahead of us, of course.

During our married years, we would occasionally go downtown for dinner at the Theatrical Grill, a popular bar/restaurant on "short" Vincent Street, which stretches only from E. 9th Street and E. 6th Street. The owner, "Mushy" Wexler, who was an important member of the "mob" was a lover of jazz and regularly brought in important performers, usually for one-week engagements. It was wonderful to be able to hear Teddy Wilson playing the piano live, and not to have to go all the way to New York to hear him. But it always annoyed me that so many people talked through the performances and didn't have the intelligence or courtesy to listen. The bar was very long, a horseshoe shaped oval with a raised stage in the middle the players had to climb up to play. The continual noisy chatter should have been distracting. Apparently, they were used to it.

One night, Maxine Sullivan was the featured singer with the Buck Clayton Combo on his first trip on the road after recovering from cancer of the lip. She was dressed in a simple tunic dress and just stood there and sang. She was wonderful. It was a terrific contrast to the girl singer in the house band who was dressed in a pink cocktail dress that looked sprayed on - and she never stopped wiggling while she tried to sell whatever she was singing. I hoped she had her ears open that week when Maxine sang. It would have been like a master lesson at a music school.

Two other things I remember about those days at the Theatrical. I don't remember and can't imagine how it happened, but I stayed downtown after work to have dinner with "Peanuts" Hucko, perhaps to be joined by Fran coming down later. He was one of the great clarinet players who later was frequently a guest on the Lawrence Welk show. He liked to play golf and always had his clubs with him when he was on the road - also his clarinet. I can't remember any of the conversation; but I suppose we talked about music and golf. YouTube has a great live performance of him playing at a concert in Tokyo where he plays "Memories of You" which Fran and I always felt was "our" song.

The other occasion was similar: Vic Dickenson, one of the great trombone players, was in town at the Theatrical and I don't know how it could have happened, but I took him to dinner.

The only memory I have of the conversation was that he complained bitterly that he was getting old and couldn't play standing, typical in a Dixieland band, for any length of time but had to play sitting down, which was some sort of blot on his character in his mind. He was still a great musician. I played one of his LPs, the Vic Dickenson Septet doing "I Cover the Waterfront" for the electrician, who was a jazz harmonica player, when he came to our house in Parma Heights to study the plans for the proposed house to be built in Brecksville. He was sitting cross legged on the floor, swaying back and forth, in time with the music. Fran had serious doubts as to his sanity - and ability. He did do the work, far more than the plans called for and no question as to his ability.

I must say the food was excellent at the Theatrical, both lunch and dinner, especially the rolls. One final Theatrical memory is the time Fran's brother, Mark, 11 years her senior, was visiting us and more for me than for him (he was very difficult to entertain) we took him for dinner at the Theatrical. The band that week was Turk Murphy, a very good west coast Dixieland band, and they were in full voice as we entered. The blast of sound was tremendous, and I think Mark who was very "square" must have been overwhelmed. But he was a good sport and probably wondered about the guy his sister had married. I don't think it affected his appetite.

Another activity that we enjoyed later in our marriage was attending jazz festivals. It started when we got a flyer in the mail from the Allegheny Jazz Club of Meadville, Pennsylvania. It was interesting but I didn't recognize many of the players and it was too expensive. The next year the announcement came and this year one of the artists was Maxine Sullivan. We decided we couldn't miss the opportunity to hear her over a three-day span of time, and maybe even get to talk to her. It was held at the Conneaut Lake Park in Pennsylvania, an old, small, amusement park with a midway, rides, and one small roller coaster, I believe. There was a small firetrap hotel on the grounds where we stayed, with a small separate building with a dance floor where the performances took place. Conneaut Lake is not a very large lake and was only about a two to three-hour drive from Cleveland.

It was a revelation: the ten or twelve performers were from the east and west coasts, many of whom had never played together before. All were first rate musicians, but because of the genre, not that well known. The sponsor, Joe Boughton, founder of the Allegheny Jazz Society, ran a tight ship, varying the mixes of the talent, and the music was nearly continuous with no intermissions and no wasted time talking. They played 45 minute-sets from 7:30 p.m. until midnight, which is a lot of high-powered music. This went on Friday and Saturday nights with additional music Saturday afternoon and Sunday morning during the farewell breakfast and it all came to an end at noon. Boughton had only one rule: No blues, which he felt could be self-indulgent and go on forever. Attendance was limited to 100-150 listeners in cabaret style seating at tables, and both the people and the performers who were approachable were so friendly, sharing their common love of the music, which made it all the more enjoyable. Not being seated in theater style added to the intimacy. Best of all was being able to actually talk to the performers when they were not on stage between sets. It was a wonderful experience. The music was so stimulating it was hard to get to sleep when we finally got to bed.

It was also fun to watch the college age servers standing at the bar between orders swaying and toe tapping to a kind of music they had never heard before, certainly not on their local radio stations.

Fran and I spent most of one Saturday afternoon sitting on the lawn in front of the hotel on the shore of the lake listening to two of the older, very well-known players, Bucky Pizzarelli, guitar, and Bud Freeman, tenor sax, reminiscing about their past. It was fascinating to be a part of that living history. Another time we wandered around the midway after lunch with Bob Haggart, the great bass player, who wrote "Big Noise from Winnetka" and "What's New." He lived in Sarasota where many other jazz greats did; and we met him several times at other festivals.

Fran was particularly fond of the trumpet playing of Ed Polcer, as was I. He was a Princeton grad and a half-owner of the Eddy Condon nightclub in Manhattan. We heard and met him for the first time at Conneaut Lake and then at almost all of the later jazz party/festivals we attended. He was very, very good; had a great flowing style that never quit. Another great discovery was Marty Grosz who played the acoustic guitar, and was related to the German cartoonist, Georg Grosz, who had work hung at the Metropolitan Museum of Art. He played fine rhythm and sang funny songs and told humorous stories. I liked his rendition of "The Chambermaid's Love Song."

I was also impressed at one of the parties by Johnny Mintz who used to play clarinet in the big bands and had to be 75 years old when we heard him. I marveled at his energy. It was hard to get him off the bandstand. He just wanted to keep playing.

I think the first time I ever heard Dick Hyman live was at Conneaut Lake, where he did a solo of "Caravan," which was remarkable. These people's recordings were virtually inaccessible then in the ordinary record shops, many recording on obscure labels privately produced, with no corporate promotion. One of the side benefits at the jazz parties was that there was always a table in the lobby displaying many of the performers' CDs and it was easy, and the only way to get their CDs. It's much different now when they almost all can be sampled on YouTube.

All in all, we probably attended ten to twelve of these festival jazz parties, many while spending our winters in Florida, notably one held every year at Easter time in Atlanta.

This was a very well-run affair, heavily attended, and attracted very high-quality performers, Bob Wilber, the soprano sax player, among them; we had dinner with him several times and got to know him. He may have been the greatest living reed player in the world at that time. He lived in Scottsdale, Arizona, in the winter and spent his summers in the Cottswolds, in England. He made an arrangement of a piece of classical piano music by Frederick Delius which I gave him; had it recorded on a CD with him leading the Toulouse Jazz Band of Toulouse, France, for whom he acted as arranger and leader sometimes. He called "my" piece "Savoy Stomp." I have the CD (it can also be found on YouTube) and get quite a thrill knowing I was responsible indirectly for one of the pieces. In the liner notes Wilber referred to me as one of his "fans" who inspired the song he wrote which is the first track on the CD.

One year, on Super Bowl weekend, we went to a jazz party in Pensacola, at the westerly end of the Florida Panhandle, stopping on the way at Tallahassee, the capital of Florida to explore it. The party was held in the old railroad station which had been converted into a Hilton Hotel. It was the first time we heard Eddy Higgins, the piano player, who knew one of my golfing friends at El Conquistador, who was a teacher and the baseball coach at Phillips Exeter Academy. He taught and coached President George H. W. Bush, "the finest young man he ever met," he said. I really enjoyed Higgins's style and talking with him; having a mutual friend made it easier.

We never went to the closest festival, which was held in Clearwater Beach, while we lived in Florida, It was sponsored by the Arbors Record Company, who have a large catalog specializing in classical jazz music. It was more expensive for the whole program and just a little too far to attend a single session, in spite of the temptation to go to hear some specific performer.

I suspect we missed some great occasions when Dick Hyman, the great "Stride" pianist (he's much more than a pianist limited to one style. He can be checked out on YouTube) was featured on the piano. He must have loved playing there because of the proximity: he lives in Venice, only two or three-hour drive south of Clearwater.

Many of the same great players appeared at all of these festivals all over the country, so we looked forward to seeing the same people but were never disappointed because of the freshness of their ideas and playing. Seeing many of the same attendees and performers, we looked forward to seeing old acquaintances again which added to our pleasure. It was like going home to visit family. As I recall the cost was in the range of $ 150-$200 per person, all-inclusive except for travel &

lodging expense. It was a great way to enjoy a short weekend get-away. These festivals originated from a private party in Denver, in the home of a wealthy individual, by invitation only, and have grown to spread all over the country, where any lover of the traditional, classic jazz may attend. It helps to get on a mailing list to know where and what to choose from.

There are even jazz festival cruises now, one as far away as Scandinavia. We took one to the eastern Caribbean featuring all Dixieland bands. It visited several islands we had not seen before and we met a Yale classmate from Connecticut who lived in the same college I did, but whom I met for the first time. It was a whole week of great music and I was mesmerized by the dancing style of one of the couples, what I dubbed the "One Step." They had been married by the ship's captain just before we left port.

They had a unique style, moving rapidly around the dance floor, emphasizing every beat. I could not take my eyes off them and wished I had that skill. They obviously were having a great time. We particularly enjoyed listening to Bob Schultz, the leader of the San Francisco Jazz Band, whom we had met at an earlier festival. His was one of the five bands, and I thought the best. Even though the music lasted for seven days, not the three-day weekend we were accustomed to, it never bored us, at least me, and we looked forward to every performance.

As always there was the opportunity to mingle with the performers which always made it special. I am very happy that in this terrible musical era of Rock 'n Roll there, are still a few oldsters and young people as well as young performers, who are striving to keep traditional jazz, which has real musical value, alive considering what it has meant to me over these past 70+ years.

During our 30 years of spending our winters in Florida, we became aware of the Sarasota Jazz Club which had about 1,500 members and claimed to be the largest such club in the world. They had a public school-educational agenda, as well as sponsoring individual performances and an annual jazz party extending over four days and held in the Van Wezel auditorium on the shores of Sarasota Bay. Many of the people we had come to know previously appeared, but the performances were on a theater stage, and the seating was in typical rows of theater seats and thus there was no chance to mingle with the performers, or to get up and wander around to relieve the tension aroused by the music, let alone dance.

It was surprising to me how many of the jazz greats lived in or retired to the Sarasota area. Perhaps it was for the same reasons we chose the area to spend our winters away from frozen Lake Erie: the amenities of a great climate, superior cultural opportunities, easy land and air transportation, and excellent medical facilities. And some pretty good restaurants.

We attended several of the individual performances when the performers were people we especially liked.

Probably the only sad occasion in all our jazz evenings was the memorial concert for Bob Haggart when most of the living jazz greats gathered together in his honor and put on a wonderful concert at the Van Wezel auditorium. Admission was free but one had to stand in line to get a ticket the day before which I gladly did. It was a wonderful tribute to a fine gentleman and a great talent.

One or two of my other jazz related memories: I was elected to man our office one New Year's Day afternoon when we closed early, and the phone rang. It was my good friend, Jack Wyse, publisher of the trade magazine, *Properties*, asking me to hold and then he put me on the line with Duke Ellington who was in town with his band to play for a private party. I couldn't believe I was actually talking with him, told him of my collection of his records, of my lifetime love of his music, said, "Happy New Year!" and begged him to "Stay well, that we needed his music." I couldn't believe it.

Some years later we went to a fund raiser for the Gilmour Academy which was held in a small shopping center in Beachwood at Cedar and Richmond Roads. The whole center was closed after 7 p.m. to accommodate the several bands and performers who did their thing without stopping which allowed attendees to rove from one location to another to sample their favorites and the others. I can't imagine how they ever assembled so much talent to appear on the same date.

The big attraction for me was the appearance of Duke Ellington and his band. We were able to wander from one performing location to the other, and we were the first ones at the Ellington site and sat on the floor in the first row right in front of the band. It was pretty cramped, and uncomfortable and we missed some other great music. We had never been to a party where you could sample various performers and wander from one to the other while eating free hamburgers. It was an interesting format and I never heard of it being used anywhere else.

One of the artists was the girl singer, Carmen McRae who was backed by the pianist, Tommy Franklin of Detroit. I liked his playing, but had never cared for her voice, and hearing her live did not change my mind.

But the big deal of the whole evening was the chance to hear the Ellington band up close. It would be closer and more intimate than Fran's Senior Prom, the week when we first met, and the Ellington Band played for the prom. Most of the couples there didn't dance much - just stood as close as they could get and listened. We were going to be even closer and with only 50 or 60 people in the room! At first it was disappointing because the Duke was not there. The band always traveled by bus, the Duke by car with Harry Carney, the baritone sax player, as his driver; they got lost and were late in arriving. When they did finally arrive, dressed for travel in clothes that looked as though they slept in them, the Duke apologized to the audience and promised to play some extra music.

A short time later he appeared, immaculately dressed for the audience and Carney took up his place with his huge baritone sax. The band was transformed and played brilliantly. Up until the Duke's arrival the band sounded like a second-rate organization. The minute the Duke appeared it all changed; and they were their old crisp, rhythmic, rich sound. The contrast was amazing. The one thing I remember was when they were doing encores; I was sitting on the floor in the front row, I asked the Duke if they could play "The Gal from Joe's," one of my favorites, featuring

Johnny Hodges, the alto sax player. I had a record of it and had loved it since my college days, playing it over and over while I was studying. He said they couldn't do it, that it was no longer on their play list. A disappointing end to a great evening.

Another of my vivid memories is the concert at Blossom Music Center one balmy, summer evening when we went to hear the New Orleans Preservation Hall Jazz Band which was very famous for playing the old genuine Dixieland jazz. They were the first half of the program. The second half was to be The World's Greatest Jazz Band, a group I had never heard play before, but which had some fine personnel.

I felt rather sorry for them having to follow the Preservation Hall group who put on a great performance. It seemed as though this second group should have appeared first to act as a warm-up act. However, as soon as the World's Greatest Jazz Band started playing, I knew that we were going to hear something remarkable. They simply blew the Preservation Hall band off the stage. I couldn't believe how good they were. Later I bought everything of theirs I could get my hands on.

The most interesting thing was that this was basically a Dixieland band which played far more than the old standby Dixie favorites. The make-up of the band was unusual in that there were single players in the rhythm section, but two players in each of the other sections. This meant that when they played a ballad or other popular song there was double the opportunity to show off the talents of the players and it made the whole experience that much richer. I still remember leaving early in the last piece to avoid the traffic jam in the parking lot, climbing up the hill listening to Billy Butterfield, trumpet, playing "What's New," the great song with great lyrics that was written by Bob Haggart, who was there playing his own creation. It was warm and uplifting and beautiful.

My listening to music still continues to be an exploration, trying to expose myself to new composers and performers who, perhaps, are not considered top tier, or well promoted, but are otherwise interesting to me - worthy of repeated listening. It's not just nostalgia for the long-gone days of the 30s and 40s. Having access to YouTube on my computer has made this search easier and more satisfying; in some cases, a source of amazement as to how I could not have known of some of the performers I stumbled on.

Of course, not having to buy a record or CD and then being disappointed, using YouTube, which is free, makes the constant search much more appealing to me.

As examples, some of the new things which I have discovered and listened to over and over, both "old friends" and people new to me are: Dick Hyman (old) and Stephanie Trick (new) doing both solo and two pianos. I never used to like the 2-piano format. It has now become one of my favorites after listening to Hyman & Trick. I listen to them doing "I'll See You in My Dreams" again and again. Incidentally, Hyman was 88 years old and Trick was 28 years old when this recording was made. It's on YouTube and it's fascinating to witness Trick's excitement and enthusiasm to have the privilege of playing with the acknowledged master of the genre. The way she keeps time with her feet is really amazing.

She also plays the greatest arrangement of "The World is Waiting for the Sunrise" I have ever heard, with her new husband, Italian pianist, Paolo Alderighi. The photography is exceptional, and the joy on her face while playing is almost palpable.

As I have grown older, I am finding that knowing the words to these songs adds something to my enjoyment. Not only do they complement the melodies, but they seem to round out the musical experience. I have actually memorized the words to two or three of the songs I like the best. I especially like Diane Keaton singing "Seems Like Old Times" from the Woody Allen movie *Annie Hall*, available on YouTube. It's as though they were written to sing to Fran and that brings a feeling of closeness.

Other recent discoveries include: Bob Wilber playing "Si Tu Vois Ma Mère" (1983); Joe Brown at the George Harrison Memorial Concert in the Royal Albert Hall in London, playing and singing the closing number "I'll See You in My Dreams." How I would have loved to have been there; something my daughter, Barb, called to my attention: Judy Collins, playing piano and singing in concert a song she wrote: "My Father Always Promised Us"; Blossom Dearie (knew the name from ads in the New Yorker but never heard her and when I did, what a revelation that was, singing solo, Duke Ellington's "Sophisticated Lady," a great introduction to her many great songs; new discovery, Paul Smith, playing in his studio for his family on his 91st birthday; Dick Hyman and Dick Wellstood, two pianos, playing "Thou Swell"; Jimmy Giuffre, reed player, with a trio, playing "The Train and the Bridge"; all the Benny Goodman small groups; all the Art Tatum and Oscar Peterson things available; and, then, not to be forgotten, Frank Sinatra singing "Goodbye." Only one word describes his performance: heartbreaking.

There is so much richness which I am afraid I will not have time to explore. Not everything on YouTube is great. One has to be selective, and one doesn't have to like something because of its category but, if my enthusiasm has not turned you off, dear reader, a little exploration could lead to many hours of pleasure and excitement.

I want to bring this long account of a life saturated with music to a close by relating two of the most shattering musical experiences in all my 96 years. The first occasion was the night, cold and rainy and we shouldn't have gone because I was coming down with a cold, when we went in to the Parma High School on Pleasant Valley Road to hear a concert given by Virgil Fox, a widely known virtuoso organist, who was also a showman. He came on stage wearing tails with a satin cape lined in red and wore patent leather pumps with red heels, enhanced with rhinestones! This proved not to be a distraction while he was playing. His playing was flawless, especially the moving *Passacaglia and Fugue* by J.S. Bach. The crowning glory of the evening for me was his encore. He played a pedal solo with incredible rapidity and accuracy. It ended with a descending passage of chords in 3rds and 4ths, which requires arching the foot to be able to strike both notes of the interval simultaneously. Open mouthed, I thought you can't physically do that. It's impossible. And at that speed. I, who had struggled with Bach's pedal solo prelude, couldn't believe it. I still don't know how he did it.

The second experience was a Thursday night concert at Severance Hall (I think it was 1968 when I would have been 47 years old) to hear István Kertész, guest conductor, lead the orchestra and chorus in a performance of Gustave Mahler's *Symphony No.2* ("Resurrection"). I was familiar with both Mahler's and Bruckner's names because classmates across the hall at Yale who were wealthy and had a collection of every symphony recorded, played symphonic music incessantly, at high volume on their Capehart record player. The sound was fine, but it was just background noise and I never was able to distinguish one piece from another or where one began and ended. It would be stretching things to say that I was acquainted with the works of Mahler.

So, many years later, this concert was the first time I would be listening to something, knowing it had been written by Mahler. The Second Symphony calls for an enlarged orchestra and a full chorus plus a contralto and soprano soloist and has five movements. It is so long that is makes up the whole program for the evening. I recall that the first 3 movements seemed fairly conventional with some very lovely melodies.

After the intermission the 4th & 5th movements began with the entry of the chorus and the two soloists singing. The words are in German and I was reading them and the translation in the program notes and was transfixed when the stunning, exalted finale came. My cheeks were wet with tears and I was literally speechless. The audience was silent and motionless for a minute or so and then jumped to their feet and erupted into cheers and applause. In the car on the way home, I finally regained part of the use of my voice. I know that Fran enjoyed the music but was more concerned by my reaction and tried to comfort me. All I can say is that no other piece of music I have ever heard in my long life has had such a profound impact on me.

I went out the next day and bought a recording of the symphony, there are many available, but it was at least a year before I could bring myself to listen to it because I feared a repeat of the emotional impact. The first time I did listen to it, it did have the same effect. It is an amazing piece of inspiration and the 5th movement is a wonderful expression of affirmation, or faith.

Finally, some ruminations on what music is and why it is so important. Because of my foregoing experiences, I bought a Great Courses class on "Music and the Brain" which I have promised myself I will listen to someday. I speculate that the professor is making a case that a special area in the brain is wired for music, that it controls and governs the perception of music; enables us, all of us, to appreciate some form of music; and that in some way is connected and influences other areas of the brain; that in the case of some highly endowed individuals enables or compels them to express themselves by becoming virtuoso performers, or composers. It is said that music is a form of language or an unseen form of communication, and I believe this to be true. I think everyone responds to music in varying degrees and in one form or another to some sort of music. And I think music can be arousing, or inspiring, or comforting. In my case, with my middling, limited talent, never of professional caliber, I am grateful for music's presence in my life. It is something for which I thank my mother every time I think of her. What would my life have been without it?

Both playing and listening, it has been a reliever of stress and a source of happiness, my escape to a more perfect realm.

I frequently wonder, granted the importance of other personal habits, if the presence of music in one's life is not a contributor to longevity. The examples of Leopold Stokowski, Paul Smith and Dick Hyman come to mind and I am sure there are many others, both classical and pop, who are out there. I consider myself a living example.

And I close with a quotation of the German philosopher, Artur Schopenhauer, which I noticed in Frank Sinatra's biography by James Kaplan, with which I totally agree.

"MUSIC IS THE ONE FORM OF ART WHICH TOUCHES THE ABSOLUTE."

# Chapter VI

## Gardening & Peony Passion

My love of gardening (which wasn't always thought of as love at the time) began at the time we started spending our summers living on Tiedeman Road, when I was fourteen years old in 1935. Mother always loved growing plants; but I don't ever remember her talking about it, nor do I remember Grandma Schmidt, who grew up on a farm, being an inspiration for me. My mother was a city girl growing up on a typical sized city lot which would have had limited space for growing things. She did tell about when she was a girl being picked up and riding in the back of a truck to pick berries on a berry farm on Dover Center Road in what is now Westlake. This hardly seems likely to be an explanation for a lifelong interest in how to make things grow. Her oldest sister, Aunt Esther, was also interested in gardening and had elaborate plantings at their home on Riverside Drive in Berea, Ohio. She was a horticulturist and knew the Latin names for every plant in her gardens, but Uncle Herb did all the physical labor. Perfectionist that he was, I remember seeing him use a surveyor's transit when he was preparing the seed bed for the lawn in their front yard. He also shoveled the topsoil against a tilted screen to sift out debris before wheeling it into place.

In our family Mother did much of the manual labor on her hands and knees (and only knew the common names for the weeds and her flowers) getting her hands and fingernails dirty. She inculcated by force, if necessary, if not by example, her love of how to make plants grow and creating beauty. Interestingly, of her four sons exposed to this regime, only the oldest (me) and the youngest, Wes, carried on this training and became gardeners when they had their own homes. I do not remember Dad taking much interest in gardening, or yard work, although there is one photo taken of him mowing the lawn, pushing a lawn mower in his rolled-up shirtsleeves after work on a Saturday afternoon.

On Tiedeman Road, we learned how to raise everything, both vegetables and flowers. I remember well the hours, usually in the morning - the afternoon was for naps and play - sweating in the sun, pulling weeds in the vegetable garden in the rear of the cottage and working on weeding the borders and cutting the lawn in the front yard.

Chemical weed control was very primitive that long ago and I only remember having nicotine sulfate to use in our hand pump tank sprayer to control aphids on the roses and thrips on the gladioli. We used to go around with coffee cans of coal oil in Japanese beetle season and knock the shiny bugs off the plant leaves into the oil to kill them. I can't remember what we used to try to kill the weevils on the bean plants, which we tried to control by blowing dry powder spray from a duster onto the under side of the leaves, best done in the early morning while the dew was still on the leaves. We learned how to find the huge hornworms, which were nearly invisible because of their protective coloring, on the tomato plants, by looking for their droppings at the base of the plants. When we located one, we knocked it to the ground and stomped on it. We couldn't do anything for sweet corn which was invaded by the fungus, "smut", except to dispose of any ears that were infected so it didn't spread. I don't remember being bothered much by rabbits, or skunks, or raccoons. Muskrats, deer, geese, and groundhogs became problems much later in Brecksville.

I remember one very unpleasant experience when my brother Russ and I were hired by the Clagues, farther south of us on Tiedeman Road, to weed their front lawn. The 'Clagues' were one of the prominent families of Brooklyn, Ohio, along with the "James" and the "Biddulphs." My great uncle Adolph's wife, Aunt Nell, was a "James." Uncle Irving's brother Frank's wife, Jesse, was a "Clague." She was undoubtedly the one who suggested us to her brother Art Clague, for the weeding job. I vaguely recall that he boarded horses, but that memory is very hazy. Our job was to weed out the plantains from the lawn, which was very large. Plantains are a very nasty weed with deep clinging roots, a cluster of broad leaves hugging the ground and a distinctive 6" tall flowering spike bearing its blossoms. Our problem was the numbers of the weeds. They were so close together we could hardly see the grass.

Mother drove us up and dropped us off and we met "Uncle Art" for the first time. I think he was about our Dad's age and wore glasses and looked fairly stern. We started in digging the weeds with a weeding tool similar to a screwdriver with a "V" shaped digging tip. We had had a dry spell and the ground was poor to begin with and very hard. It was like trying to shove the tool into concrete. We were young and conscientious and tried to pull the plants with the roots intact and not just cut the plant off at the surface. It was very slow going. I don't know whether Mother packed a lunch for us, or where we ate it and I don't remember what we did for water. Finally, the day came to an end and when we went up to Mr. Clague for our pay, he refused to pay us. We hadn't done a good enough job. I think we were in tears when Mother came to pick us up, and when she saw what had happened, she gave Mr. Clague a tongue lashing that has remained in my memory. I think she shamed him into giving us $1 each. Of course, it was an impossible job. I don't know what Mr. Clague expected. Surely, he could not have thought two kids could clear all that expanse of lawn of lawn in one day. We never went back, and I don't remember ever seeing him again.

Our experience with the Biddulphs was much better. They had a large field on the other side of the creek over the hill behind our cottage, where they raised asparagus which was very beautiful in the early morning when the rising sun was shining through the dew caught on the feathery leaves of the 3' tall plants. We did not harvest any of that, but later they grew green beans in the same area. We would cross the creek to pick beans and were paid 50 cents per half bushel basket. Mr. Biddulph, whom I do not remember at all, actually paid us, and all our backaches and sweat seemed very worthwhile and the wages were added to our joint savings.

We also learned by observing the "green" practices used by our two great uncles, Uncles Louie and Irving, who made at least part of their living by truck farming, growing vegetables for the West Side Market at Pearl and Lorain Roads, and for their table, and some of the food for their livestock.

I remember one morning watching Uncle Irving, who was gaunt and reminded me of Henry Fonda, a Hollywood movie star, trudging along behind one of his mules hitched to a shallow scuff hoe cultivator, not caring if he missed a weed or two, because this method of cultivating was not meant to remove weeds, but to conserve moisture and was called dry mulching. The objective was to slide the scuff blade of the cultivator about an inch below the surface of the soil leaving the surface undisturbed, but interrupting the capillary movement of the moisture to the surface where it would evaporate uselessly into the air. I was very impressed by this old, simple conservation practice, and added it to my bag of tricks much later when I had my own garden.

From Uncle Louie who had horses and cows and chickens, I learned the valuable lesson of adding nutrients to the soil. I remember well standing on his flatbed manure spreader wearing my galoshes and pushing the mixture of straw and excrement saved from the stable onto the land before planting. I remember how toasty warm my feet felt.

I also remember Mother driving us over the open fields on the west side of Tiedeman Road to the railroad siding where there were empty cars standing used for transporting chickens. We crawled up onto the cars and used shovels to scrape the floors which were covered in chicken droppings and sand, and then shoveled the piles into bushel baskets to get them back to our garden where it was spread judiciously. The beauty of all this is that it was free. Chicken manure is notoriously "hot." We had to be careful not to use too much so the plants' roots would not be burned and damage the plants. A little went a long way.

All this while we subscribed to *Organic Gardening* which was dedicated to conservative farming and gardening practices. I was aware from the beginning of the importance of returning natural plant and animal materials to the soil to improve its tilth and fertility; but, also, had no problem accepting the more modern ideas about land management, rotation of crops and contour plowing. It does give me pause, however, when I see pictures of nitrogen being injected directly into the soil to force higher yields per acre and some of the other mechanized methods used today in big corporation farming I am also fully aware that there are three times more people living in the U.S.A. today than when I was a boy on Tiedeman Road; an even greater increase in the population of the world and feeding the hungry is a primary responsibility of government. If modern methods increase crop yields at the expense of old-fashioned family farming, it's a price that has to be paid.

On the 3/4 acre-garden area, behind the cottage which produced about 90% of the vegetables to feed four growing boys, no small part of the family budget - we raised everything and what we grew we ate except for eggplant. Mother could not disguise it in a way to make us eat it until she invented her eggplant casserole.

This consisted of alternating layers of eggplant slices, onions, fresh tomatoes and bacon, all baked in a cast iron pot at 350 degrees for an hour. It was delicious and became a family tradition.

We ate fresh picked strawberries and raspberries in quantity, and Russ and I used to save the ears of sweet corn after we had eaten them and lay them end to end to see who had eaten the most.

I'm sure we learned some very bad eating habits and it was fortunate it was fruit and vegetable and not cookies and cake in the same quantities.

In front of the cottage which sat about 150 feet from the road, we grew flowers of all kinds and greenery in a border along the fence, a crescent shaped rock garden in front of the little fish pond, and the 3' strip of plantings along the driveway. Caring for these plants was the basis for my lifelong appreciation of flowers of all kinds.

When I was 16 years old, my mother allowed me to order, through the mail, 18 or 20 peonies from an advertisement in one of our magazines from a commercial grower, Oberlin Peony Gardens, Sinking Springs, Pennsylvania. This was an experiment. We had no peonies in our garden, and I had only seen one at Grandma Schmidt's yard in Cleveland, to which I had paid no attention. So, I did not really know what to expect. When the roots arrived in the fall, I planted them in the bed next to the driveway and hoped they would come up in the spring. I only remember two or three of their names (by this time I had come to realize the general superior quality of plants which had been bred and named) among which were "Phillipe Rivoire," "Le Cygne," and "Thérèse."

It happened that in that first year I was excited to see one large bud getting larger every day on "Thérèse". I could follow its progress on my daily trips to the road to pick up our mail. Then it happened: one day it was a tight bud the size of a pullet egg, and the next it had opened fully and it was the most beautiful flower I had ever seen. It was a loose double, flesh toned pink about 6" in diameter, and simply beautiful, especially with the sunlight shining through the petals. It was the beginning of a lifetime passion.

I do not remember having any peonies in the yard of our first home in Parma Heights, although we devoted half of the back yard to a vegetable garden with a small flowerbed between it and the house. It had several roses and other annual flowers and was intended to screen the view of the vegetable area from the living room.

We planted the usual tomatoes, corn, beans, Swiss chard, cucumbers, etc. and bordered the main area with fruit trees and bush fruits: four red raspberries, two red currant, two gooseberry bushes and four dwarf apple, two pear, and two peach trees; all this in an area of 1,200-1,500 square feet; we couldn't cram any more in; it was "fully" developed.

I remember saving our grass clippings and using them to enrich the soil, and having someone come into roto-till the soil in the spring. Having a garden brought back memories of Tiedeman Road. It was as significant for me as Christmas or the Fourth of July. Everything seemed to flourish. We filled our 13' Harder Freeze Chest in the garage with our own produce to see us through the winter.

I had one mishap with one of the two varieties of peach trees I had carefully selected: "Hale Haven," a large free stone peach common on fruit stands, with which I was familiar and the other, "Rochester," with which I was unfamiliar, but was reputed to be the sweetest of all peaches and so fragile it could not be shipped to market, and was only suitable for family kitchen gardens. Both trees grew nicely, and we enjoyed eating our first homegrown "Hale Haven" and I looked forward eagerly to tasting my first "Rochester" the next season. One could say my mouth was watering. Unfortunately, I had planted the "Rochester" at the end of the path to our 50 gallon oil drum rubbish burner (outdoor burning of rubbish and garbage was permitted in those days before the age of curbside municipal pick-up and kitchen disposal units). At the time I burned the Christmas wrapping paper and other trash the previous winter, I was expecting to taste my first "Rochester" the next summer, but the flames were so high from the burner, which was only 5 or 6 feet away from the tree and the heat so intense, it scorched the tree and killed it. I had never thought of such an outcome and brooded over it ever after. Still have not tasted my first "Rochester".

When we bought the land in Brecksville for our future home, and the house was in the beginning stages of its planning; we had decided on our architects, and before we had any idea of what shape the house would take; the thought occurred to me that I could convert the vegetable area in Parma Heights at the rear of our yard into a mini-nursery and the value of the baby plants in three or four years would far exceed the value of any vegetables we could have grown. We proceeded with that plan.

I added several bales of peat moss before having the area roto-tilled in preparation and I then proceeded to order baby plants and trees from catalogs. I remember ordering baby "Akamatsu" (Japanese red pine), two European larch, six Japanese boxwood, two American Holly, six Wisconsin willow, viburnum and euonymus. In all, I planted 300 plants in rows 15" apart with the plants 12"apart.

The most spectacular result came from a nearby nursery in Geneva, Ohio, the Girard Bros. Nursery. They offered a collection of 15 hybrid rhododendrons and 65 hardy Sherwood azaleas, 13 different varieties, white, red, pink and orchid for a total of $22.00! I expected tiny 6" single stemmed plants at that price but received beautifully formed small plants with well developed supporting root systems.

I built a lathe shade about 2' above ground level, supported on wooden stakes so the tender plants would not be sunburned, and I could place our oscillating sprinkler above the lathes to provide moisture when needed. It wasn't very attractive; and I don't know what the neighbors on both sides thought of it; but it turned out to be one of the best investments I ever made. As I recall, the total outlay was about $300. Three years later the house in Brecksville, which was only a dream when the nursery project started, was at a stage where we could landscape the foundation. We moved the 300 plants and generously landscaped 200 feet of perimeter with plants I estimate were worth $3,500-$4,000.

After 3 or 4 years had passed, in the spring, the first thing a visitor saw coming up the drive at 5320 was the blank wall of the three car garage, green Pfitzer evergreens in the background fronted by ten red and white azaleas about 4' tall, alternating red and white, a solid mass of color. It was spectacular.

Before we built the pond in front of the house in Brecksville, we had an area ploughed for a modest sized garden. We improved the soil with crushed lava rock we bought in 50 lb. bags from one of our customers who supplied the same material to local greenhouses. This modest sized garden proved to be very productive and Fran canned many jars of beans and tomatoes. I remember her mother, who was visiting at the time and who was allergic to cucumbers, being horrified at my consuming a whole plateful of sliced cucumbers prepared my favorite way in vinegar with sugar, salt, and pepper.

Among the many kinds of vegetables, we planted were sweet corn, of course. Unfortunately, we had a problem with a family of raccoons invading the corn after twilight and nibbling on each ear. It was very annoying because they did not pull a whole ear off the stalk and eat all of it, but took bites out of every ear just nibbling on a few kernels. I don't think we ate a single ear the first year of our new garden.

The next year we planted sweet corn again. However, I had read in *Organic Gardening* about a non-lethal way to protect the ears of corn. The method was to string a bare copper wire fastened to wooden stakes with porcelain insulators about 10" above the ground around the perimeter, and then to attach the wire to a capacitor and two 9-volt dry cell batteries. The capacitor would build up a charge and every second would discharge it through the wire. Raccoons will not step over a wire but will try to crawl under it, and if even one of the hairs on their backs touched the wire, they would receive a jolt of electricity and abandon their search for food. It was important to keep the grass mowed under the wire, because if it touched the wire it would ground the system and there would be no jolt.

One evening after coming home from work, I completed my installation, and then I covered the batteries with an inverted cardboard box to protect them from rain. I remember that I thought it might be wise to double check the connections of the wire to the batteries after placing the box in position, and I had to get on my hands and knees to peek under the box. I knew the capacitor was working because I could hear the discharge of electricity humming on the wire. Unfortunately, my forehead touched the wire; and I received a jolt of electricity that almost knocked me over. I was shocked! But I knew the raccoons were in for an unpleasant surprise. Later, we heard a "yip" through our open bedroom window, which overlooked the garden, and from then on, we enjoyed some very sweet corn, indeed, from our very own garden.

After our youngest daughter, Barbara, had been to summer camp at Greenfields Day Camp in Brecksville, and learned to swim, we felt it was safe to fulfill another dream of mine and build a large pond in front of the house. We would lose our garden, but I felt it would be well worth it. Fran was not entirely sold on the idea, feeling that all ponds were filled with muddy water, it would be ugly, and no one would want to swim in it. I am sure she had safety concerns. On several of my appraisal trips, I had seen ponds with clear water and felt it would be easy to convince her that her fears were groundless which I set out to do. We had to be unanimous on such large decisions, and we usually managed this without difficulty since our long-term goals seemed to coincide naturally, and our tastes were similar.

On several of my residential appraisal trips for the office, I had seen both public and private ponds that were clear, and in some cases beautiful, and definitely added value to the property. In my effort to make her feel more comfortable with the idea of us having our own pond, we spent several Sunday afternoons going to look at these ponds. One pond in particular stands out in my memory; one owned by one of our customers, a Jewish attorney, Jerry Moss, who had a summer home at the end of a ½ mile long driveway on S.O.M. Center Road in Solon, Ohio. It was a modest frame house with a wide porch overhanging the edge of his pond, which may have been 1/4 acre in size. The pond was in a very natural setting (it could have been the subject for a Kincaid painting) and had been created by damming a stream which ran past the corner of the house. When we arrived, Grandpa Jerry was in the water cavorting with two of his young grandchildren and we could see his feet clearly in 6' of crystal-clear water. It was idyllic. We had dropped in unexpectedly and I couldn't have arranged a more perfect scenario if I had tried.

This was the clincher for Fran; the next step was to contact the U.S. Dept. of Agriculture who sent one of their field men out to do a feasibility study of constructing a pond on our property on Oakes Road in Brecksville. There were two obvious problems: the land had a substantial slope, south to north toward the road, a drop of over twenty feet as it turned out, so the containment would be more in the nature of a dike than a dam, and secondly, the minimum requirement for watershed area to sustain the water level naturally, land higher than the water's surface, is 4:1. Ours was less than 1:4. Therefore, we would need an extraneous source of water to fill the pond and then keep it full. Looking down from an airplane, the pond would appear ham shaped, just as I had foreseen in the plan I had drawn for Fran the morning after the first time we saw the lot.

After checking the clay subsoil to be sure it would compact to contain the water, which it would, we proceeded over the hill to check the rate of flow of the stream there, and after being assured that the flow was constant, approval was granted. The pond was feasible; I think it was about two weeks later that working drawing plans and specifications were delivered. This was the only thing I ever received from the federal government which was free, not counting the free room and board I received in World War II.

We then located a contractor, Pete Boyas Construction Company, who proceeded to gouge out 7,500 cubic yards of earth to create a 750-footlong dike, 85' wide at the base on the far end and 24' high at that point. He did this with one bulldozer with a 12-foot blade, simply scraping and pushing the soil into place and tamping it down with the dozer treads. Thus, we ended up with an enormous hole in our front yard for which we paid $3,500. The pond had almost an acre of surface and was over 20 feet deep at its center.

The job was completed in about six weeks and then the artificial filling process began. We bought a little garden pump, about the size of a football, by Gorman Rupp, specified for intermittent use, and placed it next to the stream over the hill. Its intake and output were garden hose size. It pumped and pushed the water up a 30' hill to our Japanese stone garden behind the house and from there down to the pond. The 6" plastic overflow pipe was at the southeast corner of the pond and returned any overflow back to the stream where it had come from so none of the downstream neighbors were deprived of their share of the water. The pump ran 24 hours a day and after 31 days the brushes in the motor burned out and had to be replaced. I'm not sure, but I think it took almost three months to fill the pond to overflow. I wrote to Gorman Rupp to tell them of their little pump's performance and offered to write a testimonial, but never heard from them.

The pond provided great pleasure for us, both summer and winter. In the early years, we brought sandstone flagging from my father's patio in Rocky River when he replaced it with concrete and provided a seating area on the sand beach we had created. But it was never used for entertaining as we thought it would be. Eventually we removed it and planted grass over the whole beach area.

While the pond was filling, I built a permanent wooden dock long enough that a swimmer could dive off the end safely, and when returning could climb a ladder and not touch the bottom, if he so chose. I built a turn board at the same time, 25 yards from the dock so I could resume swimming for exercise (I wasn't getting enough exercise from mowing?) but this wasn't too successful because the water was just a little too shallow for my long arms; we applied to the State of Ohio Fish and Game Commission to receive free largemouth bass and bluegill fingerlings to stock the pond, and had to do it twice because the bass ate all the blue gills the first year because there was no cover for the bluegills to hide in while the pond was so new and the water so clear.

We trucked in sand to create a beach which extended out into the water as far as the end of the dock to make it more pleasant for swimmers (young daughters and their friends) to enter the water; our first attempt was when the lake was frozen to a depth of 12" and we proposed to have the truck back out onto the ice and dump its load on the ice where we could spread it and control its depth and area when the ice melted, but the truck could not get out on the ice, and when it tried backing over the planking we put down at the edge of the pond, there was a loud noise like a clap of thunder as the ice cracked from the weight. We had the driver dump the load on the driveway and had to spread it by hand the next spring. It was another great theory which didn't work in practice.

We planted a special grass on the downside of the dam at its highest point to prevent any erosion, and multiflora roses, which form an impenetrable barrier, along the eastern bank of the pond to prevent intrusion by any curious neighbor children. We received small trees and shrubs from one of the County programs. I remember our oldest daughter Nancy helping me plant several white pine trees at the base of the dike along the east boundary of our land. After 20 years they grew to a height of 30' and provided a very pleasant backdrop for the surface of the water. Oddly enough, while I am sure our pond met all the qualifications of an "attractive nuisance" legally, it was secluded enough and not visible from the road, that we only had one or two incidents of an intrusion. Once, two young boys came up the driveway with their fishing poles expecting to do some fishing. I intercepted them and asked if they had asked for permission to fish or had offered to do some chores to gain the right to fish, and when the answer was no, ordered them off the property. The ever-present fear was of someone falling into the pond at the deep end where there was no gradual increase in the depth as at the beach end, and a drowning could occur. I don't think I could have lived with that.

Recreationally, the pond was a great success, mostly swimming for the family. Guests tended to enjoy fishing more. Fran loved to fish, having spent summers as a girl at her father's summer place on White Fish Lake, north of Ottawa, where she had only to put a line in the water to catch a 3' pike. She never got the same excitement from trying to catch a 15" largemouth bass in our pond, but tried to arouse my interest in the sport, hoping I would experience some of the thrill she had. Not having a father who hunted, or fished, or played tennis during my childhood, I never developed any interest in those sports. He did bowl, but I never cared much for that either. It was enough for me to get a minor thrill from simply watching the fish swimming in our pond.

I remember watching a neighbor boy, Billy Richmond, who was high school age, standing on the dock and casting a gold colored, fish shaped lure about an inch long and seemingly catching a bass on every cast for an hour until he got bored and quit. Another business friend, Walter J. Smith, used to come out at twilight time to fish. He was a fanatic and unlike Billy, did not return the fish to the pond. He was fishing for his table and kept everything he caught, and he was very good. I think, over the course of one summer, he depleted the entire fish population, and when I no longer had the pleasure of seeing my fish, it was too late. I had to disinvite him.

In the winter when the pond was frozen, sometimes with 15-18' of ice, the whole family used the pond for ice skating. However, there was a problem in trying to create a smooth surface because if snow was allowed to remain on the surface for even one day, there was enough warmth in the body of water under the ice to allow it to melt at the surface which produced a popcorn effect which took all the pleasure out of the skating. Therefore, the snow had to be removed as quickly as possible and I used our Gravely tractor with the 3' blade attachment to clear a usable area near the dock. The timing had to be just right, and it didn't happen all that often. We never were able to skate over the whole surface of the pond.

I remember one Sunday afternoon, we invited our friends, the Demuths from Parma Heights, to come out for an ice-skating party. As I recall, it was one of those times when we had a smooth ice area cleared and we had a fine time with them and their three daughters who had been playmates of our children when we lived in Parma Heights. We skated until we were tired and then went up to the house. We prepared a cookout on our outdoor broiler which we brought around to the front door. I still remember how great everything tasted, eating outdoors at that time of the year, and in that setting.

My final skating performance happened on another Sunday afternoon when just the family had been skating, and all but me retired to the warmth of the den, where they all, including Fran's mother, stood at the large window overlooking the pond and watched me glide around on the ice putting on a good show for them. The climax came when the toe of my skate caught on something and I tripped straight forward as though I was sliding head-first into second base, banging my right knee in the process. I limped back to the house, ingloriously, and that was the end of my skating days.

Having a pond which covered virtually all of the front yard, did not mean that just because water can't be mowed, I was getting off lightly in the chores department. The pond required its own form of maintenance. The grass had to be mowed on top of the dike; vegetation in the water had to be controlled; traps had to be set for the muskrats who came and burrowed into the side of the dike just below water level to make their homes, which if ignored could weaken the structure of the dike; when a muskrat was caught, it had to be disposed of - a very unpleasant business; reeds grew along the east shore line, and aquatic weeds grew in any area less than 3' deep where sunlight reached the bottom, fortunately not in the areas where we swam. That problem was solved by our introducing white Amur carp which feed on vegetation. We bought thirty of them which grew to be 30-36" long and were fascinating to watch. After they had consumed all the vegetation, I had to buy Ralston Purina fish food in the form of pellets which I fed to them. I would go down near the dock with a half bucket of food and throw out one handful on the water, which they sensed and a minute later they would gather and I would throw the rest of the food out on the water (it floated) and cause a feeding frenzy. I could hear them snuffle as they fought to get at the pellets. They were a light gray color with very large scales and were sterile so there was no danger of offspring escaping to enter the waterways. I really enjoyed watching the show they put on.

During the reign of the carp, another problem arose which seriously affected our use of the pond and caused us to give up vegetable gardening later. It was the arrival of the Canada goose. I remember clearly seeing my first huge goose from my bathroom window, strutting on the driveway less than 10 feet away. I was so excited I rushed out to the kitchen after alerting Fran and called the Holden Arboretum to see what I could do to feed this poor wanderer. They recommended cracked corn which I hurried to get and which the goose totally ignored. That was the first chapter.

Future chapters were not so exciting. The lone goose soon became a flock in the succeeding years until we could watch sixty huge birds spreading their wings as the prepared to land on the pond. They were non-migratory, year-round pests; protected by Federal law, and locally by the no-shooting firearms within city limits ordinance. They left their droppings on the lawn between the water and the house, covered the driveway, and even came up to the front door. And there wasn't a thing we could do. I did read of one method which involved spraying the lawn with grape Kool-Aid. They were not supposed to like the stickiness on their feet. I tried this and it didn't work, but the grass looked funny until the next rainfall.. I bought a high-powered German air rifle which I hoped would injure but not kill them, but I never got the weapon properly sighted-in and this was unsuccessful. We bought a family of plastic swans from a supplier in Connecticut; country clubs were said to use them to deter the geese who feared swans. It didn't work. We bought fireworks, cherry bombs, on the way home from Florida, and I hoped if I could get close enough to the flock to throw a few in their midst, they might decide that our pond was off their favorite's list. I did get close enough; they retreated and then came right back at me. We never solved the problem, and it seriously affected our enjoyment of our own pond.

After the pond was completed and our garden was inundated, we moved our gardening operation to the west of our driveway. Our good neighbor, Ed Kregenow, already had a small garden in a clearing surrounded by trees on his land. And we made a deal with him to enlarge the space and have a joint garden. The result was a garden two thirds of which was on his land, and one third on ours. I would use the Gravely to plough the area in the spring and we would buy plants jointly, agree on what to plant, and care for the plants jointly. Each of us would be free to pick whatever he wanted for his family, and since we were a family of five with three growing children, and they were only two of grandparents age, we undoubtedly had the better of the deal. It all worked out; there was never any conflict, and when they sold their home, we continued the arrangement with the new neighbors, the George Hills, who had three teenage sons which caused me to shudder, initially.

We had been accustomed to years of living next to an older couple who made a home for their aged parents, a perfect situation for us. Now, our quiet was to be invaded by three young boys living next to an "attractive nuisance". Once again, I couldn't have been more wrong. The Hills were originally from Nova Scotia and still had family there. The three boys, Charley, Brian and Eric were quiet and well behaved and never set foot on our side of the driveway unless invited. In fact, on more than one occasion when it was an extremely hot day and I was well aware that their house was not air conditioned, I had to make a special trip to knock on their back door and urge them to come over and use our pond to cool off.

The boys did not receive a weekly allowance and were always available to help with jobs around our yard, and in their quiet way, I think they liked us. I remember that when our oldest daughter married, they made a twenty foot banner with the words "Good Luck, Nancy!" on it and hung it below our kitchen windows where all the after-reception guests entering the front door couldn't miss seeing it.

The mechanical help we had in the early days in Brecksville was a re-built Gravely Tractor, painted blue, which we bought at the Home & Flower Show held every spring at the Public Auditorium in downtown Cleveland. It was a walking tractor with a 36" rotary mower head, which was bolted on the front power take-off. We also equipped it with a 3' push blade for removing snow and leveling dirt, and a spring tooth harrow. All were mounted on the front of the tractor, interchangeably, as was the unique Gravely rotator plough. The plough was different because it had four rotating cutting blades, mounted on a shaft held at an angle to the surface of the ground chopping into the soil and splashing it up against a metal shield mounted above the shaft, leaving a smooth surface perfect for the seed bed, similar to that left by a Rototiller. The depth could be easily adjusted, and it cut about a 6" furrow. I always admired it and the job it did.

The Gravely had a 4-stroke 6hp engine and was started by pulling a 3/4 inch leather strap wrapped around the fly wheel and I prayed it would start on the first pull. It had a magneto to provide the spark. I learned what little I know about gas engine maintenance from taking care of the Gravely. After three or four years when the annual maintenance was done at the dealers, they convinced me to trade Old Blue in on a new traditional red model with a 9hp engine. All of the attachments were compatible with the new power source, which was a big selling point. Both Gravelys were powerful and heavy, and even with hand brakes were hard to control. After three hours of mowing grass, I knew I had had a good workout.

Later, we added a snow blowing attachment and no longer used the blade in the winter. It cut a 2' swath which meant four trips up and down the driveway, adjusting the blower to throw the snow on either side of the driveway - much easier to use than the Gravely blade. Snow disposal could be a problem. If the snow came from the north, it could drop up to 2' which it did several times. Snow from the south or west was not a problem because of the shelter provided by the trees surrounding the house. In spite of the sometimes inconvenience, I always thought winter was the most beautiful season, especially with fresh snow, looking down into the ravine from our dining room.

The last few years at Brecksville when controlling the heavy rotary mower head became too much for me and I could no longer find, or rely on, neighbor boys or high school students to do the mowing, we bought a riding mower with a small battery and an electric starter which was an incredible luxury. It couldn't get at some of the places the Gravely could, but mowing became fun and it did an acceptable job. I even got it out to ride down to the road to pick up our mail.

Our final piece of mechanical help was a Troy-Bilt rototiller which we used to till between the rows of the peonies, which were planted closer than they should have been (which meant I could have more of them) and were too close together to accommodate the Gravely. We also had a full complement of hand tools and a large garden cart, which could carry a larger load than a wheelbarrow, and had 3' bicycle type wheels. It was very convenient for transporting the peony foliage cut down in the fall, done with a gas powered weed trimmer which we used with a solid blade rather than the usual nylon cord; this was another labor saving device we acquired to stay on top of the chores that went along with maintaining such a large property without outside help.

I now come to the favorite part of my gardening life: my love affair with the Peony, which I consider to be the most beautiful flower under cultivation. I don't know if is possible for me to find words which could describe, or convey, the inner feelings they arouse in me; the wonder of seeing an invisible, underground sprout in April produce a magnificent blossom six short weeks later; the aura of oriental mystery that emanates from them. They are eager to share their beauty with us who have cared for them and waited impatiently for them to join us again each spring.

I have described earlier the impact of seeing my first "real" peony blossom on Tiedeman Road when I was 15 years old, and, looking back, it surprises me a little to realize now that although I had the opportunity in our first yard in Parma Heights, and then even in the early years in Brecksville, to pursue this passion and plant at least a few peonies, that for some reason, I never did.

It was not until the pond had been full to overflow for three or four years. We had to have a back-hoe come to remove the silt deposited by the stream in the ravine behind the house which we had dammed up to make a small pond which was the source of the water we pumped from the "little" pond up through our Japanese stone garden behind the house down to the "big" pond (and we used the opportunity to deepen and enlarge the "little" pond), that I realized I could finally indulge in my dream of owning a few peonies.

When the back-hoe was finished over the hill, I had the operator dig out an area about 50' x 60' east of the house and south of the pond to a depth of about 18," and then transport the silt from over the hill to fill in his excavation. This was the first of my many hard-earned lessons in the art of growing peonies.

My theory was that if the ancient Egyptians grew rich from growing cotton on the silt deposited every year by the Nile, this would be a great soil in which to grow peonies in Ohio. WRONG. The silt never dried out. Even though it sat waiting patiently in the sun, it retained the consistency of Jell-o; it quivered if stepped upon. It was not suitable for peonies which require good drainage and drier soil. So, before we could think of planting, we had to have the back-hoe return and remove all the silt from the peony bed and dump it back over the hill and then replace it with other soil. I do not remember where this soil came from: elsewhere on the property or trucked in from outside. At last we were ready to plant our first peonies

I had ordered 96 different named varieties of peonies from several different commercial growers from widespread parts of the country, seeking as much diversity as possible, and hoping to be a resource for growers, if a particular variety became scarce and could no longer be found in the catalogs. Two of the names I remember are Wild of Sarcoxie, Missouri, and Saunders of Hamilton College, Pavilion, New York. Professor Saunders was a pioneer hybridizer of peonies and is generally considered the Father of the Modern peony.

I don't remember many of the names in that first order, but do remember ordering "Lavender Bouquet" because of its name, hoping for an unusual lavender color; but while it was a pleasing size, it was a light, unmistakable pink; the other was a charming little white single called "Krinkled White" and I think it was the first peony I ever photographed.

The peony roots arrived in the fall and I had name tags prepared for each root (which resemble a long white radish with a brown skin and potato eyes at one end) and tried to follow the planting instructions included with the orders as carefully as I could, taking special care not to plant them too deep - more than 2" causes spindly plants and very few or no blossoms.

Then came the long wait for Spring to come to see if I had done my job correctly. These were all herbaceous peonies which, when well established will continue to produce flowers for 35-40 years in the same location. Time and effort spent in the initial planting are well rewarded. And since the Peony needs to be planted only once, its higher original price when prorated over that long lifetime of blooming, compares very favorably to the cost of planting petunias or impatiens annually on hands and knees.

Finally, when I checked the peony bed in April, I could see plants peeking above the soil and the rapidity of their growth was remarkable.

But there was a problem: only half of the roots survived. I learned another lesson of peony culture the hard way: they must have good drainage; they cannot tolerate "wet feet". Now that it was too late, I realized that the excavation of the bed had followed the natural contours of the land.

If you can picture a shallow two-pound candy box, hold it at eye level and tilt it diagonally, you can see how water would collect in the lower corner. This was what had happened in the peony bed. The bed was dug out of the typical clay soil in Brecksville and the bottom, which was impervious to water, tilted 3" or 4" from the northwest corner to the southeast corner, and the roots trapped in the lower part of the triangle turned to mush. This was a terrible disappointment, both cost wise and labor wise.

The solution was at hand and so simple: dig a trench from the low corner about 5' long, install drain tile, and tie it in to the septic tank filter bed which had sixty tons of gravel in it and its own drain over the hill. This solved our problem; we reordered the roots, replanted them and had no further trouble.

This was our first peony bed and the large number of plants satisfied my peony cravings for some time. It was the bed which, when mature, supplied the flowers used exclusively for our youngest daughter Barbara's wedding: both for the church and the reception after at the Cleveland Athletic Club.

The church, St. Demetrios Greek Orthodox, in Rocky River, Ohio, was not available on their first choice of dates, and the next closest Saturday was June 7th, which sparked an inspiration: could/would our florist use my peonies for the floral arrangements for the wedding?

On the basis of our attendance at the wedding of our friends, the Struchens' daughter, where the floral arrangements were among the best we had ever seen, my wife had employed the same florist, Michaels of Lakewood, Ohio. When asked whether he would use our peonies he was somewhat reluctant, having had no previous experience with the flower and his reputation was somewhat on the line. It was obvious he knew nothing about the peony when he called in February and wanted to come out to Brecksville to see the plants; I don't know what he thought when Fran told him there was nothing to see.

I had arranged with him to bring in baskets of flowers as they were picked to accumulate a large enough number for him to work with, and with the number required, this could only be done by using cold storage. Luckily, peonies can be picked in the half open bud stage, then kept at 38-40 degrees for up to 30 days, and at any time during that period brought out into room temperature when they resume their opening process. Michael was still dubious, in spite of my reassurances. He didn't know this was my first experience and what a gamble it was.

I arrived home from work one evening a week before the big day, and became aware of a very ominous storm brewing in the northwest, and thought it might be a good idea to pick whatever buds that were even partially open to prevent possible damage. After they were safely in the garage awaiting delivery to Michaels in Lakewood, I called him, and he agreed to stay open until I could get there - a 40 minute trip - and when I did, helped me carry in three buckets of flower which I had covered with plastic for protection so he still had not seen what he had to deal with.

However, when we uncovered the flowers before putting them in his refrigerator, his eyes opened wide and he knew we were the real deal. I think I took in three more loads of flowers, and, once again, had to wait for the outcome, something I always seemed to be doing with peonies.

When we arrived at the church Saturday morning, I was thrilled by the two large arrangements in baskets on each side of the altar for which he used three huge white double blossoms only, with greenery, in each vase, which I presumed was supposed to symbolize the holy Trinity. They were simple and impressive and beautiful.

When we arrived downtown at the CAC (Cleveland Athletic Club) and exited the elevator, we were greeted by two large basket arrangements in an arbor in which he had used all the colors available. This was early in the blooming season and the time when the hybrids bloomed with their beautiful coral and pink shades. The hallway to the dining room had several more such basket arrangements, and Michael outdid himself with several small Japanese type arrangements scattered around the lounge area. We did not use peonies for centerpieces on the tables.

Since, the Club was closed to members on weekends during June, it seemed a shame to let so much beauty go to waste, I asked the manager if we could invite the guests to take home a blossom as a souvenir, and in minutes there were no peonies left. We learned later that many of the peonies were still beautiful a week later (after having been picked 2 weeks earlier, stored in a refrigerator, and placed for display overnight in a dead air room). For years after the wedding, when I would be introduced to one of the guests, who had attended, invariably, the first remark would be: "Oh, you're the one who grows peonies!" A slightly unusual way to be remembered, but nice.

The latest occasion, when it happened again, was the celebration of the groom's mother's 90th birthday, in September 2017, which was attended by many of the same people who had been at the wedding, and again I was identified as the man who grew the peonies for the wedding. After more than 40 years, the memories were still alive. Such is the power of the peony.

I used the original peony bed, only once, to try planting peonies by seed. I think I hoped to create some super flower but knew the mathematical chance of doing so was only one chance in the millions. I left it entirely to chance. I never tried to select two plants with certain characteristics to merge into something different and then dismember the blossoms to hand pollinate them. I simply didn't have the desire to go to all that effort. It is such a long process, five to seven years, and I was already too old. I did it the lazy man's way: picking up seeds on the ground under the plants.

Part of the incentive to try the seed method was that with my first order from Saunders, as a bonus, Sylvia Saunders, Prof. Saunders's daughter who was carrying on her father's pioneering work, had included a small packet of 18 seeds along with the roots. It was part of her effort to promote the peony for the APS, the American Peony Society.

The named varieties in the catalogs are grown from root divisions of known- named varieties, not from seeds, which is the only way to guarantee that that the root received will be true to name.

This is paramount for anyone interested in competing in the annual APS exhibition, and certainly would be true for one who had fallen in love with a colored picture in a catalog and received something totally different.

In nature the seedpods burst and scatter their seeds on the ground where they lie dormant for a year before sprouting. Hybridizers, looking for improved innovations, or following some program to find a different shape, or odor, or color, using their painstaking procedures, speed the process up by gathering the seeds and placing them in a bag of damp vermiculite; placing the bag in the refrigerator until Christmas, and then removing the bag and placing it in a warm spot for three months. At that time, the seeds should have sprouted and can be planted in soil. In their second year, they will show true leaves and can be planted outdoors. The grower has gained a whole year in what is a very long process, and there is a high probability that the new plant will not be suitable for introduction to the market.

This is in contrast to a hybridizer working with daylilies, for instance, who knows in two years whether he has a new variety which he can name and introduce to the market.

Peonies take many more years. The reason for going into all this detail is that I sprouted and planted the Saunders bonus seeds and some I picked up on the ground under varieties I liked before I cut down the dead foliage for the winter. There may have been a total of thirty or forty seeds that sprouted and grew to produce flowers. They were fairly ordinary, no better nor worse than many varieties which appeared in the catalogs;

I selected the six best in my opinion and named them in honor of the most important women in my life: my mother, my mother-in-law, my wife and our three daughters. I used the full maiden names for the first three: Lydia Charlotte Gaede, Fanny Bell Niggeman and Frances Jean Thompson and the given names of our daughters: Nancy Elizabeth, Kathy Ann, and Barbara Susan. Their names are preserved in the official Registration List of the American Peony Society, something that gives me great satisfaction. Since the roots were included in the sale of my collection to the Klehm Nursery many years later, I have a faint hope that they are still living and flourishing in some corner of that far away nursery.

Before long my appetite for more peonies got the better of me, I simply outgrew the first bed. I was obsessed with having more varieties after seeing the displays at the APS shows. I persuaded Fran to let me create another bed between the driveway and the pond; this would be a larger area, about 30' wide and 250' long. We hired Brian Hill, one of our next-door neighbor's sons to plough the land and planted a crop of buckwheat the first summer to enrich the soil. Once again, I ordered plants from widespread growers, some from as far as the West coast, and for the first time in my never ending search for ever greater beauty planted some tree peonies, shrub-like cousins of the more common herbaceous peonies whose stems are not cut back to the ground in the fall. The newer American hybrids have spectacular colors, but the Japanese varieties have an additional quality that appeals to me, an air of mystery in the way they display themselves. They are exceptionally long-lived and are known to have produced blossoms for 100 years.

My first tree peony was a Father's Day gift from my daughters, purchased from Steve Moldovan, a grower in Sheffield, Ohio, and was a Japanese tree peony called "*Gessekai*" or "Lunar World". It grew to be a large bush 5' tall and 5' wide and survived being moved twice. Its blossoms were semi-double, like white satin in texture, slightly ruffled and about 8" in diameter. One year I counted ninety blossoms open at the same time, an unforgettable display. Eventually we had about thirty specimens and I would have loved to have had twice that many if I could have afforded it.

Because of their long life, tree peonies make wonderful gifts for memorials. When the husband of one of our Brecksville bridge club members died in a sail boat accident, rather than the group buying a conventional large floral arrangement with its short life, I suggested that the bridge group contribute to the cost of planting a tree peony in their yard which I volunteered to buy and plant. We did this again when she lost her son in an accident in Seattle, Washington.

Fran and I did this also, when we learned of the death of the son of Fran's seamstress friend, Corunna Feurhahn, in Hudson, Ohio. He had died at age 42 of cancer and his mother still mourned his loss. I planted one of the American hybrid tree peonies, "Age of Gold," a true yellow, which blooms prolifically, in her backyard. It was particularly touching, because the spot I unwittingly selected only because it was visible from both the kitchen and dining room windows of their home turned out to be the sand box where he had played as a child, and found her in tears in her kitchen when I came in after having finished planting.

After the death of our much loved oldest daughter, Nancy, I made arrangements with the Lakewood Park Cemetery (where her ashes are interred, and where my beloved Fran's ashes are, head to head with hers) to be allowed to plant a tree peony as a memorial. It took me two years to find a grower that had the particular Japanese tree peony variety that I wanted, "Hana Kisoi," a wonderful pink double with exceptionally beautiful blossoms and plant shape. I planted it in a spot about 15' from our gravesites and have cared for it ever since as I watched it mature. A year ago, it produced one of the most beautiful blossoms I have ever seen.

Another tradition I established was presenting a tree peony to members of the family who bought a new home. I did this for all three of our daughters and both of our granddaughters who are permanently settled in Indianapolis, Indiana and South Lyon, Michigan,. I also did the same for my youngest brother, Wes, and planted one as a memorial for my father's second wife, Mary Louise's, father, at their home in Rocky River, after her father died. Unfortunately, this plant did not recover from my father's cutting it to the ground in the fall, when the leaves had fallen, which he thought was standard procedure with all peonies and they never had the pleasure of seeing it bloom.

The tree peony I selected for Nancy's front yard at their new home in Rocky River and planted as a specimen all by itself along the walk from their garage to the front door of their house was one I had had no prior experience with in my Brecksville beds. It was named "Hana Kisoi." It was a lucky choice because the plant did well, and, because other plants did not crowd it, grew into a well-shaped, large plant. One year, Nancy counted sixty blossoms open at one time and told me that people driving by had stopped and gotten out of their cars to look at it and asked her what kind of flower this was. This was one of the reasons for choosing this particular variety for our gravesite and why I have it in my own front yard today.

With the establishment of the second bed my learning process continued. It seemed that I still had drainage problems in spite of the natural fall of the land. Some of the planting had to be done when the fall season was very wet. It felt as though every October when the roots arrived it was rainy. I remember one year when the soil was so soggy that I had to use plywood sheets to kneel on and after digging the hole, put the muck on strips of plastic mulch while trying to locate the root at the proper depth before covering it with the semi-liquid muck. It was the worst planting experience I ever had, and I was surprised that any of the roots survived.

The final total number of plants in both beds, plus those planted around the foundation and in the new bed made after adding the additions to the house was 500, including about thirty tree peonies. There were only 450 named varieties since I planted duplicates of many of my favorites, especially those that did well in exhibition. Greta Kessenich, Secretary of the APS, said once that she thought I might have one of the largest private, non-commercial collections in the whole country. Which would be interesting, if true.

I was surprised that in spite of the natural slope of the land, the new bed along the driveway still had drainage problems. I thought rainfall would run off before it could do damage, and I lost thirty or forty plants every year, which had to be replaced at some expense and, of course, the stoop labor involved. In desperation, I rented a trenching machine and dug 6" by 3'deep trenches between the rows, filled with 6" of gravel at the bottom of the trench, covered by a layer of straw to prevent infiltration of soil into the gravel, and then refilled to the surface.

While I was at it, I dug a 4' deep trench between the pond and the peony bed as a French drain to intercept any water which might seep laterally from the pond. This trench had 4' drain tile on the bottom of the trench which was then filled to within 6" of the surface with gravel. This tile was connected to the lines laid in the peony bed at the lower end and discharged into the little stream beyond the foot of the dike. This solved the problem finally. Lesson learned: Do Not Plant peonies where there is Poor Drainage. I also took advantage of having the trencher and put 4 lines of drainage tile in the vegetable garden west of the driveway.

I never planted the roots following some plan to provide an artistic mixture of color, leaf form, or size. I did try to keep all the roots from each grower separate, planting their roots alphabetically by name. This produced a random effect that I thought was pleasing.

It was quite a sight to drive up the driveway when the flowers were in full bloom and I was always mildly disappointed that more friends, or family, did not take advantage of the opportunity to see this sight, which was so nearby. I was always so busy during peony season that I never had the time to visit other local gardens, let alone travel to some of the other famous gardens in other states.

I dreamed of posting an invitation to the general public in our local newspaper to come to a "Peony Viewing at the Schmidts" evening, come one come all, one blossom of Viewer's choice free, Cookies & Lemonade. But I never had the will, or the chutzpah, to do it.

Once, my cousin, Jean Basil, brought her Berea Garden Club for visit, and once, the Shaker Heights Garden people came. I do think both groups were quite impressed.

I remember loving going down to the beds in the morning to pick blossoms, when the beds were at the height of their bloom; the excitement of seeing what a tight bud the day before had turned into; the richness of the colors in the early morning sunlight; the unforgettable, distinctive, bittersweet scent of the peonies floating in the air. I used to think I did not have to die to go to Heaven.

A few years after the second bed was well established, I read an article in the Garden Column of *The Cleveland Plain Dealer*, which told of an American Peony Society (APS) annual meeting and exhibition to be held at the Kingwood Gardens in Mansfield, Ohio, which is only about an hour's drive south of Brecksville. It sounded very interesting and I decided to go Saturday morning and take a few blossoms to enter into the competition. I was allowed to compete in the Novice Division since this was my first exhibition. Actually, since I grew more than 100 varieties, I would have to enter in any future exhibitions in the Commercial class where the blooms from my puny 500 plants would be competing against growers with acres of bloom from which to choose their entries. I did not know it at the time, but, perhaps, personal, tender, loving care of a smaller number of plants would overcome the handicap of impersonal attention to 1,000s of plants.

Everyone was very cordial. The Secretary of the APS, Greta Kessenich, an older widow lady, who had saved the Society from bankruptcy when she took over her position, took me under her wing, helping me fill out the nametags, find the proper classification for each bloom, and place the bloom in its proper place on the judging tables. It was all strange to me, and her help was invaluable. There were hundreds and hundreds of blossoms all massed on the long rows of tables for judging and the effect was overwhelming.

I do not remember how many blooms I entered in the judging or their names but do remember I could transport them all in a 12-quart basket. I do remember how thrilled I was when one of the first tree peonies I ever planted, "Souvenir de Maxime Cornu," chosen from a catalog because of its color, pale yellow with red fringe on each small petal which produced an overall orange effect, was chosen for the Court of Honor and won my first Blue Ribbon.

As an aside: "Souvenir de Maxime Cornu" is not considered one of the better varieties of tree peony in the field because it doesn't hold its blossom above the foliage. The blossoms have to be picked and brought indoors to be appreciated.

I was interested to see how this experience seemed to arouse a latent competitive component in what I had always considered to be a fairly nonaggressive nature. I discovered that I liked to win, proving in the eyes of others that I could be superior, contrary to my everyday ordinariness. I think this feeling was something my father sought all his life; that he would have been happier and more comfortable in social settings if he could have had even one blue ribbon activity in his life outside of his family and the business he founded.

I remember my response to the members of Lakeside Yacht Club who assumed I would immediately begin competing in the Wednesday club races and assuring them the only interest we had in sailing was pleasure cruising. I also remember how the very first race I entered, after agreeing "to give it a try", produced the same thrill of competition that 1 felt after winning at the peony show in Mansfield.

Actually, the competitive urge was probably always there and had probably come to life with the Thursday afternoon sailing regattas at Camp Michigania where every activity was geared to winning.

I think it's interesting that these sporting activities and other activities that involve striving to be first have never had to be contact sports for me to experience the euphoria of winning. I have always been able to find this in golf and swimming, two of my great loves, both solitary sports within a team format, where the opponent is really oneself, and success is not attained by physically dominating another individual. This is even true to a lesser extent in sailing where I was dependent on other crew members, and bridge where a good partner is necessary. Of course, winning ribbons at a flower show is the ultimate in personal performance.

It was such a solitary challenge to compete in the APS Exhibitions. There were many other exhibitors with a limited number of plants to produce their entries and we all faced the same unknowable's; would the blooms reach their peak in the opening process at just the moment the judges made their decisions; would the entry strike the fancy of the judges; would the decision of the judges, all members of the APS, be influenced by the experience of having raised the same flower in his own garden for comparison; would the temperature in the preparation room be favorable; and, most of all, what chance does an individual have competing against a large commercial grower who has 100s of any one variety to choose from for his entry. So, it was a supreme thrill for me to win the Grand Champion, Best of Show ribbon in the Court of Honor on five occasions during my years of membership in the APS.

After my first exhibition in Mansfield, for the next 20 years or so, I attended the annual meetings of the APS and entered my flowers in the competitions. In those days, although the APS, which was the custodian of nomenclature worldwide, promoted the organization as a national/international one, the Exhibitions were held in the Midwest, which made them accessible for me. I was able to transport my refrigerated blossoms, the majority of which had been stored in a florist's cooler for two to three weeks, to the exhibition without too much effort.

Today, the exhibitions are held all over the country, from, Portland, Oregon, to Richmond, Virginia, and only occasionally in Mansfield, Ohio, which used to host the Exhibition every third year.

My daughter and her husband were kind enough to take me to the most recent show in Mansfield and we both entered a few blooms in the competition (she has developed an interest in the peony, oddly enough) and we both won ribbons. I think I was 93 or 94 years old, and undoubtedly the oldest person at the show. There was only one of the members in attendance whom I remembered from my days in the APS, Don Hollingsworth of Kansas City, Missouri. He had been on the Board of Trustees with me and it was good to see him again.

After having been on the Board of Trustees for a number of years, I was elected President of the Society, serving for two years (1997-1998).

During my tenure I tried to promote a plan to self-produce an instructional video on the Peony and its Culture, which would be added to the list of peony publications for sale by the Society. My idea was to make it easy for a beginner to avoid the many mistakes I had made, and to increase the gardening public's knowledge and use of the peony. It would have been so much easier for me if such a resource had been available for me when I started. I did some checking as to the cost of producing such a video, and, assuming the cooperation of the Klehm Organization, who would have been in an ideal position to do the video-camera work at every stage: preparation of hole to removal of foliage in the fall, including feeding and preventive spraying, came up with an estimated cost of $4.50 per copy. I prepared a Story Board, suggested a retail price of $7.50 per copy, and a gift of the video at no charge to be included with each new membership, and presented the proposal to the Board. I hoped it was enough to spark some interest and start a discussion.

Unfortunately, the Board was dominated by its Secretary, Greta Kessinich (the person who had mentored me from the beginning) who showed her disrespect for the business acumen of the men on the Board, by pooh-poohing the very idea. She stated that it would be a total waste of money (there was about $75,000 in the Treasury at the time) and furthermore, no one would or could look at it. After all, who had a TV set then? This at a time when the average was two TV sets per family in the U.S. Maybe her estimation of the American male was accurate. The Board did not feel strongly enough to even appoint a committee to explore the idea and report back at the next annual meeting, and the idea died. I halfheartedly presented the same idea the next year and it died for a second time.

I think it was a sound idea and ahead of its time. The APS could have been the only flower organization in the country offering such an incentive as far as I could tell. Today, the cultural information available on the *Cricket Hill* internet site is invaluable. I would have given anything to have had access to such information when I got started.

A few years later in view of Mrs. Kessenich's increasing rigidity and the Board's inability to challenge her control, I resigned from the Board and left the Society.

But not before having won five Grand Champion Ribbons for Best of Show: Mrs. F.D.R., (my first, at Mansfield), Buckeye Belle, Pink Derby, Yellow Emperor (an Itoh hybrid), and "Teikan" (a Japanese tree peony). I think this was quite an achievement and I have always been very proud of it.

Attending the Exhibitions was always one of the highlights of the year and was highly anticipated. The preparations started in the early morning: going down to the peony beds and trying to recognize and select, (quite a guessing game) the very best blossoms at just the right state of opening - enough to predict how it might develop when fully open, but not too far advanced so that it would be too far open when judged, I wanted the pollen to be fresh when the judges examined it; cut the stem back to the second true leaf; strip the leaves; drop into a two pound paper bag with a hole pierced in the bottom; put the name of the blossom on the bag; place in water as quickly as possible; refrigerate at 38-40 degrees F until transport day.

I had so many plants that it was a problem finding a place to store the approximate 300 blooms I customarily ended taking to the Show for two or three weeks. Obviously, our old refrigerator in the garage was totally insufficient.

The problem was solved when a Brecksville friend, who owned a wholesale florist company, Cleveland Plant & Flower, at E. 9th Street & Carnegie Avenue in downtown Cleveland, allowed me to use a corner in one of his coolers in the basement of his shop. I would usually arrive in the early afternoon and carry my buckets of flowers, which had been stored temporarily in the old refrigerator in our garage, through the back of the showroom and down the stairs to the cold room. My friend never had the pleasure of seeing a blossom, only buckets of paper bags, which was his loss.

It was a big operation the morning of departure to drive down to the storeroom and carry all the buckets back up to the car and when I got home to pack the bagged flowers into a large cooler chest I had constructed from 2" thick sheets of Styrofoam. I stowed any overflow into commercial freezer chests.

We would then take off for Chicago, or Champagne-Urbana, or Janesville, Wisconsin, or Milwaukee, or Hamilton, Ontario, or even our farthest destination, Minneapolis, which was too far to drive in one day and we had to fly with fewer blossoms.

However, while we were there, we were able to visit Greta Kessenich with whom I was still on good terms and saw her peony bed and the interior of her small brick bungalow. The first floor acted as the warehouse for all the peony publications created by the Society and on sale to members and the public. There were stacks of books everywhere and it was hard to thread one's way through them.

This was one aspect of her job; she was also responsible for editing and publishing the quarterly Bulletin, which was printed by one of the members in Detroit. However, the day-to-day commercial aspects of her job were secondary to her primary passion for correct nomenclature of the 1,500+ varieties in commerce and thus the integrity of the Society. I felt that peonies were her whole life.

We also had the opportunity to visit one of my old Japanese language ASTP friends, Lou Gelfand, who grew up in Oklahoma, but who loved Minneapolis after spending two years there in the Army, married, and spent the rest of his life there. He worked for Pillsbury for a time and ended up as ombudsman for the *St. Paul Star Tribune*. I had some of the same feelings for Minneapolis and, if I had not had a family business waiting for me in Cleveland after the war, might have ended up in Minneapolis, too, and had an entirely different life.

Lou picked us up Sunday morning after the Show, about which I remember virtually nothing other than it was held in a shopping center in less than ideal conditions in the suburb, Redwing. He gave us a guided tour of Minneapolis and then of the University where we saw all of our old haunts: The Continuation Center, Shevlin Hall, the Armory, Northrop Auditorium, the famous ice cream parlor whose name I don't remember. It was a strange feeling to have those memories revived, some sad, some fearful, and many happy.

We stayed an extra day and took the opportunity, using our rental car, to do some exploring on our own, going back to St. Paul to the neighborhood where our marriage started in a rented room (uninsulated) over the front porch of a small frame house. Grandma Gossler was our landlady and lived on the ground floor with her spinster daughter, Ethel, who worked as a bookkeeper, looked like one, and quivered in the presence of a male, especially one in uniform. Her mother came from Jamaica and was very nice to us. We had kitchen privileges and access to her best china and lace tablecloth in the event we wanted to have a dinner party.

We did have such a party, attended by Mishcon, Norton, Wells, Zucker and the Steiners. I remember the main part of the menu: rolled veal roast and I made a French apple pie from scratch for dessert. After our guests arrived, Ethel, dressed to go out to a movie, contrived to pass through the living room to the kitchen through the dining room several times before she left. Grandma Gossler, who suffered from "gas" was seated a few feet away in the living room, practically at the table with us, her legs crosswise over the arms of her overstuffed rocking armchair, quietly eructing, until we managed to find her only surefire relief: Vernors Ginger Ale, which was very hard to find at that time. In desperation we learned later that Dr. Pepper would also provide her some relief. It was our first dinner party, one of many in our long marriage, and the most hilarious. The lace tablecloth with a large rent in the lace added its share to whole evening.

We actually found the house; it was still there and seemed very small. Our room did not extend over the whole width of the porch. It must also have been very small, perhaps 9' x 12', a prelude to a much larger future. The neighborhood was still decent, and I got out of the car and went to the front door, but no one was at home. The neighbor next door saw me and came over to tell me that Grandma Gossler had died many years ago, and that Ethel, who had continued to live in the house and had never married, had died just a few weeks earlier. If we had been a few months earlier, I wonder if she would have remembered us . . . or maybe only me.

Two of the Exhibitions were held in the Chicago area and it was possible to reconnect with one of my favorite *sensei* from my days in the army at the University of Minnesota, Yoshiko Uragami, with whom we had stayed in contact. She lived in Des Plaines with her aged mother, a tiny little thing. After a few polite phrases in Japanese, she relaxed and gave her approval of us, and off we went to lunch. I can still see this tiny, frail old lady and the expression on her face.

The exhibitions were much the same: arrive on Friday afternoon; if possible, scout out the work area; unpack the flowers; snip off the bottom of the stems and put them in fresh water in the glass pint bottles provided by the host; remove the paper bags; start praying they survived the trip to perform their best at 11:30 a.m. the next day; get reacquainted with friends from previous shows; go to bed exhausted from the long trip and the excitement of the coming competition; Saturday morning go to the Exhibition Hall: start deciding which blossoms have the best chance of winning a ribbon; check each bloom for proper classification by type and color using APS reference book; be aware of the time deadline of 11:30 a.m. for all exhibits to be on the judging benches; transport by helper, Fran, to the proper location on the judging tables in the main hall; blooms could be displayed singly, in groups of three in one container, or individually in groups of 10 or 25 different varieties, and a certain amount of strategy was necessary to make these selections. Also, the Court of Honor was no longer selected from the general population by the judges, but now the exhibitor had to decide whether to gamble that a sure blue ribbon on the benches should be foregone in a larger gamble to enter in the Court of Honor and not be selected and, therefore, get no ribbon at all; and then, finally, I PRAYED.

After judging which was done by groups of two or three members of the APS (anonymity was ensured by the exhibitor's name being folded back into a slot in the entry label draped around the bottle holding the bloom) the Exhibition was opened to the public who came to admire the spectacular sight of 100s of peonies in a mass display. I would wander around from table to table to see if we had won any ribbons, which we usually did. Then I would take pictures, using a tripod, of our winners, and any of the other varieties I admired and might want to add to my collection.

There were usually educational seminars conducted by APS members in the afternoon, followed by a banquet, followed by election of the following year's officers, followed by one of the primary fund raisers: a peony root auction of roots donated by members. I did this one year with a plant I did not like, but only once: digging peonies is hard work. It was sometimes possible to buy a root for less than the price quoted in the catalogs. This is how I acquired "Yellow Emperor," the Itoh hybrid which a few years later won one of my five Grand Champion Ribbons. Usually, the auctioneer was able to coax a price out of the audience far in excess of what the same root could have been bought for from the catalogs.

We met some interesting people from as far away as New Zealand and the Netherlands. One especially interesting person was Sir Peter Smithers, now living in Switzerland, but formerly Deputy Administrator of the European Union in Brussels, who gave a talk at one of the Milwaukee exhibitions. When he retired, he had been given a villa on the southern slopes of the Alps in recognition of his long service on behalf of the European Union. He established a large garden there, partly wooded, and the theory he put forth in his lecture was that gardening should be labor free. After a plant was planted, he would provide no further care. If the plant died, so be it. It was not worthy of inclusion in his garden and was not replaced.

Thinking of my gardening background it was an interesting concept. He was charming and had a wonderful English accent, was married to an American girl, and loved tree peonies. I have one of his originations in my front yard. He was a fine photographer and used an Olympus 35mm SLR. The walls in the room he used for his talk were covered with 3' x 4' color enlargements of his favorite tree peonies. They were spectacular and interesting; the enlargements were done by a company in Atlanta, Georgia. I think he said he spent his winters in the Miami area. We asked if one could purchase the photos and he said they were available at $300 for the 2' x 3' and $400 for the 3' x 4'. We had no place to display such a large picture in Brecksville and said we would think about it. One of his enlargements was hanging in the entrance to the St. Louis Arboretum, which we recognized immediately when we visited with Fran's Polar Bear friends. In spite of our mutual love of the tree peony, the one special fact in his curriculum vitae that is embedded in my memory is that he was in the British MI 6 in World War II, and sat at a desk facing Ian Fleming, the author of the James Bond stories. He said Fleming was a mad man with one crazy scheme after another.

One of the other international people we met regularly at the Exhibitions, also a tree peony lover, was a Canadian, John Simkins, who wrote a garden column for one of the Toronto newspapers. I would have liked to see his garden. The way he described it he planted his tree peonies among the trees in a wooded public park behind his house.

One thing that became apparent very quickly from having such a large number of plants was what to do with all this beauty. If a mature peony plant produced an average of five blossoms, conservatively, that would amount to a total of 2,500 flowers in a period of about six weeks. This was far more than I could share with friends and relatives. We did provide some for the Sunday services at Trinity Cathedral in downtown Cleveland, , (Fran said the odor near the altar while taking Communion was heavenly). and also to St. Matthews Episcopal in Brecksville.

We also supplied peonies for several weddings, starting with our youngest daughter, Barbara. She was intelligent enough to choose June 7th for her wedding day that I suddenly realized was the peak of the peony season. There were also the weddings of both of my youngest brother's daughters. Lauren and Lisa; the wedding of my son-in-law's sister (tree peonies exclusively); and the older daughter of one of our Camp Michigania friends, the Burmeister's, who lived in Lake Orion, Michigan. These were all gifts, of course, and I was usually able to provide five or six dozen flowers to be arranged for the occasions.

One wedding that did not turn out well was that of one of our neighbors at our first condo in Florida. Their daughter was to be married about the first of June and I thought it quite possible that none of the guests might have ever seen a tree peony blossom, since they cannot be grown in the Florida climate. I thought that if I could find some suitable blossoms after we arrived back in Brecksville, I might be able to ship a few by UPS overnight express to their flower arranger in time for the wedding and they might make the wedding something special.

I told the parents about this and brashly offered to make the attempt. When we got home to Ohio I picked about a dozen beautiful Japanese tree peonies named "Yae Zakura", bagged them as if they were to be entered in an APS exhibition, and stored them prior to the shipping date in the old refrigerator in our garage.

I did not realize that the gasket around the edge of the refrigerator door that sealed in the cold had failed and the resulting temperature was far too warm to stop the development of the blossoms. When I started packing the flowers for shipment in the special cooler chest I had bought, I checked a few of the bags and peeked to see if all was well and was dismayed to find that the petals were falling and the blossoms useless. Nevertheless, on Friday afternoon I finished the packing of everything I had picked and took them to the UPS depot on Engle Road at Hopkins Airport. I paid the extra shipping fee and shipped them for next day delivery. I hoped that one or two of the latest picked might survive and be usable, thus proving my claims of beauty for a flower they had never seen before; that I was not all talk.

But I had a bad feeling. I didn't hear from the flower arranger I had sent the flowers to. On Tuesday morning after the wedding, I called her and learned the chest had arrived on time, still chilled, but that not a single bloom had survived; not one was usable. They were able to tell from the size and color of the petals how spectacular they would have been, and what fun it would have been to arrange them. It was a great disappointment for me. I don't know if it was for our friends who had lots of other things on their minds, but they never mentioned it to me.

At some point this superabundance of beautiful flowers got to me and I began to wonder if it would be possible to sell some of them to florists. It would be an experiment that would only cost me a little time and effort, but if successful, would be more than gratifying. Not a bad gamble with little to lose. So, I decided to try it.

It was slow going at first. I had to find some florists who would agree to buy my flowers, and when I did find some, how much should I charge. I knew nothing about the florist business, where a florist got the flowers he worked with, or how much he paid for them. I had no idea what the traffic would bear and was afraid if I asked too high a price, I would make no sales. I thought I had a valuable product: locally grown, unusual, beautiful flowers, picked the day they were delivered and delivered directly to the place of business. I gritted my teeth and asked for 50 cents per stem. I never was challenged, nor offered a lower price, $5 per dozen vs. $6 asking, which should have told me I wasn't charging enough. That was what I did the first year and was happy with the results. I have no idea if I showed a profit. It was enough for me to promote the peony and spread its beauty. I called my new business venture, "Peonies, Unltd."

I used to pick in the early morning (I had retired from the family business by this time) and sort the flowers into bunches of thirteen (remembrance of selling sweet corn on Tiedeman Road?) secured by a large rubber band, and put them into two carriers which consisted of three one-quart plastic pots of water clustered around a plastic handle, which meant that I could transport about six dozen blooms at one time. It was an efficient way to solve the picking/transporting problem. When there were more than six dozen, I used plastic buckets, and many times I had ten or twelve dozen blooms riding on the back seat, and another three or four dozen on the passenger seat. It was a great incentive to drive very carefully, especially when going around a corner, or coming to a sudden stop. I guess I was lucky because I never had to dry the car out. And it certainly smelled good, an unanticipated bonus.

My other problem was educating the florists, many of whom had an active dislike of the Peony, perhaps because they had a bad experience with how they would hold up in a bouquet; a good example would be Jan Dell's, the most artistic flower arranger in Rocky River. He told me he made a large basket arrangement for a good customer for a Memorial Day family celebration using numerous blossoms of "Festiva Maxima," a large white double with red flecks, an old standard, and being humiliated by having all the petals fall after delivery and before the party. He swore he would never use another peony in an arrangement again. I tried to reason with him, pointing out that the flowers he used from his regular supplier undoubtedly had been shipped in tight bud form from the Netherlands or Israel, and couldn't compare with my fresh picked local peonies.

The ending to this story came several years later at our daughter Nancy's 40th birthday party in the backyard of her home in Rocky River, with a tent, no less, when we hired Jan Dell's to make the floral arrangements on the condition he use only the peonies we supplied. The two employees responsible for the centerpieces and other arrangements were thrilled to have such flowers to work with, but Jan Dell's, even with this example in front of his eyes, never became a paying customer.

This was the party where I, the only non-drinker among the party guests, while moving backwards, tripped on one of the corner tent guy-wires and fell, spraining my wrist so badly that my son-in-law, John, had to take me to the Lakewood Hospital Emergency Room after dinner. All ended well: my wrist was not broken; the party was a success, and the flowers were beautiful.

I started out by checking florists' addresses in the Yellow Pages and then cold calling. I would make my spiel and leave a free bloom with the florist to observe. Many would not even accept the free flower. They did not want to use anything different in their ordinary, stilted arrangements. Eventually, I found enough florists who did appreciate the peony's qualities that I had trouble supplying them.

One of my first sales was to a florist in Shaker Heights on the recommendation of my longtime friend, Lenny Himmel. He made an appointment for me to take in a sample of what I had to offer, and I took a nice selection of colors and types, probably about two dozen that first trip. Among these were three stems of one of my favorites, a variety called "Dawn Pink," a semi-double about 6" in diameter and a lovely, soft pink shade on the watermelon side.

When I arrived, two of the lady arrangers were all a-twitter; they had just received an order from Paul Newman, the Hollywood movie star, for a bouquet to be delivered to his aunt who was celebrating her 90th birthday. Paul Newman grew up in Shaker Heights. His family owned one of the early exclusive sporting goods stores, Newman Sterns, at E. 13th Street and Chester Avenue. It would not be surprising to find that he had an aunt still living in Shaker Heights.

The arrangers were wringing their hands over what to use in this very special bouquet, so I pulled one of the three "Dawn Pink" stems out of my sample bucket and piped up, "Here. This is the answer to your problem. The aunt will have never seen anything like this from a florist before." I wish I knew whether they actually used my flowers. I never had any feedback, but if they did, it was the closest I ever came to a Hollywood celebrity.

I had to deliver all over the city. There was one large florist, Segelins, at Carnegie and E. 105th Street; another on Larchmere off Shaker Square who loved tree peonies. He would take all the blossoms I could bring him. He said he always took the most beautiful one to his mother who loved them also. Another shop that would take all the peonies I could supply was located at Van Aken Boulevard and Warrensville Center Road. All these locations were quite distant from Brecksville, but I didn't mind. I was fulfilling my mission to spread the good word about an amazing flower.

Oddly, one of my steadiest customers was located right in the heart of Brecksville, and there was another florist in Broadview Heights at Broadview and Wallings Roads, both very short trips for deliveries. The Broadview Heights man, whose name I cannot remember, was the son of a member of St. Matthews Episcopal in Brecksville. (His mother was not one of Fran's favorites.) He loved peonies and as soon as he discovered what I had to offer became a steady customer.

His shop was on the ground floor of an old single-family home and he would take less than a dozen flowers. It was useful to make his shop my last stop, when I might have the dregs of the day's load left, maybe only nine or ten. I was now charging 75 cents per stem and it helped pay for the gas.

On my first visit, as was my custom, I left a large single pink called "Lovely Rose," about 8" in diameter and in prime condition; near the cash register; it would have won a ribbon at an APS Exhibition. When I returned the next day with my first order, I noticed my "Lovely Rose" over on a window seat display area in a beautiful, simple Japanese arrangement, just the one blossom near an artificial mountain on a plain black kidney-shaped mirror. It was stunning in its simplicity. I can still see it in my mind's eye. My comment to the salesperson was: "Wow! Look at what can be done with one 75 cent blossom! I'll bet he's charging $5 for that". The girl said "No, $25." After that experience I was emboldened to raise my price to $1 per stem.

Another good customer was located near where I grew up in Lakewood, on Madison Avenue just west of Bunts Road, The Cottage of Flowers. The owner knew and liked peonies and I sold large numbers to him every year. It didn't hurt my business, which I had named Peonies Unlimited, that my favorite flower's blooming season coincided with the wedding season and the high school graduation season.

I don't remember how the connection was made but I was able to supply flowers to a unique gift shop in Milan, Ohio, south of the Ohio Turnpike, which was owned by a very talented young business woman, Tracy Lake. We usually stopped there to check out her latest offerings on our trips to Detroit. She specialized in dry arrangements of wreaths and swags and had an extensive garden where she grew her own plants that were suitable for drying. She also developed a market for freeze-dried bridal bouquets which featured roses and she learned that peonies were also suitable. She agreed to pay $1 per stem and drove to Brecksville to see our peony beds and pick up her first order.

The method of freeze-drying was most interesting. She had a large freezer retort, a super refrigerator in effect, in the basement of her shop. She loaded the peonies, or other varieties of flowers, with their stems cut to a 3" or 4"length on to three or four grill-like trays (it looked like cookie dough on a sheet ready for the oven) except the flowers were exposed to subzero temperatures in the container for several hours, repeating the process three or four times until the flowers were completely desiccated. Then the trays were removed and each of the flowers was sprayed with a chemical compound that prevented them from reabsorbing moisture. After finishing this process, the flowers were supposed to last indefinitely which made them ideal for bridal bouquets. I never asked Tracy how much she charged for a dried bridal bouquet that would last forever, a very romantic concept, but she did pay me $1 per stem and ordered 300 blooms per order. I think it was a fad that faded away after three or four years and I lost a lucrative source of business. I never heard how much of the $10,000 she paid for the machine she recovered, or if she was able to find a buyer. The peonies did not have to be exhibition quality, but smaller blooms and even buds, which suited me very well, and to be honest, I was not happy with the end results; the peonies no longer looked like flowers, but more like a dried up, shriveled apples, and I didn't care for that symbolism.

Another client on the east side of Cleveland was Ingrid Luders, the premier Ikebana (Japanese style) flower arranger and instructor in Greater Cleveland. She was German, came from Chile, and was married to a neurologist at the Cleveland Clinic. I would have liked to know, having studied Japanese in the Army, how such a Caucasian background could have become interested in such an Oriental craft - and absolutely mastered it. She really excelled. It would have been hard to tell that a native of Japan had not done her arrangements,

I supplied both herbaceous and tree peony blossoms for some of her Ikebana classes and demonstrations at the Garden Center, across the street from the Cleveland Museum of Art, and stayed for one of her demonstrations and was truly impressed with her skill. She was very gracious and introduced me to the audience as the supplier of the peonies she had used in her presentation. I would have liked to take one home to show Fran.

Ingrid was instrumental in having me supply all the peonies used for the 75th Anniversary Banquet at the Cleveland Museum of Art. I think I provided about 400 stems and the Museum actually bought a large florist's display refrigerator with glass doors, after I explained that all the peonies could not be picked or delivered in one day; there would be multiple deliveries. I made several visits to the new cooler on the lower level of the Museum over a period of eight or ten days and although I had met my quota, I made one extra trip on the day of the banquet with one final load of flowers, just in case they might be needed.

The committee of eight or ten women was busily arranging the centerpieces for the 17 tables; they were obviously having a great time working with such beautiful flowers. Peonies were used exclusively with small white orchids flown in from Hawaii as filler. Ingrid, as senior in command, had the responsibility for the massive basket arrangements at the entrances and used my largest double and bomb type blossoms to great effect.

The tables were set up in the rear entrance hall of the Museum and that section was closed to the public the whole day. Fran and I were allowed to return at 5 p.m. before the banquet to see the final effect and allowed to take photos. It was truly impressive.

I was told later by Ingrid that the flowers were a huge success; that the hostess could not get the foreign visitors, Directors of many of the greatest art museums in all of Europe, to stop passing from table to table, admiring the centerpieces, and take their seats. I charged $1 per stem and had no trouble getting paid. But that was not the only satisfaction I felt: I loved the feeling that others, in this case extremely discerning individuals, responded to the same beauty I did.

My niece, Lisa, daughter of my youngest brother, Wes, started her own business on the far east side of Cleveland as a flower arranger and party arranger and used to drive all the way to Brecksville to pick up peonies. She did the flower arrangements for her sister Lauren's wedding, all peonies, of course, picked up in Brecksville by her father this time, but I think her own marriage was out of season.

I delivered peonies to the Akron area twice, once for the wedding of the daughter of mutual friends, the John Hunters. He was the chairman of a large savings and loan in Akron, and also, a mortgage loan correspondent for New York Life Insurance Company. We had much in common since we also were mortgage loan correspondents, we for Aetna Life Insurance Company. We both enjoyed playing golf, and we both owned condos in Florida not far from each other. I delivered my peonies to their florist and heard later that the flowers had made a great impression on the guests. We were not invited to that wedding so I cannot give an eyewitness report as to how she used my flowers.

The other trip to the Akron area was actually to North Canton in Portage County. I do not remember how it came about, but it was the most unusual order I ever filled. I was asked to supply a fairly small number of peonies, for use as a training aid, in a class being given for Professional Flower Judges, to prepare them to judge flower shows at County, or State Fairs, I imagine. The interesting thing to me, quite different from my usual attempt to deliver only the most beautiful examples of the peony, was the requirement that I bring examples of flawed blooms as well as perfect ones. While it felt strange that anyone would pay for less than perfection, I could understand the value to a future judge who was to be paid for her professional opinion, to have seen what less than perfection actually looks like. Especially when putting a value on the minute differences which appear in a class of flowers from exhibitors who are only going to present their very best examples. They might also be looking at blossoms used in floral arrangements based on an assigned theme, which was one of the events at the APS Exhibitions, for instance, as well as at individual specimens.

I had no trouble finding what they wanted. There is quite a variation in quality of the blossoms on each peony plant. One plant was quite capable of producing a Grand Champion and six other pretty, but flawed, blossoms at the same time. I think I tried to do exactly that as an example for the students. As a grower, it was enough for me to know they were trying their best for me.

I delivered my order to a lady instructor at a conference/classroom in a motel north of the Belden Village Shopping Mall in North Canton in time for her presentation. I remember faintly that she was pleased with the strange mixture of blooms she was going to work with, some gorgeous, some not so gorgeous.

In the later stages of my "career" as a peony guru, I was asked to be the judge of the peony entries at the annual Spring Garden Show and Plant Sale held at the Garden Center of Cleveland.. The Garden Center was one of the outstanding cultural assets of Greater Cleveland, one of the many in what I was told was the greatest concentration of cultural institutions in the world, all located on 169 acres of land: Western Reserve University, Flora Stone Mather College for Women, Case Tech, University Hospitals, Severance Hall (home of the Cleveland symphony), Cleveland Museum of Art, Western Reserve Historical Society, Museum of Natural History, Cleveland Institute of Music, and others, all within walking distance of each other. I liked the Garden Center for its classrooms and lecture halls, library, and its underground parking garage. It also had several very mature, perhaps 30 to 40-year-old tree peonies in the gardens close to the building.

It was my first experience being a judge in a non-APS event, and very interesting. This was when I learned that Ingrid Luders had no sense of humor. I made an "inside" joking comment about one of the exhibits which she had had a hand in, completely unaware of her involvement, and it did not go over well. It was one of those occasions where if I had known, I would never have made the remark. It was stupid. To my great regret I think that was the last time she ever spoke to me. Or bought any of my peonies.

Also, and once again I cannot remember how it happened, probably because of my position as president of the APS, I was asked to consult for the University of Michigan which had a project to restore the sadly neglected historic peony beds in the Nichols Arboretum and it was hoped I could identify some of the surviving plants' names (quite an honor for me and delicious for a Yalie to come to the aid of the University of Michigan). I think we must have combined a visit to Fran's mother or our friends in Detroit with a side trip out to Ann Arbor, which we always enjoyed because of the memories we both had. I remember being taken out to the peony beds which were in poor condition but with some of the plants in bloom and being unable to identify any of them positively; many of the double blossoms look much the same. I wasn't of any help at all to the University who must have had doubts as to my expertise. However, the visit was not a total loss because many memories came flooding back of our walks where our courtship began.

Towards the end of our years spent in Florida, during the winter months, Fran wanted us to stay longer, to not have to rush back to Brecksville to "take care" of the peonies. We both felt November and May were the best months of the year to enjoy the weather in Florida and less, also partly because of the lower tourist competition.

May was the time the peony beds were awaking again, and I needed to be there to till and fertilize and disbud and apply the first coat of spray. She felt that in addition to cutting short our time in Florida, missing out on the best month of the year, that the peonies were imposing too much on me physically. I disagreed. In fact I remember sitting down and estimating the number of hours I spent in a whole year taking care of the peony beds, not counting the time cutting and delivering flowers to florists, or time spent in preparation for the APS Exhibitions. To care for 500 plants I would till three or four times a season; disbud the side buds on the lactiflora plants once a season, spray twice a season; setting up the equipment and pumping water from the pond to irrigate in a dry year, possibly twice a season; and cutting down and removing the dead foliage in the fall, once, I came to a total of 40 hours, spread over five months. I was surprised and thought this was remarkable. I still do. I don't know of any other cut flower that requires so little time and attention or compares with the peony in either beauty or longevity.

Nevertheless, I assured Fran that I could give up my peony passion without regret, feeling nothing but gratitude for all the many years of joy the experience had given me, and set about trying to find a buyer for the collection. I refused to even consider digging individual plants myself - far too much hard labor and too much time required to dispose of so many plants individually. It would have taken years, been very unsightly during the process, and we might have ended up with some of the least desirable plants still trying to sell at fire sale rates. It had to be all, or nothing at all:

The only answer was to find a commercial grower, perhaps one of the advertisers in the APS Bulletin. I hoped that one incentive might be the sheer number of varieties, 450 different names, some quite rare, which in four or five years,' time could be added to the buyer's catalog listings.

I set about examining each plant carefully to estimate how many root divisions it might yield for the buyer; I assumed that his first division would produce approximately 1,500 plants, and in another three years he might have as many as 5,000 plants. In a perfect world at the prices prevalent at that time, he would have merchandise worth $50-60,000! If these assumptions were anything like what might be going through a prospective purchaser's mind, I didn't feel it was unrealistic, or unreasonable, to ask $3,500 for the entire collection, with the purchaser having the responsibility of digging and removing the plants. I would reserve the right to keep the tree peonies and the few herbaceous peonies located in the small bed on the east side of the house, created when we built the additions and enlarged the guest bedroom; also any other plants next to the foundation.

Shortly before this I learned that "Kit" Klehm, son of the owner of the Klehm Nurseries in Barrington, Illinois, from whom I had bought more peony plants over the years than from any other grower, was coming to Cleveland to give a lecture at the Cleveland Garden Center. He needed a ride to the airport after giving his talk and I volunteered to drive him. After learning who I was and my history with the APS, he was interested in seeing my peony beds, and since we had time before his plane left, we made a slight detour to Brecksville, where he looked at my beds and admired our house. He was a young man in his 20s and I think he was quite impressed, both with the peonies and the house.

Partly as a result of this fortuitous personal visit and after sending the Klehms the list of names of my peonies, the Klehms, who were the only people I ever talked to in my search (?) for a buyer, agreed to buy my collection without any haggling and I was pleased my plants would have such a good home. By this time, Klehms had moved their peony operation to Champagne-Urbana, Illinois, where they had 40 acres of peonies under cultivation. Theirs was a big operation.

They sent a foreman and four Mexican laborers to dig the plants. It was an amazing experience to watch them work. They arrived in a six-passenger pick-up truck and a large truck for transporting the plants about 8:30 a.m. The Mexican workers split into two-man teams and used steel shank square edge digging spades. They faced each other on opposite sides of the plant, drove their spades into the ground in a circle around the plant, and when done, on the count of uno, dos, tres pressed down on the handle of their spade and popped the plant out of the earth. They then set the plant aside with its name tag and went on to the next. They stopped for lunch, and Fran had made a batch of her famous Sweet & Sour Chili, which she offered to them and they politely ate, while sitting under the oak tree behind the garage. Being Mexican and used to more seriously spicy food, I wondered what they really thought of their lunch. They were very polite and appreciative, and Fran was pleased.

The foreman was not even present at the morning's digging; he had to take the big truck to a nearby dealer for minor repairs. He returned after lunch and oversaw the digging of the remainder of the plants, which was finished about 4 p.m. The men then went back to the beds to gather the plants left lying on the ground where they had been dug and put them in plastic bushel baskets which they then carried up to the big truck for loading and by 5 p.m. the job was done and they drove off to Chicago.

I never head from the Klehms whether they felt the transaction had been a good deal for them, or how the plants performed, or what happened to the "family named" peonies I had included, but have always assumed it was a good deal for them. I know they are my preferred nursery, now under the name of Song Sparrow Farms, in Wisconsin, and have bought most of the peonies planted here on Prairie Moon in North Ridgeville, from them.

I was extremely impressed by this performance in every aspect and watching the relentless effort put forth by the diggers - they never paused - it changed my perceptions of the Mexican people forever.

Thus, my Peony saga came to an end. It was important and wonderful.

Sic Transit Gloria

# Chapter VII

# Photography

One of my interests, which began after the birth in 1947, of our first daughter Nancy was photography, which was in its infancy as a popular hobby after the end of World War II. There are only a few snapshot reminders of those early days. As far as the general public was concerned, taking pictures was largely limited to the use of the simple box Eastman Kodak camera with its fixed focus and fixed lens, which limited its use to the outdoors.

Indoor photography was the domain of the professional photographer, who was visited when there was a new baby, or a wedding, or a family portrait. This was an expensive proposition and done only rarely. I remember having to get dressed up in my Sunday best, a gray flannel suit with a jacket and knicker pants with silver buckles at the knee, along with Mother and Dad and my brothers and being posed as a group in a conventional style. I was told to smile as the photographer, squatted behind his huge camera on a tripod with a black piece of cloth spread over the back of the camera and his head, finally snapped the photo. There were special floodlights, and the film was contained in large light proof 8"x10" containers, which slid in the back of the camera lens. This always impressed me. It was so mysterious.

I remember another professional photo taken of my brother Russ and me, dressed in matching sailor suits; I suspect the occasion may have been a milestone birthday, perhaps my 5th or 6th. One of these early photos of me when I was two years old and able to sit upright for the picture. This was included in the surprise 50th birthday album which Fran created for me from magazine advertisements and cartoons (and real photographs) with her own subtitles. It reveals as much of her personality as of my own and is one of my most prized possessions.

I do not remember clearly what camera we had when we were first married; it may have been a box Kodak of Fran's. I remember seeing pictures she took on vacations with her mother, and a Highland Park High School senior class trip to Washington, where for propriety's sake the girls and boys traveled on separate trains with faculty chaperones. She may have been the one who took one of my favorite photos of me sitting on the concrete bench near the rock garden on Tiedeman Road, leaning forward, elbows on knees, very pensive; one of my other favorites, which I know she took using her Kodak, is of me standing in uniform in front of their next door neighbor's garage on my first visit to Detroit to meet her mother a week after our blind date, the one on the front cover of this book. Probably my number one favorite photo is an improbable one of me taken by my college roommate with his Kodak box camera in our room on a sunny afternoon, holding the camera steady on a table while delaying somehow the shutter snap, and catching me sprawling in my easy chair, studying, holding a book open on my lap, with sunlight reflected off its pages back on my face, in a fortuitous, perfect exposure. It captured the essence of college life.

With the arrival of Nancy, it became important to me to have a better camera and we bought a smaller, more compact model made by Eastman Kodak. It was very frustrating because its limited capabilities gave it only limited use indoors. I remember one Saturday morning in our first house on Ridgewood Drive in Parma Heights when I took a photo of Nancy sitting on the floor close to the open front door with the sunlight streaming in and getting a memorable picture using outdoor light indoors.

Unfortunately, having only this limited capability camera, we have very few pictures of Nancy's childhood years. There is one I remember of me sitting in our easy chair in the corner of the living room in our apartment in Lakewood, feeding Nancy while holding her seated in my lap with my legs crossed, Nancy, wide eyed, and me with a big hole in the heel of my sock. We saved the photo, hole and all. Another favorite photo of Nancy and me is of a Sunday afternoon walk in the spring with her in her pink winter coat and leggings reaching up to hold my hand while we walked to the store. She never toddled but walked fearlessly from the beginning.

Sometime later I bought my first 35mm "candid" camera, a boxy Argus C-3. This was not much of an improvement over the Kodak, having a fixed lens and limited shutter speed and aperture. But, as I recall, it was possible to use the early flashcubes so pictures could be taken indoors, and the film came in 20 or 36 exposures, a big advance from the primitive Kodak.

The war had been over five or six years when the Japanese began to produce many inexpensive, superior 35mm SLR cameras, featuring interchangeable lenses with apertures down to 1.9, and much faster shutter speeds synchronized to flash units. Nikon and Canon became the most desirable brands because of their durable bodies and especially the quality of their lenses.

My first venture with a limited budget was to buy a less expensive brand whose name I cannot remember, but it did have a 1.9 lens, which was my goal, because I could now take photos indoors without flash. This made it ideal for truly candid shots at last to record our growing children, and opened up a whole world of possibilities in other areas.

About this time, I subscribed to the monthly magazine *Photography* which combined many informative "How to do it" articles as well as many enticing ads for new models of equipment constantly coming on the market. After a few years I upgraded and bought my first Canon SLR 35 mm camera. When I handled it in the camera shop it seemed easier to operate than the Nikon and had the added advantage of being a little less expensive.

It was the "Pellix" model which had an unusual focusing arrangement. On the traditional 35 mm at that time, the subject was seen through the viewfinder, which revealed exactly what would appear on the exposed film reflected up to the viewfinder by a hinged mirror. When the photographer was satisfied with his composition, he pushed the release button and the mirror flipped up out of the way allowing the light/image to strike the film. The movement of the mirror could possibly cause a shake of the camera body and spoil the shot with just a little blur caused by the movement.

The Pellix was different because the photographer looked directly through the mirror which did not move during the focusing and shutter releasing process, thus eliminating the possibility of camera shake. Of course, the photographer tried to remember to hold his breath as he released the shutter, and of course, at shutter speeds of 125th of a second, or higher, camera shake was not of great concern. It was probably nit-picking on my part, and I probably would have gotten good images with any other model, or even another brand, perhaps Olympus, but I had the Pellix for several years and had great success with it whether taking pictures of the family or friends, groups or portraits, or vacation scenes outdoors.

As for the business photos I needed for the larger commercial loan applications, which required more than the typical three residential photos of the subject property, subject and same side of street, and opposite side of street (try not to be there on rubbish pick-up day), the 35 mm SLR was quite a step up from the instant Polaroid I used for that purpose. The Polaroid was very convenient: I could see immediately if the pictures would be satisfactory, retake them if necessary, and saved time when time was important for an anxious client. I was never very proud of the quality. It did beat the extra day or two needed when we took conventional rolls of film to the photo finishers, the Driscoll sisters, in their small shop in The Old Arcade.

On two or three occasions, a friend took me up in a small single engine, high wing airplane and I took aerial photos of the property we were presenting to the insurance company for loan approval. It was very exciting; I did not tell Fran beforehand! I do not recall reading any articles in *Photography* on the technique involved in aerial photography and had to guess at the exposure and shutter speeds, and I only had one chance to get it right. I think I set the focus at infinity, and the shutter speed at 125th of a second. I was very relieved when I saw the results.

One flight was out of the Akron/Canton airport and I think we took photos of a proposed medical office building across the street from the Lake County Hospital. From there we traveled - as the crow flies - about 50 miles southwest to Brunswick, Ohio, for shots of a failed condominium project which our client hoped to complete as rental apartments. Sadly, neither loan was approved, and my extra effort did not pay off. I think we flew at an altitude of about 1,500 feet and a speed of 80-90 mph. And as an example of the vagaries of my memory, I cannot remember the names of the pilots with whom I entrusted my life.

The other memorable flight was from the Burke Lakefront Airport in downtown Cleveland, when another friend took me up to take a series of ten or twelve photos of downtown Cleveland for a fee appraisal (no mortgage application involved) for the Aetna Life Insurance Company. My previous experience paid off here and since the camera settings were so simple and fixed, I used my 3 x 4 Bronica with the Nikon lens, and got some stunning pictures. One in particular, is looking southeast toward the Cleveland skyline showing the ice-covered surface of the small bay in front of the Winton Place apartments on Lakewood's Gold Coast. This was one time there was no anxiety connected with the job. Aetna Life guaranteed the payment of my fee.

Unfortunately, the year before our third vacation trip to Europe, to explore France, our first to see if we would enjoy and could survive traveling in a strange country in a rental car, (it would have been 1973) the Pellix malfunctioned and had to be repaired. I remember clearly dropping it off after lunch at the Dodd Camera kiosk at the foot of the ramp leading up to the lobby of the Terminal Tower where our offices were located. I did this about a month before our departure date emphasizing to the clerk the importance of getting the Pellix back in time for our trip. A week before we were to leave, I grew worried that I had not been called to pick up the repaired camera and stopped at the kiosk to investigate and was dismayed to find that my camera had been mislaid and never sent in for repair. They were very apologetic and furnished me with a "loaner," a rebuilt Canon, better than the Pellix, but none the less, a different, unfamiliar camera. I had already invested in 25 rolls of film and would not have time to familiarize myself with its operation, let alone get an experimental roll exposed and developed before we left on our trip.

I used the "new" camera throughout the trip and considered any day that I did not take at least one roll of film a wasted day. All told, I estimate that I took 350-400 exposures, all the time praying that the camera was functioning and that I was following instructions for its operation correctly. After turning in the rental car and surviving 1,500 miles of driving in a foreign country, while packing in our hotel room in Paris (don't remember its name or where it was) to fly home the next day, I innocently remarked as Fran was stuffing canister after canister of exposed film around the edges of her suitcase, "I certainly hope that camera worked OK." She was appalled.

But all turned out well. The camera performed beautifully and there were many beautiful exposures. I remember particularly ones taken of a white columned pavilion in the gardens of Le Petit Trianon and the interiors of Le Grand Trianon at Versailles.

Photography was an important element of our trips to Europe. When I viewed the slides upon returning home, memories would flood in and I could remember exactly where I stood when taking the picture, the time of day, even feel the temperature and the wind. This remained true many years later and I wonder if it is a common experience among other photographers. By this time, I started to acquire additional lenses: a wide angle, a long and a short telephoto, and a zoom. I also experimented with multiple slave photography where several independent flash units were placed distant from the flash unit on the camera and were triggered by photoelectric cells when the main flash fired. Many special effects could be achieved in this manner, and it was particularly useful in low light conditions in large spaces such as cathedrals. I had a cable release for time release exposures, and a "C" clamp, which was screwed into the bottom of the camera and then clamped onto a door, or the back of a chair, anything immovable, once again to minimize camera shake when taking slow shutter speed exposures. The "C" clamp was a blessing because it could be carried in one's pocket and provided the steadiness of a bulky tripod and could be used to take timed exposures in the dark, relying on the automatic light reading capability of the camera to control the length of the exposure. Eventually all this equipment was stowed in a padded leather carrying shoulder bag which must have weighed about 15 lbs., This resulted in an achy shoulder after our three-week trips abroad. But I was prepared for any eventuality, photographically speaking.

The "C" clamp made it possible to take time exposures of the stained glass windows in the cathedrals and this became an obsession of mine. The use of a rental car made it possible for us to visit many, if not all of the great cathedrals in France and England, which we might not have been able to see as part of a tour group. As result, it is hard for me to name a favorite; in my memory I think I would choose Wells Cathedral in England for its inverted gothic arches in the nave and Chartres Cathedral in France for its magnificent stained glass. Each cathedral was distinctive but I tended to rank them in my mind according to the quality of their stained glass. I always felt it was sad that so much of the stained glass was destroyed in England when Cromwell's men destroyed all the lower glass which they could reach from the ground, leaving only the upper portions to suggest what we are missing today as compared to France where the windows are intact and in many cases simply breathtaking. Only once in our travels, were we forbidden to use a camera in a church in Segovia, Spain, where they sold their own photo cards to raise money for maintaining the structure. Maintaining and restoring these ancient buildings, still in use though poorly attended in most cases, is a serious challenge and most of the cathedrals had a special box for donations from tourists. We were grateful enough for the experience that we usually made a small contribution.

One other situation occurred, slightly different, when we were forbidden to take photos of the robing of the Virgin Mary in Cuenca, Spain, which is describe3 in Chapter XIV, "Credo."

My usual procedure upon entering was to look for a folding chair which could be used to support my "C" clamp, set up the camera, and proceed down the nave taking whatever amount of time was needed to take a picture of every window, ending up at the altar, then to proceed around the apse behind the altar and take pictures of any chapels, and finish with shots of the altar and lectern.

All this while Fran would be occupied taking notes. It was always so quiet and the light so ethereal that it was almost a form of worship. We always tried to show the utmost respect and do our little bit to belie the "Ugly American" image then prevalent. When we returned home from these adventures, we never regaled our families or friends with all these photos, although I was asked to present a slide show featuring the great cathedrals of England for the people of St. Matthews Episcopal Church, Fran's church in Brecksville.

My photographic activity was not limited to business and vacations. When our daughters were young, we took a group picture of them every year to enclose with our Christmas cards, the only way our out-of-town friends and relatives could keep up with their progress. We would gather them together in the living room, all dressed in their finest and the fun would begin. At that time, I didn't use flash, but two floodlights and a cable release to click the shutter. I would sit patiently waiting for all faces to smile at the same time, trying not to be cross at their antics, and it usually took a whole roll of 36 exposures to get one or two poses that we felt were acceptable.

At first, when it was just the two daughters and our budget was quite limited, we did our own developing of the negatives and printing to save money, but that aspect of photography never interested me as much as the taking of pictures, especially portraits of family members and friends. I didn't want the whole body whether one person, or a group, but to be close enough so that the face occupied the whole frame.

I had to learn to be patient, to wait for the perfect moment when the expression was at its most attractive and revealed the inner person. I learned that the best results came when using a short telephoto lens when taking portraits, which meant I would be 5 or 6 feet from the person. This seemed to result in the most faithful representation of the person's features. I always felt there was an element of luck that I was able to capture so many of our family members and friends, both posed and candid, that were good enough to be enlarged to an 8" x 10" size and presented to the subject.

I learned that some of these enlargements ended up being matted and framed and hung in a place of honor, a case of double pleasure for the recipient and the giver, with an added element of pride on the part of the giver.

I remember the time a high school friend in one of our bridge groups brought his mother out to our home in Brecksville on a sunny Saturday afternoon for a visit. Before they left, I took a stunning picture of her, standing in dappled light under the oak tree behind the house. It may have been the finest portrait I ever took.

Another time I was in the right place at the right time - an extremely important part of picture taking - at the wedding reception of the daughter of one of our Camp Michigania friends and I captured a very tender moment when the groom was holding his exhausted bride's hand in the receiving line and looking down at her as he adjusted the new wedding ring on her finger. It was a truly memorable photo.

When I knew I would be taking "people photos," I loaded my camera with film from the Seattle Film Works who bought scraps of 70 mm film leftovers from the day's shooting in Hollywood. This was specialty film produced to render superior flesh tones. Seattle Film split the film into 35 mm strips, packaged it and sold it via their ads in *Photography* magazine. I tried it and felt it produced very flattering images and used it for several years. It was a bother and took more time to have to send the order all the way to Seattle, then wait for its arrival in the mail and then send it back for processing, which they claimed only they could do, before I could see if I had had any luck. But I felt it was worth it. I took many photos of our two granddaughters when they were young and lived nearby in Chagrin Falls, Ohio, and have 3 of my favorites, 8"x10" size, mounted on stiff board sitting on my desk where I can admire them daily.

I was always frustrated that I never was able to capture the beauty that I saw in Fran's face; and over all the years of our long marriage was never pleased with my efforts. Only a handful were successful and are meaningful to me. She was never happy having her picture taken, either. On the other hand, our children probably thought their Daddy had a third eye in the middle of his forehead because he had a camera pointed at them all the time. Their faces seemed to light up with beautiful smiles when a camera was pointed at them, something I never learned how to do. I never learned how to produce a smile on demand and had to reassure the family constantly that I was not unhappy, that I just looked that way.

With the interest I had in photography and the investment in money, after our return from the first trip to France with a rental car and the close call to what could have been a disaster, I decided it might be wise to get some formal instruction.

With Fran's full concurrence, I signed up for a 12-week course on Photography offered by the Adult Education Program in Parma, Ohio. Classes were to be held at the Normandy High School on Pleasant Valley Road once a week at 7 p.m., which was only about a 30-minute drive from our home in Brecksville. The instructor was a man named Ewing, whose bushy eyebrows I remember clearly. He was probably in his 40s and I believe a professional photographer. The cost of the course was $15 and I didn't expect much for my money; feeling that you get what you pay for, and, if it's too good to be true, it probably isn't. I couldn't have been more wrong. He was a fine teacher and gave us a solid grounding in how to use a camera, as well as how to organize negatives and slides, and compose photos for special effects. After the first introductory class, we were required to bring our cameras with us to class. There were twelve or fifteen of us and the total value of the equipment in that room had to have been $3-4,000.

One of the things I remember from the class is his telling of the famous *Life Magazine* photographer, Alfred Eisenstaedt, who was sent by *Life* on a photo assignment in the Philippine Islands for an article which would be limited to a total of seven photographs. Mr. Ewing's question to the class was: "How many exposures did Eisenstaedt make to achieve seven, which would meet his artistic and professional standards?" I made the highest estimate in the class: 350, which was much too low. He took 2,500 exposures to get seven that he approved. This made quite an impression on me, and I didn't feel quite so bad about all the redundant photos I took on our European travels.

Mr. Ewing made an even bigger impression on us with his final lecture. He craved our indulgence and said we did not have to bring our cameras with us for our final class as he proposed to demonstrate what could be done with two projectors in a slide presentation. When we arrived, he had everything set up and explained that what we were about to see were slides he had taken on a vacation trip to Cape Cod the summer before with his wife and daughter. He turned the lights down and held us spellbound for the next 45 minutes with one stunning image after the other. When it was over, he gave us the essence of the whole course in two or three brief sentences. He showed us the camera he used: a simple range finder camera he brought home from Germany after the war (not a Leica) and told us that he had set the shutter speed at 1/60 of a second, the aperture at f8 and the distance at infinity. And never changed the settings the entire trip. His point: one doesn't need expensive equipment to take good pictures, one has to have taste and know what one is doing.

After this learning experience, I don't know whether the quality of my photography improved in either the business or personal fields, but I suspect it did. I now had become aware of the larger format cameras and started reading the ads in *Photography* magazine. At this point it was only a dream. I knew I could not afford a Hasselblad, but perhaps a Japanese Bronica 3x4 with Nikon lenses might be possible - someday. This became my dream.

About this time four couples of our Brecksville duplicate bridge club, the Adairs, the Sutherlands, the Cullers and ourselves decided it would be fun to go on a Caribbean cruise together.

In due course we boarded an Eastern Airline plane and flew non-stop to San Juan, Puerto Rico, where we boarded a Princess Line ship (along with a University of Michigan Alumni Travel group headed by Bob Forman, Alumni Secretary, whom we knew well from our days at Camp Michigania) and cruised all the way south to Caracas, Venezuela, and then back north through the islands, stopping at Antigua, Grenada, Martinique, and St. Johns in the Virgin Islands, before returning to Puerto Rico. It was a fun trip, seeing the islands, each so different yet with an underlying sameness.

We arrived at St. Johns on Good Friday about noon. We had a boatload of thwarted lady shoppers who had not yet been able to spend any of their husbands' money, and at last they were going to get their chance to hit the shops. This was their last chance because there would not be enough time to explore San Juan before the flight home. To their bitter disappointment, all the shops were closed because it was Good Friday, which pleased their husbands. However, I found a good camera shop open and it had the Bronica I was looking for - with a Nikon lens. It had been on my wish list for a long time, I knew the price was right, but I can't remember what I paid for it. It was lower than in Cleveland and unfortunately, after all the drama of the purchase and my high hopes for the camera, I never used it very often. It was too bulky and my Canon SLR with all its automatic features was so much easier to use. And the point of sale was too far away to return it for credit.

The family went on vacation twice to the Chataqua Institute on Lake Chataqua, New York, about a three-hour drive from Brecksville. This is a wonderful, unique place which offers a rich intellectual program for the whole family on the one hand. On the other hand, a wide variety of recreational activities, including sailing, swimming, golf and tennis; all this in a very quaint Victorian village setting; gated, and no cars allowed; no two cottages the same. One of the attractions for us was that classes were given in the mornings for a wide range of subjects for both children and adults, and among them were classes in beginning to advanced photography. I thought this might be a fine opportunity to improve my skills and having taken thousands of photos on our vacations and for business purposes, signed up for the "advanced" class.

I met the instructor who taught at the University of Wisconsin, whose name I do not remember, and tried to impress him with my qualifications and experience, and the quality of my equipment, suggesting that I was qualified for the "advanced" level class.

After patiently listening to all this back-patting, he suggested that we go out to the Plaza and he would give me a photographic problem to solve, which we did. The problem was how would I select the settings on my Canon to have everything from a nearby shrub to a building at the other end of the Plaza, 100 yards distant in sharp focus? I think I remember hemming and hawing and finally venturing that this was a depth of field problem. I used the right term but that was the only thing I did right. He finally looked at me kindly and suggested that I take the beginner's course, which I did. I endured a week of utter humiliation. I came home for dinner after working on a photo assignment, night after night, fuming at my lack of knowledge of the basic principles, or what felt like my total lack of knowledge. I wish I could remember more of his instruction. It was very valuable and dealt with the laws of optics, and once these were understood, it was impossible not to take better pictures.

The one lesson that remains to this day is how to take a picture of a flower - in my case - the peony. In my ignorance I had always opened the lens to its widest which resulted in the shortest shutter speed, especially on a bright day. The problem was that this technique produced a satisfactory photo in general, but close examination revealed a slight blurriness at the very center.

The proper way to get a crisp focus of the subject in the whole frame is the exact opposite. A tripod should be used for stability and arrangements made for holding the stem steady if there should be any breeze, and then to set the aperture at its smallest opening which results in a slow release of the shutter, sometimes taking up to 30 seconds to allow enough light to register on the film. I was amazed at the fine detail, the clarity, the richness of the color. The automatic time setting on the Canon proved to be invaluable. I used this method ever after and some of the later peony photos were gorgeous.

The only flowering plants near the instructor's office were close-to-the-ground begonias, I think, I remember getting down on my hands and knees and having a hard time arranging the tripod for something so close to the ground, and how hard it was to look through the viewfinder. This odd posture would not have fazed a passerby at Chataqua where all sorts of strange activities were going on constantly.

One of the things I really enjoyed doing was something I learned from Nancy's best friend's father, Dan Gentile. He took informal, candid photos of his daughter's wedding shower and the reception after the wedding and gave the enlargements and negatives to the newlyweds as an additional, unexpected wedding present. I thought this was a terrific thing to do, and, although I never tried to take pictures for our daughters' weddings (I was too busy), I did take "informals" at many of our friends' weddings, also at wedding anniversaries and birthday parties. I think it irritated the professional photographers, especially when I poached on their formal posings.

I used to roam the room, using my zoom lens set, at mid-telephoto length, so I could be 10-12 feet distant and capture individuals and small groups chatting without their being aware. It required a lot of patience to wait for smiling, relaxed, happy expressions fitting the occasion. Also, a good memory of whom I had already caught, so as not to waste film. When the prints came back, I would present them to the happy couple, who always seemed to be delighted with the unexpected aid to their memories of their happy day.

I think the last time I did this was the Adair wedding. Doug Adair was a member of our Brecksville Duplicate Bridge group, a golfing buddy, a member of St. Matthews Episcopal Church, had a fine voice and sang in the church choir and was the 11:00 p.m. TV news anchor for one of the major networks. He was also a horse racing buff and notoriously frugal.

He called Fran one morning before his second wedding and asked if she thought I could play the organ for the wedding. Having retired as church organist at St. Matthews several years earlier and not having played a single note since, she said she didn't think I would want to take on that responsibility.

The wedding was to take place in Peninsula, Ohio, a stop on the old Ohio Canal, a short distance south of Brecksville, in the Bronson Memorial chapel/church, which was very small, probably built in the early 1800s, and only seated about 50 people.

Doug understood her refusal on my behalf, but then promptly asked if I could act as the official "photographer" of the wedding. Fran relayed this request to me, and, feeling somewhat flattered, I accepted. After all, I had taken thousands of photos in my "career," had taken two courses in photography, and had first class equipment; he was a good friend and had seen some of my photos of the bridge group; and we had been through a lot together.

I started early on elaborate preparations; I checked that all the components of the Canon were functioning properly; actually polished various lenses I might want to use; installed a new battery; bought multiple rolls of film; and was fully prepared for the big day. The church/chapel was the smallest I had ever seen but very quaint. I used my tripod and took all the traditional poses: the Bride, a co-anchor with Doug, in her simple, white cotton dress (bought in Mexico by one of her fans and given to her) the Groom, her father, a minister, who had flown from Florida to attend, plus multiple poses of groups of family combinations.

Afterwards, there were many candid shots of the guests mingling in front of the church before leaving for the reception to be held at the Mayfield Country Club on the far east side of Cleveland, where I would continue in my role of "official" photographer. (Incidentally, I remember meeting and being impressed by Sam Rutigliano, head coach of the Cleveland Browns at that time who appeared much larger in person than on the TV screen. Shortly after meeting him I had to reload the first roll of film in the Canon and retired to the cloak room where I had stashed my camera bag with its ample supply of fresh film. That was when I discovered to my horror that I had not turned the lens the final notch when inserting it in the camera body, and therefore the flash photos taken in the church were not synchronized and the exposures, taken at 1/60th of a second in low light conditions, would be under lighted and washed out, foggy and useless.

Given all the surrounding circumstances, it had to be one of the worst moments in my life. I did load the new roll of film, made sure the lens was seated properly and took several more rolls of film, all of which turned out fine. The new battery I had installed as part of my preparations ensured that all the automatic functions of the Canon performed perfectly.

But everything on the first roll, the most important record of the ceremony, was damaged beyond repair. I went to the expense of taking the foggy, indistinct negatives to the same professional film finishing laboratory which did all the photographic work for *The Cleveland Plain Dealer* to see if they could do some magical enhancement to produce at least some idea of the event, but there was nothing they could do, and they made prints that proved it. I don't remember how I told Doug, what had happened, or if he appreciated how bad I felt, how embarrassed I was. As I recall, he was disappointed but good natured about it and we remained good friends. It helped that there were many unofficial photographers among the guests who captured what I missed and not all was lost.

I was glad for my Chataqua training when I took a photo of a white, Chinese tree peony, "White Star of China" in my collection of peonies in Brecksville. It turned out well enough to be used for the President's Christmas greetings sent to members of the American Peony Society the year I held the office, following a tradition established by my predecessors. The previous summer I had supplied some of the peonies used when Queen Elizabeth came to Washington, D.C., May 1991, on a state visit. She stayed at the British Embassy, and the first thing she saw upon entering the front door was a beautiful arrangement in the "Hague" heavy silver vase of some of my early hybrid peonies, mostly the coral pinks. The arrangements of the flowers, and indeed all the flowers used in the rooms and in the dining tents outdoors were exclusively peonies, and the other party decorations during the Queen's stay were done by Don Vanderbrook, one of my peony blossom customers, a Cleveland floral designer famous for his work as a party planner all up and down the East coast. My payment for the blooms I supplied was an 8" x 10" enlargement of the arrangement in the Hague vase.

Since I was sending my photo of "White Star of China" to my fellow APS members for Christmas and Vanderbrook had told me that the peony, not the rose, was Queen Elizabeth's favorite flower, I had the "*chutzpah*" to ask myself, "Why not send a picture of "White Star" in a Christmas card to the Queen, at the same time advising her that the first flowers she saw on her recent visit came from my garden?"

I found out the proper way to address a card to the queen from a member of our Florida condo association who came from Chester, England, and he told me that the queen responded to every card and letter she received, and assured me I would receive an acknowledgement of my card. So I composed a humble Christmas greeting, hand printed it on the card with the photo of "White Star of China" stuffed into the pocket on the face of the card and mailed it to Buckingham Palace, London, England. I did not address it to: "Queen Liz," as my English jokester condo friend first suggested.

It was one of the biggest thrills of my life when two or three weeks after Christmas I did receive an acknowledgement of my Christmas card, written by one of her Ladies in Waiting: "I am commanded by The Queen to thank you so much for the kind message of good wishes you sent to Her Majesty for Christmas and the New Year, and for the photograph of one of your peony blooms you sent for her to see. The Queen much appreciated your thought for her at this time, and I am to convey to you Her Majesty's sincere thanks." I'm glad the letter was typewritten because the salutation and closing signatures are almost undecipherable. She did type "Lady in Waiting" beneath her signature. Naturally, I kept the letter which is one of my prized possessions and kept in the photo album of my peony blossoms on the coffee table in my living room which you may inspect at any time. I sometimes wonder if I should have pursued the matter and continued to send her pictures of my better blooms in the following years. She might have asked for my advice for her gardens. Sure! I have a framed enlargement of the same blossom hanging in my entry hall. It was an exceptional blossom and an excellent photographic image.

As the years went by and our vacation trips to Europe ended because we started spending our winters in Florida after my heart attack, there were fewer and fewer family celebrations to record, I used my camera less and less and eventually decided to sell it. It was a sad occasion, the end of an era in many ways; I don't remember how (e-Bay?) or when, or even to whom I sold it.

# Chapter VIII

## Golf

I have many, many memories of my golfing life; it was almost an obsession and I spent hundreds of hours playing and practicing in many locations, and in some very unpleasant weather. It made no difference. I had to be out there trying to better my score and try to break the ever illusive 80 strokes.

I remember when our family was only Mother, Dad, Russ and me, when I must have been seven or eight years old. After dinner, the family would go to the "Big Met." Metropolitan Park operated 18-hole golf course down in the valley along the Rocky River. Mother and Dad would play 9 holes; at this time golf was considered an upper-class activity, something worth striving for, a way to join the elite. Russ and I would be their caddies, carrying their canvas golf bags, which had only 5 or 6 cheap clubs in them, so they weren't too heavy for us. We would tee their balls up with "Scotch" tees made by taking damp sand from a bucket on the tee and compressing it into a small pyramid on which we would place the ball. Dad was right handed and Mother was left handed, which was convenient since they would allow us to hit a ball once or twice, when no one else could see us; it was simple since I was right handed and Russ was left handed. I remember that Dad had a poor swing, winding up at the top and flailing at the ball, which resulted in our searching for his ball in the rough on both sides of the fairways. His swing was a carryover from the baseball he played in high school. Of course, he could never have afforded golf lessons. Mother's swing was more compact; neither swing set a good example for me. This was my introduction to the game. Big Met was a very good course and kept in very good condition, and over the years I played there many times.

1 remember the last time I ever played with my Dad; I was an adult and Dad was getting older and had not swung a club in years. I was surprised he still owned a set of clubs. We played on a gray afternoon at the "Little" Met course which was a short distance from "Big Met," and had only 9 holes: more suitable and enjoyable for beginning players. I don't remember much about our round. The score wasn't important; it was just nice for the two of us to spend an afternoon together. And it was a chance for my Dad to see how my game had developed and how well I could hit the ball.

I do not recall much about those very early days. I think I played mostly with my brother, Russ, who carried both right-handed and left-handed clubs in his bag. Having been forced to learn to write right-handed in grammar school, he would start a round of golf hitting the ball right-handed, but after two or three poor shots, and increasing levels of frustration would pull one of his left-handed clubs out of the bag and start playing left-handed. I think we used Mother and Dad's clubs.

Russ never hit the ball well enough to love the game as I did. From the beginning I seemed to have a knack for hitting the ball well, which was improved by the early instructions I received the few times I played with John McCarthy, the college student, who lived across the street from us on Parkwood Road. He was a short, compact boy weighing about 140 pounds and could hit the ball a mile. He gave me tips that were very helpful and improved my ball-striking ability: extend the club head straight back from the ball; do not lift it at the beginning of the swing. My first tip! What a thrill to hit the ball long and straight.

One summer, when we were in high school, our mother arranged for Russ and me to spend a week's vacation at the Geiger's cottage at Linwood Park. We had a wonderful time, swimming, and playing tennis, and using the hole in the fence after dark to sneak into Crystal Beach, the amusement park next door to the cottage. We had our golf clubs with us and played the 9-hole golf course on the western edge of Vermilion, Ohio; it may have been called Huron Shores. My only memory of the course is that the southern boundary was the railroad tracks of the Nickel Plate line and it was exciting when a train roared past while I was trying to hit the ball. It was a short course and I think this was the first time I ever achieved a score of 80 for 18 holes. But it didn't count because I had teed the ball up for every shot, even in the fairway. I didn't know that this was a no-no. I was young and so innocent.

I remember hitting golf balls from the field next to our cottage on Tiedeman Road in the direction of the road, sometimes over the road. I do not remember where the golf balls came from. I'm sure they were well used and had big cuts on the cover, which added to the balls erratic flight. By this time, my father, who only played once or twice a year at mortgage banker outings, had upgraded his clubs to a matched set of Ralph Gudahl clubs manufactured by the Wilson Sporting Goods Company, and I had inherited his old clubs. The one club I remember is his old driver which had the name Denny Shute on it; there was something about the shape of the head which I liked, and I seemed to be able to hit the ball well with it. It was the early days of the game and the other clubs had wooden, hickory shafts. I learned later that Denny Shute was a professional golfer from Cleveland who had won some major tournaments, including the Masters, and many years later, Fran and I played at a 27-hole golf course he owned on Route 21 (Brecksville Road) near Barberton, Ohio.

There was also a short golf course, what would now be called an "executive" course, called Roseland on Tiedeman Road south of us, near Biddulph Road. It was built around the Big Creek which ran behind our cottage. I am surprised that I only played it once or twice and remember so little about it since it was so near us, and I could easily walk to it.

This was the unlikely background for what became a lifelong passion for the game. Unfortunately, there was no country club in the picture, and thus no opportunity for instruction from a teaching professional at the beginning.

A golf swing is in some respects an unnatural movement and the muscles used have to be trained; it absolutely requires a trained observer to inculcate the proper movements. I learned that I could not make my muscles translate the words on the written page containing the tips of the touring pros into a proper motion because I could not see what my swing looked like. Even though it "felt" right, the ball did not do what it was supposed to. This was sad because it resulted in a lifelong quest for a better, more reliable, more consistent swing. For years I had to rely on tips from friends who were better golfers than I was, and the rare tips from pros on the tour which "spoke" to me that I clipped from the golf magazines I subscribed to. By the time I had to retire from the game, I had accumulated a file about 2" thick of articles that addressed what I considered my weaknesses, which used words that my muscles seemed able to absorb and respond to. When I was able to afford real lessons, I felt the teaching pro always used many different ways to describe what he wanted me to do, looking for the magic combination of words that would go through my ears directly to my muscles.

My playing "career" was interrupted by World War II and resumed after we were able to buy our first house. I played with a group of neighbors on Saturday mornings on public courses. As I grew older, I was able to play at the annual golf outings of the Mortgage Bankers Association, representing our company, at various country clubs, an exciting treat for me. I received business invitations from Land Title Guaranty & Trust Company, one of their forms of entertainment, and Jack Wyse, owner of *Properties Magazine*, a monthly trade paper, in which we advertised.

There was also a three-year layoff from playing golf while I worked on completing our home on Oakes Road. I knew myself well enough to know that I could not afford the hours required to complete a round of golf (which was an almost irresistible temptation, stealing hours from the finish work on the house) with any hope of meeting a deadline for completing the work, which was imperative because of the loan commitment secured by our company from the Aetna Life Insurance Company, which had a one year expiration date.

After the house was completed, however, my golfing adventures came into full bloom. My equipment was upgraded thanks to my father's birthday gift of a new set of Sam Sneed golf clubs made by Wilson, and several years later a birthday gift of custom-made clubs from Kosar Golf of Cuyahoga Falls, Ohio. Getting fitted for these clubs was a new experience for me. I remember making an appointment for the fitting (slightly different from being fitted for a business suit) and Mr. Kosar watching me hit innumerable golf balls into a net in his shop. After a long session of experimenting with clubs of different swing weights, his deciding that a set of clubs with a swing weight of D-5 with extra stiff, extra long shafts would be appropriate. My age, height and weight were part of the equation. The clubs had metal shafts, wood heads for the No. 1 (driver) 3 and 5, and stainless steel heads, with an unusual shape for the irons. I used these clubs for many years with some success.

I kept up with advances in golf club technology through the ads in the golfing magazines: *Golf* and *Golf Digest*; well aware of the temptations dangled before me by the promise of lower scores to be achieved by better equipment. This was a lucrative business, driven by an increasingly popular sport, as evidenced by the large number of new golf courses constructed all over the country. It was also helpful that income tax regulations during this period allowed country club memberships and business entertainment at the clubs to be tax deductions, which helped fuel the boom.

I finally succumbed when I read of a new theory: light swing-weight was better than heavy swing-weight. Up until this time I had always assumed that the heavier the swing weight, which ranged from C-5 for ladies to D-5 for men, the farther the ball would go. My game was not improving using my, by now old D-5 clubs, so I decided to investigate the lighter clubs. I remember going to a driving range with a pro shop in Fairlawn, a westerly suburb of Akron, Ohio and being invited to try the lightweight C-8 clubs made by several of the big-name golf club manufacturers. After comparing the various brands, using their 5 irons, hitting enough times with each to get the feel, and the distances obtained, I kept coming back to a name I had never heard before, Dave Peltz, who had apparently started a new company to take advantage of the new thinking, and called his clubs "Featherlight." I thought they also happened to have the most pleasing appearance. They were swing weight C-8. This was the last set of clubs I ever owned, with the exception of an occasional utility club I added to my bag, and when Peltz went out of business I bought another set of Featherlights at a close-out sale for both Fran and me to have just in case a club was lost or stolen, it could be replaced.

I don't remember the price but am sure it was in line with the other brands, and I bought a set. Later I bought a set for Fran who had been struggling with a very expensive set of Haig Ultra clubs. I do not remember where we bought them but know that we were not told the swing weight was D-5, the same as my Kosar clubs, and much too heavy for her. Her new Featherlights with a swing weight of C-5 were a revelation. She hit the ball beautifully, outdrove many of the men in the couples we played with and began to enjoy playing, even joining a women's league which played once a week.

I remember clearly my first chance to use my new Featherlights. We had planned a 10-day vacation which started out with our driving to St. Louis to attend the wedding of one of the Matthey (Polar Bear) daughters. After we checked into our motel, Fran took a nap, and I went off to a nearby driving range with my new clubs. I was amazed that my swing felt no different, except it did not require as much effort, but the ball went much farther. I was ecstatic and anticipated great things to come. I don't remember much of the wedding, except that the reception was held at the Bellerive Country Club where the Mattheys were both playing members. On later visits I was able to play the course, which was outstanding, as was to be expected.

After the wedding, we continued on the rest of our short vacation traveling across I 61 east, all the way from St. Louis to Williamsburg, Virginia, stopping in Clarksburg, West Virginia, overnight. We both loved the Williamsburg experience, and, as an additional bonus for me, I was able to play the Robert Trent Jones designed Golden Horseshoe golf course with my new clubs. I did not set the course record but noticed that I did not feel the muscular fatigue at the end of the round that I used to feel with my old clubs. This was an unexpected benefit, which continued until I could no longer play, and became increasingly helpful as I grew older.

Most of my golf was played in Ohio and Florida, but in recalling my golfing history, I was surprised to realize how many other states I have played in: Michigan, Indiana, Illinois, Missouri, West Virginia, Virginia, North Carolina, South Carolina, Georgia, Pennsylvania, New York, Massachusetts, Connecticut, New Hampshire, Maine and California. My only golfing experience in a foreign country was playing a very poor course in Stratford-on-Avon in Ontario, Canada. I missed two opportunities to play in Europe on our travels there, always a regret: once in St. Ives when a club championship caused an invitation to be retracted, and once, when the opportunity to play in Scotland with my son-in-law, John Mihocik, had to be cancelled by my recovery from a gall bladder operation. Compiling this list of states brings back many memories of courses played and the people I played with.

After our house on Oakes Road was finally completed, I have warm memories of the many times I came home from work and after dinner, picking up Grandma Bahr, the baby-sitter who lived across Oakes Road from us, and then driving with Fran the short distance to Seneca Golf Course, which had 36 holes and was owned by the City of Cleveland, although located in Broadview Heights. It was twilight golf for Fran and me and we were usually finishing the 9th hole in the dark. I remember more than once, Fran exclaiming, after the 4th or 5th hole, "I wonder if the children are alright!" Golf requires such concentration that there is not much room for anything else in one's mind. It was a wonderful, healthy way to relieve the stress of daily living. I always seemed to score better when playing just with Fran, and she often wondered out loud why I couldn't score as well as when playing with the "boys." I never quite understood either, but it was true.

Seneca came to feel like my home course, I played it so often. Many times, when it was too late for the two of us to play 9 holes, I would go to the course to practice alone. Our neighbor, Ed Kregenow, played in a regular foursome which had been together for years. They were regulars and well known to the cashier. The regular cashier knew I was Ed's neighbor, and when I showed up, when it was already twilight, would wave me through without charging me because I couldn't finish 9 holes before dark. I would go out to one of the nines and practice, hitting five balls off the tee, then hitting them up to the green and putting out for the first few holes. As it grew darker, I stopped putting, but continued to hit multiple balls off the tee until it was so dark it was hard to find them and time to try to find my way back to the parking lot. This was a great form of relaxation for me, and the practice also helped improve my game.

One of the foursomes I played with regularly on Saturday mornings, after we were living in Brecksville was formed by Oliver "Bud" Thompson, a combination attorney-CPA who was also a member of the Mercator Club, a small Midwest service club which met on Tuesdays at the Statler Hotel. Bud invited me to play with him; another Mercator member "Al" Szabo, an architect; and one of his clients, a Scottish Jew, named Arthur Barnett. He was the fur buyer for Sears Roebucks, which had only two stores in greater Cleveland at that time: one at W. 105th and Lorain, on the west side of Cleveland, and the other on Carnegie Avenue on the East side. It probably took close to an hour to get from one store to the other, and if anyone called to talk to Arthur, he was always unavailable because he was traveling from one store to the other, which made him somewhat mysterious and very elusive. He had a little bottlebrush moustache, was average size, and always impeccably dressed. We played at Landerhaven Golf Club, located in Pepper Pike, a very nice public course where tee times could be reserved, a very important factor on a Saturday morning. Arthur, who was probably ten years older than us, spoke with an interesting accent, and was always the first to arrive. The Jewish jokes he told with his Scotch accent made them funnier than they really were. He was so excited to be playing golf with us that he had to get up at 4 a.m. to prepare himself, which involved a long soak in a tub, not a simple shower, and then dousing himself in a very pungent cologne, which could be detected 15' away.

He had an unusual swing, bouncing the club shaft off his neck and re-gripping it on the downswing, producing a buggy-whip effect. This produced a slice to the right ball-flight (a banana ball) which was so consistent that he aimed at the left side of the fairway and put the ball after it finished its curved flight in the middle of the fairway. He was not a long ball hitter, but very consistent.

I played a lot of golf with Bud Thompson over the years. He joined Berkshire Hills Country Club, far east on Cedar Road, and later Acacia Country Club, closer in at the northeast corner of Cedar and Richmond Roads. Acacia was higher on the social scale than the others and a sign that he had "arrived.' He lived on Lander Road across the street from The Country Club, the most exclusive country club in Greater Cleveland.

Bud knew one of the members, Skane Bowler, who was only slightly older than us and was the President of the Western Reserve Life Insurance Company, a small local life insurance company. Skane invited Bud to play one day and to bring along a friend, and that was how I got to play that course. It was a fine course, but it was the locker room that impressed me. I had never seen such a large, comfortable, luxurious locker room before.

We had an enjoyable round and Skane said we would have to do it again. Sure enough, he invited us to play again the next year. We had changed and were in our golfing togs, eating lunch on the patio outside the Grill Room when a storm came up suddenly, with thunder and flashes of lightening in the distance. Skane's father had been struck by lightning on a golf course and Skane was terrified by it. He said very abruptly that he was sorry, but we would not be playing that day and we finished our lunch. I only played the course once; but got to use the glorious locker room twice.

Another golfing memory, is the time Bud and I were invited by the Land Title Guarantee & Trust on a three-day golf outing at the Lakeview Golf Club resort in Morgantown, West Virginia. Our hosts were Dan Crane, President of Land Title Guarantee & Trust Company, and my best business friend and luncheon companion, Roy Hausheer, V.P. We went on a Thursday and returned on Saturday. The accommodations and food were excellent, and the golf course was outstanding. The green on one of the holes was on the highest point on the course and overlooked a bend in the Youghiogheny River, two or three hundred feet below. Another hole was 600 yards long, straight down hill and was used for a ski run during the winter months.

This hole stands out in my memory because I hit two of the best consecutive shots of my life, a driver and a three wood, and my ball rolled off the back of the green. Unheard of distance for me. I had never done anything like it before. Unfortunately, the green sloped sharply to the front and my first putt rolled off the front of the green. It took three more putts. I scored a bogey, one over par instead of a very rare eagle, two under par.

On one of the rounds we were finishing in the late afternoon of a gray, threatening day. I think we may have been on the 17th hole, which was a par 4, a straight hole slightly sloping downhill, the only apparent trouble the trees on both sides of the fairway. Suddenly it started to rain and there was lightening, which seemed to travel horizontally down the fairway in the direction we were going. I thought I could smell the distinctive odor of ozone, it was so close, and I was frightened, remembering Skane's father. We put up our umbrellas. The rain was light enough that we finished the round. That was one round I was glad was over. It was folly to take such a risk.

The other thing I remember about the trip was Bud's behavior. He had recently joined Acacia Country Club and was constantly praising its amenities compared to those of what our hosts were providing for us at the resort, within their hearing. I winced and was embarrassed for him, and for being the other guest. I had nothing but good things to say about the whole experience and I was profuse in my thanks when we parted.

Bud was an only child, had reddish hair, freckles, and wore glasses. He was medium height and did not have the physique of a golfer; but he did love the game. He represented professionally, a number of the younger players on the tour, which helped him gain entrée to many courses. At some point he bought an airplane (which I never saw) and flew it all over the country, which enabled him to play all 100 of the top-rated U. S. courses in one year. An article about his feat appeared in one of the golfing magazines. I stopped playing with him after he joined Acacia because I could not afford the high greens fees I would have had to pay. It was time. We had outgrown each other.

He had a continual truculent manner about him and seemed to be trying to assert his superiority in every situation. I certainly didn't think it was very appropriate when in the role of a guest. He had a delightful wife, Phyllis and two daughters. Most of the time when we had lunch in Cleveland, which was often, I did not enjoy it. I was embarrassed by his treatment of the young waitresses, with whom he invariably became too friendly in his remarks. It was sophomoric. I was always surprised because he had two daughters, and someday one of them might work as a waitress and have to endure the same kind of treatment.

When Bud was elected president of the national (actually Midwest) Mercator Club, he appointed me his vice president-secretary, and we made annual visits to the other clubs. We always planned our visits in the summertime and were able to play golf with the local members. I remember playing the public course in Indianapolis, part of which was inside the stadium where the Indianapolis 500 Race is held every Memorial Day. The day we played our host was one of the local Mercator members, Floyd Cutler, who owned a health food store. It was a few days before the race and several of the contestants were doing practice runs. It is very hard to concentrate on hitting a golf ball with the distraction of race cars zipping around a surprisingly bumpy track at 200 mph. The noise level was growly high. I also remember the name of one of the other members, with a most unusual name, Golden Platinum Silver, a dentist, also a golfer, who must have had an interesting pair of parents. (At least one of them!)

On our many trips during his two years in office we played the Notre Dame University course in South Bend, the N.C.R. (National Cash Register) Country Club in Dayton, and a course near the Lincoln Inn, on the west side of Columbus. This was a competitive event involving members from all the clubs. One of the Columbus member's last name was Jaeger, I remember, and he was an insurance agent. Someone told us one of his customers was a young college golfer named Jack Nicklaus. I have always wished that the Columbus club had brought in a "ringer" named Nicklaus to help win the trophy. It would have been fun to be able to say, in my later years, that I played in a tournament with Jack, seeing how his career turned out.

Among the powerful memories that stand out from the thousands of hours spent on golf courses over the course of thirty years, one of the fondest is those spent with our daughter, Nancy, who took up the game after her second marriage to John Mihocik, a serious golfer with a handicap of 7-8. He was the golf coach at my old high school, Lakewood. Several times my birthday card from her included the present of an invitation to play a round of golf with her, just the two of us. I remember playing ValleyAire on State Road near our Brecksville house, twice, and once at Dorlon Park, near where I now live in North Ridgeville. These are very precious memories, and not because of the golf.

On another occasion Nancy invited me to a mixed couple's Sunday afternoon golf outing at Sweet Briar Golf Course in Avon Lake. We played only 9 holes and were probably the only father-daughter couple. There were the usual prizes at this sort of outing: closest to the hole, lowest number of putts, lowest gross and lowest net scores, longest drive, etc. On the long drive hole, a short Par 4, I was lucky and hit my drive "on the screws" almost to the green, about 240 yards, very long for me at that time, and won the prize, which I think gave great pleasure to Nancy. I remember, after eating, one of her friends approached me and asked, very politely, "Mr. Schmidt, did you use your No.3 Wood?" I think he was serious, not trying to make his friend's father feel good, and seemed a little disappointed to learn, "No, I used my driver." I don't remember what the prize was, or my score, or Nancy's. It was just great being with her.

In contrast to that sunny afternoon, I remember a similar occasion when a lady's group that Fran belonged to, which played once a week at a sporty little 9 hole course, St. Bernard, (the owner was not religious: he owned a St. Bernard dog, as well as the golf course) on Edgerton Road in Broadview Heights. The group, I do not recall what they called themselves, held their end-of-the-season outing, and invited their men to join them. We picked up another couple who lived nearby and proceeded to play the "tournament." I played very well, drove the green on one of the Par 3s, using my No. 5 wood, and ended up with a score of 35, the first and only time I ever broke par. I was seething with inner excitement. After the meal, the prizes were awarded, and I waited and waited for my name to be called. It never was. They had no prize for Low Gross!

I have pleasant memories of golfing occasions with members of our Brecksville duplicate bridge group. One weekend in early fall four couples, the Billings, Sutherlands, Adairs, and we traveled to Ann Arbor for a football weekend. None of the others had ever been to a Big Ten game with all its crowds and excitement or been inside a bowl as large as the Michigan Stadium which seated 100,000+people at that time. I think Fran was pleased that our friends would learn a little more of her background.

This was the weekend where I was stung multiple times when I disturbed a yellow jacket nest at the edge of our pond, while setting a muskrat trap before leaving on our little trip. Our baby sitter, Grandma Butts, applied liberal amounts of baking soda to the multiple stings on my waistline and face, and I must have looked as though I belonged in a minstrel show when we met the others in Toledo for dinner. We went on to Ann Arbor and checked in to our motel, and the next morning, we all played golf at the Barton Hills Country Club, which was arranged for us by friends who lived in Ann Arbor, whom we had met at Camp Michigania. I don't remember much about the course, other than seeing a deer on one of the holes.

I remember feeling very good that our friends had a little taste of the atmosphere of the campus and the town where Fran and I met on our memorable first date.

Twice, this same Brecksville group spent long weekends as guests of the Sutherlands at their country club, Canton Brookside which is a wonderful, challenging course, one of the highest ranked in the whole state of Ohio. It has a large club house with luxurious corporate suites on the second floor for the use of the Hoovers (vacuum cleaners), Timkens (ball bearings), and Beldens (bricks), all headquartered in Canton, Ohio, where we stayed on Thursday and Friday nights, playing rounds of golf in the daytime and bridge at night. For a golfing couple it couldn't have been much better, a taste of how the "other half" lived.

I also remember Canton Brookside as the site of the most expensive round of golf I never played. The Sutherlands called us at the last minute one Sunday in the early fall to see if we were free to join them for lunch and golf. We were happy to accept and enjoyed a leisurely lunch in the Grill Room overlooking the 18th hole. It was a gray day which turned into a rainy day. We all agreed that we did not want to slosh around in the rain, and instead checked out the pro shop, where everything was of the highest quality and on sale at greatly reduced prices. It was the end of the season and the Pro had marked the prices of all his merchandise down to make way for fresh merchandise for the next season. We browsed from table to table and found many needed pieces of clothing at bargain prices with the Pro gleefully assisting us. The total bill when we finally left the shop was over $300! And we were not even members of his Club.

It seemed to me that we spent much more time on the golf course with Ted and Micky Billings than the others. I remember clearly the weekend we spent at Cambridge Springs, Pennsylvania, a little more than a two-hour drive from Brecksville, just east of the Ohio border, a few miles south of 1-90. It was on a sunny Friday morning and Ted and I were in the front seat of his Buick

Riviera, dressed for golf in our balloon-sleeved golfing sweaters and golfing slacks, the fashion of the day. The women, also dressed for golf, were seated in the back seat, our clubs in the trunk.

Ted, ignoring the drop in the speed limit from 70 mph to 60 mph on 1-90 upon entering Pennsylvania, within a mile after leaving Ohio, was picked up for speeding by a lurking Pennsylvania State Trooper. As the Trooper was checking Ted's driver's license in preparation for writing up the ticket, he asked us, "Are you men golf pros?" The women in the back seat burst out laughing, and Ted and I just replied, politely, "No, we were just on our way to the Cambridge Springs Hotel for a golfing weekend (hoping the prospect for the State realizing taxes from the money spent in a local establishment would persuade him not to write a ticket). Unfortunately, he did not understand this bit of practical economics and we had to follow him to a Justice of the Peace in a nearby village where Ted paid a $100 fine (which I did not offer to split with him). I have often wondered what the Trooper's actions would have been if we had said yes, trying to bluff our way out of the citation.

The Cambridge Springs Hotel was a typical, older resort type hotel, going slightly out of fashion, along with other similar hotels: The Homestead, White Sulphur Springs, and Tides Inn in Virginia, Bedford Springs near Pittsburg, to name a few. The rooms at Cambridge Springs were very comfortable and as soon as we were settled, we took off for the Cambridge Springs Golf Course, which was just an average public golf course. I remember the number of specimen trees lining the fairways as its most attractive feature.

I remember playing very well, almost as well as I did when alone, and reaching a long par 5 hole in two strokes by using my driver from the fairway for my second shot, rather than the usual 3 wood. And then, on the 9th hole, we were all on the green and the others had putted out and I was left with a tricky side hill, downhill putt of about 6-8 feet. Ted, who had been the scorekeeper for the day, said, "Come on, Bob. You can make this," and I proceeded to do just that, whereupon Ted exclaimed, "You just shot par!" He had played with me often enough to know that this was unusual, and what it meant to me. It was the first time I ever played nine holes in 36 strokes on a regular par 72 golf course.

Sadly, it was not a breakthrough event. I then proceeded to play the second nine in 44 strokes, for an even 80 strokes, 8 strokes over par. A total of eighty strokes always seemed to be my nemesis. And trying to break that magic 80 number haunted me all my golfing days.

Another Sunday in Brecksville, Micky called Fran to see if we would like to play golf and do a cook-out afterwards; we could supply the sweet corn, as it was in season and she knew we had an ample supply from our garden. She would supply the burgers. We agreed gladly, of course, and went to play 18 holes at Pine Hills Golf Course in North Royalton, one of our favorite public courses. Very sporty.

There are two reasons for me to remember this particular round of golf. First, on the second nine there was a short par 4 hole, tight out of bounds on the right, slightly elevated green, 312 yards in length. There was a foursome on the green putting out. Golfing courtesy requires waiting for those putting out to leave the green before hitting up to the green, for safety if no other reason. We did not wait because we would have to get to our second shot, and they would surely be off the green by then. Embarrassingly, I hit the longest drive of my life while they were still putting, and my ball rolled on to the green. They were almost as startled as I was and looked up and I made some gesture of apology with my arms from where I stood on the tee box. I don't remember much else about the rest of the afternoon.

The second memory is not as pleasant. During our cookout dinner on the patio at the rear of our house, we learned that this Sunday was their daughter, Cricket's birthday. When her mother, Micky, remembered, about 8 o'clock in the evening, she hurried to our phone to wish her twelve or thirteen-year-old daughter a happy birthday. Fran and I looked at each other, disbelievingly. How could parents prefer an ephemeral afternoon playing meaningless golf with friends rather than celebrating with their daughter on her special day? I never understood and I could never forget.

I had so many golfing experiences with Ted Billings. He was responsible for my first all-male weekend away from my wife and family. He asked me to be the fourth in a foursome made up with two of his old high school friends, whom I had never met: Dr. Dick Hilfer, his doctor, and Bill Stubbs, who owned his own insurance agency. They were planning a trip to Pinehurst in North Carolina. They had reservations at the Holly Inn (I still have the receipt for my bill with its ridiculous price measured by today's standards) for three days. There were five 18-hole courses to choose from, all starting from in front of the Pinehurst Hotel where we would have our breakfasts. We would play 36 holes a day, which I had never done before, and wondered if I was able to manage, walking in the morning with a caddy, and riding a golf cart in the afternoon to spare our legs. It was in the month of March, before Ted's, a building contractor, building season began. It was a twelve-hour drive; and we would stop half-way to sleep. Fran agreed that I should go, and I remember how excited I was at the prospect, buying bags of cookies and apples, and a pint of Old Crow bourbon, which I hoped would please the others. It was a big hit!

We had two good days of weather and I remember playing Courses No. 1 and 5, but not the others. And I remember a black caddy the first day who was the best caddy I had ever had. There were lots of pine trees and woe unto you if you hit into them and had to try to hit your ball off the pine needles; they were worse than a sand trap.

Breakfast at the big hotel was outstanding (there was no food service at the Holly Inn) and I loved being able to have a custom omelet made at the buffet. Dinner was equally good, and I remember strolling through the very tiny Pinehurst Village after dinner in the balmy spring weather, and finding a small, silver Paul Revere design bowl to take back to Fran. Even though I was having such a wonderful time, I felt a sense of guilt and wished she could be there with me, sharing my happiness. My little gesture did not sit too well with the others, none of whom took back anything for their wives.

They were pleased with their winnings (small) at my expense and could not get over the fact that I, a teetotaler, would be kind enough to buy them a bottle of whiskey.

Even though it was early in the season, mild and sunny, a season which was dictated for us by the demands of the building season imposed on Ted in northern Ohio, 1,000 miles away, the weather at Pinehurst turned bad with heavy rains the third day cutting short our trip. We planned to get together again the next year. I looked forward to the excursion the whole year.

The next year we went to Pine Needles, one of the four or five courses near Pinehurst, a golf course owned and operated by Peggy Kirk Bell, a lady golf pro from Warren, Ohio. This was a smaller operation than Pinehurst with only 18 holes, and I remember nothing about it. I do remember deciding on flying from Hopkins Airport this time, and not being able to take off because of very heavy fog - at 7 p.m.! We had driven to the airport after work in Ted's car and decided we would have to drive after all, overnight, if we were to meet the others on time. We had a slight problem because Ted's car had a flat tire as we were leaving the airport. We were further delayed until we changed the tire. I remember the heavy fog all the way to Pittsburgh, driving down the middle of the Ohio Turnpike, both of us leaning toward the windshield, straining to see the white stripe in the middle of the road. It was very nerve-wracking; and we stopped someplace in Virginia and called home the next morning to tell our wives what had happened. We did arrive close to the scheduled time and did play, but once again, the weather turned bad. It became very cold and when we saw snow on the ground, decided to leave a day early. Ted and I stopped in Roanoke, Virginia, to take a break and saw a movie starring Robert Mitchum, not one of my favorite Hollywood leading men.

We four got along together very well, but, alas, that was our last golfing trip together. I blame the weather.

However, Dick Hilfer was a member of the Medina Country Club in Medina, Ohio, easily accessible from 1-71. I remember many rounds of golf played there with Ted, some of them club competitions, one of which our foursome won. This resulted in a lot of good-natured ribbing by other members of the club who accused Dick of bringing in "ringers" in order to come in first. I remember the parking lot, the patio, the first tee, and one other hole with a large pond in front of the green, but not much else about the course.

Dick was also a member of a country club in Largo, Florida, about an hour's drive north of Ted's and our condos in Florida. He always included me when he invited Ted to play in their member-guest tournaments, which teed off at 9 a.m. Once again, I do not remember much about the course; but do remember how much I enjoyed the donuts and coffee provided before the game started, the luncheon buffet afterwards; the fun we had and the memories we shared.

I remember my return to the Lakeview Golf Resort in Morgantown, West Virginia, when my good friend, "Honest" Tom Rohrbach, the electrician who wired our house on Oakes Road (and became one of my favorite bridge partners) organized a group of about 20 men to play in what he laughingly called the "Barely Open." It was my chance to reciprocate, and I invited Ted and my son-in-law, John Mihocik, to be part of the Cleveland contingent. We went twice. About this time the resort had added another 18-hole course some distance away, which was more difficult than the original 18 holes near the hotel. Two or three of my memories include rooming with Ted. His snoring was incredible and started the minute his head hit the pillow. I had never heard anything like it. I came to the realization that if I made the same noises (of which I had been accused by Fran and our children for years and I had always stoutly denied) it would explain our sleeping in separate rooms. If the sounds Ted produced had been called for in a symphonic score, he would have qualified as a virtuoso, and could have had a contract with the Cleveland Symphony.

This was another three days of all male companionship and I found I enjoyed the atmosphere very much. Perhaps I responded to a camaraderie similar to what I had known in the army and at college. I didn't feel I had to be on guard at all times or worry about doing or saying something offensive when ladies were present.

We used my car because of its large trunk which was necessary to transport four golf bags and the other necessities, and I did the driving. I remember having such severe back pain the second year that I seriously considered canceling the trip. I could hardly sit on the front seat of the car. I had rolled up a towel to put behind my back for support. It had happened once before on our return from a trip to the east coast and I remember leaving the motel in Dayton, Ohio, where we stayed the last night and going directly to Lakewood Hospital to seek treatment.

I remember stopping before we reached Youngstown on the Ohio Turnpike at a McDonald's (at which another carload of men also going to Lakeview had stopped) and remaining in the car while the others went inside. They brought me an egg concoction to eat on the way. (I maintained my record of never having tasted a McDonald's hamburger, a record that still stands proudly today.)

I was glad, for obvious reasons, that this year my roommate was John Mihocik, who had recently married our daughter, Nancy. John, who slept very quietly, had to help me out of bed and pull me to my feet the first morning, and help me dress. I remember taking some Motrin before breakfast and I'm sure John was very concerned. I wondered if I could even swing a golf club, and while waiting our turn before the first tee I practiced swinging very gingerly. It was actually more of a gentle, waving motion. That driver shot off the first tee is one of the few I can recall the feeling of: the languid, slow motion movement down into the ball (à la Julius Boros) which popped up in the air and landed about 150 yards from the tee. After about the 5th hole the pain began to ease somewhat, and I was able to finish the 18. The improvement continued for the rest of the rounds we played, and the drive home was far more comfortable, if not quite back to normal, than the drive down to Morgantown.

It seems a shame that these are the only memories that remain of two such joyous occasions, and such outstanding golf courses. Also, I have always wondered why, considering the long history of my relationship with Tommy, his part in the construction of 5320 Oakes Road, my role in the financing of his home on W. 130th Street in North Royalton by our company, the hours spent playing bridge with him, which his wife believed was the cause of his stopping drinking, the two "Barely Opens," the many contacts in the following years, why I never played a single round of golf with him. It's something I regret, something that would have put a seal on a very rare friendship.

Other recollections of rounds of golf played with friends include one played with my old high school band friend, Bruce Hardy. One afternoon after work while we were still living in our first home on Ridgewood Drive, we met at a course located close to our home (which I cannot remember the name of) at the northeast corner of Ridge Road and Ridgewood Drive, actually within walking distance of our house. I remember how badly I played and my difficulty in hitting a straight ball. This was the first time I had ever played with Bruce, who was an excellent golfer. I was ashamed of playing so poorly and was sure he would never want to play with me again. In fact, it was many years later before we did.

After it was all over, Bruce gave me an explanation of the cause on my problem. It had to do with the way I gripped the clubs. I was deliberately placing my right thumb on the right side of the golf stick in order to add extra leverage to the club-head going through the ball. This was causing the club head to "buggy whip" and arrive at the ball too soon, hence the hooks and slices and inaccuracy. The next time I played and made sure my right thumb was on the left side of the shaft at the start of the swing, I began to hit the ball straight and where I was aiming. It was so simple. I was very grateful for this tip but wondered why Bruce had waited so long to tell me what my problem was.

My other memory of this course, so nearby and so little used by me, involved an afternoon after work when I entertained (it always seemed the job fell to me as the oldest brother) one of the young men from the Aetna Life home office mortgage loan department. Senior officers were always entertained on their visits by my father and mother, as was fitting.

My guest was E.W. (Ted) Bush, a young Dartmouth graduate who lived with his mother in a farmhouse built in the 1700s in West Hartford, and was one of my favorite people to work with on my mortgage loan submissions. He was of medium height, had "bushy" blondish hair, wore glasses and had, what looked to me like bloodshot eyes. Once or twice a year the Aetna Life would visit their loan correspondents and inspect the properties on which they had approved mortgages. They would list the properties they wished to see; it was my job to arrange the order in which we drove past, me in the back seat giving Dad directions to the next property. It was actually a fun way to get out of the office, and interesting for me to see the properties consecutively that I had appraised separately in the previous six months.

At the end of the day either Dad or I would take on the responsibility of feeding and entertaining our important Home Office visitors. On one of these trips I suggested a round of golf to Ted, and we chose to play at the course near our house. Ted changed from his business suit to his golfing outfit, which consisted of a pair of old ratty, khaki golfing shorts, a sweaty tee shirt, and a pair of drooping crew sox; which looked as though they might have been lying on the floor of a locker for months. I remember feeling slightly embarrassed by his appearance when we marched to the first tee in front of a veranda full of golfers, male and female, enjoying their after-round drinks.

I thought I might have heard a faint snicker. This all changed, for the spectators and for me, when Ted briskly teed up his ball and without any practice swings, without any hesitation, hit a flat, line-drive ball about 240 yards down the middle of the fairway. I thought I could hear a hush fall over the veranda. That is my only memory of playing with Ted.

On another of the Aetna inspection trips I remember, two men came, Ted Bush and John French. No golf was played on this trip, but both men were interested in the game. On this occasion Fran was included in the entertainment, and we took Ted and John to the Embers Restaurant in Akron, Ohio, a smaller city of about 120,000 people. The Embers was one of the most highly rated eating places in a town with many from which to choose, Akron being the home of four billion-dollar rubber companies as well as the Roadway Express Trucking Company.

The Embers was housed in an older brick two-story residence, converted into a restaurant, located on West Market, the main street. It had limited seating in the rooms on the first floor, with more private seating on the second floor. At this time, Akron was again hosting one of the major pro golf tour events at the Firestone Country Club. They were busy that evening and we had to climb to the second floor to be seated. After getting settled and looking at the menu, we noticed that Arnold Palmer, Jack Nicklaus, and Gary Player were seated at the next table, not six feet away. It was very distracting; hard to concentrate on our food; and even more difficult not to lean over and ask for an autographed menu. I thought what fabulous timing!

I remember that on one of my infrequent calls on the Aetna in Hartford (when my presence might help sell one of our larger commercial loan applications) after I had made my presentation and answered Mr. Swinehart's questions, he gave the rest of the afternoon off to Ed Bush and John French. He invited us to play golf at his country club, The Hartford Country Club, which I believe was quite exclusive. We played but I remember nothing of the course except the luxurious locker room where my guest locker was next to that of the Chairman of the Connecticut General Life Insurance Company. Mr. Swinehart had been on the golf team at Williams College, and was a scratch golfer. I always regretted, that in all the years I knew him, I never had the chance to play with him and see his swing.

The other business related golf events, that I remember, are the annual Mortgage Bankers Association outings at various country clubs on both the east and west sides of Cleveland. I remember particularly the Aurora Country Club and the Elyria Country Club which had difficult holes for me at that stage of my game. One happy occasion was the MBA outing at The Chagrin Valley Country Club where I won the prize for longest drive. The golfing was always followed by a happy hour and banquet. The after-dinner speaker I enjoyed the most was my friend, Jack Wyse, publisher of the *Properties Magazine*. He had an endless supply of very funny Jewish jokes, funny in either dialect or straight English.

Jack always invited me to his country Club, Hawthorne Valley once or twice a year and I felt very much at home there. This was business oriented; we placed advertising in *Properties*, but I like to think it was more than a business relationship. I counted him as a good friend. He always arranged that the other two members of the foursome were possible sources of business for me. I remember one round we played with Fred Rzepka, one of the largest apartment builders in the city, a survivor of the Holocaust, who escaped with his family to the east, not through Portugal, but Shanghai, and ended up in Australia. He might have met Henry Kissinger who followed the same route. Fred had a wonderful, sunny disposition, constantly expressing his gratitude for being where he was.

Another of the "contacts" that Jack arranged was for me to play in a foursome with Ben Stefanski, Chairman of the Third Federal Savings & Loan Association, which was located in the Slavic Village neighborhood on Broadway Ave. on the southeast side of Cleveland. I don't know what was in my host's mind because Third Federal was one of only two savings and loan associations in Cleveland that did not make commercial loans, which was my specialty. Mr. Stefanski was about fifteen years older than me, medium height, balding, very earnest, and was wearing shorts and a see-through fishnet white golfing shirt the day we played. He obviously took the game very seriously and every shot was a major production. He gripped the club so tightly, with clenched fists, that his knuckles were white. Finally, on the 16th hole he got his reward. He hit a stupendous tee shot, and I automatically exclaimed: "Oh, Uncle Ben!", that was tremendous." He whirled around and shouted, "How did you know to call me that? That's how all my customers greet me on Friday afternoon." I then learned that it was "my friend" Ben's custom to be at the bank on Friday afternoons after 5 p.m. to welcome all his customers who were coming into the bank to deposit or cash their paychecks. He tried to promote a friendly, family atmosphere and felt a handshake from the chairman might help.

I remember another incident that occurred at Hawthorne Valley. I happened to arrive at the same time as one of the other members, Jack Goldberg, who was driving a brand new Lincoln Continental, introducing the first year of a new and beautiful body style, and parked it in the circular drive in front of the main entrance to the clubhouse. My host, Jack Wyse, told me later that it was the first car of the new model sold in the city. Goldberg was head of the family, who "owned" the Ohio Savings & Loan, and were major apartment builders and owners in Cleveland. He leaned nonchalantly against the front fender of his new possession, inspecting his finger nails, polishing them against his chest, when one of the other members came up to him and asked, "How do you like the new car?" and Jack replied in a florid Yiddish accent: "What's not ta like!" It became one of my favorite expressions and was the first time I ever heard it.

In recalling the highlights of my golfing experiences, I have come to realize how much my sailing interfered with my golfing. Both activities took the better part of a day, and sailing was only practical on weekends, so what golf I played while owning a sailboat took place during the week which meant it involved business.

It was through business that I met and later played golf with the finest golfer I ever met, Elden Papke, who lived in Wichita, Kansas. Elden was almost as tall as me, very fair complexion (he took a prescription drug during the summer months to increase the ability of his skin to tan in sunlight), played piano in a dance band to earn his way through the University of Wisconsin, had a very strong sense of honor, and was married to a lovely wife whose father invented the rotary drill head used in digging oil wells.

Elden was a sole proprietor whose occupation was finding land suitable for drilling oil and leasing it and selling the leases to oil drillers, an occupation I had never heard of. I met him when a young Cleveland entrepreneur, Owen Lavelle, came to me seeking financing for the purchase of two producing oil wells in Oklahoma, which he and Papke wanted to buy in a partnership they had formed.

On the face of it, it was an impossibility to consider the Aetna for such an unconventional form of security, but I had attended a Case Study Seminar at Michigan State University sponsored by the MBA a short time previously and had listened to an exciting speech on the final day, given by a Vice President of Northwest National Life Insurance Company, who specialized in mortgages on types of security I had never heard of before, (like a fleet of shrimp boats on the West coast). Before dismissing Lavelle out of hand, it occurred to me that I might approach V.P. Anderson at the Northwest National, whom I had complimented after his presentation and might just remember me. So I called and was put through and he told me that Minnesota law did not permit lending on oil wells, but he had always wanted to be able to do so and to let him think about the problem over the weekend and he would get back to me. He called on Monday and said he thought he had found a way to get around the law; and invited me to bring my principals to Minneapolis to present the case. And this was how I met Elden Papke, one of the few men I met after my service in the army, who began to compare to my Army friends.

After securing a commitment from Northwest National, the oil well deal failed through no fault of mine, a terrible disappointment to both Papke and Lavelle, who would have become wealthy overnight if the deal had closed, and it would have been the single largest fee ever earned in our company's history. There were several later trips to Cleveland by Papke in connection with other deals he worked on with Lavelle, who was one of the younger members of the Shaker Heights Country Club on South Woodland Avenue, in Shaker Heights, a very fine course on interesting terrain, considering it was located in a very high priced older residential neighborhood; the first nine holes stretching out along a shallow valley where the Shaker lakes are located, paralleled by the second nine returning to the clubhouse. The clubhouse and locker room were old and had a homelike feeling, and very comfortable.

I had my first chance to play with Papke on one of his subsequent visits to Cleveland, when he was invited to play "Shaker" by Owen. He had brought his own golf clubs with him and this was the first time I had a chance to see a real golfer play and see what it meant to control the ball, not just hit it. He knew what type of ball flight he wanted, whether to slice or hook his shots, and could deliberately make the ball reflect his will; it was a revelation. And he was a very good putter.

As I recall, a fellow member, Loyal Buescher, a left-handed golfer who was an attorney and the Law Director for several east side suburbs, made up the foursome. (I was allowed out of the office to have fun while my brothers slaved away in the office because it might be the source of another big loan, and this one might close.) Another member, Ed Davis, who owned a Chevrolet dealership, who had a leg injury, rode a cart behind us and kept score. Lavelle had told Davis about Papke's prowess and Davis made a bet with Papke that he could not beat par, which I think was 71. On a course he had never seen before Papke proceeded to shoot 70 to win the bet. I had never seen anything like it before.

On another of his trips to Cleveland, this time without his own clubs, I made arrangements to play Canterbury Country Club, where Howard Hendershott, an attorney who represented me when we purchased our Cleveland apartment buildings, was a member. Canterbury has been the site of several major professional golf tournaments and was considerably more difficult than Shaker Country Club. Papke was fitted out with a loaner set of clubs which had woods and irons made by different manufacturers and it took him two or three holes to get accustomed to the strange clubs. He proceeded to score one over par. Again, an exhibition and an inspiration for me.

My final memory of playing golf with Papke, perhaps in a way more impressive than my earlier rounds with him, was when he stayed with us in Brecksville on his way home from trying to do a deal with the Tecumseh Small Motor Company in lower Michigan. This time, again, he did not bring his golf clubs with him. We decided we had enough time to play 9 holes before dinner at Sleepy Hollow Country Club, only a mile away from our house and one of the most beautiful courses I have ever played, built on scenic parkland on the slopes of the Cuyahoga River valley, We had a social membership, which entitled us to play five rounds a year, and Elden used Fran's set of ladies' clubs.

Many years earlier I had bought a complete set of very inexpensive clubs for Fran at the May Company, a large department store on Euclid Avenue in the center of downtown Cleveland, hardly a country club pro shop. I remember paying $83.00 for the complete set: 1, 3, and 5 woods and 2 through 9 irons, plus wedge. I remember the heads of the woods were made of wood and painted blue. And I remember being slightly embarrassed to ask Elden to play with such clubs. Of course, they were a light swing weight, made for a woman and had short shafts to fit the average height woman, 5' 6", and Elden was 6' 3". It took him 3 holes to get the feel of the clubs with their lighter, whippier shafts, and again he shot one over par on a very difficult course he had never seen before. I couldn't believe it. I wish there had been some way that I could have played with him regularly; I'm sure it would have improved my game and it was such fun to see how easy it was for him. If he could have afforded to take the time off from his business needed for preparation, he said he would have liked to try to qualify for the U.S. Amateur Open. In my starry eyes, I think he might have made it.

Another unforgettable memory I still think of frequently is the time I was invited to be the fourth in a foursome by one of my Yale classmates, Frank Kennard, who was a Vice President at the Union Commerce Bank. We had become acquainted (I did not know him while we were at Yale) when I recognized him a few rows in front of us when we stood at the intermission of a Yale Glee Club performance. We learned that he and his wife, Polly lived in Independence, Ohio, adjacent to Brecksville, and that Polly was a friend of our Brecksville duplicate bridge club member, Micky Billings, and this led to many evenings spent playing bridge, but not to my playing golf with Frank.

It was quite a surprise when Frank called and asked if I could join him and two of his cousins from out of town, who were visiting, for a round of golf at Sleepy Hollow. He had a tee time at 1 p.m. Saturday. I accepted happily (this would be the first time I would play with a classmate and possible future regular partner) but accepted with the proviso that I had to go into the office to review and put the finishing touches on a large loan submission and then take it to the main Post Office to send off to the Aetna. I might be too late to join them and would truly regret the chance to play with Frank and meet his cousins if I could not get there on time. (Frank's wife always pronounced his name "Fronk", which jarred me every time I heard it.)

I reached the P.O. just in time to mail my package and rushed to Sleepy Hollow 14 miles away; popped the trunk and changed shoes in a rush; paid my green fees in a rush; rushed to the first tee just as my group had finished their drives, no time for introductions; rushed to tee my ball up and hit it in a rush. The first hole was 500 yards long, slightly downhill with trouble on the right side of the fairway. I hit the longest ball I had ever hit there, down the right side, and hit a 7 iron over the green for my second shot!, had two putts and my first birdie of the day. It was the start of the best, most spectacular four consecutive holes in fifty years of golfing, in front of strangers, who for a short while must have wondered who this classmate of cousin Frank's was: a Pro?

The second hole was rated as one of the toughest Par 3s in the district: 215 yards long with plenty of room on the left, but impossible trouble on the right, very intimidating. I had the honors and hit another wonderful drive, using my No. 5 wood this time. The ball ended up about 18" from the hole! Another birdie. Two in a row. Unheard of.

The third hole, a 380-yard par 4, was another very difficult one to score par on. It had a deep, wide swale in front of the elevated green, and large trees on both sides of fairway to cause trouble if one strayed to the right or left, making it impossible to reach in regulation. Again, I drove first, again straight down the middle of the fairway to the very edge of the swale, then an 8 iron to within 18" of the hole, another birdie.

The fourth hole was another long par four, much easier than the preceding holes; wide fairway and the green nestled in a pocket of large trees, making an excellent target. Once again, I hit one of my longest drives, was on the green on the second shot, and had two putts for par. I had never played four holes of golf like that before in my life.

It's too bad that I didn't make my apologies, pick up my bag and go home, because I came back to earth with a thud for the rest of the holes and became the bogey golfer that I was. I have no idea of what Frank and his cousins thought after my first four holes, and did not play with Frank again, who joined Canterbury Country Club later, until we were both retired, he in South Carolina and we, in Florida.

The Kennards invited us to stay with them, play a round on their home course, and then go to Augusta the next day to watch the Wednesday practice round at the Masters Tournament, the only time I ever saw that famous course. The azaleas were in bloom and it is a very beautiful course, but from the members' tee locations did not seem to be as difficult as it appeared to be on television; quite different from the back tees used by the pros in a tournament.

Of course, one of the drawbacks to watching golf on TV is that it is impossible to see the subtleties of the contours of the greens: they all look flat, which is far from the case. Many golf courses make up for a lack of hazards or deep rough by having impossible-to-putt greens, certainly the case at Augusta.

In recalling my many memories of the rounds of golf I played over the years it interests me that that the actual rounds, which stand out, are not recalled by the course itself, but rather by the people I played with.

I compare walking the famous Augusta National which is on TV every Spring, admiring its beauty and immaculate condition in the company of friends, the Kennards, with actually playing on the Firestone C.C. course in Akron where many PGA events were played on TV with one of the Aetna Life's auditors, John Hayer, while he was in Cleveland auditing both the local Aetna's agents records, and our records as Mortgage Loan correspondents. I remember the course as being very nice, and how fortunate that Firestone employees had free memberships and access to a course of such quality. It was easier than it appeared on TV from the regular tees with many parallel fairways which facilitated easy recovery from a sliced or hooked shot, and the famous 16th hole, a very long downhill par 5, green guarded by a pond, a birdie opportunity which the pros tried to reach in 2 shots and having to decide whether to take the chance with the water hazard. The memories of the course, which I was able to play twice, thanks to one of our residential customers, Loren Tibbals, a sportswriter with the *Akron Beacon Journal*, who made arrangements with the Pro for us to play a private course, members only.

Two things I really remember about the course are Ted Billings slicing a drive onto an adjoining fairway, his ball clearly visible from our tee, and our watching a club member foursome coming down the fairway in our direction, picking up Ted's ball, and denying Ted's challenge to return his ball. It left a bad taste in our mouths, and reflected poorly on the golf club, and its type of members, hourly wage people from the Firestone production line, who obviously knew very little of the gentlemanly nature of the game.

And a round with John Hayer, our Aetna auditor, who was an eccentric. I always thought he was Irish, but learned he was of German descent. He was extremely frugal, and had become wealthy by buying Aetna Life stock, as well as General Electric and GM and AT&T in the early 1930's, the depths of the Great Depression. He had just started his career with Aetna when they learned he had bought a large number of shares of Aetna Life stock. The Treasurer of the company called him in to question if he knew what he was doing, and to warn him he thought it was a bad idea and a mistake to be buying at that time; that he was selling his own shares of Aetna. John's response was to say that he would buy all that he could. He bought and held his blue chips, and I am sure became a multi-millionaire, yet he remained a "lowly' traveling auditor for his entire career, on the road 90% of the time; he was not interested in becoming an officer of the Company, or to sit on the Board.

He chose which companies on his rota to audit by season, rather than location. He traveled the northern half of the country in the summer, and the Southern in the winter. In this way he could travel with his golf clubs because he was a fanatic golfer, about a 12-handicap player. When I knew him, he was probably in his 50s and I knew he would be thrilled to play a course as famous as the Firestone. I even remember the day we played: December 8th, a clear, sunny, warm day, in the 60s, and very unusual for northern Ohio at that time of the year. On earlier visits to Cleveland, John, I cite this as an example of his frugality, was his pride in having measured the size of the sleeping rooms in every downtown Cleveland hotel, large or small, and settling on the Hotel Allerton, a second tier hotel, at the corner of E. 13th Street and Chester Avenue as providing the best value per square foot, down to the fraction of a cent.

After our round  about which I remember nothing, no after-image on my retina of his swing, or his score, on the way back to Cleveland, John who was ecstatic about being able to tell other golfing friends about his having played Firestone, invited Fran and me to join him for dinner as his guests to show his appreciation. I accepted and had visions of a real treat at one of Cleveland's famous restaurants. I was bubbling with excitement when I told Fran about this treat about to be enjoyed.

We picked John up at the Allerton, and proceeded to have dinner at the Stouffers Restaurant at E. 6th Street and Euclid Avenue, a very good medium priced restaurant where I had lunch frequently, but hardly Marie Schreibers, or Fischer-Rohr's, or The Continental on Chester Avenue between E 9th Street and E. 14th Street, known as restaurant row. He did pick up the check and we dropped him back at the Allerton, the best sleeping bargain in Cleveland.

Another memory involving golf on a fine country club course that I should have very positive memories of, but don't, involves the Shaker Country Club and my business acquaintance, Owen Lavelle. Owen was about 6' tall, fair complexion, very outgoing and blustery, a hail, well met type of person whose family owned a well-known, large plumbing business in Lakewood, Ohio. He was a graduate of Ohio University, in Athens, Ohio. I don't know how or where he met his wife, Patty, whose family were members of Shaker Heights society and of the Shaker Country Club.

After graduation, Owen went to work with his father-in-law (whom I never met)) in his investment banking business, Fleming & Company. As might be expected, he became a Junior Member of Shaker Country Club, which would be useful in entertaining business clients. He was very proud of the club and his membership and it appeared that the older members of the club looked with affection to him to carry on the traditions of the club.

The occasion that spoils my memory of Shaker Country Club is the afternoon when Owen invited members of a group of men with wildly different backgrounds who met once a month in the

Land Title Guarantee & Trust Company lunchroom for a bridge game after work, that I had invited Owen to join, to play golf in the afternoon, if they wished, to be followed by dinner as his guests, in the main dining room of the club house, to be followed by an evening of bridge: a perfect way to spend a day, as far as I was concerned.

Owen, the host, arranged all the foursomes, and included me in his foursome which would tee off last. Before starting, he made bets with the other three players individually, and as a team; he and I were one team. He then proceeded to bet against me, his teammate, also. We would play using our handicap ratings, mine was 16 and his, 10, giving him a six-stroke advantage over me. I do remember the 10th tee, next to the half-way house where refreshments were available, and the 18th hole, a short par 4 dogleg to the left. Up to this point Owen and I had the same number of strokes and if I beat him by only one stroke on this final hole, he would lose his bet. I managed to make my putt for a par; his drive sliced off to the right, and he made a bogey 5, and I won. His game was off, and he lost every bet he made that afternoon.

It was embarrassing to see him rush off into the clubhouse, hoping his wife would be there with enough money in her purse to pay off his bets. I don't remember how much money he lost. As I recall, the meal was excellent, and the bridge its usual challenge. But the aftermath of the golf and what Owen revealed about his character when he had hoped (expected and needed) to win enough money from his guests, taking an unfair advantage of them, (best golfer on home course) to pay for the whole day, took away a little of the enjoyment of an otherwise perfect day. I am unhappy to associate such negative memories with such a beautiful place.

I remember with such pleasure the many times Fran and I played together: the hours away from the cares of daily life, in an almost invariably beautiful setting. We played locally at Seneca, Pine Hills, St. Bernards, Briarwood, Skyland in Medina County, where she hit a drive on the 1st hole from an elevated tee down into a low area under about an inch of water from the sprinklers, and when she asked me what should she do, pick up the ball and move it?, I told her, very gravely, that she had to play it as it lay, and she proceeded to do just that with the result of a gigantic splash of water, which drenched her golfing skirt. This did not endear me to her. We loved playing at Sleepy Hollow, so beautiful and so challenging. I loved having her all to myself and usually played my very best golf with her as my only witness.

It was unfortunate that one of the Ladies' Leagues which played at nearby Briarwood on Edgerton Road in Broadview Heights, which Fran joined, was dominated by a pair of low-handicap better golfers who dictated the placement of the tee markers. There were two holes with water in front of the men's tees, which required a well hit drive to clear the water; the ladies' tee was on the far side of the water normally. The "committee", comprised of the two low-handicappers, moved the ladies' tees to the men's tee which made it impossible for all but a few (the "committee") to clear the water, leading to much frustration and many lost golf balls. Those two holes ruined many good scores. It was very unfair and not in the spirit of the game. That and the early morning starting time made Fran decide to give up playing with the ladies. I think she enjoyed the more relaxed game with me and my encouragement as long as she was able to play.

We always took our golf clubs with us on our vacations, never knowing when we might have a chance to play. We played in northern Michigan near Camp Michigania at several of the courses developed by ski resorts near Boyne City; at a course near Saginaw developed by the husband of her oldest friend in Midland, Eleanor Curry; with the Montgomery's outside of Detroit, (I could never understand why Greater Cleveland had so many more golf courses than Detroit) and once, at a course owned by Michigan State University, which had a fairway running past Meadowbrook Hall, the home of the founder of the Dodge Motor Company, Joseph Dodge, where one of our Camp Michigania friends, Marilyn Brooks, was a docent and we met her when she was sewing a button on a shirt for the movie star, Lew Ayers, who had given a talk there the night before In her imperious way she dragged Mr. Ayers from his bedroom to meet us! The only time in my life I shook the hand of a movie actor. He was charming.

I remember playing many courses in the East: Poland Springs in Maine; Toftrees in College Park, Pennsylvania; Hot Springs in Virginia; Pine Hills in North Carolina; Oglebay Park in West Virginia; many courses near Bradenton, Florida, where we were members at El Conquistador C.C. for 5 years. We also played at French Lick, Indiana, which had two courses and an 1,800 room hotel; the Notre Dame University course on the edge of the campus and in sight of the Golden Dome in South Bend; the Pontaluna Golf club near Muskegon, Michigan; the Spring Lake course near Grand Haven with the Hesses; and the 9 hole course at Walloon Lake, Michigan, where the famous golf pro Tom Watson's family had a summer cottage, and he learned to play the game with his father and brother. His father played two holes ahead of us the day we were there.

I think her favorite course in Michigan was Ye Olde Nine Holes in Charlevoix which was short and flat and tight. This is the course I remember so well because we were playing with another couple from Camp Michigania, John and Midge Campbell and while Midge was still sitting in their golf cart waiting her turn to hit her tee shot, a ball from the adjacent fairway, much too close to our tee, took one bounce at hit her squarely in the middle of her forehead. It sounded like hitting a cantaloupe with a hammer and was very scary. Immediately, a lump the size of a hen's egg formed; the skin was not broken and there was no blood, but she was severely shaken. We picked up and left the course immediately, and found that the foursome who had caused the damage had beaten us out of the parking lot and had not even reported the accident or left their names in the Pro shop. She never lost consciousness, but we took her to the hospital in Charlevoix where they checked her over and allowed her to go home. She was remarkably cool about the whole incident, but I wonder if she ever played again.

I remember wishing that Fran had just a little more confidence in her golf game, and enjoyed it more; she preferred tennis, and would come home after pitty-patting the tennis ball with the "girls" all flushed and charged up. I always thought she played a better-quality game of golf. I could never convince her of this even though she frequently outdrove the other man in our foursome. Before we were able to join El Conquistador Country Club, we usually played various public courses in Bradenton on Sunday afternoons; after we joined the country club, our playing on Sundays continued, usually with Ted Billings, who was also a member, joining us. She knew Ted well and had played with him often, comfortable with the arrangement, but could not be persuaded to play in the Friday afternoon scrambles where her long drives would have been invaluable.

A "scramble" is a 9-hole match where all four players hit drives, and the second shot is played by the other three players from the longest, or most advantageous ball. The long ball hitter does not get to hit his ball for his second shot. He hits again after the other three have hit their shots from his long ball position, and another long ball location has been determined. This format is followed until everyone is on the green. The club Pro has tried to level the playing field by mixing higher handicap players with lower ones when making up the foursomes, different every week, hoping the skills are fairly distributed, and no one team has an unfair advantage. It's a fun format, which gives newer or weaker players a chance of play with better golfers, especially women who would otherwise never have the chance to play with the better male players. It's a great way to meet other members, but a bit trying for a low handicap player at times.

The winning team is announced after all the golfers have had dinner in the Grill Room. Both Ted and I found it very enjoyable, but could only persuade Fran to play once, which was a disappointment. She wanted one of us in the foursome she played in, and this could not be arranged.

I remember only two of the scrambles. On one occasion a diminutive lady, about 75 years old, 5' feet tall, and probably weighing only about 95 lbs. was assigned to our foursome. She could only hit a golf ball about 60 yards with her driver, but she was cheerful, and determined, and a good putter. Her name was Kronheim and the family owned a several furniture stores in Cleveland, and we had bought some furniture from their store in Great Northern Mall in North Olmsted, Ohio, so we got along well.

On another Friday afternoon with a different foursome in the Scramble, on the fourth hole, which was one of the most difficult on the course with out-of-bounds (screened patios of condos) 10 yards from the fairway from tee to green along the right side, and trees and a couple of fairway bunkers 250 yards from the tee, I hit the longest drive on the fourth hole in all the rounds I ever played at El Conquistador, past the traps, probably 260 yards in the center of the fairway. The green was only 145 yards away, and none of my partners that day could hit their ball on the green. What a wasted opportunity.

There are other memories, revisited frequently, of my golfing days, I remember vividly the trip we took to Myrtle Beach with our daughter, Nancy and her golfer husband, John, joined by his son, Jeff, a wonderful young golfer. I had my quadruple bypass heart surgery on November 18th, 1985 (you will notice I remember the exact date, a rarity in this account) and Nancy had rented a three-bedroom condo for a week. I remember we flew with a layover in Pittsburgh on Christmas Day and rented a car when we arrived. Even though we flew, I took my golf clubs, and played three 18-hole rounds of golf in the week we were there, six weeks after my open heart surgery, spaced a day apart. My play was far from outstanding, I am sure, but I finished every round. And, of course, we rode a golf cart. I can only remember the name of one of the courses we played, Deer Track, and that only because the pro shop had a sale on golf shirts for $10 each. I bought two, one blue and one red, which is my favorite golfing shirt that I am still wearing 33 years later. To my mind it is a memento of playing golf six weeks after open-heart surgery. I always have thought that red was a color that faded over time; this shirt hasn't. Some might say the same of me.

I remember the only scramble I played in other than in Florida. My son-in-law John (who was a fine golfer, 6-8 handicap) invited me to play with him and another friend, Phil Gibbs (son of a Parma, Ohio, meat packing family) in a three-man scramble on a Sunday at Pine Hills Golf Club, a course which I had played often and felt very comfortable on. I think the entry fee was $50 per team and John paid the whole fee. The winning team would pocket $300.

I think John's thinking was that I might contribute with two or three long drives, setting up a second shot that might make a birdie possible. Phil who was younger than either of us and a phenomenal putter, might contribute another birdie or two. John, who was very steady, would be the anchor and counted on himself to produce regulation pars. It seemed to be a good investment.

We had just returned from a visit in Michigan where I had played very well, so my confidence level was very high. In preparation for the Sunday match, I got up early and went to a driving range adjacent to the golf course. I hit a large bucket of balls so well that I was excited at the chance to continue doing the same on the golf course where it counted. John joined me to hit just a few balls (I finished his small bucket also) and off we went to the scramble, all warmed up. Phil was already there, but was developing a headache which turned into a migraine before we teed off and no one had aspirin, or Motrin, to lessen the pain. It was so severe that it affected not only the physical control of his putter, but it affected his eyesight, with the result he was useless on the green.

Meanwhile, I had left all my long drives on the practice tee and never hit a decent drive the whole day, let alone, a long ball. John had to carry the team, which became an increasing strain on him as he observed what was going on with his partners. He rose to the occasion keeping us within reach of winning the scramble, until he, too, ran out of gas on the 17th hole (as usual, he had not eaten any breakfast and ran out of energy). With all this adversity, I recall that we finished just out of the money. Phil and I were profuse in our apologies to John, who hid his disappointment well; but also, never assembled the same team for another scramble. I still loved the scramble format but playing for money felt quite different from the friendly scrambles in Florida.

In all my years of playing golf there were only a few outstanding golfers that I recall; Elden Papke, of course; John Mihocik and his son, Jeff; and Bill Culligan, of Hillsdale, Michigan, a former University of Michigan halfback on the football team in the days of Tom Harmon. I would have expected more names in a span of more than fifty years of my playing golf; but the world is full of very average golfers. And as I always say: it takes one to know one.

The Culligans, Bill and his wife, Julie, an excellent lady golfer, and their two daughters, Marnie and Maureen, attended Camp Michigania, the family camp owned and operated by the Alumni Association, located on Lake Walloon between Petoskey and Charlevoix, in northern Michigan. They were there the first year the camp opened, as were we, and a group of six or eight couples and their children came the same week every year for more than 25 years. Many of the group's children worked as counselors and came to camp with their families after their marriage.

I remember the first time I ever played with Bill was at the 9-hole public course in Charlevoix and having to cross the main road to play two or three of the holes. Bill was short, probably 5' 8" tall, probably weighed about 175 lbs., always had a smile, had a high squeaky voice, a degree in engineering from the University of Michigan, was extremely intelligent, very gregarious, a fine bridge player, and had an amazing memory for faces and every golf hole he ever played, it seemed to me.

After our first year at Camp Michigania, I always looked forward to playing golf with him; also sailing and playing bridge. He was a low handicap golfer, and had an unusual swing, in that his hands never went above waist level, rather than the long backswing used by the pros, and emulated by most other golfers, myself included, because it was so graceful. He hit a long, flat ball for long distance. I think the reason became apparent when one saw him in his swimming trunks: the muscular development of his thighs produced his speed on the football field, and the drive and power of his golf swing. With his eye-hand coordination he was able to hit a very long ball, which I am sure surprised many opponents who only saw him in his golfing slacks.

Camp Michigania was not all play: part of the program was the invitation of two professors as guests to stay for the week with their families and give two lectures during the week after dinner, campers' attendance not compulsory. The year Michigan won the Rose Bowl, one of the guest lecturers was "Bump" Elliot, head coach of the football team, there with his family. His lectures were heavily attended, and he was invited back the next year.

He and Bill Culligan had played on the same football team at Michigan during World War II and were good friends. Bill arranged for a golf game and invited me to play in the foursome, along with another camper, Dick Brooks, an average golfer. We played at the Bayview Country Club, which was part of a Methodist summer resort west of Petoskey. One of the couples we met on a University of Michigan travel cruise on the canals of the Netherlands, the Hacketts, Bob and Jeannie, spent their summers in a cottage they owned very near Camp Michigania. Bob was a member of Bayview and was able to get us a tee time.

I remember so well how competitive Bill and Bump were, the good natured bantering that went on constantly, Bump with a sucker in his mouth at all times to help him quit smoking, and what a brilliant game Bill played. He shot his lifetime low, 71, and beat Bump by several strokes. It was really a competition between Bump and Bill. Dick and I were mere spectators and contributed nothing to the Nassau bet.

After the match, we dropped Bump off at the Methodist lodge meeting room across the road from the golf course where he was scheduled to give a speech after lunch to the local Kiwanis Club. We three returned to Michigania, and the Kiwanians delivered Bump back to camp later that afternoon.

I think Bump Elliot may have been the finest person I ever met. He was a man of honor and principle, a leader and teacher, loved his family, and if I had had sons and they were interested in sports, I would have tried my best to have them exposed to Bump's influence. I was told that one could always distinguish Elliott's players from other football players by their bearing and behavior off the field. It was a wonderful privilege to have been able to spend the hours I did with him on the golf course where so much of a person's character is revealed.

The next year Bump was invited back to Michigania and again we played golf with him; this time at the Belevedere Golf Club in Charlevoix, a difficult course, where the Michigan Amateur Open Tournament was played every year. I had played this course several times and never played well as I recall. This final time when I had the chance to play with Elliott was no exception and I have little memory of the occasion other than the warm feelings I had for a wonderful person, and gratitude for being in the right place at the right time to have such an experience.

The last time I was able to play with Culligan was at a new course in Petoskey, Michigan, built in the hills looking down on Little Traverse Bay; the course was very scenic and aptly named, Bay View. We played as a twosome and I don't remember any details of the game, other than the beauty of the course and that this might be a last round of golf with a good friend. Travel distance and age were taking their toll.

I remember two of the famous golf courses we saw but did not play- too expensive - on the only two trips we took to the West coast. We drove around the Pebble Beach Golf course, not getting much of a feel for it, but were impressed by what we could see of the other courses located on the famous "18 Mile Drive." One was Cypress Point, which has a famous par three hole visible from the road with a green jutting out into the Pacific Ocean; I had seen a large photo of this hole hanging on the wall behind our boss, Doug Swinehart's, desk in the home office of the Aetna Life in Hartford and always assumed he had played the course on one of his visits to the California loan correspondent. After seeing the hole, I hope he hit the green.

The following year we toured the Canadian Rockies where we saw the Banff National Golf Course. I actually considered playing and got out of our rental car and went into the pro shop to see if I could rent clubs and play. I could have, but the total cost for the rental clubs and green fees would have been $95, and I said, "No, thank you." We did drive a short distance to where we could look out on one of the fairways, which had a beautiful view of mountains and trees, and saw a bear on the right edge of the fairway. I think I made the right decision not to play!

While on our first trip to the West, flying in and out of San Diego, we were able to visit my old Army friend, Ray Kiser and his wife Marilyn. They were originally from Winnetka, Illinois, and had retired to Indian Wells, a suburb of Palm Springs. Luckily, since we were "dropping in" unannounced, he was at home and insisted that we stay with them until we had to leave to go home. Thus, it was that I got to play my only round of golf in California at one of the two country clubs Ray belonged to. It was the only club open because of the summer heat on the fairway grass. The other courses were due to reopen two weeks later. I remember the course as being quite ordinary and not in very good condition, and do not think I distinguished myself in Ray's eyes. I remember how good it was to see an old friend from the Japanese language days in Ann Arbor; one who shared my love of jazz and had played the guitar in the Sunnysiders Quartet in Ann Arbor.

I remember my trips when I drove alone to New Haven for my class reunions every five years. Sad to say the important thing about the Reunions was not seeing old friends again (my roommate who lived 50 miles away and my other closest friend, Ken Rosenberg, never attended), but having the chance to play the Yale University Golf Course in West Haven, the scene of my ignominious performance my Freshman year. The course is outstanding, and beautiful, and for many years was ranked in the top ten of all the courses in the U.S.A. I never scored well but it was sheer pleasure to play it. The other important thing was being able to stay with my great Army friend, Sidney Mishcon, who lived on Long Island. I was able to renew old memories, and to get to know his family. My Army friendships were much more powerful than the college friendships, and I was far more interested in keeping them alive than any friendships I had known while in college. Seeing Sidney made my whole trip worthwhile.

I remember how absorbed I was with golf; how much of my free time I spent thinking about it, wanting to improve; the frustration I felt that the tips in the golfing magazines did not seem to help. I was still shooting in the 90s when the house in Brecksville was completed and I could resume playing regularly. I could hit the ball well enough, that I felt I could be a better golfer and should be able to score in the high 70s. My problem was my inconsistency. Since I did not belong to a country club with a teaching Pro, and the magazine articles did not seem to help, I decided to look elsewhere for lessons.

I discovered that the Pro at the Seneca Golf course, a public course, only a mile or two distant from our new home on Oakes road, gave lessons. His name was Joe Salata. I remember practicing at Seneca one Sunday evening after supper, watching him show off in front of a small crowd of admirers; hitting beautiful shots in response to requests for "a slice" or a "hook", and producing the type of shot requested. When someone asked for a straight ball he would reply that's too hard! Ask for something easier.

Joe was well built, about 6' tall, 180 lbs., thinning hair and had only one eye. I never learned whether this was congenital or the result of an accident. He claimed this affected his depth perception and ability to estimate distances to the green to an extent that kept him from trying to play on the professional golf tour. I thought this was a poor excuse, and that there were deeper personality issues. He lived alone in the W. 44th Street area on the near Westside of Cleveland and was very proud that he kept chickens that supplied him with fresh eggs. I would have liked to see where he lived. He was interested in my finishing our house, but I'm not sure he ever stopped to see it.

I do not remember how many lessons I had (or how much I paid for them) before Joe felt I was ready for a playing lesson. Seneca has four 9-hole courses. No. 1 is the oldest and shortest to the west of the clubhouse. This was the course chosen for the playing lesson, where the student plays stroke for stroke with his teacher, who makes suggestions as they proceed.

The first hole is a par 4, uphill to a large green. I hit my drive first to the left side, and Joe hit his ball deliberately close to my ball. I hit a 7 iron to the green; Joe did the same. We both had two putts. I don't recall any remarks or suggestions. This continued and by the third hole, when I was still even with Joe, he started to play seriously. I matched his score for the first four holes, and then could no longer keep up with him. But I was elated. I had scored the same on four holes as a pro.

Joe had a young friend he used to play with after the pro shop closed. I do not remember him very well. His last name may have been Sullivan. He was about 6' tall and hit golf ball a long distance from what I thought was a very unusual stance. At address he placed his feet close together, almost touching, and lined them up about 30 degrees to the left. He had a full swing and somehow delivered the clubface to the ball in such a way that it flew straight, and down the middle of the fairway.

Joe invited me to play with them one Sunday evening after I had had several lessons and I found it most interesting to be playing with two golfers who were so superior to me. Rather than being intimidated, I found it a fine learning opportunity. I do not remember the score, wonder what happened to Sullivan, and wonder what might have happened if Joe had given himself a chance to qualify for the tour. It looked to me as though he hit the ball well enough and had the temperament needed to succeed. I was sorry I lost touch with him. He was my first professional golf instructor.

I remember meeting my second golf professional on one of our Michigan trips. We were on the west coast of Michigan, and I was aware of a course in Frankfort, Michigan, that I had read about and wanted to play: Crystal Downs. It is still one of the early classic designs that is competitive with more modern courses designed by a Jack Nicklaus or an Arnold Palmer. The club pro was Cliff Settergren, and I hoped that if I, a non-member of the country club could arrange for two or three lessons, he might agree to give me a playing lesson, and that way I could get to see the course.

I was able to arrange for the lessons, which were very helpful (he found that I was letting go of the club at the top of my backswing, a persistent fault, which caused the ball to slice). He had me grip the club firmly, with no sense of letting go before the downswing and I immediately began to hit straight balls. I was lucky to get the lessons, but unable to have a playing lesson (which I think would have been invaluable) because he was scheduled to play in the Milwaukee Open that weekend and had to leave Thursday. However, he did arrange for me to play the course, which I did, alone, and came away feeling I had had a real golfing experience.

I remember the next Pro I went to for help was a young lady, the teaching Pro at El Conquistador Country Club in Bradenton. Her name was Barbara Pace. She came from Painesville, Ohio, where her family owned a popular Italian restaurant. She was young, attractive and almost 6' tall, had a very pleasant personality, and I remember a compact, rhythmic swing. We joined the club when I was 65 and committed to living in Florida full time during the winter months after my heart surgery; joining the club coincided with buying our first condominium.

I had been playing El Conquistador, a for a year or so, without being able to improve my handicap because of my incessant slicing of the ball off the tee, and out on the fairway. I had used the practice range and it didn't matter which club I selected, I hit the ball to the right, where most of the trouble lay out on the course.

I remember my first lesson at El Conquistador (I only had and needed one). It was after lunch and we met in the shade of some trees to the right of the first tee. She had me use my 8 iron, and, after a few swings and observing the flight of the ball, she had me stop at the top of my backswing, and put a fifty cent piece between the heel of my left hand and the club grip, and told me not to let the coin drop to the ground. It was the same instruction in a different form that I had received from Settergren (he had me stop at the top and inserted his little finger between the heel of my left hand and the club grip) years earlier, but had forgotten. Almost immediately I lost my slice, and the game was much more fun to play.

I remember, during the time I was playing at El Conquistador, reading an advertisement in the local newspaper about a free seminar on the "Golf swing" by a golf Pro named Bill Skelly. The time and location were convenient, and I decided to see what it was all about. Skelly put on quite a performance. He was promoting greater club head speed which is necessary to achieve superior distance. He put on a skit and told us about threshing grain in the olden days in a little village. The women would use long sticks to beat the stalks of wheat spread on the threshing floor (and here Skelly used a yard stick to show the motion of the sticks the women used) and it was hard work and took a long time and was not very efficient. Then one of the women broke her stick, which did not break into two pieces, and continued with her beating and found that the far end of the stick moved much faster and beat the wheat much faster and was more efficient. The way he told his well-rehearsed story was very amusing.

At this point, he brought out two pieces of wood about a foot and a half long tied together loosely in the middle with a piece of rope, and proceeded to do the flailing motion and the increased speed of the piece of wood farther from the hand was very noticeable, producing a hum. This made sense to me, and I signed up for his course of instruction, which was given by him and his staff at a golf course in Miami Springs, on the east coast of Florida north of Miami. The course lasted five days and we stayed in an excellent motel and the food was also excellent. There were 12-15 people in the class, and the day started with lectures and then work on the practice range. I went to his course twice, and think they improved my game.

I remember playing the golf course on the last day and seeing an eagle trying to catch a fish from one of the ponds at twilight, which was exciting. The second year I remember complaining to Bill about the amount of attention paid by not only him, but also his assistants, to the lone girl in the group. She was younger and quite good-looking, and I questioned the lack of attention I was getting, and whether I was getting my money's worth (I do not remember how much the fee was, perhaps $500). Bill did give me a little more personal attention, but I don't think his heart was in it. All in all, I felt the experience helped my game. I was shocked to learn later that the girl had been murdered somewhere in Central America.

After we moved back to Ohio permanently, I played golf regularly, and frequently at a course called Mallard Creek on Route 82 in Eaton Township. John, my son-in-law, was one of the starters in charge of getting the golfers organized to play in an orderly fashion, and it added interest to have a member of the family involved in my game, even though we were not playing together. He was well aware of my constant efforts to improve my game and asked me if I would object to taking lessons from a lady Pro who gave lessons at Mallard Creek. He offered to give me a lesson as a birthday present, which I gladly accepted. I remember very little about the instructor, except that I thought she seemed very young (about my granddaughter's age). I remember wondering, even if qualified by the PGA, how much experience she could have had at her age in actually playing the game. However, I learned quickly that she was highly qualified and understood very well the fundamentals of the golf swing.

I remember how chagrined I felt when I realized that I had been playing for all my years laboring under a false conception of something as basic as how to address the ball, to set up my body prior to beginning my back-swing. The only thing more fundamental was the position of the hands in gripping the club, which I was very proud of. None of the teaching Pros, after seeing how I gripped the club, ever mentioned needed changing or adjustment.

The incorrect image in my mind as I "set up" to the ball, was of the two parallel rails of a railway track converging into a single dot at the horizon, an optical illusion. I was thinking of the green, or the middle of the fairway, as that dot (target). Of course, both targets were much closer than my imaginary horizon dot. When Missy, my instructor, pointed this out to me and instructed me to think of a line across my toes aimed at the left side of the green (the closer rail of the railroad track) and the plane of my swing aimed at the right side of the green (the rail farthest from my body) I began to hit the ball at the target I selected. The resulting stance was far more "open" than my old style; in some cases, depending on the distance involved, the imaginary line across the tips of my toes, was almost 30 degrees left of the target. I realized that my old style resulted in my aiming much too far to the right. With that stance, my body was subconsciously trying to compensate. In fact, my anatomy was pulling my arms across the front of my body at impact, which meant that the clubface was either open or closed at impact, producing slices and hooks, and inaccuracy.

This recalled the round of golf I played with Joe Salata and his young friend, Sullivan, who had such a narrow stance (feet close together), and his body lined up 30 degrees to the left, and how long and accurate he was. Of all the golfers I ever played with, his swing is the one that remains clearest in my mind. I can close my eyes and still see it. Once I incorporated the changes Missy taught me, which were not as extreme as Sullivan's stance, I became more confident in my swing, more consistently accurate, and my scores improved.

Two or three years later, during the time we spent our winters in Florida and I had subscriptions to all the golfing magazines, one of which was *Senior Golfer*, I noticed an instructional article by a PGA instructor named Don Trahan. His article was aimed at older men and women and promoted a swing friendly to older players with much less strain on the lower back. The article was illustrated, and I grasped the principal of what he was teaching immediately. I knew I had to try to get lessons from him. He had changed his teaching location and I had difficulty finding him. I don't remember how I managed to do this, but I persisted, and was able to get an appointment.

We had attended a Jazz Festival/Party in Atlanta for several years, which was held at the Doubletree Hotel in Atlanta during Easter season. Trahan's new teaching location happened to be in Greenville, South Carolina, about an hour east of Atlanta. We were able to arrange to combine the two activities. Trahan was teaching at a driving range at a country club next to an 11-story Embassy Hotel. Upon arrival we checked into the hotel, which I remember had an artificial stream with Koi swimming in it in the dining room, and after lunch, while Fran rested, I went off to meet Trahan to take my first lesson.

He was an older man, had in fact won the South Carolina Senior PGA Championship the previous year. He was about 5'10" tall, reddish hair, ruddy complexion, and a very outgoing manner. He made it easy to accept his instructions. He was finishing a lesson with another golfer and suggested that I go to the far side of the driving range and hit a few balls to loosen up.

I had been trying to follow the instructions in his article in *Senior Golf* on my own and that is how I hit my practice balls (not very well). Step one in the article used the words, "Let the club-head chase the squirrel up the tree." The reader (me) was to sweep the club head close to the ground straight back from the ball, and when the distance the club-head could go was reached, it would rise in an arc taking the hands with it until it reached the end of the swing at the top, having climbed the tree trunk.

I had been stretching too far, to a point where I was leaning backward away from the ball and could not understand why I was unable to get the results promised in the article. Unbeknownst to me, Trahan had been watching me and as we started my lesson. He quickly pointed out what I was doing wrong. I never liked his "climbing the tree" analogy. It was the only part of his article that was not clear to me. As soon as I got the feel for this new movement, things improved, and I started to hit some respectable shots.

The most important part of his concept of the golf swing was that the back-swing should end, when the club-shaft reached 180 degrees, perpendicular to the ground. The hands were to go no higher than was necessary to get the shaft into that position, not to continue past that point while cocking the wrists to increase club head speed on the downswing. There was to be no twisting of the back until the back was facing the line of flight as required by the older method. If the club head is kept square to the ball on the back swing, the hands will twist to maintain that position, and the release of the twist as the club head approaches the ball will be the equivalent of the uncocking of the wrists on the more conventional swing. Trahan claimed that club head speed was 85% with his method, compared to the speed reached in conventional teaching. It certainly seemed to be true in my case, and it certainly was easier on my lower back. We discussed Tiger Woods's swing and speculated that he would have serious back problems in the future. I wish Tiger had gone to Trahan for help early in his career.

There was such improvement in my game, and so much more pleasure, that we made the same arrangements the year following. This time he spent time on refining the improvements made the previous year. I thought the money spent on the lessons ($100/hour, very expensive) was a great investment. I only wish I had had him as my instructor twenty years earlier. I might have realized my dream of having a 5-6 handicap. After only two-hour plus lessons, I considered him a new friend.

He confided in me that his business manager had cheated him out of his retirement funds and about the concerns he had about his son D.J. (who was on the Clemson golf team and had been the NCAA national champion the previous year) had been invited to play in the Masters Tournament at Augusta as an amateur. Trahan wished aloud, very forcefully, that his son would work on his short game and not be so obsessed with the "long" ball. D.J. went on to become a professional and joined the PGA Tour, where he won one or two tournaments and won over $2,000,000 his first year, an amount never equaled after that. I searched the Monday morning sports pages to find his name for a long time. I have no idea where he is now, or what he is doing. Don Trahan has moved his teaching location, once again, to the mainland, opposite Hilton Head, South Carolina. I still have the video he made of his method that he gave me from the trunk of his car as we parted.

I remember my golfing days with great pleasure; I wish I had kept a record of every course I played, my scores, special features, etc. As it is, my memories are more general. I always marveled at Bill Culligan who seemed to be able to remember every course, and every hole he ever played. I just remembered what a wonderful time I had.

By the time we felt able to join a country club, I was 65 years old, and we chose El Conquistador in Bradenton, Florida where Ted Billings had been a member for several years. We did not join to enlarge our social life, but almost entirely to play golf. I was glad that Ted had preceded us, because if he had any influence on our decision, we were lucky that El Conquistador was such a fine test of golf. Even with playing there four to five times a week for five years, I never tired of the course and never mastered all its challenges. It seemed when I had solved one problem, another would present itself. However, I must say, à la Culligan, I think I can picture the location of my longest drive on every hole.

I never entered the Club Championship matches in my handicap division, 15-20, but played most of my rounds with Ted and two of his older friends, one of whom was married to a girl, from Lakewood, Ohio. I do not remember their names, but the fourth man in our foursome was a small man who had been a dentist, and when he bought a new set of clubs, he sold me his old No. 7 wood, a welcome addition to my arsenal.

On one of our Sunday rounds, when Fran and I played with Ted, she jumped from the cart on the 17th hole, and landed on a drainage grill in a small depression at the edge of the rough that was obscured by unmown grass, and sprained her ankle severely. It was the last golf she ever played, and I mourned the loss of my favorite golfing partner.

Soon after that, I could no longer justify the expense of belonging to a private club where only I could play (the annual fees were the equivalent of a 10 day cruise in the Caribbean that we both could enjoy) and we resigned from the club. Sixty percent of the entry fee was to be refunded upon death or resignation, and it was paid from the fees paid by new members; we had to wait two years before we received our refund. It was a great golf course, with the best (new) clubhouse in the area, a dining room overlooking Sarasota Bay, an active social program which we did not take advantage of, with a few exceptions, and a private tennis club adjacent, but no pool.

After we left the club, I continued to play at the many very good public courses and joined the Manatee County Men's Golf League. The League played two days a week, Monday and Thursday: at the County Course on 57th Street in southwest Bradenton, and River Run, the city owned shorter course on the east side of Bradenton, next to the Pittsburgh Pirate's Spring training camp. Ted continued his membership at El Conquistador. I did not get to play with him anymore except on special golf parties and getaways.

Our daughter Nancy and her husband, John, who was a far better golfer than Ted, retired from their teaching careers and bought a condo a few doors from ours in Vizcaya. John was always available for golf and we played many of the nearby fine public courses.

I did not realize it at the time, but I was nearing the end of my playing days. From the early days at the Club, I had been aware of the older members, usually five to ten years older than me in their 70s, buying new sets of clubs, or individual "hot" drivers, or the latest golf ball promising extra distance. There were constant rumors as to which equipment produced the best results. Their constant search was trying to find something, anything, that would restore lost distance. I'm afraid I looked down on these men and thought they were foolish: that their loss of distance wasn't caused by their equipment, but their age.

Five years later, I had to confront my own increased age and began to understand what the other older members were feeling. My swing was unchanged, and I was accustomed to hitting the ball 230-240 yards off the tee; suddenly I became aware that although my swing felt exactly the same, the ball wasn't going as far. No matter how hard I tried, I could not make the ball travel farther than 180-200 yards. The difference in distance between my irons, 5 iron to 6 iron for instance, had been about 7 yards. Suddenly there was no difference and I hit all irons the same distance. In fact, I only needed three clubs to play 18 holes of golf: a No. 1 or 3 wood, a 6 or 7 iron and a putter. And I had to start using the most forward tee position, which could be humiliating in itself. I began to realize that age and a lower club head speed were causing this, and it was inevitable. Suddenly golf no longer equated pleasure. It was not enough to simply be out of doors and taking a nice walk in beautiful surroundings. Even after my lessons from Trahan, when I learned to hit the most elegant golf-shots I ever had in all my golfing career, the distance I was used to seeing had disappeared. It no longer was fun. And that made it very expensive.

Another major factor in the ending of my golfing career was the onset of sciatica. The first indication that I had a problem actually occurred on a golf tee. Everything to that point (the middle of the round) had been normal, but when I was in the middle of my downswing on the tee, a sudden paralyzing electric shock ran down my right leg, and I almost fell. Somehow, I was able to get through the rest of the holes, but that was the last time I hit a golf ball. It took three years searching in Florida and Ohio to find a therapy that overcame the symptoms, which were not constant pain, but unpredictable, sporadic electric shocks down the right leg that could have caused a fall to the ground.

So, my golfing career came to an end, "not with a bang, but a whimper," to be replaced with two of my other passions: bridge and reading. I was shocked at how easily I gave up the game, how little I missed it. I would never have predicted it ten years earlier. I still have my bag of clubs, with the needlepoint head covers for the woods made by Fran, standing in a corner of the garage. I don't know what to do with them.

# Chapter IX

## Bridge

My interest in playing cards began at a very early age. I remember sitting on the floor in front of the gas grate in our living room on Parkwood Road when I was seven or eight years old, playing with cards with my brother, Russell. I can't remember if we actually played a game with a name, but we were aware of the numbers and pictures on the cards, and it was nice and warm in front of the fire.

There was no religious proscription against playing cards in our family. In our family everyone played cards, except Grandma Schmidt, who objected to card playing on religious grounds. I remember playing pinochle and sixty-six (played with half a pinochle deck) with both Grandpa Schmidt and Grandpa Gaede when we were very young. Usually, the older men played against the two boys, and when the children won a game occasionally, the older men roared with laughter. It was very exciting for Russ and me, and we tried very hard to win. I suspect that what spirit of competition I may have comes from those early beginnings. I have always liked to win at whatever I was doing as long as it was done fairly.

There were other card games, such as rummy and hearts, which we had to play with visitors because they didn't know how to play pinochle, but we didn't like those games very much. I never did learn how to play 500 or Euchre. About this time, probably 1920, a new game appeared, a variation of the old English card game 'whist': called "auction bridge". This was played with a deck of 52 cards, rather than the 48 cards used in pinochle, which had two of each face card plus the tens and nines.

Bridge started as a bidding auction. Bidding went round the table each player naming a suit and the highest bidder in the auction played the hand, the trump suit becoming the suit named in the bidding rounds by the winning bidder, the declarer. It was so long ago and so eclipsed by contract bridge that I can't remember whether it was a partnership game, or if there was a dummy (declarer's partner who lays his cards on the table face up and declarer plays both hands). This was a very simple game and became very popular.

Later in the 1930s, Harold Vanderbilt invented contract bridge, which was far more sophisticated, and became an extremely popular form of entertainment, supplanting auction bridge. It was new and did not require betting money as did poker to be interesting. It is the only card game worth playing in my opinion, and at age 98 I am still reading books on how to improve my play.

One of my earliest memories of playing bridge was when I was in the third grade and walked home from school one afternoon to find my mother entertaining three ladies, strangers to me, by playing auction bridge. One of the ladies had to leave early, and my mother ordered me to take her place and play the rest of the hands until the ladies left. I have never forgotten the mixture of pride and embarrassment I felt as they complimented my mother on my performance. They couldn't get over the fact that a nine-year old child could play cards so well. I think I made my mother proud of me that day.

By the time I was in high school, contract bridge was supplanting auction bridge, and I have faint memories of games played with our parents after dinner, but not very often.

Contract bridge was different than auction, in that there was still an auction in the bidding, but now the declarer had to make the contract he had bid to win the auction by taking the number of tricks he bid. If he "made" his contract, he scored a bonus in addition to the value of the tricks taken over the basic six tricks (book).

In this game the declarer's partner lays his cards on the table, face up, so the opponents can see them as well as the declarer, who plays both the cards on the table as well as those hidden in his hand. The declarer had the advantage of knowing where half the cards in the hand were located. His partner sat opposite him and watched him select which cards to play and in what order.

At this stage, the game was so new that few people knew how to value their hands accurately to be able to make their contracted number of tricks and there was a lot of guessing around the table, and many failed contracts where declarer "went down," which resulted in penalty points awarded to the opponents.

I remember playing after dinner with my parents and my mother, at the end of a long day, after holding three or four poor hands in a row, getting up from the table, abruptly, saying, "Time to go to bed!" I do not remember how skillful either of my parents was at the bridge table. Some of their pinochle skills carried over to the new game, so they were probably above average.

As I recall, I do not remember playing a single hand of bridge my freshman year at Yale. There simply weren't enough hours in the day. Sophomore year was more relaxed and new relationships were being established with a new group of men who would be living together for three years. A group of bridge players discovered each other, mainly scholarship students, and we played regularly after dinner at one or the other's rooms. We quickly found that we could play from 7 p.m. to 8:30 p.m. and still be able to fulfill our study obligations.

We found that we had to have a rigid time limit because we were playing simple rubber bridge in which the object was to accumulate 100 points which constituted a "game," Each trick over the minimum six tricks was worth 20 points if it was a minor suit (clubs or diamonds), and 30 points if it was a major suit (hearts and spades), with an extra 10 points for the first trick if the contract was played in no-trump; two games were required to win a "rubber." It could take hours to complete one rubber if the competition was greedy, or stubborn. So many weekday evenings ended in mid-rubber.

Weekends were different; there were not the same time constraints, and bridge was popular among the scholarship boys because no money was involved. Sometimes we went to a movie before coming back to our rooms to play bridge; on other nights when there was no movie we wanted to see, or anything else to do, we just played bridge.

I remember one Saturday night when we had one of those seesaw rubbers at the end of the evening where neither team could score enough points to win the final game and end it all. When the game did finally end, we found it was 3 a.m. and we all felt so horrible the next day that we agreed that we would establish a time limit for our games and quit at an arbitrary 1 a.m. whether or not a rubber was over. \

Thus, a pattern was established that was much more pleasurable. But I was realizing that the quality of our play was not very good and was not improving. I felt there should be a logic behind the game; that the game had a place in the world of the Ideal; that learning the logic of the game was possible and would increase the satisfaction and pleasure in playing the game. I hoped that I would find the answer someday.

I remember vividly the coming of that day: I was a junior and it was the year 1941. I had to look up something in the card catalogs that filled the nave of the Sterling Memorial Library, under the heading of "Bri" (I have no recollection of what the subject might have been, or for which course I was taking). I noticed the word "bridge" and I thought to myself, how strange to find books written about building bridges although I could see how they might be useful to an engineering student. Then I noticed the name of an author, Culbertson. Suddenly, I realized that, unlikely it might be for an august library such as the Sterling Memorial, with its 13,000,000 volumes, to have books about a subject as frivolous as bridge, a card game, but there it was.

I leafed through the several cards under that heading (I wonder how many there are today) and finally picked out three to take back to my room: the *Red Book*, by Eli Culbertson, the most famous name in the bridge world at that time; a book on odds (I can remember what the cover looked like, and that it was published in Montreal, but not the name of it (it had very few pages to read); and the shortest book in the entire category, only 89 pages, *The Theory and Play of Championship Contract Bridge* by Harold E. Simmelkjaer.

I remember feeling guilty stealing time away from my required course reading, but I read all three: skimming the Culbertson, which was much too detailed; finding the book on odds interesting, but too hard to remember; and being flabbergasted and astonished by the Simmelkjaer book. It was exactly what I felt should be written about the game and I had stumbled on it by pure chance. It was a systematic approach to the bidding that had been so sadly lacking in the games we were playing after dinner and weekends. I was sure it would work and couldn't wait to try it. All I needed was a partner. I persuaded my roommate, Gil Hunt, to read the book, which he did, grudgingly. The book did not arouse the enthusiasm I was feeling, but he was willing to give it a try.

Since the book is still available on the *Bridge World* web site, I will only give a brief description of the system, rather than go into detail with all the adjustments I have added over the years to bring it up to date. I should add that I never cared for Simmelkjaer's writing style, or many of his explanations of its application.

Briefly his system, which predated by about 10 years, the widely accepted Charles Goren Standard American system that only promoted no-trump bidding at first, calls for evaluating the hand by assigning numerical values to the honor cards: Ace = 4 points; King = 3 points; Queen = 2 points; and Jack = 1 point. Additional points are counted for more than 5 cards in a suit, and voids, singletons, and 100 & 150 honors.

Minimum number of points needed to open the bidding, counting high cards and length, is 13, and for every additional four points, the opening bid is one level higher. Partner must have 9 points to make a positive response and for every three additional points, raises partner one additional level. The partnership knows after two bids the type of hand and total number of points. When the total number of points is 25, the hand should be able to make a contract of three (nine tricks) in either a suit or no-trump. For each additional three points (a playing trick) he can jump to the level indicated immediately.

The first Saturday night Gil and I tried this new system, I kept track of the results of every auction we won. After four or five hours of play, I remember how excited I was at the results we achieved. We had bid a total of 64 tricks (probably 20-24 hands) and made one overtrick and one undertrick. Such accuracy was unheard of in the game we played.

In my mind, Simmelkjaer was validated. It was simple, had very few numbers to remember, and was very accurate. I fell in love with it immediately and found partners who agreed to use it and, in our circle, became invincible.

After my college days, my only problem was finding a partner who would try to use the system with me. Fran learned it immediately and believed in it, and we used it all our married years; the only other person who tried to learn and use the system with me was my good friend, "Honest" Tom Rohrbach, a very fine player.

I have continued to evaluate the hands I am dealt the same basic way ever since, even though my partner does not know the system, and has no interest in learning it. After evaluating my hand, I try to bid in such a way that my partner will understand the value of my hand. I must admit that I am frustrated when I observe in our duplicate bridge games now, here at Pioneer Ridge, and in past years, the number of biddable and makeable slam bids, (12 or 13 tricks) with their large bonuses, which are missed using the Standard American system with all the new-fangled conventions attached to it; I believe many, if not most of which, would have been bid using Simmelkjaer. It hurts when one realizes the rarity of slam bids, and to lose those 500-1500 bonuses!

It has always interested me to observe in the books on bridge and bridge columns I read how frequently the same contract is reached, and how much more directly and simply it could have been reached using Simmelkjaer; and it drives me crazy to hear a missed Slam dismissed with, "It's only a game."

I have never been able to understand why I have never been able to convince other players of Simmelkjaer's merits or find a regular, long-term partner who would use it with me. I have begun to suspect the way I project my enthusiasm may have something to do with it.

After college came my stint in the Army. Very few men were as fortunate as I was, never to have been in harm's way and to have spent three years in a college environment with the same group of men with similar backgrounds that produced lifelong friendships. It meant that there were always bridge players available and we spent many of our free-time hours playing rubber bridge.

I do not recall any specific games, or unusual hands, but do remember how impressed I was by my Yalie friend, Alex Norton, who grasped the principles of the game and became expert in just a few weeks. The other memory that I recall almost every time I play today is of the only Nisei who chummed with us, Trueman Kennichi Oshima, called "Osh" by us, who seemed to bid a slam every third or fourth hand and made his bid almost every time. I never understood how he did it.

After the war, I returned to civilian life, a new marriage, furnishing our first home, and the arrival of our daughters. Although we had returned to the city I had grown up in, I had no network of old friends and I remember how grateful I was that Fran was so skillful at finding and making new friends.

She had been a member of a sorority that had an active group of alumni in Cleveland, all at the same stage of their lives and seeking new friends. Bridge played a vital part in our growing social life.

We played cards with my family. We found a common interest in bridge with a few of our neighbors in Parma Heights, who led us to others of their friends. In Parma Heights, we ended up with two separate groups: neighbors and sorority couples. All the games played were simple rubber bridge. Sometime later I found business friends who enjoyed playing bridge which further expanded my chances to play.

I remember some of the names of some of the couples we played with, and think I could still recognize their appearance, but, oddly, not their strengths and weaknesses at the bridge table. Among the neighbors were the Leyavas, the Demuths, the Kellys, the Pardees; the sorority group had the Trebbes, the Hendricksons, the Hurdlebrinks, the Countrymans, my brother Ken, the Moores; the Brecksville church group had the Adairs, the Morrises, the Sutherlands, the Hayeses, the Cullers, the Billings, the Phillips, and the business group had Lenny Himmel, Owen Lavelle, Tom Clutterbuck, Roy Hausheer, Dan Crane, Bill Carter, Bill Braman, Danny Smith, and Doyle Robbins. And then there were the bridge players we met during our 30 years in Florida! I met many other faces on the neutral ground of the bridge table over the years.

I should be able to write an entire book on the hands played, my partner, and the opponents. But only one in four hands, on average, is strong enough to make game, and slams are even rarer. So, while all hands must be played with the cards dealt, most of them are a blur, quickly forgotten, impossible to remember and it would be foolish to try.

However, during the 77 years I have been playing the game, there have been a few unforgettable events involving the people or the cards.

When playing ordinary rubber bridge with friends a session lasts for 20-24 hands (2-1/2 to 3 hours). Points are accumulated on each hand until a total of 100 points is reached, which starts a new game. Two games are required to win a rubber of three games, an average score of 2,500-3000 points will usually produce a winner for the evening.

This is somewhat different, and the strategy differs, from the so-called Chicago style game where bonus points for a part score (less than 100 points) game contract, or slam are awarded each deal. The first hand no one is vulnerable, and the fourth hand, both sides are vulnerable, and the second and third hands the dealer's team is vulnerable. Vulnerability occurs after winning a game and increases the bonus or penalty points if the contract is not made thereafter. This type of scoring is the same as duplicate bridge.

The social group at Fran's church, St. Matthews, the Friday Niters's sponsored a fund-raising scheme where a group of eight couples would play, in round robin fashion, 20 hands with scores to be cumulative. Each couple would have another couple in their home (nibble food and soft drinks only to minimize the entertaining aspect) and each couple would contribute $2 per session. The money accumulated, and at the completion of the round robin the church was to receive $50 and the balance would be distributed to the highest scoring couples. This seemed to me to be a very painless way to raise money. From my point of view, it didn't hurt that the vehicle was playing bridge.

The women decided that all the couples would gather at one home to play their last round, and it would be treated as a small party celebrating the conclusion of a successful fundraiser. The final scores for each couple would be added to the earlier totals to determine the winner.

As I recall, we gathered at the Adair's home on Oakhurst Circle and our final couple were people who attended St. Matthews but were strangers to us. In all the years I played the organ at St. Matthews, I did not recall ever having seen them. I think their name may have been Anderson. We brought two decks of our regular cards, and each hand was shuffled. We sat in the same position the whole evening and played the usual 20 hands.

I have never held, before or since, such powerful hands, one after the other. I'm sure the Andersons played three or four of the hands, but every hand we played was either a game bid, or a slam. Our score at the end of the evening was over 10,000 points and we could tell the Andersons were unhappy.

We said we were going to give them the two decks of cards, which were very nice ones, and since we had finished before the others, suggested we play one more hand, hoping they would finally get a good hand; we were feeling guilty, especially Fran. They were polite and agreed, and to my astonishment, we bid and made another grand slam, (all thirteen tricks). We never saw the Andersons again. I don't remember whether we came in first in the overall scoring, and I don't remember what we had to eat.

Another similar occasion occurred in Florida at one of the regular Wednesday evening rubber bridge sessions at the second condo we bought in Vizcaya. Again, this was rubber bridge: Chicago style scoring, 20 hands, four hands per partner, random seating and random partners. In this game we put 35 cents in the pot; 25 cents of which was distributed to the high scorers, and 10 cents put into a bag and awarded to any team bidding and making a Grand Slam.

The combination of cards that make a grand slam (all 13 tricks) possible is so rare that I saw one couple split $41. Fran elected to stay home that night, so I had no one to use my Simmelkjaer system with and thus had to depend on my imperfect understanding of my various partner's style of bidding and play. One of the women, whose husband did not play bridge, was an aggressive bidder and player and liked to win. She had scored 5,000+ points, well above the average needed to win some money, and expected to come in first. I will never forget the look on her face (nor remember her name) when I turned in my score with 8,600 points, which earned me the first prize money for the evening. I was told it was the highest number of points ever scored in a Wednesday night game.

I had had another evening of one good hand after another, easy to play and, lucky that the partners I drew were among the stronger players with whom I was able to communicate. It didn't happen very often. Chance plays a very large role in every aspect of the bridge game.

One amazing combination of cards occurred in a hand in Florida at a Wednesday afternoon game at Vizcaya. I was dealt a hand with 7 hearts (A Q J xxxx) and 6 diamonds (A K Q J 10 x) and voids in clubs and spades. It was the kind of hand a bridge player dreams of. The opponents, who were among the better players, competed because they had the As and Ks of the black suits, and the final contract ended at with me playing 5 H, doubled, vulnerable and made with an overtrick. My partner had the K of hearts and the missing hearts in the opponents' hands were split 3 and 1. If my partner had indicated he had the K of hearts, I might have (should have) bid the Grand Slam, which was makeable. The bonus 1,500 points would have given us an even greater score.

In contrast, I remember a recent regular individual duplicate bridge Thursday night game here at Pioneer Ridge in Ohio. There was misunderstanding with my partner and I was inexplicably stranded in a 2 Heart contract (8 tricks) with only 4 trumps in my hand, none in partner's hand, and the opponents holding 9 of my suit declaration. The standard requirement to play a suit contract is 8 cards in one suit ideally, and occasionally 7.

Adopting my best poker face, I concealed my dismay. The opponents' cards lay in favorable positions; to be sure they had to be, and I made my contract. Everyone else played the hand at 3 No Trump and made it, so we did not get a top board score that time.

This hand was so unusual that I submitted it the writer of our local paper's bridge column, Philip Alder, who is syndicated in 200 papers, including *The New York Times* and it was published in our local *Elyria Chronicle* on June 9, 2018. I was thrilled to see my name printed in a newspaper and sent copies to friends and relatives. I suspect I may now have had my 15 minutes of fame.

I remember two early validations of my faith in the system. Fran and I used it regularly and always warned our opponents that it was a different way of bidding and explained how it functioned. I never could tell whether it was helpful to them, and we usually told them to raise a question if they heard a bid they did not understand.

When we visited Fran's mother in Detroit in the early days of our marriage, I always felt she was concerned that since I was a stranger in Detroit, I might become bored after a day or two and I might not want to visit as often, thus depriving her of the companionship of her beloved daughter. I don't think she ever realized how much pleasure I derived from simply visiting new places. She made special plans centered around making me happy to be there: dinner at the Women's City Club, cooking her favorite recipes for me, little presents, and so many other things. I cannot remember a visit to Grandma Thompson's house that I did not enjoy and look forward to.

One of the things she did almost every time we came to Detroit was to arrange a bridge game for us with the son of her oldest friend in Detroit, Charlie Bealls. Charlie's wife, Ruth, who was a nurse, was always his partner. He was about 15-20 years older than we were, rather short and chubby. I never learned how he earned his living, but Grandma Thompson told us that he supported himself in The Great Depression in the 1930s by playing bridge regularly at a card club in downtown Detroit. He was one of the best bridge players I had encountered until that time, and he and Ruth were formidable opponents.

The first time we met, I carefully explained the Simmelkjaer system to him before we started playing and do not remember any of the hands that evening, but was very pleased that when we finished playing, we young upstarts had held our own. Charlie said that he was impressed with the system, and there was nothing wrong with it. This reinforced my belief that the system worked and was very effective.

Many years later I met my friend Bill Braman's (one of my regular bridge partners) older brother, Charlie; he was in his thirties, as tall as I was, well built, and always had a twinkle in his eye when he looked at you, as if he had a secret. He was a graduate of the Western Reserve University Law School and had taken up duplicate bridge while in college. He entered many tournaments and was the youngest person at that time ever to have earned 300 Life Master Points in one year. Not only was he a fine player, he had an oversize ego.

After telling Fran about him and his prowess at the bridge table, with quite a few reservations on her part, we invited Charlie and his wife to Brecksville for an evening of rubber bridge. He had trained his wife so that their bidding allowed him to play every hand. In addition to his skill at playing the cards, he was eidetic (had a photographic memory) and claimed he could recall every card he held the whole evening, as well as the cards held by the other three players. I asked him once how he could remember so much, and his reply, with sadness, was, "How can you forget?" Too much of a good thing is a curse.

After he parked his big Cadillac, with Fran looking on, he popped his trunk and lifted out a silver trophy about 3' tall, which he had won at a recent tournament. He carried it into the house to be admired, which thoroughly intimidated Fran, which was his intention. She had been trembling ever since they had accepted our invitation. We proceeded to play.

After once again carefully explaining our system, and even though he played all the hands when their side won the bid, (using all the tricks he knew) we held our own. At the end of the evening, our scores were close. He admitted that our system had merit.

I remember how interesting it was when Charlie came to a men's game at our house on one of the occasions when Fran was in Detroit with the children visiting her mother. I think we had four tables and we played until quite late. I think everyone put in a dollar, first place with highest number of points would win $10; last place (booby) would get his dollar back. Charlie went home with his dollar and probably had a miserable time trying to play with mere mortals who didn't speak his bridge language.

We played a lot of bridge with Merlin and Jackie Jones, one of the couples at Mariners Cove, our first Florida condo. Jackie had been a businesswoman, was elected President of the condo association, and was very intelligent and fun to be with. They played bridge four or five times a week regularly and one of the games they went to was at a bridge club in Bradenton where duplicate was played. The games were sanctioned, which meant they were recognized by the ACBL and master points were awarded. I don't recall, but they may have taken lessons from a professional. They played all the latest systems, used all the latest conventions and it should have been quite a challenge for us to play with them.

Fran was close with Jackie and they arranged for us to play at their condo, or ours, frequently. I always loved to play with them, because they flaunted the latest conventions, but had so many misunderstandings or uncertainties as to whether or not their latest "understanding" was being employed, that, we, using our old-fashioned Simmelkjaer simple system (which had long since been dubbed "Schnickelfritz" by frustrated opponents) always seemed to win.

My memories of those games do not recall a single time that we did not have the winning score. I doubt that this could be true. And it was rubber bridge; if it had been duplicate where the same hands were played twelve or thirteen times with many different final contracts and many different outcomes, I do not think they would have been winners in that setting, either.

I talked my golfing buddy, Ted Billings who was a member of our Brecksville duplicate group, into to playing in one of the Manatee County Senior Organization sponsored Thursday afternoon duplicate sessions. Ted could have been a much better bridge player if he had been interested in the game. He basically played only to please his wife.

There were two sections of twelve or thirteen tables each, and we played the "Mitchell" movement where the north-south couple stays in the same seats the whole session, and the east-west couple moves in the opposite direction to the boards, which are moved to the next higher or lower table after having been played. Each of the boards is numbered and has four pockets labeled N-S-E-W to hold the hand of each player, so the same cards are played by each player in the couples sitting N-S-E-W. The big difference in duplicate, and the real test, is that the player is not competing with the opponents sitting at the table, but with all the other couples sitting in the same direction at the other tables.

This adds another dimension to the strategy in the bidding. Bidding and making a suit contract is not enough if one or more of the couples, holding the same cards, bid and take the same number of tricks at no-trump, which has an added bonus of 10 points for the first trick. Three no-trump-bid, making four (130 points) is a better result than the possibly safer contract of 4 hearts or spades which scores 120 points.

In my naiveté, when I first became interested in duplicate bridge, I thought that the greatest players in the U.S. and the great international stars, all holding the same cards would all arrive at the same contract. You can imagine my surprise when I bought a book reporting on a national tournament held in Dallas, which gave the layout of each hand and the bidding by each of the teams for every hand played. If there were 24 hands played, I found that there were 18 or 20 different final contracts, many of which I could not understand. And these were some of the greatest players in the world. It was a shock to learn that there was no perfect world of bridge; the human factor was very present.

I was surprised to see Merlin Smith at the game. His partner was his wife's father, who was 101 years old. With Merlin's known weakness at both play and bidding, and a partner more than 100 years old, I thought surely, we would be winners. As you can guess, this was not the case, and the Merlin Smith team beat us soundly. It was a sobering moment for me and caused Fran a good deal of amusement when she heard the results.

Ted and I made no attempt to use Schnicklefritz, needless to say; he couldn't be bothered. I think I went back to that Manatee County sponsored senior game only once several years later with a new partner, Barry Brown, from the second condo we owned at Vizcaya.

Another age-related memory at the bridge table occurred when Fran and I were visiting her "Aunt" Grace Niggeman (in reality her step-grandmother) in Port Huron, Michigan, where she taught English at the Junior College. Aunt Grace, who came from a very humble background and had noticeable social climbing tendencies, arranged for an afternoon bridge game with an older friend (I recall that she was 100 years old) Mrs. Andrea, who was related to the Dayton Department Store people in Minneapolis and whose son was one of their top executives. Fran and I used our high-scoring Schnicklefritz system, after carefully explaining it one more time, and at the end of an afternoon of very ordinary cards, found that we were the losers to a pair of ladies who were thirty or forty years older than we were.

As long as the mind is clear, allowances made for a certain slowness in sorting the cards (arthritis, anyone?) and the occasional memory lapses that come with old age, age itself is not a deterrent to playing bridge, which is one of its beauties as a game.

I remember the slow transition in my preferences for the different types of bridge games as I became more and more aware of the world of duplicate bridge. In the beginning, this seemed to me to be the ultimate test of skill, and the opportunity to observe the operation of one branch of the universal laws of mathematics, without having to be a mathematical genius. I started to follow the results in the big league world of the American Contract Bridge League (ACBL) who governed the game, and awarded the coveted "master points" to the winners of tournaments, as well as authorized (sanctioned) local games.

I remember the early days before the start of our monthly duplicate games in Brecksville that I became aware of large tournaments held in Cleveland. The Hotel Cleveland ballroom seemed to be the preferred venue, and I entered three of the tournaments over the years with three different partners: Bill Carter, Bill Braman, and Fran.

Considering the importance of this free time activity in my life, I am a little surprised that my recollections of the three occasions I played in large tournaments are not more detailed. My only memories of the first tournament was that it was held in the ballrooms of the Hotel Cleveland, and I was surprised at the number of tables. I now know that there were many divisions to accommodate the many types of competition and reflecting the level of skills (Masterpoints achieved). Bill Carter, one of the regular players in our monthly after dinner men's games that I played in, and I entered in the Novice section.

When we signed in the Director, an officious lady, confronted us, both young men in business suits, over six feet tall, and challenged us as to whether we were in the right division. We assured her we had no Masterpoints and had never played in a tournament before and we were allowed to register.

In fact, neither of us had ever seen a duplicate "board" before where the individual hands are stored and moved from table to table. We did not know that the "dummy" (declarer's partner) played the card called for by the declarer, and that all four cards were not thrown on the middle of the table, but kept in front of each player and we did not know that when we took a trick, the card was placed vertically in front of us, facing us; if the opponents took the trick, our card was kept in front of us but placed horizontally. When all the cards had been played and the tricks taken by each team totaled, the cards in front of each player were carefully gathered together and replaced in the proper pocket in the board so the players at the next table would play the same hands. Also, the scoring was different: each hand was a contest in itself.

I remember how embarrassing it was for us to have our opponents call the Director to our table to correct our many miscues, which slowed the play for the other twelve or thirteen tables. I'm sure we proved to her satisfaction that we were true novices, but it was such a nightmare experience that we didn't get much fun out of it.

A couple of years later, I entered the same tournament with my friend, Bill Braman, as my partner; a little more seasoned, and not in the Novice section. I remember two things about that evening: the great guru, Charles Goren (everyone recognized him) was in attendance strolling among the tables, kibitzing, which caused some excitement among the players; and there was one couple sitting in the stationary N-S direction, an older man with a younger, very pretty young lady partner. He had a stand next to their table with a bottle of champagne sitting in a bucket of ice in it and flutes of champagne on the table for him and his partner. He did not offer any to their opponents. It was a startling sight at that time and place and must have aroused a lot of speculation.

Fran and I entered the Buckeye Tournament, after my two earlier experiences, just once. I had been disturbed at both of the earlier tournaments by the rudeness and incivility of some of the partnerships. Many of the opposing couples were cordial, but there was a substantial percentage of the others who were downright rude, and openly critical of each other, as well as of their fresh opponents. They seemed to be out in force that evening and had no compunctions in criticizing, after the fact, very vocally both the bidding and the play of everyone else at the table. It was embarrassing. I felt these were super aggressive people who were very frustrated in their everyday life and who had found a socially acceptable place to vent their feelings without suffering any consequences.

After a long, stressful evening at the bridge table under tournament conditions, on the way home Fran said she did not wish to subject herself to such behavior again, and I agreed with her completely. It just was not the same as the friendly games we were used to. Thus, ended our tournament playing days, and we never regretted our decision. After three outings, I ended up with 0.038 of one masterpoint and still have the postcard notification from the ACBL to prove it.

I remember one other unpleasant evening playing bridge at home in Brecksville when we invited a widow friend, Bernice Willkom, who managed our Cleveland apartment properties and who had invited us to play golf and bridge at her country club, Chagrin Valley Country Club, many times.

She brought a fellow member at Chagrin Valley, Orrin (whose last name I have repressed) who was considered the most eligible bachelor in the club as her date for the evening. They arrived on time in his Cadillac, which because of the heavy snow, had to be left at the top of the driveway, and after introductions and drinks, we enjoyed the special meal Fran had prepared. We then retired to the bridge table set up in the den in front of the picture window overlooking our pond.

Orrin was a heavy drinker and had been indulging in his favorite drink, Scotch, ever since his arrival. Drinking did not improve his disposition and I was not pleased with the way he had been treating our friend, Bernice, who was a very sweet and unassuming person.

We played as couples for the whole evening and, therefore, I spent extra time in explaining the system we would be using (Schnicklefritz) to be sure Orrin understood how we would be bidding and urged him to ask us at any time for an explanation of the meaning of our bids. He continued to drink during the evening, and as I had observed many times when playing with my men friends in our monthly games, alcohol and bridge do not mix. Judgment is one of the most important elements in the game, and alcohol impairs judgment adversely.

By the end of the evening, Orrin was slurring his speech. We were far ahead in points, and as he arose to leave, he announced in a loud voice that he was glad the evening was over, that he did not enjoy having been cheated on at the bridge table the whole evening. We were amazed and speechless and Bernice was embarrassed.

To cap the evening off, after they had their coats on, I offered to back their car down to the road, and do as I had done many times before, accelerate up the driveway and butt my way to the top and pick them up at the front door. Orrin refused, and proceeded to back down the driveway and slipped off the drive at the lowest point, a very tricky spot, and the car was stuck. They had to trudge all the way back up the snowy driveway (an eighth of a mile) and we had to try to find a tow truck at midnight. Luckily, we did, and an unforgettable evening finally came to an end.

Of course, these three or four less than happy sessions at the bridge table could hardly diminish the pleasure I enjoyed over a lifetime, more than seventy years.

The prospect of being able to play was always the source of excitement, whether in one of our regular groups of friends, or with another couple, or being asked to play as a guest. My business friend, Owen Lavelle often asked me to be his partner at an all men's game at his Shaker Country Club, or to play in the after-work men's group, which met once a month in The Land Title Guarantee & Trust Company lunchroom, which was so diverse (it had members from all different strata of occupations: Tom Clutterbuck, Head the Mortgage Loan Department of the Cleveland Trust Company; Bud Crane, V.P. of Land Title Guarantee & Trust Company, the Italian consul, a union shop steward; "Honest" Tom Rohrbach, journeyman electrician, an employee of the Cleveland Board of Education; and many others and me).

Looking back, I think the greatest source of pleasure for me came when playing with Fran, my favorite partner, who had no objection to using my Schnicklefritz system, and was an excellent player of the cards she was dealt.

An excellent example of this, which I recall with relish, is the Sunday evening we were invited for a cookout and bridge by Herb Mercer. I met Herb when, as V.P. of the Cleveland Mortgage Bankers Association in charge of programs, I invited him to speak at our monthly luncheon meeting. He was the head of the local branch of General Electric Finance. He made very unusual loans, which made a big impression on a roomful of stodgy mortgage bankers used to typical mortgages secured by real estate.

We sat next to each other at the head table. In preparation for his introduction, I learned that he was a graduate of Harvard, the most unlikely Harvard grad I ever met; and that when he wasn't making crazy loans, he loved playing golf. He invited me to play with him and his No.2 man at his country club (the semi-private Oak Hills Golf Club in Lorain, Ohio) a difficult course with water hazards on 16 of the holes. It was the first of many such games. He had an unusual way of assessing risk: he did not propose the usual Nassau bet, which pays off for best scores on each nine holes and the total eighteen.

He assessed the risk on each hole, but did not bet on each hole, only on those holes where his risk assessment told him he had the advantage, and based on the difficulty of the hole and the skill he observed in his opponent (in this case me), would bet me a new golf ball that I could not play a certain hole in one over par. Later, he would propose similar bets depending on the severity of the water hazards. I had never heard of this way of betting before, and it was very interesting.

It was an enjoyable round of golf. I played reasonably well and afterwards in the locker room, we discovered that we both enjoyed playing bridge. He suggested that he have his wife call my wife and arrange a couples' game some evening. I readily agreed but warned him that we played an unusual system. After describing it to him briefly, he rubbed his hands together and said, "How soon can we get together!"

Mercer's house had been built by the builder for himself, and almost his entire backyard was paved with concrete in the middle of which was a large swimming pool.

It was a very warm Sunday evening and, unfortunately, the house was sited on the flight path of the north-south runway of the nearby Cleveland Hopkins airport, and the wind was from the north so the planes were coming in and going out low right over our heads.

With the heat and all the noise of the airplanes, Fran was not very impressed with Herb, and disliked him more as the evening wore on. We started an evening of miserable bridge hands. The Mercers had all the cards, and Herb gloated, calling attention to our "system," increasing Fran's irritation and desire to get the evening over with quickly so we could get back home. At about 11:00 p.m., having set the Mercers a few times and had a few good hands our scores were close, but the Mercers were ahead substantially. Fran suggested that we think about quitting because both men had to go to work the next morning and we had a long drive home to Brecksville. Herb insisted on just one more hand, and Fran gave in.

We finally had a hand where the system worked and in three bids; we bid a small slam, which if made, carried a 500-point bonus. Herb doubled promptly, as a matter of principal, he said, and Fran played the hand beautifully and made the bid.

Having proved our point, she then suggested again that we call it quits and go home. Herb insisted that we play one more hand. We agreed. Again, we had a hand ideally suited to the system, and once again in 3 bids, bid another small slam. If this were made, the bonus would be larger, 750 points since we were now vulnerable. This time Herb was quieter and did not double, and again Fran played the hand beautifully and made her bid. We had made back-to-back slams on the last two hands of the evening, and when Herb escorted us to our car, he kept muttering, "I don't understand." We had beaten them by 300 points, and they had had all the cards and he had been keeping score.

We played bridge with the Mercers several more times that fall and when we opened our Christmas card that year, Herb had enclosed the score sheet from our original meeting and made a comment on the card that I should be very thankful for Fran, as she had been "carrying me" for years.

We played bridge with our group of Camp Michigania friends, and were invited by our friends the Culligans who lived in Hillsdale, Michigan, easily accessible for us via the Ohio Turnpike, one weekend to substitute in one of their regular games. Bill was an excellent player and excelled in whatever he did. We had a great time; saw the small plant where he worked, the only product of which was the small bent tubing for U.S. built motorcars –millions of pieces of small diameter pipe bent to shape; and I had the opportunity to play Bill's home golf course, a 9-hole country club.

When we were in Camp, we soon learned we could skip the after dinner lectures by the visiting professor without attracting attention or criticism, and ended up playing bridge with one the couples in our circle of friends, Dick and Ruth Burmeister.

This became an annual activity which went on for years (we attended camp for twenty-five years) and was a source of frustration because they were the winners every year. We tried playing in each other's cabin; we tried playing with different cards; nothing worked, and we were not used to losing.

We looked forward to the camping activities with anticipation, but after a few years, the bridge with resignation. Dick was very intelligent, an engineer, an excellent golfer and tennis player and a gentle, all around nice person; Ruth was also very intelligent and sold real estate. They were stiff competition and, somehow or other, had the law of averages working for them. They lived in Lake Orion, Michigan, had two daughters and I supplied the peonies for their oldest daughter's wedding.

They had a condo in Fort Meyers, Florida, where we visited them and played golf on the executive course around the perimeter of their condo, and at a fine golf course nearby, Eagle's Nest. And bridge, of course, with the same results as in Michigan, as I remember. It was very humbling.

As I recall the years of warm memories spent at the bridge table, I can't help but feel grateful that I found an activity early in life which was socially acceptable and one in which I could excel. The memories recounted above should give some idea of what the game has meant to me.


In my long life most other card games seem to me to be merely ways to pass time with other people, trying to avoid the necessity of conversation by using cards as a vehicle of social interaction; games which require no special skills or mental effort, and have no subtleties: hearts, rummy and canasta come to mind. Poker and blackjack, which have never interested me, require a little more respect for the laws of mathematics, and a knowledge of psychology plays an important part.

I think those elements are necessary for any game to sustain the interest of an adult, and for me, bridge with its infinite variety of challenges, its subtleties, its mysteries suited me perfectly.

In my case, my interest in a game, which is more than just a game to me, a pastime, has endured for more than 75 years. The first thing I read in my morning newspaper is the bridge column; I am still buying, reading, and studying text books on bridge in an effort to improve my play and bidding skills after 75 years; although I remain stubbornly loyal to the system I discovered in college and use its method to evaluate every hand I am dealt.

The game itself continues to evolve, although the fundamentals remain the same, and there is always something new to learn and try to apply. Every chance to play is something exciting to look forward to. The possibilities are endless, and every hand picked up a fresh challenge: just like life itself.

# Chapter X

## Sailing

My earliest memory of the subject of sailing is from the days of my childhood on Parkwood Road when I learned that my playmate, David Cooper, had a father who was a doctor and owned a sailboat; I never learned what kind or what size, whether a racer or a cruising boat; but it had to have a sail and therefore was magical and mysterious to me. I believe the doctor was a member of the Cleveland Yacht Club at the mouth of Rocky River and Lake Erie. It wasn't a subject that was mentioned very often. But for some reason I was fascinated and always hoped that on some Wednesday afternoon, when all doctors took the afternoon off from their practice, the good doctor would invite his son's playmates to go for a sail. Sadly, it never happened. And if it had, I wonder if my mother would have allowed me to go.

My first real exposure to sailing came when we took a week of our vacation time and went to Camp Michigania, owned and operated by the University of Michigan Alumni Association, on Lake Walloon in northern Michigan, about 60 miles south of Mackinaw.

Among the many activities available was sailing and sailing instruction. Lake Walloon, which is reputed to be one of the ten most beautiful lakes in the world, is quite large, very deep, and has a unique and very beautiful shade of green water. The water could also be very cold, even in the second week of July which we discovered on what became our annual trips to camp for 25 consecutive years.

The lake was roughly "U" shaped with an "East" arm and a "West" arm and the largest, deepest middle section, where the camp was located on its shore. When we arrived on Saturday, we always paused at the high point at the entrance to look at that beautiful green water.

Campers could sign up for free instruction and, if already knowledgeable, to take one of the "fleet" of boats out for an hour's sail. The fleet was quite small and consisted of several types of sailboat, not in good condition after their hard use for many years by the former teenage campers.

I remember a Lightning, a Sea Scout, a C Scow, a Rebel, an O'Day, a couple of Sailfish, all about 12' to 14' long, and six Butterflies, which were the only new boats and had been donated by the builder, who was an old alum. The Butterfly was a scow type with a hull shaped like a pumpkin seed, about 10'long, could carry two people, and was very tippy. The instructors fastened a piece Styrofoam to the tip of the mast so when the boat capsized, which it did frequently, it would not turn completely upside down in the water ("turn turtle"), which made it very difficult to remove the sail underwater to be able to bring the boat back upright. The older boats were old and tired but most of them could carry four campers which helped satisfy the cravings of the large numbers of those who made sailing one of the most popular camp activities.

The first year there were two young coed instructors, Val and Peaches, who operated out of a shed where the sails and supplies were kept. They were also in charge of a power boat which was used for rescues of campers when they capsized and needed help. Our sailing was restricted to the middle section of the lake and we were ordered to sail close to the sailing dock until we gained experience which made for shorter runs of the "Crash" boat which was in constant use for the inevitable capsizes. I think the sailing staff got most of their fun from dashing to the crash boat, firing up the outboard motor, and charging off to the rescue.

The sailing area had its own dock and beach where the boats were pulled out of the water, after finishing a sail; the end of the hour was signaled by one of the staff blowing an air-horn which called us in. Another dock separated the sailing area from the swimming area.

After being taught the principles of sailing verbally on shore, we were taken out on the water to put them into practice.

There we learned about sailing "close" to the wind, how to "come about", "tacking" or changing directions to use the wind when one's destination was where the wind was coming from, the fun of sailing downwind. It was all strange and unfamiliar at first. I don't remember how clumsy I was at the beginning, or how long it took to be permitted to take a boat out alone, but it wasn't too long. I was too enthusiastic to be discouraged.

Once cleared, I would sign up to reserve a boat, any boat, for an hour the next day. It was never enough, and when I finished my hour, I would hang around the shed hoping that someone would fail to show up for his hour, and I could get his boat and go out on the water again.

I loved it and spent as many hours on the water as possible. It was exhilarating and peaceful at the same time. And, for me, there was an additional dimension: the realization that I was using the same principles that the Phoenicians used at the time of Jesus and his disciples.

It was frustrating to have to compete with the other campers for the use of the limited number of camp owned boats, and, since privately owned boats were permitted, after the second or third year we bought own small boat: a Skylark, manufactured by StarCraft of Goshen, Indiana.

It was 14' long, with a 20' unstayed mast which was seated in a pocket in the hull, and held upright by the tension of hoisting the mainsail, scow type but with a tunnel hull and two lee boards instead of a centerboard, and could carry two or three people. It was very fast. We bought a trailer to carry it to Camp and also for the few times we sailed on small lakes near home.

We made the effort to spend a Sunday afternoon picnicking and sailing at Punderson Lake, about 40 miles from Brecksville, and LaDue Reservoir near Chagrin Falls. I think we also tried one of the Portage Lakes in Akron, which had a public launching ramp. I remember it was fun, but a lot of effort, and it just was not the same as Camp Michigania. We never really pursued sailing near home. And we never attempted Lake Erie, which was the closest to home.

Thursday was Regatta Day at Camp Michigania, a great chance to demonstrate one's recently acquired skills, a chance to come in first in a competition which was important to many of the campers.

Skippers and chosen crew signed up for the race, and after lunch, met at the shed for the boat assignments and instructions for the race. The sailing staff used the crash boat to set the buoys for a triangular course taking the direction of the wind into account. After donning our required life jackets, hoisting our sails and milling around the starting line, the starting gun would fire and if no one was over the starting line early, the race would be on.

There was always a large crowd of spectators sitting on the hill leading down to the dock, cheering the contestants on. Watching a sailboat race from a distance is like watching grass grow; not very exciting. But if you were involved, it was challenging, fun, requiring strategy as to when to tack and skill rounding the marks. It was exhilarating. The racing became so popular it became necessary to have a second heat to satisfy the demand caused by would-be racers who had to be satisfied with the limited number of camp boats.

Awards were given after dinner on Friday night before the farewell party. In spite of clever skits and boisterous singing it was a sad occasion because it meant saying goodbye to old and new friends we would not see for another year, when we vowed to return the same week, the first Saturday after the Fourth of July.

Two amusing events occurred over the years in the regattas. Barb, our youngest daughter, took to sailing more than the other two girls, so we bought her a very cheap boat all of her own. It had a Styrofoam hull, similar to the material used for ice chests, a rounded bow. It resembled a shallow seven-foot bathtub; it had a short 9 foot mast and a red nylon lateen sail; it was called a Snark. It was safe for Barb and it was also very slow.

The Thursday regattas had become very popular by this time attracting a large number of spectators to watch the antics of the neophyte sailors. I sailed in the first heat in our Skylark with Bill Culligan as my crew. Bill became one of my best friends, comparable to my Army friends. He was highly intelligent, very gregarious, a first-rate golfer and a very good bridge player, but not so great on the water.

He was an engineer and felt, therefore, logically, that the shortest distance between two points is a straight line. This is very rare when sailing. When he was crewing on the Skylark, he had a tendency to sit too far forward and on such a lightweight boat with a scow type hull, it depressed the bow just enough to produce a submarining effect and we lost the race.

Being the fanatic I was, and Barb having raced in the first heat in her Snark and not wanting to race a second time, I decided to enter the 2nd heat using Barb's Snark this time. I weighed at least twice as much as the boat and with a soft nylon sail of only 90 square feet, it was hopelessly slow.

I think I was only approaching the 2nd mark when the rest of the other boats had crossed the finish line in front of the sailing dock. At this time, everyone was yelling at me, urging me to quit. The crash boat even came out and asked me if I would like to quit. The staff offered to tow me in. But I refused and, sailing downwind in very light air, sprawled out on the bottom, holding the tiller over my shoulder, slowly wended my way to the finish line, where several spectators had gathered on the dock and the hillside to watch me float over the finish line.

They had all gone back to their cabins for drinks and get cleaned up for dinner and stopped on their way back to watch the finish of the slowest regatta in Camp history. I went directly into the dining hall for the dinner I almost missed.

An unexpected consequence of this audacious exploit was that I spoiled the boat for Barb and she never set foot in it again. I don't remember if she even went back down to the sailing dock again that year. I think we may just have given the boat to the camp to add to their fleet. If we didn't do that, we must have used as a trade-in for the much better, safer, more comfortable, faster Sunfish we bought for her for Camp the next year.

Of course, that meant we had to have our boat trailer modified so that we could carry Barb's new boat on a rack above my Skylark, quite a sight. I had heard of two-house families and two-car families, but two-sailboat families?

One of the other outstanding regattas Bill Culligan and I entered, was one where we were assigned the C Scow (a misnomer- it was not a scow; it had a typical hull). It was a little larger and had a mainsail and a jib to be tended by the crew (Bill). Being the experienced sailors that we were, having done regattas before; and being as smart as we were; we decided to skip the skippers briefing before the race and assumed it was a two-lap race.

We did the regular first course in good shape, passed the finish line and proceeded to come about to begin the second lap when suddenly everyone was screaming at us that the race was over. Unfortunately, one of the lines was fouled while coming about and the boat was out of control as we tried to return to the dock. We came so close to the judges' committee boat (one of whom was filming us bearing down on them and frantically waving us off) that we cut their anchor line. The water was sixty feet deep at that point and the owner of his new anchor was not at all happy. We caromed off the sailing dock and finally were able to stop just before hitting the swimming dock. It was a spectacular performance.

The next night was the awards ceremony, where the outstanding performers in each of the camp activities received their rewards for their efforts in front of all the other campers.

With all five of our teen age daughters in attendance (hiding their heads in shame) Bill and I, wearing our balloon sleeved golfing sweaters, heads held high, carrying our golf umbrellas, proudly marched up the aisle to receive our award: a specially made trophy for each of us called "The Sinking Ship Award." It was a flat block of wood, with a sipping straw for a mast and a little rag of cloth for a sail. I saved mine for years and cannot remember what happened to it. It is one of the many wonderful memories associated with my camping adventures at Camp Michigania.

Another is of the year when "Bump" Elliot, head football coach, and his family were invited as one of the two faculty guest lecturers to give after dinner talks to those interested. He entered into all the camp activities just like an ordinary camper, including learning how to sail.

One of my most amusing memories is his sailing one of the Butterflies on his first day of lessons, about 50' in front of the swimming area and reasoning with, and finally persuading, his lovely wife, Barbara, to join him for a sail. She was reluctant and protested, "You don't know how to sail!" but somehow managed to crawl aboard while in the water, and they promptly capsized. When she surfaced, her hair looked like a poodle after a bath, and she was sputtering and furious. She had gone into Petoskey, Michigan, that morning and had her hair done. I'll never forget the look on her face. Or the sight of her ruined hairdo.

The next stage in my sailing career occurred about the time of my 50th birthday. We had been going to Camp Michigania for several years where I spent most of my time on the water when not golfing and it must have been very obvious to Fran that I was obsessed with sailing. We had been guests two or three times of our Brecksville friends, the Billings and the Puhls, on their large sailboats which they docked in Sandusky, Ohio, about an hour west of Cleveland via the Ohio Turnpike.

I remember it was on the Sunday we celebrated Nancy's husband, Paul's, 26th birthday (when he could no longer be drafted into the Army). Later, after they left and the dishes were done, I was sitting in my chair up in the den watching TV and reading when Fran came and joined me and said, "You know, you're now 50, and I think if you are ever going to, now is the time for you to get a bigger boat". I said, "Are you serious?" She replied, "Yes. But on two conditions: It must be docked here in Cleveland so we can go for evening sails to help you relieve your business tensions and it mustn't be so large that just the two of us can't handle it." And that was the beginning of a great adventure that lasted for almost 10 years.

I don't remember the details of how we found our first boat, or how long it took, but I don't remember a broker being involved. It was owned by a man named Tony Brock, who lived in Mentor, Ohio, who was upgrading to a larger boat.

The boat was a LeComte, fiberglass hull, 33' feet in length, 12' beam and 5' draft, sloop rigged, full complement of sails, and a 4 cylinder 15 hp gas engine fueled from a 15 gallon tank carved out of the keel. It was fiber glass lined that caused problems every year by the gasoline degrading the fiberglass and depositing it on the carburetor which had to be replaced. It also provided the fuel for the galley stove. It had 6' headroom in the cabin and slept four people. I think the total weight was 5 or 6 tons. It was built in the Netherlands and the quality of the workmanship in its finishing work was remarkable. It was the equivalent of the American Hinckley built in Maine, which was considered the Rolls Royce of sailboats.

This was a huge step up in size from a little 14' daysailer. But the same principals of sailing obtained. We would still be using the wind, which is free, as our source of power. We were fortunate that one of the previous owner's employees, Warren Weiant, was assigned to teach us how to manage our new boat and he became a good friend and mentor; he sailed and raced with us many times throughout the rest of our sailing days. He was even more obsessed with sailing than I was and was a wonderful helmsman, so critical when racing. I could always count on him to join us when we raced.

We docked the boat on the Grand River about 20 miles east of Cleveland (a long way from Brecksville) just tying up at a public area near the large shed where we stored the boat during the winter. This was in the little city of Grand River, which was the home of the famous football coach, Don Shula. It had a good restaurant and a food stand where we could buy fresh caught yellow perch and eat it aboard in the stern cockpit, after an afternoon of sailing, which was a new and very pleasant experience for us.

After a few weeks and having gained a little confidence out on Lake Erie, we joined a yacht club in Cleveland, the Lakeside Yacht Club, just east of the Burke Lakefront Airport, close to E. 9th Street. This satisfied one of Fran's conditions, that of being easily accessible, in contrast to our friends, the Billings, who had to drive an hour and a half to Sandusky to use their boat, and consequently, used it only on weekends.

One of the big problems in acquiring a sailboat is picking a name for it. I didn't want to go the "cute" route for a beautiful boat, choosing something like *Chapter XI*, or *Chicken of the Sea*, or *Renegade* (a particularly ugly name used by one of our Brecksville friends for his boat) or *Res Ipsa Loquiter* (used by a Cleveland attorney for his 50' Columbia, the largest boat at the club, which it was a good idea to avoid at the starting line for the Wednesday Club races).

I considered names associated with bridge: *Finess, Doubled, Notrump, Grand Slam*, but nothing struck my fancy. I then considered names associated with music: *Con Fuoco, or Presto, or Allegro, or Allegretto, or Fortissimo.* With Fran's approval, I finally settled on *Sarabande*, which was a stately court dance in the 1700s. It was a beautiful name for a beautiful boat, and it turned out to be very apt. When racing she was stately and very slow. We were always among the last to finish.

As soon as we moved from the Grand River west to Lakeside, the club members started to urge me to compete in the Wednesday evening club races which were a short triangular course on Lake Erie and usually lasted about an hour and a half to two hours. I said that I had no interest in racing, only in family cruising. They persisted and about this time I had flown to Hartford where I tried to sell a large mortgage to the Aetna Life Insurance Company. (I don't remember if I was successful).

On the flight home, I sat next to a man about my age who turned out to be very interested in sailing. He grew up in New Rochelle, New York; had an uncle who was an Admiral in the Coast Guard; and learned sailing on an Atlantic class sailboat on Long Island Sound. In the business world he was an Arborist. His name was Fred Robinson.

He was very interested in *Sarabande* and offered to crew for us. He was stocky, cheerful, very competitive, and the best helmsman I ever met, especially at the start of a race when jockeying for position to be first over the starting line and thus to enjoy the unperturbed air; most races are won at the starting line. And he brewed wonderful, iced tea.

Fred soon became our principal crew member. Between him and Warren Weiant, we attracted a cadre of dedicated, experienced crew members and we did begin to participate in the club's Wednesday evening race series..

Although not the same as the regattas at Camp Michigania, something happened I would never have predicted: I loved racing and the competition and became addicted to it.

I don't remember too much about those early races; I think we rounded up four or five regular crew (including me), everyone assembling and getting the boat ready, selecting which jib (Genoa) sail to use depending on the wind speed, proceeding to the starting area off E. 55th Street and then grinding out the race to the bitter end. Both Fred and Warren were superior helmsmen (far better than me), but no matter how hard we tried, or how skillfully we executed our strategies, we never finished in the top three. I now think the classic wine glass shaped underwater hull may have provided stability and safety, but the boat was not designed for speed, which was not what we were looking for initially, of course.

There were seldom two boats from the same builder in the races, which in the interest of fairness and an attempt to provide an even playing field, required handicapping. The boats were divided into two classes: IOR (International Offshore Racers) which tended to be big, fast, and expensive and were not handicapped; and PHRF (Performance Handicap Racing Fleet) which was a more plebeian group and did require handicapping based on boat length and weight. In the PHRF class, which we sailed in, our actual time elapsed from start to finish was adjusted to arrive at the final rankings. I was never involved in this aspect of racing, never served on a race committee, and have no idea what the formula looked like. It must have worked because I never heard any complaints about the final standings.

The second year we did one long overnight race which was initiated by our club, Lakeside. The race was called the Governor's Cup, and was attended the first year, about the middle of October, by Governor O'Neill, Governor of Ohio. The race was open to any member of the ILYA (Inter-Lake Yachting Association) and attracted boats from many distant clubs, one from Canada.

The course was due north from Lakeside to Rondeau, Canada; then west to the Colchester Reef, off Toledo; and then turning east, back to Lakeside. The distance was about 150 miles. At an average speed of about 3-4 knots per hour, this meant the race could last for as long as three days and more extensive planning was required. There are no grocery stores, or drugstores, or hardware stores out on Lake Erie. We had to plan for food and water for an expanded crew of eight or nine men who had to be divided into watches for sleeping.

It was quite different from the short Wednesday night events at the club. Also, I'm sure the crew was thinking of the "big" races: the Mackinac, the Bermuda, and the SORC (Southern Ocean Racing Circuit). I think we all had visions of sugarplums, vicariously. But it was very tiring; and I never was able to sleep well while the boat was under way - something about the sound of the water flowing over the hull and the sense of motion.

We finished dead last. We entered the next year with the same result.

One of the annual races was a one-way race, The Plain Dealer Charities Cup,(?) from Cleveland Yacht Club in Rocky River to the Mentor Yacht Club 25 miles to the east. It did not count in the Inter-Lake Yacht Association standings. It was near the end of the season and a fun occasion when one could invite wives, and family and friends as crew and relax for an easy ride with a little spice added by the competition. After crossing the finish line and entering the harbor through a narrow inlet (which had to be dredged every season) each boat was greeted with a bag of ice thrown aboard from the shore by Mentor club members, with a live Dixieland band playing in the background. We rafted off (boats tied up, side to side when there are more boats than dockside tie-ups) which required climbing over strangers' boats to get to dry land.

After getting settled, the day was finished off with a banquet, awards to the winners, and dancing. It was all very convivial and a pleasant contrast to the tensions of a "serious" race. We stayed and slept aboard after the other crew dispersed and Fred went to his home which was nearby.

Fran joined us on one of these races, which she rarely did. We sailed the boat out to the Cleveland Yacht Club Friday night and slept at our daughter Nancy's home in Rocky River, very near our mooring. Fred Robinson had driven over from Mentor and left his car at Nancy's house. We motored out to the starting line Saturday morning. We had a good start in very light air. The wind was probably 4-5 mph. Slow and not much fun on a hot, sunny day. It was strategy time; we could stay close to shore and sail a rhumb (straight) line to Mentor, hoping an offshore breeze would pick up; or we could work our way farther out on the lake where there might be a stronger breeze. The question was: would the time taken to get far off the straight line trying to find more wind (which would translate into higher speed but might not be there), and how far should we go in our search of wind before turning back east to Mentor; or would it be more or less than the time spent on the straight-line course? We chose the close to shore option which proved to be the wrong decision, especially in a slow, heavy boat. Fran, who was very competitive in her quiet way, was upset as she saw much smaller boats on our same course go zooming by. She said, "We've got to get a faster boat!"

I remember the first fall when we had to move *Sarabande* out to the shed on Grand River, a little beyond the Mentor Yacht Club, for her indoor winter storage. We chose the last Saturday in October so that Nancy's husband, Paul, and an experienced sailor friend of his (on small lakes), Larry Heidleburg, from NASA where they both worked, would not lose a day off work to make the trip. The weather was terrible: very cold, very strong east wind in our face requiring many short tacks, very choppy waves. With only three men aboard, the trip was very tiring. It was a question whether we should have had more crew to handle the boat under such conditions.

Then it became much more interesting: by the time we reached Bratenahl, only a mile or so, Larry became sea sick and was virtually helpless; that meant that Paul and I would have to adjust the sails on the many tacks. We arrived safely at the Grand River, cold and miserable, eight hours later, exhausted, and turned the boat over to the winter storage-shed people. I was not present when, later, they lifted *Sarabande* out of the water, removed her mast, placed her on a cradle and moved her into the shed with about 20 other large boats. We called Fran and Nancy who drove from Rocky River to pick us up for the long ride home.

I learned that day that there is such a thing as fair-weather sailing, quite different from the conditions we endured, which were nothing compared to what sailors endured before the days of steam, when crossing the ocean. It was just a taste for us, but one that I would try to avoid whenever possible in the future. I don't remember either Paul or Larry ever sailing with me again.

Once again, Fran was serious when she said we had to get a faster boat and we spent the fall and winter after *The Plain Dealer* race poring over *Yachting Magazine* which I had subscribed to for years, checking cabin layouts and specifications from the various boat builders, and reading the ads. The details of the search are hazy in my memory.

While we were starting our search, I do remember a trip to Grosse Pointe in the Fall to visit Fran's oldest friend, Evelyn Montgomery. Her husband Bill's father was a member of the Detroit Yacht Club and owned a racing sailboat. Bill leaned to sail on this boat and became an outstanding helmsman, his father letting him skipper the boat in the DYC races while still a teenager.

While visiting we told them of our search for a larger and faster boat and Bill was delighted to be a part of the search process. We inspected two or three boats for sale at marinas on the Detroit River and I remember the feeling I had, standing behind the wheel while moored at the dock, of an Islander 44 at how vast the foredeck was, and how would one know where the prow was when docking. In a future race we came across another Islander 44 and it was clumsy and slow. It would have been a fine boat for cruising with the family, but not for racing.

Another smaller boat we looked at, a Ranger 36 if I recall correctly, had had a leak from the head into the bilge. I couldn't imagine offering a boat in that condition for sale, and we couldn't get back ashore quickly enough.

Somehow or other, during that winter we located and bought a much larger used boat, probably through a broker, Sailing Inc., located just east of Lakeside Yacht Club, and undoubtedly traded *Sarabande* in for it. I have no idea what became of her. I remember keeping an eye out for her when we were sailing, but never saw her again. We had had her for only three seasons.

The new boat was built by Cuthbert & Cassian, located in Niagara-on-the Lake, Ontario, commonly referred to among the sailing fraternity as a C&C 39. She had a white fiberglass hull, teak deck, and a length of 39", a 54'mast (4' of additional height for racing), scimitar shaped keel weighing 6 tons, 6' draft, 9 tons weight overall, 2 cylinder Volvo diesel motor (much safer than gasoline and able to be hand cranked to start if the batteries were low). There was propane gas for cooking (stored outside in a locker accessible only from the cockpit - a much safer fuel), 15 gallon fuel tank, 6' 6" headroom in the cabin, galley, refrigerator, navigator's desk, head, ship to shore radio, depth sounder and wind speed and direction indicator at the tip of the mast, three compasses, wheel steering, a teak dining table, and could comfortably sleep seven people. In addition, she had a full complement of 9 sails: main, three Genoas, three spinnakers (three each for use according to wind speed/strength), a tall boy and a drifter. We replaced the No. 1 Genoa (the largest foresail) made by a sail maker in Rocky River on old Lake Road the second year at a cost of $1,500, which was a good investment as it increased our speed measurably. Sails were stored in the bow, which had a hatch to the deck for ease of access.

It was heaven! And she was fast and wonderful in heavy weather.

However, once again, we had the problem of finding a suitable name for a beautiful boat: new boat, new name. This time I ruled out names associated with either music or bridge, and never even thought of trying to find a name from the many peonies I had. Luckily, I read a quotation in a newspaper article from a speech made by Danton, one of the leaders of the French Revolution in which he stressed the need for "*audace*" (audacity) for France to survive. This quality seemed fitting for a boat to be used for racing, and I liked the sound of it, and settled on *Audace* as the name for our new boat. I was never sure that anyone else at the club knew the connotations, and I had to explain the meaning of this French word and its pronunciation to the crew.

I am frustrated that I can't recall all the wonderful memories of the experiences we had sailing *Audace*: the many races we won, all so similar, but each distinctive in its own way; and the cruises to the Lake Erie islands off Sandusky; and the peaceful evening sails marveling at the beauty of the lights of downtown Cleveland at night seen from the water; and how different it appeared from daytime. It is mainly a blur of constant excitement and pleasure.

I think everything that could happen to a sailboat happened to us, except having a man go overboard or capsizing. We had two collisions while racing (not our fault); ran aground at Vermilion at midnight and, luckily, were able to back off; hit a submerged log in the Cuyahoga River which bent the propeller shaft which had to be replaced at a cost of $400 - fascinating to watch how it was done; had the forestay on *Sarabande* break at the beginning of a race which could have caused the mast to collapse, which would have been a disaster; were almost blown over when a sudden squall appeared at twilight and we couldn't see it coming - we had a novice guest with us for a quiet evening sail and she was as excited as I was; had a spinnaker blow out during a race with the difficulty of retrieving it while under way. It wasn't only winning races that provided excitement.

Since we had been racing regularly at Lakeside Yacht Club on Wednesday nights, it was easy to slip into place with *Audace*. As I recall, we usually were among the top three finishers, and also in the larger weekly ILYA races. It was a pleasant change and we accumulated a bagful of trophy flags (which some skippers ran up their forestay while at dock before a race either out of pride, or to try to intimidate the other boats¨ we never resorted to this.. I think we had more blues (1st Place) than red and white. We collected our fair share of the more traditional forms of awards: pewter cups and plaques. In our various downsizing moves as we grew older, I gave the bag of flags to Fred Robinson, who was more responsible than anyone else for our winning them, and don't know what became of the other trophies which were displayed on the bookshelves in the recreation room of our home in Brecksville where only I ever looked at them.

When we started racing *Audace*, we needed a larger crew to manage the boat and provide the additional muscle needed to handle the larger sails and winches, if we were to realize the full capabilities of the boat. There were always enthusiasts (sail bums, male and female, some with more experience than others, some more compatible with the rest of the crew than others) hanging around the docks before a race and gradually we acquired a reliable group who became our regular crew. Sadly, I don't remember many of their names. On the long races where we needed 8 or 9 crew, there was always Fred Robinson, Warren Weiant, and several times Bill Montgomery, who would join us from Detroit, which gave us a huge advantage because they were all such fine helmsmen, very adept at adjusting the sails for maximum speed and able to stay on course. I may have said it before, but it is crucial to have a fresh helmsman every 45 minutes in order to maintain the level of concentration needed, which cannot be maintained for more than 45 minutes at a time. Being able to rotate three superb helmsmen gave us a distinct advantage. I do remember Clark Davies, whose wife's family had a home at Put-in-Bay, was our navigator. I do not remember the name of our fore-deck man, who was older and extremely competent, and who brought his girlfriend with him, who happened to be a genius at flying the spinnaker. Harry Bartels, a Brecksville veterinarian who loved to sail, filled in for us as extra crew when we did Bay Week. Another time we took along another member of Lakeside whose 26' boat was in for repairs as a guest crewmember. This was the race where Fred Robinson, who always started races for us, got caught over the line when the starting gun was fired. Fred was close enough that he was able to do a "dip" start (where the boat is caught over the starting line and has to come about to re-cross the line, tacking, to cross the line properly ahead of the other competitors). Fred did this so expertly that *Audace* was several boat lengths ahead of the rest of the fleet. Our guest who been sailing for a long time was astounded. He had never seen it done in a large boat before. I can remember the look on his face but can't remember his name.

I was only allowed to handle the helm in quiet, unimportant times. I was the "owner", and the crew was always aware of it, but my role was to act more as the CEO, delegating the jobs of the crew, casting the deciding vote when to tack or change course and helping with hauling lines and with the winches. Usually as a reward, I was allowed to bring the boat back to the dock after the race.

Once at Bay Week at Put-in-Bay, after a race, we were anchored out at a mooring in the bay, and I was at the wheel and gave the orders to drop the sails at the perfect time. The boat turned at a right angle and with its momentum drifted to a stop precisely over the mooring buoy. As I recall there were a few raised eyebrows.

Fran refused to sail with me alone, a violation of her second condition, and for a long time I felt that she didn't have confidence in my sailing ability. But I now realize that she was more concerned with what she would do if something were to happen to me, and she had to try to handle such a large boat by herself. Nevertheless, I always felt I was a much better sailor than the crew gave me credit for, but probably was not quite as good as I thought I was.

There was a sameness to the races; always the excitement in the preparation; being sure we had everything we could possibly need, the right charts, spare parts, batteries; and plenty of water and food, which was lavish when the Montgomery's came down from Grosse Pointe for the Governor's Cup Race with their friends, the John Bakers). Evelyn and Sadie Baker, the wives who stayed at home with Fran, supplied us with lots of goodies and lots of fresh fruit. Other skippers in their pursuit of winning did everything they could to eliminate weight on their boats, limiting food and luggage, removing dining tables, etc. Not us! We went first class and the crew knew it and I think it helped us win.

Other than the Governor's Cup Race, I suppose the highlight of the racing season was "Bay Week" which was held the first week of August at Put-in-Bay Yacht Club on South Bass Island. This was a three-day regatta of races around the island with the direction of the wind determining in which direction the island would be circled. The regatta was a highly competitive event and attracted upwards of three hundred of the best boats on Lake Erie. It was organized and run very efficiently by the host Put-in-Bay Yacht Club, of which our crew member, Clark Davies, later became Commodore.

We didn't compete the first year we had *Audace* but did so in later years. I had to take vacation time because it was more than just a weekend, which also made it a little more difficult to find crew who could fit the time into their schedules. But it was a fun experience. It happened that two of the regular crew, Warren Weiant and Clark Davies, a fellow Yale graduate and our navigator, had summer homes at Put-in-Bay, not far from the finish line for the races.

One of the years, Fran did come with us and we stayed with the Weiants. I know she joined us with the Davies children, three young daughters, for a Sunday sail and that we sailed to School House Bay where we deliberately grounded *Audace* and scrubbed the growth off her bottom to make her go faster. The children loved being part of it. I wish I could remember if Fran did any of the races with us and shared in that excitement. The children decorated their bikes with signs proclaiming "Team *Audace*" and rode around the waterfront and Perry's Monument, giving us some free advertising, and checking out the boat to see that it was still safe at its mooring spot in the harbor.

South Bass is one of a group of small islands in shallow water at the western end of Lake Erie extending all the way north to Pelee Island in Canada. It was a vacation paradise for fishermen and sailors. The islands were accessible by ferry from Sandusky and Port Clinton, and by flying into a small airport on South Bass in a Ford Trimotor airplane, a working relic of the early days of aviation. There was a state park on the north shore of Kelly's Island, and on South Bass, the Lonz

Winery, the Perry Monument and a lively tourist-oriented business district which attracted many vacationers. Clark Davies' father-in-law lived on South Bass year-round and was the island doctor. On the mainland, about halfway between Cleveland and Detroit, Cedar Point amusement park had a hotel, beach, many exciting roller coaster rides, and its own marina. Even then it attracted more than a million visitors per season. The area had something for everyone and was a great place to explore in a sailboat. I was told that the water was so shallow, less than 6 feet in some places, that it was possible for year-round residents to walk over the ice to the mainland when Lake Erie froze over in the winter.

Memories of the four or five times we participated in Bay Week are warm, punctuated by the excitement of the actual races which was enhanced by the informal activities made possible by the family atmosphere provided by having two crew members living on the island.

Bay Week always started with "Feeder Races" from the various competing yacht clubs on Friday night to arrive at Put-in-Bay on Saturday in time to prepare for the three days of racing starting on Monday. The idea was that one had to get one's boat to the site of the competition, so why not make it more interesting by racing there.

In the case of Lakeside Yacht Club in Cleveland, about 50 miles from South Bass Island, our race began on Friday night about 7:30 p.m., starting from the Cleveland Yacht Club at Rocky River, competing against the other Cleveland area yacht clubs. It was an all-night race and we expected to arrive at our destination sometime early Saturday morning.

One of the years, in very heavy weather, when one of the R Class wooden hull racing boats sank, *Audace* finished with a triple first: first boat from Cleveland to arrive in real time, first in handicapped rating, and first in our class. It was quite a feat. And, if I remember correctly, we went on to win first place in the official Bay Week race series in our class.

I remember after one of the races, while we were relaxing in one of the island cafes, overhearing one of the other LYC boats critiquing their performance and listening to their skipper exhorting his crew to do better, how they could improve; I was pleased, I took pleasure and pride, that we never felt we had to resort to such tactics. We never did practice sails to drill on various procedures, either. The *Audace* crew was experienced (except me), and just did their thing. And, I always felt we had a definite advantage having the three super helmsmen on board to spell each other, fresh after their time away from the wheel, keeping us at maximum speed, sailing close to the wind, and intuitively knowing when to tack at the right time.

We usually anchored out in the harbor to avoid the congestion of the marina and the inconvenience of having to raft off because of the shortage of dock space. Another reason was to avoid the noise of the constant partying, which went on for hours after the races. The race committee provided a power boat taxi service circling through the anchorage which made it easy to go ashore. I have a vivid memory of being up early one Sunday morning and seeing our internist, Dr. Larry Malm, an ardent sailboat racer, and a very serious professional in his office, posing on the prow of the taxi, after a night of partying, like George Washington crossing the Delaware River at Trenton, I wondered if we should be thinking of changing doctors. Of course, we didn't and were the beneficiaries of his great skill until his retirement.

The Davies' children were involved again when we had T-shirts printed at one of the local stores in "downtown" Put-in-Bay with *Audace* on the front of the shirt for anyone to see when walking towards us and a synonym on the back of the shirt in case they were curious and turned their heads to see what the meaning of *Audace* was. Twelve or thirteen of us lined up in the Weiant's backyard, including the younger "Team Audace" members, and one of the wives took our pictures both front and rear views. Some of the synonyms on the back of the shirts were a little raunchy: three of the more daring senior members of the crew chose "Balls"; on the other hand, Fran chose the more dignified "Derring-Do," as befitted the wife of the owner. I can't remember what I chose.

The year that Fran was able to join us we stayed at the Weiant cottage. It was nice not having to sleep aboard *Audace*. She chose not to race with us but enjoyed the post-race pleasures: sails exploring other nearby islands, and dinner at one of the many good restaurants within walking distance on the island. After the awards ceremony, she drove home ferrying part of the crew back to Brecksville via Lakeside Yacht Club.

Meanwhile, three of us, including Fred Robinson, had to sail back home. One year we left about four p.m. and it was a gray day with a fairly strong wind from the east in our face. We would have do one tack at a 45 degree angle to the wind to get far enough out on the lake, almost to the Canadian shore, before making the single tack to bring us back close to Cleveland, or would have to do many short tacks to stay closer to the rhumb line which was the choice we made. In either case it was going to be a very long trip. I was never comfortable trying to use the ship-to-shore radio, but it was taking so long, when we were opposite Lorain, and still had 30 miles to go, I called Fran to tell her we were safe and would be very late getting in and not to plan dinner. I think it was well after midnight when we finally arrived at Lakeside Yacht Club and put the boat to bed.

As we left Put-in-Bay, Clark Davies, who stayed behind with his family at their home on the island, circled us in his small Lyman motor boat as we set off and took some amazing photographs of *Audace* under full sail with me at the wheel. He held his 35 mm camera in one hand, steered his boat with the other and I still can't believe how sharp the focus was, considering how small his boat was and how choppy the waves were. They are the best photos we ever had of *Audace* by far. I had 3' x 4' enlargements made and presented them to the key crew members as Christmas presents. I also had smaller 11" x 14" enlargements made and framed, and they hang in my bedroom today, a daily reminder of past glory days. If only the sun had been shining!

I find it curious now, and a little sad, that none of my brothers, one of whom bought a power cruiser and joined the Cleveland Yacht Club, nor my father, ever set foot on *Audace*, or even mentioned seeing it. And none of our daughters, except Barbara, the youngest, who crewed for us twice on short Saturday morning races, seemed to have the slightest interest in our boat. I know I didn't talk about sailing or owning a large sailboat at the office where we saw each other every day.

And I certainly didn't brag about any of our exploits. I would have been happy to share the experience of sailing if they had expressed the slightest interest. It may have been that they were not as comfortable near the water as I was, and their true interests outside of the office, where we saw each other and worked together every day, lay elsewhere.

Using the boat for business entertaining was minimal. I can recall only two or three occasions when I took visiting insurance company investors for a short sail inside the breakwater after work before taking them to dinner, once with two men from our Canadian company, Confederation Life Assurance Company, of Toronto. I have no idea if this was a useful sales tool when submitting a large commercial loan for approval.

Twice we took business friends who were also social friends out for evening sails after work which involved going out four or five miles from shore, dropping the sails, and drifting while eating the picnic supper Fran had prepared; then re-hoisting the sails and cruising until it was time to return to our dock.

The one such sail that remains foremost in my memory is the time we took the Struchens, who substituted in one of our bridge groups from time to time on such a sail. Maury Struchen was two years ahead of me at Lakewood High School, was the drum major in the marching band, neither drank nor smoked, lived on Cleveland's west side all his life, and went on to become the Chairman of the Society National Bank, one of Cleveland's largest. Our mortgage company originated and serviced residential loan for the bank, and our youngest daughter, Barbara, worked at Society National at one time.

My recollection of our evening sail is of a very restful evening with just enough light breeze to keep us moving smoothly. When the evening came to an end and we had returned to our dock, Maury observed how peaceful the evening had been and how beautiful the city lights were when seen from the water.

The other midweek evening sail was slightly different. We invited my business friend, Jack Wyse and his new and beautiful wife, Bea, to go for a sail. Jack was the *Publisher of Properties Magazine* which covered real estate activity in greater Cleveland. Every year he invited me to play golf at his country club, Hawthorne Valley, usually in a foursome which included real estate owners or developers who might be useful contacts in our mortgage business. Jack was Jewish and very genial, and I believe we understood each other and were good friends. He was an excellent golfer and a great raconteur; had an endless supply of Jewish jokes which he told after dinner at the annual Mortgage Bankers Association banquets; and he was asked back to be the after dinner speaker year after year. We also placed ads in his magazine regularly. We had to. All our competitors did, as he wisely pointed out.

I will never forget seeing them walk down the dock to come on board. As I recall it was about 7 p.m. and we only had snacks that evening. Bea was wearing a very smart party dress and 3'spike heel shoes; Jack was wearing white slacks, a navy-blue double-breasted blazer with brass buttons, and a yachtsman's hat. Very sharp, very smart. It was breathtaking. I hoped they had not gone out to buy new outfits for the occasion. Of course, high heels, and leather soled shoes are a no-no on a sailboat, but Fran and I exchanged glances and didn't say a word.

Unfortunately, there wasn't a breath of air. Nevertheless, we hoisted the main and the jib sails, hoping an evening offshore breeze would spring up; turned on the motor; backed away from the dock and set out for our sail with the sails hanging uselessly. We bravely motored slowly inside the breakwater all the way past the Cuyahoga River - still no wind- and continued west to the entrance of the Edgewater Yacht Club - still no wind- turned, and motored back, sails still flapping listlessly, and after two hours of this activity returned to our dock.

When they left, they were profuse in their thanks; couldn't thank us enough for giving them one of the most exciting evenings they had ever had. I often wondered what they would have thought if we had a more typical sail in a stiff 10 mph breeze.

The contrast to that ride was the evening that we were joined by our Brecksville bridge club friends, Ted and "Mickey" Billings, who had their own 34' sailboat at the Sandusky Yacht Club where we sailed to join them for a weekend every summer. Fred Robinson was with us also. It was twilight when we left our dock and there was a 10-15 mph breeze and small choppy waves. We set our sails and decided to use the No. 3 (smallest) jib sail, which would slow our speed somewhat, (actually, quite a bit) but would make the ride more comfortable for the wives. We sailed inside the breakwater to the mouth of the Cuyahoga River and then north to the Lake and continued north to the "Crib", the city's water intake structure about a mile offshore. It was a smooth ride, and the boat was not heeling. As we rounded the crib, Ted's wife became very fearful and made such a fuss that we aborted the sail and returned to our dock. I have never forgotten or understood that performance but am sure her reasons were very complicated. Mickey was athletic and an excellent golfer and swimmer. She had been spending every weekend sailing in Sandusky with her husband, alone, for two or three years, so she was somewhat experienced and even knew a little about handling a boat. We were in no danger at any time, whatsoever.

One final recollection is of a sail from Lakeside Yacht Club to the Sandusky Yacht Club to spend a Labor Day weekend with the Billings. Their dock neighbors were spending the weekend at the State Park on Kelly's Island, and we could use their dock while they were away which could not have been more convenient for us.

We invited Fred Robinson to join us and he brought along a high school classmate, recently divorced, with whom he had become re-acquainted at a high school class reunion in New Rochelle, New York. The big attraction for her was that, if she came all the way to Cleveland, Fred could arrange for her to have her first ride in a big sailboat.

We left Lakeside early Saturday morning, very disappointed that there was no wind. We motored until noon, to a point opposite the Avon Lake power plant. Very boring. I remember Fran at the wheel; me cleaning the white plastic safety lines which were quite grimy, and I don't remember what Fred was doing: entertaining his new girlfriend, no doubt.

Suddenly, as was often the case on Lake Erie, without warning, a very strong easterly wind sprang up and with Fran still at the helm, Fred and I went forward and set our spinnaker. The wind was dead behind us and picking up speed; the lake developed long smooth swells, and suddenly we were "surfing".

Maximum hull speed, a function of the length of a boat's waterline, for 39' length, was about 7-8 knots, against the wind, and we rarely achieved that speed. We were now doing 10, 11, 12, 13 knots in a crescendo, climbing the crest of the swell, pausing, then coasting down to the bottom of the trough, then resuming 10, 11, 12, 13 knots. This went on for more than three hours. It was like riding one of the Cedar Point roller coasters. Fran had gladly relinquished the wheel to Fred, and I started forward to tend the spinnaker. Fred's girlfriend was cowering in the rear of the cockpit, absolutely terrified. I could see her white knuckles all the way from my place forward at the mast.

On a sailboat the sensation of speed feels like ten times the speed of an automobile on land. Thus, if you're making a stately 4 knots, on the water, it feels like 40 mph on land. It felt very much as though we were traveling 100-130 mph. Never having approached that kind of speed before, it was very exciting. At the same time, I was very afraid. This became terror when we could see the Cedar Point beach, the signal that it was time to take down the spinnaker and found that the line was jammed at the masthead, and we could not free it. When under spinnaker it is impossible to change course more than a few degrees and we were roaring down on the channel from Sandusky Bay to Lake Erie where the water on the west side of the channel was only 5' deep. Our draft was 6'. If we could not free the line and get the spinnaker down, slow our speed and change our course, we would cross the channel at full speed and tear the bottom off the boat.

Fortunately, just in time, with both Fran and me heaving and jerking on the line desperately, it freed up and we got the spinnaker down and back on board and we escaped a maritime disaster. Absolutely the most hair-raising experience I ever had on a sailboat.

I don't remember another thing about the whole weekend. I don't remember anything about Fred's girlfriend, whether she sailed back to Cleveland with us, or took a bus back to Cleveland, or whether he ever heard from her again. When I think of her, I wonder how she would respond to another invitation to "go for a sail," and how far she would travel for the chance.

Thinking about "flying" the spinnaker made me remember some of the other things I learned about sail handling. I learned there are no brakes on a 9-ton sailboat. The only way to avoid colliding with another boat, or running into a dock, is by controlling the forward momentum of the boat. This can be accomplished by use of the rudder.to change direction and/or controlling the attitude of the mainsail, attached to the mast and boom, and the jib foresail, which is run up from the tip of the bow to the head of the mast. It is controlled by a line running through a block pulley attached to the rail amidships closer to the cockpit. making the sail tauter or looser, using the winches for adjustment, When heading directly into the wind, if the wind flows over both sides of the sail, the whole sail will quiver; the boat will lose forward momentum, in some ways similar to applying the brakes when coming to a stop in an automobile. To get under way again, the boat has to be coaxed slightly to the left or right of the wind direction to get the airflow on the windward side of the sail. The difference in air pressure on the two sides of the sail causes the lift, which is translated into forward motion. This is the same as the airflow over the wings of an airplane creating the lift, which supports the plane in the air.

If the sails are adjusted too tightly in light air there will be a loss of speed, and the converse is true, also. The helmsman with his eye on the foresail constantly uses his judgment and orders the crew where to place the blocks; where to set the boom of the mainsail on the traveler to hold it steady; and how tightly to crank the winches to control the shape of the foresail; seeking to find the perfect combination, making adjustments constantly to use the power of the wind to achieve the maximum efficiency and speed. This requires great skill and much experience. It was a skill, which I admired and wished I had. I think I was only average, but I was the owner and allowances had to be made.

I think that the one race, that gave me more pleasure than any other, was actually meaningless in the ILYA standings. Fran had sailed with us from LYC to Mentor Yacht Club in the fun family end-of-the-season race, and we enjoyed the festivities; the crew except for Fred Robinson dispersed, and we slept on board. After breakfast in the clubhouse Sunday morning, we couldn't decide whether to cruise back to LYC or to join in the informal race back. We dithered and finally decided to do the race, although there were only the three of us to man the boat. Fred dashed up to the clubhouse to pay the $5 entry fee and by the time he returned, the race had already started. The rest of the fleet was a half-mile ahead of us when we finally crossed the starting line, the last to do so. It was a gray day with the wind coming from the southwest and the water had light choppy waves.

While Fran manned the wheel, Fred and I set the sails and we began to overtake the rest of the fleet. Fran wanted to give up the wheel, but we urged her to continue, since she was doing so well. Steering *Audace* very smartly, she got into a passing duel with our LYC dock mate's boat who had a crew of seven or eight people. They kept maneuvering in front of us, blocking us from passing them and taking our wind. She finally passed them on the leeward side, and we arrived at the entrance to the Cleveland breakwater where we had to make our first sail adjustment. We had only been able to do this because we sailed the rhumb line and did not have to tack, which was a blessing for the other two (older men) crew members. We finished first by a substantial margin with only three older people controlling a 9-ton boat under racing conditions. It was a real thrill, and for Fran, too. To have won her first race! I was so proud of her. So was Fred.

It was quite a contrast to our valedictory race, the last Governor's Cup Race we entered.

There had been some dispute with Canada about American commercial fishing in Canadian waters. This resulted in banning American boats, including sport fishermen and racing sailboats, from entering Canadian waters, in other words the northern half of Lake Erie. The Race Committee decided to do the race on a shortened course. No more sailing to the first mark off Rondeau. Now, the course would be west to the mouth of the Black River at the Lorain Harbor, then north to the easterly International border marker, one of two buoys with lights about 20 miles offshore, and then back to LYC, a considerably shorter distance than the usual one, probably only 75 or 80 miles; overnight, nevertheless.

The IOR (International Offshore Rule) boats started first, as usual, about 7:30 p.m., followed by us 30 minutes later. *Audace* was the first to reach the Lorain Harbor in our class and turned northeast to the international buoy. I was below trying to sleep in preparation for the late watch, when I heard the crew cursing that they couldn't sight the buoy but had seen the IOR fleet turn for the last leg home. They were confused as to how the IOR boats knew where to turn if they could not see the light either. The westerly light was clearly visible. I came up to the cockpit and suggested using our chart to establish the heading between the two lights, and when we reached that line, turn and sail a reasonable distance. Then, light or no light, turn and set a course for Lakeside. The crew was not convinced and so we decided to continue in our search for the missing light. We never did find the light and continued sailing northward almost to the Canadian shore before turning east to return to Lakeside. It was a very poor decision, probably the worst in all our races. We finished last. We later learned that the missing light had burned out, and the Coast Guard had not replaced it yet. This was remarkable considering that the light is an important navigation aid for the large foreign ocean freighters and our own ore freighters traversing Lake Erie.

The only disappointment or criticism I ever had of the crew, and I didn't voice it, was the dismissal of my suggestion that we make our turn by navigation, rather than by sighting of the light. I think this is what the IOR boats did. I think if we had followed my suggestion, or if I had been more forceful, we might have won another Governors Cup.

One regret during our *Audace* days is that Fran and I never did a cruise, relaxing, going where the winds took us, just the two of us. There were sensible reasons why this never happened, of course, the main one being health. I was fully recovered from my heart attack, but what if there were another one while we were under way. Could she handle a boat the size of *Audace* by herself in strange waters, drop the sails, start the diesel motor, use the ship to shore radio? I never pushed the idea.

Another regret is that we never did the annual Port Huron to Mackinaw race. Fran's "Aunt" Grace Niggeman lived in Port Huron which would have made staging and prepping for the race easier.

I remember driving through Port Huron and seeing the swarms of boats at anchor on the river that ran through the middle of town, a sense of bustling to get ready for the start. Several times approaching Port Huron from the north, I remember seeing the whole fleet under way on the Detroit River, spread out with their spinnakers flying, a very thrilling sight. I would have loved to have seen how well *Audace* would do with our regular full crew, and to be joined by Fran after the race and proceed to Georgian Bay, where Fred's family owned an island.

The logistics involved were just too much, and I don't remember even talking about it with Fred, or the crew, who would have had to take eight to ten days off from work. I would not have wanted to do the race without all of the regular crew who were familiar with the boat; would not have wanted to pick up some strange crew if one or two of or regulars had to drop out the last minute. All the planning would have been wasted. So *Audace* never sailed on the Detroit River, between Detroit and Windsor, past Alfred Glancy's mansion, never stopped at Harsen's Island to take Fran's mother's friends, the Robinsons for a sail, never felt the waters of Lake Huron or Lake Michigan, or Lake Superior, never saw Fred's Island. It would have been a dream cruise, especially if we had finished the race in the top three of our class.

One interesting experience we had occurred, when a Canadian sailor who was from Rondeau. owned a C&C 39 and sailed over to Lakeside Yacht Club, where we docked *Audace* and competed in the longer races. I'm not sure but his name may have been Campbell.

He notified LYC that the Rondeau Yacht Club was hosting a small regatta on Labor Day weekend and invited our club members to participate in the racing.

We decided to join them and sailed over on Friday night with Fred as our only crew. It felt strange to sleep on foreign waters. I don't remember how I expected us to compete with only three people aboard.

The Canadians were very cordial. I don't remember how many boats participated, but I think we only did one race and remember very little of the day. There was no clubhouse, so there was no dance in the evening as there was at Mentor Harbor Yacht Club.

What I do remember is the sail back home on Monday morning. We left early and there was no wind. We motored the entire distance until we were in sight of Lakeside. It was very warm. There were swarms of large black houseflies the whole way and two of us spent the entire day below decks very glad there were screens on the windows. The person at the helm held the wheel with one hand, and with the other, swatted the endless supply of flies. Where does a housefly come from 25 miles from shore? It was the most uncomfortable sail I ever had, and when we arrived, we had to hose down the cockpit which was red with blood from the flies

Eventually, our sailing days had to come to an end. Our financial situation had worsened due to our disastrous Columbus real estate venture; I became more and more aware of how fatiguing the long distance races were (I was 60 years old by this time); and above all, I was very aware that Fran was spending more time keeping the boat clean than enjoying time out on the water.

We put the boat on the market and accepted an offer from the Assistant Director of the Port of Savannah (I do not remember his surname, but he asked to be called "JR"). He was a passionate racer and raced in the SORC every year. This is one of the major races in the sailboat racing world, starting in St. Petersburg and ending at Fort Lauderdale, followed by an optional race to Freeport, Bahamas and back. Serious racers came from all over the world to compete.

I remember going with the Billings to a boat yard in Bradenton on the Manatee River, and watching the U.S. Naval Academy America's Cup style racing boat being towed in to dock after an afternoon's practice session in the Gulf of Mexico, a very impressive boat named *Guerriere*.

JR was looking for a "freshwater" boat (a term I had never heard before) which had never been subject to the corrosion damage done by salt water. He flew to Cleveland in February to inspect the boat; was satisfied with what he saw; a deal was agreed upon. We broke even money-wise and thus, had had the use and pleasure of a super boat for five years at no cost. I was there when the transporter loaded the boat and took off for Georgia. It was a sad day: all the more so, because after our deal was verbally accepted and before any papers had been signed, I had had two calls from a man in Seattle.

He was desperate to buy a "freshwater" boat, and offered our full asking price, sight unseen. I felt honor bound to turn him down. My Savannah buyer, JR, had driven a hard bargain; his only concession was to leave our winter storage cradle behind, for which he had absolutely no use in the Georgia winters. I later sold the cradle for $100, as I recall.

Thus ended our love affair with sailing, a decade of constant surprises, of excitement, of serenity, of challenge, of experiences impossible to be had on land, a feeling of sharing common emotions with all the sailors in the past. How fortunate I was.

A postscript: after *Audace* was gone, Fred Robinson, Clark Davies and I met on a Sunday afternoon at Warren Weiant's home in Wickliffe, Ohio, and taped all the little tips we had learned over the years about how to make Audace go fast and sent the tape to JR.

The next spring, we took our first Florida vacation and stopped in Savannah overnight. I called JR the next morning to see how *Audace* was performing for him (he renamed her *Honey II* because he had more than one girlfriend and didn't dare be specific - so much for sailboats deserving beautiful names!). He was delighted to hear from me and insisted on taking us to lunch at the Plimsoll Room, a private eating club in the Hyatt Hotel overlooking the Savannah River.

While I was getting my salad in the main dining room, JR, who had had two or three cranberry juice and vodka cocktails while waiting for us, confided to Fran that the minute he saw the condition of *Audace* he knew a woman was involved in caring for her. (It really was immaculate; we even used toothbrushes to scrub some of the smaller, hard to reach places), and he had to have the boat. He would have paid our asking price, maybe even more.

*Audace* had performed remarkably well for him in the SORC race, finishing above the middle of the fleet, quite an achievement for an 18-year old boat in its first race on saltwater. He was very pleased and thanked us for our tips, which had been invaluable and saved him and his crew a great deal of time.

# Chapter XI

## Vacations, Travel & Weekends

Vacation time was always important to me, the highlight of the year. It was the reward for having survived the daily responsibilities of family and work. Luckily, although my business life was very interesting and fulfilling, I never felt it was my main interest in life, or what defined me as a person. From the beginning my goal was to retire at age fifty and I really did not feel that I would be one of those men who dropped dead six months after retirement because his life was over; because he was not at his desk every day. Working was the price I had to pay for doing the things that were really interesting to me.

I remember an early family vacations we took when I was a child: it would have been 1928 or 1929. I remember the excitement of knowing that we were going on a camping trip, and seeing new things, and sleeping in a tent outdoors every night in a different place. I can remember my father loading the camping equipment on the car, tent fastened to the roof, and equipment on the running board on the driver's side held in place by an expandable retaining rack. The trunk was so small, I don't know how my mother was able to pack all the clothes we needed for the four of us. I think it was a 1928 dark-blue Buick.

There was a spare tire mounted above the rear bumper, and I know my father must have prayed that we didn't get a flat tire, because, in those days changing a tire was a major operation, with lugs to remove, and inner tubes to repair and jack to pump up and down to lift the flat tire wheel off the ground.

I remember only two, or possibly three vacation trips to the East coast, and at least twice that Aunt Clara, cousin Marion, and Grandma and Grandpa Schmidt followed us in Aunt Clara's Auburn, also loaded with their own camping equipment.

I regret that I don't remember more of such exciting adventures. I do remember camping at a camp-grounds close to Washington, D.C. After Dad got the center poles up and the ropes fastened to the side of the tent stretched, tied to the stakes he had driven into the ground, the folding table set up, and the folding cots we slept on set up, I was allowed to go to a swimming pool that was probably 20' x 30' but seemed much larger. It was made of heavy canvas and about 3' high and sat above ground. I do not remember anyone going with me to be sure I was safe.

I have vague memories of seeing the Washington Monument and the Lincoln Memorial, watching coins being made at the Mint, and the Smithsonian. I do remember the squirrels and trying to coax one to eat a nut from my hand while I was squatting in front of him and tapping the ground to get his attention.

On probably what was another trip I remember Boston and Lexington, seeing the House of Seven Gables, the Plymouth Rock (I was surprised at small it was) and all the pretty little white churches with their steeples in all the little towns we passed through.

I remember one night when it was raining, it was late, and we hadn't eaten. Dad was looking for some place for us to camp. At the bottom of a long hill there was a small church with a long shed open on one side of the parking area where the churchgoers put their horses and buggies during church services. Since it was the middle of the week, it was empty, and dry, and that is where we camped.

The most powerful memory I have of that night is that it was the first time I ever tasted coffee. Mother didn't have any milk for us. She set up the portable camp stove with the "white gas" for fuel, which had to be pumped up, and boiled water and made weak coffee for us to drink. She gave us a small metal, collapsible octagonal shaped cupful, which held about 3 oz. of liquid with some sugar in it, which was sweet and tasted wonderful. I can still taste it.

Another memory from one of these trips was a visit to Atlantic City where the famous boardwalk fascinated me. I remember a very large elephant (as large as a house to my young eyes) that stood in an open area near the beach. I can't imagine what its function was.

This was the occasion when we all got dressed in our bathing suits, and my mother sat me at the edge of the water and a wave washed over me unexpectedly. Some of the water got into my eyes and mouth. That was when I learned what salt water was. The ocean water was actually salty tasting. It wasn't at all like Lake Erie.

My mother also bought us some of the famous Atlantic Beach salt water taffy; but it wasn't nearly as good as that we got later at the Euclid Beach Amusement Park at home in Cleveland.

Two other sensory impressions of these trips remain in my memory: if I close my eyes, I can see a car on the side of the road with its whole front end smashed in, and a dead cow lying in the ditch next to the road. I think it was somewhere in New York state. I remember my father telling us very gravely that the driver had run into the cow and killed it. It made a big impression on me. I learned even at that age that a horse and buggy, or a cow crossing the road, moved much more slowly than an automobile.

The other memory is more amusing: we camped one night at Lake Placid, New York. It was a large campground with tents pitched in rows. We had a tent on either side of ours, and the one next to us was occupied by a preacher. In the middle of the night there was a ruckus; a skunk had gone through the preacher's tent and had sprayed the premises. The preacher was very upset; and I went back to sleep in all the fragrance.

I think it was on that trip, on the way back to Cleveland, that we stopped at the Ausable Chasm, the Grand Canyon of the East. It was quite a scenic attraction; we started at the northern, high end and walked downhill a narrow trail about a mile and a half, to the bottom and then took a bus back to our car. I don't remember much about it, but many years later we did the same thing, and it was rocky, and scenic and just as tiring again.

I don't remember much about vacations after the end of World War II and the early years of our marriage. We were very limited by the lack of a car and the second summer when we were able to take our first vacation, we spent a week at our relatives, (I don't remember how we got there) the Geiger's cottage in Linwood Park, east of Vermilion, Ohio. This was only one week and staying with family, but it meant getting away and a change in the daily routine: sunbathing on an uncrowded beach, swimming, relaxing, eating different cooking, enjoying an amusement park, a feeling of freedom.

My only specific memories of that first vacation are of the famous tennis game when Fran found some relief from the constant pain of her slipped disc and of a mental image of her sitting on the back steps of the cottage in a two-piece white swimming suit. There is a photograph of that in one of our photo albums. Although it was only a one-week vacation and only 35 miles from where we lived, it was definitely worthwhile. We knew we were going to like vacations.

After we bought our first car, an eight-year-old Pontiac, we were able to come and go as we pleased. We made many weekend trips to Detroit to visit Fran's mother and Fran's childhood friends, recently married, Evelyn Montgomery and Annabel Hess. This was long before construction of the Ohio Turnpike, or the Interstate highway system, and it took from four to five hours to go from Cleveland to Detroit. These were only weekend trips and hardly qualified as vacations but felt like mini-vacations and were a taste of the real thing.

I remember the first long trip we made to the East coast not because of where we went or what we did, which I have forgotten, but because we now had one child and were expecting a second and it was time to think of making our wills.

We spent many hours discussing terms, thinking about death for the first time at the tender age of 28, and especially whom to appoint as guardians for the children if they were orphaned by a car crash; finally settling the details, signing every page before witnesses, and feeling a sense of great relief when it was done.

I remember how uncomfortable I felt driving in and around New York City, but not where we stayed, or if we visited my old army friends, Mishcon, Zucker and Kazon. I do remember stopping for a wonderful breakfast at a little restaurant on the west side of the road in Allentown, Pennsylvania, on the way home. Fran's pregnancy with Kathy was not affected by the travel and fatigue, and we had no car troubles and arrived home safely with a feeling of considerable accomplishment. We were so very young.

After our college years and military service, all four sons joined the mortgage business started by our father in 1941. As the years of business experience lengthened and the business grew and prospered, so did the length of the vacation time mutually agreed-upon.

Eventually, we agreed that after being with the company 20 years, each of us could have a maximum of a month of vacation time with the understanding that all the days could not be taken at one time, and that no two of us could be away at the same time. These rules did not apply to Dad.

The length of vacation time started at two weeks during the first ten years of service, three weeks after fifteen years and four weeks after twenty years.

We always took every minute of vacation time we were entitled to, but the other brothers did not. I could never understand this. I remember Dad cutting short his vacations in Florida to return to Cleveland to attend a seniors' dance at a place called Brooklyn Acres, which baffled me.

In the early years of our marriage I remember Fran's mother's generosity in supplementing our meager income with gifts of nicer clothing for the children and Fran; her helping us with the furnishing of the house in Brecksville; and when vacation season came, several times renting a summer cottage on Lake Huron, where she grew up. This enabled the family to enjoy a summer vacation with her while the house in Brecksville was under construction.

She rented a cottage from an old friend, Mrs. Rowles, near Lexington, Michigan, on the shore of Lake Huron, heavily shaded by trees. It had a wood-burning fireplace for chilly evenings.

I would drive the family up and leave them for the two weeks and return to Brecksville to continue with my finish work on the interior of the house and then return to bring them back home to Parma Heights.

Once in later years, coinciding with one of my Mercator business club Annual Meetings held at Gratiot Inn, a popular resort in Port Huron, Michigan, I remember her renting a cottage within walking distance where she and the grandchildren stayed while I attended the meetings and we enjoyed the evening festivities. I particularly remember that the Inn provided a jazz quartet for dancing, headed by a fine tenor saxophonist, with whom I established a rapport by the dance tunes I requested.

Another summer Grandma Thompson rented a cabin for a week at a resort near Potawatomi, Indiana, called Wing Haven, which was only a few hours' drive from Detroit. It was owned and operated by a Christian Science couple and was very peaceful and sedate. There was a lodge where the meals were served. The guests stayed in small cabins scattered in the heavy woods on the hills above a 30 to 40-acre private lake located on the property. The water was very clear; and I enjoyed swimming in it. Fran took a movie of me swimming toward the dock and it is the only picture I have seen of me swimming. I had a very good-looking stroke, very stylish, thanks to the Yale swimming team, and could never understand why I did not go faster. I had planned on playing golf every day on the Lake James nine-hole golf course nearby, but the hills were so severe that the game was no fun and I did not return for more punishment after the first day.

Two other family vacations prior to our experience at Camp Michigania stand out in my memory. I do not remember, but suspect that my high school/Sunday school friend, Hugh

Hawthorne, whose parents owned a two-family cottage on the grounds of the Chautauqua Institute on Lake Chautauqua, New York, helped us find a rental apartment there for two weeks and we spent part of our vacation time there (1980?) with the family.

Chautauqua was a mythical place to me. I had heard of it because my parents stayed in a rented room in a cottage owned by a man named, "Pop" Steib in Bemis Point, a small town at the easterly end of Lake Chautauqua. Toward the end of the summer, Dad would take a week away from the office, bring Grandpa and Grandma Schmidt out to Tiedeman Road to look after the "boys" and Mom and Dad would go off to Chautauqua, but they never stayed there; it was too expensive. They used to stop on the way home at a dahlia grower's farm and buy a few roots to plant the next Spring. Dahlias are very pretty and come in many different shapes and colors. But they are far more work to maintain than peonies.

We loved it at Chautauqua. It was like an old Victorian village. No two cottages alike, old fashioned front porches, narrow streets with cars forbidden except for loading and unloading when moving in, an atmosphere of quiet bustle as people pursued their intellectual interests or physical activities. There were also some modern brick buildings housing the administrative office, classrooms, and the post office and general store, and several hotels, only some of which served meals: the grand dame was the Athenaeum, very stately and very Victorian, with a wonderful porch which overlooked the lake.

I also liked the ecumenical aspect of many of the religious denominations owning cottages where their ministers could stay with their families for a week, perhaps giving daily talks, or presiding at the Sunday service in the Amphitheater which held 2,000 people (?), or just vacationing. The oldest book club in the U.S.A. was on the grounds, as was the cottage of Thomas Edison, one of the founders.

Later, I learned that one of my golfing friends at El Conquistador in Bradenton, "Shorty" Follansbee, who was in his 80s had spent every summer of his life at Chautauqua from the time he was 8 years old. It was a way of life, and as addictive as we found our brief annual visits to Camp Michigania to be.

The season presenting weekly programs around an annual theme with prominent guest speakers, performers and organization was fairly short, ten weeks, and there was a resident opera company, symphony orchestra and playhouse. Many members of the Cleveland Symphony Orchestra and the Cleveland Playhouse spent their summers there.

I remember seeing one of the guest performers, the opera singer, soprano Judith Blegen, who was the soloist on my favorite record of Poulenc's *Gloria*, walking briskly to one of the rehearsal cabins, where young students practiced for the lessons they were taking.

I do not remember if our children or Fran signed up for instruction in any subject, but I did, and think I have related my humiliating and enlightening experience in the earlier chapter on Photography.

I remember renting the same apartment twice for a week, which was owned by an employee of Society National Bank who lived in Lakewood, an interesting form of investment property. It was on the second floor of a building behind the post-office/general store and had two rooms. It was a very convenient location and I recall vaguely that we had a visit one Sunday afternoon from my cousin, Doug Geiger and his family. They had attended church services in the huge open-air Amphitheater where other featured performances were also held.

In addition to our two weekly stays, we also visited Chautauqua two or three times for special programs on a daily visitor basis. Once, we attended a lecture in the evening by a well-known professor from one of the eastern schools (whose name I cannot dredge up from my memory) and the quality of his presentation and mastery of his subject was like a breath of fresh air from my college days. We went at the suggestion of Fran's friend, Dorothy Kuttler of St. Matthews, who had heard him lecture before. As I recall the lecture was held at the Hotel Athenaeum where we had dinner. It was the only time we ever set foot in the prestigious hotel. I can't remember whether we stayed overnight in one of the other newer, lesser hotels on the grounds, or made it a true day trip and drove back to Brecksville after the lecture, which was certainly feasible.

I remember another occasion when I learned of the appearance of one of my favorite Dixieland jazz bands, the Jim Cullum Jazz Band of the Riverwalk, in San Antonio. I had several of his records in my jazz collection. We arranged to stay overnight at one of the hotels and attend the concert.

Whether one lived on the grounds, rented for the season, or a week, or came for a single performance, the Institute, which was enclosed by a perimeter fence, had a central entrance where an entry fee was charged based on the length of the visit. The only thing free at the Institute was the parking, which was outside the fence enclosure. The year-round residents paid a fee for an annual pass and could attend any or all of the performances or instructional programs listed in the curriculum. We paid a nominal fee for the rare evening Cullum performance.

There was a different program offered every night, all guest performers and speakers, announced in advance in the annual program, advertised and reviewed in *The Cleveland Plain Dealer*, and the residents who had season tickets always had their sweaters, and cushions for the wooden pews in the amphitheater, and their reading material to occupy them while they waited for the program to begin.

We were seated behind a little old lady who, absorbed in her reading, was snuggled in her sweater and sitting on her cushion, in anticipation of the coming concert. I'm sure she occupied the same seat every night, on the aisle, 3rd row, right. I don't think she had any idea of what kind of music she was about to hear this night, because before Cullum and his hoys had finished their first song, she had risen to her feet and marched out of the auditorium, book in hand, cushion under arm. I could have predicted it. We, on the other hand, had driven 150 miles just to hear this particular attraction; and stayed until the last note was played.

Among my memories of the Chautauqua experience are trips to Peak 'n' Peak, a ski resort a half hour away, which had a good 18-hole golf course that I played as well as the Chataqua course across the road from the Institute. Peak 'n Perak was later managed by my cousin, Doug Geiger, who was very proud of the antique woodwork in the lobby and dining room which had been salvaged from a mansion in Erie, Pennsylvania.

We also took an afternoon tour to a nearby summer community, Lily Dale, headquarters for the study and practice of the religion, Spiritualism. We sat with an audience of 60 or 70 people and could volunteer to stand and be recognized and invite the medium on the stage to "come" to us to read our minds, or give advice on how to solve our problems. It was most interesting, and I stood and was "come" to, but with little success. I had profound worries at the time about the success of my real estate investment in Columbus, was very receptive to suggestion, but received no help.

One year I remember there was a weeklong program during the height of the Cold War which I was anxious for us to attend. It was early in the season and would not interfere with our annual trip to Camp Michigania. There was to be an array of Russian writers, journalists, musicians, and poets from the Soviet Union, sanctioned by the Soviet government, culminating on Saturday morning in a debate between representatives of the U.S.S.R. government and the Under Secretary of our State Department.

Because it was so early in the season, the Hawthornes were not yet in residence, and we were allowed to stay in the parent's suite on the first floor, rent free. I remember the mast of Hugh's son's sailboat, stored there over the winter months, lying on the hall floor all the way from the kitchen to the front door. It was a busy time for us trying to attend as many of the meetings, which were held in various locations, as we could, having to dodge the mast every time we used the front door.

The poet was a name I recognized, but would have trouble spelling, Yevtushenko. He recited some of his poetry, which was very moving, even hearing it in Russian. He spoke on the importance of poetry in the Soviet Union, which was subsidized by the state, and told of giving poetry readings during lunch hours in Soviet factories. I couldn't quite see this happening in the U.S. The debate on Saturday was very stimulating and I thought our man from the State Department acquitted himself well.

Culturally speaking, the program was a great success, so much so that it was repeated the following year with the Russians as hosts, in Riga, Latvia. We were unable to attend, but based on what they heard from us, the Hawthornes did make the trip. I do not recall Hugh every talking about their experiences.

After our two happy years at Chautauqua I remember a discussion with Fran, and our talking about the expense involved. Our daughters were getting to an age where they preferred their Day Camp in Brecksville, Camp Michigania, and Girl Scout camp to going away for vacation, and the clincher, that we were living in our own summer resort with its own lake, with even more cultural opportunities than Chautauqua, although not as organized or concentrated, and many better golf courses. Our conclusion was that maybe it was time that we should overcome my derogatory stereotype of sissies afraid of the cold up North in wintertime and fleeing to the hedonistic state of Florida, the land of perpetual sunshine. I did not feel it would cost as much to spend a month touring Florida to see what it was like, as to spend two weeks at Chautauqua. This proved to be true, but being governed by the law of unintended consequences, led to far greater expense in the long run; just as the free sailing instruction at Camp Michigania which seemed so easy led to the expense of maintaining a 39' sailboat on Lake Erie. I plan to relate my memories of our adventures in Florida in the next chapter.

My memories are very clear how our Michigania adventure began. Sometime after the first of the year we were all seated at the table eating dinner in Brecksville, and the question came up as to what we might like to do as a family for our vacation that summer. Sometime earlier, we had received a brochure in the mail from the University of Michigan Alumni Association announcing a new activity of the Association. After a year's experiment operating a "Family Camp" at Lake Douglas, the Association had bought a well-known, boy's and girl's summer camp, popular with well-to-do Detroit families, on the shores of Lake Walloon in northern Michigan, It sat on 500 wooded acres and had 1,500 feet of frontage on the lake, which was rated one of the ten most beautiful lakes in the world, and would offer every activity imaginable on the grounds except golf, all free except riflery, skeet and horseback riding, with college student instructors who also would provide care for infants in the morning; tennis, arts and crafts, swimming and sailing (instruction provided), hiking, and lectures in the evenings by guest professors, all included in a magnificent setting, three meals per day, for the modest price of $50 per adult per week and $35 for children over the age of five. There would be ten one-week sessions each year. The Alumni Association's purpose was to create closer ties among Michigan alumni with their alma mater; and it was to be absolutely family oriented. One member of the family had to be a University of Michigan graduate, and there were no age limits, nor as to size of family.

It sounded too good to be true. But Fran had misgivings: they had more to do with the possibility of the camp's virtues being overstated, and a second-rate operation being compared to the way Yale would have done it. I remember assuring her that I promised not to make any such comparison and that the price was so low that if we didn't like anything about it, we could pack up and go somewhere else and not lose very much money. We decided to table the motion.

The subject came up again in March or April, and we decided to take the gamble, with further assurances from me that I would make NO critical remarks, and we applied for the week of the first Saturday after the 4th of July. We were accepted and thus began an adventure that lasted for that same week for the next 25 years.

The first-year conditions were pretty primitive. The camp buildings were not in good condition; the whole operation was like a shakedown cruise; senior staff wandered around asking anyone they met, "Are you having a good time?" The camp was located on a bluff overlooking Lake Walloon and divided into a North camp, where the boys had been housed when it was a private facility, and the South camp, where the girls had been located. After acquiring the property, the staff went into each of the cabins which had a wood burning fireplace, and toilet room with running cold water, and open, dormitory style sleeping.

The staff erected beaverboard partitions to create space for two or three families, some with lofts reached via ladder for the older children. A common area in the middle section of the floorplan provided space for families to gather around the fireplace. Each cabin had a porch which also made it easy to get to know one another.

There were other buildings: a barn, and the dining hall with a lounge area where the evening lectures were held; a small building near the dining room where sundries were sold; sleeping huts scattered around where the male counselors lived, and next to the beach a two-story building, open for sheltered activities on the ground level, and sleeping quarters for the girl counselors above. It was called the "Crow's Nest".

I remember feeling fortunate that we were assigned to the South camp, which was far more open than the heavily wooded North; had more tennis courts; had a flag pole where one of the campers raised the flag each morning after blowing Reveille, firing his shotgun into the air, and then being surrounded by young children, and a Gazebo on a cove above the lake where, after the first year, the returning South campers, gathered for cocktails and tidbits and got caught up with their previous year's activities.

After the third day at Camp, I was wildly enthusiastic about the whole experience, the place, the people, the atmosphere, the SAILING. There was no way anyone could have gotten me to leave.

When we returned home, a distance of 480 miles to the south, I wrote a letter to the Secretary of the Alumni Association, Bob Morgan, extolling the virtues of the concept, the physical facilities of the camp, and above all the people, the campers and the staff. The first run-on sentence was a whole paragraph long. I signed the letter: Robert F. Schmidt, Yale '43.

A short time later, I had a phone call from the Secretary thanking me for my compliments; and asking if I would object to having it published in the Alumni Magazine. I was flattered and said yes. and in due course the letter appeared in the Letters to the Editor column.

The happening that followed is one of my fondest memories: Bill Culligan, who had become a close friend in that one week, called as soon as he saw the letter in the magazine and said he didn't even have to finish the first sentence to know who had written it. A copy of the letter is in my archives, somewhere.

In later years, when some of our children were old enough to work at Camp as counselors, and many did, we were told that the "Fourth Week campers" were the most active, interesting, and nicest week of the whole season. I certainly felt that the group of six or eight couples, of whom we became very fond and did things with were an exceptional group.

After a few years, the group: the Culligans, the McPhersons, the Burmeisters, the Grosses, and Marilyn Brooks, all of whom had season's tickets for the football games, gathered on Homecoming Weekend in Ann Arbor for a mini-reunion and tailgate lunch before the game. Someone bought tickets for us, and I remember parking in the same back yard of a house on a nearby side street, so crowded it was hard to squeeze our car in. I suspect the owner of the house paid most of his real estate taxes from the proceeds of his parking receipts.

Although we lived the most distant by far, we always joined them, saw the game, and then proceeded to one of the couple's homes for dinner, followed by bridge, and golf on Sunday before returning to the real world.

I was very pleased that one of the years the whole group came all the way to Brecksville for an abbreviated stay after the game. We did manage to play golf at Sleepy Hollow Golf Course, a beautiful golf course very near our home on Oakes Road.

Over a span of time as long as 25 years, the strong relationships with the people only grew stronger. We had our mini-reunions in the fall, visits to the Grosses in Toledo to hear their symphony orchestra, and visit their Museum of Art; saw the homes they all lived in, attended many of the weddings of the group's children, and were able to see their children and ours, and even grandchildren, work at Camp as counselors.

However, the activities at Camp are a blur with only a few highlights standing out from a background of consistent pleasure. It seemed the annual anticipation was never unrealized,

There was the learning of the basics of how to sail, my sail, alone, down to Walloon Village the minute I was no longer governed by Camp rules; so easy downwind, but oh, such a struggle returning through the narrows into a stiff wind, requiring innumerable short tacks. Next the circumnavigation, the exploration of all three branches of Lake Walloon, which had always been Terra Incognito with Fran aboard our Skylark the summer we had to rent a cottage on Wildwood Bay instead of attending Camp. This was because of a conflict with daughter Kathy's summer job at the National City Bank. It felt strange to "drop in" via sailboat at Camp Michigania and find it populated with strangers.

I remember taking the time away from sailing to learn how to polish a Petoskey stone and the pleasure of meeting Chip and Jane Drotos, friends of our Kathy and Stephen, while prepping for the golf chipping contest behind the barn one afternoon; and the pre-lunch tennis matches on the south Camp tennis courts, attracting a crowd to listen to Ed McPherson's Roaring Twenties manner of speaking between shots, and, of course, I remember the conflict I had between sailing and playing golf on one of the many great courses in the area. It seems that such few specific memories do not do justice to the hours of pleasure enjoyed.

One of the side benefits of attending Camp was being able to explore the areas nearby and the feeling of coming back home as we approached Camp.

We usually left for Camp, 480 miles distant, Friday night after work and got as far as Midland, Michigan, where we visited Fran's relatives, then completed our trip Saturday in time to check into Camp in the early afternoon. Many times, we were held up by a convoy of National Guard troops on their way to their summer training in Grayling, Michigan. We always had lunch at the same restaurant in Gaylord, and then passed large fields planted with potatoes, which always surprised me, and then Boyne City, the capitol of Michigan's winter ski resorts. And finally, our first glimpse of the beautiful green waters of Lake Walloon from the high point at the entrance to Camp Michigania. It was a ritual, and one we never tired of.

Once in Camp we tended not to leave it; we were there such a short time. But, if the weather was unfavorable, we would leave Camp and explore the surrounding territory.

Charlevoix was a small city with its own lake with the same name, larger than Walloon, and I remember how impressed I was the first time I saw both sides of the road approaching the city planted with a one foot strip of petunias in bloom along the curbing. The city was built around a small round lake between Lake Michigan and Lake Charlevoix, which provided a very safe anchorage for boats in a storm. There was a restaurant overlooking this lake we used to stop at on the way back from a round of golf at the Belvedere Golf Course, located to the east of the city, and it was fascinating to watch all the activity on the water.

I also remember places along the road approaching the city where we could stop and look for Petoskey stones at the water's edge. Petoskey stones came in all sizes and were found only along the shore of Little Traverse Bay. They were gray in color, and contained fossils, trilobites, which were revealed when the stone was polished. They were very popular at Camp in the Nature Center activities. My son-in-law, Stephen Kershner and his golfing buddy, Chip Drotos, used to organize trips to hunt for the stones, which they would bring back to Camp and polish. They became known as the "Gurus of the Stone."

The other preferred destination, especially for the ladies who loved the shopping, was Petoskey, west of the Camp, a little larger than Charlevoix, more established and less dependent on vacation business, although it had many fine boutique-type gift shops which did cater to vacationers and had many high priced items. The men at Camp used to dread their wives' trips to Petoskey to get their hair done. I remember being impressed by one of the shops, The Mole Hole, which had a branch in Miami Beach. Fran and I saw it the first time on one of our early trips out of Camp, and Fran returned later with a group of lady Campers and bought a piece of metal enamel ware (without my approval) created by a husband and wife team, the Brumms', of Charlevoix where they had their own shop and kilns and produced their artwork. I think I was a big disappointment to the men when I did not groan at the expense, and expressed my approval, and delight at her purchase. It now sits in my office, a "Thrush perched on Marsh Marigolds", and on another occasion we also acquired a copper sculpture of an avocet, a shore bird which resides in my living room, hiding under an end table.

This whole area of northern Michigan was a vacation land. It was hilly and covered with pine trees; there were many streams which attracted fisherman, and many small lakes surrounded by summer cottages. The roads were lined with signs advertising one craft or another and it was always interesting to stop and see what was offered, and occasionally find something of artistic merit, such as the Brumms'.

During our first year at Camp we took a day off and traveled the 60 miles north to Mackinac Island, a popular tourist destination. We took a ferry over to the island and did the typical tourist things: took a horse drawn carriage ride (no automobiles allowed on the island) on a sightseeing tour, looked down on the 9-hole golf course which had square greens, and walked the length of the porch, lined with white wicker rocking chairs of the famous Grand Hotel, which was huge for such a small place. There was a fee (to keep gawkers out) to enter the lobby, so we never saw the interior of the hotel. We did remember to buy some of the world-famous fudge to bring back to the Culligans. Bill and his friend Jack from Ann Arbor, with whom I had played golf at the Charlevoix municipal golf course the day before. They showed up on our porch at Camp Michigania after midnight, causing a mild disturbance with their loud claims for their prized fudge.

We varied our routine one year and took an extra week of vacation before camp began: we traveled east to Quebec, stayed at the famous hotel Château Frontenac where daughter Barbara charmed the Irish doorman with her red hair; had dinner at a restaurant down near the St. Laurence River; watched the parade of troops in Revolutionary uniforms the next day on the Plains of Abraham; and then proceeded westwards through Montreal (barely averting a traffic accident, the only near-call in all our travels) and then stopped briefly in Ottawa where we saw the Parliament buildings. At Ottawa we detoured 60 miles north to White Fish Lake for my only visit to Fran's father's summer home where she spent many happy summers and learned to fish. There was no one in residence so we could not see the interior, but we did look at the boathouse and dock. It brought back many memories for Fran. We then proceeded west via back roads through a national forest until we reached the little village, Trois-Rivières, on Georgian Bay, near the Mackinaw Bridge.

I remember finding a motel near the water, and after a long and tiring drive, changing into swimming suits, and my "girls" gathering together their gear and proceeding down to the beach to wash their hair in the lake water, which we were told was "soft". After they had finished, we were somewhat alarmed when a drunken Indian who had been sleeping a short distance away, got to his feet and lumbered toward us. We quickly avoided him so there was no confrontation, and the next day crossed the Mackinac Bridge back into the U.S.A. and drove the 60 miles to Lake Walloon, approaching it from the north, not the south as usual, which felt strange. Before passing through Petoskey on the way to Camp, I think we passed through the town of Harbor Springs on Little Traverse Bay for the first time. It was one of the high-end vacation spots in northern Michigan, and the political Taft family had a compound there. It also had an excellent ski resort affiliated golf course, which I played several times over the years.

Our weeks at Camp Michigania were cut short twice: first, when our first granddaughter was born, which we learned of while standing in line for lunch at the dining hall and we left camp early, very excitedly, so Fran could fly to St. Louis to be with our daughter, Kathy, and, the second time several years later when we learned that Kathy's husband, Stephen's, father had died suddenly in Decatur, Indiana, and we traveled south on route U.S. 31 through Potawatomi and Fort Wayne to attend the funeral.

Leaving Camp on Saturday was always a sad occasion. One year, a very attractive family from Detroit, the Treadwells, came to Camp during our week. They had two sons. The older brother had asthma, and the younger, Don, still in high school, about the same age as Kathy, was very good looking and taller than me, about 6'5". He paid some attention to Kathy; they wandered around Camp holding hands and it was "cute." When we left camp, we happened to take the same route as the Treadwells and happened to be directly behind their car. We had to wait to cross a one-lane wooden bridge, which allowed the two young people. much looking at each other through the car windows. while we waited our turn to cross. Later that year young Don visited us in Brecksville for a weekend, but nothing ever came of the budding romance, and they never returned to Camp and we never saw them again.

One year, we added another week's vacation at the end of Camp and rented a cottage at Crystal Lake, near Traverse City, from an Episcopal minister who lived in Berea, Ohio. It was a modern style cottage and had a front deck that extended out  over the water. Crystal Lake was unusual because it had an almost perfect circular shape and was very clear. Looking down at it from above, it would appear to be divided in half from north to south, with the westerly half shallow, and a sudden drop off into very deep water on the easterly half. The difference in the color of the water over the shallow, sandy bottom, and the deeper easterly half was startling.

The first thing we did after we settled in, we got in the car and found a marina at the north end of the lake where we could rent a sailboat for a week. This was in the early years before we had our own Skylark.

The only boat available was a small, 12' O'Day, a sturdy, well-known brand, which was very broad of beam with a less than spacious cockpit. I took command of the boat while Kathy and Barbara got onboard. We took off down the lake with a following breeze for the cottage, a distance of about a mile or so. Fran drove the car back to the cottage while we were sailing home. There were choppy waves; and it didn't take long to discover that the boat was overloaded and taking on water. There was nothing we could use to bail with; and we were slowly sinking while under way. At some point, there was so much water in the boat that it no longer responded to the helm and we were helpless as we passed our cottage while sinking. We were lucky because of the circular nature of the lake, the wind washed us ashore a half mile south of our cottage. We were never in any serious danger; and it was an exciting adventure. But after that I sailed the boat, which was clumsy to steer and handle and sluggish under sail, only once or twice, with a crew of only one. I don't remember Fran ever setting foot in the boat, and I sailed it back to the marina on the day we left, alone, without mishap. It was one of our less successful adventures while on vacation.

I remember one visit to "Aunt Grace" in Port Huron, Michigan, and going over the high Blue Water Bridge to Sarnia, Canada, for a Chinese dinner (she really preferred pickerel). I never enjoyed staying overnight in her apartment because it overlooked a switching yard for diesel locomotives and was very noisy.

I remember how good it felt to stop at Harsens Island on the Detroit River and visit Fran's mother's friends, Bill and Trixie Robinson. Their daughter, Ann, and Fran were brought up almost as sisters .They had a great cottage on the channel side of the island so it was easy to see the large ore boats gliding downstream with loads of iron ore. They seemed huge in such a narrow river, Bill had a small cabin cruiser and took us on tours which were always interesting.

Both Bill and Trixie were older, and many years later we were invited to their 70th Wedding Anniversary luncheon at a small clubhouse on the island. We had been to many 50th Anniversary celebrations, but never a 70th. It was a great occasion, and one of my vivid memories is of Trixie being helped down the hall when leaving, cheeks flushed, swaying slightly. Friends had kept her champagne glass full the entire meal.

Leaving the cottage was always difficult for the children who were probably 10-12 years old because they loved the Robinson's cockerel spaniel, Chummy. There were many hugs, followed by tears as we backed down the driveway. One year, something was forgotten, and we had to return to retrieve it, and we had gushers of tears all over again.

Because of Camp and Fran's relatives and friends in Midland and Port Huron; and her mother's connections to Lexington and Croswell; plus our friends, the Hess's summer cottage in Grand Haven; and our Camp friend, Marilyn Brook's cottage on Spring Lake near Grand Haven; and our friends in Detroit; it seems to me we spent most of our free time in Michigan in the middle and southern parts of the state.

After our many years of attending Camp Michigania, watching our children bring their children to Camp and then see them employed as counselors at camp, we began to feel a sense of guilt at the two of us occupying precious space that could accommodate a whole new family with their children; and expose them to the camping experience that had meant so much to us. So, we elected not to return. However, we continued to visit the area for many years. Our friends from the early days in Parma Heights, the Demuth's, bought a condo on the shore of Little Traverse Bay near Charlevoix, and we visited them. Our friends, the Culligans, rented a cottage on Eagles Nest Drive, next to the entrance of Camp Michigania and invited us to stay with them. Friends we met on the Michigan Alumni sponsored trip down the Danube, Bob and Jeannie Hackett, who lived in Bloomfield Hills, Michigan, owned a summer cottage and spent the summer on Walloon Lake also almost next door to Camp Michigania, and we stayed with them. Being somewhere other than where I grew up had a special appeal for me and traveling as short a distance as to Michigan helped satisfy that need.

In the early years of our marriage, we tended to explore New England, a part of the country we both loved. We usually drove (the Interstate Highway system was a blessing) which gave us more freedom to explore. We made the trip east when Fran was pregnant with Kathy, and I had my business visits to Hartford to call on the Aetna Life, as well as my Class of '43 reunions in New Haven every five years, which always included a stop in New York to visit my army friend, Sidney Mishcon. After I retired, we took advantage of being able to choose when, and where, and how long to spend on our vacations and extended weekends. I think we took full advantage of our good fortune and have no regrets about the places we did not get to explore, mainly west of the Mississippi to the Rockies: we never saw Pike's Peak, or the Grand Canyon, or Salt Lake City, or Mount Rushmore; never did a motor trip to the West coast, as my parents did with my two younger brothers. We never visited Hawaii, or Alaska, or South America, or stayed in Mexico.

The year of our 25th Wedding Anniversary, 1970, was the start of ten consecutive years of the best vacations imaginable for me. I would gladly retrace our steps, follow the same routes, stay in the same hotels and pensions, and eat in the same restaurants, if it were possible.

My brother Russ, who married in July of 1945, in celebration of his 25th Wedding Anniversary announced his first trip to Europe to retrace his steps during World War II, and invited our daughter, Barbara, to accompany them. This inspired us to do something special for our anniversary which occurred later the same year. We thought about a trip to Hawaii or Alaska, but I was more interested in historical places, and we dismissed that idea. Mexico was a foreign country, as were the countries of Central and South America, but I had no desire to travel there, and we dismissed that idea, also.

I do not remember investigating Japan and the Far East, or Australia and New Zealand, which were areas I had great interest in because of my Japanese language studies in the Army, probably because it just seemed too far with too much time wasted in getting to and from the destination, and much too expensive.

That left Europe, which we decided to do. We found a 17-day group tour of the three capitals: London, Paris and Rome, offered by the Globus Travel Agency of Chicago. The total cost per person for air transportation from Cleveland, round trip, including hotel lodging, breakfast every day, welcoming party for the group in each city, and half day sightseeing tour in each city was $472. This also included the airfare from London to Paris and Paris to Rome, from where we flew back to the U.S. It was classified as a group to justify the air fare. We never knew who the others in the group were, and only saw the group when we were picked up by the bus on the morning of the first day in each city for the guided tours of the cities. In all other respects it was as though we were traveling solo. We chose the tourist attractions we wanted to see, and the restaurants of our choice.

We had real misgivings and many discussions about such a vacation: crossing the Atlantic seemed such a long distance; in case of an emergency we would be so far away, the problem of a strange language in two of the countries; and leaving the children behind. What would we do if something happened to one of them?

We gritted our teeth and secured our first passports and hoped for the best. What we experienced was the best. On the flight home, we babbled about how wonderful it had been and how soon could we return and where would we choose to go. We could look forward to walking in the footsteps of the history of our Western Civilization.

As it turned out, our next trip was a group trip promoted by the University of Michigan Alumni Association. It was an 8-day trip leaving from Detroit, with about 100 Michigan graduates, to Vienna. All Alumni trips were accompanied by a member of the faculty, in this case, William Revelli, Director of the Marching Band, and his wife, Mary. I remember thinking what a coincidence it was that I would be taking a trip with the man who directed the opposing marching band, whom I saw for the first and only time on my trip to the Yale-Michigan football game my freshman year. We thought we should try a trip where all the arrangements were made for the traveler, including sightseeing, and we knew from our Camp experience that the fellow passengers would be compatible and interesting, and the date of the trip fit in well with the vacation schedule at my office.

We stayed at the Hotel InterContinental, and on the organized parts of the trip saw the Imperial Palace; St. Stephen's Cathedral; the State Opera House; Karl's Kirsche (a beautiful, interesting church for taking pictures in the afternoon and where I ran into the President of the Second Federal S&L of Cleveland, Arlo Smith, with whom we did business originating residential loans. He was staying at our hotel. He had a bad head-cold he picked up while attending a S&L Conference in Munich; a performance of the Lipizanner Horses in their own quarters; a performance of the Vienna Choir Boys in their palace; and when we were on our own, Demel's Coffee House, famous for their pastries and where I learned the expression *mit schlag ober*, "with whipped cream on top".

Two side trips during the week were offered: one to Budapest and the other to Saltzburg. We were lucky in our choice because those who chose Budapest had rainy days and we had beautiful sunny days. We decided on Saltzburg and the bus ride through the lake country was one of the most beautiful I have ever taken. Saltzburg was very interesting. We swam in a large swim club indoor pool, and from the number of local users, became aware of the emphasis on sports and hiking and mountain climbing in European countries. We attended a performance of Mozart's opera, *The Magic Flute* and I must confess that I didn't care for the music, heresy for a Mozart lover.

The trip back to Vienna was on a warm Sunday afternoon and the traffic was heavy. Our native guide, Frau Dorothy, a small older lady dressed in typical Austrian apparel wearing a hat with a large feather (pheasant?) decreed that we would stop at a small village for a break and a glass of wine.

We trooped off the bus onto a charming patio under a pergola, which provided some shade, and the others had their wine. Mary Revelli, who was very shy and quiet, in the shadow of her famous husband, and I asked for help from Frau Dorothy in selecting something *saft* and she ordered *Johannisblut,(John's Blood)* for us, which turned out to be black currant juice, similar to grape juice, non-alcoholic, and delicious. I have always loved grape juice but would replace it in the blink of an eye with the black currant juice if it were readily available. The only place I ever found it in the U.S. was at a butcher shop in Mayfield Heights, Ohio, operated by two German or Austrian women, I think it may have been called "The Two Sisters," which specialized in special cuts of veal. They had a small section of bottled European juices and carried *Johannesblut*. I was delighted, but it was much too far from Brecksville to keep a supply on hand regularly.

The most important thing that happened to us on this thoroughly agreeable trip was that we took a day when no special performance, or visit to a landmark, was scheduled, and discovered it was easy to rent a car for a day. Our U.S. driver's license was valid in Europe and we could use our credit card. This meant we would be free to wander on our own and not be limited to the city or public transportation. Suddenly our trip became much more expansive.

The next morning, I remember my excitement when a small blue Opel sedan was delivered to the front of the hotel and we signed the papers and accepted the keys and gingerly seated ourselves. After all, people were killed regularly in automobile accidents while driving in Europe. We were being very bold.

I had owned several small European cars at home for use in my appraisal work because of their economy and loved the way they handled, although I had never driven an Opel before; but it was a General Motors brand, and not that different. We had a map and I remember we went north of the city first to the Vienna Woods, different from forests at home. There was no underbrush in the Vienna Woods; it almost looked cultivated. Then we drove back down through the city, crossing the "brown" Danube, and stopped at the Votive Cathedral, not very attractive, (I didn't take any interior photographs) but large, which the Emperor Franz Joseph built for his brother, Karl, as a prayer to God asking Him to spare his brother from death from cancer. We were on our way south to Carlsbad, driving very sedately along the Autobahn, hugging the right side of the road, when I became aware of high beams flashing behind me in the rear view mirror, the European method of warning for overtaking a vehicle. Suddenly, a large Mercedes roared past us, buffeting our little car, in its wind stream. There were no speed limits on the Autobahns, and it must have been going at least 100 mph.

Carlsbad is a spa town with hot springs, a favorite of the Emperors, where we had lunch and checked out an arboretum; and then on west to Mayerling where Prince Rudolph committed suicide for love. There was a small church/museum there where we got out of the car and went inside. We were the only people there. Then back in the car at twilight east to Vienna where we dropped off the car at the InterContinental. Safely. We had survived our first day on the roads of Europe.

We were emboldened by this experience. On our future trips to Europe, we rented cars, which enabled us to set our own itinerary and go at our own pace. We traveled by car in England twice, France twice, Italy twice (including Sicily), Switzerland, Lichtenstein, Luxembourg, and very briefly, Germany, the Canary Islands, and Spain and Portugal. I can't remember all the brands of cars we rented, but do remember one, a Peugeot, which was quite new, very comfortable, and required new car service while in our possession. The problem was we were supposed to change the oil while we had the car. We could not figure out how to raise the hood and couldn't find a service station which had a mechanic or attendant who knew how either. Fortunately, the engine didn't seize up and we turned the car in at the end of the trip with no questions asked.

I thought it was interesting that on one of the trips the papers in the glove box of the car indicated that it was owned by a man in Denmark. I theorized that owning a car as a rental vehicle was a form of personal investment and could see the car working its way down from the north to the Mediterranean and back, earning a return on investment for its owner. It was a little different than Hertz or Avis.

On one trip we drove a Fiat, small, square and boxy, but it had more space in the trunk than the Oldsmobile Omega we had at home and got twice the mileage. The gas stations on the continent outside the large cities were usually a single pump in front of a little grocery store, much like the early days in the U .S. Gasoline was very expensive, but the exchange rate was in our favor, which made the whole adventure possible.

We stayed in a state-owned hotel in Portugal similar to a "parador" in Spain. We had one of our only scares about running out of fuel when we left in the morning, took the wrong road and after driving for miles through farmland, ended up at a dead end. The road simply ended, and we had to turn around and retrace our steps as we watched the fuel gauge near zero, wondering what we would do if we were stranded.

On another occasion in Spain we were driving within the speed limits on a rare sunny morning out in the countryside and were stopped by a pair of motorcycle policemen (dressed all in leather and wearing helmets and goggles) who asked to see our papers, and then waved us on. I was very relieved that we passed inspection because I didn't want to get mixed up with the Guardia or see the inside of a Spanish cell.

In 1973, when it was time to replace our business owned "fleet" of four Oldsmobiles. I proposed buying a Mercedes from Koepke Motors on Detroit Avenue in Lakewood, Ohio. for our trip to England that summer. We paid for the car with American dollars in the U.S. and took delivery at the factory in Stuttgart, Germany. I had read that this was possible.

It was also possible to buy more than one car. I could sign for delivery for a second Mercedes to be delivered in Cleveland. Thus, picking up my car in Stuttgart, I could drive away in my own vehicle for our vacation, and sign for a car for brother Wes who liked the idea; brother, Russ, who was in effect the Comptroller of our company, did not and was skeptical. He chose to buy another Oldsmobile. The exchange rate was favorable, and we proceeded to buy two of the smallest, simplest models: 4-door sedans, 130 horsepower, straight 6-cylinder engines. I remember that as part of the purchase package I received a certificate with a blue ribbon on it which was the cab fare from the airport to the factory.

When we arrived, I remember being taken to a long, 200-300 feet shed, open on one side, with one new car after another lined up waiting to be picked up. We were greeted by Herr Pfeiffer, dressed in a white surgeon's jacket (who might have clicked his heels) who did an inspection tour of the car, pointing out things I would need to know, before allowing us to drive off. His final caution was for us to stop at the gas station at the entrance to the factory and fill the tank with gas which only had one gallon in it. I could still remark on, if not admire, after World War II, the evidence of German efficiency and thoroughness on display in the whole transaction.

After filing the tank, we did not explore Stuttgart, which seemed like a nice city, but drove north to Heidelberg where we stayed the night and saw the famous University.

We were on our way to the English Channel and England, and passed through Luxemburg on the way to Calais, where we put our new car on the Hovercraft for which we had a reservation made for us by our travel agent in the U.S.. We drove west along the coast and I was disappointed that we never really saw any of the beaches where our troops landed on D-Day, or where the British army was saved at Dunkirk.

The Hovercraft was a surprise: it was much larger than I expected. It had to be to carry so many automobiles. I was interested in how the heavy skirts were lowered to contain the wind created by the propellers, mounted horizontally, which lifted the huge vehicle off the surface of the ground and kept it suspended while over the water.

We came ashore at a landing beach at Dover at the foot of the cliffs and were greeted by a Customs Officer. I was wearing a European style wool cap we had bought on our first trip to England, when we visited Windsor Castle and looked at some of the small shops on a side street nearby. The Customs Officer glanced at our passports and saw the name "Schmidt" and the German car we were driving and my cap and asked, "Are you German, Sir?" My instant reply was an indignant, "No, sir. We're American." I have never understood how he could have asked that question since he was looking at a U.S. Passport, unless it was an example of understated British humor. It was an unforgettable welcome to Great Britain.

There are so many memories about our trips to Europe and our wanderings that I am not going to struggle to try to sort them out chronologically, or even by country, but will be relating them as they come to me, one inspiring another.

Memories of our travels in England are many: we drove from Dover north to Canterbury where we stayed in a small, old hotel, possibly built in the 1700s, next to the main entrance of the Great Cathedral, which is very old and very beautiful. Our hotel room had a name (Buttercup?) which I have forgotten and had a wooden floor which was not level. The strongest memory I have is that the rear door of the hotel opened onto the Cathedral grounds and we were able to go out and explore the grounds after dark, which gave me an uncanny feeling. The interior of the Cathedral was very impressive and I took many pictures, especially of the stained glass windows; but it was more difficult to do the exterior because the Cathedral was so large that it dominated the surrounding shops crowded around so that it was hard to get a clear view of it. I think we had our first Chinese meal in England in Canterbury at a little restaurant across the street from where we parked the car overnight.

Our plan was to travel west along the English Channel to Lands' End in Cornwall and then proceed north all the way to Scotland, then cross to the east coast and travel south ending the trip in London. Of course, there would be side trips to the interior to visit castles, and stately homes, and other cathedrals. Compared to the U.S. England is a small place and we thought two weeks was ample time to "cover" the country. Wrong!

Except for the few U.S. Interstate, German Autobahn type highways at that time, the other roads in Great Britain were narrow with two lanes, frequently bordered by dense hedgerows and if one had the bad luck to be trapped behind a lorry, impossible to pass. We realized quickly that we would be lucky to see the southern half of England.

Life was further complicated because our Mercedes was built for the American market with the driver seated on the left. This did not make driving on the wrong side of the road in England easy and Fran developed a stiff neck from turning to see if I was clear to turn, or pass. It was a great relief when we turned the car over to the transport company in London to ship home without a ding on it. I was fascinated to learn that the car was not shipped from London, but Antwerp. Since it was late in October, it had to be unloaded in Baltimore, not Cleveland as I had expected, because of the possibility of the St. Lawrence River freezing.

A final comment on the Mercedes: simple as it was, it was the best and most exciting car I ever drove. Every time I sat behind the wheel; I felt a thrill. Whereas the Oldsmobiles "wanted" to go 70 mph and then felt dangerous above that speed, the Mercedes loved to go 85 mph with perfect control. After flying to Baltimore, I picked the car up at the docks, and drove to Cleveland in less than six hours. It was a thrill.

The only negative aspect of owning a Mercedes was the cost of maintenance. The engineers did not have ease of maintenance in mind when they designed the car. We were misled by Koepke Motors who told me the maintenance cost for a Mercedes should average about $200 a year. In our experience it was $200 every time we had the oil changed. We tried other dealers, foreign car repair specialists, and never solved the problem. The vehicle was on our Company's books at $9,000, which included the purchase price, shipping from Europe, excise tax and insurance. I turned it in to the Company when I retired 9 years later, with 100,000 miles on the odometer; it was sold for $4,500, a 10-year-old car with 100,000 miles, retained 50% of its value.

I remember my surprise at seeing palm trees in the towns near the Channel, and we had to stop overnight in Essex to have the 500-mile check-up on the car and re-torqueing. We saw the cathedral. (I think of all larger masonry churches as cathedrals, even when I know they are not the seat of a bishopric) which was not as large as Canterbury, but beautiful and went to see a movie, *Day of the Jackal*, that night, a good thriller, and the only movie we ever saw on any of our trips.

Other memories are of stopping at the quaint little fishing village, Mousehole, and staying at a bed and breakfast in St. Ives.

We had one of the best meals I have ever had in a small restaurant there: Le Chaperon Rouge, recommended by our landlord. It had only five or six tables; the husband, formerly a sous-chef at The Connaught Hotel in London and his wife, (they were French) who took the orders and served the meals were the owners. We had Megrim sole a fish found only in the Irish Sea. It was the most delicious fish I have ever tasted, and in a most unlikely place.

I remember standing on the edge of the bluff overlooking the ocean at Land's End and feeling overwhelmed by the volume of water between us and home in Ohio.

Other memories: a small hotel outside of Bristol where the hostess who registered us had just come in from riding and was still wearing her jodhpurs and riding boots; of the plains of Salisbury; seeing the Druid Circle and wondering how those primitive people were able to hoist the horizontal stones which must have weighed tons, onto the upright stones. And why?

The Salisbury Cathedral, nearby, is one of the larger cathedrals and stood by itself surrounded by open fields, which is great for picture taking. We were there for our first Evensong service and watched the line of little choirboys dressed in their crimson and gray robes process into the choir stalls. Then, we listened to the ethereal sound filling the vastness of the cathedral's space, their voices singing old sacred music. The boys all attended the cathedral's school of music and ranged in age from 10 to 18 years. The different sound of the unchanged voices of the youngest members produces an effect different from that of a church choir with mature female soprano voices. I think I remember Fran saying they were adorable, not one of her usual adjectives. I thought they were, too, but also probably full of little boys' mischief.

We tried to attend Evensong services as often as possible. They were always at 5 p.m. and were all music, no sermon or homily, and usually sparsely attended. The sound of the young voices in a great cathedral space, reverberating off all that stone, remains with me and is something I yearn for.

In our journeys we arrived in Worcester, north of Bristol, about 5 p.m. and got our first glimpse of that cathedral, which was across the street from our hotel. We enjoyed the lounge, where dinner was ordered off the menu and drinks served. before being seated in the dining room as where the first course of our dinner was being placed on our table as we were seated, which is a very civilized way of doing things, I thought. The lounge had windows from floor to ceiling and comfortable seating. The facade of the cathedral was floodlit; and the view was spectacular.

We toured the cathedral the next morning, and I do not recall anything special about it. We visited the Worcester china factory later, which was most interesting. They manufactured not only fine porcelain dishes, but also stylized figurines (such as a foxhunter jumping a fence). The quality standards were very high because there was a large bin in the workshop where the figurines were being handmade, where the imperfect pieces were thrown. It was almost full.

We also passed through Winchester and saw its cathedral, which did not appeal to me. At the entrance to the city, there was a statue of King Arthur, whom legend says was born there. I'm not sure, but I think this was the cathedral that had a chapel, which was a large room dominated by a round table to seat King Arthur's twelve knights.

We stopped in Bath and saw the Basilica and the Roman baths, which were a remarkable engineering achievement for their time. We had lunch there, and I remember seeing The Royal Crescent and the impression it made on me; how it brought back memories of the period of English literature I studied in college.

The Royal Crescent was a shallow curved row of what we would call, nowadays, townhouses, all the same style, creamy white, 20 or 24 residences. In my head, I could hear horses and carriages and see men in top hats and cravats and swallow-tail coats, and ladies in long dresses with umbrellas unfurled.

I remember the morning we saw the cathedral at Wells. It was a soft, sunny morning and the walk from the parking area to the church was past the Bishop's residence, which sat back on a wide, very green lawn and was simple yet imposing. The cathedral itself seemed smaller, but what I remember most, and what makes it my favorite of all the English cathedrals we saw, was the interior, which had inverse Gothic arches of stone supporting the roof over the nave which produced a shape like the outline of an hourglass. It's hard for me to describe; but it made a great impression on me. It is the only cathedral of any we saw in all our travels that I can close my eyes today and still see clearly. I do not remember the stained glass, which I am sure I photographed, as I always did, but I do remember those arches.

We spent a day on the way north, crossing the bridge at Conway to pass into Wales, and were immediately aware of the unusual spelling of the place names. We saw the castle, Caernarfon, which was huge, and where, since the 1300s, the heir to the throne of England is crowned Prince of Wales. The trip back into England was through a scenic valley and I remember stopping in Chester and seeing the cathedral, but what I remember more clearly, was an unusual central market arrangement. As I recall there were two or three floors of parking above the retail section, which made shopping for groceries and everyday necessities very convenient. I had never seen anything like it before; in effect, a shopping center built into a parking structure.

We continued to the east and visited a stately home near York, the most northerly point in England we reached. Fran was more interested in the stately homes (probably to get ideas for decorating); and I was more interested in the cathedrals, their stained glass windows. We progressed to York, spending most of our time in York at its cathedral. It was my understanding that York was the second most important cathedral in England, after Canterbury, and I was disappointed. In my mind every cathedral was a photo opportunity, and I took hundreds of slides of all the cathedrals we saw in England, and on the continent. York seemed very austere and cold, cavernous, and I did not care for the stained glass. We continued south to Lincoln, which seemed more welcoming and stayed the night. I remember using the C-clamp attached to my camera to take pictures of the facade of the cathedral, which was floodlit, and the next morning taking a photo of the Rose window from the interior, which was justifiably famous and very beautiful.

On our way south to London we stopped at Blenheim Palace, the birthplace of Winston Churchill, and my remaining impression is one of a comfortable place to live in spite of its enormous size; and that it had an organ, which I would have loved to slip away from the tour group to play a few chords. Of course, I restrained myself.

We stopped at Oxford, which was of great interest to me, because I thought the residential college system at Yale had probably originated at Oxford. I remember entering the famous Bodleian Library, which I had read about, and peeking into the entryways of several of the colleges, my camera on the ready.

It was at the entry to All Soul's College that we had an unusual adventure. There was a sign saying: "No Admittance," and a porter on guard in his office. I dared to walk just past his post to try to sneak  a photo of the inner courtyard. As I was focusing, I was approached by the porter who said, "No, no. No photos allowed." He was overruled by a Don in robes, who was entering at that moment. He asked us who we were, and a conversation ensued, which resulted in his inviting us to join him in his office. After, he had given us a brief tour of the college, the chapel, the Christopher Wren sundial, the library and the dining hall, it all seemed familiar, even his office. It reminded me of an ancient Pierson College. We must have chatted for nearly an hour and learned that he taught law, specializing in the South African legal system. He had lived in Shaker Heights, Ohio, at one time and had visited Yale. He told us the College was immensely wealthy and owned about half of the downtown real estate in Oxford. He explained the English educational system and was so cordial. I wish I could remember his name.

Thus, ended our touring in England. We never saw the Lake Country or Scotland. Finding a place to sleep was more like France and Spain than Italy and Austria because the only accommodations we could find were hotels, or motels. In Italy and Sicily, Austria, Switzerland there were always gasthouses or pensions offered by private individuals. It seemed to me these were less expensive and provided an opportunity to interact with local people. We drove the new Mercedes about 1,500 miles and by the time we finished our trip and said goodbye to our car, I had become somewhat accustomed to driving on the wrong side of the road.

Probably the most interesting hotel we ever stayed in was in the Cotswolds area, near Cheltenham, where we had lunch. I did not realize at the time that it was the location of the British communications and cryptography operations in World War II and that it had a famous race course; I had not yet read any of the Dick Francis novels.

We found a small hotel in a very small village, Castle Combe, which was very quaint. I think the hotel may have had only eight or ten sleeping rooms on the second floor, had a lounge but did not serve food. What I remember (with horror - what if there had been a fire?) was the narrow stairway to the second floor. It was hardly wide enough for one person at a time to climb  and very steep, almost like climbing a ladder. I had to push Fran from behind to get to our room and drag our suitcase behind me.

The other memory I have of Castle Combe, which was a photographer's delight, was that there was a highly rated restaurant a short distance from our hotel. We made reservations and it was obviously a very fine establishment. When we ordered I was feeling expansive, and we ordered a bottle of wine for Fran, rather than the usual glass, after carefully checking the wine list. When the wine was served and Fran tasted it, she made a face and said there's something wrong with this. I called the waiter over, and he called the sommelier, who sniffed the cork, tasted, and declared there was nothing wrong with the wine. We did not take that bottle with us to be stowed on the back seat of the car as we had done before. It was an expensive lesson, and I am positive the sommelier felt we were "American cousins" who had no taste and had no recourse. He had the added benefit of getting rid of a bottle of "corked" wine that should have been thrown out.

After dropping off the Mercedes for shipping to Cleveland, we spent a few days in London doing tourist things; visited the Tate Art Museum with its wonderful collection of Turners and the National Art Museum, but not the British Museum which I always regretted. Of course, we visited St. Paul's Cathedral, designed by Christopher Wren, so different from the Gothic cathedrals we had seen. While we were there and I was busy getting my photographic record, Fran was seated close to the altar dictating her notes into her recorder. She noticed a group of Japanese tourists following their guide, and trailing the group, Ernie and Janet Ellenberger, close friends from Brecksville. We had no idea they were in Europe. They had just completed a trip to Scandinavia and were stopping off in London to meet a daughter, who was apprenticed to a goldsmith in Germany, and came to England to see her parents.

We arranged to meet them at Westminster Abbey at 5 p.m. for the Evensong service before going to dinner. The by now familiar service was beautiful and attended mostly by tourists. After the service, the organist played a short concert, showing off the great organ, which had something I had never heard before: a 32-foot pedal stop. The organs I was familiar with never went lower than 16 feet. The 32-foot stop produced tones so low that I thought I felt the whole building tremble. Somehow, meeting old friends from home, unexpectedly, and hearing that magnificent organ, was a fitting end to an unforgettable adventure.

We took our trips to Europe in the years 1970 to 1981, usually in early June or October, trying to avoid the worst of the tourist crush during the summer school vacation period. Four of these trips were guided tours: three conducted by the University of Michigan Alumni Association: our first, the trip to Vienna in 1971, then a trip down the Danube in 1980, and a trip through the waterways of Holland in 1981.

The fourth trip was with strangers who had joined the same discount travel club we did which was headquartered in Michigan and departed from Detroit. It was a last-minute decision on our part and our destination was the Canary Islands, owned by Spain, a popular destination for northern Europeans in the winter season. The islands were not at all what I expected: lush tropical islands. They were extremely dry, an extension of the Sahara Desert off the coast of Africa. We landed at Gran Canaria, the largest island of the group; the accommodations were fine, modern mid-rise hotels built by the Spanish government, and we rented a car for a day to explore, but found the perimeter road was so short - there were no interior roads - we turned the car in early. I remember the most vivid green spot we saw on the whole island was a golf course a short distance from our hotel which was watered with tertiary treatment effluent. I remember two side trips flying to two of the other islands in the group: on one we rode camels, and the other a drive along the coast and saw beaches of black sand.

This was the place where after dinner in a restaurant near our hotel, after finishing our meal, we were approached by a photographer trying to get guests to let him take their photograph and then buy a copy from him. His gimmick was that he had a small pet monkey, which he threw on Fran's lap. The resulting photograph reflects her horror and astonishment perfectly. It was our least enjoyable travel experience, mainly because of the uncomfortable, old, chartered DC-9 airplanes used to get us to Gran Canaria, and back home. We landed on one of the Azores Islands, 1,000 miles east of Portugal on the flight home to refuel, and can say we visited the source of Madeira wine – at least the airport.

Our other vacations in Europe were usually 3 weeks in length plus a weekend and started the year after our trip to Vienna. The year was 1972, Kathy had graduated from the University of Michigan with a degree in Fine Arts. She wanted to travel to Europe and tour the great art museums with a friend, Dale, a classmate. who was engaged to a boy who was doing a walking tour of Ireland at the same time the two girls would be on their trip. They would meet in Paris and spend a week there before returning home together. It is a sign of how different things are now that we agreed to allow this. I can't imagine permitting a daughter, aged 22, to travel abroad, essentially alone, under today's conditions.

We consented, and rationalizing, to reduce the expense of the trip, bought an Opel 4-door sedan for her in Cleveland to be picked up at the factory in Russelheim, Germany by Kathy. I was proud that she would even attempt this, going through all the formalities at the factory, driving away in a strange car in a strange country with a strange language, shy Kathy. She would drive the Opel for three weeks, and then we would meet and take over the car and drive it on a trip of our own for another three weeks. The unpaid rental for six weeks would offset the price of the Opel.

Their plan was to drive south all the way to the Riviera on the Mediterranean, and then work their way north to Paris, visiting art museums as they progressed. We would meet them at Chartres; about 50 miles southwest of Paris, take over the Opel, and the girls would take the train to Paris and meet Dale's fiancé and return home together, after enjoying the delights of Paris, especially the Louvre for Kathy.

Unfortunately, the fiancé fell to his death while climbing a cliff in Ireland, and our reunion in Chartres was not a happy one. Dale's minister had volunteered to be there in Chartres to break the terrible news, since there was no way to contact the girls while they were on the road. We met him at Idlewild Airport, traveled on the same plane, and took the same train to Chartres. Somehow, the girls overcame the shock of the terrible news, and cut their trip short, flying home with the minister the first flight they could get from Paris. I don't think Kathy ever got to see the Louvre, the pinnacle of her trip.

I remember the special sadness of our farewells when Kathy gave us the keys to the Opel. She was on her own to complete her trip. We were about to begin our experience of wandering in a foreign country in a strange car we owned.

We spent the first day, a Sunday, in Chartres. We went to the church service at the cathedral, and I remember walking down a long gravel walk to the church, and passing a drunken peasant, wearing rubber boots, curled up, lying on his side on the ground sleeping off his drunk under a bench: hardly a desirable first impression of one of the greatest architectural masterpieces in the world, as we were to learn shortly. We planned to return in the afternoon to see the church without the crowds of people, and I could take my pictures of the stained glass, which I already knew was remarkable.

When we returned from lunch, we noticed a sign advertising a guided tour-lecture in English lasting an hour given by a Malcom Miller. We thought it might be a good idea to get some background before I started taking pictures. This turned out to be a wise decision because Mr. Miller was an English scholar who had devoted his life to a study of the cathedral. We learned a great deal about cathedral architecture in general and Chartres specifically: the relationship of the exterior sculptured figures to the figures in the stained glass. Considering the literacy level of the worshippers, they could learn the lessons of the Bible from seeing pictures, rather than reading Scripture. It was a wonderful lecture, and we came back for a second, different tour and lecture later that afternoon. His two lectures added to our appreciation of the cathedrals we saw everywhere immeasurably.

As a footnote, while we were living in Florida many years later, we learned that Mr. Miller was giving a lecture in Sarasota, which we attended eagerly. It was a pleasure to listen to such a dedicated person with an encyclopedic knowledge of his subject. His presentation was humble, and charming: his enthusiasm, contagious.

I loved the pictures of the stained glass I took; it was hard to believe such colors could be achieved in the 14th and 15th centuries. I think the stained glass we saw at Chartres was the most beautiful of any that we saw in all our travels; and since it was our first real trip, set the standard for everything that came after.

We traveled north from Chartres. I remember stopping for lunch and using my French for the first time; placing an order for a ham sandwich, using a long forgotten word *jambon* (ham) and being a little surprised and pleased that that was what was delivered. As my "ear" for French became more accustomed to hearing it, confidence in my schoolboy French increased and after the second week I felt I could get along speaking French quite well. I felt the French people appreciated my at least trying to use their language, even in Paris.

Out first destination was Le Mont-Saint-Michel on the coast of the English Channel. As a photographic icon, it probably ranks with the Taj Mahal, and our first view of it, seemingly floating above the fields was unforgettable. We were able to cross the causeway at low tide and park the Opel safely. When the tide comes in is when Le Mont St. Michel becomes an island. We found a room in a small hotel at the base of the mount and had dinner across the street at La Mère Poulard's Restaurant. It was a dinner I will never forget, and I relive it frequently. When we entered the dining area, we were led past a fireplace at least ten feet long with a roaring fire. For some reason, I ordered an *omelette*, and it was by far the finest I have ever tasted. Folded over it was at least four inches thick and covered the entire plate. I do not remember anything else about the meal. After we finished, I watched the *omelettes* being prepared at the fireplace. There was a young man beating fresh eggs from crates stacked against the wall in a large copper kettle about the size of a kettle drum in a symphony orchestra. He used a long whisk and had a jazzy rhythm, and a right forearm that reminded me of the comic strip character, Popeye. The chef used a cast-iron skillet with a 6' handle into which he put a 3" cube of fresh dairy butter, and when it was melted, the frothy eggs. I asked him how many eggs there were in one of the omelettes and was amazed when he said two. The combination of fresh farm grown eggs, fresh butter from the nearby farms, and the smoke from the burning fire produced a flavor I have never tasted anywhere else in the world. The first thing I order in a new restaurant is a fluffy omelet, and I am continually disappointed. When we eventually arrived in Paris, I remember ordering an omelette for lunch at the Café Fauré on the Champs-Élysées (I remember the name because Gabriel Fauré is one of my favorite composers) and it did not compare with that of La Mère Poulard.

One of the benefits of traveling alone, especially in a rental car, is the freedom to spend as much time at a tourist attraction as one wants; deciding which to visit from the multitude of choices listed in our trusty Michelin guidebook (we liked Michelin best) knowing that we would probably never see it again; not to be herded along to the next attraction to suit the guide's timetable. This is true of an individual site, or a whole region.

Also, we enjoyed the luxury of being able to sprawl with our luggage in our own car and picking our own lodging for the night (we devised a plan where one of us picked the hotel or pensione every other night. To make it interesting, we competed to see which was the nicest room and lowest price: often $15-$17 per night, including breakfast and free parking. We had fun shopping every day after breakfast for the makings of our lunch to be consumed outdoors in a park, or next to a stream; going from one small shop for the luncheon meat or cheese, to another for freshly baked bread, and another for a sweet - hopefully a macaroon for me.

Before we left Le Mont-Saint-Michel, we climbed the spiraling pathway, houses and shops on both sides, to the Chapel with a spectacular view at the very top of the Mont. It was low tide so we could leave and with a dry car we drove south to the Loire Valley to visit as many of the famous *châteaux* as possible. We started at Angers, close to the mouth of the Loire River, where it flows into the Atlantic Ocean. We worked our way east zig-zagging back and forth across the river and explored eight or ten of the most famous *châteaux*. The beauty of the buildings themselves, and the settings were overwhelming, and have become a blur in my mind. I have difficulty understanding how such beauty and structural integrity could have been produced so many years ago. How did they do it?

When I see a picture of Chambord, or the gardens of Villandry, perhaps on the back of an expensive deck of cards, or remember the smaller, more human beauty of the Château de Menars, on the north side of the Loire River, the home of Mme. Pompadour, it brings back memories of a fantastic week, ending at the city of Orléans to the east, where there is another large cathedral with beautiful stained glass, dedicated to Joan of Arc  Sainte-Croix.

We visited the cathedral late in the afternoon and I remember one of my better photos of the sunbeams slanting across the nave, illuminating motes of dust in the air, with the altar, mysterious, in the far distance.

This is also where we had dinner in a restaurant close to our hotel, which was around the corner from the cathedral, and I observed the waiter bringing desserts, which I learned were called *profiteroles*, to a table of plump, older ladies. *Profiteroles* are one of the famous European desserts; along with *charlotte Russe* and *pêche Melba* and are a pyramid of small cream puffs, about an inch and a half in diameter, slathered with chocolate sauce. I had my first of many at a restaurant in Grenoble, France, which was the farthest point south we reached.

We had to cut our planned weeklong exploration of the Loire Valley short, because on the second day, after seeing the Château in Saumur (not one of the prettier ones, built more for defense) in the late afternoon, while I was parking the car in the hotel garage, Fran went up to the room and being very warm and headachy, took two aspirin with a sip of water from the tap. We had been warned never to drink the water and always had bottled water with us, as well as a bottle of wine on the back seat of the car for Fran for our lunches. By morning she was violently ill (Montezuma's Revenge) and it was obvious we would have to find some place to stay until she recovered. I checked at the hotel desk and they suggested the Château d'Artigny, not too far distant. I called and using my best French, reserved a room after checking the price (in French).

We found the Château d'Artigny without difficulty but I was disappointed in a way when I found we would not be staying a structure built in the 1500s but in a modern, very accurate version of one of the old châteaux, built in the 1920s by René Coty, the founder of the cosmetic empire, who lived there until his death. It was sold and converted into a hotel after World War II, when it was occupied by the German High Command.

It was extremely luxurious, almost decadent, and while Fran was recovering, I wandered the grounds and the building and ate my meals alone. The doctor who called on her prescribed syrup of Coca Cola, which did the trick, and two days later we were back on the road. When I went to pay the bill, I learned that I had misunderstood the price quotation (given in French), and they were the most expensive lodgings we ever enjoyed, anywhere. If I had heard correctly, I am sure we would have looked elsewhere. Fran didn't have much fun and never really even saw the hotel.

We continued south from Orleans and I remember passing through Clermont-Ferrand where the Renault Motor automobiles were manufactured; farther south in mountainous country I had my first experience of driving through switchbacks; I remember mountainsides blooming with yellow Scotch Broom, and after reaching Grenoble, turning north to pass through Aix-les-Bains, on the way to Switzerland. There we saw Geneva, Zurich, Lucerne, Lausanne where the Chillon Castle can be seen from the road. We had lunch one day in Interlachen, located between two Swiss lakes, and as we approached the restaurant were greeted by the blaring sound of the Charley Barnett big band playing "Skyliner" thru the loudspeakers, one of the records in my collection. It brought back memories of home.

This is where we learned of another, new to us, European custom. There were two young backpackers seated at the next table. The waiter brought rolls and water before our meal was served, and one of the young people very politely asked if they could have a roll. Of course, we offered the basket of rolls and they took some. They left before we did, and when our bill came, I found that we had been charged for each roll that was missing, whether we had eaten it, or not. From then on, we guarded our rolls that were always fresh and delicious with our lives.

While we were in Switzerland, we had to "climb" a Swiss alp. I remember before calling it a day, driving to the parking area for the Jungfrau, a very high mountain, and speaking to a Japanese tourist who had just come down from his visit, complaining of altitude sickness, which gave us some concern. The next day we went to Mt. Titlis, about 12,000 feet high, bought our tickets for the cogwheel train and were not impressed with the local people with their skis and ski poles who were very free with their elbows as they tried to get ahead of us for a place on the small car. The cogwheel train took us up to a half-way point where we switched to a gondola car and went the rest of the way by cable to the ski area near the top of the mountain.

It was mid-June and a clear day, a great day for taking photos, which I did. I found a spot where I was able to take a 360 degrees panorama of the surrounding snow-covered peaks. We were probably at an elevation of about 11,000 feet but seemed to have no difficulty in breathing, contrary to our Japanese friend the night before.

There was a small café at the gondola landing with a fenced in area where there were many people sunbathing, reclining on chaises, the men bare to their waists. It was a sunny day, after all, but there was also a steady stream of skiers whizzing by on their way down the slope. It was incongruous and I will never forget it.

I will also never forget the lunch we had after we came down the mountain. We drove a short distance away and found a nice spot for our picnic lunch next to a fast rushing stream about three feet wide and a foot deep. The water had a milky appearance and made a rushing noise. I do not remember exactly what kind of sandwich we had that day, or if I had a macaroon for dessert, but I do remember putting my hand into the rushing water up to my wrist and withdrawing it instantly because it was the coldest water I had ever felt. It must have been melt from the glacier at the top of Mt. Titlis. My hand was numb in 10 seconds. I wonder what the water might have tasted like.

I remember seeing the huge water fountain in Lake Geneva, and our difficulty of breaking out of the traffic pattern at rush hour to get to our hotel and the room we had (with a view of the lake) on the fifth floor. The elevator only went to the fourth floor and we had to climb stairs to get to our room on the fifth. The view was from a very small window in a clothes closet. I also remember the small, gilt wind-up Neuchâtel clock we bought at the gift shop in the hotel, which we still have, although I no longer bother to wind once a week, just enjoy having it to look at to bring back memories.

I don't remember Zurich, except as a bustling good-sized city, but do remember leaving there to travel south to Lichtenstein, a very small principality, largely owned by one ancient family. The whole country is about 2 miles square and issues its own stamps. It has a well-known art museum in the family castle. I had read an article about the museum in *Time Magazine* some time before our trip. While we were there, we checked it out. It was a disappointment. It was not very large, and the pictures were second rate. We were only in the country because, our youngest daughter, Barbara, who had told us about a country she saw on her trip with her cousin, Debbie, the summer before, whose name started with "L." When we returned home, we told about our excursion down into Lichtenstein, and she said, "Oh, No. It was Luxembourg." This elicited a feeble chuckle on my part.

On our progress northwards and westwards toward Paris, we passed through the Champagne district, and I realized for the first time that wine is named for the district in which it is produced; also, jam: we passed through Bar-le-Duc, which answered one of my questions.

When we approached the city of Reims, I was surprised to see a familiar American name on a French building: the Andrew Carnegie Public Library. We stopped to see how this could be and learned that after World War I, Andrew Carnegie, who was the Secretary of the Treasury of the U.S., immensely wealthy, donated the money to build the library. It was yellow brick and reminded me of a similar building in the Slavic Village area of Cleveland.

The main attraction in Reims is the famous gothic Cathédrale of Notre Dame, which we explored, and I took my usual pictures. I think I remember walls hung with huge tapestries, and I do remember the main entrance because we have an interesting painting of it done in an Impressionistic style by a neighbor of Kathy and Stephen's in Chagrin Falls. We saw so many cathedrals during our travels that I find it difficult to remember one from another, and their distinguishing features. The blur is wonderful, however.

As we traveled west, we were running out of time and passed, but did not stop at the Château de Malmaison, home of the Empress Joséphine Napoleon, on our way to Fontainebleau.

It was at Fontainebleau that I first realized the virulent anti-Semitism of the French. We approached the Palace on the main road from Paris and were impressed by the elaborate entrance. There were railroad tracks next to the road and a stop for the trains, a spacious boulevard and a great many monuments of French heroes. It was an impressive introduction to one of the great museums of the world, a taste of what awaited us once we entered the château itself.

We found a small hotel on a small street (quite a contrast to the grand main entrance) at the rear of the château, and while Fran was settling in, I took the opportunity to take some late afternoon pictures of the exterior of the château and the grounds. According to our trusty Michelin guidebook there was a rear entrance to the grounds right around the corner from our hotel.

I found it without difficulty, and as I was about to enter, I noticed a small plaque, about 12" x 15" mounted on the brick wall (in a very inconspicuous position, easily missed) which was a memorial to the Jews in World War II, who were sent to the extermination camps in the east by the Nazis with the cooperation of the French. The contrast to the splendor of the main entrance was overwhelming, and, unfortunately, that is how I remember this beautiful château.

The Palace of Versailles, about 18 miles west of Paris, was our last stop before dropping off the car. It was interesting to see how royalty added to the original palace. I was unprepared for the scale of the palace: the main structure, the stables, the housing for the servants, the huge cobbled-plaza. It was a small city. The only memories of all this that remain of the interior are of the royal chapel, and The Hall of Mirrors.

My most lasting memory of Versailles was of my first sight of the Grand Trianon, after leaving the original palace and passing through the surrounding, manicured gardens. It was slightly elevated, one-story only, and resembled a pink marble Greek temple, not a royal palace for relaxation. Our tour took us from room to room, each with two doors on the left, outside wall at the corner of each room for entering and leaving, giving the feeling of rooms off a long corridor.

I have never seen anything more beautiful anywhere, each room surpassing the previous one: beautiful carpets, and delicate, elegant furniture and walls covered with beautiful paintings, all coordinated in exquisite taste. The elegance and harmony created by the French designers was overwhelming. Photography was permitted, which surprised me, no flash allowed, and I don't know how many exposures I made. After seeing this, the royal palaces in Austria and Spain, and even England, though beautiful in their own way, were unsuccessful attempts to keep up with the French.

I remember the feeling of relief I always felt, after having traveled so many miles safely in a foreign country, when we turned in our car and checked into the hotel where our travel agent had made reservations for us. We used the day provided for rest and relaxation to see our final sights. On our final day in Paris, a Saturday, we were walking, and I was looking for a bookseller's store.

I had finished all the reading material I had brought from home and was hoping to find an Inspector Maigret novel by Georges Simenon in French. The store we found was quite small and happened to be across the street from the Élysée Palace, the official residence of the President of France. I remember it was close to noon, and many large Citroën limousines were lined up in the forecourt and stopping to pick up dignitaries at the front door, where the President (?) was saying farewell.

I asked the proprietress (in French) for directions on how to find the famous La Madelaine Church, Grecian temple style and if it was within walking distance. I knew the church was only a short distance from the shop of Durand & Fils, music publishers.

I wanted to see if I could find some organ music. I loved the distinctive size of their sheet music, which was larger than that published in the U.S., about 11" x 14", and on stiff cream-colored paper: very unique. I did find a copy of César Franck's *Trois Chorals*, which was one of the first large pieces I learned to play on the organ, and eventually played each of the chorales for church service at St. Matthews in Brecksville.

Madame said that the church was an easy walk and astounded me by locking the front door of her store, on a Saturday about noon, and walking us to a corner a block away and pointing out the direction we were to take; this in a big city where the French were reputed to look down their noses at the barbaric U.S. tourists. It was a long block, and an unexpected courtesy.

It happened to us another time in Paris when we were puzzling over a wall-mounted map of the Metro, the underground rail system. A young man saw our confusion and approached us and politely asked if he could help. We were obviously tourists having difficulties in his city and he came to our aid. Once again, I was able to use what French I had, and I have always wondered, poor accent and all, if this had an effect on the French citizens' attitude toward us. The people we interacted with in the countryside were unfailingly courteous and helpful and in the big cities, as well.

One final memory of the sights of Paris was our visit to the Sainte-Chapelle, a part of the royal palace on the Île de la Cité, quite near Notre-Dame Cathedral. The entrance for the public on the street level is unprepossessing, a large room with a low ceiling, perhaps 7' high, painted a dark blue and dappled with stars, then a short climb up the stairway to the chapel.

I will never forget my first sight of this magnificent room. It took my breath away, and I heard gasps as other tourists saw it for the first time. The walls are beautiful stained glass, from floor to ceiling, fleche style, equaling those of the Chartres Cathedral, but here the walls are entirely glass. . I have never seen anything so beautiful, so inspiring, before or since.

On our flight home I remember excitedly discussing where or next trip should be.

We decided on Italy. This would be our fourth adventure in Europe, and our travel agent, Larry, at the National City Bank arranged for us see northern Italy for our three week vacation, flying into Milan, picking up our rental car and staying the first night at a small hotel on Lake Como. The start of our trip was inauspicious.

We arrived at Idlewild with time to spare only to learn that our Air Alitalia airline flight was delayed for mechanical reasons. Instead of leaving at 7:30 p.m., they were estimating 9:30 p.m.; we decided we had better get something to eat and had a terrible meal in the airport. When we returned to the Air Alitalia lounge, we were told that there were further delays, and estimated departure time was now 12:30 a.m., and that we would be taken to a restaurant and a meal provided.

At this point, I could see losing an entire day of our precious vacation time and left to check out leaving earlier on one of the other airlines. I checked Swiss Air, which had a flight leaving immediately for Zurich, but we would have to take a train to Milan to pick up our rental car and there would be no gain in time; and Air France had nothing useful. Back to Alitalia and our free meal. There were two busloads of people and we were taken to a Howard Johnson restaurant nearby. So much for an outstanding free dinner at a famous Italian restaurant.

The flight was not crowded and very comfortable. Unfortunately, there were two or three Italian families with babies who fussed and cried the whole flight, and we did not spend a restful night.

It was a shock we were unprepared for to see soldiers armed with automatic rifles and guard dogs patrolling the Milan airport. We picked up our car (without need for their protection). I don't remember what make car of it was, but think it was a little Fiat 4-door sedan, much smaller than the Oldsmobile Omega we had in Brecksville, but with a much roomier interior and trunk.

After checking into our hotel and before resting until dinner, we checked out the public dock and then took a walk on the road next to the lake, which was beautiful, and on the way back to our room passed the hotel Villa d'Este, a famous, very expensive old resort hotel with its own dock on Lake Como. Lake Como was large enough to have a small passenger boat service which circled the lake and stopped, on schedule, at the many villages on the shores of the lake. We napped until dinner and chatted with a young German couple who were sitting at the table next to us in the dining room, who spoke English and who were returning home to Germany after a year of working in Italy.

Finally, after a very long day, we were ready for a hot shower to get rid of our travel grime, and sleep without babies wailing. We discovered not only was there no hot water there was no water at all. Repairs to the water mains were being made at the next village north of our hotel, and our supply was therefore cut off. I had to go down to the reception desk and buy a bottle of water so we could brush our teeth. But it was all right. We were in Italy. We did not expect everything to work perfectly, or everything to be on time.

The next morning when I connected my electric razor, I found there was no electricity. I shrugged and solved my beard problem at our first stop on the autostrada (similar to our interstate highways but more scenic) on our way to Genoa. Here I received another shock (no pun intended) when, after shaving in a trucker's cubicle, I went into the plaza to buy a bottle of drinking water and was amazed to see a full bar: serving wine and liquor, open for business, with several male patrons present on an early Sunday morning. I could not believe that the State would sanction the sale of liquor on a limited access highway. It was not very reassuring.

After this shaky introduction to the splendors of Italy, there were no further surprises, only one great experience after another. Another benefit to me in traveling independently was that we were isolated, dependent only on each other; we could not speak the language, read the newspaper, or watch TV; had to pray the merchants were giving us our correct change. We could concentrate on the history, the beauty and each other.

We drove south through Genoa, Siena, Pisa, and stayed in Florence for two or three days in a small hotel, with a public parking garage nearby where we stored our car while we were there. On the way, we saw all the typical tourist sights: the Leaning Tower (we ate lunch sitting on the lawn of a park while waiting for it to topple); in Siena we saw our first churches built with contrasting bands of colored marble, so different from the gray stone Gothic style we had become accustomed to; Florence, home of the Medicis was an overload of historical, visual places of interest. I remember seeing the Uffizi Museum, and the Pitti Palace and the Galleria dell'Accademia, where the famous statue of David is located. I took many pictures of this perfectly proportioned, more than life-sized statue and have a clear memory of its impact. However, I also remember noticing the big toe on one of the feet, which was stained dark brown by floodwaters when the Amo River, which runs through Florence, overflowed its banks one spring, which brought me back to reality.

I remember the kindness of the hotel proprietor in Florence (he owned and operated the small hotel), who, when he learned that our next destination was Venice, offered to and made reservations for us at another small hotel two bridges over canals away from St. Mark's Square.

I remember the now familiar regrets at having to leave a wonderful place too soon, wishing we could spend a week or a month there, an impossibility, knowing that we would probably never be there again, and the same bittersweet feeling every time we drove away from a city. We left Florence after driving up a hill to an overlook point and sitting there looking out over the city spread below us.

Then it was on to Venice, all the way across the peninsula, through Bologna, lunch at Padua, and finally the parking structure where we left the car on dry land before taking the vaporetto (water taxi) to our hotel, carrying our luggage.

I have decided that I am not going to try to remember or describe all the wonders we saw on the trips we made to Europe. There are simply too many and this is not a travel guide. My memory has difficulty with the chronology, and I am afraid there is an overload. The reader must assume that we saw most of the major tourist attractions on the route we took, relying on our guidebook not to miss too many. It was impossible to see everything on the limited amount of time we had each year, and I confess the memories tend to blur into a montage.

I get great pleasure in my reading when a place I have visited is mentioned and described and I am transported in my mind back to the time we spent there. Another problem: I fear that I was concentrating on the photography, not the subject, so my memory imprint may not have been as strong as it could have been.

Venice was an incredible experience, unlike any place we had ever seen; almost unreal in its beauty, and certainly hard to believe real people lived there and had jobs and families and children who went to school.

One vivid memory remains of seeing well-dressed young couples on a sunny Sunday afternoon with beautifully dressed young children enjoying themselves in St. Mark's Square, the children feeding flocks of pigeons who, knowing a good thing, fluttered and hovered over them.

Another example of the contrast between the old and the new is the evening we took a water taxi across the Grand Canal to one of the famous churches (name forgotten) which, from St. Mark's Square, looks as though it is floating on the water. It has many priceless paintings hung on its walls and was very beautiful. This was one of the few times I was persuaded to climb stairs and we climbed, with a monk in attendance, all the way to the top of the bell tower which provided a fantastic panoramic view of the city. So much history! And if one looked down on the neighboring property, a school, one saw a group of boisterous boys playing soccer.

I remember every time we walked to the Square as we passed over the second bridge looking to our right and seeing the Bridge of Sighs, part of the Doge's Palace where prisoners of the State went over a canal from their cells directly to the Palace's interrogation rooms. The Bridge of Sighs, which is more an elevated enclosed passage from one building to another than what is normally thought of as a bridge, was only about 50-yards from where we walked over our bridge, always in shade, ominous, brooding. It gave me the shivers when I thought of its purpose. We actually took the same steps some very unhappy men took centuries ago when we toured the Palace and had to see the prison cells.

Some of the more personal memories of Venice include: getting used to canals as streets and taxis as motor boats; our gondola ride, passing under the Rialto Bridge; seeing the home where Robert and Elizabeth Barrett Browning, English poets, lived; the Cipriani Hotel where the famous Harry's Bar is located; and after wandering the maze of canals, the return to the dock with its distinctive poles. I was surprised at the size of the gondolas and that the canals were shallow enough that poles could be used for propulsion, although there is a brace at the stem where the gondolier stands and uses to lever his pole in a sideways motion to propel the boat and to steer it, rather than sticking the pole into the bottom mud and pushing.

The big surprise was to see a cruise ship anchored in the Grand Canal (the main thoroughfare) off St. Mark's Square. I didn't realize the Grand Canal was that deep, and my youngest brother, Wes, told me that when he was in the navy their ship anchored there, also.

One morning when we were out walking, we came across a German TV company making a film which involved a very beautiful actress being helped into a gondola close to the Rialto Bridge by a handsome leading man, both in period costumes. I was within telephoto distance and took a great many pictures (surprise!) including their retreat to their trailers or standing around for makeup repairs during breaks in the shooting. It was the closest I ever came to a Hollywood film set.

One of the things we did while exploring St. Mark's Square was to ascend the Campanile Tower. I can't remember whether we climbed, it's very tall, or took an elevator. I think the latter, because I have never liked climbing steps and have always avoided them, if possible. We recognized one of the other tourists, having seen him in a restaurant. We struck up a conversation and learned that he was from Seattle, traveling alone, and his name was Klink, the same as Colonel Klink of the *Hogan's Heroes* TV series. We had lunch with him, but never saw him again.

We took a motorboat cruise to some of the islands in the lagoon and were aware that the skipper was very careful to stay within the channel markers because the water is very shallow, especially at low tide. We never saw the famous Lido Beach, a popular resort area (on what would be called a barrier island in Florida) at the mouth of the Venice Lagoon, but did visit Murano, Burano, Torcello and Sant'Erasmo. We were fascinated by the glass factories on Murano where we could watch the glass blowers puffing their cheeks and working their magic on molten glass. Many years later, while living in Florida, we bought a dining room chandelier, which was made in Murano. It is unusual and, I think, very beautiful and it still hangs in the dining area where I now live.

One of the nights after our island cruise, we went to a highly recommended restaurant on a narrow street to the left of St. Marks's cathedral. It was named Trattoria Do Forni, two forges (?) and there were two restaurants with the same name facing each other across the narrow side street. We chose the one on the right side and I had one of the best meals I have ever had. It was so good we went back the next night and tried the restaurant on the left side of the street.

My main course was called *Tortellini a la San' Erasmo*, and probably originated on the island we had visited the previous day. The creamy sauce was assembled at the tableside by the waiter, who then poured it over the pre-cooked stuffed tortellini. It was so delicious; I couldn't get enough of it. I have never seen it on a menu since. I do not remember what I ordered the second night at the same restaurant across the street, but it was not as good as my *Tortellini San' Erasmo*.

Three things remain in my mind from our wanderings on foot through the narrow streets and over the many bridges: we were shopping on the left side of St. Mark's Square and were aware, suddenly, of a small parade of boisterous people holding banners and singing and waving flags. It was election time, and these were members of the Communist party making their presence known, trying to get votes. We had to duck into a shop entrance to avoid being swept into the marchers. They were not marching out in the huge, open square, but in the covered passageway in front of the shops; I was very pleased to see a music shop in our wanderings, and since I was always on the lookout for something new to play for church services at St. Matthews, I went in and found several pieces of music by composers I was not familiar with, music publishers I had never heard of, and easy enough for me to play. I brought several things home with me; we ended up for lunch at a restaurant on the west side of the Grand Canal on the day a bomb had exploded in a trash can at an automobile manufacturing plant in Turin, a Communist stronghold, and everyone in the restaurant attributed it to the Communists as part of the their election campaign.

This was the restaurant where Fran needed to use the restroom and found that it consisted of a hole in the ground with no seat but ceramic footprints indicating where one's feet should be placed while squatting. It reminded me of using a latrine in the field in the army; it was only semi-private, and I had to stand guard at the door. This in one the greatest tourist attractions in the world. It was a "cultural" shock. Obviously unforgettable.

I don't think I should neglect recalling a few memories of St. Mark's Cathedral which is one of the great cathedrals of the world. Unfortunately, the façade was under repair and hidden by scaffolding with bamboo screening for safety reasons. The front entrance was open, and we were able to see the interior. It was very different from the churches we had seen in France and England: there were no stained-glass windows. We climbed to the second floor and looked down on the floor we had just walked over, unaware then of the many-colored marble inlay patterns, which immediately became obvious. Then we looked up to see the upper walls of the church which had portraits of the saints in mosaics so detailed that it was almost like looking at a photograph. These were surrounded by a background of all, plain gold mosaics pieces which reflected and magnified light. Seeing this for the first time was an amazing, awe inspiring experience.

After reluctantly leaving Venice, we drove up into the Dolomite Alps, and spent a night at a pensione in Cortina d'Ampezzo, where one of the winter Olympic games was held. The only memory I have of Cortina is looking out of our bedroom window through the scrubby trees and seeing one of the decaying concrete retaining walls for one of the sharp curves on the bobsled run. We walked over to examine it before we left the next morning. It looked pretty steep to me for such a sharp turn. And now, after all these years, it was crumbling.

We had done northern Italy and loved everything about it and decided to do southern Italy next. On that trip, we flew into Rome and drove to Naples. I remember stopping to take some pictures. When Fran got out of the car, she was wearing a skirt and was carrying my camera on her lap, didn't feel its presence, and as she turned to open her door it slipped off her lap and dropped to the ground. I was horrified; it was our first day on a three-week trip and I had a lot of film with me. The question was: had the lens with its complex structure been jarred so that it would no longer focus or had the automatic feature on which I was so dependent been damaged. We would not know until we returned home.

I remember being uncomfortable when we started driving down the outer, westbound lane, of the two-lane Amalfi Drive. With very scenic views of the Tyrrhenian Sea on the right, it was a very narrow road carved out of the side of a mountain with a sheer drop of about 300 feet in some places to the sea below; with inadequate guard rails (in my opinion); with many curves and limited lines of sight. I was very relieved when we finished that portion of the trip. It only lasted about an hour, but it gave a new meaning to the term "cold sweat."

We didn't explore Naples. I only remember a large parking area at the docks, and driving our car up onto a large ferry, which would take us overnight to Palermo, Sicily. After driving our car into its parking spot in the ferry, we checked into our room, then had dinner ashore, and back to the boat to our small stateroom. We woke up the next morning in Palermo, a large city on the northwest corner of the island, which is quite large and roughly shaped like an isosceles triangle with its base facing Italy.

We drove our car off the ferry into rush hour morning traffic and had some problems finding our way out of the city, but no trouble, thereafter, following our plan to circumnavigate the island counterclockwise. My first memory is of the mosaics we saw in the Cattedrale di Monreale the first day.

Before we planned to see Sicily, I had some misgivings: it was the home of the Mafia and controlled by families of gangsters, according to what I read and saw in the movies; it was an accepted way of life and I was a little uneasy at being exposed to that risk; and it was supposed to be one of the poorest regions in Italy. I was prepared to see sights of extreme poverty and being resented as a relatively wealthy tourist. We were warned to be especially cautious if we stopped in Catania, on the eastern end of the island because it was the headquarters of the Mafia, and crime was "rampant" there.

We spent a week on the island and never saw any signs of poverty, or any evidence of the "mob." Cities were clean, roads good, and there were more Grecian ruins in good condition than in Greece because of fewer earthquakes, we were told. The most outstanding temple I remember was at Agrigento, on the south coast, and known as the Temple of Concordia. Except for having no roof, it is intact. My recollection is that it was at the head of the Valley of Temples where several other temples in various stages of ruin were standing.

We found a small hotel in the modern section of Agrigento, not knowing that our room looked out at the Temple of Concordia, which was about 200 yards away, and floodlit at night. I was able to take several pictures of it floodlit. thanks to the automatic feature of my camera. It was truly impressive and conveyed a powerful feeling of ancient history. The next day before we left, we watched a young, modern-day couple's wedding ceremony performed on the front steps of the temple, white dress and veil, and all.

I do not remember the names of the towns we passed through along the coast road. I do remember about mid-island leaving the coast and driving up into the mountains to a small town recommended in our guidebook, which was an interesting drive, dead-ending at the town which was quaint, and turning and retracing our ride down the mountain to the coast and continuing on to Syracuse. I remember that it was a Sunday and the bed and breakfast we stayed at did not serve dinner, so we had to go out and find a restaurant.

I remember having a main course dish of a local fish I had never heard of before and feeling lucky that it was a mild tasting variety that I was able to enjoy.

Syracuse is a very old city and was a powerful rival of Athens which dominated the region long before the time of Christ. I'm sure we saw many old ruins, but do not remember what they were; one, perhaps, a huge stone amphitheater built on the side of a hill.

I have a slight feeling of shame that the strongest memory I have of Sicily is my discovery of what has become my favorite Italian food, Carbonara. I rarely see it today in American Italian restaurants, but it was on the menu in every restaurant in Sicily.

It is a pasta dish in a cheesy, creamy sauce with bits of Italian Ham and a few peas. There seemed to be a slight variation in the preparation in the various restaurants where we had it. It made me think of American potato salad, which is a common household meal in the U.S., with as many variations as there are cooks. I think we had carbonara at least once a day in Sicily and never tired of it. I wish it were more available in the U.S., and always sample it when I do find it.

We continued northward and, in spite of the warnings, did stop in Catania. I left Fran alone in the car while I went, feeling very uneasy, to find food for our lunch; then continuing north to Messina, where we boarded another ferry for the three or four-mile ride through the historic Strait of Messina. I had always been curious to see since reading about Scylla and Charybdis and the Sirens in Homer's *Odyssey* in my college days. It was a short, uneventful ride: no rocks with tempting females or swirling currents that day.

When we disembarked at Calabria, we had planned to explore the southernmost part of the toe and heel of Italy and went as far as Croton, where Pythagoras, the mathematician/philosopher had his academy. But after a look at the poverty and a glimpse of the Ionian Sea, we decided to give up that plan and headed back up the west coast of Italy to Rome. This meant driving the stretch of the Amalfi Drive, which was not nearly as intimidating when driving north on the right lane next to the mountain. I remember stopping in the city of Amalfi and climbing a long series of steps up to a church which looked out on the Tyrrhenian Sea.

There had been a wedding and the newlyweds had just departed, as we climbed the steps, which we found littered with candy coated almonds that had been thrown instead of the rice. we were accustomed to at home in the U.S. It seemed to me to be an extravagant custom and I had to resist the temptation to pick up one of the almonds to taste it to see if it was real.

I remember staying overnight in Rapallo, a small town in the hills above the Bay of Naples, where Gore Vidal, the author, owned a villa. We stayed overnight in a small hotel in a very comfortable room with a balcony overlooking gardens. We had dinner in the dining room and were attended to by the owner of the hotel, who told us the property had been in his family for generations (he had a prominent Roman nose), and there were vineyards on the land from which they made their own wine. He was very proud that one of his regular customers who featured his wine was a restaurant in Manhattan. I can't recall the name of the wine, the hotel or the restaurant. What I remember most was the dessert, which he prepared personally, and was his specialty: a runny, lemon soufflé served warm on a dessert plate with bits of the whipped egg whites showing. It was delicious. Eating in Italy was always an adventure, and we looked forward to every meal.

It was a slight shock when passing through the city of Sorrento on the Bay of Naples to realize how close it is to Mount Vesuvius and to realize this was the city in the old Italian song, one of my favorites, "Torna a Sorriento" ("Come back to Sorrento") Dean Martin's version of which will settle any questions as to his talent.

I remember the surprise I felt after we had toured the remains of Pompeii, easily accessible on foot, to proceed to another victim of the eruption of Mount Vesuvius, the city, Herculaneum, to find the excavations were ten or twelve feet below the level of the street we were driving on.

We also spent a day on Capri, off the coast of Naples. It is a small, very pleasant island famous for its Green Grotto, a small cave at the edge of the island, entered by rowboat and we had to duck to avoid hitting our heads until we were inside. Then, looking back out the entrance, the color of the water was a beautiful shade of green. We had to take a high-speed passenger ferry to get out to the island; and were picked up off-shore from a floating dock. On the way, we passed a villa built into a steep cliff with a small cove for swimming. We were told that it was owned by Sophia Loren, who was not in residence.

Unfortunately, after we landed at the little port on the island, we hired a very old man who assured us he could row us from the docks the mile or so to the grotto. It was a very small rowboat, barely large enough for the two of us, and was equipped with oars, not an outboard motor. I believe our Captain was asthmatic. About half-way there, he had to stop. We sat until a friend of his in an empty rowboat, returning to the dock, took over from our man and completed the trip.

After seeing the grotto, we were able to climb a hill to a road where there was a bus line which took us into the city. Along the way we passed Hadrian's Villa, the summer residence of the Roman Emperor who built the Wall across Great Britain. It was very open to the breezes and had fine gardens. The city was touristy, but not too much so because of its smallness and the bother in getting there from the mainland. I thought it would a very pleasant place to spend two or three months on vacation.

Eventually, we arrived in Rome and had to drive in its city traffic, which was a challenge, more aptly, a nightmare. It seemed that Roman motorists used their horns instead of their brakes. We turned our undamaged rental car in at the agency which was conveniently located a street away from our hotel, the Hotel Flora. I know that our travel agent at the National City Bank in Cleveland knew we were on a budget in all our travels, and could never understand why he booked us into the Hotel Flora, which was one of the most luxurious and most expensive hotels in Rome. We could afford to stay there only one night and after lunch the next day tried to find something more affordable. We located a small hotel a half block from the Hotel Hassler Roma, at the top of the Spanish Steps, another famous hotel and even more expensive than the Hotel Flora.

We had arranged to meet Fran's oldest friend and her husband, the Montgomerys of Grosse Ponte, Michigan, who were on a guided tour of northern Italy with their friends, John and Sadie Baker, for lunch at the Hassler. I remember what a pleasure it was to spend time with old friends in a foreign capital. It was such a once-in-a-lifetime experience: so exotic. We had had many meals with these friends back home in the U.S. They had come to Cleveland to sail in sailboat races with me, and we had visited them many times in Detroit to visit and play golf. This meeting in Rome was different, had a special quality about it. Part of the feeling was the sheer improbability of it. I remember our lunch in the Hotel Hassler dining room looking over the rooftops of Rome.

After lunch, they inspected our find and they marveled at the amount of space. We had found a small commercial traveler-type hotel on the same street a block away, no glamorous lobby, or dining room, I do not remember its name, but our room was more a suite, having a spacious entry, a sitting room, as well as a sleeping chamber and gorgeous Italian tile bathroom. I think it cost about a quarter of the rates charged at the Hotel Flora. Of course, there was no dining room in the hotel, but we had the added bonus of being able to hear the lions roar at night at the Rome Zoo, which was nearby.

I remember one of our few unpleasant experiences in our travels, which happened when we returned to our hotel by taxi about 10 p.m. and I felt the driver grossly overcharged us. I went in to the hotel to change a travelers' check into lira, and after explaining our problem to the clerk, an older man, he came out to the street and denounced the driver, lectured and threatened him, and secured a large reduction in our fare.

After our first meeting with our friends from home, they were kept busy with their tour group. We saw little of them, other than a dinner together on the Piazza del Popolo, one of the famous Roman squares, at a Spanish restaurant, which featured performances of flamenco dancing. When we returned home we could share experiences at the dinner table of our days spent in Italy while visiting them in Detroit. Same personnel, different venue.

Other than the typical tourist sights: St. Peters Basilica, the Vatican, the awe-inspiring Sistine Chapel, the Coliseum, the Trevi Fountain, the Spanish Steps, the Forum, the Tiber. there is also a powerful memory of the contrast with modern times: the Via Condoti, the Rodeo Drive of Rome, one expensive shop after another. We strolled past the Bulgari jewelry store and I was impressed that there was an armed guard standing at the entrance to the showroom. Fran needed a new winter coat and we found a shop, which had been recommended. We left the store with a full length, light brown leather coat with a mink collar, which fit perfectly and was very elegant.

We took a guided tour bus trip to the Villa d'Este, which is famous for its water garden. I don't remember the interior of the villa being anything special, but the palace was at the edge of a steep hill, possibly 100 feet high. The whole side of the hill was landscaped and water from a stream at the top of the hill was fed to a series of different, interesting fountains irrigating the shrubs and flowers.

The view from the bottom of the hill where there was a grotto, dark and damp, was spectacular: to see so many different fountains spraying the plants. It was worth the trip. On the way back to our hotel the bus stopped; and I bought a couple bunches of grapes which were yellow and almost as large as plums. They were delicious. As I was enjoying them on the way our hotel, I wondered what they had been sprayed with, and when, and would my foolishness be costly. Luckily, there were no ill results.

I remember the ride on the bus the day we left, in the late afternoon to the Leonardo da Vinci Airport, and how it seemed all the buildings on the route had the same mud colored stucco exteriors. I wish I were not color-blind so I might be able to give a more exact description of the color: more yellow than buff, ochre, perhaps. The sun at that time of day warmed the color, trying to make it more attractive, but the apartment buildings were monotonous, and shabby, not at all indicative of what lay behind or ahead of the wonders of Rome.

There were more contrasts at the airport, which was built in an almost flamboyant ultra-modern style. In preparation for the long flight ahead of us, non-stop to Idlewild in New York City, I paid a visit to the men's room, and was surprised to find a line of men standing next to each other using a common porcelain trough. While I was waiting my turn, a cleaning woman came into the room, which was very large, with her mop and pail, and nonchalantly began mopping the floor. It was a cultural shock. I cannot remember whether the airline we used was Alitalia, but do remember it as comfortable, and how much time we spent talking about our next trip abroad.

One of the incidents, which occurred at the end of the earlier trip to Venice the year before, we left the Dolomite Alps and went along the northern shore of Lake Constance, and ended our day in Freiburg, Germany. Another example of the operation of chance in our travels. I remember parking the car a block away from the center of the city, and leaving Fran in the car, while I went searching for lodging on foot. We alternated nights finding a place to sleep, and it was my turn this night. I found a gasthaus with a room for us on Cathedral Square (which was actually an oval). It was owned by a young German couple who were very cordial and welcoming. Our room was on the second floor and looked over a small balcony at the cathedral, about 100 feet away. The cathedral is famous for the intricacy of its spire which appears lacy when looking upward at the sky from the interior.

The hotel had a fenced-in area in front for outdoor dining in good weather facing the cathedral, and when we came down for dinner on this pleasant summer evening in June, we asked if we could sit there. All the tables were occupied except one table for six which had two German men seated at the end closest to the church, reading their evening paper and smoking pipes, wine glasses at hand, but no food. Our host asked if it was permissible for us to sit at the other end of the table, and they readily agreed. After we were seated and had ordered our food, and a white sparkling wine for Fran (the only time she ever ordered something like that in all our travels) the two men spoke to us. They were our age, and one was burly and resembled Max Baer, the heavyweight boxer, the other was more ordinary and could have been a university professor. One of the great, old universities is located in Freiburg.

I reconstruct the conversation that followed frequently in my mind but am not sure of the exact wording. One of the men, the professor, I think, asked if we were British, or American. "American," I replied. "Where are you from," he asked. "Cleveland, Ohio," I said. He said: "Ach! Shteel und chemicals." After that exchange, they went back to their papers, and we ate our dinner. When we were finished and getting up to leave, the professor suggested to Fran that she not drink that kind of wine, but rather a strong wine of the region. Then we left and they bid us goodbye and safe trip home. They couldn't have been more correct, or polite.

After dinner, we walked around the cathedral, which is quite large, and noticed an old building next to our hotel, built in the 1400s, still in use, and in very good condition. It was the Hochschule für Musick, and there had been a concert that evening. We walked in as the concertgoers were leaving to see what the interior looked like. Then off to bed. I think this was the first time I ever slept under a duvet: it was like having a cloud for a blanket. After breakfast the next morning, while Fran was getting ready for the rest of the day, I took my camera and went out to get pictures of the cathedral. It was Tuesday, market day, and the "square" between our hotel and the church was crowded with stands selling everything imaginable and crowded with shoppers. I found the front doors to the church locked, so I walked around the exterior. I could hear the organ playing through an open window. I knew someone was there. I persisted and found a small door on the east side of the church open and ventured inside. I'm glad I did because the stained glass was very good, and the organ was playing. After finishing my photography, I went up and stood by the organist. He was preparing for a concert that night (another opportunity that had to be missed) and I learned that the organ had been built in the 1700s by Silberman, a contemporary and friend of J.S. Bach. It had a magnificent sound in such a large space and had a rank of pipes mounted on the east wall above the windows, which the organist could control from his position at the main keyboard. He could play either or both at the same time, an early example of surround sound. I told him that I was a church organist back home in the U.S., but he did not invite me to play. The American organist, Diane Bish, has a program in her series on Great Organs of Europe on You Tube, which is how I learned that there are pipes on all four walls of the church, controlled by the main keyboard at the front of the church, and there is a view of the hotel we stayed in as she did part of her narrative from the front steps of the church.

After joining Fran, I remember wandering around the old city. Some of the shops had a mosaic symbol embedded in the cobbled walkway in front of the door designating what it was. I remember a mortar and pestle in front of a drug store. Also, I was interested in the gutters along the sides of the streets: the city was built on a high point and a stream diverted, so the gutters had a steady stream of water 24 hours a day removing debris without the need of street cleaners.

The University of Freiburg, one of the oldest and most prestigious in Germany and Europe, is located in the city but we did not see it. It does not sit on one campus, but the various schools are in scattered buildings around the town.

We did pass by a gun shop that had a gorgeous (I am no gun lover) double-barreled shotgun on display in the window with a beautifully engraved gold- plated breech with a price tag of $4,500.00. I took a picture of it through the window to show our Brecksville friend Karl Culler, a huntsman, showing him that we appreciated the high culture found in Europe and to make him envious. I'm sure he would have spent a lot of time in that shop, if he had been with us.

When we left Freiburg, we drove northward on an autobahn along the Rhine and soon came to a bridge over the river where we crossed. We were on our way to Strasbourg, which I thought was a German city, but we were greeted on the other side of the river by two gendarmes wearing the typical French *kepi* hats. I turned to Fran and said that I had never been so glad to leave a country in my life. We had been under no threat whatsoever, had been treated with the utmost courtesy and kindness, and yet I was haunted by the remembrance of our two dinner partners the night before.

I was certain that they had been involved in the death camps, and the Holocaust was a deep-seated obsession of mine from the time I learned of them when I was in the army. I felt that most Germans were complicit, and the real horror for me was that had I been born in Germany, I might also have been, by choice or force, a part of it, goose-stepping and "Sieg Heil-ing." I was fortunate to have been born in Cleveland, Ohio, and only to have a faint feeling of shame for my German ancestry. That a country that had given so much to humanity: a strong Catholic population, home of Martin Luther and the Reformation, Goethe and Schiller, Beethoven and Schubert, could degenerate in a period of fifteen years to the level of destroying 6,000,000 human beings. The feelings of horror are never far from my thoughts.

I am convinced that most Germans knew or had heard about the camps and most were secretly glad that their Jewish problem was being solved. They were helpless, were they not? There was nothing they could do to stop it. Relatively few actually saw the atrocities, or participated in them directly, so the knowledge was based on rumor. But they knew what was happening. I still see our two German tablemates in Freiburg, smoking their pipes, and smoking their cigars, all very peacefully on a warm June night.

Other memories of our brief forays into Germany are of passing through Partenkirchen in the Bavarian Alps on a Saturday and seeing a small German oompah band playing on the square; staying overnight in Innsbruck where the host was a ski instructor and had competed in the Olympic games; looking down to see, from a road high above, in the distance "Mad" King Ludwig's fairytale castle, Neuschwanstein, which we did not tour; and then on to another of his castles on the Chiemsee, near Munich. This castle, the Herrenchiemsee, was modeled on the Grand Trianon at Versailles, and never finished, except for several rooms.

The story was that Ludwig never spent one night there. The Chiemsee is a large lake, about 80 square miles, and no powerboats are allowed. We were taken on an electric motor-powered launch to the island where the castle was built and looking to the south saw 50 or 60 sailboats under full sail in a mass. It was a spectacular sight. I couldn't understand how there could be so many sailboats on such a small lake, or how much fun it would be to navigate in such traffic.

In the Salzburg area, we toured a salt mine with an underground lake. Salt was like gold in Medieval times and ownership or control of salt conferred power, enough to challenge the Pope in far off Rome. At the entrance to the mine, which was dug into the side of a mountain, the same as a gold or coal mine, we had to don yellow raincoats and wear crash helmets. We clambered around various levels and finally were rowed across an underground lake to return to the entry. I remember dripping water and cold, and poor lighting.

We visited Hitler's "Eagles Nest" hideaway/retreat. The approach was through a long tunnel with an elevator to the top of a small mountain. I don't remember much of the interior, but it was possible to go outside and tour the grounds. We did this. I remember sitting on the edge of a cliff, looking out over a beautiful landscape, and having large crows flutter up to beg for bits of the sandwich I was eating. It was lunch time for me, but it was always lunch time for them.

I do not remember why but think that we flew home from Munich the next weekend after seeing the castles. I remember staying in a hotel; noticing many Turkish migrant workers near the railway station which made me uneasy; seeing the famous town hall with a large clock on the face of the tower where figures marched across the face on the hour. I remember the great cathedral, rebuilt after World War II with very interesting modern stained glass. We must have taken a guided tour of the city because I remember stopping at the Pinakothek Art Museum and being very impressed with the size and quality of their collection. My mind is blank as to how we got to the airport, or whether we flew to Schiphol or Heathrow to fly back across the Atlantic.

I have many memories of our longest trip to Europe, a month in Spain with a rental car. It was the year after we decided not to attend Camp Michigania, and it was the only time we used up our allotted 30 days of vacation time all at one time. Fran had read James Michener's *Iberia*, much of which could be used as a guidebook for historical places to visit. She carried the book with her; it was recognized by many of the merchants mentioned in the book when we stopped in their shops. We chose the month of April, which included Holy Week (Easter) which made our trip far more interesting than a more typical tourist trip in June or September.

I do not remember how we flew to Madrid, or the airport, but do remember our arrival at the Hotel Plaza for our first night's lodging and wondering, once again, what our travel agent, Larry, was thinking: he booked us into the most expensive hotel in Madrid. After our first night, we found a more modest businessman's hotel, the Hotel Victoria, on a square near the Plaza. We stayed the second night there and our rental car was delivered the next morning. We also made reservations at the Victoria for the last three days of our trip after our driving days in Spain were ended.

Spain is a large country and based on our experiences in England, our ambitions for seeing all of Spain were more realistic. We chose to explore the southern half of the country, traveling in a flattened circle clockwise from Madrid.

Our first destination was the city of Toledo, southwest of Madrid: lots of history, and our first "parador," a kind of hotel. We had learned of the paradors and looked forward to staying in them. They were a chain of hotels in all parts of the country, operated by the government which created them by renovating historic palaces, monasteries, convents, etc. (Preserving ancient buildings dating back to the 13th and 14th centuries and promoting tourism at the same time.) The ones we were able to stay in were the most interesting hotels we ever encountered; the prices were a bargain, the accommodations superb and the food outstanding. Unfortunately, the parador in Toledo was closed for repairs, so we had to stay in a conventional hotel.

If I recall correctly, we had time to do some shopping in Toledo and stopped in a gift shop, which happened to be mentioned in Michener's book. The proprietor recognized the book immediately and took an interest in us. After we bought a small *intaglio* dish, he offered to close his shop and show us the city. So, we rode in his car and had a free, personalized guided tour by an individual who obviously loved his city very much. We stopped for coffee on the way back to his shop; he even invited us to join him for dinner before we parted to return to our hotel. It was a great introduction to a foreign country.

The next leg of our journey is described in a later chapter, Chapter XIV, "Credo".

After our experiences in Cuenca and leaving Úbeda, we drove south to Málaga and then proceeded westerly along the section of the Mediterranean known as the Costa del Sol. I was anxious to see the city of Marbella because one of our Brecksville friends, "Micky" Billings was a close friend of Francy McCreery, wife of Bob McCreery, who owned the bank in Brecksville which was later bought by Central National Bank of Cleveland.

We first met Francy when she drove Micky up to our house on Oakes Road one afternoon in her Daimler sports car with the top down, the only one I ever saw. We knew Micky had visited Francy for a week in Marbella in a condo she owned there. That was our connection to Marbella, which was a very popular winter vacation area for northern Europeans, and for Americans because of the very favorable exchange rate, even more than the warm sun and the beaches.

We had our usual makings for lunch and sat in our car looking out at the sea. It was a very windy, chilly, gray day and I remember feeling sorry for the tourists we saw walking the beach bundled up in jackets and sweaters, and wondered what it was costing them to escape the same weather back in Sweden, or Denmark, or Scotland.

We visited most of the important places and were constantly impressed with the Moorish influences we saw. The weather continued to be unfavorable, cloudy, cool and drizzly enough to make the traveling uncomfortable but not impossible. I remember going down to Cádiz hoping to be able to see the coast of North Africa, but it was not quite clear enough. We did see the cathedral where Columbus worshipped before one of his voyages, but the church was undergoing major repairs and I couldn't even see the interior from the entrance. This was where I found an olive vendor in an outdoor market, while gathering supplies for lunch, and bought a plastic bag of bits and pieces of green olives that were the most delicious I have ever tasted.

Holy Week, the week before Easter, was an important travel time for native Spaniards and complicated finding lodgings for the night. We learned after luckily finding a room at our second parador to make reservations in advance, for the remainder of the trip. We were not always successful in trying to guess what our itinerary would be and times of arrival. I am surprised, considering how impressed I was with the paradors, that I cannot remember which of them we stayed in, or their cities. (Unlike Italy, Austria, or Germany, where we had to stay in a hotel every night.)

We saw and heard other evidence of Holy Week other than the "floats" we first saw at Cuenca. One evening in Granada, we saw a procession of twenty or twenty-five young women, dressed all in black, wearing black mantillas, holding candles, walking silently in single file down the hill from the Alhambra, followed by a similar number of men dressed all in black, wearing black dunces' hats, the leader holding a cross aloft. It was very solemn. Later, in our hotel room, high on a hill, with the window open, we could hear a lone voice chanting a lament as the procession of floats passed by. We were told that these singers were hired by families for this occasion only. It was haunting to hear such sadness.

We did not realize how important Holy Week is in Seville, so were lucky that we chose to be there on Maundy Thursday, the night of the huge procession of all the floats of the parishes that processed to the cathedral where the Bishop blessed each. There were folding chairs set up on the square around the cathedral and we had to pay $1 for a seat. It was a painless way to observe the festivities for what I expected to be a very solemn celebration. Each float was preceded by its parish brotherhood, and followed by its women's organization, all in traditional costume: the men in black robes, pointed "black dunce hats," barefoot, many carrying crosses, and the women: all dressed in black, long skirted dresses and mantillas. I was surprised and a little offended by the levity. Small children kept darting out into the street begging for candy from the marchers. It was incongruous to see a barefooted, robed, hooded man pull up his robe and dip into the pocket of his business suit to give a child a piece of candy. I began to appreciate it was the end of Lent, and a time for rejoicing. We lingered after the long procession ended; watched the floats disperse to their home parishes through very crowded streets, filled with merrymakers; very much aware of the smell of burning candles and the hypnotic effect of the swaying floats on the flickering candles mounted on the corners of the floats.

I remember our seeing the sun for the first time in many days in Seville, as I was approaching the cathedral through the cloister that was planted with orange trees, which were in bloom. I associated the sweet odor of the orange blossoms with the vastness and beauty of the cathedral. We were told it is the largest cathedral in the world. Worshipping in such a space would be awe-inspiring.

Other memories of our stay in Seville are of our having to move from the hotel we stayed in the first night to another because of the flood of visitors for the Holy Week procession the next night, and being fortunate to find another room on the other side of town. After checking in to our second hotel, we went out to explore our new neighborhood. Fran was startled and a little afraid when, turning a corner, she almost bumped into a man already dressed in his black robe and hood for the parade that evening. It was her first sight of such an apparition, and she was not prepared for it by Michener's book.

Before we left Seville, I remember doing something we had never done before on any of our trips: we took a tour of the city in an open carriage drawn by a horse. It was warm and sunny and a very pleasant way to see the city.

Other memories of this area of Spain are of the strange cathedral in Cordoba which was originally a mosque and converted into a Christian church when the Moors were driven from Spain; going out of our way to find a huge bird sanctuary mentioned in Michener's book, *Iberia*.

This was the only recommendation of his that was not too worthwhile. It was just a vast expanse of brush, and we didn't see any birds.

We were very near Portugal, which my business friend, the architect, Keith Haag of Cuyahoga Falls, had strongly recommended that we visit. He is the friend who gave us a valuable travel trip: take all your old sox and underwear with you on your trip and discard them rather than washing them and re-wearing them, thus creating space in your luggage for mementos you acquired and wanted to bring home. He also pointed out that while the exchange rates made Spain an inexpensive place to vacation, Portugal was even less expensive.

So, we decided to spend two or three days in a neighboring country. We entered Portugal from the south and drove through Lisbon, noting the gambling casino as we passed, and drove north up the coast. I remember a very colorful fishing village, Sintra; seeing the Shrine of Our Lady of Fatima; staying in a pousada, the Portuguese version of a parador, in Óbidos; I remember the shock of seeing the hammer and sickle on an election sign at a sharp curve on the roadway; and the shock of seeing a group of women at the edge of a stream washing clothes by pounding them on stones. It was like time travel.

We re-entered Spain at Mérida and wound our way eastward back to Madrid; seeing the walled city of Avila, the tomb of Franco at The Valley of the Fallen, and the cathedral at Segovia, which I remember only because taking pictures inside the cathedral was forbidden. I remember being mildly annoyed, and think it was the only church we ever visited where I did not leave an offering when leaving in the box provided for maintenance and upkeep, usually prominently displayed at the entrance to the church. I am not too proud of that today.

This trip was so much longer than our earlier ones that it felt almost like returning home when we arrived back in Madrid to the Hotel Victoria to find our room awaiting us. I remember starting to feel uneasy after the third week, after being away so long, worrying about the children and what was happening at the office. I set the alarm for 3 a.m. and got up to place a call home. I remember some slight difficulty with the International operator in Spain, but finally was able to talk to my father who reassured me that all was well. It was a relief and made the rest of our stay more enjoyable.

I don't remember how we spent our last days in Madrid. I remember being warned to stay off the streets by the concierge at the hotel because of a large parade down the main street in front of the Plaza Hotel staged by the Communist party, celebrating the First of May. I remember visiting the famous Prado Art Museum. On Sunday afternoon, the day before we flew home, we took a trolley to the bullring at the edge of the city to see our first and only bullfight. We only did it out of a sense of *de rigeur*. Neither of us enjoyed it. I was not impressed with the pageantry, and do not see how bullfighting can be classified as a form of sport. My sympathies were all with the bull.

In our travels, I remember two or three things that required adjustment from the way we were accustomed to doing things: in France, and also Spain, we couldn't get used to the long lunch hours. Everything closed at noon including museums. Shopkeepers and guards went home to eat and returned at or 2 or 3 p.m. This interfered greatly with our sightseeing program. And, in Spain, I couldn't get used to the standard hours for the evening meal in restaurants, which started at 10 p.m. The restaurants were open for business earlier, but no one was there but the waiters. This worked to our advantage when we arrived at 7 p.m. and never had a problem finding a table. I remember one restaurant near our hotel where we arrived at 7 to a large, beautiful room of carefully spaced tables with white linen tablecloths, a centerpiece on each table, of an electric lamp like a candlestick with a shade and the shades were pink, which cast a glow on the room. No other illumination was necessary. This was visible from the street, and very inviting. We were the only patrons; it was lonely, but the service was outstanding, and I had my first taste of garlic soup, very tasty.

On our last night in Madrid we decided to splurge after another successful trip and took a taxi to a restaurant famous for being a notorious haunt of Nazi diplomats during World War II (I wish I could remember its name). After we were seated, the waiter brought a cushion on which he placed Fran's feet (under my watchful supervision) a custom begun during the war years, when fuel was scarce and floors were drafty and cold. No longer necessary, but certainly distinctive. This was something I have never seen before or since. We then proceeded to have an excellent dinner. It was expensive and after settling the bill, we had so little Spanish currency left (not wanting to receive Spanish currency as change from cashing a $50 travelers' check the day we were leaving) we walked back to our hotel, a distance probably equivalent to walking from E. 105th Street and Carnegie Avenue to the Cleveland Public Square; a walk I would never attempt at 10 p.m. I remember how comforting it was to walk the quiet streets of Madrid seeing police patrolling wearing their distinctive, shiny tri-corn black leather hats.

Spain was our last European vacation driving a rental car and wandering. We visited Europe four other times on guided tours for shorter periods of time, usually one week plus a weekend. As I grew older, I found that traveling with a group was also very enjoyable. Driving was exhilarating with its sense of freedom and adventure; but it was also stressful and fatiguing. I recall clearly, the sense of relief every time I returned our rental car without damage; I was waiting for our luck to run out.

One of our short trips, solo, particularly meaningful to me since one of my favorite courses at Yale was Classical Civilization, was a promotion by Olympic Airways to fly to Athens, stay there for the weekend; then board a ship and visit islands in the Aegean Sea; return to Athens and spend three or four days ashore. We signed up for this trip and it is one I would like to repeat, not only to revisit the Parthenon and the National Museum, but to take more side trips in a more leisurely manner.

The tour people crammed so much into the long day trips, from the eight in the morning pick-up at our hotel to our return at eight in the evening that it was too tiring. When we went to Mt. Olympus (which was very interesting and we visited the Oracle of Delphi we could have stayed overnight and completed the trip the next day. It would have been much more enjoyable.

Our all-inclusive package included our hotel, the Hotel Amalia, a business traveler's type of lodging only a few blocks from Revolution Square and the far more luxurious hotel, The Grande Bretagne, in the heart of Athens. One thoughtful touch: Monday morning, the date of our departure: a representative of the shipping line came to our room and collected us and our luggage to put us on board our ship, the *Stella Solaris*, a medium size cruise ship, carrying only 300-400 passengers and very luxurious. The ship left from Piraeus, a city that serves as the port of Athens and was some distance from our hotel. I remember how grateful I was that we did not have to struggle with getting a taxi and going through the boarding procedures by ourselves. Our shepherd was about our age and came from Crete; he was also on hand for our debarking procedure at the end of our cruise which was an additional nice touch.

I remember a slight complication in the itinerary described in the promotion: we were unable to visit Ephesus in Turkey because relations between the two countries, always prickly because of ancient conflicts, had flared up and no direct contact between the two countries was permitted. Cairo was substituted as the main attraction and, instead of sailing east to the coast of Turkey, we went due south to Alexandria, close to the mouth of the Nile. I was not too disappointed when a trip to Cairo was substituted. One of my business acquaintances, the Chicago Mortgage Loan correspondent for Aetna Life, Ferd Kramer, loved Egypt and said he could spend the rest of his life in the National Museum in Cairo, so I looked forward to that with great anticipation.

We were aware of three Frenchmen, about our age, who talked of renting a car to make the trip to Cairo, which turned out to be a wise decision. They rented a Mercedes, left early, saw the sights in Cairo, and were back on board our ship in time for dinner.

We, on the other hand, booked a tour along with a busload of shipmates. We rode on an uncomfortable, cramped bus the 110 miles to Cairo, following the road next to the Nile, where I saw my first lateen sails. I was surprised at the size of the boats, at least 50-60 feet in length, and masts 60-70 feet in height, clearly visible from the road as they moved silently, mysteriously downstream.

Our bus driver reluctantly gave in to the demands and threats of a passenger sitting in front of us, whose husband suffered from some urinary disability, and we stopped at a small mud building and the passengers trooped off the bus seeking some relief. It was so primitive and so filthy that the women refused to use the facility, out-of-doors in back.

We completed our trip in the parking area for the National Museum about 20 minutes before it closed for lunch. We were rushed past a few of the exhibits, just enough to know that there was much more to see. I was disappointed in how poorly the beautiful, ancient objects were displayed, and how shabby the whole museum was. I don't remember ever having a chance to tell Ferd Kramer of my disappointment.

After this brief stop at the museum, the bus took us to the east bank of the Nile to a Sheraton Hotel for lunch. It was very modern and reeked of home. As soon as we disembarked from the bus and entered the hotel, there was a mad rush for the restrooms.

Feeling human once again, we were ushered into an American style dining room, set up with round tables seating eight; we could have been in New York - or Cleveland. There were rolls and a large bowl of green salad dressed with a very tasty dressing on each table. Before we started passing the rolls and salad, I asked a waiter for San Pellegrino bottled water, which he brought. I think we were the only people at our table that did so. The rolls were delicious, and the salad and dressing were equally so. I think the meal was something similar to beef bourguignon. It was all very tasty.

After another trip to the restrooms, we re-boarded our bus and proceeded to visit the other tourist attractions of Cairo.

It was strange to find the famous pyramids and the Sphynx so close to a modern city with millions of inhabitants. It was as though leaving Cleveland Public Square one no longer took notice of a huge monument - the pyramids or the Sphynx - thousands of year's old, sitting on the edge of Rocky River. The poverty we saw was severe and depressing, and I could not get used to seeing horse drawn wagons and carriages with rubber tires using the same roadways as taxis and buses and modern day autos.

I remember the great pyramid: we were not allowed to walk, but had to pay a fee and were forced to ride a camel from the entrance to the site of the pyramid, a distance of about 200 yards, all the while Fran had to fend off her camel driver, who was leading the camel on foot, who kept trying to touch her. I was perched precariously on top of my camel and could not come to her aid. I remember being impressed with the immensity of the pyramid; that its sides were not smooth; the huge stone pieces were clearly visible; and that the narrow tunnel leading up into the interior of the structure to a tomb was very claustrophobic.

We were driven by the Sphynx late in the afternoon and only saw it from the bus; were not given any dinner; were abandoned by our first driver who hopped off the bus at the outskirts of the town to go to his home; and was replaced by a new, inexperienced driver.

We returned to Alexandria by a more direct inland road, which had no signs of life, in pitch-black darkness. About half-way back to Alexandria, there was a disabled car on our side of the road with an individual waving at our bus to stop. At this point, one of our fellow passengers, Robert Schmidt, CEO of the Redwood Corporation of America, who was very wealthy (he wore John Lobb bespoke shoes made for him in London), charged to the front of the bus, and fearing being kidnapped and held for ransom, threatened to throw the driver out of the bus if he stopped. This had never occurred to me and was very exciting. We roared by the stranded motorist without hesitation.

When we arrived in Alexandria about 9 p.m., the driver did not know the way to the docks, or how to find our ship, which was a little disconcerting for a bus load of very tired, starving passengers, who had had nothing to east since lunch. Eventually it all got sorted out, and we did find the ship, where there was food awaiting us.

We left the harbor at Alexandria the next morning, passing again what passed for the Egyptian navy, little more than patrol boats, on our way to the first of our Aegean islands, Rhodes. At the dinner table the night before arriving, I suddenly felt very queasy, and had to excuse myself, and remember staggering, lurching my way back to our cabin. The raw salad in Cairo had struck. I never felt so sick or weak in my life.

I think I was the first of the Cairo bus group to come down with the illness, but everyone else did. The ship's doctor saw me and prescribed powdered charcoal among other things. I was able to be on deck and see us enter the harbor at Rhodes the next morning. Alas, The Colossus of Rhodes, one of the seven wonders of ancient history is no longer there. I was not well enough to go ashore, but Fran was, and she did the tour and handled the photographic responsibilities. She had a small adventure when she could not find her way back to the ship and feared it might leave without her. She was at a high point above the city, and realized that if she just walked downhill, she would come to the water. So, it all ended well. However, the next day she came down with the illness, and could not go ashore at Delos, but felt well enough in the afternoon to do so at Mykonos, our next island.

Delos was the island where all the city-states of Greece had their treasuries and was uninhabited but covered with the ruins of the temples where the wealth was stored.

There was one caretaker couple living on the island as guards and since there was no dock for a large ship, we had to take a tender into the island. Our boat held ten or twelve people healthy enough to go ashore, among them the wife of Robert Schmidt, the hero of our return from Cairo. Her name was Rose, and she was from the Murphy family in Detroit who were the owners of the downtown office tower, the Penobscot Building. She was very open and friendly and when she ran out of film allowed me to give her one of my spare rolls.

I remember the color of the water. Until then I had never seen such a beautiful clear blue. When the sun was shining, one could see clearly to a depth of 50 or 60 feet. All the ladies on the tender were oohing and aahing over the color. At this point, seizing a golden opportunity, I said something like, "Oh, come on. Every time the caretaker on the island sees on his schedule that a ship is going to bring people ashore, he gets up early in the morning and spreads 50 gallons of blue dye from his boat into the landing area and that's why it's so blue." The women, wide-eyed, exclaimed, "No.... Is that true," and I winked and I'm not sure I made many friends that morning. But it was a rare opportunity, one not to be missed.

Delos was littered with stone remnants from the past. I remember a roadway from where we landed leading up to the temples. The roadway (wide path) was lined with the ruins of the treasuries, which were temples and sacred and therefore safe from raids by rival cities. There were a few largely intact statues of lions or leopards on each side guarding the way. It was a quiet, sober place that gave pause for reflection.

The next island was Mykonos, much larger than Delos and inhabited, only a short distance from Delos. After lunch, we went ashore. Fran had recovered enough to chance it, although we were both a little shaky, and I remember feeling that our Cairo experience put a damper on the rest of our trip. We just didn't seem to have our usual energy.

I loved Mykonos, as I did all the islands we visited and would have liked to return to stay for a week or two. We actually checked out rentals while there. I thought an ideal vacation might have been to stay on one island after another, starting with Mallorca and Ibiza off the coast of Spain, then Capri, off Naples in Italy, Corsica and Sardinia, and on to Corfu off the west coast of Greece and then on to the islands of the Aegean Sea.

There was a stretch of buildings on Mykonos built so close to the water that it was referred to as "Little Venice"; there were windmills on a hill overlooking the harbor, very picturesque; and we admired the most famous inhabitant on the island, "Pete", a live pet pelican, perched on the back of a chair on the patio of a famous café where we stopped for iced tea. There was also a number of dead octopi there, about 3' long, hanging out to dry. I remember the older women, dressed all in widow's black sitting in doorways of their dazzlingly white-washed homes, with all the wood trim around windows and doors painted a bright blue.

We went ashore on Crete, a larger island and toured the castle with its natural air conditioning system. The guide told us proudly that the Cretans invented air conditioning. I was intrigued with the Palace's pillars, which tapered from wide at the top to narrow at the bottom. Frank Lloyd Wright may have had these unusual pillars in mind when he designed the famous Johnson & Johnson building in Racine, Wisconsin. The only other place I remember seeing this type of pillar was the new Main Library in Sarasota, Florida.

Then on to Santorini, where we again had to use a tender. The ride into the landing from the ship was interesting because there were bits of pumice floating on the surface of the water. I remember trailing my hand in the water to see what the floating particles were and being surprised that it was a form of stone, which had enough air trapped in it to float, and not some form of vegetation. The harbor at Santorini is actually the crater of a volcano, which erupted 2,500 years ago; is very deep and surrounded by a sheer cliff 200-300' above the surface of the water where a little village is located.

To reach the town we had to ride a donkey up a steep hill on a roadway cut out of the mountain. (We learned later that the other side of the island slopes gently down to a beach). We lined up on a platform similar to a loading dock for a warehouse, and patiently waited our turn for our donkey to be led by a native for mounting. We did not have to climb up to the saddle, but rather sat down on it, which was a blessing. The donkeys were not young and vigorous like the mules I had worked with in my army basic training, but were very old and skinny and small, my feet almost touched the ground. My mount was very forlorn and, I think, asthmatic. He wheezed with every breath all the way up the steep path to the top of the hill. I felt very guilty at the load he was forced to carry. We had to stop half-way up the hill for him to catch his breath.

The little village at the top was typical dazzling white houses with blue trim, a few small shops and a church and had a spectacular view of the round harbor below with the *Stella Solaris* at anchor and a further view of the blue Aegean spreading into the distance. I don't remember riding back down the hill after our tour of the village. In fact, I'm sure we walked and felt sorry for the donkeys we passed going up the hill with the burdens they had to carry.

My recollections of Athens upon our return are of an evening meal with Fran in a restaurant looking out on the Acropolis. It was twilight time and we had seats next to a window. I remember sliding the window open and mounting my camera on its C-clamp, fastening it to the sill, and taking pictures of the Parthenon, which was floodlit and to which we returned to tour in daylight. When I had my course in Classical Civilization at Yale my freshman year, I never dreamt that I would one day walk in the footsteps of those ancient Greek heroes.

The sight of the Greek soldiers marching guard on Revolution Squire, at the tomb of their Unknown Veteran, in their ridiculous uniforms with tutu type skirts and pompoms on their boots brought mixed emotions. I was shocked at the smallness of the national cathedral, the mother church of the Greek Orthodox national religion. Both the size of the structure and its location seemed very insignificant to me. Touring the great cathedrals of France and England had not prepared me for this.

We spent time, not nearly enough, in the National Museum, which was full of beautiful artifacts and statuary. I remember particularly the beauty of the gold death mask of Agamemnon. It has always been a marvel to me that such beauty could be created such a long time ago. I think it is humbling to realize that the need and the drive to create manmade beauty has always been a part of our human nature and is still with us.

On one of our days back on the mainland, we took a day trip to the Peloponnesus and saw from a very high bridge, looking from a height of about 500 feet, the modern day Greek equivalent of the Panama Canal: a straight canal dug five or six miles long, cut through a mountain, to shorten shipping routes, making the southern half of the Greek peninsula an island.

We stopped in Corinth, at the mouth of the canal, and saw the spot where St. Paul was said to have preached to the Corinthians and went on to our ultimate destination, Agamemnon's Tomb, an igloo shaped building. One of the ladies did not want to make the long walk to the tomb and stayed behind, sitting on a bench, knitting. Fran, who was a wonderful knitter herself, struck up a conversation with her and found that she was from Lorain, Ohio, now living in Manhattan. Her husband was a maritime attorney in a large firm that numbered Aristotle Onassis as one of its clients. After touring the tomb, I bought some small oranges and shared them with the others; they were small and the sweetest I have ever tasted.

We sat with them on the bus, and at a table when we stopped for dinner at Nafplion, a very beautiful city, which had been conquered by the Venetians in the 18th century. It had many of their forts still in existence. One of these occupied an entire island in the middle of the harbor and it was fascinating to look at it while eating; it seemed to float on the surface of the bay like a drop of oil on water. We sat with our new friends (I cannot recall their names) and heard about a business meeting he had aboard the Onassis yacht in Manhattan, which impressed all of us. The tale was told very modestly, and when finished, Fran had another of her wonderful moments and volunteered that we had been on Onassis' jet. This aroused the attorney's interest until Fran delivered her punch line: we had flown to Greece on Olympic Airways, owned by Onassis.

This did not destroy a new friendship, and after our return to Athens, we had dinner with them; and they invited us up to their second-floor suite in the Grand Bretagne Hotel overlooking Revolution Square. It was very luxurious - much different from our hotel, the Amalia - and we watched the Orthodox Easter celebration with them from their large balcony overlooking the square. Each of the four corners of the square had a large censer, with incense burning, which we could smell from our front row perch (best seats in the house). While we watched, military bands playing solemn music for the occasion; followed by units of the military in dress uniform, entered from one corner of the square and processed around the square; followed by civic dignitaries, and finally the clergy in their gorgeous robes and unusual headgear. It was a long, colorful parade and very impressive.

Final memories of our trip to Greece: we hired a taxi to give us a half-day tour and, at my request, he drove us by the ship works where the Olympic Yachts were built. I was familiar with the boats from *Yachting Magazine* but had never seen nor competed against one. Then the driver proceeded another 30 or 40 miles to Cape Sounion, where he proudly showed us the ruins, many of the columns still standing, of a temple of Poseidon, Greek god of the sea, looking from a high point, surrounded by water on three sides, out over the Aegean Sea. It is a lingering visual image and a fitting farewell to our encounters with an ancient, still pertinent civilization.

Our last two trips to Europe were very enjoyable even though we were not wandering in a rental car. They were guided tours offered by the University of Michigan Alumni Association where we were a part of group of 75 or 80 Michigan graduates on week-long cruises down the Danube and the canals of the Netherlands. This is a great way to travel, sleeping in the same bed every night, only packing and unpacking once, fascinating scenery and good food, in the company of people with a shared background, and guided side trips under the watchful care of a representative of the University. And no rough seas.

The first trip on the Danube (which is not blue) was during the Cold War and we sailed on a Russian riverboat flying the hammer and sickle, which took a little getting used to. The boat was built in Austria and the workmanship was very high quality. I speculated that the Russians did not waste their precious resources on frivolous activities, when they could be bought and then put to use earning coveted foreign exchange. We spent a lot of time trying to guess who the KGB representatives were among the crew.

My memories are of the shock of passing between soldiers on the dock armed with automatic rifles when leaving the boat to tour Bratislava in Czechoslovakia and having our group tailed by two furtive individuals in cheap orange business suits who listened to every word said by our guide; my wonder that such a small city had its own opera house in the "old town", and the sight of a beautiful, sinuous, white concrete bridge over the Danube.

The next stop was Vienna, which felt like coming home for us; we had stayed there twice already, and had half a day, a night on the boat, and another day to explore before proceeding down the Danube to visit Budapest in Hungary, Bucharest in Romania, and Belgrade in Yugoslavia.

My recollections are that the cities were and had been beautiful, reminding me of Paris somewhat, but grimy, shabby, dingy, not very prosperous. The most startling contrast in what we saw to what we took for granted back at home was on the bus trip to Bucharest, which is about 60 miles east of the Danube. We drove through farmland and I saw men plowing huge 100-acre fields walking behind horses. I wondered if this was the best the Romanians could do after 70 years of total government control under the communist system.

We had to wait for three or four hours aboard our boat while the Hungarian army held military exercises practicing amphibious cross river assaults. And we had been warned that we would be boarded as we entered Yugoslavian waters by customs officials to check our passports. Unfortunately, because of the delay up river, we were awakened about 2 a.m. and had to have our passports collected, held in the purser's office until we debarked at Belgrade, the most modern and western of the cities we had seen so far, and I was relieved when our passports were returned to us without comment.

We ended our voyage at a dock in Russia on the Black Sea, where we boarded a modern cruise ship built in France but owned and operated by the Russians. 1 can honestly say that I was on Russian soil, but only for a very short time.

We ended our trip in Istanbul (Constantinople), Turkey, having arisen at dawn to see the approach to the city from the foredeck of our ship while passing through the famous Strait of Bosporus. Istanbul was another very old, poor and dirty city, and dangerous. There was political unrest at the time; and we saw armed soldiers guarding the gas stations where there were long lines. I remember the telephone poles at street corners with literally hundreds of telephone lines converging at each pole. I would not have wanted to be a telephone repairman.

We were warned not to stray far from our hotel after dark. We did get to see the enormous Hagia Sophia Cathedral, which had been converted to Muslim use when the Ottoman Turks conquered the city; the great Blue Mosque; and the Topkapi Museum, which was the former royal harem and loaded with beautiful porcelain.

When we were docking on arrival, I noticed another cruise liner with a group of University of Iowa passengers starting on the same kind of cruise we were completing, but going up the Danube, rather than down, and I remember thinking how much more pleasant it would have been to end our trip in Vienna.

One of the most important plusses of our two river cruise trips with the Michigan alumni, was meeting two couples who became friends and with whom we enjoyed a lasting relationship.

On the Danube trip, we became acquainted with Frank and Connie Daly. I remember being somewhat surprised to learn that Frank was a graduate of the University of Massachusetts and finished his career as head of the Engineering Department of General Motors. I had always assumed that G.M. recruited its people from the University of Michigan, or their Northwood Institute in northern Michigan.

He had to get permission from the State Department to take this trip because it was behind the Iron Curtain, and he night have had industrial knowledge valuable to the Russians and they might have taken an "interest" in him. His private passion was short wave radio, and after his retirement they moved to Cape Cod, which surprised me.

But Cape Cod's climate is usually mild in the winter because of its proximity to the Atlantic Ocean. He became very active in volunteer rescue at sea work. Another advantage he pointed out was that all the cultural activities of Boston were readily available. He did not play bridge.

His wife, Connie, had a delightful personality: charming, warm, witty, outgoing, and caring. Her chief extra-curricular activity was playing competitive duplicate bridge, and I am sure she had a great many Master Points. She had a regular partner and they competed in ACBL sponsored tournaments all over the country. After their retirement to the Cape, they helped us find a house to rent for a week of our vacation time on two occasions; and invited us to dinner at the home they had bought for their retirement. One of my regrets is that I never had the chance to play bridge with her. We exchanged Christmas cards with the Daly's for years.

On our last European trip, the following year, "Windmills & Waterways of the Netherlands" another of the guided tours sponsored by the Alumni Association, we met Bob and Jeannie Hackett of Bloomfield Hills, Michigan.

Our meeting was slightly unusual: when boarding the plane in Detroit, following the rules of the Alumni Association we were seated in order of our graduating class, the lower the year, the closer to the front row of seats, which was a nice concession to the older passengers. (It would probably be called "FIFO" in accounting parlance.) This held true when boarding buses also, and everyone was good-natured about it.

Shortly after takeoff, and being seated amidships, the stewardess asked me if I might be more comfortable changing seats to one in the first row next to the bulkhead, where there was more legroom and an unoccupied seat. Fran said: "Go", and I jumped at the chance; excusing myself, gingerly I eased myself into the window seat, stepping over a lady. This was how I met Jeannie Hackett. Or didn't meet her. I excused myself for any inconvenience, but neither of us said another word, even when leaving the plane. I remember how unusual the situation was and hoped I had chanced on a lady who did not indulge in idle chitchat and treasured her privacy.

We landed in Brussels and immediately boarded a bus for Bruges. My only recollection of Brussels was of a large square surrounded by impressive buildings and then hurrying on to Bruges, which is an extremely interesting old city, a former sea port now 15-20 miles inland, where we spent the night on board our river-boat.

The next day we had a guided tour of the city, a boat ride on one of the canals, and visited the Beguine, which was a residence for Catholic women who were not nuns, founded in the 18th century. My recollection is of a "U" shaped red brick two-story building with a large forecourt.

We found ourselves at the back of the group with the Hacketts. We introduced ourselves, and Jeannie remarked how grateful she was that I was not a chatterbox, because she had a nasty headache and was very tired on the plane. I had lucked out and we spent much of the rest of the trip seeing sites together as couples. I remember how smooth our cruising was (no rough seas), and how interesting the Netherlands was. We would have liked to return and tour by bicycle, no hills.

Our cruise ended at Remagen on the Rhine River, the site of an important battle in World War II. Before boarding the bus that would take us to Amsterdam for the last 3 days of our trip, we stopped at a small military cemetery at the side of the road, probably 200 graves, each marked by simple white stone slab incised with the soldier's name - they were all Canadian and Polish - all with a two or three word touching phrase inscription chosen by the family.

I can't remember ever being so overwhelmed; and went back to the bus in tears before the others. 1 believe that every man who boarded that bus had tears in his eyes. We had never seen any of the large military cemeteries on our other travels, those with only American graves, so I do not know if I would have reacted in the same way. But although this little cemetery was quiet and unassuming, it was sufficient to trigger some very powerful emotions.

We did not finish our cruise on canals, but rode a bus from Remagen on the Rhine River, site of one of the ferocious battles in World War II to save the bridge so the Allies could cross into Germany near the end of the War, to Amsterdam, another fascinating city.

We were there two or three days and I remember rides on the canals; the unique facades of the old buildings; a visit to a royal castle away from the central city which was just a simple, unpretentious, large frame house; eating an Indonesian meal called *rijstafel*, which reminded me of a Swedish smorgasbord; learning from the local guide, who had a direct connection to the University of Michigan, how the Dutch survived starvation during the Nazi occupation by eating tulip bulbs, roasted, fried, boiled – prepared in every way imaginable - I didn't know they were edible (daffodils are poisonous), and I wondered what a roasted tulip bulb would taste like; I remember two art museums, the National, where the famous Van Dyke *Night Watch* hangs, and especially the Van Gogh Museum where all the paintings are by Van Gogh and I was able to take a close-up photo of every painting.

I remember how indifferent I felt about getting on a bus to go look at tulips blooming, and what a shock it was when we finally walked through the Keukenhof Gardens. The bus passed through Haarlem, 15 or 20 miles from Amsterdam, and stopped for a photo opportunity along the way at our request.

We could see fields of bulb plantings, and large piles of what turned out to be hyacinth petals, cut off so all the plant's energy would be used to produce larger bulbs; we got off the bus to take photographs and although the fields were a quarter of a mile distant on the other side of the road, the distinctive scent of the hyacinths was very powerful.

I do not think any description of the Keukenhof Gardens could prepare anyone for what awaits them. The commercial growers of bulbs plant literally millions of (mainly) tulip bulbs on 80 acres of parkland every year, showcasing their latest hybridized creations; they plant them in masses, by the hundreds with name tags for identification, in case you might like to order a few, and the effect of the masses of color, blossoms all the same height and shape and color is simply overwhelming, I had exhibited in many peony exhibitions, visited a dahlia convention in Cleveland, visited Kew Gardens in London, and seen the gardens at the Chateau at Villandry in the Loire Valley, but never anything like this. I never wished more fervently that I was not colorblind, so I could enjoy the colors the way Fran could.

We were on a schedule and were to be back on the bus at 3:30 or 4 p.m. so I cut short my viewing, because there were booths scattered throughout the gardens where bulbs could be ordered.

I was so excited that I remember finding a piece of paper and a pencil and drawing a circle representing the inner circle of the driveway of our house in Brecksville. I calculated the area of the circle, and using 6" spacing, how many bulbs it would take to fill the space, and got as far as starting to fill out an order form when we were called back to our bus. So we never planted any Keukenhof tulips in Brecksville. However, this turned out to be a blessing. We were spared. I was prepared to have invested $400-500 in bulbs, and, once back in Brecksville, was able to get some named variety Darwin bulbs for a lot less on sale at the Wilson Feed Mill nursery supply house on Canal Road in Sagamore Hills, where I bought salt for our water-softener and fish food for our pond.

I selected the bulbs carefully by height and color, and bought nine dozen bulbs, carefully planted them around the foundation with nametags and then waited to see what would happen the next Spring. I was dismayed when only nine bulbs survived; the rest had been eaten over the winter by moles and chipmunks.

'Windmills and Waterways' was our last trip abroad, but we had other cruises originating in the U.S. Our first was a Caribbean cruise with three of the couples from our Brecksville duplicate bridge group, the Adairs, the Cullers, and the Sutherlands, on the Cunard "Princess" line, flying Eastern Airlines non-stop from Cleveland to San Juan, Puerto Rico.

I remember when gathered at the boarding gate in Cleveland, standing back with the others while Doug Adair, who was a very popular TV newscaster, was swarmed by fans seeking his autograph while his wife looked on, ignored, with us from a distance.

When we arrived in San Juan and were waiting in line to board ship, Fran and I looked up to see Bob Forman, secretary of the University of Michigan Alumni Association whom we knew well from our weeks at Camp Michigania, waving down at us from the deck of the ship. He yelled at us to get our attention and pointed out that if we had been a part of the group of alumni he was shepherding, we would already be aboard. I do not recall interacting with any of the Michigan group on the cruise, but I do remember encountering Forman at the gambling casino on the top deck when I explored the ship. He spent all his spare time playing roulette and did well. So, after observing his system, I was tempted, and told myself that if I lost more than $20, I would quit.

Fran also had a $20 limit but she played blackjack and lost it all the first night I played the roulette wheel the first two nights, not knowing what I was doing, but suddenly was $73 ahead and it seemed so easy. I should have quit while I was ahead because my $73 was all gone by the end of the week, plus another $20.

It actually was an inexpensive way to learn a valuable lesson. One interesting memory of my introduction to "bigtime" gambling was the casino personnel: they were known as the Chesterfield "boys", and all were young and good looking, and dressed in white tie and white tails. It was all so elegant.

The first port on the cruise was Caracas, Venezuela, with landing at La Guaira, the port for Caracas, about 15 miles away, and a ride on a funicular to the top of a steep hill where we boarded a bus to tour the city. I only remember a racetrack and the ride back down the hill to the ship in a bus.

The tour then proceeded to Grenada, Antigua, Martinique, and St. John's in the Virgin Islands, returning to San Juan for the flight back to Cleveland.

In all we took four cruises during our travel years: three leaving from Fort Lauderdale, which made it easy for us since we were already in Florida, and the fourth cruise was with a group of Akron people, which sailed from New Orleans.

Each of the islands had a different character, but there was an underlying similarity. The real reason to take a cruise was not to explore historic sites, which was a large motivation for our trips to Europe, but for the weather, the being on the water, and the luxury and relaxation. And the food. I came to feel that it wasn't necessary to leave the ship to have an enjoyable time. I would like to have had the time and money to be able to do Mediterranean and Scandinavian cruises, which would have had the additional dimension of experiencing history interesting to me, face to face.

On our first cruise on the Princess I remember docking at Grenada and seeing a group on the wharf holding an unmistakable, large UofM banner to greet the Association group on board. I wonder what special activity they planned for their short stay. We established a pattern for each island: dodge the locals selling souvenirs on the dock, find a taxi, split into two couples and hire a taxi to take us to explore the island; check out the port city, usually the capital, back to the ship, rest, drinks in one of the cabins before dinner; then go to the entertainment provided onboard, or play bridge.

The second or third night, having witnessed the degree of poverty and living conditions from the taxi, Jan Adair was obviously very disturbed. She could not square what she saw with the life her children had.

The discussion continued at the dinner table, and Carl Culler and I both pointed out that the way of life she saw was all the natives knew, and that there were some good things about their lives. There was the wonderful climate, and apparently fruit free for the picking, and it was the only life they knew. She became so upset that she left the table; and we did not see her for the rest of the evening. I think this was the beginning of a deep depression that continued the rest of her life. She could not accept Carl's and my viewpoint and had little patience with us. This continued after we returned home and was a subject we avoided whenever we were together.

We arrived at St. John's, Virgin Islands, the only U.S. island we saw, the day before our return to San Juan, Porto Rico. All the women were anxious to explore the shops and were frustrated by not having been able to spend much on the other islands. Unfortunately, it was Good Friday, and all the shops were closed. Fran and I saw what looked like a topaz ring that I would have liked to investigate in a jewelry store window, but the store was closed.

On the other hand, I found a camera shop open and this is where I bought the Bronica camera I had been looking for. And all the liquor stores were open. We bought six or seven bottles of liqueurs that were duty free and lasted us for years after we got home. We flew home on a stretch DC-9 and watched while they loaded the plane for take-off. It looked as though there was a half-acre of bottles of liquor waiting to be put in the plane's hold. Plastic was not used for bottles then, so the weight of the glass and liquid must have been considerable, and I worried about the plane getting off the ground. The runway ended at the edge of a cliff, a sheer drop of 20 or 30 feet to the water. When we finally did start down the runway, it was the only time I remember being fearful on the take-off of a plane. I think we were only about 10' in the air when we passed over the edge of the cliff. Obviously, we got home safely, or I wouldn't be writing this.

Except for the cruise leaving from New Orleans, we used the Holland American Line, which had mid-sized ships, and Indonesian crews who were very well trained.

On the last of these trips we took a Jazz cruise. It featured a part of the western Caribbean we had not visited, and we stopped at the Cayman Islands, where I did not open an "off shore" bank account, and Jamaica, which was a disappointment because I had heard so much about it and it seemed rather lackluster. The Montego Bay resort area on the north coast might have seemed more prosperous.

The main attraction for us was the music on board: there were five Dixieland jazz bands, all excellent, and after an evening performance in the Crew's Nest, a bar on the top deck, which was private, the bands continued to play on the pool deck where other passengers could listen and dance.

One of the bands was Bob Schultz's San Francisco Jazz Band, which was probably the best of the five, and we had heard him at the Atlanta Jazz Parties we went to every year. It was fun to talk with him about the earlier parties. He played cornet and sang some of the songs. Fran requested her favorite; "Sweet Emmaline" (which I didn't think much of) and he sang it for her twice.

The first night in the Crew's Nest we got there early to get good seats and Fran struck up a conversation with the lady sitting next to her while I wandered off to talk with Schultz. When I returned and got settled for the music, I found that Fran had discovered that her new friend's husband had gone to Yale, was in my Class of '43 and, furthermore, had lived in Pierson College. They were Dick and Nancy Schneller and lived in Essex, Connecticut. He had been a Senator in the Connecticut legislature for ten years. I had absolutely no recollection of ever having seen him at Pierson, and was amazed, because we were there for three years together and there were only about 100 people in our class in the residential college. It made the voyage much more fun and more interesting. meeting someone with something in common. They had one of the luxurious patio cabins on the upper decks, and we were invited there for drinks before dinner, ate many meals together, and listened to the music together. He was as hooked on jazz as I was.

The other very powerful memory of that cruise is of one of the jazz couples who danced every dance in a style I had never seen before: they seemed to glide, moving rapidly, effortlessly and punctuated each beat with a step and moved rapidly around the floor (deck). I couldn't take my eyes off them, simply sat and stared in amazement and wished I could do the same. Fran finally told me to stop staring: it was embarrassing.

They were from the San Francisco area and had joined the cruise to hear the Schultz band with whom they were very familiar. The interesting thing was that the Captain of the ship had married them on board ship before we left for their honeymoon cruise. They were about our age, and I spoke with the male partner (I do not remember his name) and asked him how he had learned to dance in that style and he said that no one had taught him, he had just started doing it. It was obvious his new wife loved it. I wish there had been time for him to teach me.

The day before we returned to Fort Lauderdale, after we passed Guantanamo Bay on the tip of Cuba, barely visible to the west, the ship stopped at the private island owned by Holland American Lines, Half Moon Cay, and we all went ashore by tender and swam and picnicked. As much as we did with the Schnellers and as well as we got along together, we never heard from them again. So much for the Old Blue ties.

The cruise from New Orleans was different because we sailed south from New Orleans on a Russian ship as far south as Honduras, and then returned on basically the same course back to the homeport. The weather was so unfavorable at Honduras, where we would have had to use a tender to go ashore, that we stayed on board and the ship turned northwest for the return leg of the trip.

1 remember stopping on the southern leg and going ashore at Playa Del Carmen to take a bus tour to see Mayan ruins inland. The buses broke down both coming and going, and it was hot and rainy, and very tiring, but the ruins were impressive and well preserved. I thought the stadium where a form of polo-basketball was played was interesting and the pyramid was too steep to climb. It was a long day. There was obviously a viable civilization present, but the beauty, if there is any, was too crude and harsh, and never appealed to me and I had no interest in it then, nor do I have any today.

I remember more of our time onboard the ship, *The Azerbaijan*, a Russian cruise ship, crewed with young Russian people who could have been college students. It was very comfortable, and the food was good. They actually offered beginner's lessons in the Russian language.

There wasn't much for the ladies to buy in the ship's gift shop. The one item I remember is the nesting Matryoshka Russian dolls, which I had never seen before. On the final leg before we returned to New Orleans, we stopped at Cancun on the tip of the Yucatan peninsula, which I had heard of as a vacation resort destination. I remember going to a beach, but do not recall whether we swam in the Gulf of Mexico. After seeing what little we did of Mexico, I failed to see what the attraction was, and determined never waste precious vacation time in Mexico, when there was so much of Europe we had not been able to explore.

This vacation was also different in that we were with a group of strangers. The group had taken an annual vacation together for several years, and when one of the couples could not make it, one the group, Tom and Lois Linak, members of St. Matthews in Brecksville, proposed us, and the price was so reasonable, we were glad to accept.

The common denominator in the group was that all the men were engineers with Goodrich or Goodyear Tire Companies. They were a very congenial group; a lasting friendship resulted with Walt and Mary Brodine, of Hudson, Ohio. We played bridge with them regularly, and I played golf with Walt. His hobby was making miniature dollhouse furniture to scale. He also was responsible for the design and all the finish work for the new Christ Episcopal Church addition in Hudson. His design and workmanship were remarkable, something I was especially able to appreciate after my experience in doing the finish work at our home in Brecksville.

We also had in common that they had three daughters, one of whom lived in Hudson and had a lovely singing voice.

I attended a recital she gave in the church, which was especially meaningful because of all the work her father had done on the interior, and remember meeting Walt's mother, for the first and only time. Mary disliked her, and I could see why. She dominated her (only) son, was imperious, and spoiled every family gathering, according to Mary.

On this occasion she barely acknowledged me, who was introduced to her as her son's very good friend, and when her granddaughter came up to greet her grandmother, couldn't find one complimentary thing to say. I was embarrassed to witness this with Walt standing next to me.

We did not return to Cleveland with the others on Saturday, but stayed on to explore New Orleans, which, with my love of Dixieland jazz, I had heard so much about.

My recollections are of a very old, very historic city, still very vital. I remember the lacework iron grillwork on the second floor balconies of the hotels; the music at all hours on Bourbon Street blaring from the open doors of the clubs; what a shock the Preservation Hall was, the home of the famous Dixieland band, where there were no seats, but one stood crowded together to hear the old time players do their thing. It was a small frame building, little more than a storefront the size of a two car garage. The night we were there "Sweet Emma" Barnet played the piano and the Humphrey brothers, Willie and Percy, played trumpet and clarinet; all were in their 70s and 80s.

When they took their break, a small boy in the audience, about twelve or thirteen years old was invited to come up on the stage and play the piano. As I recall, I was impressed, and I think his name was Harry Connick, Jr., who became a well-known band leader when he grew up. We were there at the beginning of one career and celebrating the impending ends of others.

We had breakfast at Brennan's and had their famous "Bananas Foster; dinner at Antoine's; fresh beignets at a street vendor near the St. Louis Cathedral; listened to a performance by Pete Fountain at his club, which was a very tourist oriented, business-like performance: it was theater seating and patrons were herded in and out for each of the 45 minute sessions; saw the famous cemetery where all the graves were above ground because of the high water table, just the opposite of the cemeteries we saw in Switzerland, where graves could not be dug because of there was no soil, only rock.

And then we flew home to Cleveland Monday afternoon, having had a very enjoyable and interesting experience.

We had one other short vacation which involved a ship: We decided to explore Nova Scotia, partly because our neighbors in Brecksville, the Hills, were from Nova Scotia, and their oldest son, Brian, had returned there after getting his college degree at Kent State. There were relatives still living near Truro where he leased a large tract of forest from the government on the condition that he harvest timber for two or three years.

We drove to Portland, Maine and took a ferry overnight to Halifax. I only remember a few of our experiences: we basically drove around the perimeter of the island clockwise, stopping first to take photos of the famous Peggy's Cove, near Halifax. The weather was foggy; and I got two pictures of small sailboats, one with a red hull, lying at anchor in still water, which I liked enough to frame and hang in my office. As we progressed northward on the Cabot Trail, a very scenic route, I was shocked and depressed to see whole forests of dead spruce trees, still standing, gray and sullen, killed by an infestation of the spruce beetle. I remember seeing the fortress at Louisbourg near the end of our circumnavigation.

Our other highlight was our meeting Brian Hill, our young neighbor from Brecksville, for dinner in Truro. I remember how pleased I was to see Brian again; he was very shy when he lived next door to us, and his college work, and being independent and, loving the outdoors, doing logging work for a living, seemed to have raised the level of his confidence in himself. After dinner he took us to the Tidal Bore, which is a long curved creek, almost dry at low tide, connecting to the Bay of Fundy, where there are very high tides, and we settled down by the empty river to wait for the tide to come roaring in, filling the river. Alas, the tide was not very high that night, and we did not hear any roar of the water or see it fill the riverbed.

Brian apologized for our disappointment when we said goodnight and I think that was the last time we ever saw him. He took a job with an accounting firm in Niles, Ohio, when he returned to the U.S., after he had his fling at trying to support himself by selling raw timber he had to cut down himself in Canada. When he visited his mother next door, his time with her was so precious that we didn't get to visit with him.

After our night in Truro, we crossed into New Brunswick and spent some time in Saint John where the tide levels regularly rise and fall more than 20 feet. We saw docks on stilts twenty-five feet in the air with a boat with very long docking lines floating at the foot of the dock. Unfortunately, we could not wait for the tide to come in, so we never saw the phenomenon of some of the highest tides in the world.

This was the trip when we were able to pay a visit to my best friend at Yale, Ken Mason, who lived on the coast of Maine. We stayed in a small B&B in Blue Hill, where the proprietors were away at a wedding when we arrived. As instructed in a note left at the reception desk, we checked ourselves in. The next morning we called the Masons who were about three miles east in Sunset, Maine, about 15 miles east of Bangor, on the coast overlooking the Atlantic. The result was an invitation to have lunch with them and a chance to meet his charming wife, Cherie. He gave us a tour of his home, which had been built by a retired general in the Army and was very well built and very comfortable. It had a detached 2-story 3-car garage where Ken, long retired from Quaker Oats, did his writing on the second floor. We also walked down to the water and inspected his little Sunfish sailboat, which he was learning to sail. I admired that he was on salt water and had to be aware of the tide, which is not a factor on Lake Erie. Cherie was an ardent gardener, but unfamiliar with peonies. I proceeded to hook her on them, pointing out several favorable locations where they might be planted, which she did. I think I sent her a tree peony as a thank-you gift, She thanks me every year in their Christmas card.

After we left, reluctantly on my part, we drove back through Blue Hill to Bangor, about 15 miles due west from Sunset. While we were filling the tank, I thought it would be wise to make a forward reservation for the night. I remember my dismay at being informed at motel after motel that it was Columbus Day holiday, when Manhattan emptied out every year to travel north to see the colors, and that there were no vacancies. One motel suggested that we park overnight in their parking lot and sleep in our car and they would provide blankets for us.

We stopped for dinner in Portland and made more calls to motels without success, and, finally in desperation, called Fran's childhood friend, Nancy Jarnis, one of the Polar Bears, who lived in a suburb of Boston (and whom she had not told of our trip).

As is always the case, there is never enough time to see all the relatives and friends in a city when traveling with a limited time budget on vacation. It was a relief when Nancy graciously - we would be arriving between midnight and 1 a.m. - offered us a bed. So we had a brief visit before retiring; a fine breakfast the next morning; a tour of her small but interesting garden (after their fifth child was in grammar school, Nancy earned a degree in Landscape Architecture at Harvard) and a long drive home to Brecksville.

In our long marriage, there was never a year that we did not take every minute of vacation time that we were entitled to, until Fran's health precluded traveling.

In addition, in most years I was able to squeeze in an additional business oriented two or three day trips for myself. We were always searching for something or someplace new and different, and fortunately we both had the same urge.

I remember our three stays on Cape Cod when we rented a cottage for a week or two. The first was one built by Bill Wrenn, the Episcopal minister from Brecksville, who had taken a job as a counselor at Tufts University, in Boston. All I remember about the cottage was its modest size, and how uncomfortable the beds were.

Cape Cod's size and distance from Boston were a big surprise to me. I had always envisioned a narrow spit of sand with a narrow road down the middle; instead, I found a massive amount of land, heavily developed, dotted with small towns with familiar English names, and separated from the mainland by a shipping canal.

I remember the house we rented, found for us by the Daly's, who had retired to Cape Cod: 2 stories, large enough to entertain, and Fran inviting the Jarnises and the Dalys for evening meals. There was a fish market nearby and I could get fresh halibut which was easy to prepare and wonderful.

I remember Jack Curtis, one of my roommates in Ann Arbor, who grew up in Japan with a Japanese *ama* to care for him. Japanese was a second language for him; and he served as an interpreter at the surrender of the Japanese, graduated from Princeton and became an architect. He invited us to Sunday lunch at his home, which was built in true Japanese style on the south shore overlooking the Atlantic. He served us bluefish, which was delicious. I was fascinated that his house had an outdoor bathroom, with an *o-furo,* a large wooden soaking tub like a 5' tall barrel, typical of houses in Japan. I never thought to go that far when I instructed our architects in Brecksville.

I remember playing golf on several of the courses which were uniformly good. One of them was on a high point overlooking both Cape Cod Bay and the Atlantic Ocean and had one hole with a mausoleum on the edge of the fairway containing the body of the founder of the club. I was also impressed with the city of West Denis golf course, a very fine layout, where, if you were a resident taxpayer, green fees were free.

I recall getting up early one morning to take the bus into Boston with the Dalys to attend a matinee performance of the Boston Symphony in Boston Symphony Hall, a large rectangular space, very plain. No comparison to Severance Hall in Cleveland. I do not remember what they played, but that they compared favorably to the Cleveland orchestra. (Smug, smug.)

It was a long but easy bus ride, and the symphony, the art museum and other programs provided by the many universities in Boston, together with the usually mild winters, made Cape Cope an unexpectedly attractive retirement destination. In two of the years, we took the ferry from Woods Hole to Martha's Vineyard, and Nantucket, both very interesting islands and understandably popular places to vacation or spend the summer, if money was not a problem. We stayed overnight at Nantucket, the larger of the two islands, and saw a play in their summer theater playhouse. I also remember that on our first visit, Bill Wrenn took us on a guided tour all the way to Provincetown on the tip of the peninsula. We stopped on the way and watched pods of whales a mile or so offshore in the Atlantic, my first sighting of a whale.

After our two-week trips to Europe and our one-week vacations at Camp Michigania, in the late 1960s and the 1970s, we had another week to spend. Most of the time we went to the New England area. I remember showing Fran New Haven; having dinner with my roommate, Gil Hunt and his wife in Vernon, Connecticut, a short distance north of Hartford, where he taught English in his old high school; visiting the Aetna Life home office; seeing Miss Porter's School for Girls in West Hartford; going north in Vermont past Lake Champlain, and coming back down south through New Hampshire, and buying the highest grade maple syrup (which was almost white, a surprise because I always thought that the darker the color, the better the flavor); going down a road in the Pocono Mountains in the fall with brilliant sunlight filtered through a canopy of golden maple leaves, a sight I will never forget. On another trip having the misfortune to visit the famous Grossinger's Resort Hotel, the kingpin of the Borscht Belt, on Yom Kippur, a Jewish high holy day when the restaurant was closed and we were lucky to get a kosher sandwich in the hotel coffee shop.

On one of our trips we stopped in Williamstown, New York, and saw the well-respected Williams College Art Museum. I was interested because both of the men I worked with most closely at the Aetna Life were graduates of Williams College. Also, one of the art professors, George Heard Hamilton, I worked for at Yale, had become the Director of the museum, which I did not know at the time.

On another trip with the children, we stayed for a week at the old resort hotel in Poland Springs, Maine, home of the famous mineral water. There was an 18-hole golf course that was never very crowded, and Kathy and Barbara tried to play, not very successfully. I never pushed any of my daughters into learning the game, which meant so much to me, something I find hard to understand today. We also became acquainted with another older couple from New Jersey, whose name I do not remember. He was a psychiatrist at a New Jersey State Mental facility, and we played several rounds of golf together. The TV night show host, Jack Paar, had his private studio on the grounds, but I don't think we ever saw it. We took one afternoon and went to a nearby lake to try to learn to water ski. As I recall, the girls succeeded in getting up into skiing position, but their father could not get out of the water to a standing position no matter how fast the towboat went or how hard he tried. It was quite a spectacle,

I have fond memories of that trip and remember the food at the hotel as being exceptional, but the bottled water from the Poland Springs that was marketed nationally had a mineral, medicinal taste and after one sip I could not drink it.

We had other memorable vacations with the children. We bought a share in a new resort called Out Island Inn on one of the islands in the Bahamas, Great Exuma. It was developed and promoted by a group of dentists from southern Michigan, among them, Jim and Marge Harrison, who was a sorority sister of Fran's. It was a paradise with balmy temperatures, steady trade winds and incredibly beautiful water. The inn was located at the edge of a "sound" and was protected from the open waters to the east by Stocking Island. It had a fresh-water pool and a separate dining room.

The only return on our investment was taking advantage of an owner's privilege of a free week's stay with family once a year. We took advantage of this two years in a row during Kathy and Barbara's spring breaks from school, before Kathy went off to the University of Michigan.

I remember that we learned of the assassination of Martin Luther King while we waited in the Miami airport for our flight to Nassau, where we took a Bahamas Airways DC-3 to Great Exuma a distance of about 110 miles. I have never seen before or since such beautiful colors as in the shallow waters surrounding the many islands.

I remember my first impressions of Great Exuma as not being very prosperous, a sleepy place with a different pace than back home in the U.S., but the great dignity of the people; my learning to snorkel and the amazing array of tropical fish on the reef 50 yards from our rooms; the yellow-birds who came to the railing of our porch to nibble on the sugar we sprinkled for them there; sailing the Inn's Sunfish with the wind steady in one direction for hours at a time, in water so clear it was impossible to tell if it was 3 feet or 20 feet deep; of hiring a guide to go bone-fishing, which was a was a waste of money (we later saw our guide, after our second visit, in the airport in Nassau on our way home, where he had a job as a porter and carried our bags to the plane); the dusty half mile walk to the capital, Georgetown, the sides of the road littered with trash, and the little group of native women weaving straw hats in the shade of a huge tree; the movie star Errol Flynn's 120'sailboat with a badly damaged stern moored at the government pier; meeting the Detroit financier, Alfred Glancy, who spent the winter at the Inn, and was kind to us.

I took a picture of him in his swimming trunks displaying a large Bahamian lobster (an oversized crayfish, all tail). He was a graduate of Princeton and a contemporary of Jimmy Stewart. He loved it there (may have been one of the investors) and was very critical of the management and the native housekeeping when an epidemic of dysentery swept through the guests - we had to get a native doctor for Fran, who was shocked when he dispensed pills from a bottle onto his sweaty palm and gave them to her to take. She did recover quickly, so he knew what he was doing. He was from South Africa.

Her bout did not spoil our vacation; many years later Alfred Glancy was murdered in the kitchen of his mansion on Jefferson Avenue in Grosse Pointe, Michigan, overlooking the Detroit River. It was rumored that he interrupted a drug deal involving his son.

The second year, I sailed with a man named McNitt, who was chairman of one of the big pharmaceutical companies. It was an interesting resort, very relaxed and informal, and almost criminal when the Back Bay Boys in Nassau who controlled the islands, were thrown out of office and replaced by a native government lead by a man named Pindling, a graduate of Harvard (we were there during his campaign). The new government imposed so many new regulations that required so many ill-equipped native employees in management, staff and record keeping, that the dentist developers of Out Island Inn lost the property. Our investment was lost; and we never heard what the final outcome was. I only know our money was gone, and the only return on our investment was the two "free" vacations we had at the resort.

My final memory of Out Island Inn is of our last trip home, flying off the small airstrip in a 12 passenger Beechcraft twin-engine plane (Bahamas Airways had gone bankrupt) with Barbara and Kathy in the seats behind us, looking down at the beautiful colors in the water, tears streaming down their cheeks. They did not want to leave such a wonderful place.

I have so many memories of another family vacation, the trip East to look at colleges. We loaded the trunk of the car with our bags, each daughter in charge of her own little suitcase, loading and unloading every day without directions from us, and set off to visit eastern girls' schools campuses when Nancy was beginning to think of college.

We traveled on Route 20, the northern route, to Cornell and Wells College in the Finger Lakes region in New York, then Smith College in Northampton, Massachusetts, where I had had so many good times, and then on to the Boston area to see the Wellesley College campus, and Radcliff. At that time these were all schools for girls exclusively, the coed movements in the Ivy League had not yet begun, and I was secretly hoping that Nancy would like one of the girls' schools.

I remember one of the motels we stayed at in Springfield, Massachusetts. We were all in one room in a two-bed unit, and a foldaway cot was brought in for Barbara, who was the youngest, 11 years old, person in our party. All was well until she tried to get into bed whereupon the cot collapsed, folding up and trapping her inside. The expression of dismay on her face, and her cries for help are permanently lodged in our family history.

After seeing some of the sights in Boston and the Harvard and M.I.T. campuses, we traveled south to New London, Connecticut, where the Connecticut College for Women is located, where I had also gone to parties when I was at Yale.

We ended the college portion of our tour by stopping in New Haven, getting out of the car, and showing the girls the Yale Campus, and my room in Pierson College. Graduation and Reunion weekends were over, so the campus was technically closed, and had a hushed air about it, but the porter allowed us inside the Pierson courtyard to look at No. 1480 from the outside. I do not recall the girls ever talking about the impression Yale made on them. Today, I am curious about this.

The main purpose of the trip having been accomplished, we continued on and stayed the night at the Barbizon Hotel, overlooking Central Park, in New York City. Here we had two rooms, and Barb did not have to endure another bed collapse.

It was drizzly weather, and we went to Mama Leone's Restaurant for dinner. This was a famous Italian restaurant, very popular with tourists. The only thing I remember about the food is that it was very plentiful, and there was a waffle-like cookie dusted with powdered sugar that was served after the meal. Barbara loved the food and ate so much that the button fastening the top of her skirt popped off which caused a small problem walking back to the hotel.

I also remember that as part of the daughters' education, I insisted that we go to see a revival of one of the classic comedians' movies of the silent movie era, Harold Lloyd, (others were Buster Keaton and Charley Chaplin). I do not remember the title of the movie, but the highlight was Harold clinging desperately to the minute hand of a giant clock on top of a skyscraper with no visible means of escape as the minutes ticked by. I don't remember how he escaped his predicament, but I thought it was pretty funny, a view not shared by my daughters who thought the whole picture was a waste of time.

We ended that trip in Washington, D.C.: I remember being led to our room at the Marriott Motel by a bellboy on a bicycle; touring the White House; the glossy leaves of the tall magnolia trees; trying to feed a squirrel on a lawn; seeing the Mint; and looking out over the Potomac from the sloping lawn of Mount Vernon. We were running out of money, the mark of a successful vacation, but had time to see Thomas Jefferson's fascinating home, Monticello; the campus of the University of Virginia which he designed and then tired, but satisfied, back to Brecksville.

Thinking back on the vacation trips we took when I was seven or eight years old, and the constant fighting and bickering with my brother on the back seat, I couldn't get over the contrast with our daughters who behaved beautifully the whole trip. It was a pleasure to be in their company.

I remember our two trips to the West coast in consecutive years: we flew to San Diego and rented a car and thus did not see the interior of our country or feel the vastness of the area between the Mississippi and the Rockies. We had planned a third trip that would have explored Texas, Arizona, Oklahoma, Colorado, Montana and Utah by car, but it never happened.

We did follow the coast north from San Diego, stopping to see Hearst's Castle, San Simeon which I thought was grossly overrated; drove the Big Sur; never left the highway to see Los Angeles; stayed in San Francisco, again a disappointment except for the waterfront, the cable cars, and Gump's department store where we bought a beautiful Sevres glass bowl. We did not try to see my cousin, Marion, in Palo Alto, and I did not realize that my army friend, Dick Thomas lived in a suburb north of San Francisco Bay.

We did see the redwoods in the Muir Forest which was worth the whole trip, explored the wine country, and passed through Sacramento on the way to Lake Tahoe; we slept in a condo in the hills above Reno and checked out Harrah's Casino there, our first and only visit to a gambling den, but did not place a bet or feed a slot machine. It was dinner time and we swept through the gambling area to the restaurant.

From there we drove down the west side of Lake Tahoe which is very beautiful; resumed our way south on an inland route; stopped in Fresno to see picked grapes lying on trays between the rows turning into raisins, drying in the sun; and were fortunate to spend our last days with another army friend, Ray Kiser, in Palm Springs, which made the whole trip worthwhile.

After our trip, I still could not understand the lure of California. I remember landing at Hopkins Airport in Cleveland to see the most beautiful sunset I have ever seen, more beautiful than anything we saw on our trip except the redwoods.

I have very warm memories of Palm Springs and of our few days with the Kisers, who lived in Indian Wells. We were so fortunate to find them at home; I had not told Ray of our trip to the west coast and assumed they would be vacationing themselves where it was cooler.

A few years earlier they had stopped at our home in Brecksville on the way south from Chicago to Pine Hurst to play golf and seemed glad to have us stay with them. We had a guided tour and saw Frank Sinatra's compound, the Eisenhower heart clinic, slept in a guest room with a picture of Ray playing golf with President Ford (Ray said he always addressed the president as Mr. President, not Jerry), and I played golf at one of the clubs he belonged to, my only round of golf in California.

The bond created from our mutual experience of studying the Japanese language was very strong, very similar to finding a bottle of ice water in the middle of a desert when dying of thirst. It was wonderful to relive our time together in Ann Arbor.

The next year we explored the Canadian Rockies, again with a rental car. We flew to Calgary, and went all the way north through Alberta to Banff National Park where we saw moose feeding on the shrubbery of a motel, Lake Louise which was very scenic, and we had lunch (I remember a huge of bowl of fresh red raspberries, buffet style so one could take all one wanted,) and the Icelandic poppies in pastel colors outside on the terrace. We took a bus to the Glacier National Park and I walked out on the ice, tasted melted water on the surface that was 300 years old, and spoke to two young girls, Japanese tourists, using the remains of what I remembered of my army Japanese. They tittered politely.

We wended our way south and ended in Vancouver where we spent three days. When I turned in our rental car, I found there was a $300 surcharge drop-off fee. I rued that we did not know this and had not done the trip in reverse, thus avoiding the fee if the car was dropped off in Calgary. Nevertheless, I found that I preferred Vancouver (not so hilly) to San Francisco.

At that time, there was a heavy influx of Chinese from Hong Kong, who could acquire Canadian citizenship with the transfer of a substantial sum of money ($500,000?) into a Canadian bank. They were fleeing Hong Kong in anticipation of the Communist takeover. Their wealth was driving the price of Vancouver real estate so high that the middle-class natives could no longer afford to live in the city. The Chinese would buy two adjoining houses, tear them both down and build a mansion in the middle of the combined lots. I remember one of our tour guide bus drivers pointing out one of the mansions. He was bitter. His daughter, a schoolteacher, had been forced to leave the city resulting a long daily commute to her job.

I remember visiting the Chinese Cultural Center. One of its attractions was an authentic, typical upper-class Chinese home, fully furnished, walled, and built around an inner courtyard, with a pond, and could have been moved from Beijing.

On the grounds of the Center there was also a large community center building housing a basketball court and on the upper floor, a gallery for displaying Chinese art.

Always on the lookout for scrolls *(kakemono)*, we inspected the paintings carefully and were impressed with one of the artists, in particular: Margaret Ho Chinn. Her work stood out but was either marked NFS or Sold. When we were leaving, I stopped to ask if she was a local artist, and if so, could I have her phone number because I wanted to know if she had anything else to sell. The receptionist would not give me her number, but took ours, and said she would have Mrs. Chinn call us. I thought we would never hear from her, but she called that evening, and we arranged to meet her the next day at her home.

We took the ferry across the bay to Richmond, boarded a bus, got off where instructed and were met by Mrs. Chinn, who was petite, probably in her 40s, and very attractive. She drove us to her home, which was a typical frame subdivision house with a built-in two-car garage that she had converted into her studio and was where she taught her classes in Chinese brush painting. She had many completed paintings for us to look at, but we did not see anything that we wanted. They were mainly landscapes or lotus leaves floating in a pond, and the colors would not have worked in our house in Brecksville.

She was unfamiliar with peonies, at least as a subject for her painting, which surprised me since the peony has been revered for centuries in China. I promised to send her some of my color photographs of my peonies and promised her that they would be an inspiration.

We discussed price and her painting something for us on commission. Then she invited us into her living room and offered us tea and a piece of her homemade Harvest Moon cake. It was close to Halloween and apparently, the Chinese have a fall festival celebrating the harvest season. I remember the cake well: it was a loaf cake with the yolk of a hardboiled egg baked into the center, and when the cake was sliced the egg yolk was cut in half and represented the harvest moon. It was delicious and we thought the custom was charming.

Before we left, we arranged for her to paint something for us now that she knew us and send it to Brecksville, which she did. Our problem was that we didn't like it and we returned it, fearing that she would be offended and have feelings of "loss of face," which is a characteristic of the Chinese. I think she was hurt because we did not get a Christmas card that year. After all, she was considered the outstanding Chinese Brush painter, male or female, in all of North America. Her works were on display at the Chinese Gallery in Ottawa, and she had established a school of brush painting in Vancouver.

As I recall nothing happened for two or three years. Fran was to have a milestone birthday, and the thought occurred to me that it would be fun to surprise her with a painting all of her own.

I had our daughter, Nancy, acting as my agent, contact Margaret again. Fran and I had long since stopped giving each other personal gifts for Christmas or birthdays, and just seemed to drift into finding something beautiful for the house, where our tastes coincided; remembering our personal celebration in that way.

We brought back things from our trips to Europe, and the Sevres glass bowl from Gumps in San Francisco; the Japanese cherry blossom picture in the circular matting from Neiman Marcus in Florida; the Kerman Oriental rug in front of the fireplace from Haig Avedisian of St. Matthews, and the Robert Laessig woodland painting.

I think it was a very sensible arrangement after the "honey moon" years of our marriage were over; it skirted around my picking something not to Fran's taste, that she would have returned to the seller; or being reduced to exchanging checks with instructions to go find something you like for yourself. That was hardly the tradition I grew up in, where much thought was put into finding my idea of what the perfect gift was, and the recipient was obligated to like it, and use it, and cherish it, while possibly hating it. This new way was hard for me to get used to but resulted in what I think was a home with many beautiful furnishings.

In due course Margaret sent Nancy three color 5"x7" photos of paintings of peonies which she had painted for our approval. Nancy and I conspired to pick out the one we thought the best. When the painting arrived, I think Fran really liked it.

It is a spray of pink peony blossoms and was hung over the fireplace in our Brecksville house, and now hangs in my office. In addition, Margaret painted a small peony blossom with a personal inscription using Chinese characters to Fran wishing her a Happy Birthday, (translated on the reverse side). So, all ended well: my check cleared, I could sincerely praise her for her painting, and the exchange of Christmas cards resumed. I followed her career for a while, and then a Christmas card was returned for wrong address which worried me. Recently, after a long search on Google, I found that she apparently is still alive and still teaching, offering classes, as of August, 2017.

After 3 days in Vancouver, I remember the ferry ride to Victoria Island, quite a surprising distance, and staying at the famous, recently renovated Empress Hotel, overlooking the harbor. I remember high tea at the hotel, something we had not done before, in Canada, or England. The formality, the protocol reminded me of the tea ceremony in Japan which I had heard so much about, only on a grander scale, and without any spiritual content.

The highlight of the stay on the island was our tour of the Butchart Gardens, which are world famous and rightly so. They seemed as large as the Keukenhoff Gardens we had seen in the

Netherlands, which had concentrated on tulips. The Butchart's flowerbeds rotated their plantings seasonally and were in constant bloom, and immaculately cared for.

There was a restaurant on the grounds; and we had dinner there in order to stay for the evening tour of the lighted gardens. The colors of the flowers were different under the artificial light (at least to me), and slightly mysterious. It was very impressive and a great way to end the day.

We were disappointed when we had to leave Victoria, because I had been looking forward to riding on the catamaran-type ferry to Seattle, which was out of service for repairs and we had to use the much slower conventional ferry (eight hours instead of four) which meant arrival at midnight instead of 8 p.m.

I remember being very favorably impressed with Seattle. We rented a car for a day and saw Lake Washington, but not the University, and had to choose between looking at Mt. Shasta, or going the opposite direction and driving though the rain forest around the Olympic Peninsula. We chose the former. I have always regretted not seeing the Olympic peninsula as well, which I think might have been more interesting than Mt. Shasta, which was impressive, viewed from a lookout point. We flew back to Cleveland and landed in anther gorgeous sunset. It could have been the ending of a travelogue.

I am glad that we had a chance to see a little of Seattle. Our granddaughter, Katy, is now employed at Amazon in Seattle, and having seen where she and my great grandsons now live makes her feel a little closer.

Other long weekends involved our annual get-togethers with Fran's four oldest childhood friends which began in 1991. I remember when Cleveland was the destination for the initial meeting.

It was interesting showing attractions in my hometown to our friends that I had either ignored, such as a cruise up the Cuyahoga River to see and admire the 32 bridges of all types spanning it and necessary to get from the east side of town to the west side, or things I did not know existed, for instance the Cleveland Greenhouse where all the annual flower plants are grown for the city parks. I assume it was the same for the others when they were the hosts in their cities.

Highlight memories are of ascending the Saarinen arch in St. Louis next to the Mississippi River, the Gateway to the West, and the Belle Rive Country Club; the long climb up from the beach of the icy cold Lake Michigan in Grand Haven, Michigan, at the summer cottage of the Hesses of Chicago; a train trip into Chicago from Grand Haven, Michigan, to visit the Museum of Art to see an exhibit of Pierre Renoir, personally escorted by Mary Barbara, the Hesse's younger daughter who worked in the museum; a visit to the Botanical Gardens and Sculpture Park established by the Meijer grocery chain family in Grand Rapids, dominated by passing by or under a replica of a huge bronze statue of a war horse by Michelangelo when leaving the park, and the many evening meals at the Win Shuler restaurant in Grand Haven (amazing quality for such a small town).

In Detroit, I remember touring the Ford Museum in Dearborn and lunch at a superb Arab restaurant afterwards, as well as wonderful evening meals at the Dearborn Inn. In Boston, in addition to our own personal resident guides for all the history in that city, there was lunch at the famous Durgin Park Restaurant, which we had sampled before, and is truly exceptional; we went north to the Jarnis's summer cottage in Eastman New Hampshire, and, after lunch, at the nearby Dartmouth Inn, I finally got to see the Dartmouth college campus, alma mater of our Brecksville friend, Phil Sutherland, and my Sunday school classmate, Dave Bortz.

While our activities at these annual reunions were always interesting and enjoyable, the real incentive to make the effort to see each other as a group every year was what I can only describe as a feeling of *gemutlikeit*, (defined in the dictionary as "cordiality, agreeableness, friendliness, congeniality) all synonyms describing exactly what I felt.

Every year when we parted after our farewell breakfast, I gave thanks for the good health of ten people all in their 70s which allowed us to gather together and prayed we could all be together the next year. It was the equivalent for Fran to the feelings that I felt when I saw my old army friends from the Japanese language program.

After 10 years, the charm was broken when our oldest member, Lee Matthey, died, followed by Annabel Hess and Bill Montgomery in the next few years. The surviving spouses continued to come, but it was not the same. Now, as I write this, only Nancy Jarnis and I survive. I consider myself very fortunate to have had this experience, (I thank Fran for it), and hated to see it come to its inevitable end. Sic Transit Polar Bears!

There were many other long weekends over the years. Fran indulged my passion for classic jazz/swing music by joining me at Jazz Party weekends, which started for us at Conneaut Lake Park, in Pennsylvania, for several years and continued after we started spending our winters in Florida by our attending a very well run party organized by Phil Carroll at the Doubletree Hotel, north of Atlanta, Georgia.

In addition, there were many, many short get-away trips, some solo, some with Fran, and many business related. I remember having a few days of precious vacation time left one year and Fran and I just taking off to Lexington, Kentucky, with our golf clubs, hoping that the fellow Aetna Life correspondent in Lexington could arrange a round of golf at his country club. (I didn't even know his name, had never met him at any of the MBA meetings, or if he even played golf).

We did have an adventure when we stayed overnight in Granville, Ohio, where Denison University is located. We tried to stay at the Granville Inn, midweek, but they had no rooms available. They put us up instead at the owner's private home about one mile east of the Inn. The owner's name was Sallie Baxter, and she was a nationally known equestrienne. We slept in her trophy room on the second floor of her mansion, and I remember the next morning being introduced to one of her friends, an actress visiting from New York.

She showed us her barns where she kept the prize cattle she bred, and there was a photographer there that morning taking pictures of one of her prize bulls for publication. I remember seeing him employ one of the tricks of the trade to enhance the appearance of his subject: he rubbed a bar of soap along the bull's spine to control any stray hairs which might distract a viewer's appreciation of the beauty of the bull's profile.

I remember being disillusioned to learn that blue grass is not blue; I do not know what I expected, but it was just ordinary lush green. The Aetna correspondent was out of town, so we played golf on a public course, stayed in the Campbell Inn next to the famous horse auction house, and drove through the University of Kentucky campus at twilight, which was pleasant.

On the drive back to Cleveland we stopped for dinner at a trout club in Newark, Ohio, and had fresh caught trout for dinner on the recommendation of two of my Cleveland customers we happened to meet after breakfast at the Granville Inn.

It was the only trout that I have ever tasted that I liked, and the club gave us a copy of the recipe they used to prepare it, which involved white wine and breadcrumbs. Fran never attempted to use the recipe for one of the largemouth bass from our pond, which could not have been the same as a freshly caught trout from a running stream. We never tasted a fish from our pond in all the years we lived in Brecksville.

We had golfing weekends with our Brecksville duplicate group, once in southern Ohio at the Hueston State Park at the suggestion of Karl Culler; on the way back to Cleveland we stopped for dinner at the historic restaurant, the Golden Lamb in Lebanon, Ohio, and inspected the five or six bedrooms named for Presidents on the second floor of the Inn where U.S. presidents had slept.

Another time, which we arranged, we drove to Ann Arbor with members of the Brecksville Duplicate group, where we played the Barton Hills Country Club and saw a Michigan football game, the next day.

One year in late fall, Phil Sutherland arranged for us to play golf at a country club in Meadville, Pennsylvania, which is not far from Cleveland, cold and wet, we had to find a store to buy rain gear, and played a very uncomfortable round. We were lucky that it was only a nine-hole course. We also had a golfing weekend with one of the couples, the Billings, in Cambridge Springs, Pennsylvania. And the bridge group was invited to spend a weekend at Canton Brookside Country Club in Canton, Ohio, in luxurious corporate suites by the Sutherlands, who were members there. Fran and I were also treated to a midweek stay at a country club in Mt. Union, Ohio by the Akron office of the Land Title Guaranty & Trust Co.

I also remember the many trips I took without Fran for business, traveling to Hartford to present a loan application in person, or to New York or Chicago to attend mortgage or appraisal conferences.

Every fall at World Series time, Dad and I would fly to Chicago to the Mortgage Bankers' Association Fall Conference at the huge Stevens Hotel where we attended the programs sponsored by the MBA for the benefit of the members, and spent as much time as possible in the Aetna Life suite where most of the men we dealt with were in attendance and we could talk with them, one on one.

I remember two of the Society of Residential Appraisal conferences in Chicago and New York that I attended with my friend, Bill Braman. Bill loved to walk; and we covered many miles in both cities on foot.

In Chicago, one night after dinner we walked west on Rush Street almost to the city limits before turning back. As we neared the downtown business district, we were lured into a strip bar out of curiosity and stayed only a very short time. Being the father of three young girls, I was deeply depressed by the dancers, not at all the effect intended. We left very abruptly.

In New York, Bill and I stayed at the Hilton for the meetings, and the highlight of the trip for me was an invitation to dinner for us at the apartment (a co-op near the Metropolitan Museum of Art) of Del Zucker, my old army friend from the ASTP in Minneapolis, who had finally married. We walked, of course, and it was a long walk, and on the way passed a florist's shop.

I thought it might be a nice gesture for us to bring our hostess some flowers. It was the end of the day and the only thing the florist had left was a small bunch of ranunculas, a small cup shaped flower on a fleshy stem in vivid pastel colors, which we bought and presented to Del's wife, Frieda, a delightful person with whom I immediately felt at home. She was warm and gracious and welcoming. And I felt Zucker had been wise to wait as long as he did to marry.

A short time later, the other guests arrived: first Sidney Mishcon and his wife, Peppi, and then Phil Kazon and his wife, Mimi, whom I had never met.

The minute Mimi entered the apartment she saw the flowers, rushed over to admire them, ignoring everyone in the room, and exclaimed, "Oh! Ranunculas! They're the "in" flower this season!" She was petite, dark haired, beautifully dressed, and proceeded to dominate the evening with tales of her exceptional daughter, her work at the Women's Wear Daily which was the "in" trade fashion paper, the problems they had with their maid who stole some jewelry from her before they left for a trip to Vermont to visit Phil's family, reporting the maid to the police, and a year later finding the jewelry in a shoe box on the top shelf of her closet where she forgot she had hidden it. It was quite a performance. Bill watched on in amazement,

Sidney and Del, who had seen this before, were dismissive, and Phil, her husband, puffed away on his pipe and seemed to be bemused. It was an unforgettable evening.

It was wonderful to have a whole evening with three of my best friends in the army, and to have Bill observe why they occupied the place in my heart that they did. I don't remember what Frieda served, but I was glad that the only flowers in the florist's shop that afternoon happened to be ranunculas.

I remember many other solo trips over the years, all with pleasure and excitement. I went back to Yale every five years for the Reunion weekend, driving my small foreign model car, a French Simca the first time, and taking my golf clubs.

Fran accompanied me only once for one of these Reunions and got to experience firsthand how things were done in the Ivy League. She saw my old haunts and my rooms, the library and gym, and, most impressive of all, met Frank Ryan, the Athletic Director at that time, and former quarterback of the Cleveland Browns.

My brother, Wes, Class of '53, attended the only Reunion he ever went to when I returned for my 25th. I picked up him at his home on Esther Drive in Highland Heights in the early morning. It was a pleasure for us to make the long drive together.

However, he did not enjoy his experience and never went again. He did not have armed service friends living nearby like I did. There never seemed to be many of the men I associated with while I was in school at the Reunions: never my roommate who lived only 50 miles away, or my best friends, McGoldrick and Mason. If I didn't get to see them, the trip was not in vain because I always stopped in New York and stayed with Sidney Mishcon and his family, which made the whole trip worthwhile; this was the real reason for my going.

I remember other solo trips to Hartford for business reasons, when I called on the Aetna Life to try to sell a commercial loan, and similar trips to Galveston, Philadelphia and Toronto to call on our other insurance companies. I particularly enjoyed the people in Toronto at the Confederation Life Insurance Company, who had a slightly different air about them. I loved being taken to lunch at the Army & Navy Club, it made me realize I was in a foreign country.

I enjoyed visiting Galveston, a very interesting city located on a large barrier island off the coast of Texas about 60 miles south of Houston, which still showed scars left by a major hurricane 30 years earlier. It was the headquarters city of the American National Insurance Company, founded by the Moody family.

I had met their vice-president in charge of mortgage loans, Ray Wilson, at the Case Study Seminars sponsored by the MBA at the Kellogg Center at Michigan State University. These were two weeklong seminars featuring unusual types of financing and requiring intensive study and were very stimulating. They were held in early December with a year interval between the two courses.

The Kellogg Center was a small modern hotel built by the University on campus and used for training students in MSU's Hotel Management courses. It was in fact a giant classroom. Students performed all the duties and functions of the Center/hotel, and I was surprised at how efficient and well trained they were.

Getting to know Ray in classes and working with him on some of the Case Studies, and going out in the evening after class and dinner to the Boom Boom Room Bar & Grill, led to my asking if I could submit an occasional loan application to him although they already had a correspondent in

Cleveland. He agreed, but I never had much success with the Company: either they could not approve my application, or they would approve it, and I could not get my customer to accept their offer. We never closed a loan with them.

One of my trips to Galveston was at their invitation as their guest at a conference for their loan correspondents to inform us of their latest policies and to get to know one another better. We stayed in a large downtown hotel the top floor of which also served as the home of Shawn Moody, scion of the founding family, at that time the CEO of American National (looking after his family's interests). We never saw him, of course.

The program was well organized: serious business in the morning, lectures and then relaxation with lunch in the officers' dining room, and a tour of a local brewery followed by a seafood buffet in the late afternoon. The only things I remember are the luncheon and the tour. As one of the new loan correspondents, I was pleased at the chance to make an impression because at lunch, each table seated eight men, one of whom was a senior officer of the company. The officer assigned to my table was the Treasurer, not a mere vice-president.

We were all seated waiting for him to appear, when we were told he would be delayed because of an overseas phone call. At this point one of the legs of the chair I was seated on collapsed, spilling me over backwards onto the floor. It was an embarrassing spectacle with waiters rushing over to help me to my feet and carrying in a new chair. Shortly thereafter, after I was sitting calmly in my place, the Treasurer appeared. I have always suspected he would have remembered me more clearly if he had been there to witness my performance.

I remember how impressed I was with the size and scope of the brewing operation, I don't recall the name of the brand, but there were a lot of huge, shiny vats and lots of piping. I do remember the buffet in the lobby after the tour which was dismaying to me because of my dislike of seafood (as opposed to fish) which I had never tasted as a child, and that was the only thing there was to eat. There were large amounts of every seafood imaginable and I was lucky to settle on one I could tolerate and actually like: crab-claws, which I had never seen before. They were long talon-like claws with a lump of white meat at one end, nestling on a bed of ice, very easy to grasp and dip in a cocktail sauce. Perhaps, it was because they were chilled, that I liked them.

Recalling the Case Study Seminars and my trips to Galveston brings back memories of one of the fellow students who was from Houston, Texas. Dick Adkins, who also happened to be a long-time loan correspondent for American National. He was one of the few people I ever met in later life that I felt had qualities equal to my army friends. He had curly hair, a twinkle in his eye, dimples, and always had a smile on his face; he had a cherubic look - my image of a choirboy - mischievous. He also had an endless supply of off-color jokes that were made even funnier by his appearance.

Dick was extremely intelligent, resourceful, and tried to coach me in my approaches to American National. On my few visits to Galveston, I always stopped (I had no choice) in Houston, and Dick would meet me at the airport in his Cadillac convertible. We would go off to have lunch.

This was how I became acquainted with catfish, which I had never tasted before: an unlikely choice for me, I was amazed. I loved it. Even though a long distance separated us, we stayed in touch and tried to help each other with mortgage problems until my retirement, after which I lost track of his career.

I have hazy memories of a trip to Iowa to inspect the completion of construction of improvements to a Neisner retail store, with an absolute net lease securing a mortgage on behalf of a lender (American National?) for one of our Cleveland customers, Elmer Babin, in Sheridan (?), Iowa. I remember the trip as a happy adventure, a chance to get out of the office to a new area of the country. I remember flying to Des Moines, renting a car, finding my way to the property in a small town, and finding everything satisfactorily completed. The only exact memory of the whole trip is of my return to the Des Moines airport at sunset and driving through swarms of soft-body, flying insects that smashed on the windshield, coating it so thickly that I had to stop at the side of the road every few miles to scrape the windshield with the edge of my credit card.

Looking back over these pages of memories of leisure time away from work at the office, necessarily compressed as they are, it almost feels as though I was out of the office more than I was in it, away on exotic business trips. I fear my brothers felt that all I did was play, but I know this was not the case. The last 15 years of my business career I was entitled to only twenty days per year out of the office on family vacation time, time monitored very closely by my brother, Russ. The memories I have related here, gathered together in one consecutive narrative, may tend to give a false impression that all I did was play, but the memories are powerful, spread over a period of 30-40 years, of great experiences and exciting new places to explore, meeting interesting people, new challenges to solve. All this for an individual who began life as an introverted, shy, insecure boy. I truly cherish my memories; I think they represent more than just a "good time."

The final leisure time memory I want to share with you is probably my favorite. It involved my (our) immersion for a long weekend in an exotic culture, very different from the environment I grew up in, or the married life we lived as adults. This was not a trip to Iceland, or Bora Bora; it was being the houseguests of one of my Jewish real estate developer customers, Saul . . . . .for a President's Day long weekend in February, in his condo in Miami Beach, Florida. This would be our first trip to Florida; it could have been a fairy tale from the Brothers Grimm.

I have only faint recollections of my first meeting with Saul. I believe he was brought into our office seeking financing for a shopping center to be built in Rocky River, a couple of blocks east of Westgate Shopping Center, a well-established center on Center Ridge Road, where we had financed several office buildings with the Aetna Life.

I think he was brought in by a very fine Austrian immigrant architect, Adelbert Kleine, who had an option on the land and hoped to realize a profit on the land as well as earn an architect's commission for drawing the plans and supervising the construction, which would only be realized if the center were actually built. I was enthusiastic because I felt we could keep the entire loan commission/finder's fee, a rare event, which would be substantial for a loan in the $2-$3 million range.

I was persuaded to take an application, my first for the new company, to American National in Galveston, in person. I agreed to go, all expenses paid, and secured an appointment to present the application to one of the men in the mortgage loan department. I was well treated and got to see some of the sights in Galveston, and the loan was eventually approved. I kept track of my expenses, and when I returned gave an accounting to Adelbert, who had advanced $250 to cover my expenses, and returned $10 or $15 plus change to him, which astounded him. He fully expected that I would find a way to spend all his money. He said, "Only with the Schmidts!" which I thought was a great compliment.

Alas, while I was spending my time and effort to secure the necessary financing, Saul had been busy talking to other "friends" in the lending business and found a better offer elsewhere which he accepted, and, thus my first effort to place a loan with the American National was a failure, and Rockport Center was built without my help.

Saul was an interesting character: about five or six years younger than me, 6' tall, very fit, beautifully dressed, and presented himself as a bashful, country boy who didn't really know what he was doing and needed help to get what he wanted. I expected to hear him say, "Aw, shucks!" as he switched a blade of hay from one side of his mouth to the other. (He wore alligator shoes and carried an Italian men's purse). I found it was impossible not to like him. In the course of later visits to our office seeking advice and "help", I learned that he came from Mansfield, Ohio, was married, and had two sons; that he owned the largest shopping center in Mansfield, a major interest in a fast food chain, and his crown jewel was an office building in Harrisburg, with a twenty-five year absolute net lease to the State of Pennsylvania, as close as one could get to owning a risk free U.S. government bond, but at a much higher rate of return.

When he learned that we had a common interest in golf, he invited me and my wife to spend a weekend in Florida with him and his wife in their condo in Miami Beach, and to be sure to bring my golf sticks so we could play at his country club, The Fontainebleau, which I assumed was owned by the famous hotel of the same name. We had never been to Florida and it was not too difficult to persuade Fran that this was something we should do. I also suspected that he had something else in mind that he needed "help" with, which could result in some business for the office.

Saul met us at the Miami airport about 7:30 p.m. and on the way to his condo we stopped at a marina where he took me to meet a friend who lived on a large sailboat. I was interested because the only sailboats I was familiar with were 12-15 feet long with one sail: this was a ketch with two masts and large enough to live on, probably 45'- 50' in length. I don't remember anything about the owner of the boat or the reason for Saul's stopping to see him. It was an interesting beginning, a preview of what was to come.

This was our first visit to Florida and we were wide eyed at the palm trees, and the balmy temperature in February as we crossed the bridge in Saul's Mercedes convertible with the top down to the island and saw Saul's high rise condo building, which stood across the street from the Fontainebleau and Doral hotels. I think his unit was on the fifth floor.

We were greeted at the door by Ruth, Saul's wife, and her best friend in the building, Ruth (I do not remember her last name - she was married to a retired circus clown). I will refer to her hereafter as Ruth II. I think Saul sent us on ahead while he parked the car. I remember some initial confusion while we introduced ourselves. I remember wondering if Saul had even told his wife he was bringing guests, let alone that they would be staying for two or three days, or that they were *goy* (gentile). Ruth was at a loss and Ruth II took over ushering us in and seating us. Ruth simply did not know what to do. She was the most helpless person I ever met. She must have had a housekeeper and nanny to raise her children in Mansfield because she did not seem even able to boil water. Saul, or Ruth II had to do everything for her. She was a lovely person, but it was hard for us to know how to behave around her. Saul arrived and promptly took their dog out for a walk.

When he returned, he showed us to our guest room, which was not at all what I had expected. We were put in a large pantry type room with two doors to the hall and the kitchen, and no windows. It was an interior room where they kept their dog (I cannot believe that I do not remember what kind of dog it was, except that it was large) in an attempt to control the noise from its constant barking, which infuriated the neighbors who complained to the condo board on a regular basis. It was fortunate that neither Fran nor I had a dog dander allergy problem. Knowing what I knew of Saul, I did not find this kind of treatment demeaning: we were "friends" and, he felt, almost a part of his family. I do not remember what we actually slept on, probably some sort of roll-away beds, or if the dog reclaimed his home whenever we were not in residence while there.

The condo was unexceptional with decent sized rooms - I do not remember how many bedrooms it had, two, I suspect, each occupied by one of our hosts, or how many bathrooms, or which one we used, or how accessible it was from our "guest" room.

Looking out from the living room windows, one saw the facades of the Fontainebleau and Doral hotels blocking a view of the Atlantic Ocean except for the narrow open space between them.

One unusual feature of the condo was that there were five telephone lines to the suite, and it seemed as though one of them was always ringing. Saul received a lot of phone calls. This caused a problem because the phones were scattered in various rooms, and every time a phone rang, we had to drop everything and try to locate which phone was asking to be answered. Many times it was buried between the cushions of the sofa in the living room. It was like a Marx Brothers movie *shtick*.

I do not remember many of the small, ordinary details of our stay. I think we were able to sleep peacefully, but I do not remember where the dog slept; I don't remember what the breakfast arrangements were, except I am sure Ruth did not do what preparation there was, that was Saul's department; after all, we were his guests.

Saturday we were to play golf at Saul's country club. This was in the midst of the first OPEC oil embargo, and there were long lines at gas stations at all times. Saul was thoughtful and considerate and went out early - at 6 a.m.? - and had the Mercedes' tank topped off. We left for the club about 10 a.m.. Top down, back over the bridge to the mainland, and toward the airport.

This was when I began to realize that something was wrong with our whole trip: Saul didn't know how to find his country club! We had to stop, on a Saturday morning, on a national holiday weekend at an office park, where he was lucky to find an office on the second floor open and came back and said we were all set to go. He just couldn't remember which direction to turn.

We turned to the left to the airport and proceeded on a road along the southern boundary of the airport and two or three miles west of the airport, turned right on an unpaved gravel road with incomplete two-story condo buildings on both sides of the street, cement block walls not yet stuccoed, windows without glass: it could have been a prison. After two or three hundred yards we turned right again on a narrower gravel driveway.

We had arrived at the Fontainebleau Country Club. The clubhouse where food and drinks were available was a house trailer sitting on cement blocks with a latticework skirt to give some feeling of permanence next to another trailer which was the pro shop where the greens fees were paid. It was a bit of a shock, but Saul was his breezy self and unconcerned.

He left me sitting on the open-door sill of the Mercedes while he went off to make the arrangements for our play. I was not to worry. The Pro was a friend of his. Before he left he gave me a file folder from the back seat and asked me to read it, and suddenly it became clear why I had been invited:

Saul had been brought in to complete a stalled condo development in Hollywood, Florida. His fee was to be a free unit, and any excess in financing funds after completion. My fee would be 1% or 2% of the amount of the mortgage. He had devised a scheme to leverage the amount of money from the financing. His idea was to split off the recreational facilities, which were located between the condos and the highway, the clubhouse, the pool and the tennis courts, and finance them separately.

The security for this proposed financing would be the land and buildings of the split-off recreational part of the property itself, including the income flow from the captive condo owners who would be obliged to pay a monthly fee for the privilege of using their own property, and have the added pleasure of thinking about their situation every time they turned off the main road to get to their condo unit. It was an outrageous idea. I wanted no part in it.

If I had known what was in his mind, I would have never agreed to come to Florida, and to bring my wife? Furthermore, the concept was unfinanceable. I may have been a wizard mortgage man in his mind - after all hadn't I found a mortgage for his Rockport Shopping Center for him,

456

which he didn't accept (was this his attempt to compensate me for that loss?) but I was certain there wasn't a financial institution in America that wouldn't be laughing all the way to the front door as they were showing me out, and wondering if I were serious, and if they could trust my judgment on any future deals.

While I was skimming through Saul's file, I happened to look up at the practice green, about 30 feet in diameter, where four of the biggest black men I had ever seen were warming up. They had to average 6' 6" and all were wearing knitted golf caps with a pom-pom on top. I felt slightly intimidated.

Saul appeared shortly afterwards with our lunch: two hotdogs with mustard and said he had fixed it with the Pro that we could go off ahead of the black foursome on the practice green. Which we did. I don't remember much about the course, which was new and wandered around between the unfinished buildings, and was flat and uninteresting. Saul was not much of a golfer, and that day, neither was I.

After we finished the round, Saul decided we would "take a steam" at the Doral Hotel health club where he was a member. It was after 5 p.m. and the club was closed, but an attendant was still there and Saul, who was not a member, but a "friend" of the attendant, talked his way into our using the sauna. I have never enjoyed steam baths, but this was part of the whole experience.

We met Saul's mother, an 80-year-old lady, for dinner with Fran and Ruth at a popular Jewish deli/cafeteria, and after the meal Saul drove us to a busy intersection where he dropped his mother off to cross the street alone to get to her apartment. I remember Fran and I looking at each other questioningably. I do not remember how we spent the rest of that evening.

The next day was Sunday and Saul left early in the morning to attend to business at the condo in Hollywood, leaving us alone with Ruth. I think Fran walked the dog again.

Saul and Ruth's son was engaged to a Lutheran girl, a *shiksa*, and her minister was vacationing in one of his parishioner's condos in Miami Beach. He had invited himself to pay a visit Sunday afternoon to meet the parents of the man proposing to marry one of his flock to check them out. I now understood Saul's urgent business in Hollywood. Poor Ruth was left alone to face this awkward situation.

Except that Ruth would not be alone: she had Ruth II at her side, as well as her two new gentile friends from Cleveland. She was buffered on both sides of the religious front.

The minister rang the bell to the condo on time, and it was Ruth II who volunteered to open the door to greet him. He was not alone: he had brought his wife and daughter, a 12-year-old, with him, which did not make things easier for Ruth. Now she was supposed to entertain three strangers instead of one, and this only two days after getting used to two strangers as her house guests.

We ended up in the living room after the introductions had been made with the minister and his family seated on a sofa under the front window. Ruth, Ruth II, Fran and I seated opposite, a coffee table separating us. After a half hour of very stilted conversation, Fran asked Ruth if she could help by getting some refreshments from the kitchen. I will never forget Ruth's look of gratitude as she silently beseeched Fran to take over.

While Fran was filling the drink order and bringing it in on a tray (Ruth could never have remembered what drink went to whom, and might not have known if she even had a tray) the minister, who was sitting opposite me and was obviously puzzled by my presence, bluntly asked me about my religious background.

This was an unexpected question and about on a par with asking a stranger how much income he paid tax on. I remember feeling uncomfortable and then telling him that I had been raised as a Christian Scientist but had drifted away and did not know how I would be classified now. He digested this information, and the afternoon went on.

Eventually, the minister and his family got to their feet and took their leave. No sooner had the door closed than Ruth II, who had overheard the question about religious beliefs, turned to me and hissed, "I don't like that man. He had no right to ask such a question." She was definitely my friend.

The sequel to this episode is that Saul's son and the girl did marry. Saul and Ruth hosted a reception some months later at their condo in Beachwood, Ohio, for all of Saul's "friends" to meet the happy couple.

We were invited to the party and while we were dancing. Saul, who had invited his secretary, a very attractive younger woman, to come all the way from Florida for the occasion, and was dancing with her, stopped to talk with us and told us how happy he was to be surrounded by all his "friends." I had noticed that the V.P. in charge of the mortgage loan department at the Union Commerce Bank, and several of the title company executives who also apparently qualified as "friends." However, I doubted they had ever been houseguests.

On Monday afternoon Saul learned that three pairs of special order green alligator shoes could be picked up at the Neiman Marcus store in Boca Raton and invited us to come with him. It was a fairly long ride, but interesting because we had never been in Florida before. We had never been in a Neiman Marcus store before, either, and were amazed at the luxury and the prices.

This was the occasion when I had located an oriental painting of a branch of cherry blossoms framed with circular matting in the Fine Arts department on the second floor. When Fran came to get me to leave, I was standing in the entrance to the fine arts department and told her I had spotted something she could see from where she was standing. She glanced around and pointed immediately at the painting, which was hanging at the far corner, and we bought it as a memento of our trip to Miami Beach.

Saul showed me his new shoes, which resembled clunky Foot Joy golf shoes, not sleek Bally imports, and explained he had bought three pair because he wanted one for each of his condos so he wouldn't have to pack them when he traveled. He had a small condo in Manhattan, two condos in Florida, one in Beachwood, Ohio, and, of course, his homestead in Mansfield. All his homes were fully furnished and stocked with clothing, so he only needed minimal luggage when they travelled, a great convenience.

That evening we were to go out for dinner at a popular eating place with live entertainment. Saul said we would be impressed with the quality of the young Cuban couples who would be there.

When we strode up to the Maître d' Saul was informed that he did not have a reservation. Saul then proceeded to browbeat the Maître d' insisting his wife had made the reservation that very morning. The conversation became very heated, and I was so embarrassed by Saul's performance that I retreated to the cloak room. I did not want to be associated with him.

The result was that Saul prevailed, and as we were led to our table, a very attractive young Cuban couple were denied their reservation, and I wondered if it was their table we were seated at. The rest of the evening is a blur. I do not remember who walked the dog when we got back to the condo. I kept thinking about that young Cuban couple, and where they ended up eating.

One other memory that did not involve me is of Fran's telling me about going shopping with Ruth.

Ruth had bought an *etagere* found for her by her female interior decorator. It was standing in a corner of her living room and its shelves were empty and needed to be filled with tasteful *tchotke*, or other objets d'art. Of course the interior decorator would have to pick these things out for Ruth, who had to have help in picking out the shade of her lipstick for the day, and it wouldn't hurt to have Fran with her sense of taste along to help in the selections. So, Fran and Ruth were standing in front of the building when the decorator drove up in her Rolls Royce to pick them up. Fran finally got to ride in a Rolls.

Fran also had an opportunity to visit Ruth II in her boutique dress shop and Ruth II lamented that Fran did not live in the area so she could model clothes for her. I think I remember that Fran bought a summer dress as her memento of an unforgettable weekend.

Over the years there were many other weekends: attendance at the Mercator Club annual conventions in Akron, Columbus, Dayton, and South Bend, once extending the trip by spending 3 days with Bud and Phyllis Thompson at French Lick, Indiana, a famous mid-west resort with an 1,800 room hotel and 2 golf courses. In the sense that they were both in the State of Indiana, it was on the way to the Culver Academy on Lake Maxincuckee, Indiana, the site of the convention that year; our many trips to the annual American Peony Society exhibitions in Illinois, Wisconsin, Minnesota and Hamilton, Ontario, as well as nearby Mansfield, Ohio. Then there were the weddings of friends' children in St. Louis and Michigan; stays at the Tides Inn and Williamsburg in Virginia; hosting dinners with friends at our rental house on Cape Cod where we entertained the Daly's and the Jamis'. Each had its own memory attached to it, but nothing compared to our weekend with Saul and Ruth in Miami Beach.

# Chapter XII

## Sunny Florida, et seq.

My memories of the steps leading up to our spending almost half of our married life in Florida are confused. I recall that we decided to explore the feasibility of spending the winter in a warmer climate the year after our last University of Michigan guided tour of the canals of the Netherlands . We talked about cost and effort and health risk as we aged; and decided to see if we would see the same advantages that our friends had discovered, who were already spending their winters in Florida.

Our Brecksville friends, the Billings, who had bought a condo on the Gulf of Mexico a few years earlier promoted the idea enthusiastically. I think the year was 1981 or 1982, when I would have been about 60 years old, and we planned to spend a month exploring. I remember it as February. We planned to travel southeast to the eastern coast where we would pick up 1-95, and our first stop would be Asheville, North Carolina, to tour the famous Biltmore mansion; also to see what the campus of the Asheville School, a highly regarded prep school for boys, looked like.

 It was quite a shock to arrive at the Biltmore Mansion, which was well worth seeing, to find 2" of slush on the ground (not supposed to happen in the South) and then be unable to get directions the next day to find the famous Asheville School from our motel clerk. I wanted to see the school because it was where my best friend at Yale, Ken Rosenberg, learned to write and the school where the great American novelist, Thomas Wolfe, received his training.

It was also the prep school attended by all the men in the McPherson family from Camp Michigania. We only saw a few of the buildings from the main road as we left town and I was not impressed. However, Biltmore did manage to impress us, slush or no slush.

The next stop was Andersonville, South Carolina, where we visited the Linak's, friends of Fran's from St. Matthews Episcopal Church in Brecksville, who were the couple who invited us to join them on the Russian cruise departing New Orleans. They had moved there permanently after Tom's retirement, and we were again shocked to see the ground covered with snow this far south. I began to wonder if there was any advantage as far as weather was concerned in vacationing in the South.

The distances surprised me on this first trip: we finally joined I-95 at Savannah and had to pass through the whole state of Georgia before we even reached Florida. (I thought Florida began after South Carolina.)

The trip was enlightening because in our travels down the east coast all the way south to Key West and then back north along the west coast to the Bradenton-Sarasota area we were exposed to all the various types of housing solutions imaginable.

We stopped to visit Fran's sorority sister friend, Marge Harrison, in Palm City, across the river from Stuart, Florida. They had retired from southern Michigan and lived year-round in a frame, two-bedroom house, which was very spacious. They were experienced sailors and were on a river (St. John's?) which provided quick access to the Atlantic Ocean. Their cruising sailboat (33-34'?) was docked about 50 feet from their front porch.

Our next exposure to life in Florida was a little more luxurious. Fran's friend, Janet Ellenberger's husband, Ernie, had a wealthy brother who lived year-round in a large home on the ocean near Pompano Beach. His lot extended over Route A1A to the Intracoastal waterway, and he had a small, what amounted to a museum, on the land between A1A and the Intracoastal with a large collection of mechanical music boxes, which were destined to be donated to the Smithsonian. I had never seen anything like them. They were all sizes and shapes, some going back to the Revolutionary War period.

Before Ernie's brother and his wife moved to their present location, they had lived in a luxurious high-rise condo in a large two-bedroom suite in town. They kept this as a place for friends and relatives to stay when visiting them, and our friends were staying for a month. We stayed the night with them and got a taste of upper scale living in Florida.

I remember the house the brother moved to as being just off the beach and the Atlantic Ocean, very large, and that as one entered the foyer, one was greeted with a spotlighted 4'-5' built to scale model of an ocean going tugboat with a functional diesel engine, which had been built by his brother, Ernie, and was destined for the Smithsonian, also. I was impressed with the meticulous , beautiful workmanship.

Our next exposure to the different styles of lodging in Florida came when we stopped to visit with our daughter, Nancy's in-laws. They were living in Pompano Beach in the smallest rental apartment I had ever seen. I doubt it had 600 square feet, with two bedrooms which were about 9' x 9'. It was in an older post World War II neighborhood.

This was temporary as they planned to move into the spacious house occupied by their daughter and son-in-law (when they moved into the million-dollar house they were building on the same parcel of land). The land was in Pompano Beach adjacent to the Hillsboro Cove Club, a well-known private club and on an outlet to the Atlantic Ocean. It was a very large house, I would guess about 5,000 square feet, which we had a chance to inspect.

It was impressive, and it was also remarkable that Rick, the owner, was personally attaching the flooring on an elevated porch with stainless steel screws. It had beach frontage and their children were able to walk right on to the beach. The son-in-aw, was a very likable young man, who operated a motel on the beach in Fort Lauderdale, which we also saw.

By this time, we had begun to understand the lure of balmy weather in wintertime. On our way to Key West, we stayed overnight in a motel on Key Largo, the first of the large keys south of Miami. Its gimmick to attract tourists driving by was a display of the original small boat, probably about 16' long and very narrow, used in the movie *African Queen,* sitting in the parking lot near the road. As far as I could tell, it was authentic, and not very big.

We enjoyed driving over the bridges from one Cay to the next because of the variations in color of the water in the shallows that were so beautiful, and reminded us of the colors we saw from the airplane taking us from Nassau to Great Exuma in the Bahamas. We stayed two or three nights in Key West and saw all the typical tourist attractions, and then worked our way back north along the coast of the Gulf of Mexico, passing through Naples for the first time. I remember staying in a motel on the beach in the Fort Meyers area and actually stopping to inspect a new condo for sale in Venice, but we did not like the floor plan.

As planned, we ended our "tour" by staying for a week in a rental apartment, the "Bali Hai", across the street from the condo owned by our friends, the Billings, in Holmes Beach, Florida. Holmes Beach takes up the middle third of the barrier island, Anna Maria. Anna Maria Island is the northernmost of the three barrier islands off the coast of Bradenton and Sarasota, about midway in the Florida peninsula. It opens to Tampa Bay to the north.

There were height restrictions on the island so there is only one condo development with more than three floors on the whole island. It was a very quiet place, most streets built up with modest size one-story cement block ranch style homes, all within walking distances of the beaches, which were wide and uncrowded, in contrast to the more popular Siesta Key or the exclusive Long Boat Key, whose residents made access to their beaches difficult.

We stayed in a typically furnished, vacation apartment and learned the plusses and minuses of renting space for a month or two, and at the same time, were exposed to the benefits of ownership because we spent most our time with the Billings who drove us all over the area, selling us on the advantages of Sarasota-Bradenton. They were glad to see someone from home, as were we, and I think they hoped that we would do as they had and decide to buy and spend more time in Florida.

The Billings's condo development was called West Winds and their unit was on the second floor. There was no elevator, and no restroom at ground level where the pool, covered parking and storage lockers were located. There were two eight-unit buildings, four units per floor. Theirs was in the building away from the beach and the rooms were arranged in a row off a corridor from front to rear, similar to the shotgun houses in Key West and New Orleans. I estimated that their two-bedroom unit had about 1,000 square feet, which was on the small side. They had a screened porch on both ends of the suite, which was a very nice feature. The units were comfortable; the residents around the pool, which was between the two buildings, were very friendly.

However, I was not impressed with the floor plan. Given the size of the parcel of land, I don't know how else the developers could have squeezed sixteen units on the amount of land available.

It was built by two friends from Chicago, Joe Wenckus and Eddie Price, who were not in the building contractor/developer business. Their two companies were involved in the production of the Sears-Roebuck catalog. They spent their winters in the condominium they created with the customers who bought their product, which could have been uncomfortable, but wasn't. From comments made by Ted Billings, the smallness of the community made for difficulties in operating the condominium in compliance with the condo laws of Florida and enforcing rules and regulations. The pool of people available to fill officer positions on the condo board was very small, and it imposed a burden on the few who were willing or able to perform the duties required by the State.

When we learned that we could rent a unit at West Winds for a month for less than an apartment at the Bali Hai for two weeks, we signed up promptly for the next year, and returned to Brecksville wondering what it would be like to spend a month in one place in Florida.

We would be occupying a unit identical to the Billings, but in the building facing on the beach on the second floor across the landing from the suite occupied by Joe Wenckus, whom we got to know very well.

This was a very nice suite: the front porch overlooked the Gulf of Mexico, and the rear porch looked down on the pool. Fran loved the color of the water and it was wonderful for us to be able to leave our suite and walk out directly to the beach, just to be able to swim, or sun bathe, or walk the beach, feeling the warm water roll over our feet and find an occasional shell to add to our collection. There were never very many people present; occasionally a fisherman standing in the surf, casting.

On one of our walks we saw a fisherman's bucket with a pompano he had caught. On our first trip to New York we had been warned that pompano had an unusual flavor and we never tasted one. It was a flat fish like a flounder, fairly rare, perhaps 15" long, which lived on the bottom in shallow water. Many times, we saw live starfish near the edge of the water, sometimes with one of the legs missing (which we were told would regenerate). There were also repulsive blobs of dead jellyfish which would wash in with the tide, which we carefully avoided. Luckily, we never encountered a live jellyfish while we were swimming which could have resulted in painful stings.

We loved sitting on our porch and watching the sunsets out over the Gulf, and marveled at the enormous flock of birds, probably a mile long, which would gather every night and fly in a long line like a ribbon at twilight north to the bird sanctuary in Tampa Bay. I never learned what the name of the bird was.

I knew they were not pelicans, which cruised along the shoreline coasting on spread wings, constantly diving head first from a height of 15 or 20 feet, bills closed, opening their mouths as they reached the surface of the water to catch their dinner. Endlessly fascinating. And then there were the flocks of gulls, several varieties, coming and going, some quite large, some quite bold, and some very raucous. It was quite a change from bundling up and using the snow blower to clear the driveway in Brecksville.

Thus, our history in Florida began. After the first year at West Winds, we rented the same unit from Wenckus for two and then three months until 1986, after my heart surgery, and became thoroughly acquainted with the Bradenton area; we learned where to shop on the mainland, where the best early-bird restaurants were, opened a Florida bank account on Anna Maria, and I explored the many golf courses.

Our life in Florida was divided into three chapters: our rental phase, and then the two condominiums we bought, each in a different area of Bradenton. Each move involved changing our patterns for shopping and eating; and each resulted in getting to know a different group of fellow snowbirds. In general, many elements remained the same, but each group of people was different, and my memories of Florida are highlighted by the people more than the place, although the places were very nice

After our first two winters vacationing in Florida, we got to know and were accepted by several of the other owners at West Winds: Wenckus and Price, with whom I played golf; Bob Bird, from Chicago, Ted Billing's across-the-hall landing neighbor, who was an agent for Lloyd's of London, liked to vacation in Cape Town, South Africa, and also liked to gamble on Jai Alai at the fronton in Tampa where we accompanied him several times.

His wife asked me to look up the Japanese character for 'bird' in my Japanese-English dictionary. She had a signet ring made using the character as a seal for his birthday. There was also Rolf Berg and his wife from Minneapolis.

Wenckus, Price, Berg and Billings bought a small (24'-26'?) cabin cruiser with a very small cockpit and used it to go fishing out in the Gulf of Mexico 15 or 20 miles offshore. They also located an artificial reef, but I do not recall that they ever had much success. At least there was no holding up a giant fish to have pictures taken when returning to dock.

Hunting and fishing were not a sport for Ted; they were a method of putting food on the table. I watched him as he probed for clams at the Anna Maria pier, and looked for live shrimp n a nearby creek; he had more luck with the clams. Ted took us for two or three fishing trips close to shore. With its shallow draft, we could go almost anywhere in Sarasota Bay and Perico Sound. It was interesting to explore familiar sights on land from the water, which was also true with our sailboat on Lake Erie. However, my lack of success in ever catching anything did nothing to arouse my interest in fishing as a sport.

The Four Musketeers (!) used to take a week-long trip on their boat (I do not remember its name) every year. I do remember how disgusted Ted was with the others on their trip down the coast to Fort Meyers, up the Caloosahachee River to LaBelle, where there was access to Lake Okeechobee. They drank too much; and their behavior was adolescent.

They got as far as Lake Okeechobee, hired a guide but didn't catch any fish and the boat was small enough that with four men aboard for a week it was overcrowded. I think they decided to spend one night on the trip home in a motel in LaBelle, to try to get a good night's sleep and a much-needed shower. Having played golf with the men regularly, I was glad the boat was so small that I was not invited. I remember that Ted only did this sort of thing once or twice and then used the boat personally thereafter.

I remember that it was nice to have a friend from home to play golf with who was also retired and always available. There were many fine public courses in the area, including the Manatee County course in Bradenton and the city owned River Run golf course on the east side of Bradenton adjacent to the Pittsburgh Pirates' winter training facility.

Both of these courses sponsored men's and women's leagues. At this early stage in my golfing experience in Florida, probably the finest layout I was able to play was the new River Wilderness Golf Club in Parish along the Manatee River, a little further east and north of Bradenton on one of the old roads to Tampa.

As it was establishing itself, it operated on a semi-private basis, which meant an up-front fee plus daily green's fees for the "member" and his guests. Joe Wenckus took advantage of this and frequently took Ted and me there to play.

The touring pro affiliated with the new course was Paul Azinger, a Bradenton native, and the club pro was Gary Geiger, no relative of my cousins in Lakewood.

The course opened for play in 1984, and in 1985, I took a few lessons from Geiger. In the course of getting acquainted I learned that Azinger's father was about to have open-heart surgery and was spooked at the prospect. Geiger wondered if I would be willing to talk to Azinger senior about my experience with its excellent outcome, and I said, "Of course," gave him my phone number, but never heard from him. Two or three years later, our friends from Brecksville, the Pete Forsters, invited us to sail with them on their 34' Caliber sailboat to the Bradenton Yacht Club on the Manatee River for the club's Sunday brunch.

While waiting in the line to select our food, I noticed Paul Azinger standing in line ahead of us. After we were seated and finished eating, I went over to the Azingers' table and explaining why, asked Paul how his father's heart procedure had turned out. Paul said, "Just fine." and introduced me to his father who was seated at the table. It was minor thrill to speak to a touring pro.

We became very comfortable with the Bradenton area as we returned to it every year, and as our stays lengthened it felt more and more like home. After the sixth or seventh year, having survived my heart attack and open-heart surgery in 1985, and the death of my father in 1988, ( I learned of his death while sitting in our living room at West Wind); and felt the awful sense of loneliness with both parents gone, it was not difficult to decide to buy a home in Bradenton and spend half the year in Florida.

My doctors had advised me not to try to function in temperatures below 40 degrees, which meant I would be at risk every time I cleared our 1/8th mile driveway of snow in Brecksville, a three-hour task. Furthermore, if we became Florida citizens, which we did, there would be certain tax advantages.

Before returning to Ohio, after my father's funeral, we began a serious search for a home in Florida, looking at both used and new single homes, and the many condominiums on the market. We were drawn to one new condo development in Cortez, a small, quaint old fishing village on Cortez Road, one of the two roads from the mainland to Anna Maria Island.

The development, called Mariners Cove, was on the Intracoastal Waterway and each unit had a dock on one of the small canals on the property, which could handle a boat up to 38' in length. While we had no intention of ever owning another boat, boat storage space along the coast in marinas was very scarce and expensive, and we felt that owning our own dock might be a selling point when the time came that we had to sell our unit.

Five of the proposed six buildings on the parcel were completed with 12 units in each building. The living space was reached from an elevator in a lobby off the parking and storage locker areas on the ground level. The units were large, had wood burning fireplaces, and the top (3rd) floor had a circular stair to a mezzanine/loft under the roof gables. The suites at each end of the building had about 2,400 square feet and the other four suites on each floor had 1,950 square feet. All the suites had glazed patios overlooking the water, which made the units seem even larger. The property was at the end of a peninsula, was gated, had a pool and two tennis courts. However, there was no clubhouse. Landscaping was excellent and everything was fresh and new.

We decided to make an offer, contingent on our finally securing the permanent financing of the apartment projects I had bought in Columbus, and the builder accepted the offer with the contingency and invited us to stay in one of the unsold units which they had furnished as a model for as long as we liked to be sure this was the place we wanted to make our new home. We took advantage of this and stayed in a unit with the same floor plan as ours in Building 1 on the upper floor of Building 5 for two weeks in October when the weather was still quite warm.

We had determined that we would try to join Ted Billing's country club, El Conquistador, where I had played many times as his guest, and if we had been refused, it might have made our decision to buy our unit at Mariners Cove more difficult. In fact, because of delays in securing my permanent financing for the apartments in Columbus, we had to withdraw our offer for Mariners Cove twice, which was embarrassing, and it was not until 1989, that we were finally able to close the deal, and at age 68, I was able to join a country club, fulfilling a lifetime dream.

I wonder at the kind of memory I have. It is certainly voluminous and contains many specific details about events, ancient and current, but there are aspects of it that baffle me: how is it that I cannot remember the financial details of so many of the important events of my life? I do not, cannot, remember what our house in Brecksville cost to build or listed for or sold for; I do remember that we sold the "back" six acres of the land for $135,000: why does that number stick in my memory, but not the other numbers?

I remember that we paid $13,950 for our first house in Parma Heights and sold it for $18,000. But I cannot remember what the purchase price was for any of the apartment projects I bought, either in Cleveland, or Columbus. I cannot remember what the purchase price was for our unit

(#113) in Mariners Cove, or how we financed it - who the lender was, or the interest rate, or the loan amount. I know we refinanced it at least once to secure a lower rate because I can remember how different the closing procedures were in Florida where the parties met face to face in the title company's attorney's office. The same is true for the sale of Mariners Cove, and the financial details for either of the two condos we bought later at Vizcaya. Why does my mind refuse to recall the dollar details that were positive, or negative.

I remember clearly my father driving down streets in Cleveland and being able to recite the details of a mortgage he had made years before. I was never able to do that; my mind does not work that way.

One of my strongest memories of Mariners Cove was the feeling of intimidation I felt as we pulled in under the building for the first time to unload our humble Oldsmobile and drove past a Rolls Royce, a Mercedes sport convertible, a Porsche, and a BMV. I had to wonder what we were getting into.

We proceeded to settle in and buy the necessary furnishings. Since we did not sell our home in Brecksville in order to move to Florida twelve months a year, we did not bring any furniture with us; there would be no dark, old style reminders of the North. We would be starting out, once again, 44 years later, almost as newlyweds, and I pointed out to Fran that she no longer had budgetary constraints, but could indulge her taste and have fun while doing so.

There were excellent furniture and furnishing stores in Sarasota and we spent a lot of time and money at Robb & Stuckey's, and Kane's stores which specialized in modern design and very high quality. We also stopped in High Point, North Carolina, both going to and coming from Ohio, where we found our beautiful Henredon dining room set and other pieces at discounted prices. I remember how discouraged we were at not finding a dining room set with so many to choose from which we could agree on in either Sarasota or High Point.

Almost in desperation, at the end of the last day, at the last showroom in High Point, climbing down the stairs to the basement of the store, we saw from the steps, over at the far end of the room the set we both instantly knew was the one we had been looking for. It was dark ebony rosewood, oval shaped, Empire style and manufactured by Henredon, a very fine name.

We bought the table, six oriental chairs and a chest, and had it all shipped to Mariners Cove. (I do not remember what we paid for it.)

I also remember being very pleased to find an unusual TV cabinet which, being only four feet tall, was not a large living room focal point. It was rather compact, about 4' square, enclosed with glass doors. It was supported by a one-half inch square metal tube framework which housed the TV set, and provided room for other electronic components, record or DVD storage. Most interesting was that the vertical and external flat surfaces were vitrolite, a form of glass, which came in many different colors, one of which was coral, which matched colors in our new sofa; even more interesting was that it was manufactured by a company, which had "Engineered" in its name, located in Napoleon, Ohio, south of Toledo.

I mention "Engineered" because my only complaint about this otherwise handsome, practical piece of furniture is that it was not well engineered. The horizontal tubing support at the bottom of the cabinet was not strong enough to support the weight of the TV set and one of our early visitors the first year, sitting opposite the TV, asked innocently if the cabinet wasn't sagging.

Which it was - and I had not noticed; I had to measure the distance from the floor to the bottom of the cabinet and get a piece of wood at a lumber yard and find a way to fasten it to the bottom of the middle of the cabinet to provide support and correct the manufacturer's engineering. In spite of this, the cabinet was one of my favorite pieces of furniture in our new home.

I remember how enjoyable it was to take my mandatory, post-operative walks in the morning in January and February in my shirt sleeves; and occasionally be so warm that I had to get in the pool after my walk up to Cortez Road (about a half mile) and back to cool off.

Our unit was on the first floor above the parking, No. 113 (Building No 1, 1st floor, 3rd unit from the left) and had spacious rooms laid out in an efficient plan with both the living-dining room and the master bedroom opening to the glazed porch overlooking the Intracoastal Waterway between Anna Maria Island and the mainland and about a mile wide at this point.

I preferred this view after sundown because the far shore lit up with lights of the condos there; on the beach at West Winds there were no signs of life except the occasional shrimp trawler, or the running-lights on a merchant ship four or five miles off-shore making its way to the port at Tampa.

The fireplace was functional; and we burned Australian pine logs two or three times when it was chilly. Australian pine is not indigenous, not a true pine and surprisingly dense and heavy. I remember how surprised I was when I picked up my first piece, about 3" in diameter and 2' long and could hardly lift it. It burned to a very fine ash, which made it easy to keep the fireplace tidy.

The suite had three bedrooms, the third usually used as a study or TV room, or for guests, and had two baths. I remember the steady stream of guests, curious to see what we had done, the first year. It was exciting, but a lot of work. Over the years four of my army friends stayed with us, or visited (Hermon Wells, Bud Klauser, Lou Gelfand, Jack Seward; Sidney Mishcon bought a condo on Long Boat Key about nine miles from Mariners Cove after his father died. He had spent a month during the winter for years with his father at Bal Harbor on the east coast, and also had a sister living in the Miami area, so I was surprised when he settled on the west coast - and thrilled.

I remember looking forward to seeing my cousin, Jean Ridenour, every year. They stayed at the same place on Siesta Key, which we never saw, and would call and come up to Cortez to have lunch with us and spend the afternoon visiting.

Her sister, Ginny Fischrupp, and another cousin, David Gaede, happened to be in the area at the same time one year. We suggested, having been there before, that we all gather at the Mighty

Wurlitzer Pizza Parlor, which seated about 200 people, picnic table style, in Ellenton for lunch and hear requests played on the organ.

We had to pay an admission fee and then select our food and carry it to one of the long tables. The organ, which was a theatrical rather than church organ, with many unusual stops for special effects (banjo, bird calls, coach horns, chimes, snare drums etc.) which were mounted on the walls and spotlighted when they were in use, rose to stage level with the organist playing.

This was one of the two "mighty" Wurlitzer organs remaining in the U.S. and had been moved from Indianapolis. There were two organists alternating performances daily, and they bragged that they had never failed to play a request correctly Many of the requests were for college fight songs, or golden oldies. I tried to stump him by requesting something classical and requested the "Toccata" from the Widor's *Fifth Symphony*. He remarked that he didn't often get such a request and proceeded to play it very well. I think the cousins were impressed and had a good time. Jack Fischrupp said that it was the best $15 he had ever spent.

One of my warmest memories is of a visit from my brother, Russ, on his way home from visiting his daughter in El Paso. I pointed out to him that he could fly back to Cleveland via Tampa at no extra cost and we would be happy to pick him up at the airport and bring him down to Mariners Cove. He could stay as long as he liked.

The things I remember of his visit are the slow walks we had around the grounds, talking over happy memories of growing up together and his relaxing on the chaise longue on the porch looking northward over the expanse of calm water of the Intracoastal toward the bridge on Manatee Avenue which led to Anna Maria. He was still recovering from the amputation of the little toe of his left foot caused by diabetes, and soaking his foot in warm salt water in a bucket he carried with him.

I think his visit to Texas, where he had a chance to meet his two grandsons for the first time, was stressful because his daughter who had become a born again Christian was urging him to change his lifetime religious beliefs. I can still hear him saying, "It's so peaceful here." I remember how glad I was to be able to provide this brief respite from his troubles.

He had met a distant cousin, who was widowed, the granddaughter of our great uncle, Uncle Louie, and they had decided to marry. I had had dinner with them in Lakewood before they made their decision and approved of Elaine very highly. Now, the year after Russ's solo trip to El Paso, they were returning to El Paso hoping to secure the approval of his daughter of the proposed marriage, and for him to see his grandsons for the second time. I believe he was 70 years old and had serious health problems.

Debby, his daughter, said that if the marriage went forward, they would be welcome to visit the grandchildren, but that she would not be present. I was appalled at this Christian behavior.

Following precedent, they stopped at Mariners Cove on the way home and we had a fine visit. The memory I have of this visit is of our going up to Ruskin, half-way to Tampa, to show them the mature Del Webb community there, which we had checked out in our own search.

When we arrived, Elaine realized this was where she sent Christmas cards to one of her former bosses who had retired. Russ was already, after two short visits to Florida, thinking of buying something and moving to Florida permanently. We stopped at one of the houses for sale and inspected it. It was a smaller two-bedroom house; and he was already thinking of where their furniture would fit; and found an alcove where he could put his Hammond organ. I thought this much too hasty and suggested that they check the rental pool, and rent a house for a season before taking the major step he was thinking of, that the community was large enough that there would always be something available to buy or rent.

They did marry, very happily, but his health did not improve and two years later he died without a chance to realize their dream.

In spite of the lack of a clubhouse at Mariners Cove, there was a social life, which consisted of private parties, usually attended by people in the same building, and poorly organized "pool" parties at cocktail hour, hosted by one of the buildings, where people from all the buildings mingled. The condominium was not large enough to employ a Social Secretary, who would arrange various forms of entertainment; it fell to individual wives to make things happen.

Some of the wives enjoyed playing tennis and met regularly in the morning when it was cool to play, which led to fairly regular bridge games, which led to going out for early bird dinners at restaurants offering reduced prices before 5:30 p.m. This is how I remember our social life developed. Of course, for the first few years we still did things with the West Winds friends, especially the Billings.

Frequently, social obligations were discharged by having a couple in for dinner, followed by conversation or bridge; sometimes a couple would host a dinner party for ten or twelve people in a private room at their country club. The Egbert Beall's, owners of the Bealls Discount Store chain, members of the Bradenton Country Club, who were Building One people, did this every year, something we looked forward to. Another Building One couple, Gordon Hartman, retired V.P. of the Tropicana Orange Juice Company, and his wife Billie Sue, who had a broad 'Gawja' accent and was one of Fran's tennis/bridge friends, owned a 50' cabin cruiser built in Hong Kong, and gathered three of the Building One couples and cruised to a nearby restaurant on the waterway for a Christmas dinner, having lavishly decorated the boat with holiday lights. I remember how huge the boat seemed and admired Gordon's skill at docking it. I also remember having the only grouper (fish) I ever liked on that occasion.

There were a number of interesting people in our building: the Beall's, Egbert and Tapa, in a large end unit; the Ferries, retired V.P of Liberty Mutual Insurance Company; Charley and Ginny Cook, a retired Colonel from the Air force; the Shircliffs; Marvin and Judy Langer; Dana and Susan Weinkle, who were both doctors, an ophthalmologist and a dermatologist, (younger than the rest of us, and owners of the Porsche and BMV parked next to us). Later, after Harry Ferries's death, the Beall's daughter, Beverly, an executive in the family business, bought that suite and lived there, close to her parents.

The most vivid memory I have of a party held at Building One, was one given by the Ferries who must have had a lot of practice when Harry was carrying out his duties at the Liberty Mutual Insurance Company. It was interesting when I learned that Ann, who was delightful and a minister's daughter, was a scholarship girl at Cleveland's prestigious Hathaway Brown School for Girls, and later married in the chapel of the Congregational Church on the campus of Western Reserve University on Euclid Avenue in Cleveland. We arrived on time to find their front door open, but our hosts were not present. Instead there were detailed instructions on an easel for each of the couples to carry out: set the table, fill the water glasses, put the roast in the oven, make the salad, set the table, etc. It was quite a lark, and precisely at 7 p.m. (they had been at the movies) as promised, our hosts walked in their front door, not having lifted a finger to prepare for their party. We proceeded to have a very good time; it was the most unusual form of entertainment I ever saw, before or since. Of course, the guests returned the favor: someone who had gone to camp when a kid suggested "short sheeting" the Ferries' bed. Harry and Ann spent a lot of time trying to find who the guilty parties were.

Overall, I remember our time at Mariners Cove as very pleasant. I think both of us filled our time doing things we enjoyed: lots of golf (more than ever before) and bridge and interesting people. We became acquainted with Frank and Nan Gilloon in Building Five, he was a retired judge from Dubuque; Jack and Teasley Denison in Building Four, he was a graduate of Princeton and former diplomat; Charley Rauch in Building Three, a retired banker from New Haven; Steve and Peg Foldes from Cleveland, where he had owned a chemical company; Joe and Judy Hanrahan from Norwalk, Connecticut; Fred and Gene Schaaf from Columbus, Ohio, a retired V.P of Nationwide Insurance Company, who was responsible for the construction of Nationwide's new main office building in downtown Columbus; and Merlin and Jackie Jones, she was a former business woman and elected for a term as President of the condo association.

My disillusionment began when the builder gave up his control of the Association upon completion of the construction, although there was still one building, No. 6, to be built. The initial officers after the condo owners took over were exceptional: Bill Jackson, President, Joe Callen, V.P., and Steve Foldes, Treasurer. These were highly intelligent men with business experience in the real world. They suspected and found deficiencies in the construction - the stucco was less than a half inch in thickness in many places, and various other problems, and when they were unable to get a settlement from the builder, proceeded to sue him, who, typically, built each of his projects as a separate corporation which meant that any recovery would be made from the project alone. His other assets were immune from attack. The suit dragged on for two or three years and eventually a settlement was reached.

During that time the Board decided it was necessary to make a special assessment for all the owners, and at the meeting, I pointed out that the proposal was substantial enough that some of the widows might be forced to sell their unit. After the assessment was passed, I brought this up with Fred Schaaf, who was a member of the Board, and was shocked at his lack of sympathy (he had always seemed such a nice person) when he said, very cold bloodedly, "If they can't afford to live here, let'em move."

We were beginning to feel some pressure from problems with our Columbus apartments and for the first time I began to wonder if we really belonged at Mariners Cove.

Then I remember Charley Cook who lived on the second floor of Building 1 inviting me up for a chat. He was head of the Grounds Committee and was resigning in disgust at the criticism of the way he was doing his job, which I found no fault with at all. He was proposing me as his successor and cautioned me not to take the job unless I had complete autonomy in all aspects of my duties and reported only to the President of the Association. In due course, I was appointed after having written a letter to the Board outlining the conditions under which I was willing to serve, coached by Charley. I then went to the library and proceeded to study how to grow plants in Florida and which plants to use in landscaping, the necessity of pruning vegetation because of its rapid growth., etc.

While I had no problems with how to make things grow up North, this was a different world. One of the most important stipulations in my letter of acceptance to the Board was that all complaints or suggestions from owners should be referred to me directly for disposition - I should have the opportunity to solve problems before they came to the attention of the Board, the Board not making decisions that were my responsibility, which happened to Charley constantly.

I recall that shortly after being appointed, on my conditions, that we had a violent storm and the grounds were littered with limbs blown off some of the trees, and I went out and spent an afternoon picking up and removing the debris in preparation for the regular lawn mowing. I don't remember any other special activity needed. But before we left to return to Ohio for the summer, I do remember giving specific instructions for work to be done around the guardhouse and before we left was shocked to see trees being trimmed, authorized by the Board without my knowledge, in spite of my having made such an issue of just this sort of behavior. As soon as we got back to Brecksville, I wrote a letter of resignation to the Board. My career was a very brief one.

The original officers of the Association at the take-over from the builder were an exceptional group of men, and after the legal struggles in trying to have deficiencies corrected, and trying to defend themselves from some of the very vocal critics, within a year the President, Vice President and Treasurer sold their units a moved elsewhere. I understood their frustration and disappointment, having observed the same type of activity when I served on the Brecksville Planning Commission.

I remember my feelings of foreboding as to whether we wanted to remain in Mariners Cove, which increased when a new President was elected, a woman named Jackie Jones, who was very competent and had the messy job of finishing up the loose ends of the lawsuit against the builder, which entailed more legal fees for the Association. She faced the hostility and criticism of the same group of bystanders who claimed they could have done a better job than the original officers. She was not only a woman, but a Jewish businesswoman, and I always wondered if her job was not made more difficult by a smack hint of deep-seated anti-Semitism in some of her critics. Fran was a good friend of Jackies, and we played a lot of bridge with them. Unfortunately, her husband (it was a second marriage for both) was constantly offering his help, acting as an unwanted deputy, trying to ease her burden, and his manner was annoying, even to me. Eventually, Jackie's term ended and feeling unwelcome, within a year they too sold and moved to another nearby condominium.

I recall about this time that one of Fran's tennis partners, Judy Hanrahan, who lived on the second floor of Building 5, suddenly moved to another condominium, Vizcaya of Bradenton. I had heard of Vizcaya on the golf course, praised by a roofing contractor, as one of the best built, best buys in the area, After the Hanrahans were settled they invited us for dinner and extolled the virtues of Vizcaya.

Vizcaya was a different kind of condominium; it had 34 two-story buildings, on a 35-acre parcel of land, at grade above flood plain level, Spanish type architecture with Spanish barrel tile roofs. There were four or five different floor plans, and the ground floor units each had a walled patio garden. All had a glazed porch the width of the unit. The buildings were "U" shaped, had 8 units each, and the floor plans were excellent. There was covered parking. The buildings were clustered around four small lakes, which provided a view of water from each of the units. The main entrance, across the street from the fairways of El Conquistador Country Club, led to a large two story clubhouse, where the condo office was located, as well as a very large common room, looking out at one of the nicest pool-deck areas I had ever seen, a card room, storage, restrooms accessible to the pool, and on the second floor meeting rooms and a billiard table. This condo was large enough, 272 units, that the monthly maintenance fee could allow for having a professional manager on site. There was a six-foot masonry wall surrounding the property and a keypad gate at the guardhouse provided security. There was also a rear entrance from a side street. There were no tennis courts, but public ones nearby. The property was basically square and served by a circular road with condo buildings on both sides of the roadway. I had never cared much for Spanish, adobe, red tile roofed architecture before, but Vizcaya's style appealed to me immediately.

The Hanrahan's unit was on the second floor and made a fine impression. When we returned the next fall, Judy was excited and called Fran to tell her there was a very attractive ground floor unit that had just come on the market, and urged us to investigate, which we did. We made an appointment and met the owner, Sue Collins, who was moving back north to be near her daughter. My recollection of my first impression was of the kitchen which had grape colored painted walls with white cabinets, and a view from the living room that looked out over a little Japanese arched bridge to a little lake beyond. Fran would have a view of water, which she loved.

It seemed like a perfect unit for us, I had no difficulty turning my back on Mariners Cove. Fran looked at me and I looked at her, and we knew that this was the place for us. I immediately had visions of someone else beating us to Mrs. Coleman with an offer and tried to assure her that we were very serious. We made an appointment to return that evening with an offer and a check. She agreed not to show the unit to anyone else and we did return that same evening and made an acceptable offer, meeting her asking price (which I do not remember). We both agreed that the first thing we would do to improve the unit was to change the color of the kitchen; who ever had heard of purple kitchen walls? Within two weeks we learned to love our purple kitchen and would never have dreamed of changing the color and our northern visitors agreed with us.

We loved the view and our small private patio, which was shaded, and large enough to allow me to do some gardening when I was not on the golf course across the street struggling to lower my handicap. The Hanrahans were in place, and we met many new friends at the bridge table. This was something that was not possible at Mariners Cove with its lack of a clubhouse. There was a group of between 35 and 40 people who enjoyed the game and we played twice a week, Tuesday afternoon and Thursday evening. We used the small card room on Tuesday afternoons, and the large common room Thursday nights when there were more players. The games were informal and presided over by Shar Kenney who came from Detroit. She did not like duplicate bridge and, therefore, we did not play duplicate bridge.

Many of the men bridge players also played golf, so I had readymade golfing partners after we resigned from El Conquistador. While members of El Conquistador, we did enjoy meals in the new clubhouse with its spectacular view of Sarasota Bay, and the Sunday brunches and holiday banquets, which we usually attended with Ted Billings and his sister, who made her home with him after the death of his wife. The fact is that we took advantage of very few of the social activities at the Club. Ultimately, after Fran was no longer able to play after her accident, I felt the $5,000 annual expense of the membership was too expensive for one member of the family for only half of the year and would pay for a cruise, or some other trip, that we both could enjoy.

After two or three happy years at our first unit, I learned that one of the largest suites was coming on the market. The owner, a widow living alone and a chain smoker, had died and her daughter, the executrix of the estate, who lived on the West coast, was anxious to sell. I stopped to look at it after a round of golf and told Fran we should look at it. I thought she would like its larger size, and its better view of its larger lake (we would be giving up our Japanese bridge, however). Although there would be substantial remedial work to be done, we decided to make an offer, and learned there was a competing offer on the table. Ours was accepted and in due course Unit 12-E became ours. We faced two problems: it was May. We wanted to be back in Brecksville to care for my peonies and needed to ready the new unit for occupancy. The previous owner spent all her time in bed, smoking constantly, and the whole suite reeked of stale tobacco smoke. The upper third of the walls and ceilings were stained orange from the smoke. We hired a painter to paint the interior, and he had to spray paint a primer coat of sealer to kill the odor and keep the orange stain from bleeding through the new white paint. (I remember his young girl assistant's first name was Dakota.)

Our other problem was having to sell our present unit in the short time left before we had to leave to go back North. We decided to try to sell without a broker, and, if unsuccessful before leaving for Brecksville, list it with a broker to sell while we were back in Ohio. I bought "For Sale" signs to put out at the corner of the street and in front of the main entrance to Vizcaya, and almost immediately we had an offer at our asking price (again, I do not remember the dollar amount). The couple making the offer turned out to be our competition for 12-E! We met them at their home in the Sarabay neighborhood, a very well-established older area anchored by the Sarabay Country Club.

It was a very attractive home with an additional lot. I remember some beautiful stained-glass windows. They had a signed sales agreement, and it was in escrow waiting to close. They insisted on a contingency in their offer to us, that the sale on their present home had to close to provide the funds to close our deal. Having seen their home, I felt comfortable with this and we sat back to wait for the completion of our sale. A week later our purchaser called, she was in tears, and said that their buyers were having trouble getting their financing, and that our closing had to be delayed. She begged us to grant them time for their deal to close.

We agreed to wait, kept F-26 off the market, and finally, in the second week of June our buyer called us to tell us that they could not go through with our deal; that their buyer had failed to secure his financing. She was broken hearted. So were we. We now had to find a broker and try to sell a property while 1,300 miles away. And during the worst time of the year to sell condos in Florida. We listed it, but the broker could not find a buyer; we did not renew our listing with her. After our return to Vizcaya in October, week after week I drove up to the entrance to Vizcaya to post my "For Sale" signs on the tree lawn (not on Vizcaya property, forbidden in the by-laws). We were making two mortgage payments every month and were glad when a buyer finally appeared. It was a single woman with some kind of back problem who wanted to move to Bradenton where her brother lived and was a C.P.A. During negotiations she seemed very nice, but turned out to be very difficult, so much so, that at the closing, the title company attorney, where customarily closing documents were signed in each other's presence, placed us in separate rooms so we would not have to speak to her. From the moment she moved in her behavior was so distrustful, demanding and antagonistic and violent that she became the most disliked person in Vizcaya. I don't think our friends were very happy with our choice of buyers.

Our furniture from Mariners Cove fit nicely into the new unit which had only two bedrooms, but a more defined, larger dining area which had one mirrored wall above built-in storage cabinets. The mirrored wall at the end of the unit made it seem larger. The master bedroom was larger than Mariners Cove and had separate side by side his and her bathrooms; his with a large stall shower in his and hers with a fake marble oval bath tub set at an angle into a one piece square in the corner of the room-very dramatic. Both baths opened on to a screened patio in the patio garden enclosed by the 7' privacy wall. There were also two walk-in closets. The smaller bedroom was distant from the master bedroom, which provided complete privacy and had its own bathroom with tiled stall shower. The large square living room and the dining room had wall to wall, floor to ceiling sliding glass doors, and the porch was also glazed, floor to ceiling. I thought it was a great floor plan, an improvement over Mariners Cove. We were very comfortable there.

The only problem we ever had was with the sliding glass doors on the porch, which, because the ceiling was sagging from the overhead weight, made it impossible to slide the doors. Since it was a structural problem, it was the Association's responsibility to repair, which they did. We had to wait our turn because there were several other units with the same problem. When they opened up the area at the bend in the porch after propping up the support beam with an adjustable jack, I could see the cause of the problem: The engineering, if there was any, was very poor and, essentially, the whole weight of the upper porch was supported by three ten-penny nails and the frame of the sliding glass panels. If it had collapsed while someone was sitting on the porch below (us) there could have been serious injury, or even death. I couldn't believe it.

At Vizcaya we only had three neighbors. Each building had two entrance courts with stairs to the two units on the second floor, which also provided storage area for the ground floor units. At both 26 F and 12-E, we got along well with our neighbors, but did nothing with them socially. The closest we came was with our across to the courtyard ground floor neighbors, the Eldridges. He was an avid tennis player with knee problems and I used to see him off to his game at the El Conquistador Tennis Club, hobbling with his knee braces; he was a talented color pencil portraitist; she was very diminutive and always well dressed. They were the first people I ever met who drove one of the early Toyota electric Prius models. They invited us for cocktails several times and I was always impressed how well their decorating worked and how different it was from ours. He and I agreed that I would tend the courtyard plantings and I volunteered to put up and take down the Christmas wreaths, which I adorned with lights. The upper floor owners were content with this arrangement and everyone gladly chipped in with any cost involved.

Our first upstairs neighbors were very agreeable at 12-E. I don't remember their names but do remember that he had a heart attack and by-pass surgery. Two weeks after he came home to recuperate and we had not seen him, we climbed the stairs to visit him. I was shocked at his appearance and told his wife that I thought he should be back in the hospital. He did recover, but they moved to a new home off the fairways at El Conquistador that was on one floor, with no stairs. I think it was climbing the stairs at Vizcaya, which were quite steep that forced the move. Climbing the stairs could have caused his heart attack.

The new owners above us were a younger, unmarried couple and were noisy. They had violent fights, which we could hear clearly. When I would bump into him in the courtyard on his way to work, several times he attempted to apologize, carefully avoiding the reasons for a need to apologize, by telling me of his background, and about his grandfather who, according to him, was one of the founders of the Bethlehem Steel Company. I do not remember their names.

These neighbors were quite different from the couple who lived above us at Mariners Cove, who made an entirely different kind of noise: the tap-tap-tapping of high heels. Marvin and Judy Langer lived above us. He was an entrepreneur from Detroit, possibly an investor in the Mariners Cove project, bought a unit for his mother in Building No. 5, played golf with us, and was married to a younger woman who was, or tried to be, chic. She had a flamboyant figure that she was very proud of and showed off whenever in public. I think Marvin was very proud of her. She was a very nice person and passionate about nature; when it was proposed to remove the Australian pines near the buildings and docks, she formed a committee to protest and hired an arborist from the Shelby Gardens to lead the committee on an inspection tour and then give his professional opinion as to the wisdom of removing the trees. Of course, being a professional and knowing the reputation of the trees, he recommended removal. Before that could be accomplished, there was a violent storm. A 50' Australian pine at the entrance to our canal and docks, within 30' of Building No. 1. blew down. It fell parallel to the canal and if it had fallen 10' to the left, it would have destroyed three boats docked there. As it was, it did severe damage to the docks. A short time later Judy could no longer hear the breeze rustling in the pines, and we came into a large supply of free firewood.

The Langers bought their unit, No. 213, pre-construction and had several upgrade improvements installed: they had the wall between the master bath and master bedroom removed, and had a huge hot tub replace the standard tub and increased the size of their stall shower. The hot tub was open to the sleeping area and dominated the room. In all my appraisal experience I had never seen anything quite like it.

Marvin also went to considerable expense to import a special black ceramic tile from Germany to cover the floors and counter tops. Their color scheme for their decoration was black and white, Judy's favorite decorating color combination. To get around the condo by-laws that required all second-floor units have carpeted floors to soften any sound transmission. The Langers, who never intended to carpet their unit, went to the additional expense of laying his black tile over cork under-flooring, which must have been very expensive, to provide sound proofing. This was obviously unsuccessful because we could clearly hear Judy moving around their unit in her high heels, which she must have worn at all times. It wasn't really annoying for us, but when we mentioned it to Marvin, he couldn't believe it and came down to our suite, had Judy walk around upstairs, and listened, and had to agree that the cork did not do the job.

They were very proud of their decorations and had us up for dinner once or twice. I confess that the only things I can remember of the decor was the dining room light fixture, which was a satin floor lamp in the form of a palm tree. The lamp had a curved trunk about 3" in diameter with the light bulbs concealed among the satin palm leaf foliage leaning over the table. The other thing I remember are the black tile countertops in the kitchen. The black tiles were different, more expensive, because the black ceramic glaze was baked over a black clay base, not the usual beige bisque color.

I remember one unfortunate incident when Marvin came down to see what was wrong in our suite because something had leaked through our floor onto his Lincoln. He was worried that its finish might be damaged. We found out that it was our dishwasher: a gasket had ruptured; and the leak was dripping from the exposed plastic piping on the ceiling of the parking area, directly over the middle of his car. The residue was white, chalky and very obvious; but did no damage for which I was very grateful. Another incident involved Judy's convertible Mercedes sports car. She had the car parked in the space next to ours with the top up, and thieves came by boat up to the front of our building, with its open parking and slit the canvas roof and stole her radio. The condo property had limited access by land with a guard at the gate 24 hours a day, but the whole perimeter of the property was open to shallow water and vulnerable.

My memories of our thirty years in Florida are of a very pleasant way of life, enjoying the mild weather, meeting and making new friends, being visited by friends and family, and visiting friends on both the east and west coasts, and exploring the whole area. There were no shadows until the last ten years when our oldest daughter, Nancy, died of cancer in our presence, and Fran injured her shoulder, which was never successfully repaired. Age began to take its toll and the annual commute from Ohio to Florida, traveling the same routes became monotonous, and more dangerous for me who did all the driving, boring. We discovered, with the help of our children, Barb and Pete in Cleveland, and Kathy and Stephen who had retired to Tampa, that it was not all bad to get on an airplane and arrive two and a half hours later non-stop at our destination, rather than spending 2 1/2days and driving for 20 hours.

I recall how frequently I felt grateful that I did not miss Brecksville as soon as we arrived in Florida, usually around 5 p.m., stopping for dinner at our favorite Italian restaurant, The Trattoria, before going on to unpack and open up our condo and vice versa. I did not miss Florida when we were back in Brecksville. I remember how pleased I was that both Nancy and John and Kathy and Stephen when they retired, decided to settle in Florida. Nancy and John actually moved into Vizcaya, and Kathy and Stephen bought a home in Weeki Wachee, on the west coast about 50 miles north of Tampa, for the last few years of their careers and then moved to Tampa, so Stephen could finally indulge his passion for horses at the Tampa Downs Race Track. I like to think that their observation of our happiness may have had some influence in the making of their decisions

Memories, highlights, compressed to be sure, of thirty years of the daily routine of living, are of visits of friends and family: the annual visit of Kathy and Stephen with our two granddaughters, Liz and Katy, during their spring vacation from school, watching them enjoy swimming in our outdoor pool in the winter; going to see the Lipizanner horses perform at their winter quarters; driving all the way to Homosassa Springs to see the feeding of the manatees, and the other animals, the hippopotamus and the 14' long crocodile; and the trip to Disney World, where Katy, who was only about 4 years old wanted to go back home before the first day was over because she was tired - her legs were shorter them ours- and she wanted to get back to swimming in the pool.

Nancy and John Mihocik, her second husband, who were both high school teachers, also had spring breaks, and visited us. John, who was the golf coach at Lakewood High school, especially enjoyed having the chance to play so early in the season and we explored most of the public courses in the area, and later enjoyed playing El Conquistador, the private club we joined after my heart attack. Nancy loved playing tennis, which was easy with nearby public courts, and they could take long walks together without jackets or boots - in the wintertime. While John and I were on the links, Fran and Nancy were able to have precious mother-daughter time together. And after they moved to Vizcaya upon retiring, Nancy would stop off for brief visits on her way home from a committee meeting or sunning at the pool and would visit. I remember how nice it was to be sitting, relaxing in my chair, to have my adult daughter stop to talk with me for a few minutes on the way home to prepare dinner. Those were happy times.

I remember visits from army friends: Bud Klauser, who was a Trustee of DePauw University and attending a meeting of the Trustees in Sarasota; Lou Gelfand, who vacationed at the Colony Club on Long Boat Key, and Hermon Wells, who was checking out the area for retirement. And we were able to do things more often with the Mishcons who spent the winter at their condo on Long Boat Key; playing golf with Sidney on the Gulf side golf course, and having dinner with them at the wonderful Italian restaurant The Osteria at St. Armands Circle.

One time we met the Mishcons for lunch after not having seen each other for a year or two during which time my weight had ballooned up to near 250 lbs., and on first sight of me in the parking lot while opening his arms for an embrace, greeted me by saying, "*Bamba* (my Army nickname), Oh, sturdy one!" This is one of my warmest and fondest memories.

I also remember vividly a visit from Jack Seward, another army friend, and his wife, Jeannie. He called me from Houston and said he was doing some research on "springs;" that he was coming to Sarasota to give a lecture and was inquiring about Arcadia Springs, Homosassa Springs and Crystal Springs. I think he thought these were places where one could stay in a small hotel and soak in hot spring water, as in Japan. I disabused him and invited them to stay with us for a few days and he accepted. Fran had me ask him if there was anything special about their diet, especially as he was married to a Japanese native. He assured us there was nothing special. Two things happened when we opened the front door to his knock: he apologized in advance if they should speak to each other in Japanese in our presence, they would not be saying anything derogatory about us - they were truly bi-lingual and it was second nature in their marriage; and secondly, he told Fran that he was diabetic, which she was unprepared for, which did not endear him to her. His wife was a former model in Japan, diminutive and beautiful, now working at Neiman Marcus, representing Shiseido in the cosmetics department. I don't remember a thing of what we did, or how long they stayed, but that it was wonderful to have an army friend as my guest to reminisce with. Jack was part of the University of Michigan ASTP group, had been in the CIA during the occupation of Japan, and was an author: he had published 23 books, half of them written in Japanese for the Japanese market. Remarkable. I do not know if he was disappointed that the springs were not hot; or if that was the real reason he called me.

One year our friends, the Sutherlands of our Brecksville Duplicate Bridge group vacationed in Englewood, south of Venice, and invited the Billings and us down for a day of golf; one year our next door neighbor in Brecksville, Shirley Hill visited her brother, Ralph, from Nova Scotia who was staying at Lehigh Acres, east of Fort Meyers, and we drove down to take her to lunch. On another occasion, on our way to the east coast we stopped in Naples and had lunch at the Royal Poinciana Golf Club with my friend, Maury Struchen, and saw his condominium, which he had owned for many years. It was very nice, but humble compared to the new style being built at the time. We also drove down to Fort Meyers and stayed with Jim and Marge Harrison from Gull Lake, Michigan: she was one of Fran's sorority sisters and they had moved from their single family house we saw on our first trip to Florida on the east coast to the west coast at Pelican Point, south of Fort Meyers, to a very fine condo development, making their easy life even easier.

I remember how excited Fran was when she learned that one of her closest childhood friends, Julia Matthey, one of the Polar Bears, was going to visit one of her sisters in Fort Meyers. We arranged to drive down to pick her up, spent some time with the sister and her husband who were retired dentists from Michigan, and brought her back to stay with us a few days - I can't remember if it was at Mariners Cove or Vizcaya.

I don't remember what we did to entertain all our out of town guests but suspect that we took them on the same sight-seeing tour of the Sarasota-Bradenton area that the Billings took us on when we came to Florida the first time. We became quite good tour guides.

We visited with Frank and Polly Kennard three or four times. He was a classmate at Yale although I did not know him there, and Polly played bridge with the ladies in Brecksville. They were both golfers. They rented a condo in Englewood for a month; and invited us come down and stay. The condo had its own golf course but was so large that reservations had to be made two or three days in advance, and foursomes were selected by computer. Frank was not too happy about the situation and could only play once or twice a week using the system, not what he was looking for, but found that by hanging around the pro-shop, he might be able to fill in for a no-show. He could not get a time while we were there, so I carted my clubs all that way for naught.

Another year, we met them at the Calloway Gardens in Georgia, 60 miles southwest of Atlanta, and had a good time. The gardens are justly famous; huge display of stately Amaryllis and a long drive around a large lake on the approach, heavily planted with Azaleas in full bloom. We met them again at their condo in South Carolina, played golf at their course and the next day went to Augusta to watch the practice round of the Masters golf tournament, the only time I ever set foot on that famous course, even more beautiful than it appears on TV. Their retirement home was near Clemson University and we drove through the campus, which was nothing exceptional except that all the roadways had orange paw marks, Clemson's symbol, instead of yellow center stripes.

On the west, (Sun) coast, where we lived, we visited friends from Ohio and Michigania at Fort Meyers where Lenny Himmel had the use of his sister's condo for a month. He was a real estate agent and longtime friend from Cleveland; he had me as his guest at The Temple's Brotherhood Week banquet every year, which was always inspirational, and we played bridge as couples whenever we were together. I remember loving being at their home in Shaker Heights for Sunday dinner during corn season, Lenny picking a few precious ears from his tiny garden along the north side of his garage. After dinner, sitting at the bridge table, we'd be interrupted by a constant flow of "drop-in" callers, their children and friends, just wanting to see what was new; how they were doing. We were accepted as part of it all. There was a warmth in this Jewish household that I never experienced with our "westside" friends, who were much more formal in their lifestyle. I wonder if the advent of the iPhone has changed this pattern. I hope not.

Our friends, Dick and Ruth Burmeister of Lake Orion, Michigan (our nemesis at the bridge table at Camp Michigania) invited us visit them at her sister's condo in Fort Meyers, twice. The condo had an executive course around the perimeter, which was fun for us all to play. Dick and I went to an excellent public course nearby to play. Dick was deceptive: he was quiet and unassuming, but a brilliant engineer, a fine golfer and an excellent bridge player. He also did well at sailing and tennis, which he learned at Alumni camp. He and Ruth arranged for us to use her sister's condo with Nancy and John one year, which was very generous. On that occasion we toured the Ford Museum in Fort Myers, which was well worthwhile. It's hard to believe that Henry Ford, Thomas Edison and Harvey Firestone all spent their winters in Fort Meyers at the same time.

Our friends, Bob and Helen Hendrickson of Rocky River, members of the Friday night Gamma Phi Beta bridge group, rented a condo on Marco Island south and east of Naples for a month and invited us to spend a weekend with them. The condo was on an upper floor in a high-rise building and the views were spectacular, another corner of Florida explored.

I have many memories of the trips we took to the East coast. From our starting point in Bradenton we learned there were three routes to the east coast: go north on I-75 to Tampa and take I-4 to the east coast a short distance north of Daytona Beach; take S.R. 70 south of Sarasota and go east all the way to the coast, passing the northern edge of Lake Okeechobee on the way to Stuart; or continue south on I-75 to the Tamiami Trail (S.R. 41) to Naples and then east to the Ft. Lauderdale area, which was the route we took for our Caribbean cruises. This took us through the Everglades and led to the docks and parking garage for the cruise ships in Ft. Lauderdale. Upon our return we took advantage of being on the east coast and went north on I-95, and visited friends: Fran's mother's friends, Bill and Trixie Robinson in Stuart, and twice stayed overnight with Fran's sorority sister, Ginny Phillips and her husband, Bill.

Also, using S.R. 70 to reach the east coast we spent a weekend with Hugh and Jane Hawthorne, old friends going back to high school days in Lakewood, spending their summers at Chautauqua, who bought a condo in Vero Beach, next to the public beach parking lot. If I remember correctly, we made that trip twice, the first time climbing the levee for Lake Okeechobee to see a disappointing expanse of empty water. After sailing on Lake Erie, it was not very impressive and once one has seen a broad expanse of featureless water, one has seen them all. We passed the southern tip of Okeechobee on the way to West Palm Springs for Fran's shoulder operation, but never bothered to stop and see if the southern end of the lake was as uninteresting as the northern end. It is essential to the Everglades, however, and is famous for its bass fishing.

While visiting the Phillips, I remember going to visit my cousin, Don Geiger, at his winter home on Nettles Island. I remember his waiting for me at the gate of their development, a high-end trailer-park, very common in Florida, which was very security minded, and being impressed with his double-wide manufactured home. On another day, we stopped to see Don's twin brother, Doug, on the mainland in a very attractive home they rented for the season in Palm Harbor across the Intracoastal Waterway from Nettles Island. I remember seeing the TV/movie star, Frances

Langford's ocean-going yacht, about 100' long, at anchor on the river, parked in front of her famous restaurant.

We maintained our friendship with Merlin and Jackie Jones after they moved away from Mariners Cove and made their final move to St. Augustine to be closer to her son. I remember how my first impressions of St. Augustine changed after staying there three or four days as a guest and seeing the town through the eyes of a resident.

We took many day trips to St. Petersburg to the art museum where my outstanding memory is of seeing the glass works of the artist Dale Chihuli for the first time. In addition to colorful creations of all sizes and shapes on display scattered around the Museum, part of the installation at the museum was a room with a ceiling of his pieces, and one lay on the floor looking up to see the colorful exhibit, which was backlit. We went more than once and took our granddaughter, Katy, to see it when she visited us during spring break from the University of Michigan. I remember eating lunch across the street from the museum, at an interesting restaurant every time we visited the museum, including Katy's visit when it rained; we had to close the window next to our table.

For several years, I went to the Bay Shore VA medical facility on the Intracoastal water way on the west side of St. Petersburg, to get my prescription drugs at discounted prices. I was able to visit and have lunch with my cousin, Marilyn (Gaede) Bayer and her husband who lived in Seminole, only a mile from the VA clinic.

There were other exhibits in St. Petersburg advertised in the Bradenton newspaper and we went to see outstanding exhibits of Egyptian and Russian works of art displayed in a former department store. Anytime we were in St. Petersburg we always tried to eat at Colombo's Restaurant on the Pier, which was on the third floor of a very unusual building in the shape of an inverted pyramid. The Pier was probably a half mile long, jutting into the Bay, wide enough for parking on both sides of a roadway to the end. It was a big tourist attraction with many shops selling souvenirs. The restaurant provided a view of sailboat races and landing and take-off of small planes across the bay from the busy Whitted small plane airport. St. Petersburg also had an old-fashioned airport from the 1940s which could handle large modern jet planes. It was supplanted by the much larger, modern Tampa International which, in my opinion, is the best designed air terminal I have ever seen. The older field was smaller, the buildings were one story, and had surface parking only, but still had flights from larger cities in the north, especially economy fares. Anytime we could meet someone coming for a visit at the St. Petersburg field we much preferred it. It was closer to Bradenton and easier to get into and out of.

I remember spending the day with Clark and Mella Davies, one of the crew members of our sailboat, *Audace*, who had bought a small home in Gulfport, a suburb of St. Petersburg, on Tampa Bay. They took us to lunch at the St. Petersburg Yacht Club where Clark had an honorary membership because of his position as Commodore of the Put-in-Bay Yacht Club in Ohio.

We had visits with Bob and Dorothy Demuth at the home they bought in New Port Ritchie, on the same street as her brother, on the West coast. They were among our oldest friends from our early days in Parma Heights. They had three daughters (contemporary with ours) and we spent a week in the Adirondacks with them the year our daughter Barbara, was born. He had his own company, which he sold to a Swedish corporation when he retired, and they moved to Indianapolis, where we also spent a weekend with them. They had a summer place on a nearby lake, Raccoon Lake. Bob was a self-made man who grew up in Kansas and rode a horse to school. I don't ever remember hearing how they met. He was Methodist, and she a devout Catholic.

When our daughter's husband, Stephen, both librarians, began to fear for the future of his job because of failure of tax levies in Illinois to support public libraries, they decided to move to Florida. He found a job as the Assistant Director of the Pasco County Library System, 50 miles north of Tampa on the west coast; Kathy could not take a job in the same county because of the nepotism policy in Pasco County, and was lucky to find a job in the Hernando County Library System. She was no longer as the Children's Librarian, which had always been her position.

The two counties are adjoining so they tried to locate a home midway, and found one in Weeki Wachee, where Weeki Wachee Springs (home of the mermaids) is located, which we had visited several times before they moved to Florida. I remember on our first visit watching the performance of the underwater mermaids in their fishtail costumes, the young girls breathing through plastic tubing while doing underwater ballet which we watched from a room with a plate glass window like an aquarium. Weeki Wachee became a State Park and we never visited it again after the children moved there, and I do not know if there are still mermaid performances.

Kathy and Stephen's house was on a large lot and very spacious. It had a third bedroom at the rear of the house, which I used when we visited, and a screened patio and small pool. It was a two-hour drive from Bradenton on Interstate and toll roads, and we visited them two or three times a year. When they reached retirement age, they moved farther south to Tampa, near the Tampa Bay Downs Racetrack. It was fun seeing this part of Florida. There was a famous Greek restaurant, Pappas (I remember the Greek Salad with American potato salad on the bottom) in Tarpon Springs, which is a very interesting historic community, about halfway between Weeki Wachee and Tampa, famous for its Sponge Pier and for its Sponge Festival, which we never saw.

We took several days to attend a Jazz Festival in Pensacola, a distance of almost 500 miles from Bradenton. We followed the coast and stayed overnight in Panama City. It was "off season" and there were only two or three motels open; we were lucky to find a Radisson Inn mid-rise motel where we had a room on the ground floor. It was a new experience the next morning to walk out of the rear door directly onto a beautiful sand beach. We allowed extra time to do a little sightseeing and thought Tallahassee, the State capitol, was a very attractive city. I remember the Governor's Mansion, and driving up a hill to what turned out to be Florida State A & M. As soon as we realized where we were, on a black campus, we felt like intruders and we turned around and drove back down the hill. Tallahassee is built on seven hills and quite a contrast to Rome.

We also drove north out of Tallahassee into Georgia where we saw a famous collection of beautiful camellias in bloom; there were many different colors and they were scattered about the estate of a former Cleveland industrialist, whose name I do not remember. (When I had to buy a corsage for a date for a formal dance, I always tried to find camellias rather than the usual gardenias with their heavy scent).

Farther north, on the same road to Thomasville, Georgia, after the Festival we had time to visit the Pebble Hill Plantation, a very interesting museum today. In the 20th century it was owned by the politically powerful Hanna family of the Cleveland 400, who turned it into a hunting-shooting plantation. I was particularly interested in it because I had heard one of my classmates at Yale, John Butler, who was an investment banker in Cleveland, and was married to the daughter of George Humphreys, Eisenhower's Secretary of the Treasury, talk about spending a week at Pebble Hill shooting grouse and pheasant, with his father-in-law.

We used I-10 to go west through Tallahassee to Pensacola. I don't remember much about the city, but knew of its importance, as a Naval Air Station training base, and that there was a naval air museum there. I spent the afternoon before the start of the Jazz Festival at the museum, which was filled with historic fighter planes, and other historically important items, which I found very impressive.

The Festival was held in the old train station depot, which had been converted into a Hilton Hotel. The transformation was very well done, and after our experiences in Europe where so many buildings hundreds of years old were still occupied and in use, I remember how pleased I was that an older building in this country was not torn down and replaced with something modern. I remember the floor of the lobby was small, white hexagon tiles, which "dated" the structure and I thought a little unusual. The Festival was very well-run and we heard some wonderful music and saw many performers with whom we were already familiar.

After Pebble Hill we went directly back to Bradenton, stopping to spend the night in Lakeland where we watched the Super Bowl.

Over the years we went to the center of the state two or three times to Orlando to Disney World with the Kershner Family and visited it on our own to see Epcot Center, which I much preferred to Disney World. There was also an outstanding park nearby, undoubtedly sponsored by the Chinese Communist government of three-quarter scale models of the outstanding tourist attractions of that country.

There was an amazing model of the Imperial Palace in Beijing, and the famous gorges. We liked it so well we visited it several times and took Ann Robinson, Fran's friend from Ann Arbor and Katy, our granddaughter when she was in college, when they visited us at Vizcaya. It was a fine day trip via I-4. And there were two excellent Chinese restaurants on the grounds.

We visited the Villages. I had heard a great deal about The Villages and was disappointed by what we found. One of John Mihocik's friends and the Polar Bear Jarnises bought there and seemed to like it. It seemed so artificial. It had several golf courses and the usual infrastructure and had already grown to a population of about 15,000 people, but I could not see what the reason, the attraction, was to buy there. The Jarnises had retired and spent their summers in Eastman, New Hampshire, and winters in The Villages and were perfectly happy there, until they had to move back to Ann Arbor to live in an in-law suite in a beautiful new home built by one of their daughters. I much preferred our Sarasota area with all its benefits.

Two of the years while they were living at Vizcaya, we spent a Christmas weekend with our daughter, Nancy, and her husband John in Mt. Dora, Florida, in a Bed and Breakfast we found on the Internet. I had heard about Mt. Dora from our neighbor in Brecksville, Ed Kregenow, who spent two weeks there every winter.

Mt. Dora was a small town, which could have been transplanted from New England, very unusual for Florida. It was built around a square, which was filled with large trees. These were lit with strings of Christmas lights for the holidays and it was like walking in fairyland to stroll through the square after dinner. There were many shops for the ladies, several restaurants, and a very good golf course nearby for John and me to spend our mornings playing golf.

We also took a trip to Key West with John and Nancy. We had been to Key West two or three times before and enjoyed the city very much. I remember how much Nancy, who taught French at Rocky River High School and was fluent, enjoyed using her French with the innkeeper at our Bed and Breakfast, but not much else of what we did: probably the President Truman winter White House, Hemingway's residence, the Mallory Pier at sunset, and the Lily Pulitzer fabric shop.

I remember on one of our early trips to Key West, on the way home, stopping for lunch at a small restaurant on one of the Cays halfway to Largo and having my first piece of authentic Key Lime Pie, which was unforgettable; and stopping at an amazing orchid farm in Homestead, Florida, the city which was destroyed by Hurricane Andrew some years later.

I remember how our life settled into a routine of daily living varied only by our shopping and eating patterns that changed when we moved from our first condo to our second and third at Vizcaya, neighborhoods only five or six miles apart.

We moved bank accounts, switched from Albertsons to Publix for our groceries, were happy to find a Piccadilly Cafeteria, Sonny's Ribs, Olive Garden, and Miller's Amish restaurant close to Vizcaya, and Primo's Italian restaurant near the airport on the way to Sarasota, where there were many other choices available.

We had a complete set of doctors, both in Ohio and Florida, but found ourselves changing hospitals from Blake Memorial in Bradenton to Sarasota Hospital in Sarasota, and even changing the doctors and specialists for their more convenient locations in relation to Vizcaya. I was surprised somewhat to realize what a difference five or six miles made. When we checked out the huge new Lakewood Ranch development, another seven to eight miles east of Vizcaya, which got underway about the time we were deciding to leave Mariners Cove, it was so large and so far on the east side of Sarasota that to have moved there would have felt like moving to the east coast.

I remember how pleased I was with the variety of cultural life in Sarasota, almost the equivalent of Cleveland. The Sarasota Symphony Orchestra was renamed the West Coast Symphony Orchestra under its new conductor, Leif Bjaland, who transformed it into a first-class group. The orchestra performed Thursday night dress rehearsals (we had subscription seats and sat next to a couple from North Royalton, Ohio) at the Manatee County Community College auditorium (300 seats, ample free parking) almost in walking distance from Vizcaya. Their Saturday night performances were at the Van Wezel auditorium in downtown Sarasota.

The Van Wezel Auditorium was located on the shore of Sarasota Bay and it was delightful to go out on the terrace overlooking the Bay at intermission time. Its architecture was unusual, supposedly influenced by Frank Lloyd Wright, in the shape of a cochineal shell, and everything was purple: roof, walls, interior, carpeting, and upholstery on the seats.

It presented a wide variety of entertainment every night from October to May. The Cleveland Symphony performed there as well as other symphony orchestras. Many popular artists appeared. I remember going to hear Andy William, in his white suit, do his Christmas program one night.

I also remember going on Thursday nights occasionally to hear travelogues and found it interesting that this was one type of entertainment permitted to Mennonites/Amish people. There was a large colony of Mennonites on the south side of Sarasota with several good Amish restaurants. One had to be careful driving because of the many three-wheel bicycles. There was usually a row of Amish ladies seated behind us wearing their bonnets. Tickets could be bought for the whole season, or for individual performances, which is what we did.

Van Wezel was also the place where the Sarasota Jazz Club, said to be the largest in the world with 1,500 members (we were members) put on its annual festival in April. It was also the place where the Club staged a free Memorial Concert in tribute to Bob Haggart, after his death, who had retired to Sarasota; he was a true gentleman and one of the great jazz bass players. He also painted and composed; he wrote "What's New" and "Big Noise from Winnetka" and was a co-founder of The World's Greatest Jazz Band. Van Wezel has 1,700 seats and it was SRO that night; with great older jazz artists from all over the country playing, as well as the great name jazz artists who had retired to the area. An unforgettable emotional experience.

The campus of Florida South University spans the Tamiami Trail requiring a pedestrian bridge over the Trail and, The Ringling School of Design, very well known, was a short distance south. On the west side of the Trail extending all the way to Sarasota Bay was the Ringling Estate where the Ringling Art Museum is located adjoining the Asolo Theatre, a medieval theater dismantled in Italy and bought by Ringling, then reassembled inside a new outer shell on the grounds of his estate. We went to many plays there and it was fascinating to park on sand under palm trees, and enter a horseshoe shaped theatre, the stage at the open end, with three tiers of stalls surrounding the seats on the main floor. It had an exotic feel, watching performers on a stage that had had actors and actresses saying their lines from the same stage 500 years earlier.

On the same grounds there was the Ringling Circus Museum, very interesting, a good restaurant, and the Ringling Mansion, Ca'd'Zan, which sat on the edge of Sarasota Bay and had Venetian type gondola mooring poles recalling the waterfront at St. Mark's square on the Grand Canal in Venice. It was a place we visited infrequently, but always tried to show our guests.

Sarasota also had its own opera house with a month-long season every year. I saw two productions, Saturday matinees, that were of very high quality; one was the rarely performed, for good reasons, *Le Wally*, by an obscure Italian composer. It had only one beautiful aria, which was at the core of a movie I had enjoyed years before, *Diva*, which starred the soprano, Wilhemenia Fernandez, who sang the aria which I found unforgettable, several times during the movie. It was the only reason I went to the opera which was otherwise boring.

The Shelby Gardens just south of the downtown business section of Sarasota is famous for its orchid collection, which we admired many times. It was an old estate, the house converted into a museum and there was a walk around the perimeter next to the Bay. Sarasota was also proud of its modern library with its Cretan columns, and an entry to the children's wing through a gigantic floor to ceiling tropical fish aquarium.

There were two ways to get to Sarasota from Vizcaya. One could go straight down the Tamiami Trail, which was faster, to get to downtown, or further south to the Sarasota Hospital and medical office buildings, and then on to Venice; or it could be reached by crossing over the Intracoastal to Long Boat Key via the Cortez Road bridge, a more scenic route, viewing the Gulf of Mexico on the right and all the impressive condo buildings being built among the existing older residences and resorts.

During the "season" there was a steady stream of traffic on the two-lane road. Taking this route, one left Long Boat Key by crossing a bridge over the inlet from the Gulf to the Intracoastal Waterway to St. Armand's Key, looking down to the right from the bridge at Beer Can Island where there was public parking, which made it a popular picnicking spot. Fran and Nan made it an annual tradition on her Spring Breaks to enjoy a shrimp salad picnic lunch there.

After crossing the bridge at Beer Can one was on St. Armand's Key and proceeded to St. Armand's Circle. This was a large circle with shops and restaurants on the outer perimeter, and the interior of the circle landscaped with walks. It was a very popular destination and always difficult to find a place to park. It was a must on our guided tours for our visitors. One left St. Armand's by a causeway to downtown Sarasota and the Sarasota Yacht Club was located there. We were guests at the club several times. It did not arouse any desire on my part to get back into boating. Better to admire from afar.

Sarasota offered everything a major city had to offer, but on a much smaller scale.

Long Boat Key was an interesting example of NIMBY. Periodically the residents wrote letters to the editor suggesting toll booths at the two entrances to the island, on Gulf of Mexico Drive, a State highway, to charge a fee and hopefully discourage sightseer traffic; also, the notices of

Access to the Beaches, which by Florida law were open to the public, were carefully concealed by shrubbery, and parking along the road was forbidden. As a result, the miles of beautiful beach were largely deserted.

I remember a fine restaurant located at the northern end of the island, L'Auberge du Bon Vivant, which we treated ourselves to frequently, as well as several other first class restaurants, and we went to an art exhibit at The Longboat Key Art Society, which was very active, to admire a sculpture done by Mimi Mishcon, the wife of my army friend.

There were two outstanding golf courses on the island, both visible from Gulf Drive, the older on the Gulf of Mexico side of the road, and the newer course along the Intracoastal Waterway. I remember one round I played with Sidney, just the two of us, which was very pleasant, and that afterwards, when we were relaxing in the clubhouse, he gave me a copy of a small book on golf instruction which he had written and self-published under the pseudonym, "Sandy MacTavish". It was not very useful technically, but heavy on the philosophy of the game, and written in a charming style. I have it somewhere among my memorabilia.

I remember playing the newer course with a different group, two of whom were graduates of Princeton. One lived at Mariners Cove, the other in one of the older one-story condominium developments on the island, Spanish Main, (very Spanish-style architecture) on the Intracoastal side of the road. His next door neighbors were the parents of Dave Peltz, the PGA putting guru for players on the tour, and manufacturer of the golf clubs I was using. I have no idea of how often he visited his parents, but it would have been interesting to have run into him and tell him how much I enjoyed using his clubs, the best set I ever had.

I think one had to be an owner to be a member of the country club, which included both curses. I much preferred the older Gulf-side course and did not like the newer course, only playing it once or twice..

I remember a couple, Bud and Marge Lobdel, whom we met at a dinner party given by the Kenny's, Bob and Shar, at Vizcaya, who became very good friends. They were from Connecticut; he was a graduate of M.I.T. and retired from Aramco; and they had lived in Arabia for many years. Marge and Shar Kenny were close, old time friends, loved playing bridge and Marge had serious macular degeneration in her eyes. I recall that there were six couples at the party, and that the main course was a whole planked salmon, eyes and all, about 36" long, which I do not know how Shar got in her oven. Fran was amused at my predicament because I am not fond of salmon, something about its flavor, and would never order it in a restaurant. If only it had been Cobia or Amberjack!

When we were leaving Marge turned to Fran and said she would give her a call. And a few days later she did so! She invited us to a performance of the Island Players in Anna Maria City at the northern tip of the island. They had two sets of tickets for the season and loved the little theatre ambience; and taking friends to share their pleasure. The performances we saw were always quite well done.

One of the characters in one of the plays was an attorney, and the role was played by a real attorney from Cleveland, Zol Cavitch, partner in the law firm Familo, Cavitch & Durkin, a large law firm with offices on the 14th floor, the, same floor in the building where we had our offices.

Our mortgage company had made the mortgage for him on his home in Shaker Heights. He was only about 5'6" tall, wore glasses and had a beautiful speaking voice. He did much of the work in our estate planning. It was great fun to see him perform and to talk with him after the performance. I think Marge was impressed when she met one of the leads in the play. As I recall the Cavitches stayed in Clearwater during the winter season, which would have been a fair distance south for him to drive for rehearsals and performances. It was far enough away that we never saw him except that one time on stage, and that was happenstance.

The playhouse was an old, converted frame single house, which seated at the most about 100 people. The seats were from an old movie theater and every seat in the house was close to the stage. Occasionally we would meet the Lobdels for dinner at a seafood restaurant on the island on the way to the theater, but more often, we would meet them at the theater. Bud drove one of the very large, old Cadillacs from the 1960s. He was a small man, very quiet and a complete contrast to his wife who was very outgoing. She was slowly going blind but did not let it affect her desire to be active and surrounded with people. She loved to swim; and they lived year-round in the Westchester Condominium, on Long Boat Key, on the fifth floor, a modest sized unit, in an older building, overlooking the Gulf of Mexico. She swam every day in the gulf and then would finish her swim in the condo's fresh-water pool.

They had us for dinner and bridge many times and then Bud died. It must have occurred during the summer when we were in Brecksville, because I do not remember attending his funeral services. That put an end to our bridge games, but we still called Marge and would pick her up and take her out for lunch at a nearby restaurant, which made excellent omelets. They had a daughter who lived in Sarasota who was a great help, and gradually our visits faded away. I thought it was interesting that Shar Kenny, who introduced us to the Lobdels at her dinner party, and whom I saw at least twice a week at the bridge games at Vizcaya never mentioned Marge, or inquired as to whether we had seen them recently.

Between the Mishcons and the Lobdels, we did get a taste of what it was like to live on Longboat Key. My army friend, Lou Gelfand, and his wife spent two weeks at the Colony Tennis Club, a very popular resort for tennis players, with an outstanding restaurant where we had dinner with them. There were several other very fine restaurants where we used to go for special occasions. So, Longboat Key was part of our life in Florida: a fun place to visit, although I would not have wanted to live there.

During our years of living in Florida, we met many couples whom we always enjoyed being with, having things in common, shared memories; some relationships lasting longer than others. Being absent six months of the year complicated life in many ways; trying to remain active in church affiliations, organization memberships, dual sets of medical professionals, keeping up with the death toll. Maintaining casual friendships, new and old, was one of the complications I was most conscious of, both in the South and the North.

On one of our trips back to Ohio we went north on I-95 along the east coast and stopped overnight at the Tides Inn, a very fine resort hotel, in many ways nicer (it was smaller and there was personal attention from the owner) than White Sulphur Springs or the Homestead. It was located in Irving, Virginia, near the mouth of the Rappahannock River, and had both dockage and a golf course across a creek. Also, cookies and milk at the head of the stairs on the way to bed. They also had sunset cruises to the Chesapeake Bay on a converted vessel, a Canadian naval Corvette, and "cove" cruises on their own cabin cruiser, which revealed many beautiful homes hidden from the road but clearly visible from the water. I also liked their custom of assigning a dining table and the same waitress for all the meals for the length of the stay. It was considerably less expensive than the Homestead. We had stopped here several times, so it was like home for us.

It was a stopping point for boaters on their way to their summer sailing waters in Maine, and I remember once looking down at the docks from our window on the second floor and marveling at two Hinckley 52' sloops, the Rolls Royce of the sailing world, (about a half million dollars each) tied up bow to bow. I had never seen one before and had to see them up close.

I remember rushing downstairs and then proceeding nonchalantly to the docks, hoping to strike up a conversation - salt water sailing vs. freshwater sailing, racing records, etc. and the merits of our piddling C& C39'.

All I learned was that they were out of Virginia City, on the way (husband, wife and teenage daughter handling a 52' sailboat) to Bar Harbor, Maine, where they spent the summer. I speculate that, of course, they would probably only be under sail when conditions were moderate; and motor the rest of the time. So, I saw a Hinckley up close, and later saw where they were built in East Harbor, Maine, but I was not invited aboard, a great disappointment.

On one of our stays at Tides Inn, we were seated at a table for two next to a couple, John and Erma Lenane, with whom we struck up a conversation. He was Irish and very witty, I responded to his remarks immediately. We seemed to speak the same language. Erma was very pleasant. I recall that John and I sat across from each other, making it easy to converse. It turned out that they lived on Siesta Key, although they were originally from New Jersey. They invited us to their home on Siesta Key for dinner which we did several times, always enjoyable. I'm sure we had them up to either Vizcaya or Mariners Cove for equally enjoyable evenings. But this was one of those relationships that just seemed to die out, and we lost touch with them.

Siesta Key is fairly large and heavily developed with many hotels and condos on the Gulf side, but only one main road running north to south between the two bridges to the mainland, and the traffic during the day was terrible. Many times one had to wait so long to turn left against the steady stream of opposing traffic that, a turn to the right to find a stoplight in the opposite direction was the smart move to make. And, yet this was where my cousin Jean Ridenour and her husband came, and her sister, Virginia, year after year to spend their Florida vacations. The beaches were famous but always crowded, and the contrast to Anna Maria to the north was striking. I would never choose to spend my precious vacation time on Siesta Key because of the congestion.

The key next south to Siesta Key, but not accessible from Siesta, was Casey Key, which I found very interesting. It was much smaller and probably not more than 150 feet wide at its widest point. It had a one-lane road running its length, and only enough depth for a building lot for houses on one side of the street. I remember there being only a total of twelve or fifteen houses. It seemed very remote, far from a large city, private and secluded. It was the closest to my idea of what a Florida key should be of any of the keys or barrier islands we saw while we were in Florida.

The longest couples' relationship that developed in our years is Florida came about because of Fran's attraction to a dried flower/wreath boutique shop called Naturally County in Milan, Ohio. It was owned and operated by a young businesswoman, Tracy Lake, on a piece of land large enough to hold her shop, a hangar and landing strip for her husband's airplane, which he used in his construction business, the gardens where she grew her own flowers for drying, and her home. It was a very popular destination and always crowded when we stopped on the way home from Detroit, or on a special trip for something specific that Fran wanted. She would also repair and revive her old, dried arrangements with fresh material.

Tracy freeze dried flowers and used them in bridal bouquets as perpetual mementos. I sold many of my peony blossoms to her (she did not require exhibition quality blossoms) and she came to Brecksville to check out my peony beds before we started doing business. I was very happy with the arrangement because she paid full price, 75 cents per stem, for what I considered "culls".

When Tracy learned that we spent our winters on Anna Maria Island where her head horticulturist had a condo, she suggested that we meet. Thus, we met Don and Rosanna Strauss at their condo on Anna Maria, which was located immediately after arriving on Anna Maria island from Bradenton on Manatee Avenue (S.R. 64). The condos were modest: frame, two story with five or six units per building scattered on a peninsula with great views of the Intracoastal Waterway and the Skyway Bridge over Tampa Bay.

I do not remember where our first meeting took place, but think it was at their first condo. They later moved to a larger unit, closer to the water and with a better view. We quickly learned that Don had to give up dentistry because of a bad back which kept him in constant pain, and that Rosanna loved her job being in charge of flower production for Naturally Country. They had a son who had a small sailboat and Don crewed for him.

They spent their summers in a manufactured home on a canal in a development opposite the entrance to East Harbor State Park on Catawba Island, near Sandusky, Ohio. Their home there was beautifully finished and maintained and sat on a piece of land about 30' x 50'. I remember how lush his grass was when we first saw it and couldn't believe that he fed it with kitchen leftovers, including Coca Cola. They had their own dock about 20 feet from their front door, and Don had a small cabin cruiser, possibly 24', which he used for walleye fishing. He had two other friends who lived in the development and owned their own boats, and the three men alternated using one another's boats three days a week, and from what I observed, really knew how to catch walleye. It was almost a commercial operation. Don always brought a large freezer chest filled with enough walleye to last the season, kept cold with dry ice when they drove to Florida.

Although the Strausses did not play bridge, what pleased me was that we seemed to fall into the category of old friends very quickly.

After the lack of social activity at Mariners Cove, it was very welcome to us to be included in many of the organized activities of the Strauss's condo association and we met several couples and got to know them well (I do not remember their names). We were included when the group went to Tampa for a matinee performance of *The Phantom of the Opera*, which was outstanding, and followed by a meal at an unusual restaurant nearby. On another occasion we were included with the group when they took a tour of Sarasota Bay in a glass bottom boat that scooped material off the bottom of the bay and brought it aboard for us to sort out to see what we could find. It was not as icky as it sounds and was most interesting. We also toured the Selby Gardens with them and admired the orchid collection.

One year just before our return to Ohio, Rosanna called Fran and invited us to a Walleye chowder meal with their friends at their condo. The chowder was Don's specialty; and he did all the preparation. They were anxious to use up the walleye they had been unable to finish eating before leaving. I was not too enthusiastic because I didn't think I liked fish soup and chowder is fish soup. I was very wrong. It was simply delicious and a great way to end another season in sunny Florida.

After our return to Ohio, we continued to see the Strausses for many years. They came to Brecksville for a weekend and we took them to the Rain Forest at the Cleveland Zoo, which I knew would be of great interest to Rosanna. They had us up to East Harbor to stay overnight and we went to concert at the Lakeside Resort given by the Ohio State University Big Band Jazz band, which was spectacular.

One morning while we were in Florida Don called me. He was very excited and had something he wanted to show me. This was rather unusual because most of our get-togethers were arranged by the women. When I arrived, he showed me a birthday gift he had received from Rosanna: Web TV.

This was a very simple form of computer marketed by Microsoft, and was limited to access to the Internet, sending and receiving e-Mails, and using the search engines. And it only cost $300 This was my introduction to the world of computers that was still very new.

Two of the men at Mariners Cove, Joe Hanrahan and Joe Callen had impressive computer set-ups, which cost thousands of dollars, which they used for computing in which I had no interest, and of course, the cost was prohibitive. However, I was very impressed with Don's new toy and its capability to show pictures in color.

When we returned to Brecksville, I told my son-in-law, Pete, about WebTV and I also checked out prices of various brands, etc. \

He called one morning and said he was at the RCA warehouse in Maple Heights, and they had a WebTV for $200.00. I asked if it included the keyboard, and he said it did, did I want him to get me one. Since it was $100 less than anything I had been able to find, I said yes.

I was very happy for the next several years with the new world that had opened up for me. Eventually Microsoft discontinued the WebTV system, and that led to my daughters getting me the rebuilt HP Compaq desktop computer which I am using to write this project. At age 90, I undertook to learn how to use a real computer. I have learned much and still have much to learn in the process of writing this autobiography, but it has many capabilities in which I have no interest.

Our relationship with the Strausses lasted longer than any other originating in Florida, and I think of them as a very caring, gentle couple. They sold the condo in Florida, and the home at East Harbor, and moved to Virginia to be close to their children. We were reduced to exchanging Christmas cards. Don passed away several years ago and a few months ago, at the invitation of her daughter, I sent a congratulatory birthday to Rosanna, recalling many of our fond memories, for her 90th birthday.

There are so many memories of the good times in Florida, that it is impossible to recall all of them. Many are mere fragments, others as vivid and complete as though they had happened yesterday. I have a huge sense of gratitude that my life unfolded in such a way that half of my married life took place in Florida.

After the adventure of the first few trips from Ohio to Florida lost its glow - there were only three routes to take - the getting there became a chore, a price to be paid, and boredom became a risk. We usually settled on taking the westerly route (I-75) going south, which enabled us, after turning south at Chattanooga, to stop in Dalton, Georgia, a well-known carpet outlet city (we bought carpeting for both Florida and the addition to 5320 Oakes Road there).

After negotiating the traffic around Atlanta, the second day, I remember stopping at the Outlet Mall in Valdosta, Georgia, practically on the border of Florida. We knew that that night we would sleep on our own beds in our own condo. The final proof that we had arrived was to have what became our traditional come to Florida meal at one of our favorite Italian restaurants, The Trattoria, on Cortez Road in Bradenton.

I should point out that at this time we owned three cars, two small, one large, one of which was left in the garage in Ohio, while we were in Florida, and one left under a canvas tarp as cover in our parking spot in Florida, while we were in Ohio. The third car was the large one with as large a trunk as we could find. We found both Lincoln Town Cars and Buick Roadmasters had trunks rated at 22 cubic feet, and when under way both the trunk and the back seat were filled to capacity. We learned this was necessary because of the length of our stays in both places, in spite of leaving much of our clothing behind. Part of the clothing problem was the season: It was always summer in

Florida year-round, and summer in Ohio, when we were back north. We never did resort to a station wagon, or SUV for transport and never had an overcoat in Florida.

When it came time to replace the Oldsmobile we had driven for many years, I was tempted by the new model of Lincoln Town car, which I thought was very handsome and had a 22 cubic foot trunk. We were unable to find one which had a passenger side airbag (airbags were just coming on the market) and one had to pay extra for the protection of the passenger, which was important in our case because of the distances involved and I, as a matter of course, did all the driving, and Fran was the passenger.

After hours of frustration spent touring dealers' lots and hours wasted in showrooms, on a Saturday afternoon, I called our old friend, Mike Fogliano, who sold us our "fleet" (4 vehicles) Oldsmobile's for Schmidt Mortgage Company when he was a salesman at A.D. Pelunis in Lakewood.

Mike now had his own small business buying and selling all makes of cars. After telling him our requirements, he called back in an hour and had found just what we wanted at a dealer in Lorain, Ohio. It was even a light blue, one of my favorite colors. Mike arranged for me to talk with the manager of the dealership, who lived in Parma, Ohio.

When I told him we lived in Brecksville, he asked if he could call me back. A few minutes later, he called and said there would be a limousine at our front door at 9 a.m. Monday morning to pick us up and take us to the dealer about 35 miles west in Lorain. I protested that that was not necessary, but he insisted, and since we had never set foot in a stretch limousine, I did not refuse. Since we had had a Rolls Royce (bringing our yardman) and a BMV 700 series driven by our cleaning lady at our front door on the same day recently, I wondered what our neighbors might think of this latest mode of transportation.

At 9 a.m. our limo came up the driveway. We were waiting for it, and I was dressed normally, but we planned to drop off some lamp shades for repair on the way back from Lorain in the new car, and Fran had tied a babushka over her hair to protect it, and was carrying a large vinyl sack containing the lampshades over her shoulder, and looked very much as though she had just gotten off the boat at Ellis Island.

The driver was very proud of his vehicle; a Lincoln stretch limo, and showed us all the amenities: hot coffee and rolls, mini bar, TV, privacy window between the driver's seat the passenger compartment, mobile telephone, and on and on. With a regal flourish we boarded the limo, which was so long the driver had to "back and fill" several times before he could negotiate the driveway circle in front of the house. As far as I know the whole performance was wasted on the neighbors. I don't think a single one saw any of the performance. I do not remember the name of the dealership, or our driver.

I told the driver that this was a very nice way to travel and would he mind stopping off in Toledo so we could impress our friends there and he said, "Of course." and he would have..

But we left the Ohio Turnpike at Exit 9, Lorain-Elyria, About two miles from the dealership our driver called them to let them know our ETA: 5 minutes, and in due course we arrived, to be greeted by the Manager, Sales Manager and Service Manager.

When Fran exited our coach, she noticed a limousine, the same as the one we had just arrived in, parked a short distance away in the line of used cars for sale, and seizing the opportunity, bless her, brightly announced that she had changed her mind and that, pointing at the other limo, is what she wanted.

After some mild consternation, we went in to close the deal for a car we had never seen. All went smoothly, and when the cost of repairs to the computers on board was explained, I did something I had never done before: I bought an Extended Warranty for $700+ and paid for it monthly.

It turned out to be one of the best investments I ever made. With our garbage bag of lampshades on the back seat we drove off, waving goodbye to our new friends, and as we crossed the curb to the roadway there was a slight bump and one of the speaker grills mounted on the door fell off. This meant we had to turn around and have our first service on the car, to the embarrassment of the dealer.

Sad to say, it was not the last special service needed for the car. Lincoln-Mercury lost thousands of dollars in repairs under the extended warranty for what was undoubtedly the finest, most luxurious car we ever owned. I can't remember how many times the car had to be towed into the shop.

The first time was after sitting in our garage for three days unused after arriving safely from Lorain, one of our daughters and her husband stopped in for a visit and, of course, I showed them the new car: unfortunately, the battery was dead, and it had to be towed in to the nearest dealer near the Cloverleaf at Rockslide and Brecksville Road for service.

Eventually, they discovered that when the glove compartment door was closed, it did not turn off the light.

We were also embarrassed by the alarm system going off without cause while we were at Mariners Cove. I had to go down in the middle of the night to be sure there had been no break-in and turn off the alarm, which was very loud, and I am sure disturbed our long-suffering neighbors. It was finally discovered that replacing the lock on the trunk solved that problem. When it came time to replace the Lincoln, needless to say, I did not rush out to buy another one, but we turned to Buick and their Roadmaster model which also had a 22 cubic foot trunk, and had wonderful service from it, and replaced it with our first SUV, a Buick Renaissance.

On our return trips to Ohio, for variety's sake, we would leave I-75 at Ocala, have lunch at a wonderful restaurant there, Carmichael's, and then proceed northeast to I-10 to Jacksonville where we joined I-95. We only stayed on I-95 all the way to Washington two or three times and then back to Cleveland via the Pennsylvania Turnpike.

On the last of these trips, using I-95, we continued all the way to New Haven. I had missed my 65th Reunion the year before in 2003, and I wanted to stop and visit my army friends: Bud Klauser, in Charleston, S.C., and after seeing his condo unit and having lunch with him and a member of my class at Yale and on the swimming team, Jack Puleyn, we got back on I-95 to Philadelphia to visit Hermon ("Orson") Wells, at Kendal House in Kennet Square. This was the first Kendall House we had ever seen and we admired it and what it had to offer, had dinner at a restaurant looking at a building which had a large sign painted on it, proclaiming "Kennet Square, Mushroom Capital of the World", and stayed over nigh in a motel. . .

I have warm memories of Wells with whom I shared the dubious pleasure of learning Japanese. We saw the famous gardens at Kennet Square the next morning, and because of a rare occurrence, the need of car service, had a chance to see our first Ikea store, very impressive, and had lunch there in their restaurant in the store building.

We continued on to New Haven, arriving after dark, and managed to get lost in a poor section of the town. I remember how relieved I felt when a young woman in a gas station offered to lead us downtown to our motel, which she could not find! We had the street address, but the name of the motel was different. She even called her husband for help. The reason for the confusion: the motel had been sold and the signage changed the day before we arrived, which the desk clerk failed to mention when we checked in with her for our late arrival. We finally sorted out the problem and it was a very convenient location at the edge of the main campus.

The next day we had lunch with George Atwood, the man in charge of our Yale Charitable Trust who took us to an outstanding restaurant across the street from the Yale Art Museum. Afterwards we walked through the Old Campus and Fran saw where I lived as a Freshman, and the beautiful Sterling Library. We ended our tour at the Whitney Gym where George left us, and she saw the Exhibition Pool, used for our swimming meets, and saw my picture in the team photo for the Class of 1942 on the wall outside the entrance to the pool. How young I was, and how strange our blue silk tank suits look today.

While Fran slept in and prepared for the trip home, I got up early and had time to play what I knew would be my last round of golf on the famous Yale Golf Course in the hills of West Haven. Fran never got to play the course, and I never had a chance to play a round there with my son-in-law, John Mihocik, who is a fine golfer. I think he would have been impressed; it is beautiful and has stood the test of time. My final score was a minor triumph. I remember my elation at breaking 90, a considerable improvement over the 139 I scored 66 years earlier.

On this trip home we did not go south through Manhattan to use the Pennsylvania Turnpike, or I-81, but rather, due west through Danbury, Connecticut, and used the Middle Tier Throughway across New York. This took us through Coming, New York, the home of the Steuben Glassworks. We stopped to tour the museum again which was filled with beautiful glass art ware,, not only Steuben. And then we watched the glassblowers perform their magic. I have always found handling and shaping molten glass fascinating. I fear it is an art form which is disappearing along with the manufacture of buggy whips. It was a nice trip home. Perhaps, our best.

Our more usual route was to leave I-95 near Savannah and go west on I-16 to Columbia, South Carolina, where I-77 ended at that time. Both the east and west routes were about the same length, 1,230-1,250 miles, but quite different in character.

On the easterly route we passed through North Carolina where I admired the massive plantings of wildflowers between the divided highway and on the berms. To come around a bend in the highway and have acres of wildflowers in bloom open up before us was breathtaking. I remember looking forward to using the West Virginia Turnpike on this route. It was built through very mountainous terrain and I don't know how the engineers maintained the maximum grade regulations. There were several tunnels, which helped, and many curves, and something of interest everywhere one looked.

Traveling the eastern route took us near Hilton Head Island, a very popular vacation area. We spent a week there on one of our early vacations. My good friend, Roy Hausheer, V.P. of Land Title Guarantee and Trust Company, my most frequent business luncheon companion (our offices faced each other across Superior Avenue in the early days and we could signal when we were about to leave the office to meet for lunch).

Roy and his wife, Helen, had been the guest of Roy's boss, Dan Crane, President of Land Title Guarantee and Trust Company, on Hilton Head, and when Roy retired he followed his boss there, bought a home and joined the private country club. The constant pressure of the tourists on the island was too much for him, and after two or three years, he moved to Ocala, where we visited him. I remember him fretting about an armadillo that had torn up his foundation plantings.

Roy's wife died of heart disease and Dan Crane, who was a heavy smoker, (he used to lay his lit cigarette on the grass next to his ball, before every drive, and also on every later shot from the fairway), died of lung cancer. Roy married Dan's widow, Harriet, who was a lovely person. They sold both their properties and bought a condo in one of the communities on the island, and we visited them there.

Later, Harriet died, and Roy stayed on the Island and moved to Seabrook House, which was a very elegant, assisted living establishment in the middle of the Island. We visited him there, too, stayed overnight, and had dinner in the excellent restaurant. It was interesting to see husband's pushing their wives in wheelchairs to dinner from their nursing wing rooms, my first experience observing this. I had no idea what the future held in store for me.

Roy was ten years older than I am, and I do not know for sure, but I think his health failed and he moved to Washington to live with his daughter. We lost touch and no longer received our usual Christmas cards. When I contacted Seabrook House, they were unable (or unwilling) to help me with a current address.

While living in Florida, having friends and family visit gave us opportunities to explore many of the attractions that Florida had to offer: Crystal Springs with its amazingly clear water, seeing the sunken Grecian temple used in a James Bond movie from a glass bottomed boat, feeling it could be touched, although it was 20 feet under water; the mermaids at Weeki Wachee; the water-ski performances at Cypress Gardens; the white Lipizzaner horses performing at their winter quarters in Sarasota; the tryout performance of new acts for the coming season of the Ringling Bros. Circus in Venice; having dinner at the original Colombia Restaurant in historic Ybor City (cigar making capital of the U.S., east of Tampa),; polo matches at Lakewood Village - it's very exciting to be sitting on the ground next to the playing field and have two or three huge horses come thundering down the sidelines trying to get to the ball; major league baseball training camps and preseason games. I remember watching the Pittsburgh Pirates play a game in Bradenton with Joe Wenckus and spending a day in Lakeland with my sons-in-law, John Mihocik and Stephen Kershner, at the Cleveland Indians training facility and seeing them play. I do not remember who the opposing team was.

There was also Disney World and Epcot Center in Orlando; Busch Gardens in Tampa; driving to Tampa with the Billings and the Birds to watch "jai alai" matches and bet on them at the Fronton; the sunken gardens in St. Petersburg we used to tour when we visited Fran's sorority sister, B.J. Carlson and also a similar garden in Sarasota which had a collection of wildly colored parrots; Sea World and the Pelican Man, who rescued injured birds; and the manatees, especially Snooty in his private pool, chomping on lettuce and carrots fed to him by his keeper, swimming alongside him at the Bishop Natural History museum in Bradenton. In 30 years, we saw a lot of what Florida has to offer but only scratched the surface.

Thinking back on these memories as I have recalled and related them here, I fear that the reader may feel that only sunny, happy things filled my days; and this was largely true in the early years. But as we grew older, age began to become a force to be reckoned with and some clouds began to appear. We did all the normal check-ups with the skilled doctors we found in Florida. I had a "trigger" finger repaired by a hand specialist who came from Chicago and attracted patients from Europe. Finding patients was not a problem; he liked the weather. The few problems I faced were well handled and I was very impressed with my new cardiologist.

Fran had never had any serious physical issues except a varicose vein operation early in our marriage, the slipped disc which seemed to take care of itself, and the glass vase shattering and cutting the tendons on her ring finger. She spent most of her time kissing me on my way into an operating room.

However, she injured her right shoulder using a trowel to weed the circle in the driveway at the entrance to St. Matthews Church in Brecksville in preparation for our middle daughter, Kathy's up-coming wedding. The dirt was as hard as concrete and she caused permanent damage to her right shoulder. The whole family went down to the church and helped the truck driver unload and install the new pews which arrived two days before the wedding. And I washed the high entry windows of the church.

I am not going to recount every detail that remains in my memory. Much of it is too painful; no point in rehashing such unpleasantness and reliving the pain and suffering.

This is true regarding our oldest daughter, Nancy's struggle with cancer. If my memories are correct, Nancy's ordeal begin about the year 2001, when she stopped at our condo late one afternoon (John was still on the golf course) and she was hardly able to breathe. I persuaded her to let me take her immediately, not to wait for John to get home, to Blake Memorial Hospital where they drained a liter of fluid from the area between the sac containing the lungs and her ribs and kept her overnight. When we visited the next evening, she waited until John was out of the room, and then told us very solemnly that they had found cancer cells in the fluid. It was a terrible blow, but she was confident that she could overcome the disease: her sister, Kathy, had just survived breast cancer, and her best friend from high school days, Danni Gentile, had also overcome cancer.

Nancy had been part of her support team and was already planning how to assemble her own team from her friends at Vizcaya. Furthermore, the Moffitt Cancer Center that serves the whole southeastern part of the U.S., located on the campus of the University of South Florida in Tampa was easily accessible via I-75 and only an hour's drive away.

Nancy was referred to Moffit by the doctors at Blake Memorial Hospital in Bradenton, and we took her and John to her appointment for admission. It is a very impressive institution. She liked the doctor assigned to her immediately. John, who was in deep denial from day one, suggested a round of golf with her doctor at a nearby golf course, hoping to gain a more personal interest in his new patient.

I think we visited again two days later and learned that hers was a very rare form of cancer, peritoneal cancer of the lining of the sac containing the intestines and reproductive organs; no single large tumor which could be removed surgically, but many small nodules. Nancy responded well to treatment and was put on a course of chemotherapy which required that she stay in Florida that summer while the treatment was working. It was apparently successful; and she tolerated the chemo well. I remember a photo of her and one of our neighbors at Vizcaya Para-sailing above the Gulf, towed by a powerboat.

I also remember our whole family gathering that fall at the holiday season and all of us going over to Holmes Beach on Anna Maria where there was an Arts & Crafts festival in progress. I remember because I bought a leather belt, handcrafted for me on the spot, for which I paid $10 and am still wearing every day.

We had put up our artificial Christmas tree in the corner of the living room and I think this may have been the year that Fran decorated it entirely in pink, using hand-tied pink satin bows as decorations. We sat around the tree after dinner and exchanged presents, and Fran and I had this terrible feeling that this, her 56th, was to be Nancy's last Christmas.

Earlier that fall we were dismayed when symptoms returned, and Nancy had to reenter Moffit, and now it was learned that she suffered from ovarian cancer, which did not respond to chemo, and when Moffit could do no more for her, she was sent home to Vizcaya.

I can envision clearly, the second bedroom in their condo set up as a hospital room thanks to Hospice, a wonderful support. There always seemed to be a vigil of three or four of her friends to fetch things and run errands and take care of her patio garden.

She was in constant pain and a morphine pump was used, administered by the Hospice people.

There was a steady stream of friends, family, and former students from all parts of the country and she was able to say goodbye to many friends and relatives. She was able to manage her final days with grace and dignity, which she had promised herself, and succeeded in doing for which I was proud and grateful.

One Sunday morning after her return home, I walked the short distance to their condo for some trivial reason or other and found John, who still had hopes that she would be one of the few who recovered from this terrible disease and they would play golf together again, helping and encouraging Nancy to walk around the living room to regain her strength. It was lucky I happened to arrive when I did because she was nearing collapse, and it took both of us to get her back in bed safely. I believe that was the last time she left her bed, and John finally faced his reality.

A few weeks later she had her 56th birthday and Fran and I took a little 6" birthday cake over to celebrate, hoping she could get a bite down. She tried, but it was a mistake. At this point the only thing she could tolerate was wiping her lips with a mini foam paintbrush dipped in ice water.

After her second return from Moffit, at Fran's suggestion, she went over to their condo at midnight and spent the nights trying to comfort Nancy and allow John to get some sleep. I remember spending most of my afternoons sitting in their living room listening for her call for help, for more morphine for the pain and brushing her lips with ice water. By this time, it was obvious to me that the end was drawing near. I remember the bitterness I felt at being so helpless, and my wonder at how a beneficent Deity could allow such suffering.

Two or three years earlier I had started a poem for Nancy on her birthday, trying to the express the depth of my love for her, what it meant to me to claim her as my child, and my pride in her accomplishments. For some reason I was unable to finish it. I now retrieved it and was able to finish it and I think, I am sure, the inspiration was her impending birthday and her health. As Fran and I observed, first-hand, our impending loss, Fran wrote a long letter to Nancy. She never discussed its contents with me, and I never had a chance to read it, which is one of my great regrets.

We took the letter and the poem with us to her birthday "party" and asked John to read them to her when he thought she might be able to understand. John has no recollection of this or of the letter or the poem. The letter was never found, and my poem was discovered at the bottom of a pile of magazines on a bedside table.

Nancy's loss was made more terrible for Fran for not knowing whether her final words to her daughter had been heard or understood.

Perhaps we should have been more insistent and read our farewells to her ourselves even though she would have undoubtedly been unable to understand.

Fran's not knowing if her letter had been read was devastating to her and she never got over it. I think it was the beginning of a deep depression, which she could not overcome and led her to new medications by her Florida internist and treatment by psychiatrists in Ohio. I remember the many times I naively urged her to think positively, to feel gratitude for all the good in her life, to no avail. In my own way I was as unrealistic as John, holding on desperately to beliefs that might ward off, or reverse the inevitable.

I remember how endless the days seemed. Nancy's worsening condition, the uncontrollable cries caused by the pain, the faint, sickly, distinctive odor, associated with cancer, called "ascites" I was told,. when entering the front door of their condo (I hope I never smell it again), all made me silently beg for her release. I was actually praying for the death of my own daughter. I remember feeling horror for such a wish and a little shame at being able to rationalize it.

On June 6th, 2003, two days before Fran's birthday. John called about 1 p.m. and said we should hurry over because he thought the end was near and felt we would want to be present. We dropped everything and when we arrived found four of the posse sitting in the living room, Nancy in her bed, pale and comatose.

We gathered around her bed and Fran held her left hand, I, her right, and John was at the foot of the bed. At 2:15 p.m. Nancy took her final breath, and a great spirit left this world and was free at last. I remember feeling an odd mixture of terrible loss, and relief that the suffering was at an end at last. It was the first time I had ever been present at a death and I pray I will never have that experience again. I now could say with absolute authority that no parent should ever have to bury his own child.

I don't remember how we ever walked that short but very long distance home, but later that afternoon John called and asked if we would like to come over to view Nancy's body before the undertakers removed it for cremation. We both refused. We had seen the deterioration of her body, and now needed to replace those images with memories of the original vital, exuberant Nancy we were so familiar with.

We helped John select the burial urn to contain her ashes which he transported back to Ohio. It was such a tremendous personal loss for him that he could not face planning a memorial service for Nancy, and only agreed to one after we told him that there would be, had to be, a memorial service, which we would plan and pay for, if necessary.

John enlisted his brother Bob's aid. I remember meeting John and his brother at his brother's church on Dover Center Road in Westlake, where we met the minister who would preside. She was a young graduate of the Yale Divinity School and I felt very comfortable with her, and with her help.

On July 31ˢᵗ, the service was held with a reception afterwards. It was the largest memorial I had ever attended and when it was concluded and we were leaving, I remember feeling a sense of comfort and satisfaction that Nancy's contributions to her community had been properly recognized.

John arranged for the interment of the urn for which we were not present. Their grave is head to head with ours, which I had not realized before, and I secured permission from Lakewood Park Cemetery to purchase at my expense, and plant a Japanese tree peony about 15 feet from our two gravesites as a memorial. A well-established tree peony will live and bloom for up to a hundred years, and I thought this a very fitting form of memorial: something beautiful for generations to come to admire and give pause for reflection.

I selected a variety named "Hana Kisoi," an example of which Nancy had in her yard on Erie Road in Rocky River, which bloomed so profusely that motorists passing by stopped to inquire what is that? I remember how frustrated I was at the difficulty to find a grower who had a "Hana Kisoi" in stock. It took me two or three years, but finally the plant arrived and was planted.

It is now mature and a year ago produced one of the most beautiful peony blossoms I have ever seen in spite of growing in excessive shade. It is a large, loose double blossom, deep flesh pink, and both the bush and the blossom have an oriental air of mystery about them.

I have aroused the interest of the head groundskeeper at the cemetery and he has taken over the care of the plant now that I am no longer able to do so. The bush/shrub is large and easily grown. I have always thought its shape was intriguing, almost like a natural version of a professionally shaped bonsai miniature tree.

As the years passed in Florida, Fran had cataract surgery on both eyes, a tooth implant, and physical therapy for her shoulder. On a Wednesday morning she drove to one of her regular therapy sessions, which took place at Blake Memorial Hospital in Bradenton in a building separate from the hospital, but adjacent to the parking area.

When she walked to the car after the session, she tripped and fell between our car and one of the doctor's cars and damaged the same shoulder again. She could not regain her feet for a long time and when she did, returned to the physical therapy building that she had just left. Wednesday was her regular bridge game day in the afternoon at Mariners Cove, and I usually took the opportunity to go to the DeSoto Square Mall for lunch and a movie. Luckily, Fran was able to call me just before I left, and I was able to join her at the hospital.

The wait for a person in pain to be seen by someone on the medical staff was endless, and in fact the first person to see Fran was the hospital's attorney. X-rays were taken and the doctor said that there was no break but recommended that she see an orthopedic specialist. Fran's pain was severe and constant.

The next day we went to the orthopedic man who took one look at the x-ray and said there was, indeed, a break and pointed out the line on the x-ray that even we could see. She was referred to Dr. John Moor, who was the Chicago White Sox team physician while they were in Sarasota for spring training.

From this point on my memories, especially the chronology, are a jumble. I know that Fran underwent four procedures in four years involving her shoulder, enduring the pain, while dealing with her depression, and never complained.

Dr. Moor recommended a half shoulder replacement, which involved removing the natural knob at the end of the femur in the shoulder socket, and replacing it with a metal one at the end of a short stem, which would be embedded in the femur. He performed the surgery at Doctors Hospital, a smaller private hospital on the Tamiami Trail near Cattleman Road. I was very impressed with the amenities at this hospital; it had many small touches to make the patients feel more comfortable.

The operation was a success; and we went to Dr. Moor's office (walls covered with photographs of baseball players) for a course of physical therapy for several weeks. The pain persisted and she did not regain the use of her arm for which Dr. Moor had no explanation.

We then went to another orthopedic man for a second opinion who took x-rays that revealed that the stem of the new knob was not aligned properly and the angle the new knob met the socket was causing the pain and the slow recovery. He recommended more surgery to correct the problem. It was now May and we were planning the departure date for our return to Ohio. I had just received a diagnosis of cancer of the prostate and before deciding to have that surgery done in Florida, we decided we both would consult with the Cleveland Clinic as soon as we could after our return to Ohio.

Fran saw Dr. William Seitz who did an exploratory operation to determine the condition of the shoulder joint, followed by a conventional whole shoulder replacement at a later date. I saw Dr. Arthur Cieske at the main campus who confirmed the findings of Dr. Curtis in Florida, and after hearing the same three options for treatment; surgical removal of the gland, radiation treatment which meant three trips a week for six weeks, or radioactive seed implantation which was done in a single procedure taking about 45 minutes, I opted for the latter. The only drawbacks to the radiation route were the resulting incontinence, which was a nuisance, and not being able to hold our first great-grandchild, Hattie Mae Whiteacre, when we visited later that summer. I was not allowed within 6 feet of the child because of my radioactivity, which decreased 50% every two weeks.

Dr. Seitz performed the first of his two surgeries on Fran's shoulder successfully, and she went to regular physical therapy sessions at the old Lutheran Hospital on W.25th Street and Franklin Boulevard, which was a convenient location for us to reach from our small condo in Lakewood in the Clifton Boulevard and W. 117 Street area.

Seeking an answer for Fran's continuing pain Dr. Seitz, a year later, performed an exploratory operation to determine the condition of the new joint and the rotator cuff and deltoid muscles. I think he came to the conclusion that there was nothing more he could do for her. Meanwhile, Fran's pain persisted, and I continued to perform all household duties, which had begun when Fran came home from the first operation at Doctors Hospital in Sarasota. I did her nails and even ironed my knit shirts in the beginning.

While these health issues were being faced, many other things were happening in other aspects of our life. My apartment investment in Columbus was not doing well and, under constant pressure, I made many poor decisions that led to its ultimate foreclosure.

I was forced to change the management company by the FHA, which I should have done immediately after the acquisition, but I was operating under my theory that more could be accomplished with honey than vinegar, and I stayed with the original management company far too long. Along the way the FHA seemed to become my adversary, forcing me to do things I might otherwise not have done. I think they were accustomed to dealing with large builders and were not accustomed to dealing with an individual investor, although the rules and regulations called for the same treatment for both categories of ownership.

When the day came that foreclosure and loss of the property was imminent, I remember how bitterly I faced up to the reality that I was not going to be a hero to my children; I had hoped to do one more tax free exchange and if that had happened, would ultimately have left each of the daughters more than a million dollars after our deaths.

Now, a family meeting was called at our estate planning attorneys' office, attended by my entire family, attorney and C.P.A. also, and we undid thousands of dollars of planning, establishing trusts, etc., and faced up to the IRS attempting to recoup the accelerated depreciation I had been taking which provided the tax shelter we had enjoyed for so many years. This was when I learned that in spite of there being no personal liability for the debt and nothing to fear from the holder of the mortgage personally, the IRS was standing there with its hands out waiting to recoup all those years of depreciation - at one time, if possible. They were the unseen enforcers.

At the family meeting it was decided that everything in my name had to be transferred to Fran, my Trusts, dissolved, and then we would have to wait and see what the IRS would do. In the end they did nothing; the paper losses were so large that no taxes, which could have been confiscatory, were due.

We had begun to feel that in spite of our planning on being able to spend our old age at 5320 Oakes, and designing the house so that we could live comfortably on the ground floor, after 40 years, maintenance was becoming too heavy, and I could not find people to keep the yard the way I wanted it, so we decided to downsize.

As part of the new financial strategy, we established a Charitable Remainder Trust with Yale University as the beneficiary, with myself and Bernie Mandel, my attorney, as the managing

Trustees. The house on Oakes Road was the largest asset in the Trust. My theory was that if the IRS tried to take our home away from us, they would have to deal with Yale and its legal resources, rather than an individual.

We were not very successful in operating the Trust; its value decreased every year, and after two or three years I persuaded Yale to take over the management. They could see that based on our record in a few years there would be nothing left in the Trust, which was paying us income based on the declining value of the trust every January 1st. This meant that 5320 Oakes had to be sold before we turned the Trust over to Yale because any real estate held in a Yale Charitable Trust had to be free and clear.

Thus, in addition to all the other stress in our lives, I had to face the loss of what I felt was the defining element of my persona, the wonderful house in which I had invested so much thought and personal effort. The most bitter pill to swallow, disregarding the evidence of the passage of time, was that the broker we employed could not find a buyer. No one else saw in the house what I did. I had delusions that the house would be snapped up the minute it hit the market which turned out to be far from the case.

In preparation for this major change in our lives, as one option, we had checked out rental apartments and discovered that one of the major Westside apartment owners, the Zaremba family, had several locations where they would lease a fully furnished apartment, with cleaning services provided, for a six month term. We seriously considered doing this but did not like the idea that we would probably not be able to have the same apartment the following year after our return from Florida. We considered renting a large ground floor unfurnished apartment on an annual basis in a development on Stearns Road south of I-480, where we could leave our things while we were in Florida, and come back to the same place every year.

But, in our searching we had seen a free standing, basementless, Bob Schmitt built condo at Mills Creek West, off Center Ridge Road in North Ridgeville. (Our company had provided financing for Bob Schmitt Homes in the same area many years before.)

The house was 12 years old, built around a patio, lots of glass but complete privacy, had a fireplace, skylights in the kitchen and master bath, and this was what we settled on. It was known as a zero-lot line condo and the west wall was one foot from the lot line and had no windows. The master bedroom was at the rear and looked out on trees and the rear of a wooded lot. The house had many built-ins and had some of the same feel that 5320 Oakes did, on a smaller scale.

I remember vividly our experience with Bob Schmitt, the builder. I knew him from our business, but he was my brother, Russ's customer. He was probably the best builder of mid to upper-range homes in the entire state of Ohio. He refused to build a home with a basement, feeling he could provide equal storage area for less money above ground. He used non-union labor, who worked as teams for all the trades. The FHA appraised his homes for more than the sales price, which was unheard of.

One could pick out a lot, sit with Ed Schmitt, architect, Bob's brother, and have a house designed to meet one's family needs, and move into an 1,800-2,500 square foot house six weeks later. Every house in the subdivision was custom designed so there was homogeneity, but variety was achieved by the different elevations. No two homes looked the same.

We wanted to replace the carpeting in our new home before moving in and after the old carpeting was ripped up, and before the new laid, we visited and noted immediately a serious crack in the concrete floor running from the corner of the patio, the narrowest point in the house, southwest through the hallway, the corner of the laundry and the master bath. No expansion scoring had been used and the crack, caused by shrinkage of the concrete, was jagged and a half inch wide. We pointed this out to the broker who had no way of knowing, was shocked and said she would report it to the builder. A few days later we were asked to be at the house so repairs could be made.

At the appointed hour, I saw a Cadillac drive up, pop the trunk and a well-dressed individual appear, wearing an ultra-suede sport jacket and gabardine trousers. He took a 5-gallon bucket out of the trunk with tools in it, and when he came to the door I recognized him immediately: it was Bob Schmitt, himself, come to do the repairs personally on one of his twelve-year-old houses.

He got on his hands and knees and filled the crack with some sort of epoxy material, scraped off the excess, mixed up some mortar and troweled it over the crack. I couldn't believe it. He came back two or three days later and finished the job.

I remember two surprises connected with this transaction. One of the brokers who came to see 5320 Oakes with the thought of possibly listing it was Bob Schmitt's daughter, who was a real estate broker, and had sold many of his homes, and had to be very familiar with contemporary architecture.

I remember sitting with her in our living room, after having done her inspection and telling her the story of how it all came about, but she did not like the house and turned down the chance to list it. I never understood this. Perhaps it was the four living levels, after being accustomed to a single level living produced by her father.

The other disappointment was the first appraiser, whom I knew casually from my membership in the Society of Residential Appraisers. He was highly regarded; and I was appalled at his lack of imagination when he turned in his appraisal with a ridiculously low value.

He had used the standard residential appraisal method accepted by the banks and savings and loan associations for typical houses on typical residential lots, ignoring the replacement cost per square foot determined by the quality of materials used and the age and condition. and relied on "comparables." In this method the appraiser finds three recent sales of similar properties, makes adjustments for time of sale, and location, averages the numbers and arrives at value.

There were no comparable properties in Brecksville at the time of his appraisal; so, he had to go far a-field, and one of his comparables was a large Gothic style house in Independence, Ohio.

When I questioned his opinion and asked how he could use the "comparable" method when none of his comparables were similar in any way to our house, he had no answer. Instead he asked how I would have done it, and I said, "Cost per square foot less depreciation," depreciation taking into account age of the structure and its physical condition. He replied that that would have required too many adjustments. I just looked at him and said, "You didn't have to make any adjustments on your comparables"?

I then turned to my friend, Bill Braman, who did a massively detailed appraisal with a much more realistic value, which we were able to use to establish the value of the Charitable Trust. I know I saved a copy of this appraisal but have not referred to it and do not remember the final value. The endowment people at Yale accepted it and we proceeded to try to sell the house.

If any evidence of the vagaries of memory were needed, I offer as an example my complete lack of memory of the details of the financial side of our many real estate transactions. My memory is a total blank as to the final sales price of our Oakes Road house. I do remember finding the records I kept during construction and the cost of the addition and other capital improvements over the years and being surprised that it totaled about $250,000, with no value allocated for my three years of labor during the construction period, or later years' exterior painting. I don't know where the money came from.

And, yet I cannot recall the sales price when our broker brought us a deal a year after the house was listed for sale. I cannot remember the various refinancings, and I cannot remember the price we paid for the North Ridgeville condo, or how it was financed.

To me, this is very odd. I think it's strange that I do remember selling the rear six landlocked acres of our land in Brecksville for $135,000 to developers, and paying our neighbor, Ed Kregenow, $1,500 for a strip of land along our westerly lot line to round off our frontage on Oakes Road to 300 feet, which enabled us to create two sub lots with 100 foot frontage for sale, if we chose.

After several years of very comfortable living in our Bob Schmitt condo on Cedar Branch Circle, and getting to know North Ridgeville where my cousins, the David Gaedes grew up; two of our daughters, Nancy and Barbara bought condos in the same development and we had the pleasure of their being our neighbors. It was a joy having them so near.

We had one further downsizing in Ohio. We were spending fewer and fewer days in Ohio, which strengthened our position as citizens of Florida for tax purposes, and a reverse mortgage on that condo helped our financial picture there, I felt our cost of maintaining a permanent residence in Ohio was disproportionate. It was a reality that was hard to accept. We started a search for a small apartment to lease, or a condo to buy, and ended up buying a condo on Clifton Boulevard in Lakewood, Ohio, a short distance west of W.117th Street. It had about 600 square feet, two elevators, was on the fourth floor, and had an underground garage which was great for storing our Ohio car over the winter, and it had a swimming pool on the 7th floor, and a very nice party room In addition it was an extremely convenient location.

In this instance I do remember the sales price: $64,000, which we thought was a bargain. And I remember getting our mortgage from First Federal Savings & Loan Association of Lakewood, an 80% loan, but I do not remember the interest rate. The loan officer's sister lived in the same building.

Later we made a Home Equity loan to buy our daughter, Barbara's, father-in-law's Cadillac, after his death (owning a Cadillac was a dream I never had). Thus, at age 80, I was returning to live in the city I grew up in and was pleased that the city had remained so viable, and it was fun for me to drive through areas I had walked in as a teenager, going to school, or the library, or on a date. It was not fun to live so close to the church I had grown up in and loved with its unusual architecture and see it abandoned and slowly decaying.

We bought when the real estate bubble was getting ready to pop and when it did, we found that we could not sell the condo for anywhere near the amount of the mortgage balance.

We had to default on the condo mortgage. Although all my business life had ingrained into my thinking that debt is sacred and a promise that must be kept. I felt we were among the little people who were victims of a gigantic fraud; a market manipulated from top to bottom, starting with the real estate broker who located the unwitting buyer who was told he could own a home with no down payment and needn't worry about his credit; who never had the realities of the simple mathematics of how interest is computed or how long it takes to pay off 5% of the principal on a 100% mortgage with a 30-40 year term; to build even enough equity to pay a broker's commission; let alone understand, if he did get an explanation from the broker or mortgage lender before closing; to the appraiser; to the mortgage companies; to the title companies; and to the investment bankers on Wall Street, who made more money than all the accomplices combined by packaging these mortgages according to yield and selling them as bonds, guaranteed by the government (FHA and FNMA) so no one could lose, including the ultimate owner of the mortgage.

Except the homeowner when the bubble burst. And he didn't lose many dollars because he hadn't put any in and didn't have enough time (8 to 10 years) to accumulate 5% of the loan in the form of reduced debt. He just lost his home where he and his family lived. Thus I rationalized the decision to default: not very admirable. But we were operating under the old, honest guidelines with a 20% cash down payment to lose and the bubble bursting should not have affected us. But it did.

While all this was going on, our daughters, very aware of our increasing age, had been subtly suggesting that perhaps it was time to stop driving the long, boring distance to Florida and back every year and we should try flying. Kathy and Stephen had decided to leave Illinois with its terrible financial situation, with financing of libraries at risk and found library jobs on the west coast of Florida about an hour north of Tampa.

They pointed out that Barb and Pete could take us to the Cleveland airport and get us on the plane, and they would meet the plane in Tampa and drive us down to Bradenton and see us settled in. At this time Continental Airlines had non-stop service between Tampa and Cleveland at a very favorable time of the day. We were persuaded. And after our first flight decided that this was the only way to go back and forth; why hadn't we done it sooner? Two and one-half hours in the air was an excellent trade-off for two and one- half days driving, and less risky.

I don't remember what year we initiated this plan, but I do remember the last year we used it. In 2010, I happened to notice an article in the *Bradenton Herald* telling of a new shoulder procedure being done on the East coast of Florida in Atlantis, near Palm Beach. It was a reverse replacement in which the socket of the shoulder was moved to the arm, and the ball was attached to the body. According to the article a 70-year-old man had been able to resume playing handball after the procedure. I learned later that the procedure was done in Cleveland and was surprised that Dr. Seitz at the Cleveland Clinic had not proposed it to Fran, after she did not regain the use of her arm and was still in constant pain.

I contacted the doctor, Dr. Howard Routman, and made arrangements to drive to the east coast for a consultation to see whether he felt Fran would be a good candidate. I remember being quite impressed with him and his staff. His offices were in a medical office building adjacent to the new Robert Kennedy Medical Center, a very large, new (two-three-year-old) hospital, where Fran's procedure was finally done. I remember clearly his report after the procedure was finished successfully that her pain was gone, which he had predicted, no matter what the outcome regarding her use of the shoulder. I remember thanking him profusely for restoring my wife to me.

I remember staying in a motel in West Palm Beach, the night before the procedure, because of its name: The Barefoot Postman. (This was the name of one of the first movies I ever saw; before the railroad was extended down the east coast of Florida there was a postman who walked the beaches barefoot, delivering the mail, from St. Augustine to Miami). After the procedure we stayed in a Marriott in a suite that was almost as large as a single-family home, which was welcome because we had to stay for a week until she could have her post-operative checkup.

On the way home to Bradenton, we learned of the death of Dad's second wife who had been suffering from dementia for several years. This meant the dissolution of my father's Family Trust and disposition of the funds, which posed a different kind of problem for us: how to invest the proceeds. I had not been following the market since the time of Fran's mother's death, and certainly did not want to invest in real estate again.

It came to me that the Swiss franc annuity we had purchased years before was probably the best investment we ever made, and why wouldn't it make sense at our age to try to find another Swiss annuity. We were successful, and together with the inheritance dollars and scraping together most of our other cash, we bought a second, smaller annuity which will pay quarterly dividends in a fixed number of Swiss francs, and used to purchase US dollars and deposited in our local bank account until the second of us dies.

I remember that after we returned to Vizcaya, although the persistent pain Fran suffered disappeared, she spent increasing amounts of time in her bed. She lost interest in things about her and I had trouble in persuading her to go out once or twice a week for an Early Bird special, which she had previously looked forward to. She showed no interest in TV and no longer enjoyed reading. It's awful to contemplate that she was aware that there was something wrong with her mind, and that she was afraid she might suffer the same fate as her childhood friend, Annabel Hess, who died from Alzheimer's. Worst of all was not being able to use her shoulder.

At this point, I attributed her behavior to the lingering effects of her grief over losing Nancy seven years earlier. I continued trying to encourage her and thought if she could drive again, it might restore some interest in her life.

One afternoon, after lunch at the Piccadilly Cafeteria, I drove to the empty parking lot of the Community College near Vizcaya, stopped the car, helped Fran get behind the wheel and she drove in circles and backed up, stopped and restarted the car. She did so well I allowed her to leave the parking lot and drive home to Vizcaya where she negotiated the security gate and parked the car in our spot. It was the last time she ever drove. Her success did not produce the stimulus I had hoped for, arousing more interest in her surroundings, perhaps to venture out on some errand or other. It was a great disappointment; and I continued my household chores and caring for her.

Fran started taking Zyprexa, a very dangerous new anti-depressant on the market, in addition to the other medications she was taking for depression, prescribed for her by her doctor, Dr. Linda Maynard, who was originally from Saginaw, Michigan. Fran was comfortable with her since she was from a neighbor city of Midland, and was where Fran had her dental work done when she was a girl. The new drug was not effective (I was glad when her use of it was discontinued) and Fran started spending 20-22 hours a day in bed, only leaving her bed to use the bathroom and come to the kitchen table for meals. This continued when we returned to Ohio.

Now, our daughters who were watching over us and who had orchestrated my giving up driving to Florida, not insisting but allowing me to come to my own conclusions, exposed us to the idea of leaving Florida permanently. In the year 2010, we left Florida, as usual, about the first of June, with reservations for our return in October, and flew back to Cleveland.

We never did return to our condo in Florida, which our daughter, Kathy, closed up for us, and after a long search, Barbara bought this new, large, luxurious house on Prairie Moon in a Del Webb established adult community. I lease it from her, and the rent is the total of her carrying cost.

This was necessary because of the damage I had done to my credit rating when defaulting on the mortgages on our condo in Lakewood.

It seemed that no sooner than our housing problem was solved, that a new search started seeking a suitable nursing home for dementia patients.

I remember how concerned I was that the amount of time Fran spent in bed was affecting her muscle tone and ability to walk. I urged, cajoled, even threatened her constantly to get out of bed and use her Rollator to walk around the house. I remember observing her, eyes half closed, trudging around a circular path in our house, our large, new house.

Shortly after our arrival we made an appointment for Fran to see her new Ohio internist, Dr. John Geraci, who is also Barbara and Pete's doctor. She was barely able to walk to the garage and almost collapsed getting to the car, and I was barely able to save her. Dr. Geraci took one look at her and immediately called St. John's Hospital which is located almost across the street from his office; and arranged for her to by-pass the Emergency Room and be admitted directly into a room. I realize now that she was very close to death that day.

I think she was in the hospital for a week before she was stabilized enough to go to a nursing home for re-hab. Barbara and Pete had scouted various nursing homes near us and I went to look at their first choice, the O'Neill facility on Center Ridge Road about four miles from our new house in Pioneer Ridge. It seemed very suitable and Fran spent the next six weeks there recuperating and rebuilding her strength so she could return home. Sometimes Fran was in her room, a single, fortunately, napping; other days she would be in the physical therapy room and I would return her to her room after the session. Then she would nap, or I began reading aloud to her, which she seemed to enjoy.

She was highly motivated because she was able to understand that she would not be released to go home until she could walk unassisted from her room to the therapy room, a considerable distance, and get into our car unassisted. She persisted, passed her tests, and returned to our new home on Prairie Moon where she fell into her old habit of spending all her time in bed.

We were able to keep doctors' appointments, get her hair done once a week, and more and more infrequently, I was able to persuade her to go out for dinner. Among the doctors she saw were two psychiatrists, one at the Cleveland Clinic, a Dr. Sanitato, who was Italian not Japanese, and a Dr. Sung, who was German, not Chinese. She also saw a lady psychologist. None of the visits and counseling or the medications prescribed seemed to help.

A week prior to her hospitalization I remember how much I looked forward to a 90th birthday party for me at the Pioneer Ridge lodge, arranged by Barbara and Kathy, who came from Florida, to attend. I had been playing bridge for several months with the Pioneer group, who were very friendly, and it was suggested that I also invite them to come to the party, as well as family and friends. It was catered and held in the party room at the lodge.

I remember that our daughters had bought a new outfit, a suit dress, red, for Fran and it was lucky they were there because it was complicated for Fran to get into, and, if it had been up to me, I don't know if I could have done it. It was red, one of her colors and she looked her best. We borrowed a wheelchair from Pete's family and Fran sat in it the whole party and tried to carry on conversations with the guests. I remember her face seemed to be a frozen mask as she exchanged peasantries. This was the only time any of my new bridge playing friends ever saw her, and, I regretted so much that they had not known Fran in her prime, or known the person capable of creating the album celebrating my 50th birthday, which revealed her sense of humor, and we had brought to the party.

I remember the difficulty finding a hairdresser for Fran. After a few attempts at a nearby salon in Elyria, I knew she would be happier with Nadja, her old Lebanese operator in Cleveland on Clifton Boulevard near W. 117th Street, near our old Lakewood condo. So, we made the long drive from North Ridgeville to Cleveland every week until she had to enter the final nursing home.

As time passed my responsibilities, which I undertook gladly, increased. I stopped ironing tee shirts, and I no longer tried to find new recipes which might arouse Fran's interest in food.

The unceasing, 24-hour a day responsibility began to take its toll on me, and, to provide some relief, we found a home care person, Shirley McKenna, who came three times a week for four hours, on my bridge days, Monday evenings, Tuesday afternoons, and Thursday evenings. I would eat at a nearby restaurant and then play bridge for three hours which required intense concentration. It did provide some relief, but I always felt guilty and worried, even when I knew that Fran was being watched over by a professional caregiver.

Dr. Sanitato, the psychiatrist at the Cleveland Clinic, had suggested that we see a specialist in Lakewood and the result of that encounter was a diagnosis of dementia, the first time I had heard that word used which changed my whole attitude toward her situation. Now that I realized (and should have much sooner, being well aware of the condition of Fran's childhood friend Annabel Hess, in Chicago) that Fran was helpless to control her behavior and still lucid enough to be terrified at what her future would be, my care for her took on another dimension.

We were still living at 9125 Prairie Moon, but I was now 92 years old and not as physically capable as I was at an earlier age. Three things occurred that made a permanent change necessary.

I was awakened one morning about 6 a.m. by a loud voice, that of our next-door neighbor, calling out from inside our house; he had found the front door standing open. His wife had discovered Fran in her nightclothes pushing her rollator across their backyard toward a large retention pond. She rushed out and stopped Fran from tumbling down into the pond, and we got her back into bed. After that I made sure to turn on the alarm system every night, so that if a door was opened when I was asleep, theoretically I would have been awakened in time to prevent another "stroll".

The other two incidents involved falls. They occurred in the master bathroom, which has a clay tile floor, and the master bedroom, which is carpeted. Our pattern was that after I fed Fran her dinner and made sure she was comfortable; I would go into the living room and watch TV or read.

As I recall, the first fall happened when Fran had gotten up to go to the bathroom without alerting me and on her way back to bed her Rollator tipped sideways and she fell face first on the tile floor, ending up with her head against the cabinets, her nose bleeding profusely, and she had a large abrasion on her cheek. I heard the crash and rushed to help and after she was back in bed persuaded her that we should go to the Elyria Hospital Emergency Room for her to be checked out. I remember getting into the car and wondering where the hospital was located. I had seen it in my rare visits to Elyria, but the streets are not laid out in a regular grid plan, and I had a general idea, but no certainty. Again, I failed to call 911, and do not know why.

As it happened, I went north to Sugar Ridge Road, which becomes East Broadway after crossing S.R. 57 and continued on westwards and found the hospital easily, almost as though I had known where I was going. The Emergency Room was not busy at that time of night, and it was a great relief when Fran checked out all right: no concussion, but a broken nose, which they tended to and we were released to go back home.

The next fall was probably a year later and more serious. Again I was sitting in the living room watching TV 20 feet away from Fran's bed, and she had used the bathroom without alerting me, and was returning to her bed when once again the Rollator tipped over and she fell between the foot of her bed and her vanity. Once again, she broke her nose, and lay there, bleeding, crying feebly for help. When I finally heard, I don't know how much later, I rushed in to find her lying on the floor, her head in a pool of blood ten-twelve inches in diameter. I don't remember if the bleeding had stopped. (I was not smart enough to call 911.) It was a terrific struggle for me to try to help her back into bed. I no longer had the physical strength to do what would have been easy for me 10 years earlier. Once again, we went to the ER, with no arguments on her part. There was no concussion; and they treated her broken nose.

Sometime after recovering from this second fall, in one of her lucid moments, Fran talked to me seriously and said that perhaps it was time for her to go to an assisted living home. I had dreaded having to make this decision by myself, and I agreed that maybe it was time.

Barb and Pete had located a dementia facility in Olmsted Falls, Kemper House, devoted entirely to the care of people in various stages of dementia. They took me to inspect it and I was very impressed. It was located off Bagley Road about 10 miles from 9125 Prairie Moon, an easy drive, and I could use I-480 in bad weather to reduce road risk if necessary. This was important to me as I planned to spend as much time with Fran as possible, visiting every day, which I was able to do except for two occasions when there was too much fresh snow and I was allowed to stay overnight sleeping in a recliner in her room.

We thought it might help her for there to be something recognizable from her old world as she entered her new one. We brought pictures from home, which we were allowed to put on the walls, and brought our own TV set and bought a small table and chairs for me to use while eating after feeding her. I bought her a cell phone with family phone numbers programmed in it, so she would not feel isolated, but she was unable to use it. Her closet was filled with her clothes, and the nurses' aides dressed her every morning, but it did no good.

Kemper House was an attractive, newer structure, brick, two stories, a large rectangle with an attractive, usable courtyard accessible from the dining room. It had single and double rooms on both side of a corridor, which created a loop. It was perfectly safe for those residents who were able to, to roam freely since they always returned to their starting point. It had all the modern safety and security systems; so, I had no qualms about Fran being found wandering around in the parking lot. Before my decision was made, I was invited to meet the staff and to have lunch in their conference room and I thought the food was very good.

I remember vividly the day, July 24th, 2013, when I put Fran in the car, suitcase packed with her belongings, her favorite dresses and blouses, and I watched the garage door come down as we pulled away. Although we were allowed to sign a resident out for a visit, or to go to a restaurant, I realized with finality that this was the last time she would ever see her home at 9125 Prairie Moon, and probably the last time she would ever ride in our car. I don't remember her looking back as we drove away, or any particular interest in the route we took to Kemper House, which she was about to see for the first time.

Her first room was on the first floor, for which I was grateful, a double with a silent occupant I never saw or heard. It was across the hall from the dining room.

When I came for my first visit the next day after lunch, I found Fran in a group of twelve to fifteen occupants celebrating 'Christmas in July' on July 25th, on the front porch, singing Christmas Carols, which, somehow, I found reassuring. Sometime later, Fran agreed to go on one of the regular Wednesday afternoon 'Mystery Bus Rides' destination unknown but ice cream at midpoint. I was disappointed that she did not like this because of physical discomfort from the Kemper vehicle, and could not wait to get back to her bed. I was disappointed that this part of Kemper's program to provide mental stimulation for its residents was unsuccessful in our case.

Within a week a single room on the first floor (No. 126) became available and Fran was moved into it, and this was where she spent the rest of her days . It was fairly spacious, looked out on a natural setting at the rear of the building, and had a large closet, a kitchenette with an under-the-counter refrigerator and sink, but no cook-top and a large, private bathroom with stall shower. It was as far away from the dining room as possible, which meant a long walk for me when I brought her evening meal to her..

A pattern was quickly established: I remember in the early days joining Fran in the dining room for lunch once or twice but she did not seem to welcome this and the nurses-aides brought her to the dining room and helped her eat her food. I would appear after my lunch, in the early afternoon and stay through the dinner hour until she was readied for bed about 8:30 p.m. At this stage she had lost interest in my reading aloud to her or watching TV. I could not even get her to watch the Laurence Welk Show on Saturday night which had been one of our favorites.

In the first few months, we did go to the dining room for dinner. The nurse's aides would help Fran into her wheelchair; and I would push her down to the dining room, where we would find a table for two in a corner. She did not want to sit at a larger table with six or eight strangers.

There was a steady progression downward, however, and soon she refused to go to the dining room; and I started bringing her meals to her in her room and had to feed her. She was happy with this, and I would often stay in the room and eat the same meal at the little table next to the sink/refrigerator.

Many times, I went back to the dining room and sat at a table with the other residents who could feed themselves and had the same meal they did. One of these ladies lived in the room across the hall from Fran's room, and her son came every evening to feed her and in good weather wheel her out to the front porch where they would stay until bedtime. He was a snowplow driver at Cleveland Hopkins Airport. One of the other ladies at the table was Edna, who was still quite lucid. I used to sit next to her and heard the story many times of her growing up on a dairy farm and stories about her father. I don't think she ever had a visitor. There were not many daily visitors on the first floor.

I remember how surprised I was at the change in my attitude about nursing homes after Fran entered Kemper House. I had inspected and appraised two nursing homes located in Akron during my business days and was appalled at what I saw and was depressed for days afterwards.

I also accompanied Fran when she visited her fellow member of St. Matthews church, and bridge playing friend, Diane Obenauer's mother in a nursing home in Sagamore Hills. The few times I went with Fran and walked down the hall to the mother's room I cringed at the cries for help. Diane's mother was not suffering from dementia and was lonely because all the other residents were.

Diane's mother loved to play Rummi-Cubes and Fran would play with her. The mother liked to win and was not above some minor cheating to make that happen. She thought she was fooling Fran and that made it more delicious. I thought it was a great kindness that Fran gave up an hour or two on a Sunday almost every week to make these visits and know that Diane appreciated it.

From the beginning, I had none of these feelings when Fran became a resident of Kemper House. I was so impressed with the skill and care of the attendants, the obvious evidence of their ability to provide the necessary care, and the concern shown for the residents made a great impression on me. And I found that I had great sympathy for the residents. It was not offensive to see patients, helpless in wheel chairs with large bibs around their necks, the same faces night after night, being spoon fed by nurses-aides, who I knew would do their best to care for and protect Fran, something I could no longer do alone.

One exciting incident took place on one of my afternoon visits. One of the male residents was a small wiry man who wandered the halls singing in a Welsh tenor voice. I had noticed him in the dining room. His room was two or three doors from Fran's. The door to Fran's room was open and I was leaning over the bed straightening her bed covers, or helping her drink some water, when the little Welsh man entered the room, thinking it was his room, and attacked me, actually punching me, screaming, "You leave my wife alone." The nurses-aides appeared very promptly and subdued him quickly. I had put my arms up to protect myself, but did not try to strike back at him, and it made me wonder about my legal status if I had. I never found out if a visitor could protect himself if attacked by striking the resident or subduing him with force. The nurses told me that he died a few days later and I was no longer to worry.

One very disturbing thing happened to Fran while she was at Kemper House. I received a phone call one morning while still at home telling me that Fran had slid out of bed and fallen to the floor and was in pain. She was taken by ambulance to an orthopedic clinic in Westlake and evaluated. It was determined that she had dislocated her left hip, which they were able to reset without surgery. I went to the clinic while she was still there and met a Chinese doctor, Dr. Liu, (or Lew) who was a hip specialist. He said the problem was that Fran's left hip socket was congenitally malformed and there was not enough upper lip on the socket to retain the femur, and it was likely to happen again, and, if it did, surgery would be necessary, which he would be very reluctant to perform, given Fran's age and condition.

I asked if there were some sort of brace, which could hold the femur in place, and he gave me the name of a medical supply manufacturer in Lorain, Ohio, that might have something. After Fran was returned to Kemper House, I called the company in Lorain and they sent a man to examine Fran the next day, and the day after that he returned with a brace which he custom fitted.

It was steel and held in place by straps around her rib cage and her left leg above the knee, with a cushioned pivot joint at the hip, which applied pressure laterally to the hip joint and kept the femur in place.

This was a mixed blessing: probably no surgery, but almost total immobility. It meant Fran would spend the rest of her life lying on her back, unable to roll over or lie on her side. I hated the contraption. State law forbids patient restraints and Kemper Houser's solution to the problem was to bring in a separate twin-bed size mattress and place it on the floor next to her bed, which was lowered to its lowest setting. Thus, if another slip occurred, the fall would be to a soft surface and only a drop of about 6 inches. This was a nuisance when trying to provide assistance or feed her, the mattress had to be slid away from the hospital bed, or tilted up against the wall at the head of the bed, but it was a practical solution to the problem and there were no further falls from bed.

Her involuntary cries of "Help!" or "Help me!" became more incessant. It was very difficult to sit three feet away from Fran, having just rearranged her blankets, or given her a drink of water, and not know what to do or how to help. The nurses-aides responded on their patrols and when they asked how they could help, received no reply, only a continuation of the cries for help.

After three or four hours of this, I had to escape, and would go out to a chair in the hall and try to read. I think by now it was after the first of the year, and I foolishly kept hoping to see improvement. In my defense, the daily visiting brought me too close to her condition. The incremental deterioration of Fran's mental condition was so gradual that the reality did not register with me. It became more difficult to get her to eat, which was a major concern. Her weight had dropped from 165 to 106 pounds.

One of the older nurses, Helen, who administered the meds before dinner and who had a mother suffering from dementia, took me aside, and asked if I had considered calling in Hospice. I had never thought of this and did not know it was available in a nursing home. I thought it was for cancer patients sent home from the hospital to die.

She said, "No. It was available at Kemper House," and it did not mean death was immanent; that there was a patient with asthma on the second floor who had Hospice care for almost two years. She said that Medicare paid for any charges, and that the Hospice care was in addition to the regular nursing attention provided the patient by Kemper House. I thanked her and went to the office immediately and signed up for the service.

There was a team of two younger women from Hospice who were on the premises every day. They took over, the younger immediately trying to establish contact and a relationship with Fran, who appeared to like her.

The next day Hospice had a far more comfortable, larger wheel chair delivered, and from then on, when I took Fran for a ride around the corridor loop, we would stop at the corner nearest to her room where there was a built-in aviary with five or six live love-bird couples in residence that I found fascinating, but were of no interest to her. We used the luxurious piece of equipment, but usually, by the time we reached the dining room, half-way back to her room, Fran would be pleading to return to her bed.

The first week of April 2014, was particularly trying. On Monday she cried for help incessantly, moaned constantly, thrashing around in bed kicking off her blankets, which had to be replaced. She was unable to respond to my pleas or commands or those of the nurses-aides. However, on Tuesday, she had a quiet day and ate the complete dinner meal, even part of a second ice cream cup, and I was much encouraged.

Wednesday was a moderately restless day. I was told that she had refused to eat either breakfast or lunch, and I was unable to get her to touch her food at dinner. We spent the evening quietly and the nurse's aide came to get her ready for bed as I was putting on my jacket to leave.

Fran seemed to be asleep already so, I was surprised as I was tip-toeing out the door when she called out "You didn't kiss me goodnight." This was a first. She had never said anything like that before.

I responded quickly, "I can take care of that easily," slipped off my jacket and went over to her bed. But instead of going to the head of the bed and leaning over the headboard to give her the usual peck on the cheek, or forehead, I moved the twin-bed mattress away from the hospital bed, and approached her face on.

I rearranged her blankets which she already kicked off, tucked them in between the bed and the wall, and leaned over and asked, "Would you like your hands outside or under the covers?" She squirmed a little, and said, "I think under," so I tucked the covers under her chin and bent over for her goodnight kiss.

She was more lucid that I had seen her in months. And she invited me to kiss her on the lips, something I had not been able to do for years, literally. I will never forget how warm and velvety soft her lips were, and how tender. It was a lingering kiss, and when it was over I told her, "I love you so," and she replied, "I love you, too."

Then it was time to leave and I told her briskly, "I'll be back early tomorrow after lunch, and it's Thursday but I'll stay through dinner. I'm not playing bridge on Thursday nights anymore until your appetite comes back and you start eating again." Then I moved the mattress back into place, put on my jacket and left.

The next day, Thursday, started out typically. I stopped somewhere for lunch and then proceeded to Kemper House, parking in a handicapped spot at the front door. When I entered\, the first thing I saw was my son-in-law, Pete standing with one of the staff in the lobby, and with a sinking feeling, my first thought was that after that wonderful period of lucidity the night before, Fran had fallen again and broken something, or maybe had a stroke.

But, I learned quickly, that it was much worse. Fran had died an hour before. Kemper was able to reach Barb and Pete on their cell phone at their dentist's office before any work had been done, and they rushed from Lakewood out to Olmsted Falls, arriving only a few minutes before I did.

From this point on my memories are very hazy. After seating us in the conference room where we met the staff on our first visit and had lunch, we were told that Fran was taken to the dining room for lunch and had to be rushed back to her room because of severe respiratory distress, unable to breath and the respirator used to try restore her breathing failed, and she died surrounded by the nurses trying to help her. An hour later and I would have been there, and possibly Barb and Pete.

An hour later I do remember clearly being asked if I would like to view the body and declining, at which point Barbara said she did want to view the body and I did not want her to do that alone so we both were taken to the room with which I had become so familiar.

The wheelchair had been removed, the bed moved to a position with the head against the wall, and Fran looked as though she were peacefully sleeping. Her hair had been combed and her mouth was open as it usually was when she slept. Barbara and I sat, she at the foot of the bed, I at Fran's right side and contemplated and remembered.

Before we left I leaned over, one last time, and kissed Fran's forehead, which was cool and damp with sweat as the body heat dissipated, a terrible contrast to the night before, such a short time ago. This is the image I see when I look at the blank area of wall above my television set: the bed at right angles to the wall, with the figure of a small body of an old lady lying on it. If I close my eyes, I still see it after five years. The image is very clear; and I try to avoid looking at that area of wall above my television set.

I remember how mixed my emotions were when the reality of the news and the final viewing of the body set in. A numbing sense of loss, an uncertainty as to how I would go on living without her, but also an enormous sense of relief and joy that Fran was at last freed from the prison of a failing mind and body. The image that immediately came to mind was that of a picture I had seen of a Forest Ranger releasing a large bird from captivity and rehab, tossing it high, watching fly back to its home and its freedom.

Barbara and Pete were wonderfully kind to me; arranged for one of Pete's brothers to bring my car to their home; took me home with them where I stayed for a week while I tried to adjust to my new reality. The training I received from my mother, and the Army, plus ten years of doing all that was needed to care for Fran had prepared me to live alone, but it was a little hard to imagine what that would feel like.

I would still be sitting in my chair in the living room watching TV, but the difference would be that Fran would not be physically present in the next room lying in her bed, sleeping. I did not know what to expect. As a matter of fact, I did not find it difficult. My gratitude at her release from her suffering was so great that to adjust to a new routine, albeit a strange one in that I had only my own needs and desires to account for was not difficult.

The time spent previously attending to her needs now was available for thought and contemplation. The thoughts about the implications and reality of infinity which had been evolving ever since I wrote the earlier chapter of this book, Credo, now made me realize that the words in our wedding vow "Till Death do us part" were only partially true. I would forever be denied Fran's physical presence, but I know that her unique iota in the vastness of infinity, her spirit, which came into being at the instant of her conception cannot be destroyed because it is a part of infinity. Her death was ordained by her lifespan, and death is the change that released her from the diseased husk of her physical bounds to her true spiritual reality, consciousness intact, which is a part of an ever-expanding infinity. I find these thoughts to be very comforting, and, in a strange way, exciting.

I had cause recently to go through the body of poems I have written over my lifetime, and among them are two I wrote specifically for Fran as gifts for two important occasions: our Wedding and our 50th Wedding Anniversary. We had a discussion about a subject unusual for us, while driving somewhere, about our differing beliefs which reflected our different early religious training about the "afterlife" Since this is my story and I am the one telling it, I think I will include the 50th anniversary poem, written almost 25 years ago. I think its foretaste of where my thinking has led me today is interesting.

*Robert F. Schmidt*

## *PROTHALAMIUM*

*In that dark silence of the stellar deep*

*Whither my soul its lost mate shall seek,*

*Without aid of accustomed sense for guide,*

*Lost, lonesome, incomplete, wand'ring, searching,*

*Endless rooms of endless eternities.*

*Till surely, Oh My love, at last love shall be drawn*

*To its lost love again: two souls made one.*

*And all the promise of that first sweet promise*

*Shall be kept.*

*October 27, 1995*

For several weeks after I returned home, I continued to return to Barb and Pete's for my evening meal and I remember how comforting this was.

After a time, gradually, a routine was established: leave the house for lunch at one of the rota of restaurants I discovered; read while eating; bridge three times a week; brunch with Barb and Pete on Sundays, usually at the Blue Sky restaurant on Center Ridge Road at S.R. 57, where I had the same meal every time, a bacon & cheese omelet, much to Pete's amusement; dinner at home while reading; reading and TV until midnight; then read for an hour and lights out, the end of one more day. It was very humdrum and gradually the initial pain of loss and separation lessened.

I am ashamed and can't understand why I remember so little of Fran's funeral. I believe Barb and Pete took me out to St. Matthews in Brecksville for the Palm Sunday service three days after her death. We met the minister, the Reverend Stephanie Pace, who couldn't have been nicer or more accommodating had we been long time parishioners.

The traditional Episcopal funeral service was held in early May after Rev. Pace returned from a trip. I remember seeing many of the friends who had attended services at St. Matthews when I played the organ. We arranged for a professional organist to play for the service, a young woman, who was very good, but I don't know how we found her. There was a small reception in the Great Room after the service, and then the family and the Rev. Pace proceeded all the way from

Brecksville to the Lakewood Park Cemetery in Rocky River, where our daughter lies in a grave next to ours. I don't remember if this was when the burial urn was interred, or later in July when we had a graveside Memorial service, which the grandchildren, who could not come to the funeral, attended. It had to be under a canopy because it was raining, and I remember scattering ashes from a small hand-sized urn provided by the funeral director around the base of the tree peony I had planted as a memorial for Nancy, that would now serve as a memorial for Fran, also.

After the brief service, which was presided over by the Rev. Pace, who made the long trip from Brecksville to Rocky River again, everyone drove back to Barb and Pete's home in North Ridgeville where there was food and drink for everyone, and warm memories of Fran's extraordinary life were recalled.

Thus, a long life of 69 years together, faithful to each other, loving each other, with three children to be enormously proud of, a life full of rich memories in a beautiful home and widespread travels, came to an end. Now I am left in the sixth month of my ninety-ninth year as I write this, alone, in another beautiful home, surrounded by pictures of my wonderful family, and many beautiful mementos of our life together. And I think constantly of infinity and what it means.

# Chapter XIII

## Business Career & Investments

Any reader of this chronicle will notice that my accomplishments in the business world, such as they may have been, rank last in importance to me by being placed near the end of the chapters dealing with the things I enjoyed doing the most. All my life I remember reading stories of men whose business careers were the most important thing in their lives, taking precedence over every other aspect of their life, who were lost without their work and who died six months after their retirement.

My attitude from the beginning was totally the opposite of this. I hoped my job would be interesting, thank goodness the family business was not a butcher shop. That it would produce enough income so that I could provide a comfortable life for my family, and that there would be enough left over to allow me to indulge in other activities which were of real interest to me.

I remember feeling very grateful that there was a job waiting for me when I left the army; that because of my father's business background, there was also a suite in an apartment building he had bought as an investment which was ideal for me and my new bride to start our married life.

I can remember sitting at the breakfast nook table as a kid and listening to my Dad and Mother discussing some deal my Dad was working on, always involving real estate. My parents never had any desire to invest in the stock market, and certainly did not have enough money to do so if they had wanted to.

These early experiences which included getting to meet Mr. Fraser, Dad's boss, probably laid the foundation for my future career.

My father graduated from a good west side Cleveland high school, West Tech, in 1918, at the end of the First World War. There was not enough money in his family for him to go to college and he started his business life as a bank messenger. When A.D. Frasier started his mortgage company, my father was one of the first five men he hired. I remember a few of the names of the others, but not their duties: Byron Beum (a calligrapher); Harry Chandler; Mrs. Wilmot, (Mr. Frasier's secretary). Over the years Dad rose to become Vice President and Secretary of the A.D. Fraser Mortgage Company. I think the company must have been one of the early mortgage loan correspondent companies. Mr. Fraser had been able to secure contracts with several insurance companies to find real estate investments for them, and service the loans after they were funded, collecting the interest and principal payments monthly and remitting them to the holder of the mortgage. I remember hearing insurance company names like Metropolitan Life (the Met), Life of Virginia, Lincoln National, Midland Mutual and Western and Southern. These were only names to me at the time and I certainly did not understand the workings of the mortgage lending business at that early age. But the background was there, the foundation laid.

Dad had been in the business for about 20 years and had built a loyal following of real estate investors, mostly Jewish, many of whom he had helped save their properties from foreclosure during the Great Depression. Mr. Fraser had promised Dad that he could buy the company when he retired, and Dad was counting on it. However, I recall him talking about incidents at the office, both personal and business, which did not measure up to Dad's standards and he blew "the whistle;" his being a "teetotaler" did not help endear him to the others in the office either. I suspect that he was admired at the same time he was disliked.

I remember the company's office was on the fifth floor of the Guardian Bank building at Euclid Avenue and E. 6th Street. I can remember Dad, when I was six or seven years old, taking me with him on a Saturday morning (men worked half-days on Saturdays in those days) to sit outside the window of his office on the soot stained 30" wide stone sill overlooking Euclid Avenue to watch a long parade of Shriners (in Cleveland for their national convention) marching down Euclid Avenue in their colorful costumes, shiny balloon pants and turbans. Another Saturday, he took me to his office, undoubtedly, to get me out from under Mother's feet, and took me to Ander's Cafeteria on the second floor, at the corner of E. 4th Street and Prospect Avenue, a very popular eating place. I remember the delicious mashed potatoes with gravy.

In May, many years later, the Ander's son (one of four high school seniors that included Dick Neale and John Morgan from Shaw High School in East Cleveland) and me, were taken to the Sub-Frosh Weekend at Cornell University in Ithaca, New York, by a Cornell grad who was one of Dad's business friends. Cornell offered a degree in restaurant management, and Anders was the only one in our group who went there. The others had scholarships to Yale.

One day in the Spring of 1940, nearing the end of my freshman year, my weekly letter from home told me that Dad had either quit working at Fraser Mortgage or had been fired, I have never been sure exactly what happened.

This was very scary news. I can remember worrying how my parents could pay my college expenses with my brother, Russ, about to join me at Yale with a scholarship of his own. Would I have to quit school and get a job to help support the family? Even with the scholarship and mandatory bursary jobs, which paid for our meals, there was still the room rent and travel expense and fees to be paid, and for the two of us this would amount to $700-$800 minimum per year.

I remember sitting at the top of the stairs listening (when I was supposed to be in bed) to Mother and Dad, sitting next to each other on the sofa in the living room, worrying about what it meant for Mr. Fraser to have hired a man from Elkhart, Indiana, to take over many of Dad's duties. Did it mean that Mr. Fraser was changing his mind about selling his company to Dad after he retired? The man from Elkhart lasted less than a year, but immediately there was another threat: a man named Bill Miller who had two sons Phil and Bill.

I remember hearing that shortly after Miller was hired, he sat on the corner of Dad's desk and told him that if he thought he was going to get the company, he was wrong. He, Bill Miller, was going to be the new owner. I'm sure that was when Dad started looking for another job or thought of starting a new company of his own. He had learned how the mortgage business worked and had 20 years of experience. And plenty of motivation.

At this time Cleveland was the fifth largest city in the U.S. and headquarters for 34 of the Fortune 500 companies; its economy was strong; and it was growing. The Aetna Life and Casualty Insurance Company, with headquarters in Hartford, Connecticut was looking for representation in the mortgage market in northeast Ohio, where one of their largest insurance agencies was located. They approached one of Dad's old friends, Charley Braman, who was the mortgage loan correspondent for Connecticut Mutual Life Insurance Company.

The Bramans had three sons and a daughter and lived on Bunts Road in Lakewood, the street next west of Parkwood Road where we lived. I remember walking with my parents on a warm summer evening down Parkwood to Franklin Boulevard, west to Bunts Road and then north a half-block to the Braman's house for a visit.

Mr. Braman told the Aetna man, R. Douglas Swinehart, that he was having trouble supplying Connecticut Mutual with all the business they needed and that he did not want to take on another company. He could highly recommend someone, however, and suggested that he look up Frank Schmidt, hardworking, honest, Cleveland native with 20 years experience, who was looking for a new job. Mr. Swinehart, a graduate of Williams College, met Dad, liked what he saw, admired the family with two boys at Yale, and offered the correspondent position to Dad. And that is how what became the Schmidt Mortgage Company came into being.

The first office was No. 418, Leader Building at the corner of E. 6th Street and Superior Avenue, across the street from the Federal Reserve Bank and the Cleveland Public Library. It was a very small office with only 2 rooms, and an entrance off the elevator lobby.

It must have been a tremendous struggle at the beginning. The Aetna provided no support for their new correspondent and Dad had to buy the office furniture and supplies, run the business and find the mortgages which would provide the income to support his family and the new business.

There was no portfolio of existing mortgages to provide servicing income and there was no money with which to hire solicitors to find new loans, nor to hire a secretary. The new business was dependent on friends Dad had made at Frasers bringing him their business. Mother came to the office to do the typing for loan submissions and served as Dad's secretary and Dad operated the business from his personal check book, before he was required to open a commercial account, choosing National City Bank, where his old friend, Paul Minter, was head of the mortgage loan department. It was really starting a business from scratch, and remarkable that it succeeded.

It was understood, although no demands were ever made or pressure applied, that when World War II ended that my brother, Russ, and I would come to work for Dad in the new business which had survived and was now three years old.

Russ, who had worked in the office during the summer months while still in high school and was expert at the inside work of record keeping, so important to maintain the relationship with the Aetna, joined the company as an employee about 6 months before I was released from the Army and joined him in the outer office with its two desks and one sitting chair. Mother was at last released from office duty.

I remember how impressed I was with Russ's memory. He seemed to have a knack for being able to put a customer's face, or some other distinguishing characteristic, an unusual name, or strange occupation, with the loan number assigned by the Aetna.

In the beginning, monthly payments were hand posted with pen and ink on stiff yellow cards supplied by the Aetna, broken down to the amount charged for interest and credited to the principal which became the basis for the calculation of the nest month's interest. It was uncanny how Russ, if a name was mentioned in some question, could call out the loan number and go to the card. The pile of cards was growing thicker by the month, and we began to feel we were making a contribution to the business, which no longer was so dependent on Dad's old friendships developed at Frasers.

In all my thirty-three working years, I never had to create a resume, or fill out a job application form. My starting salary was $50 per week, which required some careful money management on Fran's part. We had a system for budgeting which involved taking an agreed amount of cash and putting it into an envelope with a designation written on its face: Rent - $50, Food - $50, Lunch - $15, Movies - $5, Church - $8, etc. It was supposed to add up to $100 every two weeks, and after the first week we found ourselves borrowing money from one envelope to put into an envelope that had become empty. My mother, when she heard of our budgeting plan was amused and told us that there would never be a "normal" month, and she was right

Our pay came directly from my father's pocket. Every time we were paid, it meant that much less for him and the rest of the family, now with two younger brothers. This remained true when we were granted small raises as the years passed. I am very hazy as to the occurrence of raises, but I know they happened.

Dad's philosophy was to keep the wages just adequate enough to cover ordinary family expenses. If money accumulated in the "wages" account, he would pay out a bonus, if possible, every 6 months. If it had all been paid out every month, it would be frittered away, whereas a six month accumulation might be $1,000 or $1,500 and something significant could be done with that.

Russ had some experience in the business, but I had none and had to learn everything fresh. I had never taken a course in Economics in either high school or college, and had no idea of how the banking system worked or understood the investment pressures on insurance companies where the premium dollars just came rolling in month after month and had to be invested safely and at rates high enough to keep the promises made in the policies being written.

It was boom time after the war/ During the War, the only investments available to the insurance companies were government bonds which paid a paltry 1%-2%. It took years for the insurance companies to replace all the war time bonds at higher rates, which started at 4% in 1946 and gradually moved higher in the 1950s.

The redeployment of the bonds fueled a huge pent-up demand for everything from nylon stockings for the women to business suits for the men, appliances and automobiles, and especially housing of all kinds for the millions of young men returning home and starting families, and, of course, retail space to sell the products that would now be coming off the production lines instead of planes and tanks.

I learned by standing at Dad's shoulder as he took an application, how to learn critical facts of the customer's finances and employment, and the details of his house purchase. Later, once an application was signed, I would take Dad's dictation as he spoke (no Dictaphones in our office) writing the submission letter to the Aetna. If it was a residential mortgage ($20,000 maximum loan, with at least one-third cash down payment [verified] and a maximum term of 15 years).The letters always closed with the ritual: "submitted with our recommendation at 4 ½% gross, 1/2% servicing fee, at 101. This meant that the Aetna would pay us 1% of the loan amount at the closing and our earnings would be 1/2% of 1% of the interest paid every month , More than half the time we had to pay all or part of the 1% fee to an insurance agent or attorney, or other "finder."

The real "bread and butter" of our income was not from the loan fee, but from the portion of the interest paid monthly and was the servicing fee, typically ½ of 1%. As the size of the portfolio of loans that we serviced increased, our income increased proportionately. It grew to a size that supported five families; and was able to pay bonuses. In other words, it was a profitable business. And it required no capital investment from us.

 Very soon, as part of my training (it wasn't called that - it wasn't called anything) Dad would pick me up in front of the Leader Building at the Superior Avenue entrance. I would have taken the street car to arrive at work at 8:30 a.m. Dad would drive down later to pick me up, but he was always late, and I remember how irritated I would get wasting time waiting for him to pick me up.

We did most of our work in the eastern suburbs of Cleveland, which was a fertile market of upper class homes, the kind the Aetna preferred, especially Shaker Heights. I observed how Dad announced our presence to the housewife to appraise her home, who may or may not have been told by her husband that we were coming. And then, using my college degree, I held the tape measure while he measured the exterior dimensions. We would then enter the home. I do not remember ever being challenged by the trusting housewife. Once inside, I filled out the appraisal card supplied by the Aetna, drawing the first floor plan on the grid on the card, as we inspected the interior, noted the type of heating system and other amenities, and the general condition of the property.  In my first ten years in the mortgage business, I estimate that I may have gone through this process and inspected from top to bottom 2,500 houses, small and large, new and old, (we made a mortgage on a home in Hudson, Ohio, owned by John Brown (of the Harper's Ferry Raid fame during the Civil War, which was being remodeled to bring it into the twentieth century.)

Soon Dad gained confidence in me and I started taking applications and then appraising the house and writing the submission letter to the Aetna by myself, well aware that Aetna came to Cleveland every six months or so to inspect the loans they had approved. Woe if they thought there had been any misrepresentation on our part because there was a clause in the Aetna contract which required us to buy back any disapproved mortgage upon their demand. This never happened to us.

We tried to have our loan submissions arrive at the Home Office early in the week, hoping for approval in the loan committee's regular Friday morning meeting. Friday afternoons were anxious times in the office as we waited to hear if a loan submission had been approved as submitted, thus requiring no further negotiation with the borrower.

After a loan approval it was part of my job to prepare the mortgage documents, the Note and the Mortgage which was to be filed in the County Records, and the Disbursement Order, which instructed the title company how to disburse the proceeds. on forms supplied by the Aetna, whose legal department checked my work very carefully.

It was not just the financial aspect of a deal for our company; it was hard not to develop empathy for an applicant after seeing his home and learning of his family and financial life. It was a pleasure to call our client and give him good news. I always hated the part of the job when I had to call with bad news: that an application had been turned down, or had conditions requiring more down payment, usually. which happened occasionally.

My having progressed to this point meant Dad could spend more time in the office cultivating his list of friends in search of the larger commercial loans. He also took me on appraisal and inspection trips to look at apartment buildings, office buildings, and shopping centers so I would become comfortable in handling larger loans.

I also accompanied him when he took Mr. Swinehart on his inspection trips to look at the larger loans Aetna had approved. We were fortunate that Aetna would consider residential hotel loans and leasehold loans as well as the more conventional types of income properties which gave us an advantage since our competitors did not have companies that would.

My job on those occasions was to prepare a 3" x 5" card for each loan to be inspected with all the basic information and then arrange them in the most efficient order to be inspected.

I did the same when the residential inspection trips were made by the younger men in the department. Inspection seemed to be defined very loosely – it involved our driving up to the house, or apartment building, and watching the home office men compare what they saw to the photographs in their file.

However, on the larger loans of over $1,000,000, such as the Alcazar Hotel in Cleveland Heights, a prime residential hotel, I remember Mr. Swinehart went into the hotel and was briefed on the operation by Charley Reinholt, the Manager, a long time friend of my father.

Generally, with 35 or 40 properties to see in one day, I don't remember any of the younger men, E. W. Bush, John French, or Jack Walsh ever getting out of the car. If the loans were all residential, Dad usually stayed in the office and Russ got a chance to get out of the office. I would do the driving and he would use the cards to pick out the next property to "inspect". I remember having a good feeling of accomplishment, seeing that many properties consecutively, rather than one by one, as the applications came in. It made a very attractive picture in my mind of the work that had been done in which I took great pride.

For many years, my father signed all the appraisal cards, which established the value on which the loan amount was based. With my inexperience he may have thought this would be reassuring to the Aetna. But gradually, he began to let me sign the appraisals, especially if he had not seen the property.

Finally, I was allowed to handle a large income property loan, an older apartment house, on my own: negotiating the terms of the Application, doing the Appraisal alone, then writing the Submission Letter with its accompanying Explanatory Notes and photographs. and if approved, preparing the mortgage documents for approval with the other closing papers by the Home Office attorney, William Aschaffenburg, Esq. a graduate of Oxford University, who escaped from Germany just in time in 1938, and spoke English with an upper class English accent enriched with traces of his German ancestry.

My first was a refinance, and the amount was $300,000.00. It was a large three-story brick apartment building with 100 suites at the corner of E. 103rd Street and Chester Avenue, which was one of the major routes from downtown Cleveland to the easterly suburbs and carried heavy traffic at all times. The Cleveland Clinic, University Circle with all its cultural institutions, several large residential hotels, Western Reserve University, and Rabbi Abba Hillel Silver's The Temple with a congregation of 3,000 families were all within walking distance. Today, I do not remember the names of the borrowers, two old friends of Dad's. But I do remember the thrill of having my first big loan approved. Maybe there would be a future for me in the mortgage business, after all.

There were many positive features in the little-known mortgage business. Several of the large life insurance companies maintained offices locally, staffed with home office employees. Others, including the Aetna (fortunately for us) operated with local people on a contractual basis to supply them with suitable investment opportunities. Since we were using Aetna's inexhaustible funds to commit for closing loans, we did not have to supply any funds of our own (which we did not have). Even construction loans which required advanced payments at various stages of construction could be closed, using a local commercial bank who would supply the necessary funds during construction, secured by the commitment of the Aetna to pay out the entire principal amount upon satisfactory completion of the project, which the bank could rely on.

I found that I enjoyed dealing with interesting and highly intelligent men (for the most part) knowing that I was playing a vital part in the real estate world, residential or commercial. It was good to know that I was being helpful to both the lender and the borrower, and it was hard for me not to take a personal interest in the principals, each with his unique background and story which I came to know. I took approvals or disapprovals very personally, which was not very professional.

I enjoyed the opportunity to get out of the office to investigate a loan inquiry. We considered northeast Ohio: Cuyahoga, Lorain, Erie, Medina, Summit, Portage, Geauga and Lake Counties as our exclusive territory, in which Aetna would only accept loan applications from the Schmidt Mortgage Company.

This was a large area for two men, Dad and me, to cover, and in the late 1950's, as an experiment, we opened a small office in the First National Bank Building in Akron, Ohio, the county seat of Summit County, and headquarters for the four largest tire companies in the U.S., as well as the national trucking line, Roadway Express.

We hired an older man, an Akron native, Bob Kocher, to do what I started out doing in Cuyahoga County: find good residential loans and, with any luck, good commercial loans. It was never very productive and after two or three years we closed the office. In reality, the bulk of our business came from Cuyahoga and Lake Counties, although we did make some nice loans in Summit County, and Kocher did have a hand in some of them. I carried the key to the men's restrooms in the First National Tower on my key chain for years although it didn't get much use.

The business grew and we needed more office space, and actually hired our first female secretary, Agnes Fertal, who was very intelligent and a hard worker. She was recommended by our cousin, Ellsworth Holden, who taught commercial courses at James Ford Rhodes High School.

Our first move was to a larger office on the same floor of the Leader Building, No. 458, and then to 459 across the hall, which had just been vacated by the Cleveland Browns who moved their offices to Tower B of the Cleveland Stadium.

We had loans to some of the Cleveland Browns: "Frosty" Froberg, General Manager; Harold Sauerbreei, Publicity; Nate Wallach, V.P., as well as several of the players who used to walk across the hall to make their monthly payments during playing season when they were in town. I remember Ed Ulinski, a guard, as being very unassuming and very nice to talk to. I also remember riding the elevator with Lenny Ford, one of the ends on the team and at 6'5", 250 pounds feeling absolutely dwarfed by this massive man standing next to me.

Our next move was to take a ten-year lease on a much larger office on the 19th floor of the Terminal Tower, overlooking Cleveland's Public Square. When that lease expired, we needed more space and moved once again to the southwest corner of the 14th floor of the East Ohio Gas Building at E. 9th Street and Superior Avenue. This was an 'L' shaped space and Dad, although retired at age 70, still came into his corner office (which we kept unoccupied as long as he lived) to take care of his personal affairs. It seemed that every ten years the business grew, reflecting the efforts of the now mature, older brothers, and the addition of the two younger brothers, to a point where there wasn't enough space for another desk. The demands for shelf space in our file storage room grew larger and larger.

I was producing a fairly steady supply of commercial loans as Dad's productivity declined (his friends were getting to retirement age, and he could no longer face the rejection of a loan he had originated and recommended, by a young employee at the home office who might be half his age, a feeling I did not understand at the time, but came to appreciate as time passed by).

Russ' role become more important to the growth of the business. Aetna stopped making residential loans on single family homes, previously a large part of our loan volume, probably in the late 1960s or early 1970s, which meant that the role of dealing with FNMA and Freddy Mac, quasi government agencies, the source for money for such loans, became more important and this became Russ's domain. He also arranged for us to originate and service loans for a local savings & loan, which was most unusual. He hired solicitors, priced and packaged loans for sale to the government agencies, thus ensuring the continuity of that part of the business, which only required compliance with the government rules and regulations and certain financial standards on our part, all of which he mastered, in addition to his duties as office manager, and *de facto* Treasurer of the Company.

Our youngest brother, Wesley, joined the company after his service in the Navy, probably 1966, and took over duties which had been performed previously by Russ. He soon became expert in remitting the monthly funds due the Aetna with perfect accuracy.

I am pretty sure at that time the payments were still recorded as they were received on the ledger card supplied by Aetna for each loan, residential as well as commercial. I am not sure whether Wes ever had more than one girl who worked for and with him. Hand posting became too tedious, and error prone which required much time to find and correct, and the accepted step up in the mechanical process of this recording of records was to go to the National Cash Register system which used typing and a machine to print out the numbers on another card.

Wes had become interested in the IBM punch card system and proposed that we go from hand posting directly to the IBM system. It was all very mysterious to me, and I remember Aetna's auditor, John Heyer, saying that it was impossible.

Far from it. Wes was able to find used IBM equipment and set up the system. I can remember the sound of the machines clacking away processing the punch cards. It was a wonderful solution to having to hire more and more girls to process the numbers. Furthermore, it could be used for reminders of insurance renewals, and at the end of the year each loan's monthly cards could be run through the machine to produce a record to give the customer for his income tax returns, together with the amount of real estate taxes paid and the information on insurance coverage. I never heard what John Hayer thought of this success.

After Wes proved that his idea was feasible and a great boon for smaller companies such as ours, he wrote an article which appeared in the national monthly magazine, *Mortgage Banker Magazine*, published by the MBA in Washington D.C., of which we were very proud. I remember hearing Dad brag to a friend at lunch how one of his "boys" had written an article in a national publication. Again, I never heard of any acknowledgement of this accomplishment by the Aetna Home Office.

An interesting event involving this aspect of the business occurred when Dad and I, attending the fall meeting of the MBA in Chicago at the Stevens Hotel, happened to be riding down an elevator with Jay Zook, President of the Zook Mortgage Company (bitter rivals whom Dad was indirectly responsible for putting into business) by having turned down a chance to take on the New York Life Insurance Company account, when the Land Title Guarantee & Trust Company (who serviced the account during World War II)& gave it up and offered it to Dad.

Dad said the same thing to them that Charley Braman told Mr. Swinehart when he said he was having trouble supplying Connecticut Mutual with all the business they wanted, politely refusing the Aetna account and recommending Dad.

Russ and I looked at each other, groaning. Dad had just doomed us to smallness, limited our chances for growth. We were giving up any leverage we had with the Aetna. We were missing a chance to grow in a time of great growth, and the opportunity to choose which source of money to approach for every inquiry we received. Zook got the account and many years later sold his company to Mellon National Bank.

I loved the mortgage business. I loved and was proud of the relationship with what I considered the highest quality insurance company in the U.S. I loved the excitement of being part of Aetna's network of loan correspondents, people I could call on for information and trust, knowing I would do the same for them if called on. I loved having been able to acquire the knowledge which could produce large sums of money for the "office," i.e., to my father and my brothers. I loved being exposed to interesting people, to interesting real estate transaction before they became public knowledge and the situations which arose which required problem solving. I loved all this and still being able to be home for dinner with my family almost every night.

However, as time passed, I had an uneasy feeling about our relationship with the Aetna, our primary source of money. Dad had allowed the responsibility for commercial loan production to pass into my hands and it was now my responsibility to make that part of the business grow. Too many of our applications were being turned down. And loans turned down by the Aetna were being made by other life insurance companies, which meant to me that it was not my judgment that was at fault, but something at the Aetna. Of course, every inquiry or loan submission represented a substantial mount of time and work for which we received no compensation.

At the Aetna we were competing for Aetna's dollars with much larger and more powerful loan correspondents located in larger, more prosperous cities with better growth: Draper & Kramer, the Chicago correspondent, and Galbreath Mortgage in Columbus, Ohio, very aggressive, who flew the head of Aetna's mortgage department to Paris for the horse races at the famous Longchamps Race Course, where John Galbreath had one of his thoroughbreds entered, and of course, the monster Coldwell Banker Company in Los Angeles who covered the whole west coast, plus Arizona and later bought the correspondent for the whole state of Minnesota. These companies not only covered more territory but provided services other than mortgage lending: real estate brokerage, property management, development of major projects, appraisal and inspection services, all of which were in-house sources of business. Aetna also had a very active correspondent in Washington, D.C., a very old city, but a vibrant growth area. I should point out that it was a bitter disappointment when one of my applications was turned down: I was not paid for all the hours spent in preparation and investigation. We were unable to compete in the services provided area and had to rely on the quality of the mortgage loan applications we were able to produce. I remember telling myself that if I were sitting at a desk in Hartford, and had two applications on my desk for identical properties, equally strong credit, one located in Atlanta and the other in Cleveland, and I could only present one to the loan committee on Friday, which would I choose. I knew the answer, and my only solution was to work harder. And rely on a record of never having had a foreclosure.

I remember seeing the hand writing on the wall and the need for us to try to find additional companies to represent when I attended a meeting at the "invitation" of the Aetna of their Mid-Atlantic Correspondents in Silver City, Maryland, a suburb of Washington D.C.

The main speech of the first meeting was given by a new Vice President of Mortgage Loans, James Daly, now head of the department, a young man (younger than me), who had been a senior officer of one of the large Chicago banks. He was replacing R. Douglas Swinehart, our mentor, who was retiring. Daly may have been giving his first of such speeches. I remember how excited, how jubilant he was. He wanted to share with us the best news we would ever hear. He had been promised by the Treasurer of the Aetna Life that the mortgage loan department's allocation of funds available for investment in the upcoming annual budget was to be increased from one billion to four billion dollars, a huge increase. No loan was too large for us in the coming year! Our job was to find suitable, high quality investments and to lay them on his doorstep. We had never had such an opportunity before. He implied that approvals would be easy to secure. He also announced that the minimum size application Aetna would now consider was to be raised to one million dollars.

I remember the sinking feeling I had when I asked myself how the smaller correspondents, located in smaller cities like Waterloo, Iowa, for example, which was probably fully supplied with post-war, modern commercial property, with no possibility of demand for more space. And I remembered the number of inquiries I had looked at the previous year in the $300,000-$500,000 range, perfectly sound investments, possibly owned by Aetna life insurance policy holders, who would no longer have access to Aetna premium dollars to finance their investments. How could a correspondent take advantage of this largess in a saturated market? I thought I heard a great rushing noise as the Rust Belt premium dollars were being sucked out to finance the growth of places like Honolulu, Atlanta, Houston, Los Angeles and Washington, D.C. This was a great plan for Aetna who could invest four times the money in the same number of loans without increasing the size of their loan processing staff. Furthermore, bigger deals should be more exciting.

After Daly's speech, there were one on one meetings with the Home Office staff. I remember being dismayed by my being assigned to sit down with Bill Russell, whom I had met only once or twice before when I visited the Home Office. I knew that he had lived in Cleveland after World War II and taught grammar school in Bay Village, Ohio. But as far as I knew he had never worked on a case I had sent to the Aetna and was not familiar with my work, or the general Cleveland area. I remember getting right to the point with him, telling him I was getting concerned that so many of my applications were being turned down. Was I doing something wrong? He was very reassuring and said that my work was just fine; and I should just continue doing as I had been.

I then asked him something that had been on my mind for a long time. I asked him if Aetna kept any records of loans that were turned down, or any records of serious inquiries made by their correspondents. He said no. I said that was unfortunate from my point of view because it was a record not only of productivity, but of time, effort and hard work done on Aetna's behalf. I told him I could document having sent $50,000,000 of such inquiries or applications to Aetna in the past twelve months, and the refusals were all the more discouraging because many of those loans were subsequently made by other insurance companies. I had to assume that the loans were an acceptable type of security for an insurance company to hold. I pointed out that my record of failures was beginning to affect our reputation, to say nothing about our loss of income. Everyone in Cleveland would agree that we were a fine company and that I was a good "mortgage" man, but what was the point of wasting time dealing with Schmidt Mortgage Company? They can't get anything approved. Russell seemed unconcerned, patted me on the back, and urged me to be patient, and to keep up the good work!

Two other alarming events occurred about this time. Dad and I were invited to call on First Union Realty, an REIT, whose prize possession was the Union Commerce Building, in the heart of downtown Cleveland. They were considering refinancing their mortgage and wondered if we thought the Aetna would be interested. Dad looked at me and I looked at him, and we said yes simultaneously. The Union Commerce Building was the largest office building in Cleveland at the time, in a prime location, the heart of the downtown business district at the northeast corner of E. 9th Street and Euclid Avenue. And to make a mortgage on it would be a tremendous feather in our cap. The loan amount they were seeking was $15,000,000, and our fee would be substantial, perhaps $75,000 or more. We were dealing with a V.P. of the Trust, Jack Frost, who was charming. He asked simple questions about how we would proceed and who would be a man senior enough at the Home Office to handle such a large loan. We gave him the name of R. Douglas Swinehart, our mentor. As soon as we left his office Mr. Frost called Mr. Swinehart and the upshot of our conference was that Aetna made the loan without our services, the first time they had ever dealt directly with a borrower in our area. Mr. Swinehart was very casual about the whole affair. He told Dad that we should have gotten a signed application while we were there. It was a devastating experience.

Mr. Swinehart may have had some second thoughts; because he called and talked to me. He asked if I would be interested in doing the appraisal they needed for their file to support the loan amount. Aetna would pay me (Schmidt Mortgage Company) a $15,000 appraisal fee and I was assured of getting it. This put me in an awkward position. If I turned down the assignment, would it look like the deal was too large for me? Would it confirm a suspicion in the Home Office as to the superiority of the larger correspondents? Would it mean that I didn't have enough confidence in my ability to take on the responsibility for such a large appraisal, or our Company was unable to handle all aspects of real estate financing, services their other correspondents in Chicago and the West Coast were able to provide without question?

After a lot of soul searching of this sort, I accepted the assignment and spent the next eight weeks almost full time during office hours, and then staying downtown through the dinner hour until 8 or 9 p.m., as well as Saturdays and Sundays working on the project. (I could see our sailboat, operated by the crew, setting out on the regular Wednesday night race from my office window.) It was by far the most time consuming, complicated appraisal I ever attempted. Not only was there the sheer size of the building; there was also a parking structure across Chester Avenue with direct access to the Union Commerce building by an underground tunnel under Chester Avenue. This was a great convenience because without the tunnel, anyone doing business in the building would have to walk a city block on E. 9th Street, the windiest street in the city. The income from parking revenues was of a different nature than the ordinary office rentals, and the income derived from the Union Bank of Commerce, the building's largest tenant, to say nothing of the income from the Midday Club, an eating club that occupied the entire top floor or the retail income from the small retail shops at street level. And the tunnel provided no income per se, but surely its convenience had some value. It was a complicated puzzle assigning values to these varying types of income and a further complication was that a small piece of the land under the main building at the northeast corner was held under a 100-year leasehold.

One of my friends rented a small high wing airplane and we flew out of the Burke Lakefront Airport, so I could take colored photographs of downtown Cleveland, orienting the subject property to the other office buildings and its location on the grid of streets. I remember taking one exposure looking southeast from the Winton Place high-rise apartment building located on Lakewood's Gold Coast on the near westside of Cleveland looking toward the central business district, a view over a small bay in front of Winton Place still partially covered by ice from the winter freeze of Lake Erie near shore. I thought it was a very successful (and lucky) photo. I had the usable photos enlarged to 8" x 10," and mounted, with three or four sheets of glassine plastic hinged over the photo with streets and buildings identified on separate sheets. I thought the graphics added something to the appraisal.

Once again my memory seems to have difficulty in dealing with numbers, but the culmination of my career as a mortgage loan man, probably, was this appraisal, which, ironically, had nothing to do with my processing a commercial loan application. I worked alone and started to keep track of the extra hours spent at the office outside regular office hours (48) and asked for and received the equivalent in unpaid vacation time: the brothers could hardly object because I had agreed to their receiving double pay for the vacation hours they spent working in the office.

The appraisal was approved and accepted by the Aetna, the final appraisal amount signed with fear and trembling: $23,000,000.

The second warning that change was coming, in addition to the Aetna's being willing to deal directly with a customer (if he was large enough and powerful enough) was to learn that they had approved a loan submitted by the Galbreath Company (our rivals and their correspondent in Columbus) in the Akron area, which we considered part of our exclusive territory. I found this very alarming.

One of the perks that went along with the commercial loan part of the business was the occasional chance to travel. I remember being taken to New York by one of our friends from the Ostendorf Morris Company, who lived across the street from Russ, in a big old frame house, one of the original mansions, overlooking Lake Erie.

The Ostendorf Morris Company was one of the oldest commercial real estate brokers in Cleveland and was trying to sell a clay mine in New Jersey, across the river from Manhattan to the Rockefeller interests. The clay was used for making bricks which were used nearby in Manhattan for all the building going on there. We flew (at Ostendorf Morris' expense) to New York and I had the rare experience of sitting in the office of the Rockefeller's financial advisers and observing how they analyzed deals that were brought to them. I was appalled. They seemed to have no concern for what their actions could do to human lives. I don't remember the name of the advisor company, or the location of the building where the meeting took place, or the location of the mine, except that it was near water and very close to Manhattan. I do remember calling Aetna and being assured that the quality of the credit would be the basis for any loan requested, not the quality of the clay. The mine was owned by one family, who owned the majority of the shares of the company, which was listed on the Over the Counter Stock Exchange. For some reason, this complicated things; for the investment adviser, but made it interesting for him to move his chess pieces (people) all over the board. We flew home that afternoon, and the only benefit other than being out of the office for a day in an exciting situation was the unforgettable lesson I learned of the unimportance of human beings. I found out later that the deal was never made.

Closer to home, on another occasion, I was taken to lunch with the CEO of the Babcock & Wilcox Company (industrial boilers) in Barberton, Ohio, west of Canton. Once again, I was the faceless mortgage man, the source of the money, and sat quietly at the far end of the table. The CEO, whose name I cannot remember, and his entourage of six or seven men showed up about 30 minutes late. I then observed a performance of a little man who could have portrayed Napoleon, and certainly acted like him. He loved to display his power. The performance was unbelievable. I wondered how a stock exchange listed company could stay in business with leadership such as I observed that day. I do not remember what the money they were seeking was to be used for – some plant expansion, perhaps, and they were exploring using their real estate as collateral rather than the more usual issuance of bonds. Nothing ever came of that afternoon.

Another powerful personality I met in Akron was the son of the V.P. in charge of international sales of the General Tire Company, one of the big four tire makers at that time (my Dad always bought General's when he had to replace tires on his car). The son was married to the widow of the Chairman of the Friden Business Machine Company and claimed to have a net worth of $15,000,000 on an application I took for an Aetna loan. The widow's new husband had convinced her to consolidate their real estate holdings to locations within the U.S. I remember that they were in the process of selling a ranch in Paraguay at the time.

Our Akron employee, Bob Kocher, and my architect friend, Keith Haag, who was not only a talented architect, but also a very astute businessman, brought us together and I took an application for $400,000 for a small two-story office building on West Market Street on Akron's west side. This was an unusual building design because it employed prefab concrete exterior walls which were delivered by truck, unloaded and then tilted up into position to form the exterior of the building.

I met my new customer at his offices in a bowling alley (!), in Akron and as part of Aetna's form of application, filled in the financial information in which he stated his net worth to be $15,000,000 which was very impressive. I think it was the largest individual net worth I had ever processed. When I was finished and before he would sign the application, he insisted on calling his attorney and going over the "boiler plate." He picked up the phone and said, "Hello dere, Calhoun," and proceeded to read every word in the fine print parodying the dialect of the popular radio show (Amos and Andy). By the time he was through I was practically rolling on the floor. Later, I also heard him do an imitation of Winston Churchill, which was remarkable. He had a rich baritone speaking voice which he knew how to use.

As I recall, this $400,000 loan was the first commercial loan application we originated in Akron and Kocher, who would receive a bonus if it was approved, was as anxious as was I. I flew to the Home Office in Hartford to present it in person. I remember sitting at Mr. Swinehart's desk while he went through the application. When he got to the section dealing with net worth of the applicant, he asked me if I had checked the $15,000,000 figure and I confessed that I hadn't (How could I? Why would Mr. A lie)? I would have been impressed with a figure of $3,000,000, an amount far in excess of that needed to support a loan of $ 400,000. Mr. Swinehart looked at me in his kindly way and said I wouldn't last ten minutes on Wall Street. Nevertheless, the loan was approved; and Keith Haag's unusual exterior wall system was used, and I was there to watch the panels tilted into place and bolted to the steel frame.

Sometime later when John French, one of the brilliant younger men at the Home Office with whom we dealt regularly, was doing one of the regular Home inspections, we were persuaded to meet our Friden-money customer, Mr. A, at his home in Sharon Center, west of Akron. He was a horse fancier and had a large indoor riding rink building as well as the usual stables and fenced outdoor training facilities. After passing these, we came to an attractive, large, ranch-style house, were ushered in, seated and while getting acquainted, his wealthy wife, who had spent the afternoon doing volunteer work at a hospital and was still in her uniform, called out to say she was home, sticking her head around the corner of the room where we were seated. At this point Mr. A did not introduce her to his guests, but, rather, treated her like a servant in front of three strangers, and ordered her brusquely to bring drinks. This was happening, presumably, when he was trying to impress a source for financing their real estate with an inexhaustible supply of money. I had not seen this side of him before and was shocked at his treatment of his wife. John French looked at me, and I looked at him, and that was the last time I tried to do business with Mr. A.

As Mr. Swinehart suspected, the wife's money was tied up in Trusts to which her husband had no access, but with which he could claim an acquaintanceship.

Much later (I recall it being 1980 when I was 59 and had been in the business 33 years) I received a phone call in the morning from E.W. Bush, one of the younger officers in the mortgage loan department of the Aetna, with whom I had played golf and enjoyed working with on loan submissions, asking if my brothers and I could join him at Cleveland Hopkins Airport where he had a private conference room reserved. Of course, I said yes and that we would take the Rapid Transit from our building and would be there within the hour. This was most unusual and had never happened before in all the forty years we had represented Aetna. There had to be a reason for all three of us to be present and it couldn't be a good one. Fortunately, Dad had retired a few years earlier and did not have to be present.

My memories of that meeting are very sketchy. I think Bush was very succinct and simply announced that Aetna's business model had changed; that in accordance with our contract with Aetna, and with no fault on our part, Aetna was exercising its option to cancel their contract with Schmidt Mortgage Company. They appreciated all the years of loyalty, but we would no longer represent them. After the turnover of the portfolio, we would no longer receive servicing income, and they would compensate us for that loss. They invited us to determine a fair value for such loss and relay the amount to them. He then closed his briefcase and left us to call on some of the other smaller correspondents with the same message no doubt. What an unpleasant job to have to do! Our ride back downtown on the Rapid was very quiet. There was no discussion. I knew there could be no appeal. At least they had sent an officer to deliver the edict.

I set about figuring out what I thought the fair market value at 6% would be for the remaining life of each of the Aetna loans we serviced, and when I delivered the amount (which I do not remember) Bush thought it was too high and I should have used 4% in my assumptions. I pointed out that at his amount we would be better off doing the servicing and watching the monthly amount dwindle to zero, since we could no longer submit loans to replace the monthly shrinkage. Bush prevailed, as if there had ever been any doubt.

In the end, the Aetna was not the buyer; using the lower price forced on us by Aetna established by Aetna, we were forced to sell at that price to the Columbus correspondent, Galbreath

Mortgage Company. I cannot believe that I do not remember the details of such a momentous event: not the value I established, nor the amount Aetna agreed to, nor how the transfer was effected. I assume we had to turn over all the files, but simply do not remember how it was done. All contact with the Aetna ceased and I never heard what happened to the careers of the men I had been working with for so many years.

I do remember that in a vindictive frame of mind, I bought one share of Aetna Life & Casualty stock so I would receive their annual statement. And I found it interesting that under the old business model there had never been a foreclosure in Aetna's history, but under the new model of large loans and large regional correspondents, that within a few years the statements showed $250,000,000 of foreclosures and non-performing loans which meant that interest was not being paid. However, it was small satisfaction.

The moment I heard Bush's news, I knew it would cause a major change in my life, and that it presented me with an opportunity to leave Schmidt Mortgage Company at last. For several years I had not enjoyed my work which had become impossible because of the high interest rates imposed by the Federal Reserve Bank under Paul Volcker. The rates were so high (18%- 20%) that it was impossible to apply them to net income when appraising and arrive at a value that could support a mortgage of any size. In fact, I believed that if Congress passed a law requiring every bank and insurance company in the U.S. to "mark to market" the real estate assets on their balance sheets, which would have been a fraction of the amount of dollars invested, every bank and insurance company in America would have been bankrupt.

In addition to the inability to make new mortgages, and losing the Aetna account, with the passing years there had been an increasing amount of friction between the brothers. Some of the glow I felt from my role of being the oldest son and responsible to some extent for the well-being of my younger brothers no longer existed. Looking back on the situation, family friction was the price paid for the privilege of continuing my childhood by seeing my younger brothers every day, as opposed to working in a large corporate environment where vicious corporate politics were common.

Our corporate agreements provided that we could not be fired, nor have our pay cut, and that retirement at age 65 was mandatory. I insisted when these agreements were made that it be possible for a stockholder to retire before age 65 at a 2% discounted value of his shares per year. There had to be some way to escape the Company, which brother Ken, did at age 40, at a 50% discount of the value of his shares determined by a complicated formula treating different sources of income at differing rates, on December 31st every year. The Company would repurchase the retiree's stock over a ten-year period, monthly, at no interest. This was an attempt to protect the viability of the Company, and to provide for a replacement of the retiree.

Well aware of this and knowing that if I simply sat at my desk and collected my regular pay check, it would bankrupt Schmidt Mortgage Company within a year, I wrote a long letter of resignation and gave it to my brothers. I think there is a copy of it somewhere in my papers. This was not as hard to do as one might think. First of all, it was the right thing to do. I felt that the residential side of the business with its secure source of money could survive without my commercial mortgage business, and Fran and I stood a good chance of not being hurt too badly financially. I never told anyone, not even Fran, perhaps, but I had always had the dream of retiring at age 50 as my golfing friend, Ted Billings, had done.

Many years earlier as our oldest daughter, Nancy, was about to enter high school, I recall discussing the foreseeable financial challenges we faced as a family with Fran, whose mother was still living: the probable burden of paying out of state tuition for college and, hopefully, for three weddings. This was when I learned for the first time after about twenty years of marriage that Fran would inherit a substantial number of shares of Dow Chemical stock upon the death of her mother from a Trust established at the time of the divorce of her parents in 1931,  When I learned the rough terms of the settlement, I questioned more than ever the propriety of a couple using the same lawyer to represent both sides of a marriage in a divorce proceeding, especially when in such a small town they were friends moving in the same social circles. The settlement was heavily in favor of Fran's father, and Fran's mother agreed to accept only 600 shares of Dow Chemical stock. Because of the social stigma of divorce in those days, she felt she had to leave her family and friends in Midland; and with custody of her daughter decided to move to Detroit, leaving behind to her former husband the home built for and given to them by her parents as a wedding present. She had been brought up in the genteel tradition and had no marketable skills with which to find a job, with only a few shares of GM and AT&T of her own to supplement the Dow Chemical income. One of the unfortunate features in the divorce settlement was that Fran's father, who was still responsible for Fran's college education, was named the Trustee of the Trust and Fran's mother was dependent on him to send her dividend checks promptly, which he frequently failed to do, putting terrible financial pressure on her mother who was living day by day very close to the edge. Shortly after his subsequent marriage to his secretary, Dr. Thompson left Midland, Michigan, to go to Freeport, Texas, to become manager of the Dow Chemical Hospital there, leaving behind his son, Mark Edward, Jr., eleven years Fran's senior, age nineteen at the time, to live with his two maiden aunts. All this history is hearsay, of course, but a fairly accurate picture of the situation, as I put the bits and pieces together over the years from hearing Fran talk about her relatives in Midland.

With all this in mind I suggested to Fran that I try to find an apartment house to buy, as my father had done before I went away to college. Fran was always dubious about real estate as an investment, her background making her more familiar with the stock market, and being familiar with the success of Dow Chemical, which never failed to pay a dividend and had several stock splits. Nevertheless, she agreed that I should proceed.

I mentioned this to my friend, Bill Braman, and he knew of a building for sale at the northwest corner of Detroit Street and West Boulevard in Cleveland. This seemed to be a good location, close to downtown Cleveland, on a bus line, and a short walk to the first stop from downtown on the Cleveland Rapid Transit System whose westerly arm ended at the Cleveland Hopkins airport, about a twenty minute ride from airport to central business district, and passing under the Terminal

Tower hub, gave access to the east side of Cleveland near the lake, and to the Shaker Heights area to the south.

It was a 34 suite, 4-story walk-up building with a courtyard off the lobby, built in the late 1920s, buff colored brick, not red, which pleased me and its only drawback that I could see was that the parking was poor, only a limited number of spaces in front of the building on West Boulevard and a few at the rear of the building, none that we could assign or control. However, many of the tenants might not have cars, relying on the excellent public transportation available, and it was a style very similar to my Dad's building where we started our marriage.

The building appeared to be in reasonably good condition and occupancy appeared to be good; neither the tenants vacating, nor the custodian bothered to remove names on the mailboxes when a suite became vacant; this was the first time I had seen this trick. All the boxes had names in their slots. We had very little money to invest, and I conceived the idea of installing an elevator opposite the front door to overcome the 4-story walk-up stigma. This would enable me to create a pro-forma income statement with increased rents projected and possibly justify a loan large enough to buy the property with the $15,000 down payment we were able to scrape up.

I would go to my friend in the mortgage business, Jim Cozzens, and the Citizens Federal Savings & Loan of Painesville for the mortgage and hire Fran's sorority sister friend's husband (from the Friday night bridge group) the architect, Tom Moore, to draw the plans for the elevator to be installed as a condition for securing the mortgage. I knew he had just done something similar for an existing building in Parma recently, thus his estimate of the cost should be very good.

We proceeded to make an offer on this basis which was accepted; and the loan was approved using my pro-forma income statement. After the title passed, I learned to my dismay that there was a 25% vacancy and that the custodian had very carefully avoided showing me any of the vacant apartments, many of which were in very poor condition. And I found that Moore's estimate of the cost of the elevator was grossly low; all of the contractors he suggested quoting much higher prices. In desperation I had to find a contractor on my own, something I had never done before and was fortunate to find a contractor just starting in the business, Nacy Panzica, who quoted a price that fit our budget and he did a fine job, completing the job promptly with no cost overruns. I called him after the job was completed, and since his bid was so much lower than the other contractors, said that I hoped he had made some profit. He said that he didn't make as much as he hoped, but that he did make a profit. I saw his name frequently on jobs in the years that followed, always with a warm feeling, and believe he had a major contract for improvements at the Cleveland Hopkins Airport. We remained friends with the Moores, but Tom never apologized for his poor advice, or gave any indication that he was aware of the stress I suffered.

I began looking for a new custodian immediately, and do not remember how I found a classmate at Lakewood High School, Walter J. Smith, who was struggling in the real estate business. He agreed to move into the custodian's suite with his wife and take over the management. He did a remarkable job, and eventually redecorated and repaired all the suites, not only those that were vacant at the time of purchase. This consumed any excess rental income, so the only advantage to me was the gradual increase in value due to improving the building, and the tax advantages due to the depreciation expense (paper losses based on the size and age of the property, not like actual cash spent for paint and plumbing supplies) which were allowed and approved by the IRS. There was no big increase in cash for us to spend on personal items or travel. All excess cash was reinvested in improvements to the building.

We never solved the parking problem. There was a building next door on Detroit Street occupied by a religious publishing company which had a large, fenced in, paved parking lot at the rear, padlocked at night, and I was never able to come to some arrangement with them for our tenants' use of their lot after 6 p.m. There was also a small, unimproved vacant lot at the corner of Detroit Street and West Boulevard which was designated as a City park, part of the Cudel Grant from the early days of Cleveland's settling, before Detroit Street was built which bisected the area designated as parkland. If we could have come to some agreement to lease the land from the City, it could have accommodated ten-twelve cars, accessed from the curb cut on Detroit Street to the rear entrance of our building. Unfortunately, I was never able to get the Parks Division of the City of Cleveland to see the benefits of my plan, which would have taken some of the pressure off our tenants in their search for a place to park their cars overnight on the city streets.

One of the main reasons for me to undertake such a risky investment was Dad's adamant stand against having our company establish a pension plan which would have tied the bonds between the brothers even tighter, always one of his goals. His sons, to whom he had given their shares in the original partnership, were to arrange for their own retirement just as he had. Before finalizing my deal, I disclosed my plan to Dad, the methods I was using, and what I hoped to accomplish. I don't know if he ever visited the building, or even drove by, but he had no objections. I do not remember telling my brothers of my plans, and don't think Dad did either, all three sons still being in the business.

About this time, Russ also bought a small apartment building on Clarence Avenue, just north of Detroit Street in Lakewood with a high school classmate, Chuck Huffman as his partner. He kept his deal secret from the rest of us including Dad, and it turned out badly. I never understood why none of the brothers ever took advantage of the knowledge I had acquired in valuing real estate. Perhaps they didn't trust me; thought I would try to horn in, or steal their deal; or they didn't have any confidence in me; or, never having had the slightest interest in my part of the business, had any way of knowing the quality of the advice they would have received. Whether or not I would have approved of the purchase price, etc. of Russ's deal, I will never know. As far as I know, the younger brothers never looked to real estate as a type of personal investment to supplement their income or provide for their retirement.

While the equity was building up in our first apartment investment, Nancy went off to the University of Michigan, and Fran's mother passed on, a very sad occasion for Fran and me. I hope I have recalled the memories earlier in this account of her last week at our house, my seeing the silent owl, her talisman, on the white oak behind our garage, our taking her to the Cleveland Clinic main campus, and after visiting the last afternoon, going home only to turn around to rush back when the Clinic called, and arriving thirty minutes too late to be with her when she passed ; then a few days later picking up Nancy in Ann Arbor on the way to Lexington, Michigan where the brief services were held.

After three or four years of the increasing value of our West Boulevard property, we could consider using it as collateral to buy another apartment project, which was part of a plan I was beginning to formulate. I would never be able to start a business to provide jobs for three daughters, but perhaps I could accumulate enough real estate to leave each of them a substantial estate to secure their financial future after I was gone.

I located an apartment project for sale on E. 222nd Street in Euclid, Ohio. It had 92 one and two-bedroom suites in six two-story buildings, and was situated on a large parcel of land providing a parkland type of setting. The financing was unusual and required a temporary second mortgage and personal liability. But in spite of the additional risk, it seemed worth doing.

After the deal closed, the improvement of the property began all over again, building up equity for the next step in my plan. I now owned 126 rental units on opposite sides of the town and did not feel I could take the time necessary to manage the properties, a personal investment, from the office, as Dad had done. I hired a professional management company, owned by Bernice Willkom, the widow of one of Dad's old business friends. She was honest, extremely competent and hard-working. I have always felt she was responsible for much of the increase in the value of the properties.

At this time, it was possible to do a tax free exchange in real estate, where, if the property to be acquired was larger than the property being traded for it, no tax was due on any capital gains. This fit in nicely with my grand plan, which ended with my actual tax free exchange of the Cleveland properties which I had owned for about eighteen years and seen the original $15,000 investment grow to $1,100,000 in equity, for two much larger rental properties with a total of 304 garden type and townhouse units on two parcels of land about a mile apart on the east side of Columbus, Ohio. I had considered a few properties which were much farther away, Louisville, Kentucky, and an office building in North Carolina, and remember how grateful I felt that the final choice was only 100 miles from Brecksville, in Columbus, an easy two hour drive. More details of the transaction are related in Chapter XIII.

Other perks arising from my income property loan part of the business included brief trips to look at unusual loan opportunities, or to attend conventions or visit the lender's home office – we eventually ended up representing three other smaller insurance companies: the Provident Mutual of Philadelphia (we were never able to find a loan with sufficiently high credit to submit to them); the American National of Galveston, Texas, whose V.P., Ray Wilson, was in charge of their mortgage loan department, whom I met at the Case Study Seminar at Michigan State University (we did secure an approval for a shopping center from them but could not persuade our customer to accept it); and Confederation Life of Toronto, Canada, who sought us out because of Cleveland's proximity to Toronto, which would make inspection trips to inspect a loan inquiry one day affairs for them. We did secure a commitment for an unusual apartment to be built in Lorain, Ohio, designed by my friend, Keith Haag, owned by an inexperienced but impressive retired, diminutive Army nurse and her twin sister, a property she lost because of a misunderstanding she had with the architect regarding inspections during construction. That loan never closed.

The most exotic deal I ever worked on involved flying to Minneapolis to visit the Northwest National Insurance Company home office, and ultimately, securing financing for the purchase of two producing oil wells by two young entrepreneurs, one from Cleveland, the other from Wichita, Kansas. It would have produced more tax-free income over a period of the nineteen years remaining life of the wells, approximately $60,000 per year, 23% tax free, than any other large loan we ever made for the Aetna. It was a tremendous disappointment for me when the deal fell apart on the closing table.

It was even more disappointing was to learn at a later Yale Reunion, while chatting with George Pillsbury, a classmate I never saw while at school, that I should have called him in Minneapolis. Northwestern National's president was his brother, John Pillsbury, also a Yale alum, who might have been able to save my deal by insisting on Northwest finding another banking partner for his insurance company, a key to the financing. It was the Wichita bank partner that Northwest National had selected who backed out at the last minute which killed the deal. This was the closest I ever came in 35 years to seeing some positive financial benefit to my Yale education.

Other interesting opportunities offered themselves because of the nature of the mortgage business. One morning I had a call from my insurance agent/sailing friend, Bob Busha, who invited me to join him at an investment banker's office to hear a presentation on the advantages of Swiss banking by a visiting Swiss banker. As a result of this we later opened a small savings account at a small Swiss bank, Ubersee Bank of Zurich. It was exciting to diversify in this manner.

Several years later, after the death of Fran's mother, and following the generally accepted advice of investment professionals to diversify and not have all one's eggs in one basket, while spending the winter in Florida, we flew to Nassau to attend a seminar exploring Swiss investments presented by the Jorg Lattman Company, a Swiss brokerage and agency company

Faced with the problem of diversifying (what seemed like a good opportunity which arose when the IRS permitted, if not encouraged, in an effort to stimulate the market) a new type of mutual fund which would hold only shares of stock in companies which had been locked up in family's investment portfolios for decades because of the huge capital gains tax, which would accrue if the shares were sold. In order to free up this segment of the market, the IRS, or the Treasury, proposed a tax-fee exchange wherein the long-held shares could be traded for shares of the same value in a new issue of a mutual fund created for this purpose, tax-free, and future tax liability would be based on the share value at initial offering.

All the large brokerage houses established such new mutual funds and attracted family shares to take in trade as expected. I found a highly regarded mutual fund company located in Pittsburg, which I remember had "Federated" in its name, and we proceeded to transfer roughly one-third of Fran's Trust funds into this new entity. When the fund was fully subscribed, I remember seeing 2700+ shares of Dow Chemical listed among its assets and knew immediately they had to be Fran's.

What started out well turned into a disaster a few years later when the Pittsburg company sold the fund to a west coast brokerage house, who proceeded to loot the portfolio. Their scheme was to sell the blue-chip securities in the new fund and use the proceeds to replace them with worthless penny stocks they created. The State of California took an interest, prosecuted, and a Trustee was appointed to recover the lost money. It took seven or eight years before we recovered all the principal, but we had no earnings, or chance of appreciation in the stock price during that time. We were lucky to recover as much as we did. If I recall correctly, the state appointed Trustee named his recovery fund the "Pegasus Fund."

When we investigated the Swiss opportunity, we stayed in a hotel on Paradise Island in the Nassau harbor and I remember how hot and humid it was. The event was well organized and well attended. After the various presentations, we were taken to a small conference room and heard further explanations from one of the executives. The result of this indoctrination was that we took a portion of Fran's Dow shares and bought a Swiss franc annuity issued by a Swiss life insurance company, Ticino Life, which was a single premium, immediate pay policy, guaranteeing quarterly payments of a fixed number of Swiss franc for life, until the second of us died. If we both died before fifteen years, payments to our beneficiaries guaranteed for the remaining years of the fifteen year period.

Our intention was not to speculate. My plan was that the diversification process would be in investments which surely would fluctuate, but when one asset was down, the other would be up, and, hopefully, our principal would be preserved. At this time, every Swiss franc was backed by gold held by the Swiss central bank, and therefore, far more secure than the U.S. dollar which was backed only by the promise of the federal government. Furthermore, the rate of inflation between the two countries was widely different, the Swiss rate being much lower than then U.S. When the insurance company followed our instructions and converted our francs into U.S. dollars, there was the possibility of realizing some gains from a stronger currency buying a weaker one as well.

This advantage is lost today because the Swiss have joined the rest of the world; their franc is no longer backed by gold, one for one, and they can print as much money as they wish to, and have lowered interest rates to negative territory I still receive the same number of francs every quarter and have not been hurt thus far.

The bulk of the rest of Fran's trust money went into the annuity; the balance was used to buy 23 ounces of physical gold at $139 per ounce, if I remember correctly (which we never saw) stored in a vault in Zurich, shares of a South African diamond mine, of an Australian gold mine, and the small savings account at the Ubersee Bank in Zurich. If we had stayed in Zurich overnight on one of our trips to Europe, it would have been fun to drop in on the bank and chat with the manager about the bank and world affairs.

All these investments moved counter to the U.S. market and were liquidated at a profit (never the intention) and sunk into my Columbus apartment projects much later in a vain attempt to prevent their loss.

Of all the investments made over the years, the real estate and other types of speculations done in partnership with others, driven by a lack of a company pension plan, and an attempt to secure our future in our old age (most of which were unsuccessful) the Swiss annuities have turned out the best, with no skills or experience needed, and are the major source of my retirement income, thanks to my long life, having long outlived the actuarial assumptions.

I have rueful memories of some of the offbeat ventures I became involved in, which fortunately, were small enough that I did not feel the need to tell Fran about. The first was the purchase of a small vacant lot in Elyria, Ohio, near Griswold Road and the Midway Mall and Holiday Inn for which I arranged the financing, so I had some familiarity with the location. My partner and finder of the deal was an Akron attorney friend, Dick Sternberg. I recall paying my half of the $1,500 price for it and had hopes that it might sell for $5,000. It was owned by one of Sternberg's clients. The lot never sold and may well still be vacant and for sale, 60 years later.

I repeated this process with Sternberg on another piece of vacant land on the west side of Akron, with the same sad results. My advice: Do not buy vacant land as a speculation.

Some of these ventures entailed more than just losing the purchase price money. My good friend, Elden Papke, of Wichita, Kansas, whose profession was persuading farmers in Oklahoma, Texas and Kansas to lease the subsoil rights under their farms to drill for oil. He found what he felt was a sure-fire bet: it was a lease on a piece of land adjacent to very successful producing wells 300 yards away. He proposed to form a partnership to drill for oil himself and invited (persuaded) me to be one of his partners. He arranged for a loan from a bank in Wichita to pay for my share (and co-signed the note without my knowledge) and the drilling proceeded. Fran had full knowledge of this deal.

The drilling proceeded and I received weekly reports by postcard as to progress. All very favorable, and it was very exciting, but when the well reached the producing zone, we learned that the rock structure around the well had narrowed to a state that pinched the shale so tight that although there was oil there, it was impossible to pump it to the surface.

This was one investment that I told Fran all about, the risks, but the huge payoff if there was success. She suffered along with the rest of the family to the extent of the monthly loan repayment which went on for several years. I always felt a little guilty that I never told her about the Sternberg gambles which required relatively small amounts of cash which would not be missed; and would have had far smaller payoffs than part ownership of an oil well.

Not all the opportunities that presented themselves because of the nature of the mortgage finance business were benign, as you may have surmised. I met an Akron customer, Harry Sugar, former CEO of Alsco Aluminum Siding, when I refinanced his midrise luxury apartment building on Portage Trail in Akron across the road from the Portage Country Club, the premier country club in Akron. It was a $1,500,000 loan which was submitted and closed in December. This speed was unusual; and I remember having the feeling that Aetna wanted to be sure to use up all their annual allocation of funds for the year. If you are the Head of the Department, leave no funds unspent.

I had to appraise a completed, fully occupied structure and never saw the plans, which I frequently did in this kind of situation. The building was a copy of one built in Miami, the plans for which were not drawn by an architect, but by a famous "designer," whose name I cannot remember. Today, I suspect Harry may have bought the plans for $1,000 (or less), thus avoiding the expense of an architect's fee and the benefit of architectural training, and architectural inspection during construction.

After the loan closed, I began to discover flaws in the design, which were invisible to an appraiser. While the exterior, white brick, was attractive, and the suites very spacious, the building had been built with double concrete floors to control noise transmission, with an 8" space between the ceiling of the suite below and the floor of the suite above. There was no vertical separation of the units so that the tenant in the northwest corner of the building could smell what the tenant in the southeast corner was having for dinner. Furthermore, each pair of suites shared a laundry room which was not vented and became so hot in the summer that the tenant's maids balked at working in them.

The worst flaw that I worried about the most was the attached underground garage, which had a parking deck for its roof. When I checked it out later, after I became aware of the other defects, I saw that the concrete deck/roof of the garage was supported by steel "Ls" bolted to the exterior cement block walls, rather than having the slab rest on the cement block walls, which were already tilting outwards from the pressure of the weight of the slab, and at a certain point would allow the deck to slip off the "L" and collapse. I used to wake up nights worrying about this. It was very shoddy construction; and I am surprised, or am I, knowing Harry, that the city building inspectors and the contractors allowed the building to pass inspections. Cost cutting was evident everywhere if the appraiser (me) had looked for it. Fortunately for me and the tenants, what I feared never happened, and the Aetna never registered any disapproval.

I don't think Harry ever expected me to be able to get his loan approved, and when I did, I became a "source" for any kind of financing he needed. We became "friends" and were invited to his home on Yellowstone Road in Bath, Ohio, for dinner. I played golf with him at his country club in Montrose, a suburb of Akron. He was a very interesting person.

He invited me to join him and two other men in a partnership to find a location in Cleveland to build an automatic car wash. He was planning to start a chain of car washes using washing equipment that he would manufacture. Automatic car washes were the latest thing and he wanted to be ahead of the crowd. Profits would be even larger since we would be producing our own washing equipment. The other partners would be Jack Krontz, an employee of the Jay Zook Mortgage Company, our mortgage banking rival, who was to be the location specialist, a specialty of his, and a younger man, a distant relative of Harry's who would be the day-to-day manager of the chain of car washes.

Krontz found a piece of vacant land next to a Shell gas station on Carnegie Avenue just east of E. 30th Street, which I thought was a very favorable location because of the amount of traffic Carnegie Avenue carried. We leased the land from Albert and Robert Levin, prominent Jewish real estate investors and philanthropists. I believe the lease was for a five year term, renewable.

I have absolutely no memory of securing the financing for the building, where the money came from or how much, but all went well and the simple rectangular cement block building was built, the equipment (which Harry bought, and did not manufacture) was installed but did not function well and the business rapidly failed. The building was abandoned; and I was left as the only partner, willing and able to pay the ground rent, honoring our obligation which went on for two or three years. The others refused to pay their share, offering heart rending reasons for their inability to pay. Once again, my family suffered because of my ambitions - or was that foolishness? Robert Levin, who was an attorney, told me later that the only reason they had ever agreed to the lease was that I was one of the partners. Small consolation! The final blow was to learn that the young man who was to be our business manager, not only had no money, but had a criminal record in New Jersey and had spent time in prison for sex offences against a minor. The warning signs were there: Harry habitually cut corners, and Fran, who met Krontz only once, took an immediate dislike to him and warned me not to trust him. I only met the young man from New Jersey once and did not have much chance to gain an impression of his character. My lesson: follow your gut instincts, but before investing any money. Investigate.

As to entering into a partnership with my brothers outside of the mortgage business, I had no desire. I felt that in some respects we were too close to one another already. However, if I learned of a perfect deal which required no cash and no personal liability, such as the one my customer had where he leased an office building located in Harrisburg to the State of Pennsylvania for 25 years, absolute net with no personal liability, the perfect real estate investment, I would do everything in my power to secure such a deal for the four of us. It would be the fulfillment of a dream I had from childhood, instilled in me by my parents. Unfortunately, there were not many deals of this nature in the market.

The closest I ever came to one of these "perfect" real estate investments was when Ted Miller, a stockbroker specializing in insurance company stocks, with Joseph, Mellen & Miller, on our floor of the East Ohio Gas Building, dropped in to my office one morning and asked whether I thought we could finance the sale leaseback of the home office of the Celine Life Insurance Company, of Celine, Ohio. I assured him that with that quality of credit it should be possible, and that I would like to investigate with the thought of forming a partnership with my brothers to be the purchaser, leasing the property back to the insurance company for as long a term as they desired, the rent being the equivalent of the mortgage payments plus a small negotiable percentage, 1 or 1 ½% for us, the owners. In effect they would be borrowing several million dollars at 4 or 4 ½%. I would want a firm contract in hand before approaching our source of the money. In effect, Celine could write their own ticket, and the amount of money they would receive from the sale would be determined by how much rent they were willing to pay. They were a fine, highly respected insurance company located in an attractive small town and it would have been the perfect deal for the brothers. Ted said he would see what he could do but was unable to sell the idea to his client and nothing ever came of the inquiry. I am sure my brothers were as disappointed as I was.

Another opportunity, somewhat similar, arose when, with the brothers' blessing, I tried to start a "wraparound mortgage" real estate mutual fund. I spent many hours creating a prospectus which outlined that advantages of having a fund able to approach property owners and lenders with check book in hand with the ability to make, in effect, a second mortgage without the disadvantage of its much higher interest rate. The fund would make a new mortgage in a face amount large enough to include the new money and the old first mortgage, not simply a traditional second mortgage for the amount of the new money. In this way the fund would earn the new interest rate, only slightly higher that the existing first mortgage rate, on the funds they supplied, but would also collect the difference of the two rates, old and new, while the fund continued to pay the old first mortgage payments. The leverage could be spectacular. I had visions of calling on all the Aetna correspondents and making "wraps" around all their larger loans.

I do not remember how I found the New York investment banker, but do remember sitting in his Manhattan office with a young man my age at Roosevelt & Company, in business since the 1920s, investment bankers, similar to Goldman Sachs, or Lehman Bros. While getting acquainted, I learned that he was a Yalie and had lived in Saybrook College across the street from my college, Pierson, which made things a little easier for me. They agreed to study the proposal, and I was invited back, and this time was taken to the offices of one of the most prominent law firms in Manhattan, Paul Weiss Rifkind, of which Arthur Goldberg, Supreme Court Justice, had been a partner. I was terrified of large legal fees and was assured that I need not worry. Things went along well, and when I was expecting to get the approval, I learned that Roosevelt & Company had gone bankrupt a few days earlier. My deal collapsed with their collapse. A huge disappointment, indeed. It would have provided growth we needed, and been a large diversification from our original business, into one we were already prepared for. And it could have dwarfed our original business. It might also have given us some leverage with Aetna.

The maddening thing was that within a few days I received a phone call asking me to attend a meeting in the offices of Al Lerner, later the owner of the Cleveland Browns. I was informed that Lerner and a local attorney were about to launch a "wraparound mortgage" mutual fund. He wondered if there were any loans in our Aetna portfolio which might be suitable candidates. I can't forget that he smoked a big stogie the whole meeting. The thing that bothered me, other than the odor of the cigar smoke, was that there was not a single individual in the prospectus for the proposed fund, which actually came into being, who was in the mortgage business or had any connection to mortgages.

In such a long life there were bound to be many disappointments, some large, some small, some from outside sources, some self-inflicted. Many seem insignificant today. I don't think I recalled them daily at the time, keeping them alive, using them for motivation. But there are vestiges. The worst are buried very deep and writing these pages has helped me come to terms with the worst of them, to find explanations which make the memories easier to live with, and even to forgive. Writing this autobiography has made it possible to find peace and I am very grateful for that.

I remember freeing myself from the terrible sense of inferiority I struggled with as a teenager and having the goal of earning enough to have a secure old age, of never being a burden to my daughters, and in fact, of leaving them enough so they would never have to worry. Luckily, my marriage was to a person who shared these goals; and we were always future goal oriented. All our lives together we had champagne tastes and a beer budget.

After securing the well-being of my immediate family, I had similar desires for my three brothers. These feelings were fundamental to me, always in the back of my mind. If I succeeded, it would be proof to the world that a teenager's *angst* is a poor predictor of his future.

I believe it was less than a year after we lost the Aetna account before I realized what a profound event that was in my life. I began to realize that it was more than an ordinary man losing an ordinary job, packing up his belongings in a cardboard box and carrying them out the front door for the last time on the way to his parking lot.

After all, I was leaving the only job that I ever had and one that defined an important aspect of who I was, with no assurance that a career interrupted, if not ended, could be easily transferred. I was 59 years old and never checked to see if a bank or other mortgage company would hire someone with my qualifications at that age. I had no doubts that conditions in the money markets were such that it would seem to make finding a job in my field impossible for the foreseeable future.

With unjustified optimism – if conditions were such that no one would hire me – why should a new company I would start succeed? If I had been more realistic, I would have asked myself: Would I hire me?

Without the benefit of hindsight, I started a new business with minimal investment: I converted Kathy's old bedroom on the lower level of 5320 Oakes Road into an office, using the built-in desk I had made for her, bought a filing cabinet, and got a separate phone line. I had stationery printed, designed by an old friend from our Leader Building days, Joseph Guillozet, which designated me as a "Mortgage Consultant," a loose enough designation to cover any kind of deal I might ever find. The office was the most delightful I had ever had: small and cozy, window at grade level looking out on a Japanese stone garden with its pond and the large stone at the edge of the ravine. It's too bad no one else ever saw it.

Before I started the venture, I promised Fran that I would not be the stereotype retiree, under foot and demanding her attention, showing her ways how to do her job better. I assured her that her life would go on just the same as if I were still leaving at 8:30 a.m. every morning to go to the office, although the office was only one floor below.

I told her my brave plans for my personal discipline: up every morning at 7:30 a.m., practice the piano for an hour, do my two mile (eight laps) walk up and down our driveway, and then start using the telephone at 10:00 a.m. when I could expect unretired men to be at their desks. I planned to maintain old friendships by going downtown two or three times a week for lunch, and then come home to my new office for more phone calls and work till 5 p.m. And I would not have to endure rush hour homeward bound traffic anymore.

Within a few months all my admirable plans were a shambles: the phone never rang, and I soon had it disconnected; I stayed in bed later and did not practice or walk; I found that my old friends had forgotten I existed and that the few lunches I initiated were too expensive because the downtown parking fees cost more than the lunch. But the hardest thing to assimilate was the fact that the business had changed radically and was becoming dominated by new methods of financing which were controlled by the big banks in New York and Wall Street investment bankers. The mortgage business was no longer the same and I was obsolete, thirty years of experience, worthless.

Nevertheless, my days were full, and frequently, I wondered how I had ever had time to go to work at the Schmidt Mortgage Company. I can honestly say that I never had a boring day. Please do not ask what I did with the days. I do not remember. But they were filled for the most part with activities that I enjoyed. I looked forward to each new day with anticipation. However, some of the days were not enjoyable at all, as you will see.

The final memory I wish to recall falls in the category of "self" inflicted. When I think of what this writing project has turned into, I think of the movie *The King and I* with Deborah Kerr and Yul Brynner. One of the great songs in the movie is "Getting to Know You." With a slight change in the title to "Getting to Know Me," it could apply to all the preceding pages, the reason for recounting the hundreds of memories therein. However, I have not saved the best for last. It is a rare day that I am not haunted by this memory.

It is concerned with my Columbus real estate venture. After the rocky start caused by the overnight change in interest rates by the F.H.A. the day after the transfer of title, things settled down and I remember a feeling of near elation when driving alone, at having achieved ownership of 304 rental units in a good location off Morse Road in Columbus, and, if not in Cleveland, close enough to visit easily. Although I realized the financing problem was hardly solved, I had visions of doing one more tax-free exchange in ten years or so.

We furnished one of the suites with rental furniture and used it on my/our periodic inspection visits. We provided our daughter, Barbara, and her new husband, Pete, with the use of an otherwise vacant suite rent-free as long as Pete finished his education at Ohio State University. We were able to provide a suite for Doug Adair when he took his new job as an anchor TV newsman in Columbus; we used our suite when we went to one of the early Memorial Golf Tournaments at Jack Nicklaus' golf course in Dublin, Ohio; we stayed in our suite after returning at midnight from a one-day vacation with a vacation club at the Greenbriar Resort in White Sulphur Springs, West Virginia, to see the Christmas decorations and have dinner, as guests of our manager couple, Ray Casto and Gloria Humphreys.

However, I acquired the property in 1981, and it took three years to secure the permanent financing which involved unbelievable stress, hardly mitigated by the fun things mentioned in the previous paragraph. I had a mild heart attack in 1984, and because of a worsening condition, quadruple by-pass surgery in November of 1985. When I had recovered, Fran and I had long discussions about real estate with its constant problems, management at a distance, and our future, and we decided to put the property on the market. We would cash out and enjoy a stress-free life.

With the favorable financing I had finally secured, there should be many buyers hungry for the leverage of a 9-3/4% interest rate on over $5,000,000 of conventional financing at 18% - 20%. In my mind the financing was more valuable than the vehicle of the brick and mortar. I do not remember the details, but we did receive an offer procured by Ray Casto, the manager, I believe, who oversaw the improvements required by the FHA loan. A price was agreed upon but when it came time for the closing, the buyers raised the question of the disposition of the Depreciation Reserve Fund which the FHA loan documents required. These funds, a small percentage of the physical value of the property. had to be deposited in a separate bank account monthly and had grown to $60,000. It was only after this money had been deposited and all other expenses paid, that the owner was allowed to take any income for himself.

In my mind this was turning an accounting, paper expense into a real dollar expense just like monthly utility expenses, and if the apartments had been financed with a conventional insurance company loan, no such cash deposits would have been required, and I could have enjoyed the $60,000, spending it on things other than repairs to the buildings. The estimated life for each category (roof, wiring, plumbing, etc.) varied and the amount designated for many of the categories of remaining life might be as long a 30-40 yeas, long after I would have disposed of the property. The account, now $60,000, was guaranteed to grow at a fixed rate monthly with no limit in size.

This became a matter of principle for me and I refused to give the account to the buyers, as they demanded. They would have to fund it and then watch it grow, unspendable, as I had done. But, because of a matter of "principle," with a cost of approximately $60,000, and my stubbornness, I lost the opportunity to cash out with $1,100,000 and freedom from the risks associated with owning real estate and the constant stress. The otherwise favorable financing was not enough for the buyers.

I do not recall anyone: my father, my attorney, Casto, the manager, or Fran offering advice, pointing out my folly. I'm sure there was no one who could have persuaded me to change my mind, because in my mind it was a matter of right and wrong. I was not about to give away

$60,000 of my dollars. I could not see that the Reserve fund was part of what the buyers were buying, just as they were buying the land and the brick and mortar; that it was a totality, part of the whole FHA financing package which had attracted them in the first place; and they were not trying to outsmart me, or take advantage of me.

I have spent countless hours dreaming of how different our life might have been with a nest egg of that size. How much might have been left after 20 years? Or what might it have grown to? Would I have been wise enough to put most of it into more Swiss annuities, stress free, risk free? What might have remained to pass along to our daughters?

Recalling such unhappy memories, which have been a burden in my later adult life, now that I am older and not suffering through the events as they happened, I finally have let go of the loss of the Columbus apartments and what seemed at the time to be a betrayal by the Aetna, a company in which I took such pride. I realize now that I was not at fault and that they were doing what a large corporation must do: change its business plan with the changing times in order to survive.

Any misunderstandings with my brothers I now attribute to a lack of knowledge of what my part of the business consisted of and what I had to do to get a loan approved. I am sure that our order of birth also played its part. Today, I am able to submerge any feelings of hurt or disappointment, and remember all the good times we had growing up, and revel in the pleasure I felt for over 30 years of seeing and working with my brothers every day, an incredible span of time in today's business world, in a sense extending our childhood by our working together and seeing each other every day.

I think of my next oldest brother, Russ's first visit to our condo in Mariners Cove and what the serenity he felt meant to him, and our last time together the day before he died, reminiscing over fond memories of growing up as allies. I think of my relationship with my youngest brother, Wesley, our discovering so many common interests and a common outlook on life which has led go a warm appreciation of each other. I think he is aware of the admiration I have for him. Although we now live fifty miles apart, we have lunch together regularly.

My third brother, Ken, passed on a short time ago and spent most of his business life in the South after he left our company. He remains a mystery to me.

As to the Columbus real estate, there were many good things connected with it, overshadowed by many years of problems, a changing rental market, an increasing hostility on the part of the FHA who ceased being cooperative and finally forced a change in management which I should have done years earlier, one of the examples of my poor judgment.

I met and dealt with some very fine individuals in Columbus: Tom Kohr, President of Kohr and Royer, Griffith, and Kevin Showe, of the Showe Real Estate Company, with whom I became a partner briefly, when they took over the management and almost succeeded in a new financing plan that would have saved the property. Always in the back of my mind was the thought, the fear, that I had undertaken a project beyond the capabilities of a mid-western high school boy. A classic example of *hubris,* perhaps. I have stopped blaming myself for the bad memories and bad judgments and am glad it is all so far in the past and am grateful for the healing that has taken place with the passage of time and this writing.

After writing more than 500 pages. I now consider myself an amateur writer, not an author, since imagination does not play any part in my story. At the start as an amateur, I had uncertainties and misgivings as to whether my story would be of any interest to others than members of my family. However, I felt encouraged when I took the time from my writing to read three recently published memoirs. The first two by Anne Fadiman and Jamie Bernstein related memories of what it was like to grow up with a famous father. The third was by Christopher Buckley, son of Bill Buckley, and it was about growing up with two prominent parents.

At the start of my project I was very aware of the number of names I included of ordinary people, playmates, schoolmates, neighbors, that would just be names, no chance of a reader ever reading about them elsewhere, or meeting them, but, hopefully, their inclusion would add authenticity and color. I was happy to see that reading names of prominent people I would never meet in the Bernstein book, and lists of names of exotic wines I would never taste in the Fadiman book took nothing away from my enjoyment of the books with their many other qualities, and this served as a source of encouragement to me. I recommend to any reader any and all of the three memoirs.

I do not remember when my fascination with the idea of infinity began, but it was very early in my life, probably in Sunday School. But the older I grew, especially as my writing project progressed and the proximity to death grew nearer in tandem, the subject invaded my thinking. I took some time off from my writing and delved into the subject. It was heavy going. Among the several books I explored I could not find a simple guide as to how to think about infinity, and never finished any of them. Thus, my conclusions, undoubtedly not original, feel as though they are my own, and I am sure would be criticized by a philosopher or theologian as simplistic and thoroughly puerile. No matter. My ideas and conclusions are a comfort to me, and I have now reached an age where I feel free to disclose what formerly have always been my most private thoughts

As this project progressed, and as more and more time passed, I became more and more aware of my first attempt at writing, of what I called the "Credo," Chapter XIV. I found as I grew older that my beliefs were evolving into something beyond the beliefs in "Credo," which are still part, if not the basis, of my thinking. As my time on Earth became more limited, I began to think more and more of Infinity and of Deity, and the final Chapter, No. XV reveals where I stand now in those beliefs with which I have become very comfortable. Since infinity encompasses literally all of creation, animate and inanimate, there is room for my earlier beliefs that have served me so well.

In my reading I seemed to notice the use of the word "infinity" in articles frequently and it bothered me that it was used so casually. "Infinite" or "infinitely" are not in the same class as "nice," or "warm," or "sunny," or "gloomy." They convey a more profound meaning and are not simple intensifiers. I hope I have not been guilty of this. I liken this to the almost flippant use of the word "trillion" today. There seems to me no effort to examine the true significance of either word. I feel it would be so beneficial for the world if more attention were paid to the deep meaning of "infinity."

I think of Paul's letter to the Corinthians where he said, "Now we see through a glass darkly, and then face to face. Now I know in part, but then shall I know even as also I am known." I always liked this verse, there was something about looking "through a glass darkly" that spoke to a silent part of me. I think writing this autobiography with its overview of a lifetime; and now the contemplation of the ending of my story have made the hours spent in writing very worthwhile to me.

I find the way my mind works interesting. I have watched three or four of the 21 day free meditation series offered by Oprah Winfrey and Deepak Chopra; and found that when my mind was in state of relaxation it was not empty as it was supposed to be, but filled with music, especially Poulenc's *Gloria*, for instance, or the final movement of Mahler's *Second Symphony, The Resurrection Symphony*. I would seem to experience a great, calm sense of release. On other occasions I got the same feeling from visual images that float before my eyes. I think of the photograph of my daughter Nancy parasailing with our neighbor in Florida her last summer, and after the shock of Fran's unexpected death, the image of the Forest Ranger releasing the raptor after its rehabilitation, exulting in its return to its freedom.

Lately, I have been thinking about the "horizon." I have a confusing picture in my mind of standing on the shore of a large body of water, staring at the distant horizon, or driving down one of those western highways with the mountains in the distance and feeling frustration that I can never reach my horizon. It is always receding; and the distance remains constant. I take this as a metaphor for life that is always seeking something unattainable. When I think of death and my concept of what it is, that it is not the end of existence; I believe we are not doomed to nothingness. Death is a change in our existence after we have incubated on earth a sufficient time to be released to our mature form, whatever that may be, surely spiritual, at last free to explore infinity. I believe absolutely that death is not the end of existence, but a form of change. The metaphor that occurs to me involves the horizon: at the moment of death we finally reach our horizon and can see beyond. With all infinity to explore it has to be glorious.

When I undertook the writing of this project, I did not impose on myself the discipline of a professional author. I am thinking of Hemingway, and others, who forced themselves to write a thousand words every day or arose at 6 a.m. and sat at their typewriter until they had produced the magical 1,000 words. I was struggling how to operate a computer and had many hours wasted correcting a beginner's errors. I tried to find days when I could count on two hours of uninterrupted time to type, which for me was the equivalent of one page composed, typed, corrected and printed. Although there were many days I did no work on my "project" at all. But this was not all bad; it allowed me to continue my regular reading habits, more or less, and I found many inspirations.

Now it has come to an end, and I think these last few pages have been a strange way to end a chapter on business and finance. Maybe, you, the reader, will see a connection.

In my ordinary reading during this long period of composition (almost four years) for which I have been spared, I was constantly noticing ideas that were inspirational, or puzzling or thought provoking. A few I noted and saved:

"Do not remember the former things or consider things of old. I am about to do a new thing. Now it springs forth, do ye not perceive it?"

the *Bible*

"But memory does not require the writing of history."

Author unknown.

"To tell a long-lasting story....to create something that endured, to be alive somehow as long as someone would read my books."

Susan Orlean, *The Library* page 310

"Bless what there is for being,

That singular command

I do not understand.

Bless what there is for being

Which has to be obeyed, for

What else am I made for,

Agreeing or disagreeing."

W. H. Auden

"I have realized that the past and the future are real illusions, that they exist in the present which is what there is and all there is."

Alan Watts

Perhaps the most concentrated, productive thinking I did about infinity happened at the new Cleveland Clinic Hospital in Avon Lake, Ohio in February 2019. It was the time that most of the bits and pieces of my previous reading and thinking about infinity came together. It was also the time that I became convinced that the practice of meditation can have profound effects on our physical bodies, although it is apparently the mind we are dealing with.

On the day I was to leave, my blood pressure was taken before lunch and it read 150 /96, which was very high for me. After lunch I decided not to start reading something new and spent the next two hours drifting in and out of a light sleep in my recliner chair in the warm sunlight (the room faced south and overlooked I-90). In a short while I was drifting in and out of a light sleep, my mind started going over the thoughts that had been accumulating about infinity and I started to write them down on a piece of paper, much of the writing hard to decipher today even with a magnifying glass. I still have that piece of paper, kept in anticipation of the conclusion of this project.

One final blood pressure was taken a half hour before I was to leave, about 2:30 p.m., after my meditation/resting, and the reading was 96/58. I thought this was remarkable and called it to the nurse's attention, who said she thought the drop was probably a result of my state of total relaxation. I think it was a form of meditation and just as an off-color remark can cause a blush on one's cheek, meditation can affect the circulation and heartbeat. I had never had this experience from any of the meditation series offered by Oprah Winfrey and Deepak Chopra on the internet. The subject matter of my thoughts may also have had something to do with it.

The insights I gained from that memorable afternoon are to be found in the final chapter where my story must draw to a close. I would like to take a break from my labors. I do not want the fourth corner of my puzzle finding me at my computer trying to recall some smaller, more distant memory that might add a touch of color to the puzzle that has been my life.

# Chapter XIV

# Credo

Note: This is the first chapter written of my autobiography started two years before undertaking the main project. You may be interested in the growth of my thinking during the writing of this story.

A question in a letter from an old friend in Kansas asked if I was a "Christian" and did I have a "Personal Savior." I asked myself: Could I be classified as a "Christian" and not have a personal savior? I did not have an immediate answer and do not know how I should be classified now.

At my age, 95+, I no longer feel such a question is intrusive or too personal, and I suddenly realized that no one, family or friend, knows what I believe or why. Since I have so much to be grateful for, maybe, in the short time I may have left, it might be of interest for me to organize my thoughts and put in writing for those who follow, what I have evolved into, although I do not know the classification. So this is meant to be a testimonial to a long life that has felt the loving hand of Deity from childhood on, who lives in a world of gratitude, and who, in spite of inevitable omissions caused by an imperfect memory, wishes to reveal as complete an overall picture as possible.

My story begins with my being about six or seven years old and remembering being taken each Sunday to Sunday school at Fourth (or Sixth?) Christian Science Church on Denison Avenue on the west side of Cleveland. Services were held in the basement of an unfinished building at that time. Needless to say, I remember nothing of this experience or of my earliest Sundays at Fifth Church, at the corner of W. 117th St. and Lake Avenue, where we started going sometime after our move to Lakewood when I was two years old (1923).

It was at Fifth Church Sunday School that I started to absorb my early religious beliefs and training. It was at my mother's insistence, something basic in her concept of being a good mother, that required regular attendance. I remember sitting on little chairs in a circle in a large open room under the main auditorium, entered by walking down a ramp. There was a small stage at one end of the room where the superintendent conducted the service and where the piano for singing hymns was located. I remember being the only one in my early classes asked to read the Bible, where we learned the usual Bible stories and memorized the Lord's Prayer, the Ten Commandments and the Twenty-Third Psalm. Later, probably about the tenth grade in high school, I remember playing the piano for the whole Sunday School to sing the hymns and also some prelude music before classes began to signal it was time to start getting serious and be quiet. Much later I worked as a janitor in the summer when the two regular janitors took their vacations. I loved that church, which was of such unique architecture, octagonal shape with a dome, with blue velvet upholstered theater seats instead of pews. It was an honor to help preserve its beauty and dignity, and I loved the quiet of being alone there.

As far as I know our Sunday School teachers were recruited from the congregation; and I don't know what training they may or may not have had. As I grew to high school age, I remember two outstanding ones, Mr. Malin and Mrs. Irene Fenton. From a very early age, we were taught a definition of "God" as well as memorizing the Lord's Prayer and the Twenty-Third Psalm, and gratitude for Mary Baker Eddy, the founder and discoverer of Christian Science. Christian Science at that time was a radical new Christian denomination, with very different beliefs. It was anathema to the standard, accepted denominations, especially Roman Catholicism.

Mrs. Eddy taught that God is Life, Truth, Love, Mind, Principle, Soul and Spirit, Infinite and Eternal, Omniscient and All-Powerful, Perfect. Therefore, His creation could not be otherwise. In no way could He have created evil, or matter, or punish His own ideas, His own creation. We were taught to believe the first verses of Genesis that "God created Man in His own image." We were taught that we are His idea and reflect His image; that the sickness and sin that we see and experience around us are illusion; a mist that arose from the earth; that Jesus was the most perfect of all mortal men, a worker of miracles and our way-shower; that the same miracles performed by Jesus could occur today by using Mrs. Eddy's discovery of divine healing which was considered a form of insanity by the conventional denominations. This is and was pretty heavy stuff. It led to the stereotype in the minds of the conventional churches of a strange sect that forbade turning to doctors or medicine for healing of sickness; that forbade the use of alcohol or drugs or tobacco, even coffee or tea; that had no marriage or funeral ceremonies and a very unusual form of communion service (without wine) and only twice a year. So, there was no smoking or drinking or going to doctors and that made me very strange to my peers. It added pressures to a young teenager who was the oldest child, the first to face social challenges; painfully shy, insecure, and secretly ashamed to be different. In spite of the teachings of my church, I felt I failed not only in the healing of physical problems, but also the more intangible social ones. These feelings began to lessen in my second semester at Yale when going from one class to another in the beautiful new spring greenery, I suddenly realized that this magic place, Yale, did not think I was a freak: indeed, they thought highly enough of me that they were actually paying me to attend in the form of my scholarship.

Christian Science had no trained, professional clergy with degrees in Theology. Instead, it had a formal order of service prepared by the Mother Church in Boston, members studying and hearing the same "lesson" worldwide, led by a First and Second Reader elected from members of the congregation for three year terms, I believe. Selected passages from the King James version of the Bible were read by the Second Reader (usually a woman); explanatory passages of those verses were read from the Christian Science textbook, *Science & Health with Key to the Scriptures,* read by the First Reader (usually a man). The "sermon," thus, was a series of six daily lessons, which were to have been studied at home during the week by the congregation, who then came to church to hear what they had been studying made more clear by the more inspired readers. These lessons followed an annual unchanging rotation of subjects and were prepared by the Mother Church in

Boston and published as the "Quarterly," in various languages and used around the world. The study at home during the week was a form of very strict discipline. There was no place for the individual thoughts or interpretations of a school trained theologian. It all seemed very austere and intellectual when I was allowed to attend services upstairs after "graduating" from Sunday school at age sixteen.

However, doubts had begun for me after an experience in Mrs. Fenton's Sunday school class. She was the finest teacher I ever had. She insisted that we study the daily lessons and actually gave us written questions to answer the following week based on the weekly lesson. One Sunday one of her questions was: "Is Christian Science the final revelation of all Truth?' I innocently answered "No! It can't be because God is Truth and is Infinite. His creation is constantly expanding; and his Truth is growing and expanding with it and finding new ways to express itself". This from a fifteen or sixteen year-old! She was stunned and I think slapped my cheek lightly and then started a vigorous refutation defending Mrs. Eddy, and her teachings, which we were expected to acknowledge and accept without question.

I do not recall what it was, or could have been, but it did not satisfy me, and was the beginning of my doubts. These were not assuaged by my many sincere, hopeful attempts at healing physical problems mentally, which did not work. They never did. But I was encouraged to keep trying and the blame was always on me because my "understanding" was deficient.

I remember once trying to help a girl, a fellow Scientist from Sunday school, recover from a cold so we could attend a picnic, and I failed. Of course. On the other hand, I do not remember any specific attempts for personal healings (cold sores were a fairly constant problem, interfering with my clarinet lessons) and it may be that Christian Science was providing an unwitting, general protection for me, imperfect "understanding" or not. For instance, the first pill I ever took (a salt pill) was at age twenty-two in the Army before a 35 mile "hike" on a very hot day and I had a terrible time. I didn't know how to swallow it.

I went away to college still an earnest student of Christian Science with the blessings of my parents, their friends at Fifth Church and Mrs. Fenton, whose son, Doug, was a half-year behind me in high school and won the scholarship to M.I.T. that year. I still believed and practiced my early teachings although there was not enough time to read the Daily Lessons with my scholarship dependent on so much assigned reading, three hour's bursary work every day and other activities including organ lessons which required an hour's practice daily. Then there was marching band, swimming team, etc.

I joined the Christian Science Society at Yale, overseen by a Practitioner from Manhattan, Judd Stilson, assigned by the Mother Church in Boston (to ensure the purity of the readings?). I was elected Reader my junior year. This meant that I had to prepare readings from the Bible and Science and Health textbook. This was as close as possible to being able to express personal ideas or beliefs, albeit through the words of the texts, in that I had some choice, praying they were coherent, read them and then conduct the testimonial (acknowledgment of healing demonstrations of all kinds – usually a long period of empty silence) portion of the meeting. All this was modeled on the regular Wednesday night services at the regular Christian Science churches. I think we met once a month, fifteen or twenty of us.

One other event while at college stands out in my memory. While I never took a course in religion, I did take one in philosophy, about which I recall very little. One piece in my puzzle occurred in my Freshman English class where we read the *King James Version of the Bible* as literature for a month. While discussing the Flight from Egypt and the Crossing of the Red Sea in class, one of the students scoffed at the whole story and was silenced when the instructor asked him where the idea had come from? To cross at that perfect place and at that perfect time? This fit in nicely with my belief that God is Mind and manifested in ideas. I found it comforting and reassuring. The questioning student was silenced and had no riposte..

Much later, reading the daily letters between Fran and myself, which covered the period from our meeting until the fifteenth year of our marriage (we knew within a week something serious had happened) I told her of my daily experiences at basic training at Fort McClellan, Alabama. I can't get over the help my Christian Science background was to me, doubts and all. I know the other men survived the rigors, but I also know it was easier for me, I think, because of my early religious training, in spite of the invidious doubts that increasingly crept into my thinking.

Before our marriage in 1945, Fran and I had many discussions about religion, knowing that with such different backgrounds, problems could arise. Her religious background was Roman Catholic on her father's side and Episcopalian on her mother's. She did have a neighbor boy in Detroit who was a Christian Scientist; and her mother had a landlady who was a Christian Scientist. She had some familiarity with the religion, at least as to how the religion affected personalities. Fran agreed to "try" to learn what Christian Science really was, at her own pace and on her own terms. However, she wanted assurance from me that if we married and she was unsuccessful in her attempts to change her beliefs, that I would raise no objection to turning to doctors and medicine for help for any children we might have. In my doubtful state of mind, still hoping for her "conversion" while I was trying to deal with my own serious doubts, I had no trouble in agreeing with her. And so it was.

The first year of our marriage she developed severe back problems which we later learned were caused by a slipped disc. She actually worked with a Christian Science Practitioner who attended Fifth Church where we went the first few years. But the Christian Science "treatments" were unsuccessful; and her pain continued. Oddly enough, relief came not from medicine, but an incident on a tennis court, where I had cajoled her into playing with me on the theory that it couldn't be any more painful. While stretching to return a ball, something popped, and the pain did in fact decrease. No conscious attempt on our part to employ the "healing" power of Christian Science. Perhaps the presence of a general power for good?

So, perhaps now with this background, it is time for me to start enumerating what I believe is evidence of "God's Hand" in my life. I had arrived at the age of twenty-five with doubts as to my religious training, about the apparent reality of my physical, material body (when I pinch it, it hurts) even the very existence of God; how to reconcile this with my belief in a spiritual reality. How can this perfect God, Spirit, whom I acknowledge and worship, operate in a world He could not have logically created? Ever since my 20s, to this day, I have searched for the answer, for insights on this problem, which goes all the way back to the Greek philosophers.

In my 30s and 40s, I read a lot of science fiction and had my eyes opened to some of the far-out ideas floated, which have since come true. *Star Wars, Star Trek, 2001* in the movies and TV provided more bits and pieces in my search. Are there other worlds in the cosmos with knowable life; could there be other dimensions; does the definition of infinity include an infinite number of universes; is it true that if one can conceive an idea, it can be true? This sort of thinking and searching in my reading was going on constantly. What I was looking for was a positive answer to the question: does God exist? I needed something to reinforce the shaky foundation of what faith I had.

About this time the comments of a Christian Science Sunday school teacher in Brecksville provided the final blow. I had been taking the children to Sunday school (their mother did not accompany us - although she was not in any way hostile and was probably glad the children were getting some sort of Christian teaching, even though she could not accept the teachings), one of the Sunday school teachers answered one of my daughter's questions as to why her Grandma died, by saying that if my mother had been a better Christian Scientist, and her beliefs had been stronger, she would still be alive and with us. I couldn't believe anyone could be so insensitive to say something like that to a grieving nine-year-old who naturally came to her Daddy for reassurance. That, plus the difference between words and actions of other Christian Science members of my family resulted in my giving up any further study of Christian Science, let alone attendance at church or Sunday school. I was probably about thirty-five at the time. Shortly thereafter their mother began taking the children to her Episcopal church which was a new "Mission," of which she was very proud to be one of the original nine members. It started as a very small group meeting at the children's' grammar school in Brecksville.

Here I must confess to what was surely the most shameful, hurtful thing I did to my dear wife in all the 69 years of our marriage. Her name must have been in the central records of the Diocese and someone on the organizing committee appointed by the Diocese (known as "downtown") called on her in Brecksville to enlist her support in founding a new church in Brecksville. I don't remember being present, but she told me about it and all I could see was endless calls for financial support. We were still struggling somewhat with three daughters and a large new house and I didn't feel we needed this undoubted additional expense, especially for something I couldn't believe in.

An army friend's younger brother, in Cleveland on a business trip, contacted me and was invited to dinner. Afterwards, we were sitting in the living room, chatting, and the subject of the new church came up and I vented, in front of a virtual stranger, meeting my wife for the first time, calling into question the sincerity of her beliefs since we had lived down the street for eight years within walking distance of a well-established Episcopal church and she had never set foot in it. All this ugliness, the strident voice, the looks of rage, just spewed forth, and even I was embarrassed when I finished. Fran was stunned and embarrassed, as well, and I can't imagine what our friend must have thought. Somehow the evening ended and no more was said. But Fran did become one the nine Founders and the first lady vestryman, of which she was very proud. And I spent the rest of her life trying to make up for my unspeakable behavior that night.

An opportunity arose to begin my "payback." when a substitute was needed to play the organ for a Sunday service,. Fran, knowing that I had played piano for Christian Science services and had had organ lessons at Yale, very timidly and reluctantly came to me and asked if I would consider helping out. This was at a stage where she actively disinvited me to accompany her and the children to her church or church functions (such as potlucks or picnics), could not tolerate my disparagement of the intellectual content of her beliefs, or my active hostility. I look back on those days with horror at my behavior. I don't understand where it came from. Undoubtedly someplace very deep down. I pointed out that it had been twenty years since I had touched an organ, that I didn't know the Episcopal order of service nor how to play the chants. But I would try my best, if that would help, and pray that I would not embarrass her. I got through the service somehow or other, limp and sweaty from the tension. Do I look back now and see the Hand of God, giving me a second chance? You bet I do. After that first Sunday I substituted several times and then the new church was built with a larger Baldwin electronic organ, and the regular organist was in Hawaii the Sunday of the Dedication of the new church. It fell to me to play for that first service, which was attended by the Bishop, who knocked on the front door with a large Cross before entering; the Mayor and Council members and every seat was filled. I had grown to play that first service with respect and affection. In fact, I played an extra closing verse of one of the hymns, all alone, and apologized to the Bishop afterwards. He just chuckled. This was just one more step in a long series in my attempts to seek forgiveness and redemption for my earlier outburst.

It was the beginning of a wonderful period of my life that lasted about five years, where I was actively serving God. I was broadening my understanding and acceptance of other beliefs, ending the Sunday before our oldest daughter's wedding, when I retired. There was a wonderful sense of fulfillment, a feeling of being where I was meant to be. And always, the chance of improving my image in my wife's eyes, and just maybe, giving her a small feeling of pride.

I actually listened to the sermons carefully, trying to find ideas which had some correspondence to my early Christian Science training. I was critical of the use of the *Revised Standard Bible* which lacks the poetry and majesty of the King James version. The changes in translation to make the message easier to understand and more accessible to today's worshipers never once improved or changed my understanding (when I compared them to the same passages as they were read to the small King James version given to me when I entered the Army).

On Saturdays, when I took a break from my final practice for the Sunday service, I often found myself in the Rev. Wrenn's office and we would engage in very friendly discussions about religion. He was most interested in my curious background. He was a wonderful Pastor and a pleasure to work with.

On one occasion, I told him that I listened very carefully and critically to his weekly sermon which I found interesting and useful, but always had an empty feeling because God was constantly referred to and I had no idea what his concept of God or Deity was. I told him that if he could not tell me what He is, he surely could tell me what He is not, nor could be. My recollection is that this comment caused a deep intake of breath, in shock. The result came a week later in his sermon, the finest he ever gave in those five years, on Prayer. It was very powerful, very moving and I had tears in my eyes when it ended. As we left, I said, "That was for me, wasn't it?" And he just nodded. I have tears now as I proofread this. I now regret that I never asked him for a copy, or his notes which I am sure he must have had.

Another incident revealing my strange religious background occurred when the new altar arrived and on my break the Rev. Wrenn, who was immensely proud of it, invited me to go with him to look at it closely. It was a large coffin shaped box made of walnut and had two bas relief carvings on the face, somewhat impressionistic. He asked me what they signified to me. After a few minutes' thought, I told him: 'The Burning Bush and the Living Rock.' He was stunned because, of course, the correct answer was: the 'Sheaf of Wheat' and the 'Bunch of Grapes,' both very traditional Christian symbols. I don't know what this says about my beliefs, other than the importance of the Old Testament to me.

Finally, when I look back at my long life, the most gratifying thing I ever did, even more so than completing our home in Brecksville, was to play the organ those five years for St. Matthews Episcopal Church (I played gratis, and spent hundreds of hours in practice and preparation) mainly the feeling of being a part of a Community and of the service itself, of actually being of service to God, and occasionally to add a spark of inspiration to one of the parishioners. But also, to have the opportunity at the same time to prove to my wife that I was changed for the better; and she was the inspiration for making me a better person.

Now, to go on to some of the many incidents which made me increasingly aware of the presence of God in my life.

After the general early background which I am sure had many instances of God's presence starting with parents who were hardworking and loving and principled, the first event that I think of as an epiphany was the amazing coincidence of meeting the girl who was to become my wife and lifelong partner. I have told the story many times and still re-tell it to myself in my quiet times before drifting off to sleep. There were so many coincidences, so many improbabilities. How could I live only a few blocks distant from her for a whole year, her senior year, without our paths crossing? How could she waste two precious weeks overcoming her stereotypical image of a "Yale" man before agreeing to our blind date, surely a waste of her precious study time? My main reason for agreeing to the arranged meeting was to listen to my jazz records, which I had with me in Ann Arbor, on a better sound system. I was not looking for a wife the last week of my stay in Ann Arbor. It was too late for that. Her reasons ultimately must have included curiosity. However, looking back, we were both ripe for what happened. I had a recent failed love affair, was twenty-four years old, and had "sized up" every girl I ever met (not many) since high school and even before, by asking myself: could I live with this person for the rest of my life? Could I adapt to her requirements for a lifetime? I'm sure this attitude was learned from my parents. I'm also sure Fran must have hoped to meet someone in her four years on campus who would satisfy her requirements for a lifetime commitment, especially in light of the outcome of her parent's marriage. She dated many boys but was probably hampered in her search by World War II and the smaller pool of men present on campus. She was twenty-two and very wise for her years.

So, the stage was set. It was a Tuesday evening, probably 7 p.m. (May 22, 1945, as I learned later from our letters) that I was led to the Gamma Phi Beta house by my army friend, Ken Pierson, to meet the unknown. She appeared promptly (good); was very attractive (good); brunette (good); tall and slender (good); very gracious and we sat down and played a few hands of bridge (very good); took a break to go to a nearby soda fountain; remarked about how cute a young boy seated down the counter was and then back to the sorority house to dance to my music. I don't know what she must have thought about it. I'm sure it was her first exposure to real jazz. But she was game and held her own by telling me of her favorites: Tommy Dorsey, Harry James, and Benny Goodman, all of whom I thought were OK, but terribly "commercial," not in the same league as the small group jazz I loved. I don't remember how the evening ended. I do remember how shaken I felt, and how excited, and absolutely terrified that I would do something or say something that would make me lose her. I already knew, after the first half hour, that she was the one that I had been searching for. I knew already that this was the girl I wanted to marry and spend the rest of my life with.

She agreed to another date the next day and every day thereafter and I never stopped talking, trying desperately to convince her that I was for real, and not just a serviceman trying to take advantage of a coed.

We were to graduate from Language School on Saturday. She would not let me break a date with the daughter of one of my favorite Sunday school teachers for the Company party at the USO on Friday night, but did allow me to break the date (a first for me) for her Senior Prom, so I could take her to her Senior Prom where we danced to the music of Duke Ellington, my favorite Big Band. That's how it worked out. By the end of the week she knew I was for real and was beginning to feel the same way. I had two week's leave before reporting to Fort McClellan, Alabama, and spent the first week visiting my great friend, Sidney Mishcon, in New York where we visited 52nd Street every night to listen to real live jazz. Then I returned to Ann Arbor for the Prom, slept in an empty room on a mattress cover in Tyler House, our old quarters; went to Detroit to meet her mother whom I instantly took to; then home to Cleveland. Fran came to Cleveland to meet my family. By this time, we had agreed we were serious and very much in love. The parting, when I had to leave, was a sad one. The first of many.

What are the odds of such a chance meeting, in such a short time frame, under wartime pressures, enforced separations, different backgrounds, lack of money and all the other things that could go wrong, after only 21 dates, resulting in a marriage, completely faithful on both sides, that lasted almost sixty-nine years until her death in April, 2014? You may attribute this to nothing more than blind chance, or sheer luck, but it happened to me, and I do not. I think this is one way in which God has manifested Himself in my life.

The second event had nothing to do with my emotional life. We had been married for about twenty-five years; had our three daughters, beautiful in every way; successfully completed the building of our unique house in Brecksville; had our ten year span of wonderful vacations in Europe, loving the joys of discovery while wandering by rental car. My father, who founded our mortgage business in 1941, which we (all four sons) were expected to join, and did after leaving the service, was of the old school and felt that each of us should provide for his own retirement, as he had by buying, perhaps, a small apartment house. He felt our income, which he had initially provided from his own pocket, was ample for us to make our own investments to take care of our old age. All this occurred at a time of great growth in real estate, and the economy, making up for the time lost in winning World War II.

I followed his example, taking advantage of financing conditions in the market at the time, investing a small amount of money to acquire a small apartment building in Cleveland, followed a few years later by a larger building in Euclid, Ohio. This was a market I knew more about than any other thanks to my specialty in the mortgage business. It provided extra income and generous tax benefits as well as possible capital gains. With three girls to educate and possibly three weddings to pay for (hopefully), this seemed the logical way to go.

After starting out very modestly in the Cleveland market, reinvesting the income in improving the properties, and taking advantage of the strength of the post-war economy, I was able to use the tax laws and trade the Cleveland properties for two much larger properties in Columbus in what was known as a tax-free exchange. This appeared to be the answer to arrange for a secure old age. It had the additional advantage of being able to leave a substantial estate to be divided among my daughters. So, on the basis of my analysis and my business experience, the deal went forward and closed at which time it became irreversible. To my horror, the very next day the FHA announced a rate increase, part of the Reagan/Volcker plan to bring inflation under control. As a result, the financing of the trade we had been counting on disappeared. That began a long period of unbelievable, unrelenting stress. I was caught in a bear trap. Evidence of the Hand of God? Hard to rationalize. It was the beginning of a 3 years search for a solution, unsuccessful every step of the way, and increasingly stressful, facing the loss of all that we had worked for and achieved to that point.

Finally, I discovered an FHA program that might solve the problem and made application in Columbus at Buckeye Federal S&L where I knew the CEO from his days in the business in Cleveland. Also, the head of his mortgage loan department had been a former employee of the local FHA office.

The Columbus apartments were two separate properties under the same ownership about a mile apart, and at the time of the trade, financed with three different life insurance company conventional mortgages. None of them would consider refinancing their loans for the new purchaser because of the rate changes going on in the market. The new FHA program we were attempting to use to solve our refinance problem was operated on a blind auction process, nationwide, I would be competing against desperate borrowers in Chicago and Los Angeles and San Francisco, for instance, with a total authorized dollar amount far short of the nationwide demand. The program interest rate was so low compared to the conventional, uninsured market and the term allowed so long that the program was bound to be vastly oversubscribed. The financing itself was worth far more than the brick and mortar.

I had applied to The Buckeye Federal S&L people who proposed to file an application for two mortgages, one for each property, and while I am no mathematician, I knew that in the face of the competition, it had to increase the odds of failure hugely. And, if only one application of the two happened to be approved, it would not solve my problem. So, I suggested that Buckeye Federal file a single application for a single "blanket" mortgage, one mortgage deed covering both properties, which they did, without much hope of success and after a lot of tedious, hard work.

This was the background for our leaving on our desperately needed first vacation in Florida. I believe it was February. We left, car loaded and with my briefcase filled with the Columbus files. The interesting thing to me now was that I had bought a tape recording of the Francis Poulenc "Gloria" with Judith Blegen singing the solo part, and rather than listening to jazz as we usually did, we binge listened to the "Gloria", playing it over and over again, absorbing the Latin words: *Laudamus te, Benedicimus te, Domine Deo*, (We Praise Thee, We Bless Thee, Lord God). I still sing them to myself, frequently, before drifting off to sleep. Eventually we arrived in Key West, a fascinating place, and after lunch, without much hope, once again, after many earlier calls, I called Buckeye Federal from the back storage room of one of the shops while Fran shopped, prepared for the worst and learned our application had been approved under Section 221d4, Substantial Rehab for $5,146,000. They were amazed and I was overwhelmed with gratitude and relief. Our problem was solved. I later learned that the amount approved was the largest single loan in all of Ohio and Michigan.

Now, once again, I am no mathematician, but what are the odds? How can this not be considered the Hand of God intervening by some unknown mechanism in human affairs? I choose to think it is, or was, and my gratitude is and was boundless.

In connecting the dots in my life, I find it intriguing to remember one of my favorite teachers, my 6th grade teacher, Mrs. Henrietta Pagan, whose husband was a sergeant in the U.S. Army, stationed in China. I think she may have been there with him. Her experiences made her teaching of geography, especially mysterious China, very vivid and we were all very impressed with the Chinese although I doubt that I had ever seen a live Oriental person at that point.

I do not recall any other contact with Oriental matters. I did study Latin and had French all through high school and Yale, which surely has some connection to my love of language and words and reading. When my Army Basic Training was completed, my next step as a college graduate was to qualify for the linguistic side of the new ASTP program since all the OCS schools were temporarily closed. When I arrived for my interview to determine if I was qualified in French, I was helped by an enlisted man who just happened to be a fellow Yale grad (How odd! Right time, right place?) was accepted and sent to the University of Minnesota, where French was not offered, this being the Army. The languages taught there were: German, the Scandinavian languages, and Japanese. We were allowed two choices for the language we would prefer to study, and no one elected Japanese. The Army's solution to this dilemma was to take the men with the top 120 scores on the Army AGCT test we all took when inducted and fill their quota that way. And that is how I became a Japanese scholar, which may have saved my life.

Ultimately, after a second year of study at the University of Michigan, I met Fran. I had acquired a skill so valuable (Japanese was the only language that survived the cancellation of the ASTP experiment) that I was spared the fate of the other linguists who became infantrymen in the Battle of the Bulge, where with inadequate training and equipment, under very unfavorable conditions, they had heavy casualties. It took so long to learn this most difficult language that the war ended before we ever completed our studies, and I was spared. I have always felt that I was guided on this strange journey by some Higher Power and I am still trying to find a way to express the gratitude I feel. As a side benefit, I learned to love Japanese art and poetry, and architecture. And Japanese tree peonies! The house we commissioned and built in Brecksville was full of Japanese influences, and this long before Oriental architecture became a fad in the U.S.

It's hard for me not to give credit to God for saving my life, leading me to my lifelong mate, and an amazing circle of fellow language student friends. But then, maybe it was just luck.

Now, before I recall the next to last great epiphany in my life, I want to provide some background. Going back to my very early religious training, it is important to remember that Christian Science was on the defensive. It was a new religion (some said cult) radical in its beliefs, and aroused the hostility of the older denominations, especially the Roman Catholics with their "idolatry" and "worship" of the Virgin Mary. Christian Science was looked down upon, became very ingrown and struggled to maintain the purity of their new beliefs to give them the time to be appreciated and accepted by the outsiders. Any hint of worship of the Virgin Mary was unthinkable. I fully subscribed to this, of course. However, in my outside reading I was exposed to Mary in literature and was aware of the 19th century movement making her role more and more important in Catholicism. I always resisted this and reinforced my beliefs by going back to the Christian Science definition of God (I just checked the Glossary of the Christian Science textbook and was rather surprised to find there is no definition of Mary, but of many others, including God, Jesus, Joseph, Judah, etc. Obviously my earliest and later training made it very difficult for me to assign any importance to the role of Mary in theology other than the Virgin Birth, the mother of Jesus, in my worship of God. To hear the expression Holy Mother of God troubled me. God can have no mother and Jesus is not God.

My concepts of Mary started to broaden after being exposed to my wife's background, playing the organ for her church and listening critically to the weekly sermons which explicated a different concept of Deity. But not as enlightened as the Christian Science concepts. I was growing older and hopefully more tolerant and open-minded. One enlightenment occurred in a conversation I had with one of the Cleveland brokers in the Columbus real estate transaction, an older man and a very devout Catholic, which I deeply respected. I can't remember how the subject came up; the only thing I do remember is that he referred to the Virgin Mary not as the Virgin Mary, but as the "Holy Mother", and this became very meaningful to me.

Now we are at that part of my journey, my fifth decade, when we traveled to Europe for our vacations: England, France, Italy, Switzerland, and Spain; where we visited every cathedral we could on our route, going out of our way if necessary, taking copious color slides of the architecture and especially the stained glass windows. This was always done quietly, unobtrusively and with respect. If there were conditions allowing us to intrude in this way, or outright prohibitions to taking photographs, we obeyed and respected them and their different customs.

The great revelation for me came at the beginning of our month-long trip to Spain, our longest, which included Holy Week  On our second day with our rental car, we left Toledo south of Madrid, after stopping for luncheon supplies, and visiting the royal summer palace in Aranjuez, we continued east to Cuenca, an interesting, ancient town, very defensible, built on top of a rock formation resembling enormous boulders where the original town is located and where the cathedral is situated. After we checked into our hotel in the lower, new part of town, since the constant drizzle had stopped, we decided to visit the old square and the cathedral. The cathedral is not large or beautiful and the stained-glass disappointing. What was interesting was that eight or nine people were busy preparing and dressing a figure of the Virgin Mary on a large "float" for the Good Friday procession. Every parish has its own float which is carried on the backs of laborers, where, after processing through the city, it enters the cathedral to be blessed by the bishop on Good Friday.

In our ignorance, I believe we stumbled on one of the most unusual floats of all the many floats we saw later. There was something special about the likeness of the kneeling Mary, gazing up in adoration at a lace-draped cross, being dressed in fresh white linens, holding rosary beads and with a long, black velvet cape with a border of gold frogging that draped from her shoulders to cover the rest of the float. The love, and care, and devotion of the workers was palpable.

The float was probably 8' x 12' and probably weighed more than a ton. It was carried on the shoulders of ten-twelve laborers who raised it and lowered it to the ground to rest every ten feet or so on the signal of a marcher at the rear corner of the float. There were large silver candle sticks at each corner which were lit, and the up and down swaying movements of the float caused by the way it was carried were hypnotic. And to see fifteen or twenty floats processing in the darkened streets filled with revelers celebrating the ending of the Lenten season, with only the candlelight and the swaying was an amazing experience for us, which we witnessed a few days later in Seville.

The Cuenca cathedral was also unusual because the second float (there are always two) which depict Christ in some pose, usually hanging from the Cross, was the only one we ever saw of Christ Recumbent, having been taken down from the Cross and lying on the ground.

After I had captured all the stained glass and circled behind the altar, and photographed the new black cape, I was now ready for the interesting part, photographing the process of robing Mary. Fran met me with the Spanish gentleman who was in charge and we were informed we could take no pictures until the robing was completed. I was very disappointed, but obediently put the camera back into its carrying case and we sat in a pew, freezing, for possibly an hour before we fled outdoors to explore the square and find a place to eat. I am pleased to this day that I was never tempted to sneak a forbidden photo. There was just too much respect for the reverence I saw and felt.

The workers chose the same restaurant we did. Afterwards we returned to the cathedral where they finally applied their finishing touches; and I was allowed to climb a stepladder and take my photo. I used multiple flash units because of the amount of space and the total darkness. The enlarged result now hangs in my living room where I am writing this account. In all the rest of the cities where we saw the Virgin Mary floats, we never saw another Virgin Mary as beautiful as "our" Virgin Mary.

Today I wonder: Why did we choose to stop in Cuence that particular day? There were many other cities we could have chosen. How did we happen to pick the day of the robing? A day earlier we would have missed the entire event. A day later it would have been all done and might as well have been a postcard.

The next day we drove further east and then south to the small city of Ubeda. It has a beautiful old city square dating back to the 1400s. It was going to be our first chance to stay in a *parador*, which is a state owned and operated hotel, usually a restored and rehabbed ancient palace, or monastery, or school. We found it without difficulty and while Fran was busy unloading our things, I walked a fair distance on a gravel path to register. To my dismay the uniformed clerk said they were full, and they had no vacant rooms. It was the Holy Week holidays and travel was heavy. Another younger couple carrying a young child were told the same. We would have to find a room in a hotel in town. I walked back to the car and told Fran the bad news and we repacked the car. As we were starting to back up to leave there, was a knock of my window and it was the clerk who said there had been a cancellation and we could have the room after all. Ten minutes earlier, the young couple with the child would have been first in line for the cancellation. I turned to Fran and said to her, "See? If you treat the Virgin Mary with reverence and respect, she will look after you." The room was large and beautifully furnished, the beds comfortable, the bathroom fantastic and dinner was delicious. And it was very reasonable.

Day after day for the rest of the trip we experienced fortuitous events, more so than in all of the other trips we ever took. And it was the beginning of my real awareness of the presence of someone or something, call it "Holy Mother Mary," if you will, in my life. I recall being taught an early childhood prayer: "Father-Mother God, lead my little footsteps up to Thee". I think of it as the essence of motherhood, operating much the same as the laws of mathematics, always there to be called on to help solve problems, always there to reveal the right path to follow. But I still have to take the responsibility for my decisions and actions and for any risk for following or applying these insights. No way that it would be done for me.

I am now up to the eighth decade of my life, still searching for reassurance, proof that Deity exists, in spite of all the positive events described above. Reading Mortimer Adler's *How to Think About God* was a very positive experience for me. Once again, I unintentionally stumbled on it by reading William Buckley's book about his "Firing Line" TV program (which I never watched) while recuperating in the hospital from my carotid artery operation. I loved his answer to the question for which the only answer is "God." The question is why is there "Something," rather than "Nothing?" And the only possible answer is "God." Along with this persistent longing for reassurance as to the existence of Deity, was a less urgent concern about the existence of an afterlife. My understanding of Christian Science teachings is that when this life ends, we wake up to a new level of experience on the road to perfection, solving problems in new existences until finally we reach perfection and are able join Him. Logically, if there is an infinite, spiritual Creator and we are part of his creation, we cannot cease to exist simply because to our human understanding we have experienced a change in our state of being caused by Death. Nevertheless, I was still searching for some form of reassurance that this concept was true.

This came to me from an experience after my oldest daughter's death in Florida to which I was a witness. Given that the cause of death was cancer, I was able to be grateful for her release from her suffering, although questioning how this plan of release could be attributed to an All-Loving, All-Powerful and All-Knowing Deity.

I have never spoken to anyone, nor shared, the experience I am about to relate, especially immediately after witnessing her death, for fear that I might be considered demented by grief, or suffering from a hyperactive imagination brought on by my grief. None of this type of reason is valid, or adequate. I had the experience; and it was shattering and very beautiful.

After her ashes had been interred, about thirty days after her return to Ohio, I stopped at the cemetery frequently when passing by to grieve and to give thanks for having had the privilege of having Nancy be a part of my life. On this particular day I was standing at her grave, communing and praying, looking eastward in the near distance when I became aware of a luminous, holographic type of image with sparkling energy outlines and it was the bust of Nancy, our daughter. The absolute, breathtaking thing was not the fact of an image appearing, but the ineffable, otherworldly expression on her face.

I felt she was telling me in the utter silence that there was a future after the change of death and that I had nothing to fear. I do not know any words, in my large vocabulary, that can do justice to that expression. The very inability to find a proper word to describe the expression on her face is proof to me that this experience was real. It was in fact Nancy, not a product of my imagination. Her image was utterly loving, peaceful, and knowing - a special knowledge she wanted me to know, and share with me: that I was safe in my beliefs and had absolutely no reason to fear the future or the change that is called Death. Gradually the image faded away and I was left weak and shaken, and sad because I knew this would never happen again and I would never see her again while on this Earth.

This was the end of my search for reassurance. I know there is a Supreme Being, the only Cause of Creation. I know that Life and Love are Infinite and Eternal; that my individual life is part of an endless striving for perfection. And after many lifetimes ending in deaths (changes) only to be born again to strive again for perfection until there will be no barrier left to keep me separate from my Maker, a part of whose perfect creation I am.

There, you have the whole picture of where I stand and perhaps a glimpse of how I arrived at this place in what I consider a remarkable life, the major events that shaped that life. Not everything was good, or outcomes easy to accept or understand, and if I give credit to God for all the good He has allowed me to enjoy, I must also realize that I did not always see the path before me and allowed ungodly actions to obscure the way. But the right path was always there and for the most part I was led back to it. I thank and praise God and am overwhelmed with gratitude.

*Laudamus Te, Benedicimus Te, Domine Deo*

It is for you to say whether I am a Christian, or not. I still do not know and I am not sure if is of any importance.

Robert F. Schmidt, amended August 25, 2021

# Chapter XV

## Conclusions - Delusions

Since I started this project by writing two of the later chapters first, perhaps it is fitting that I write the concluding chapter before I write the two last chapters of my story, "Florida" and "Finances," before I come to the end of my story.

After all, having seen what started as a memoir turn into an autobiography and voyage of self-discovery, it seems to me that if I have learned anything at all about myself, having already written almost 600 pages (single spaced) about myself while this process has been going on, I must have learned all that there is to know about me and nothing new or startling will pop up that would require going back to add to the contents of this final chapter.

The initial impetus to begin what has turned into a major project was a simple question asked by a close friend's widow who was concerned about the state of my spiritual well-being. I struggled to answer her questions: "Was I a Christian?" and "Had I accepted Jesus as my personal savior?" It became apparent to me immediately that answering her questions, that forcing myself to clarify my beliefs at age 95, was more for my benefit than hers. It took so long to reduce my thoughts to paper that when, with some misgiving as to whether I would offend her, a born-again Christian, I sent my "Credo" chapter to her. It arrived on the day of her funeral services. So, there was never a chance for a dialogue to develop. Her daughter, who read the chapter, wrote that after reading it, she felt she knew me better than she did her own father, which I found touching, and reassuring..

A year or so later, after having seen and held in my hands a book of the poems I have written over my lifetime, self-published at the instigation and with the help of a dear cousin, Sue Bauer, I felt emotions of pride and satisfaction which I had not expected. Apparently, this was something deep-seated and a need had been satisfied.

When my daughters again urged me, as they did periodically, to write my story for their benefit and that of my great grandchildren, leaving some record of what it was like to live almost hundred years ago, I finally agreed. So in my 95th, or 96th year I began at the beginning, and once started, have found the same sort of satisfaction I felt when Fran persuaded me to build a dollhouse for my older granddaughter (which I resisted vigorously) but once started couldn't wait to resume work every day until it was completed. The final product was sheer pleasure. Completing the house on Oakes Road produced the same feelings. In this writing it has been the same. I regret the unavoidable interruptions in the writing process and want to live long enough to see it finished to feel that same pleasure again.

I have never had a conscious goal of living to a certain age, say 100 or (110?) and have never lived my life with some rigid regime to attain such a goal. I am grateful that my mother was interested in nutrition and inculcated in me a love of vegetables and fruit (made simpler by our summers on Tiedeman Road); that my parents insisted on adequate sleep for a growing adolescent (I hated having to go to bed at 7:30 p.m. every night until I was a junior in high school with the exception of summertime, 8:30 p.m.); that they encouraged music and reading, which helped me satisfy my insatiable curiosity; that they believed in the value of higher education. I have a theory, unprovable, that the four years of intensive physical training demanded by the Yale swimming team, has contributed to my long life, and that my love of music also has contributed to my long life. I also believe that having a positive attitude, expecting good as a birthright, is a fundamental factor in a long and good life.

The beginning of this project came about against the backdrop of my experience of caring for my beloved wife during the final years of her life, living with the devastation of dementia and observing firsthand the daily disintegration of a wonderful mind; the fading away of all memory of a wonderful life; how I wish she had been able to write her story. How I wish my parents and brothers had written their stories. How such memoirs would help me understand the person and the lives they lived by their revealing the truths of their experiences the way they remembered them. I have learned that there are many facets to truth and each of us reflects a different aspect of it, which makes it the only truth for ourselves. I am left so curious and will never know.

So, in part, since so many of my memories are still clear, I almost feel a sense of obligation to share those memories of the different world in which I grew up. But there is also the hope that in the selection of which recollections to record (the very deliberate choice of which to relate, and which to omit) as well as the choice of the words used to describe the memories, will serve to reveal my true self, if that can be done, given my omission of many negatives. I do not believe recalling unhappiness, or failures, of which there were relatively few in my life, would improve the overall picture of who I am. This is a deliberate action on my part, contrary to what we were taught at Yale in our Freshman English class, where the object in our writing was to conceal the identity of the author.

I was shocked when I realized as I was writing how lonely I have been for most of my life, with the exception of the proximity of living with my wife, and my three years in the army, ironically; how I have always been driven by an inner need to please my mother, having to earn her love, and more than that, having the same feelings about the other women in my life: my wife and daughters, my mother-in-law; how I have always hungered for understanding and acceptance from others; and how much I hope that some unknown reader may put enough of the pieces of the puzzle of me together and say: "I know him! I understand him. I wish I had known him when he was living."

After completing the chapter on my early life, I began to think of my story as a gigantic 10,000 piece jigsaw puzzle spread out on a table in a public place, partially completed, waiting for passers-by to be tempted to try to move a piece to a partially completed cluster or island of pieces scattered about within the outline of the puzzle. Perhaps this is a poor analogy because a jigsaw puzzle is two-dimensional, a life is certainly not.

First I had to find all the pieces (memories) with straight edges to piece together the outline, (childhood, teens and adulthood) and the corners (three thus far, the fourth will signify my death, which will close the boundary of the puzzle); then to begin to assemble clusters or islands of pieces (memories) of the same color and patterns, which is the easy way to do any jigsaw puzzle. It would be an easier task if there were a picture in color on the cover of the box the puzzle came in standing at the edge of the table to refer to, an impossibility in my case. My hope was that the clusters would grow larger and larger and begin to interlock, making a fairly complete picture. Unfortunately, this is a very large puzzle, and even if all the clusters could combine into one picture, the remaining half or two-thirds of the ten thousand piece puzzle would be background: monochrome sky with or without clouds, rolling wheat fields or, calm or raging seas, and with no specks of contrasting color in the background to provide clues, almost impossible to assemble.

Thus, I began to realize that although I was supplying the pieces, some colorful, if I succeeded in my project, I was bound to fail because of the whimsies of memory. I knew as I completed every page that there were critical, important details of every incident that I was describing which my memory could not recall, so, not only were the memories incomplete, but there was a huge number of memories I could not recall at all, nor determine if they had been stored alongside those I did recall. Reconstructing what must have happened is narrative fiction, not memory. If I were going to be unable to arrive at a true picture of myself through memory, what would others make of my story?

I wish I had words of wisdom derived from my long life that might help anyone whose goal is a long life to reach his goal. I have a few thoughts and theories but do not think I should presume that age alone confers a right to issue dicta. I was taught at an early age that being of service to others was a source of satisfaction and my experience tells me that this is true; I was taught to leave any place that I used in better condition than I found it. This was sometimes burdensome after a picnic. Above all I was taught to feel a sense of gratitude for all that was done for me and given me, and, I would say this has consciously governed my life.

I can recommend moderation in all things; never eating or drinking anything that would affect the working of one's mind; listening to one's body's signals and responding quickly when the body tells you something needs fixing; allowing oneself time for adequate sleep and eating healthy foods. I think having a positive attitude is fundamental in life and has helped me to look for good in all things; and to realize that every coin has two sides (and an edge) and that even in the worst case, something positive can be found. I think it leads to health and happiness to look for good in all things and expect to find it.

Considering how annoying and irritating some of the mantras of mine were to my wife and my brothers at work in the office, I hesitate to lay them before you. When I thought it appropriate, I would insist: "Be specific!" identify *with specific detail";* or, "Penny wise, Pound foolish", also

"All that glitters," all of which elicited eye-rolling and loud groans. After many years of these tiresome reactions, I tried to stop these automatic responses that my listeners found so irritating with questionable success. I know that Fran was hurt many times to my great regret, when it happened to her, either privately, or in a social setting.

I have always been fond of Oscar Wilde's wit, especially his advice, "The only way to overcome temptation is to give in to it;" in the case of my passion for peonies, the advice did the opposite. Otherwise, in many instances, it was very accurate.

And early in my search for answers to the big questions of life, I came across the Silver Rule, the obverse of the Golden Rule: "Do **not** do unto others that which you would **not** have them do unto you," which I have always thought was the more practical approach to living one's life and making important decisions and suited my rather passive nature. It is certainly far more achievable by the average person.

This all leads me to the stereotype of the group of aging, little old Jewish men, who never attended religious services (except the High Holy Days) when younger, meeting at the temple every morning to pray. Their approaching death has caught their attention and maybe it wouldn't be such a bad idea to finally pay some attention to God.

In my case with the little time left to me, I find myself impatient to cut through the chaff I observe around me as I search for the answers to my own questions about the meaning of life as I try to simplify it, and what my role was supposed to have been in it. No one conventional source of such wisdom has provided an answer to my lifelong quest. In that lifelong search, I have been able to find a piece here and a piece there in my own real-life puzzle and have come more and more to a conclusion which satisfies me, realizing how intensely personal this subject is and that it is not intended as an answer for others, who also may be troubled and searching and dissatisfied, certainly not an attempt at persuasion. What follows is simply what I believe as well as I can describe it. It has to do with Infinity.

I had only one course in Philosophy in college and never one in Logic, which I think would have been invaluable. Thus, I have no confidence that the thoughts I have on Infinity are logical or coherent or will withstand philosophical rigor. All I know is that I am comfortable with the answers that I have found although they may seem muddled and inconclusive. I am also comfortable knowing that if infinity is what I think it is, muddled thoughts or not, they are a part of an infinite existence which has room for imperfection, an insight denied me in my earlier years.

I do not have sufficient intelligence to organize the thoughts that have accreted from so many sources over so many years - intimations from my observations of nature, scattered thoughts from my reading, personal experiences - into an orderly, easily understood system. I wish I could. All my life I have tried to find "systems" which make solving problems quicker and would have made my life easier in its every aspect, whether work or play. I do feel that efficient use of time multiplies time, allowing more to be accomplished.

I can only hope that what follows is not so disjointed to a reader as to be unintelligible as I piece together the fragments of ideas that have been floating in my brain for all these years, and increasingly, while writing this story: the hints, the clues, the intimations, the haunting example of metamorphosis, the beginning of my early religious training, which is described in Chapter XIV, written more than four years ago. The simple act of the writing of this autobiography stimulated the search for more satisfactory (for me) answers. I fear such answers as I have found are incomplete, inconclusive or inconsistent, but that that may also be one aspect of infinity, which includes all, is, as a matter of fact, all. I do not have the strength of mind nor the training to explain the thoughts that have accumulated from so many scattered sources over so many years to form my concepts into a simple, ordered statement of a proof of Infinity. I can only hope that what follows is not so disjointed as to be unintelligible.

In recent years I have become more and more conscious of the vastness we are a part of, both on a micro and macro scale. I have read somewhere that there are 80 billion molecules in each of our bodies which are dying constantly and regenerating; if I multiply 80 billion by the approximately 8 billion individuals living on planet Earth, the number of particles invisible to my limited senses is unimaginably large; my mind cannot comprehend such a large number, even equipped with a brain containing billions of neuron connections itself.

Modern science has given us the Hubble Telescope in space, multiplying our limited senses, which reveals millions or billions of galaxies, each having millions of star systems, and again the enormity of the numbers cannot be comprehended by the human mind. Even in our current economy where, until recently, one billion was accepted as a metric of magnitude, it has been supplanted by the number, trillion, and we now think in terms of "trillions," which for most people, is just another word. But, somewhere, in my reading I learned that counting one second at a time, it would take 12,000 years to reach one billion, and 32,000 years to reach one trillion, six times the length of mankind's recorded history.

To me these enormous numbers are intimations of Infinity, a concept I can barely grasp, although I am a part of it. It is all-inclusive, unending, and without limit; the result of a creative principal which underlies all existence; the underlying law which by its very nature must create and expand. Infinitely.

Because of the limitations of our human senses all cultures, including ours, have sought to understand and explain something so much greater than themselves, and as the ages passed, conceived ideas of Deity, or Creation, which have given them limited access to the underlying laws and universal power that keeps the universe functioning.

Just recently a thought occurred to me (where do they come from?) and I found the small pocket-sized *King James Bible* given to me by my church when I entered the Army in 1943. In the Judeo- Christian culture I grew up in, the story of Creation in the first chapter of Genesis in the *King James Bible* was the accepted version for our times. I re-read the first Chapter of Genesis and was once again impressed with the beauty and power of the language: we have had no new change of this story, which is 5,000 years old, i.e. that God created heaven and earth, the seas and land, all the creatures therein and on the sixth day he created man. And He saw that it was good. And on the seventh day, He rested from his labors. The question that popped into my head was: What did God do on the eighth day? God is the only Creator and I do not believe creation was complete for all time on that sixth day. I believe His Creation resumed on the eighth day, that in fact it never ceased, and will never cease.

I do not believe there is, or can be, any limit to Creation, no boundary that could contain it. I believe existence is infinite.

If infinity by definition encompasses all, it helps me understand a problem which has bothered me from my youth when I could never quite grasp, how a Creator who was spiritual (not physical) could conceive of, let alone, create His opposite: flesh and bones, dirt and water, skyscrapers and prison camps, evil, his opposite, a world I could see and feel. The analogy I am now comfortable with is that infinity consists of light, but also includes darkness, one aspect of infinity; that light is perceived when it dispels darkness; that light requires darkness, which is necessary to define Light, to define itself; that the stars remain in their place, invisible while the sun shines and we cannot see them. And even though the sun is always shining, in a sense, we are living in a shadow, constantly seeking the light and finding little pieces of evidence of that pure light when we experience love of one another, feel the flush of success when overcoming an obstacle, when perceiving or creating beauty, be it a sunset or a perfect peony blossom.

I believe that principles, laws if you prefer, of mathematics and physics, which must be the same everywhere in all of Creation, are an analogy for the principles underlying creation; that they apply to everything, animate or inanimate, everywhere in creation, and are accessible to any form of consciousness, waiting with infinite patience, and are longing to be used. The laws discovered by Euclid are still true and in use daily. We do not have to pray to Euclid to ask permission to use his laws. The laws governing creation are just as accessible.

I do not believe it is necessary to be able to understand the Laws of Creation to enjoy their benefits, to be able to fill a blackboard or a whiteboard with symbols which "prove" how the laws of creation operate, any more than it is necessary for a second grader to know, to understand the Theory of Numbers, and the more abstruse theories of mathematics which are universal, to be able to use those laws in his daily life.

We are given, born with the knowledge, that these laws exist, that they are ever operative, that without them there would be chaos, that they function for our benefit to the extent of our various levels of intelligence.

Thus, I do not feel that my inability to "prove" infinity's existence, logically or otherwise, is of any concern. Just as a second grader knows that 2 + 2 equals 4, and he can count on that always being true, I know that Infinity is real, and that I am an infinitesimal part of it.

I have been troubled, in view of my understanding of infinity, by a lack of any memory of a previous existence. Suddenly, I have realized that I had no previous life, that I am a part - an iota - of the ongoing creation; that my physical conception, that new spark of consciousness, brought about an addition to infinity in its inexorable expansion, and that once I became this infinitely small grain of sand, or drop of water, I became a new part of infinity; and once created, I was indestructible; that each of us is a separate infinity (remember the 80 billion molecules) part of an ever expanding, never ending, limitless creation, no boundaries, no horizons. I believe that the Creator, once having created something, cannot by His very nature, uncreate that something.

Therefore, I believe what we call Death here on Earth at our present level of consciousness is a change of substance, the termination of a natural span of time, varied by species and individuals in each species, of an innate consciousness, partially matured by our time on Earth, ready for change. Since nothing once created can be destroyed, the changed "iota" retains its identity as a unique part of infinity. Death is Change, not destruction, the first step in an endless journey.

I believe that this surviving "iota" of consciousness, along with all other forms of consciousness, ever seeking the pure Light, yearns to join its Creator at the center of His expanding creation, and knows that it will require many eternities to reach that destination.

*Veni Creator Spiritus*

# Acknowledgment

I would like to thank my daughters, Kathy Ann Kershner and Barbara Susan Pappadakes for their quiet encouragement as I progressed in the telling of my story. It was at their urging that I began. I should include my cousin Carolyn ("Sue") Bauer for her encouragement; my granddaughter Elizabeth Whiteacre, whose practical advice about publishing matters has been invaluable; a special thanks to Alex Rosenberg, who allowed me to proof read three of his manuscripts in preparation for publishing from which I learned a great deal about my own project and who has been a constant source of encouragement from the beginning;. A special thanks to Pete Pappadakes and to Barbara, hiss wife, for whom I have special feelings of gratitude for having listened to my almost daily woes in dealing with my constant computer errors, many times droppjng what they were doing to come help me solve my computer's glitches. Special thanks also go to my friends, Mark Grabo and Otto Miller, and my new friends and neighbors, Al & Genine Bednarski, computer gurus in their own rights, who have saved me vast amounts of time correcting my missteps as I learned how to use a computer. I am grateful for their interest and support, and for the fact that none of them requested daily progress reports.

I want to acknowledge and thank the staff of BookLocker, my publisher, Angela, Ali, Brian, Richard, Todd et. al. for their infinite patience in dealing with an inexperienced, first time author. They have been the "icing on the cake" of my project, making the publishing part of the project a pleasure.

Printed in the USA
CPSIA information can be obtained
at www.ICGtesting.com
LVHW081028071023
760467LV00012B/230